THE WORLD MONEY MAZE

THE WORLD MONEY MAZE

National Currencies in International Payments

ROBERT TRIFFIN

New Haven and London | Yale University Press

1966

To my unborn grandchildren

and to the world we should be building

for them and their friends

Acknowledgments

The author of this book is not Robert Triffin.

It is, rather, the tidal wave of stimulations to thought and challenges to action in which my generation has found itself engulfed and immersed ever since the First, and particularly the Second World War. My role, in writing this book, has been merely to register and transmit to others my own reactions to these varied impulses from the outside world.

My thanks should therefore go, first of all, to the crises and challenges with which our life has been confronted, and particularly to those which I have tried to recount and interpret in this volume.

They should go, secondly, to the people and institutions which made my task easier by educating and persuading me, or which made it harder but more creative by spurring me to disagreements and controversies. I mentioned only a few of them in the dedication of my book on *Europe and the Money Muddle,* and would add many others today if I did not fear to brand them as "fellow travelers" on a path still regarded as revolutionary, irresponsible, or even downright sinister by their more orthodox colleagues and superiors. I should, however, make an exception for some of the more imaginative and constructive participants in the marathon debates on international monetary reform and regional monetary integration: Per Jacobbson, Pierre-Paul Schweitzer, Otmar Emminger, E. van Lennep, Henry S. Reuss, Robert V. Roosa, M. W. Holtrop, Raúl Prebisch, Felipe Herrera, Javier Marquéz, Paolo Baffi, Rinaldo Ossola, Milton Gilbert, Marcus J. Fleming, Xenophon Zolotas, Reginald Maudling, Valéry Giscard d'Estaing, and, neither last nor least, President Charles de Gaulle, among the officials; Jean Monnet, Fritz Machlup, William J. Fellner, Pierre Uri, Jan Tinbergen, Maxwell Stamp, Karl Deutsch, James Tobin, Sir Roy Harrod, Harry G. Johnson, Peter B. Kenen, Albert Kervyn, Alexandre Lamfalussy, Fred Hirsch, Tibor Scitovsky, Victor Urquidi, Richard N. Cooper, Walter S. Salant, and—why not?—Jacques Rueff, among the main gadflies outside the official family. I trust that the length, and especially the composition, of this list will dispel any suspicion of identification of their views with mine, and that its arbitrary concision will adequately explain the absence of many, many other names with as good, or better, claims for inclusion.

My third debt is to the ivory tower which has so generously under-written my freedom of thought and expression over the last fifteen years, and provided me with skeptically provocative and enthusiastic groups of students, an incredibly efficient, accurate, and smiling secretary, Mrs. Julie Hovey, and a university press which tries valiantly to carry over into such a rebarbative volume as this some, at least, of the qualities which mark its unequaled performance in artistic publications.

Finally, I cannot refrain from crediting the happy and relaxed family life which I owe to my wife and our three sons, and which left me free—too free at times?—to devote my thoughts and energies to the problems discussed in this book.

ROBERT TRIFFIN

Yale University
March 1966

Contents

Introduction

THE READER BEWARE!
or
A CONFESSION OF BIAS

THE DOUBTFUL MERITS and undoubted shortcomings of my peculiar brand of economic theorizing derive very largely from two of its characteristics. It tends to be politically oriented and to derive its main inspiration from empirical observations rather than mere internal logic.

My analysis of international economic problems has thus concentrated primarily on the broad policy issues raised by contemporary developments in this area, such as: (1) the dollar shortage of the early postwar years, and the dollar glut which succeeded it; (2) the initial frustration and sterility of the IMF (International Monetary Fund) attempts to establish international rules for monetary cooperation, and the spectacular success of the OEEC (Organization for European Economic Cooperation), EPU (European Payments Union), EEC (European Economic Community), etc., in developing such cooperation on a regional basis as a necessary prerequisite for effective cooperation in the broader framework of world-wide arrangements; (3) the recurrent crises of the key currencies—sterling and the dollar—triggered by the haphazardness and vulnerability of the so-called international gold-exchange standard.

These problems, and others, have been amply debated by the economic profession without ever producing agreed answers that might carry conviction with the policy-makers. These divergent views between men of unquestioned competence and good faith may be explained in a variety of ways. Logicians stress the different assumptions and value judgments that underlie the reasoning of different economists. The choice of assumptions, however, often seems to be dictated by their fitness to predetermined conclusions, rather than vice versa. Psychoanalysts have long told us, indeed, that man's logic is primarily devoted to providing *ex post* rationalizations for his instinctive choices and behavior, rather than used *ex ante* to derive "objective" conclusions and guides to action.

The advocates of automatic mechanisms for balance-of-payments adjustment, for instance—such as the "restoration" of a mythical gold standard—are primarily motivated by a deep distrust of the inflationary proclivities of most forms of government intervention in economic life. The enthusiasts of flexible rates, on the other hand, may

3

also be recruited from the ranks of *laissez-faire* economists, weary of any kind of government interference with individual freedom and market forces. Many of them, however, are inspired by a totally different ideology, i.e. by the desire to strengthen the ability of their own national government to choose and implement desirable domestic policies, without undue inflationary or deflationary pressures arising from foreign, less well managed, economies, or from ill-conceived advice or disciplines emanating from such international bodies as the IMF.

In fairness to the reader, I should therefore clarify at the outset my own "biases," even though I may personally cherish the illusion that they are rationally derived from empirical observations and sound analysis of the concrete problems discussed, and deeply rooted in broader scientific and philosophical generalizations of our human experience.[1]

I regard our major economic crises and breakdowns, as well as our political ones, as reflecting our inability to coordinate our individual and collective—particularly national—decisions in such a way as to make them mutually compatible, and thus effective, in a growingly interdependent world. The very preservation of individual freedom has always required a minimum of mergers into collective decisions insofar as the decisions of any individual interfere, for better or for worse, with the freedom and fate of others. While many decisions may be left to the discretion of the individual, many others have to be coordinated at the level of the family, the firm, the town, the state, and so on.

The institutional arrangements embodying and implementing this fact of life always tend to lag far behind the need for ever broader coordination arising from increasing world population and from the growing intercourse between men and groups of men made possible, and necessary, by technological developments in transportation, mass production, mass communication media, and means of mass destruction.

The formation of national states has marked, in this regard, an enormous step forward in the evolution of mankind, and probably remained for many centuries the only form of world organization that

---

1. If this were not considered "out of bounds" in a modest and narrowly economic investigation such as the present one, I would refer the reader to the writings of Pierre Teilhard de Chardin (e.g. *The Future of Man,* New York, 1964) and Jean E. Charon (*L'Homme à sa découverte,* Paris, 1963).

was needed, or could realistically be aimed at, under then existing forms of technology. This stage, however, has long been past. The international spread of business cycles demonstrated, well before the atomic bomb, the inability of national states to ignore the impact of their nationally "sovereign" decisions upon other states, and to make themselves independent from the sovereign decisions of others. National borders and the patriotic emotions needed for their support were once a factor of progress, as they replaced outworn frontiers between counties and dukedoms. They have long been, by now, a source of economic waste and mass murders and might even precipitate tomorrow the collective suicide of mankind.

This does not mean, however, that all decisions left today to national governments will soon have to be handed over to a world government. Transitional, and even enduring, compromises will be sufficient to answer real needs for international coordination, and remain desirable to preserve a maximum of freedom for smaller collectivities. Even if a world-wide government is formally established some day, its jurisdiction should remain limited to those decisions for which such a framework has revealed itself indispensable, or at least worth the difficulties and real costs entailed in arriving at joint decisions among so many interested participants.

The task that confronts us is not to choose between alternative forums for collective decisions, but rather to delineate the minimum jurisdiction that needs and can be assigned to broader and broader collective groups, and the maximum jurisdiction that may be safely left to smaller collectivities, and to the individual himself.

Descending now from these broad generalizations and lofty heights to the more pedestrian problems dealt with in this volume, I may summarize my preconceptions as follows:

(1) International monetary and balance-of-payments problems are created largely by the incompatibility of the objectives and means assigned to different national policies, and orders of priorities, by legally sovereign, but actually interdependent, countries.

(2) Such differences are partly irreconcilable, at least at the present stage of understanding of economic experts, governments, parliaments, and public opinion, and the costs which they entail must be accepted as the inescapable price of living with our own limitations.

(3) We must strive, however, both to reach a better understanding of the problems and to disentangle from existing knowledge and prejudices the maximum degree of harmonization of national policies

and of shifts in institutional jurisdictions that may be achieved at each point of time.

(4) This will involve gradually increasing mergers of legal and *de facto* sovereignty between nation states through various forms of intergovernmental commitments as well as of supranational institutions.

(5) This process of interpenetration and mergers of sovereignties cannot, and need not, proceed uniformly and simultaneously, at the same pace, between all nation states: regional groups, such as Benelux, the European Economic Community, the Central American Common Market, the Organization for Economic Cooperation and Development, etc., need and may be able to negotiate and implement a closer degree of economic and political integration than is yet feasible, or even indeed desirable, on a world-wide scale. Yet all nations and regional groups should also recognize the need to organize, as fast as possible, these broader forms of cooperation to the full extent required by their actual interdependence.

These broad guide lines may sound commonplace, and susceptible of contradictory interpretations by each policy-maker. They are. The specific contents which I have given them on concrete issues are detailed in this volume, and may be judged by the reader in the light of his own preconceptions and of the events which later confirmed, or infirmed, my own diagnoses, prognoses, and prescriptions.

To Read or Not To Read?

Guideposts for the Avid Reader

The problems of international settlements are shaped by two totally different but closely interrelated sets of factors.

The first relates to *national* developments and policies affecting the over-all pace and structural direction of production and expenditures in the various countries, their impact upon the balance of payments of each, and the feedback of surpluses and deficits, and of their monetary settlements, upon the future course of economic events and policies in the countries concerned. Part One centers on these national aspects of international imbalance and the process of "intercountry" adjustments, which lie at the core of most textbooks on international economics.

The second set of factors has received far less attention from the economic profession until very recently, but today dominates international debates and negotiations. This is the world-wide impact of the institutional framework of international settlements and reserve creation upon the over-all pace of economic growth and the ease or difficulties with which national imbalances can be financed or corrected. Parts Two and Three review the evolution of our international monetary system and the reasons which have prompted, particularly since the end of World War II, a growing degree of concerted policy harmonization and institutional changes and integration, both at the world-wide (Part Two) and at the regional (Part Three) levels.

Each of these parts begins with a few articles of a general theoretical or methodological character, and continues with articles reviewing, in that light, some of the major crises and controversies of the postwar years. Most of them have been published before in a wide variety of American and foreign periodicals, but a few reproduce private papers and memoranda buried in the archives of the organizations or individuals for which they were written. The origin of each paper is indicated either in the text or in a note at the foot of the page.

Finally, I have relegated to an Appendix a study which I would like to salvage from total oblivion, but which did not quite fit the general style and continuity of the volume, and merely listed others which only an occasional student might wish to consult.

Shortcuts for the Hurried Reader

I cannot but sympathize with the hurried reader, confronted with this undigestible mountain of pages, on a variety of topics, old, new, or even futuristic. Just as I tried to shorten his way, some years ago, through *Europe and the Money Muddle*,[2] I shall now try to guide him, even more sparingly, through *The World Money Maze*.

In Part One, let him merely sample either Section 1 or Section 3 of Chapter I, forget about the forgotten dollar gap, and even about the rest of Part One, with the possible exception of Section 3 of Chapter III.

I would like him, of course, to devote a little more time to the burning and perennial issues discussed in Part Two, but shall not hold it against him if he feels satisfied with a glance at Section 3, B of Chapter V, Section 2, A of Chapter VI, Section 1 of Chapter VII and, alas, the whole of Chapter IX.

I shall let him off lightly, in Part Three, with a quick perusal of

2. Yale University Press, 1957; see pp. xv–xxi.

Section 2 of Chapter X (possibly Section 3A of Chapter XI), and hardly need warn him against meandering into the Appendix.

He should, on no account, however, miss a CONCLUSION whose briefness is probably unparalleled in the literature.

Finally, the most allergic and hurried of all my laymen readers may find most of what matters to him in the final section of this introduction.

An Apology to All

I cannot close without apologizing for the controversial tone of some portions of the text, and particularly for an occasional, but deplorable, "I told you so" type of remark. I was personally involved in many of these controversies, and have—probably mistakenly—tried to recapture the atmosphere of the times in order to enliven what might otherwise have been a fairly dull account of issues long dead and forgotten, but which will reappear, again and again, in a different garb, over the years to come.

Academic economists and government experts are human. They are the prey of emotions and of passing fads and events which inevitably color their advice and decisions. Let us admit candidly that objective economic analysis fades out at times before psychoanalysis in any realistic explanation of the course of our economic, as well as political, affairs.

EXPLAINING THE GIBBERISH

Balance of Payments

The *balance of payments* of a country is a summary of all its residents' receipts from abroad—from exports, investment-earnings, etc. —and payments abroad—for imports, travel, investments, etc.—over a given period of time.

Although the two should equilibrate each other in the long run, they do not from day to day, or even from year to year. The difference—*surplus* or *deficit*—is made up by the country's monetary authorities in the following fashion.

Each country's resident usually wishes to be paid in his own national currency for what he sells, and can only pay in his national currency for what he buys. Commercial banks normally act as brokers

---

A glossary for the layman, written in late 1963, of some of the technical terms most used in current discussions of the international monetary problem.

in the process, exchanging the currency paid out by the buyers for the currency needed by the sellers.

When a country's residents' total payments abroad exceed their total receipts from abroad, the country's commercial banks run out of foreign currencies, and replenish their stock of these by purchasing them from the country's *central bank,* i.e. from the institution charged with the issue of the country's national currency (The Federal Reserve System in this country).

Convertibility and International Reserves

In order to preserve the free *convertibility* of the national currency into foreign currencies at stable exchange rates, the central bank must, in turn, hold an adequate stock of *international monetary reserves.* Under the *gold standard,* these were traditionally held in gold metal, all central banks standing ready to sell their national currency for gold, and gold for their national currency at a fixed price ($35.00 an ounce today in the United States). Under the *gold-exchange standard,* most central banks keep varying proportions of their total reserves in so-called *key currencies,* or *reserve currencies,* widely traded and acceptable in world markets. Only the pound sterling and the U.S. dollar have so far been used for this purpose to any significant extent.

As world trade and international capital transactions increase in volume with the liberalization of former trade and exchange restrictions, and the growth of production itself, the pool of international reserves necessary for the functioning of the system must also increase from year to year. The desirable pace of such increases, however, bears little or no relationship to the sources from which this pool is now most erratically fed: Western gold production (less than 10 per cent over the last five years), U.S.S.R. sales in Western markets (7 per cent, but rising sharply at the moment as a result of Russian wheat purchases), IMF transactions (5 per cent), and U.S. net reserve losses (79 per cent).

International Agreements

A host of international agreements have been concluded since the war in an effort to remedy the worst pitfalls of the system.

The most ambitious and promising created, in 1944, the *International Monetary Fund* (IMF), which groups today more than 100 countries, and aims at helping each of them to preserve, or restore, the free convertibility of its national currency into any and all foreign currencies at stable exchange rates. To assist it in this task, the Fund has been endowed with considerable lending resources, derived primarily from fixed capital subscriptions by each member. The 1962 *General Arrangements to Borrow* aimed primarily at reconstituting, in case of need, the Fund's badly depleted resources in the Continental European currencies. The participating countries—the United States, Canada, the United Kingdom, France, Germany, Italy, the Netherlands, Belgium, Sweden, and Japan—are known as the *Group of Ten.*

The *European Economic Community* (EEC) is in the process of merging into an economic union free from tariff and other restrictions among member countries: France, Germany, Italy, the Netherlands, Belgium, and Luxemburg. It may develop in time into a political and monetary federation.

Bilateral swap and other agreements have been negotiated in the last two years between the U.S. and other major financial powers, primarily as an attempt to ward off or slow down foreign central banks' conversions into gold of our bloated short-term dollar debts to them. Massive gold conversions of such debts might otherwise so deplete our gold stock as to endanger our ability to preserve the free convertibility of the dollar into other currencies at the present exchange rates based on a gold price of $35 an ounce.

The Forthcoming Examination of the World Monetary System

A long-range study of the international monetary system was launched at the 1963 IMF meeting, but will involve both a study by the IMF staff and simultaneous explorations by high-level officials designated by, and reporting to, the finance ministers and central bank governors of the Group of Ten.

PART ONE

Balances of Payments

Always Balance . . .

or Never

I HAVE GROUPED under this intriguing title a number of papers whose main focus is on the problems raised by national balance-of-payments disequilibria in an interdependent world, and the policies—cushioning or adjustment—appropriate to deal with the many different causes from which such disequilibria may arise.

The first four papers (Chapter I) are very general in character, and unrelated to current events. They deal primarily with broad theoretical and policy issues and with the methodology of balance-of-payments statistics.

The others, on the contrary, were inspired by concrete developments in the world situation, and particularly with the sharp reversal in the world's dollar problem.

Chapter II may reawaken for the old-timers forgotten emotions elicited at the time by the rearguard fight of the "structural dollar shortage" theorists and policy advisers against the accumulating evidence of growing U.S. deficits and foreign countries' surpluses in international payments.

Chapter III is composed of two papers dealing specifically with U.S. foreign trade policy, at two widely separated points in time.

Finally, Chapter IV deals, in much broader terms, with the major disequilibria in world payments of the last five or six years, and particularly with the crucial role played in these disturbances by speculative capital movements closely associated with the latent crisis of the two key currencies: sterling and the dollar.

This last theme provides a transition to the second part of the volume, devoted to the weakness imparted to our present international monetary system by its reliance on these *national* currencies as *international* reserve media.

Chapter I: Financing and Adjusting Imbalance

1. ADJUSTING FEATURES IN THE MECHANISM OF THE BALANCE OF PAYMENTS AND EXCHANGE RATES

The Inevitability of Balance

PROFESSORS of international trade like to shock their students by denying the existence of any balance-of-payments problem. All balances of payments are always adjusted, in all countries and at all times, irrespective of the state of the economy and of the policies followed by the country concerned or by its trade partners.

Paradoxical as it may sound, this statement is, of course, perfectly correct. It does not, and indeed could not, deny the existence of possible deficits or surpluses on current account, i.e. of a possible imbalance between a country's foreign income and its expenditures abroad on goods and services. It asserts merely the obvious fact that any current account deficit must necessarily be offset by the liquidation of international reserves or other foreign assets, or by foreign loans or gifts, including the involuntary gifts resulting from permanent defaults on the part of the debtor country. Similarly, current account surpluses are inseparable from an equivalent accumulation of international reserves and investments or foreign grants by the surplus country.

This universal and inescapable type of international balance has no more virtue, however, than the accounting balance implicit in all double-entry bookkeeping procedures. Yet it may be used as a point of departure for a second observation which has a real bearing on the problem of balance-of-payments adjustments. Come hell or high water, a country's foreign deficits on current account cannot possibly exceed the external means of financing available to cover them, i.e. the amount of international reserves and foreign investments on which the country is able and willing to draw, *plus* the amount of foreign grants and capital it is able to attract and willing to accept. The maximum deficit

---

Foreign Economic Policy, Hearings before the Subcommittee on Foreign Economic Policy of the Joint Committee on the Economic Report, Eighty-fourth Congress, November 9, 1955 (Washington, D.C., 1955), pp. 134–42.

that can be incurred will inescapably be limited to this sum, irrespective of the wisdom or folly of the country's policies.

Financing versus Adjustment

Some people may delight in pointing out that one of the implications of this statement is that the deficits of foreign countries in the postwar era would have been adjusted and corrected far more speedily than they were in fact if we had not made their continuation possible by our own foreign aid programs. This is true, but tells us nothing about the levels of trade, production, consumption and investment at which equilibrium would have been attained, nor about the political consequences which might have ensued, nationally and internationally.

Current account equilibrium in a country's balance of payments is neither the sole nor the best form of adjustment in all cases. It may be perfectly rational and legitimate for a country to regard as desirable a current account deficit which can be financed through capital imports and which will permit a faster rate of reconstruction, investment, and economic growth than could be attained on the basis of its domestic savings alone. International investment certainly played a significant part in our own economic growth as well as in that of other countries in the nineteenth century.[1]

An important objective of national and international economic policy should be to recreate conditions which will stimulate once more an adequate flow of international development capital, and facilitate therefore the financing, rather than the elimination, of desirable balance-of-payments deficits.

Yet there are limits to the amount of indebtedness which a country is, or should be, prepared to incur in this manner, and there are further external limitations on the amounts it will be able to borrow abroad or to procure from previously accumulated reserves and foreign assets. The deficit on current account may be smaller, but cannot possibly be larger, than this. In some manner or fashion, foreign earnings and foreign expenditures will have to adjust to a level equal to, or smaller than, the maximum deficit which can be financed from available foreign assets, borrowings, and grants. The real question is not *whether* this adjustment will take place, but *how* it will take place.

---

1. It might be observed in passing that British capital exports alone are estimated to have averaged 4 per cent of national income in the years 1870–1913. At current rates of national income in the United States, this would correspond to net capital exports of more than $10 billion a year.

I take it that your Committee's purpose in calling for this discussion today was to compare the various alternative ways in which this inescapable adjustment may come about, either through market forces or through government policies.

Alternative Paths to Adjustment

Broadly speaking, adjustment may be reached in three different ways: through deflation, through devaluation, or through various types of trade and exchange controls. The question that immediately comes to mind is which of these three adjustments is the most desirable either from the international point of view or from the point of view of the country concerned? Although often debated in economic textbooks as well as in more popular writings, this is, I think, a nonsensical question. You might as well try and get from your doctor *the* best prescription to cure a fever, without letting him first diagnose what may be the cause of that fever. A balance-of-payments deficit is only one of the most easily perceived symptoms and results of more basic maladjustments which may differ widely from one case to another. The cure must be fitted to the disease, in economics as well as in medicine, and there is no universal and ideal panacea for all balance-of-payments maladjustments.

I shall limit myself here to a brief and necessarily highly simplified discussion of four major types of balance-of-payments deficits.

To Cure Cost-Price Disparities. First, the deficit may have resulted from the excessive rise of price and cost levels in the country concerned in relation to price and cost levels in the rest of the world. This will have both stimulated imports and discouraged exports and will have produced balance-of-payments deficits, accompanied by a contraction in economic activity and employment.

This type of case is the one which has been most extensively investigated by economists and which underlies most of their prescriptions for balance-of-payments readjustments.[2] Let us see how the three corrective mechanisms mentioned above—deflation, devaluation, and controls—compare in this kind of situation.

The traditional remedy was to let prices and wages be forced down under the market impact of foreign competition, external deficits, and

2. This overemphasis has been unfortunate for the analysis of postwar developments, where deficits were accompanied by full or overfull employment and could not be explained in terms of price disparities alone.

the ensuing contraction in employment, incomes, and money. This readjustment could be accelerated, if need be, by additional "deflationary" monetary and fiscal measures curtailing the volume of outstanding bank credit and disposable incomes.

Although effective from the balance-of-payments viewpoint (at least under the famous *ceteris paribus* assumption) this kind of readjustment also tends to contract still further economic activity and employment, and therefore to elicit social and political resistance to it, as long as the process has not been fully completed. Moreover, under modern economic conditions, wage rigidities may offer nearly insuperable obstacles to full adaptation, with the result that balance-of-payments equilibrium may only be reached through the impact of permanent unemployment on incomes and import demand. The bulk of economic opinion has therefore come more and more to reject deflation as the best method of balance-of-payments adjustment whenever it is likely to require drastic cost reductions to drag on for a long time, or—worse still—to remain incomplete and perpetuate unemployment as a balancing factor in the country's international transactions.

The method of readjustment which now finds most support among liberal economists in such a case is that of exchange-rate readjustments. A devaluation of the currency will tend to stimulate exports and reduce imports, while releasing at the same time expansionary, rather than contractionist, forces in home demand for domestically produced goods.

Both deflation and devaluation, however, have met with strong objections among less orthodox circles which see a third, and better, way out in trade or exchange restrictions. Their objections to devaluation are bolstered both by a controversial analysis of its probable effects on the devaluing country's terms of trade[3] and by the fact that repeated currency devaluations will shake confidence in the currency, discourage domestic savings, stimulate capital flights, and may in the end bring about a total collapse of the monetary system.

If imports and other foreign exchange expenditures can be reduced directly by tariffs, trade, or exchange controls, the country will be able to close its balance-of-payments gap with a smaller volume of exports. Export prices, therefore, expressed in foreign currencies, will not

3. Although generally raised against devaluation, the same objection would also hold to a considerable extent against policies aiming at a reduction of domestic prices.

have to be forced down so much as they would under the alternative policies of price deflation or exchange-rate devaluation. This "terms of trade" advantage, however, must be weighed against its disadvantages. The contraction in export activities—accepted and even advocated by the proponents of trade restrictions—may involve very costly and difficult readjustments in the country's trade and production pattern. This first disadvantage will be particularly felt by small countries, in which important sectors are heavily dependent on foreign markets for the bulk of their production.[4] Specialized export resources may not be quickly and easily shifted into the lines of production previously satisfied by imports. Moreover, insofar as it does in fact take place, this substitution of domestically produced goods for the formerly imported goods—and of domestic markets for foreign markets—may involve heavy sacrifices in terms of long-run productivity and living standards.[5]

As for the objections which can legitimately be raised against repeated currency devaluations, they would also tend to apply against a continuous tightening of trade and exchange controls. If devaluation or controls must be resorted to repeatedly to maintain balance-of-payments equilibrium, the source of the trouble is not in the current level of price and cost disparities, but in the reasons underlying the continuing tendency of domestic prices and costs to rise further and further above price and cost levels in foreign countries.

To Cure Overspending. This brings us to a second possible diagnosis of the balance-of-payments deficit, which fits far better than the first the characteristic features of the postwar years. Foreign deficits, in this period, have most often been accompanied, not by unemployment, but by full or overfull employment. Effective demand for consumption and investment was in excess of the maximum amount of production which could be obtained from full employment of the deficit country's resources. Under such conditions the pressure of excess demand was

4. A recent study estimates that production for exports accounts for as much as 40 per cent of total industrial production and employment in Belgium, and more than 80 per cent of production and employment in the basic iron and steel industries. See "La Place du Commerce Extérieur dans l'Economie Belge," *Bulletin d'Information et de Documentation* (Banque Nationale de Belgique, August 1955), p. 94.

5. It may also be noted that this whole "terms of trade" argument should have nothing to do with the existence or absence of a trade deficit, and should only bear on the determination of the optimum level of trade under equilibrium conditions.

bound to find an outlet either in foreign deficits or in inflationary price rises at home, or both, whether or not domestic prices were competitive with foreign prices. As long as excess demand persisted, any measures which successfully eliminated the foreign deficit would also aggravate domestic inflationary pressures, and any measures which successfully suppressed domestic inflationary pressures would aggravate the foreign deficit. Only the removal of the excess demand itself could provide a valid answer to both problems.[6]

It is here that the crucial role of internal monetary mechanisms and policies emerges most clearly, for an excess of expenditures over current production income can only be financed, in the end, through the monetary system itself. Individuals or firms can, of course, obtain such financing from one another through the capital market or the sale of real assets. For the community as a whole, however, such transactions necessarily wash out, and an over-all excess of expenditures over production incomes can only be financed (a) from foreign disinvestment or borrowings, (b) from borrowings from the banking system, or (c) from a drawing down of cash and other liquid assets held on the banks.

The excess demand of firms or individuals, however, can result in an actual excess of over-all spending over production incomes only if the net sum of these three methods of financing allows the community as a whole to *satisfy* the excess demand through an excess of imports over exports. Alternatively, the excess demand may be *thwarted* by internal price rises which restore balance between expenditures and incomes through nominal rises in the latter. In this event, the price increases reflect the fact that the pressure of excess demand has been directed toward the home market itself, and that the resources procured by some individuals to finance their own excess expenditures have not been paid out abroad but absorbed within the community itself. For instance, individual cash disinvestments, spent domestically, have merely resulted in a reshuffling of total cash holdings rather than in an over-all contraction for the community as a whole. Finally, the excess demand may also be thwarted by comprehensive trade or exchange restrictions, price controls, and rationing, which also restore balance between actual expenditures and production, but

6. Let us remember, however, that the excess demand, and foreign deficit, need not be entirely eliminated, but only brought down to a level compatible with available and desirable means of financing the external deficit.

perpetuate latent inflationary pressures in the form of a forced accumulation of inactive cash balances.

Let us now consider in turn these three methods of financing, their impact on the balance of payments and the alternative ways in which the deficit may be adjusted to the available means of external financing.

(1) The liquidation of foreign assets by individuals and direct borrowings abroad by them provide at the same time (a) the means to cover the external deficit on current account without drawing down the international reserves of the banking system, and (b) the means to cover, from foreign sources, the excess internal demand for goods and services without unleashing domestic inflationary pressures. Such transactions may be regarded as desirable or undesirable by the monetary authorities, and various types of controls may be instituted by them over such foreign borrowings or disinvestments. In any case, the process need not involve, as long as it lasts, either balance-of-payments difficulties or uncontrollable inflationary pressures for the economy.

(2) The drawing down of cash balances and other liquid assets previously accumulated on the banking system raises a different kind of problem.

Such assets may actually be drawn down in order to purchase from the banking system the foreign exchange resources necessary to cover the external deficit arising from the excess of national spending over national production. As long as the international reserves of the system are adequate to cover such withdrawals, the process can continue without involving inflationary pressures and without endangering the external stability and convertibility of the national currency.[7] The very contraction of cash balances will tend progressively to slow down the process and to bring to an end the excess of expenditures over production incomes.

Difficulties may arise, however, long before this stage is reached, if the liquid balances outstanding are in excess of "normal" requirements and have previously been built up by domestic bank credit rather than by foreign surpluses and the acquisition of equivalent gold and foreign exchange resources by the banking system. Fluctuations in the ratios of liquid assets to national income and to interna-

7. On the contrary, the danger that may be involved here is one of deflationary pressures and unemployment.

tional reserves are worth watching, from this point of view, as a gauge of the vulnerability of the monetary system to cash disinvestments by the public.

Let us consider the case when international reserves have clearly become inadequate to satisfy the public demand for conversion of its liquid balances into foreign exchange. How do trade and exchange controls, devaluation or deflation fit this type of situation?

(a) Trade and exchange controls may, of course, reduce the outflow of foreign exchange for imports and other transactions. If excess liquidities are substantial, however, and the controls have to be maintained indefinitely, the public will be less and less likely to hoard the cash which it is thereby prevented from spending abroad. The controls, particularly on capital flight, may become more and more difficult to enforce. Insofar as over-all spending abroad can be effectively controlled, demand will turn toward the home market. This may initially stimulate production but if, or when, a level of high employment has been reached, the shift of demand from imports to home-produced goods will exert upward pressures on prices. Rising prices will both curtail foreign demand for the country's exports and induce producers to sell in the domestic market rather than in foreign markets. Thus, foreign exchange receipts will decline and the controls on imports may have to be tightened further. This spiral will continue until rising prices have curtailed sufficiently the purchasing power of existing cash balances and restored a "normal" ratio of such assets to national income at the new, and higher, level of prices and costs. Prices may then cease to rise, but the controls will have to be retained indefinitely. We thus come back to a situation in which the balance-of-payments difficulties can be ascribed to international price disparities, and the analysis outlined in the preceding section of this paper becomes relevant.

Price rises may, of course, be more or less effectively controlled by an extensive system of internal price controls and rationing. If this is done, however, the overliquidity will not be reabsorbed, and rationing will also have to be retained indefinitely. The disadvantages of such policies—aside from the administrative burdens involved and their interference with our traditional concepts of freedom—are the same as those already discussed. They entail inevitably a curtailment of productivity and living standards for the community as a whole.

We must observe, however, that if excess liquidities are of moderate magnitude they may be absorbed in time by the normal growth of production. Moreover, if foreign prices and costs are themselves rising, it will be possible to reabsorb excess liquidities by allowing a parallel rise in domestic prices and costs without endangering the country's competitiveness in international trade. Both of these factors did, indeed, help correct to some extent the overliquidity inherited by European countries from excessive rates of monetary expansion during the war and early postwar years.

(b) Currency devaluation does not, by itself, readjust the level of liquidity. It may only do so if internal prices are allowed to rise. The readjusting effects of devaluation in this case do not lie in an improvement in the country's competitiveness through a lowering of its prices in relation to foreign prices. On the contrary, if domestic prices are prevented from rising, nothing will be achieved toward the elimination of overliquidity, and the devaluation may then result in a needless and costly deterioration of the country's terms of trade. The justification for the devaluation in this case lies in the need to preserve the country's competitiveness in spite of the rise in prices necessary to reabsorb excess liquidities.

(c) Finally, both controls and currency devaluation may be avoided by a direct cut-down of excess liquidities through monetary and fiscal policies. The so-called "monetary purges" of the postwar years, and particularly those of Belgium and Germany, tried to achieve this result overnight by the temporary blocking, long-term funding, or outright cancellation of a large portion of cash holdings and other liquid assets. Slower methods were applied, or at least officially endorsed, in other countries where reliance was placed on budgetary surpluses, a progressive contraction of bank credits, etc. The over-all results of these measures, however, are not impressive. Downward liquidity readjustments, like downward price readjustments, are difficult to carry out in practice if large cut-downs are required and can be implemented only over a long period of time. If the readjustments cannot be effected reasonably quickly, price increases and currency devaluation may be preferable to a long-drawn-out process of deflation.

(3) The third method of financing excess demand, the expansion of bank credit, differs radically from the other two in that it is not subject to the same absolute limitations. In the absence of voluntary, legal, or administrative restraints, the process can continue indefinitely and lead in extreme cases to a total collapse of the monetary system.

The reasons for the failure of either trade controls or devaluation to effect a satisfactory adjustment in this case are identical to those which we have just discussed, but are greatly reinforced by the inexhaustible character of such inflationary financing. As long as it continues, trade controls will have to be tightened further and further in order to adjust foreign expenditures to a constantly declining level of foreign exchange receipts, as the diversion of inflationary pressure from imports to the home market accelerates the increase in domestic prices. Repeated currency devaluations will then become unavoidable, in spite of trade controls, to preserve even a trickle of exports. Ultimately, the acceleration of price increases and currency devaluation may lead to a total currency collapse, as happened in Germany and several Central European countries after the First World War.

At first view, internal price controls and rationing offer a third, and more attractive, way out. In practice, their efficacy is also likely to break down if a persistent inflation of credit and money forces an ever-increasing tightening of the controls, thus confronting the administrative authorities with ever-growing difficulties of enforcement, and the political authorities with increasing opposition on the part of the public. Again, this may lead in the end to another form of currency breakdown like that experienced by Germany after the Second World War. Official prices had probably been better controlled and enforced in Germany than in any other belligerent country, but ration coupons, cigarettes, nylon stockings, etc., had in fact replaced the Reichsmark as an effective currency unit. Transactions increasingly took the form of barter deals, and incentives to produce or sell became nearly nil when payment could only be expected in the form of further additions to large, and unusable, cash balances rather than to scarce goods or ration coupons.

Neither devaluation nor trade controls nor rationing can provide valid alternatives to monetary restraints in such a situation. This is not to say, of course, that the whole burden of readjustment should always be placed on monetary policy alone, nor that monetary expansion does not have a role to play in the process of economic growth, and particularly in a fight against depression and unemployment. In the situation of acute scarcities which accompanied and followed the war in many countries, the distribution of scarce resources between consumption and investment, among various types of investment, and among individual consumers, could not be left to market forces, or handled through feasible instruments of monetary and fiscal policy, without running the risk of considerable delays in essential reconstruction and investment needs, and of starvation levels of consumption for many people. The distribution of scarce resources in accordance with socially accepted criteria of essential needs, rather than with individual desires and purchasing power, was the real justification for trade restrictions, exchange controls, and rationing during this period. This, however, did not absolve the monetary authorities from all responsibility in the matter. They faced the double task of restraining the over-all expansion of credit so as to minimize inflationary pressures and of directing such expansion toward the most urgent and essential needs of the economy.

As production recovered, however, and the harmful effects of direct controls upon productivity and incentives became increasingly felt with the passage of time, public policy gave more and more attention to the restoration of market mechanisms of internal and external adjustment. Unlike many of my colleagues, I incline to think that the delays experienced in that respect were due in many cases, particularly in Britain and the Scandinavian countries, to the slowness of liquidity adaptations rather than of exchange rate adaptations. In dollar terms, British and Norwegian prices, for instance, had risen *less* than United States prices between 1938 and 1947, but the ratio of money to GNP had grown to about 164 per cent of prewar in Britain and 200 per cent in Norway. Exports were not held down so much by a lack of foreign demand, due to uncompetitive prices, as by the impact of overliquidity on internal demand.[8] This overliquidity could have been reabsorbed—and was largely reabsorbed later—by domestic price increases curtailing the real purchasing power of liquid balances and restoring a more "normal" ratio of cash to incomes. Currency devaluation might then, but only then, become necessary to restore price competitiveness in world markets. Coming as they did much in advance of price increases, and accompanied as they were by concurrent efforts to prevent them, the devaluations of sterling and the Scandinavian currencies in September 1949 contributed for a time to a needless deterioration of these countries' terms of trade, without correcting the overliquidity which was one of the primary factors of their balance-of-payments difficulties.

8. In the British case, this overliquidity was also reflected in the size of sterling balances held abroad. These financed "unrequited exports" which similarly absorbed exportable capacity without contributing to the United Kingdom's foreign exchange receipts.

To Combat the Spread of Foreign Deflation and Restrictions. Price
uncompetitiveness and the financing of excess demand by current
monetary expansion or excess liquidity are not the only causes of
balance-of-payments deficits. Foreign deficits may also arise from a
contraction of exports resulting from a decline in economic activity
and employment abroad, or from the adoption of various measures of
trade and exchange restriction by a country's trade partners.

Both of these factors played a major role in the balance-of-payments
difficulties of the 1930s. If these had been due to international price
disparities or to national inflationary policies, we should have witnessed
a simultaneous increase in the deficit countries' imports and decrease
in their exports. What took place in fact was a simultaneous decrease
in both exports *and imports,* ranging in most countries from 60 to 80
per cent between 1929 and 1933, associated with a wave of international deflation and unemployment. United States national income contracted by more than one half from 1929 to 1933, unemployment rose
from 400,000 to nearly 12 million workers, and expenditures abroad
on current and long-term capital account declined by about two
thirds. Under such circumstances, national deflationary policies might
well bring temporary relief to the balance of payments of a country,
but would also contribute to the spread of the depression. On the
other hand, national anti-deflationary measures would tend to aggravate exchange losses and force a country to try and protect its
vanishing foreign exchange reserves through devaluation or restrictions. The effectiveness of these measures on the stimulation of exports would be largely nullified by their tendency to spread from
country to country. Individual countries could always control and
contract their import levels, but their efforts to expand exports could
always be thwarted by other countries' actions. Thus, in practice, the
unavoidable readjustments in the balance of payments were primarily
effected by a reduction in the volume of trade and the sacrifice of the
advantages of international specialization and of an economic allocation of the world's resources.

From a purely national point of view, this was a perfectly rational
and largely unavoidable way to deal with the situation. The benefits
of international trade become illusory if the pattern of production
which they imply makes a country highly dependent on excessively
volatile export markets. Recurrent unemployment in the export industries may involve social and economic costs out of proportion with

the advantages derived from international trade in the more prosperous export years.

The maintenance of a high and growing level of economic activity in the United States throughout the postwar era, together with the gradual liberalization of our tariff policies, has greatly contributed to creating, in this respect, an environment totally different from that of the 1930s. Yet full confidence in the benefits of freer trading policies may not be established on the basis of unilateral, and always reversible, action by one or a few countries. Multilateral and reciprocal agreements are necessary to hasten and consolidate progress toward the removal of excessive trade barriers. Experience, as well as economic analysis, amply demonstrates that regional agreements (of the OEEC-EPU type) and world-wide agreements (of the GATT-IMF type) may both be of great value in this respect. It is with some regret that I must leave aside this aspect of the problem, which will be debated before your Committee in later hearings.

Policies for the Surplus Countries

I have concentrated so far on the readjustment of balance-of-payments deficits rather than of balance-of-payments surpluses. Our own problem, of course, has long been of the latter sort, and we have solved it in a great variety of ways.

In the 1930s, and particularly following the devaluation of the dollar in 1934, we cashed our over-all surplus in the form of an unprecedented accumulation of gold reserves: nearly $11 billion in six years, of which more than $3 billion was accumulated in 1939 alone. This gold avalanche, however, was linked primarily to an unprecedented inflow of capital to the United States. Our current account surpluses were far smaller in the 1930s than in the previous decade, as foreign countries contracted sharply (by about two thirds from 1929 to 1933) their expenditures on our goods and services, under the double impact of the world deflation and of their losses of foreign reserves. Certainly, these two forms of adjustment—huge gold flows and a sharp contraction in trade and economic activity—were about the worst possible solution of the problem, for us as well as for foreign nations.

The postwar record contrasts sharply with that of the 1930s. Instead of accumulating surpluses in the form of gold reserves, we financed them overwhelmingly through large-scale government loans and grants to foreign nations. The major arguments for this policy were certainly political rather than economic, and I don't propose to discuss them here. The fact is that, in spite of current account surpluses totaling nearly $37 billion over the nine years 1946–54,[9] our gold reserves increased by less than $2 billion, an increase more than offset by a $5 billion growth in our short-term liabilities to foreign countries.

Our financial aid to foreign nations was certainly the main prop in the maintenance of our high export levels (more than twice prewar in volume and four times prewar in dollar value) in the initial postwar years.[10] It also contributed, however, to the rapid recovery of production and export capacity abroad. Foreign countries' exports to the United States this year [1955] for instance, ran close to twice their 1938 volume, and five-and-a-half times their 1938 dollar value. Ever since the end of 1952, our tapering levels of foreign assistance have been matched by almost equal rises in foreign countries' gold and dollar assets.

This closing of the so-called "dollar gap" through increased American imports is certainly preferable to the two alternative forms of adjustment: (a) the continued financing of a high level of U.S. exports by huge grants of foreign aid, and (b) a contraction of U. S. exports brought about by foreign deflation, devaluation, or trade and exchange restrictions.

The rise in our imports is the result of the recovery of production and exportable capacity abroad, of over-all monetary recovery and exchange rate adjustments by foreign countries, of the high and growing levels of economic activity at home, and of our trade liberalization policies. All of these factors are beneficial to us as well as to others. The trade liberalization policies pursued by our country for the last twenty years are too often defended on altruistic or political grounds, as if they represented a concession by us to our foreign allies. They correspond in truth to our own direct economic interests, particularly in times of high economic activity verging on inflationary pressures.

A final method of adjustment should be mentioned. This is foreign investment. There is no doubt that American capital can accelerate economic development abroad and bring benefits to our own investors as well. Once more, this question can hardly be discussed without

9. This figure does not include military transfers under aid programs.

10. Our $11.6 billion surplus on goods and services in 1947 alone was just about equal to the total gold reserves and official dollar holdings of foreign countries at the end of that year ($12.2 billion).

bringing in political considerations alongside of economic considerations. Yet, on economic grounds alone, there is no lack of opportunities for profitable foreign investments on a scale substantially larger than that of recent years. The obstacles to private initiative in this respect are well known. They are gradually being removed today, and the acceleration of this process through various domestic measures as well as through international negotiation, agreements and institutions should be regarded as a legitimate and fruitful task of American economic policy.

Summary

(1) Deficits may be desirable and may therefore call for *financing* rather than readjustment.

(2) They will in any case always be limited, as a maximum, to available means for their *external* financing. The question is not *whether,* but *how,* this adjustment will take place.

(3) The crucial role of monetary policy in such adjustments results primarily from the fact that external deficits impinging upon the monetary and banking system also presuppose some form of *internal* financing by the system itself.

(4) Public opinion has shifted radically since Bretton Woods from an exaggerated concern for exchange stability to an equally exaggerated faith in the virtue of exchange-rate adaptations. Such a solution fits particularly well the classical case of deficits due to *uncompetitive price and cost levels,* usually inherited from a *previous* era of monetary inflation, and accompanied by domestic deflationary pressures.

(5) Devaluation does not, by itself, remedy two other causes of foreign deficits which have played a large role in postwar balance-of-payments difficulties and which explain the simultaneity of balance-of-payments deficits and domestic inflationary (rather than deflationary) pressures during that period. The first is the case of a *persistent financing by bank credit and monetary expansion of a level of over-all demand in excess of current incomes and production capacity.* The second is the *financing of such excess demand out of the redundant cash balances inherited from a previous inflation,* unaccompanied by corresponding price rises. The most appropriate readjustment of such deficits obviously lies in the control of current inflation in the first case, and in the reabsorption of excess liquidities—through price rises, or monetary purges or other techniques of disinflation—in the second

case. As long as such solutions are not applied, any measure which successfully contains the foreign deficit can only result in an aggravation of the internal inflationary pressures, and vice versa. This is true of devaluation as well as of trade and exchange controls.

(6) Deficits may also arise from *foreign,* rather than national, maladjustments or policies. They may be due, for instance, to large-scale deflation or unemployment abroad or to the adoption of trade and exchange restrictions by other countries. The elimination of the deficits through *national* policies can only be achieved, in such a case, through measures which contribute to the further spread of deflation, devaluation, and restrictions. The balance-of-payments maladjustments of the 1930s must be explained primarily in these terms, rather than by the inflationary policies of the deficit countries.

The only alternative to deflation and restrictions in such a case lies in concerted efforts on the part of all, but especially of the major, countries to restore economic activity and employment at home, to eschew restrictive trade or exchange policies and to facilitate and encourage similar action by others. The postwar record of U.S. performance in this respect is highly satisfactory. We have maintained economic activity at a high and growing level, and followed on the whole a consistent policy of progressive trade liberalization. We have also backed and supported international cooperation in the pursuit of these aims by the United Nations, the International Bank for Reconstruction and Development, the International Monetary Fund, the General Agreement on Tariffs and Trade, the Organization for European Economic Cooperation, the European Payments Union, etc. One may regret, but should not wonder, that this dispersion of efforts has led at times to divided counsels and to some amount of confusion regarding the coordination of national, regional, and international policies, and of trade, exchange, and financial measures, in the achievement of our broad objectives in such a wide and complex field.[11]

11. The views expressed in this paper are documented in considerable detail in the first two chapters of *Europe and the Money Muddle,* pp. 1–87. They also inspired the statistical methodology presented in the first section of the Appendix.

2. THE ADJUSTMENT MECHANISM TO DIFFERENTIAL RATES OF MONETARY EXPANSION AMONG THE COUNTRIES OF THE EUROPEAN ECONOMIC COMMUNITY

The ghost of the "closed economy" assumptions continues to dominate economic theory, even in discussions of such "open economy" problems as those involved in the international mechanism of balance-of-payments adjustments. One is free, of course, to define words as one chooses and to identify "inflation" with price rises rather than with the excess demand—or, in monetary analysis, excess financing—which prompts such price rises and is in turn absorbed by them. In a closed economy, little damage is done by this choice of terms even though it entails a lack of parallelism with the usual definition of the opposite term "deflation" in terms of a contraction in production and employment rather than prices.

In an open economy, however, price increases constitute only one of two alternative, as well as complementary forms of adjustment to domestic inflationary pressures. The other is the direct impact which excess demand—supported by excess financing—may exercise *directly* upon the balance of payments, without waiting for the further, *indirect* balance-of-payments deterioration resulting from changes in the price level. In the short run at least, and a short run which may well embrace a period of several years, balance-of-payments deficits may, under certain conditions, constitute the main channel of adjustment to inflationary pressures and reduce correspondingly the extent of domestic price increases.

This distribution of inflationary pressures between the domestic economy and the balance of payments will be vitally affected both by the degree of "openness" of the countries under consideration and by the degree of integration which links together their national economies; and it is utterly naïve and unrealistic to assume, as is often done tacitly, that such integration is nil between areas divided by a political border, but absolute between regions subject to the same political sovereignty. This lack of realism becomes all the more apparent—and fatal to economic analysis and policy—at a time when

Prepared in collaboration with Herbert Grubel, this paper was published in *The Review of Economics and Statistics*, XLIV (November 1962), pp. 486–91. The authors gratefully acknowledge helpful suggestions and assistance, especially with the computations, by James Tobin and Harold Watts of the Cowles Foundation at Yale University.

the economic significance of political borders becomes increasingly blurred by regional arrangements such as OEEC, EEC, EFTA, Benelux, etc., some of which may, but only gradually, merge several countries into a single economic, or even political, union.

Even in the absence of such explicit commitments to economic integration, the maximum range of divergencies between national price levels is likely to be severely restricted among neighboring countries (1) with broadly similar, and therefore competitive rather than complementary, structures of production and trade; (2) whose mutual trade accounts for a substantial share of GNP; (3) with relatively low —or even simply relatively stable—levels of trade and exchange restrictions on such trade; (4) with stable exchange rates among each other.

The simultaneous fulfilment of all four of these conditions rules out any wide divergency in the evolution of national price levels. Differential rates of national inflationary pressures then tend to be deflected into the countries' balances of payments, increasing the deficits (or reducing the surpluses) of the more inflationary (or less deflationary) countries of the group. Such a situation can persist only so long as the balance-of-payments deficits can be financed, but such financing may be available in fact, for considerable amounts and for a long time, if the deficit countries have ample monetary reserves or can maintain sufficient confidence in the future of their currency to attract large inflows of foreign private and official capital and of assets previously accumulated abroad by their own nationals. Under favorable conditions, these international adjustments may approximate very closely indeed the mechanism of adjustment between different regions of the same country.

The main differences are that (1) convertibility and exchange-rate stability can never be trusted to be as irrevocable between independent countries as they are between regions of the same country; and (2) major inflationary pressures depend on the performance of fiscal, monetary, and banking institutions, and these are ultimately subject to national control, preventing wide and persistent discrepancies between regions of a single country.

Within the same country, therefore, differential rates of inflationary pressures will be limited in their amount and duration, will be absorbed primarily by interregional balance-of-payments disequilibria rather than price divergencies, and these disequilibria will be financed by corresponding capital movements.

Between different countries, on the other hand, inflationary pressures may differ more widely and persistently. They may also be absorbed very largely, at first, by balance-of-payments deficits rather than price increases, but the capital movements necessary to their financing are likely to dry up, or even to become maladjusting, if investors begin to doubt the ability of the authorities to maintain either exchange freedom or exchange-rate stability. The gradual exhaustion of the inflationary country's monetary reserves will then force either a readjustment of the rate of credit expansion to sustainable levels, or impose recourse to devaluation or trade and exchange restrictions. Only then can differential rates of inflationary pressures become reflected in major divergencies between national price levels rather than in balance-of-payments disequilibria.

The Variables

The present paper endeavors to test, in this light, the degree of integration achieved by the six countries of the European Economic Community in the years preceding the coming into force of the Rome Treaty. It is based entirely on the methodology and estimates presented in an OEEC volume on *Statistics of Sources and Uses of Finance, 1948–1958,*[1] to which the reader is referred for further elucidation of the concepts and methods used in this study.[2]

In a closed economy, total expenditures for consumption and investment (X) would be identically equal to production income (Y). Any increase of expenditures over the previous year's production income $(X - Y_o)$ must be accompanied either by price changes $[(p - p_o)y]$ or by volume changes $[(y - y_o)p_o]$ preserving the identity of X and Y. Thus,

$$X - Y_o = Y - Y_o = (p - p_o)y + (y - y_o)p_o \qquad (1)$$

Monetary analysis centers attention on the creation of the additional means of payment, or changes in the income velocity of money needed to finance the excess of expenditures over production income.

Additional means of payment can be created only by the monetary and banking system, either through an expansion of its assets (A)—that is, domestic loans and investments—or through the conversion

1. Paris, 1960. See particularly Tables 1.a of *Country Statistics* in Part II, Section B, and the *Technical Appendix* in Part III, Sections A and B.

2. See also in the Appendix to this volume the text of the internal OEEC paper which initiated this inquiry.

into money (M) of other, somewhat less liquid, liabilities of the system.[3] Monetary "bank financing" (F^b) is thus defined as the increase in (necessarily domestic) bank assets (A) over and above the concurrent increase in bank liabilities (L) other than money, and is in a closed economy, but in a closed economy only, identical with the increase in money itself.

$$F^b = A - (L - M) = M \tag{2}$$

An excess of expenditures over production income may also be financed, however, by "dishoarding" (F^m), that is, by a reduction in the ratio of money to GNP. If we designate such ratio by

$\mu = \dfrac{\Sigma M}{Y}$, we may write

$$F^m = (\mu_o - \mu)Y = \left(\frac{\Sigma M_o}{Y_o} - \frac{\Sigma M}{Y} \right) Y \tag{3}$$

Total monetary financing (F) in a closed economy is the sum of bank financing and dishoarding. It is related to changes in expenditures and in GNP prices and volume through the following formula:

$$F = F^b + F^m = \mu(X - Y_o) = \mu(p - p_o)y + \mu(y - y_o)p_o \tag{4}$$

Two further variables must be introduced, however, when we pass from a closed to an open economy.

The first is the country's import surplus, or external deficit on current account (D). Formula (1) above now becomes:

$$X - Y_o = (p - p_o)y + (y - y_o)p_o + D \tag{1a}$$

That is to say, the excess of current expenditures over the preceding year's production income will be absorbed by—or will absorb—price rises, production growth and/or a deficit in the balance of payments on current account.

A new variable must also be added to monetary financing, to reflect "external financing" (F^e), that is, net borrowings or disinvestment abroad—including net grants from abroad—by the nonbank sectors of the economy. Our financial equation, incorporating both F^e and D, now becomes:

$$F = F^b + F^m + F^e = \mu(p - p_o)y + \mu(y - y_o)p_o + D \tag{4a}$$

3. For the sake of international comparability, M is generally defined as the sum of coin, currency, and demand deposits owned by resident firms and households. A somewhat broader definition of highly liquid claims—including near-money—may prove preferable for the analysis of developments in a single country.

In other words, total monetary financing will be absorbed by, or will absorb, price and volume changes of production, *plus* the external deficit on current account.

Let us finally note that the foreign exchange settlement of the deficit on current account will differ from F^e by the amount of changes in the *net* external assets (N^e) of the banking system. We may write $D = F^e - N^e$. We must also redefine accordingly "bank financing" (F^b) as the increase in *domestic* bank assets over and above the concurrent increase in the banks' *domestic* liabilities other than money. Changes in the money stock are no longer identical with F^b, as some of the new money arising from bank financing may spill abroad through balance-of-payments deficits in excess of F^e. The definition of F^b in (2) above now becomes:

$$F^b = A^i - (L - M) = M - N^e \qquad (2a)$$

where A^i represents the increase of the *internal* assets of the banking system and N^e the increase ($-N^e$, the decrease) in its *net* external assets.[4]

The Computations

In order to facilitate intertemporal and especially international comparisons, the variables discussed above, and also a number of others, are uniformly expressed by the OEEC study in percentages of the preceding year's money supply. National estimates for each of the five EEC countries (Belgium and Luxemburg being grouped together), for simple arithmetical EEC area averages, and for the United States, for the seven years 1951–57 were fed into an IBM computer to test for all possible relevant correlations. In order, however, to test more precisely the relationships between *divergent* monetary and economic developments *as between* the five countries of EEC taken as a relatively integrated area, the same process was repeated for the national *deviations* from the EEC average.

4. The relationship between F^b, M, and N^e may be expressed indifferently in the following three forms:

(a) as above ($F^b = M - N^e$), meaning that bank financing must be absorbed either by an increase in the cash retained by borrowers, or by their net purchases of foreign exchange from the banking system;

(b) as $M = F^b + N^e$, meaning that money supply may expand as a result of an increase of internal bank financing or of net purchases of gold and foreign exchange by the banking system;

(c) as $N^e = M - F^b$, meaning that the changes in the net gold and foreign exchange assets of the banks reflect the difference between the increase in internal demand for money and the amount of bank financing.

Third and fourth sets of calculations were then made for the years 1953–57 alone, in order to exclude the years of the Korean crisis dominated by wide movements of external origin and during which recourse to trade and exchange restrictions was much greater than in the following period.

The accompanying table presents a brief abstract of the results deemed most relevant to the elucidation of the questions raised in the introduction to this study. The critical value for five degrees of freedom at the 5 per cent level of significance is .75 for the observations relating to the 1951–57 period and .88 for those relating to the 1953–57 period; it is .83 and .93 respectively for the 2 per cent level of significance, and .87 and .96 for the 1 per cent level. Coefficients above the 1 per cent level of significance are underlined in the table.

Interpretation

(1) The "openness" and "interdependence" of the six countries, even before the entry into force of the Rome Treaty, is evidenced by:

(a) the high correlations between national monetary financing and import surplus for each of them[5] taken separately (lines IA, 1–5);

(b) the much lower, or nonexistent, correlation between national monetary financing and either price changes or production changes (lines IB and C, 1–5);

(c) the low, or nonexistent, correlation between national price changes and import surpluses (lines III, 1–5).

(2) For the EEC area *as a whole,* however, a significant correlation appears between monetary financing and prices, as the degree to which monetary financing "spills out" through balance-of-payments deficits, instead of affecting the area's own price level, is much smaller for the *relatively* self-contained EEC area as a whole than for the individual member countries (line IB, 6).

(3) The *relatively* closed economy of the United States shows even less relationship between monetary financing and the balance of payments than the EEC area (line IA, 6 and 7), but no relationship either between monetary financing and prices (line IB, 7). In contrast to the EEC, monetary financing appears to be related in the United States to production rather than prices (line IC, 7). The main, but not the only, explanation for this contrast may be in the fact that inflationary

5. Only five areas are listed, as many Belgium and Luxemburg data are available only for the two countries together which have long formed a Monetary and Economic Union.

Correlation coefficients between:	Absolute changes		Deviations from EEC area mean	
	1951–57	1953–57	1951–57	1953–57
I. Total monetary financing (F) and				
A. *Import surplus* (D)				
1. France	81	95	90	97
2. Italy	70	94	92	99
3. Germany	97	98	99	99
4. Netherlands	98	97	96	97
5. Belgium-Luxemburg	−6	58	93	94
6. EEC Area	83	83		
7. United States	−5	33		
B. *Prices* (p)				
1. France	91	95	83	85
2. Italy	75	19	54	90
3. Germany	85	33	15	26
4. Netherlands	71	88	83	62
5. Belgium-Luxemburg	61	17	−7	−65
6. EEC Area	94	99.7		
7. United States	63	−18		
C. *Production* (y)				
1. France	−6	45	39	57
2. Italy	21	69	2	27
3. Germany	80	84	98	99.5
4. Netherlands	−20	−81	−18	−73
5. Belgium-Luxemburg	75	9	−23	−10
6. EEC Area	17	4		
7. United States	95	90		
II. Internal monetary financing (F^i) and				
A. *Import Surplus* (D)				
1. France	75	95	77	95
2. Italy	48	90	90	99
3. Germany	96	98	97	98
4. Netherlands	93	88	88	89
5. Belgium-Luxemburg	−40	−31	67	38
6. EEC Area	86	85		
7. United States	−19	17		
B. *Decline in banks' net foreign assets* ($−N^e$)				
1. France	85	94	95	97
2. Italy	9	87	91	99
3. Germany	76	94	97	98
4. Netherlands	98	97	97	96
5. Belgium-Luxemburg	−14	47	81	69
6. EEC Area	58	43		
7. United States	−1	−5		
III. Prices and import surplus (D)				
1. France	52	80	56	90
2. Italy	18	11	23	92
3. Germany	74	18	6	13
4. Netherlands	63	77	69	45
5. Belgium-Luxemburg	−80	−70	−39	−85
6. EEC Area	70	81		
7. United States	−70	−95		

pressures were far greater, during this period, in EEC than in the United States. The EEC area was much closer throughout to full employment, or even overemployment in some countries, leaving price rises as the main absorber of excess financing, while production and employment could rise more markedly in the less fully employed economy of the United States.

(4) This explanation may find some confirmation in the similar correlation between monetary financing and production in Germany (line IC, 3), where production increases could be fed also by drawing both on a less fully employed labor force and on a large flow of immigration from the East.

(5) The only country in which the calculations strongly suggest the existence of a correlation between monetary financing and prices (line IB, 1) and between prices and the balance of payments (line III, 1) is France. This conforms to expectations as France was the only country in the group to reintroduce stringent trade restrictions during the period under study, thus diverting inflationary pressures from the balance of payments to the internal price level.

(6) It might be suspected, of course, that the high correlation discovered between total monetary financing and import surplus could be due to the fact that "external financing" (F^e) contributes both to the size of total monetary financing (F) and to the ability of each country to finance its import surplus. In fact, however, lines IIA show that correlations remain relatively high even if one excludes external financing and considers internal financing alone. They are even higher, if one relates internal financing to the decline in the banks' net foreign assets (lines IIB). This is, of course, extremely significant, as a constraint on policy. Other calculations (not reproduced here) confirm the absence of any systematic relationship between external financing and import surpluses, and the existence of relatively good correlations between "bank financing"—excluding "dishoarding" as well as "external financing"—and import surpluses.

(7) Finally, and in accordance with our initial hypotheses, the expected correlation between monetary financing and import surplus is somewhat higher for the period 1953–57, which excludes the wide exogenous disturbances and tighter trade and exchange restrictions of the Korean crisis. It is also much more marked in the "deviations from mean" columns than in the "absolute changes" columns, as the latter do not isolate the impact of differential rates of expansion as among

the six countries only—which is the main topic of this study—from the impact of developments and policies in the rest of the world.

Tentative Conclusions

Too much weight should not be put on the results just described. They are based on relatively few observations and could be vastly improved by additional, but unfortunately time-consuming, work. The EEC area average, especially, and the national deviations from it should better be computed on the basis of aggregative data for the area as a whole rather than of the simple arithmetic mean used in the calculations. Other OEEC countries could also be included in the investigation, and the data brought up to date.

Imperfect and tentative as they are, however, the results give some support to the hypotheses stated in the introduction of this paper. The five countries of the European Economic Community, with wide open economies, a high degree of economic integration, stable exchange rates, and relatively low and declining levels of trade and exchange restrictions among them, exhibited, as early as the 1950s, many of the characteristics of *interregional*—rather than international—adjustments as described by traditional economic theory. Divergencies between national monetary policies were primarily reflected in the balance-of-payments experience of the countries concerned, rather than in prices of production trends which were closely linked together by influences pervading the area as a whole. Excessive expansion by one country tended rapidly to spill into larger deficits, or smaller surpluses, rather than in stronger internal price pressures or production growth. Independent *national* monetary policy by any one of these countries could therefore have relatively little influence on the evolution of its own prices, production, and employment levels, as long as it kept its exchange rate stable and observed its OEEC trade liberalization commitments. Monetary policy, under these conditions, could only become effective within the framework of the area as a whole.

In the absence of a sufficient degree of *ex ante* coordination at that level, balance-of-payments deficits would force the more inflationary countries either to readjust their policies *ex post,* or to resort to devaluation or restrictions, unless they succeeded in financing their deficits from previously accumulated reserves or from induced private or official capital imports. Restrictions were indeed reintroduced by France, and followed later by a devaluation of the franc. Yet the over-all results of this study show how successful the relatively mild forms of cooperation embodied in the OEEC-EPU system were in circumscribing such breakdowns of regional integration and substituting for them (a) large, readjusting, movements of private and official capital, predicated on (b) the acceptance of residual adjustments in over-all fiscal, monetary, and credit policies.

We should also note, however, that the large over-all surpluses of the area as a whole with the outside world contributed both to moderating the size of the balance-of-payments deficits of the more expansionist of the OEEC countries, and to making it easier for their OEEC partners to finance them out of their growing gold and foreign exchange reserves.

The accelerated implementation of the long-term provisions of the Rome Treaty in the commercial field—up to the full elimination of remaining quantitative and tariff restrictions on mutual trade, and the complete merger of commercial policies, tariff duties, and other restrictions toward the rest of the world—may be expected to sharpen even further the characteristic features of the adjustment mechanism among the EEC countries already discernible before the entry into force of the Rome Treaty. The effectiveness of independent *national* monetary policies will become less and less, and the forces impelling a shift from national to Community policies and institutions will become greater and greater, in the monetary field as well as in the commercial field. The full implementation of the explicit clauses of the Treaty in the field of trade will thus entail inevitably a growing harmonization and integration of monetary policies and institutions, far beyond the explicit clauses of the Treaty itself.

Finally, the record analyzed in this paper should prompt us to reconsider the theory of balance-of-payments adjustments and to recognize the actual gradation from the limiting case of *intranational* regional adjustments within a single country, at one extreme, and the theoretical model of *international* adjustments of our textbooks, on the other. Adjustments among the countries of the European Economic Community already seem to be, and are likely to become increasingly, closer to the first than to the latter. Other country groupings may exhibit a similar trend, depending on the degree of interdependence already forced upon them by market forces, or consciously adopted by them through international policies and agreements.

3. Groping for a Consensus

A more appropriate title for this section might well be "stumbling on a consensus." Our major purpose was not to reach such a consensus, but to identify and understand our disagreements regarding the major defects of present international monetary arrangements and the major remedies proposed by the critics.

In fact, however, the confrontation and discussion of the various underlying assumptions which logically explain these differences proved most useful, not only in increasing our understanding of—and empathy for—divergent viewpoints, but also in eliciting from most of us some appreciable shifts from our original positions, converging toward a far greater consensus than any of us expected, or would have dared to hope.

We felt that the brief summary below might be of some interest to the public, and demonstrate the very usefulness of the apparently tedious and academic exploration of disagreements which is the main topic of this report.

It cannot be stressed too strongly, however, that convergence, or consensus, does not mean unanimity; that it allows for a different emphasis on the relative importance of the points stressed below; and, most of all, that the somewhat dissentient views grouped together, for convenience' sake, at the end of this section may well prove more correct in the end than those reflected in our "consensus." Scientific issues cannot be decided by counting heads.

With these reservations and qualifications, an extensive agreement emerged from our discussions on the following points:

(1) That the use of international reserves and borrowing to finance balance-of-payments maladjustments may be highly desirable, or totally inappropriate, depending on the sources and nature of the particular disequilibrium in point. Financing should not be a substitute for desirable adjustments, nor unnecessary adjustments a substitute for inadequate finance.

(2) That a realistic appraisal of avoidable or unavoidable mishaps

---

Although primarily devoted to the problem of balance-of-payments adjustment—and included here for that reason—this paper also deals with the issues of international monetary reform discussed in Part Two of this volume. Prepared, in the course of a sleepless night, as a first draft for the International Study Group on International Monetary Arrangements, it was substantially revamped and shortened in the course of the Group's following deliberations. See *International Monetary Arrangements: The Problem of Choice* (Princeton, 1964), pp. 101–07.

and imperfections in the actual carrying out of domestic adjustment policies should lead us to some shift of emphasis in exchange-rate policies and institutions in the direction of speedier and smoother adjustments, when desirable.

(3) That the mechanism of international reserve creation should be more consciously oriented than it has been in the past toward adjusting the volume of reserves to noninflationary growth rates in the world economy, and toward eliminating the major sources of instability characteristic of the present system.

(4) That the protection of the large outstanding foreign-exchange component of the world reserve pool against sudden or massive conversions into gold metal should receive a high order of priority at this juncture.

The Problem of Adjustment

(1) The optimum balance-of-payments pattern to which adjustment should be directed clearly depends on the relative stage of development and capital endowment reached by the various trading countries at a given point in their history. This should determine ideally: (a) a desirable, and feasible, rate of net capital exports from the more to the less developed countries; (b) corresponding, and offsetting, surpluses on current account for the first countries, and deficits for the latter.

(2) In practice, this optimum pattern can only be approximated at best by any country of the real world, at any one point in time. Undesirable disequilibria might be measured by unrequited net reserve gains or losses (including foreign borrowing). A strong distinction should be drawn here, however, between three types of such disequilibria: (a) temporary disequilibria, arising from crop failures, movements of private capital and inventory fluctuations associated with different phases of the cycle among trading countries, and reinforced by consequent interest-rate differentials; lags in producers' response to changes in tastes (car fins) or technology; etc.; (b) deficits or surpluses currently generated by the simple spillover of purchasing power from the more expansionist countries to the less expansionist countries; (c) more obdurate and persistent disequilibria resulting from "built-in" disparities in the international cost pattern of the trading countries and reflected in: (i) either persistent disturbances of the "ideal" or "normal" current-account pattern defined under (1)

(b) above, as long as these can be financed; or, (ii) persistent deflationary pressures and unemployment—or recourses to trade or exchange restrictions—in the undercompetitive countries, matched by persistent inflationary pressures in the overcompetitive countries.

(3) In practice, again, these three types of disequilibria are rarely met in their pure form in the real world. They tend indeed to merge into one another, the second being a frequent cause of the third, and the third a frequent factor in the first. Neither is the proper diagnosis of an actual disequilibrium as falling clearly under one of the three types, rather than the others, particularly easy to make, especially in its earliest stages. Yet such a diagnosis is of vital importance to a proper choice of the remedy to be applied:

(a) Temporary deficits and surpluses should be cushioned by adequate reserves and/or financing, rather than corrected at the expense of unnecessary and costly disruptions in employment and/or price and cost levels—under fixed exchange rates—or in the international pattern of exchange rates.

(b) "Spillover" types of disequilibria can and should be corrected as rapidly as possible, through better policy harmonization between the more expansionist and the less expansionist countries, aiming at sustaining maximum rates of growth while stifling inflationary excesses. Excessive and automatic financing facilities might encourage undue delays in necessary harmonization by inflationary countries. In other cases, however, insufficient reserves or financing would force deficit countries to align their policies on those of deflationary countries, or to depreciate their currency, or to resort to trade or exchange restrictions.

(c) Finally, deficits and surpluses arising from moderate disparities in the international price and cost pattern might possibly best be met if such disparities can be effectively corrected, over a reasonable period of time, by appropriate "income policies" (i.e. by slower wage rises than productivity increases in the deficit countries, and higher wage rises than productivity increases in the surplus countries). If, however, such policies prove ineffective, or if the disparities to be corrected are of considerable amplitude, exchange-rate readjustments would be nearly unanimously accepted today by economists as the most appropriate remedy.

(5) There is, therefore, no panacea fitting all causes of balance-of-payments disturbances. This consideration should rule out automatic

financing as well as complete and automatic "nonfinancing" (i.e. fully floating exchange rates) of all balance-of-payments disequilibria, irrespective of their origin.

In cases of uncertainty, the real costs of financing (i.e. the dangers of imported inflation) should be weighed against the real costs of premature or unnecessary adjustments in the national economies concerned and in the international pattern of prices and costs.

This conclusion has a direct bearing on our views as to the proper orientation of the large "credit reserves" component already incorporated into the present world reserve pool. Such credit reserves, and later additions to them, should help finance in nonautomatic fashion—except for moderate, short-term overdrafts—the temporary disequilibria discussed above, under conditions stimulating the harmonization of national policies around maximum, noninflationary growth rates. The system should limit as severely the right of a deficit country to drop inflationary IOU's into the world reserve pool, as the right of a surplus country to force deflation, currency devaluation, or trade restrictions upon its partners by extracting excessive amounts of gold metal from it in settlement of its surpluses.

The Process of Reserve Creation

(6) Reforms of the international monetary system should aim at three major objectives:

(a) To orient future increases in the world reserve pool in such a way as to facilitate the attainment of maximum, feasible growth rates, and of desirable, attainable expansion of international trade, and to combat pervasive inflationary pressures in the world economy.

(b) To invest the large and constantly growing "credit reserves" component of the system in such a way as to cushion temporary disequilibria in the members' balances of payments, to give deficit countries the breathing space necessary for the proper diagnosis and implementation of desirable readjustment policies, and to stimulate a better harmonization of such policies around the objectives discussed under (a) above.

(c) To eliminate the present sources of vulnerability of the present system, described in other parts of this report, and particularly those arising from sudden or massive shifts from one reserve medium into another, i.e. among different reserve currencies and between such currencies and gold metal.

(7) The attainment of these objectives would obviously be im-

possible if all countries insisted upon retaining and exercising in fact their present—and already largely theoretical—right to convert into gold metal larger proportions of their total reserves than is compatible with the present world stock of monetary gold and with the modest accretions of new gold now derived from Western production and Russian gold sales.

This fact is now widely accepted by responsible monetary officials. Voluntary restraints and *ad hoc* cooperation by central banks have been buttressed in recent years by a complex array of overlapping arrangements of a short-term nature, and have succeeded so far in their modest attempt to meet the recurrent crises triggered by the system itself. More organic and permanent reforms are obviously needed to ensure the longer-run viability and efficiency of our international money order.

(8) Each of many various alternative solutions has its own merits and defects from the various points of view under which they were examined, and which are discussed at length in other parts of this report. The consensus that emerged among most of us, however, favored the broad line of approach described in this report as the "Centralization of Monetary Reserves," as best designed to meet all three of the objectives set out in paragraph 7 above. In brief, reserve deposits with the IMF—in agreed proportions to each country's global reserves —should serve as the keystone of the system, and be substituted gradually for the use of national currencies as international reserves. They would carry the same guarantees now attached to all IMF assets and liabilities, and be freely usable for all international settlements. They would obviate the need for the periodic quota increases, which flood the Fund with superfluous amounts of some currencies while leaving it short of other currencies most needed for its operations.

(9) The global amount of deposits held with the Fund would not be affected by settlements among members, and could be used in part for investments in IBRD obligations or similar types of securities, and in part in the traditional lending operations of the Fund. Most of the much enlarged and growing resources derived from the conversion of currency balances into Fund deposits should, however, be primarily invested in the major financial markets actively engaged in overseas-development lending. Compensatory transfers of such investments from one market to another—to cushion temporary disequilibria in accordance with the criteria mentioned in Section I—would strengthen their ability to perform their traditional long-term lending functions

with far less risk of endangering their own liquidity than is the case today.

An Orderly Transition

(10) The huge short-term indebtedness inherited by the reserve-currency countries from their support of the gold-exchange standard over nearly half a century poses a particularly grave problem at this time. Agreement on its importance and urgency and on the broad lines of a favored solution has been virtually unanimous among the conferees in attendance at each of our four meetings.

(11) The choice of a centralized reserve-deposit system as the most appropriate one for the long-term problem of an orderly system of reserve creation inevitably entailed a similar choice with regard to this transitional problem. A clear preference was thus expressed for the conversion of such national currency reserves into liquid, gold-guaranteed deposits with the Fund.

The corresponding obligations assumed by the currency-reserve debtors toward the Fund would carry similar guarantees, but be subject only to gradual amortization of no more than 5 per cent a year, to be exercised at the option of the Fund, and only insofar as such amortization would serve, rather than hinder, the broad objectives of international monetary stabilization.

———

This dry summary of the consensus that emerged from our deliberations does not imply, in the least, that these are the only points on which substantial agreement could be found, nor that other views were not solidly affirmed and persuasively argued by some of us.

On the problem of balances of payments, for instance, the arguments of some in favor of faster domestic adjustments and more rigid stability of exchange rates contrasted with those of others in favor of slower adjustments, and of others still in favor of fully flexible exchange rates. Another point which was amply discussed was whether cushioning finance should be sought primarily in private capital movements, stimulated by more exchange-rate flexibility and/or adjustments of interest rates, or in official capital and reserve transactions.

On the reform of the international reserve system itself, opinions ranged also from the utilization of gold alone as a reserve medium to its total exclusion from the world reserve system.

Finally, most of us would regard a system of multiple-currency reserves as a possible alternative to the full centralization of reserves, and as indeed nearly equivalent in practice, if central banks' decisions about the composition of such direct holdings among the various currencies could be coordinated sufficiently continuously and rapidly to serve the same purposes. This unfortunately appeared immensely difficult and complex in view of the multiple choices which this would involve as to the precise mix of individual currencies to be transferred by each participant to every other participant, either for the settlement of imbalances between the countries concerned, or to offset opposite temporary movements of speculative funds from one currency to another. Most of such transfers would be unnecessary in a centralized reserve-deposit system, whose total liabilities—and assets —would be left unchanged by deposit settlements among members; disequilibrating private capital movements could be far more easily offset by simple compensating transfers of Fund investments between the countries involved in such movements.

The main argument in favor of the multiple-currency system lay in the escape it might offer from the difficulties associated with the exact determination of voting power in a centralized deposit institution. Most participants felt, however, that a greater decentralization of the IMF structure, recognizing the complementary role of emerging regional monetary organizations, such as provided for in the Rome Treaty and in the Central American Monetary Union, might help in the solution of this problem.

Another possibility, which seemed worthy of further study to many of us, would be to provide for some safeguards against real or fancied abuses of majority rules in the lending operations of the institution by granting additional votes to *surplus* countries, suffering simultaneously from *inflationary* pressures, and to *deficit* countries suffering from *deflationary* pressures.

Alternatively, any country which persistently lost, or gained, reserves at an excessive pace should be given more leeway, and even encouragement, to appropriate exchange-rate changes.

Preference should be given to the first procedure when the *same* inflationary (or deflationary) pressures prevail throughout the world economy, thus calling for a slowdown (or acceleration) of Fund lending. Exchange-rate readjustments, on the other hand, would be more appropriate when deflationary pressures in the surplus countries coincide with inflationary pressures in the deficit countries.

4. The Presentation of United States Balance-of-Payments Statistics

(1) Any user of balance-of-payments statistics should first of all recognize his immense debt to Walther Lederer for his untiring labor and excellent judgment in presenting us for many years with detailed and comprehensive estimates of our balance of payments in a form which has become a "classic" in the field.

I would like, most of all, to congratulate him for his unparalleled integrity and self-effacement in resisting the temptation to force his own analytical predilections upon us, and in giving us instead a presentation which lends itself admirably to any recasting and re-arrangement that may suit our own tastes or needs, rather than his. This is a rare virtue, of which I might readily admit myself incapable, were I in his place, but which is indeed the essential prerequisite of his job.

(2) My task today, however, is to try and spur him to some innova-tions, which I feel would facilitate even further my own life and, I hope, yours as *users* of his estimates. In an effort to be as constructive as possible, I shall eschew mere questions and negative criticisms, and venture concrete alternatives which I hope deserve exploration. In doing so, and especially in attempting to fill in my suggested categories with actual figures, I am deeply conscious of the many pitfalls which face any *user* trying to parade as a *builder* of statistics, particularly when he does not have at hand all the sources and time necessary for the job. I shall be sticking my neck way out as a most con-venient target for your, and Walther's axe. And I shall indulge my most unconventional and controversial personal tastes, predilections, and prejudices.

(3) We all agree, of course, with the basic proposition that no single presentation of the balance of payments can serve all the multiple purposes of the analysts and policy-makers and that what matters most is that the basic table of the *Survey of Current Business* present available estimates in sufficient detail to permit as many dif-

---

American Statistical Association, *1961 Proceedings of the Business and Economic Statistics Section* (Washington, D.C., 1962), pp. 51–57. Some of the suggestions presented in this paper, particularly the substitution of "official settlements" for the *Survey's* "over-all balance" concept, have met with wide acceptance, even in official circles. See, e.g., *The Balance-of-Payments Statistics of the United States,* Report of the Review Committee for Balance-of-Payments Statistics to the Bureau of the Budget (Washington, D.C., April 1965).

ferent regroupings of items as may be needed for different purposes.

Yet no presentation of balance-of-payments estimates—not even that of Table 2 of the *Survey*—can be completely neutral. Table 2 chooses to emphasize the balance on goods and services, with and without transfers under military grants, and even more what has come to be designated as our "over-all balance," i.e. changes in our net international reserves, arbitrarily defined as our official gold and convertible currency holdings *minus* our liquid liabilities, public and private.

This is undoubtedly a very significant and meaningful concept, and I would be quite ready to defend Walther Lederer on this point against most of his critics, and especially against those who would like to count our private short-term assets abroad as part of our reserve assets. While I shall propose later a different measurement of our net reserves, what I mostly regret is the overemphasis placed by the *Survey* on this single aggregate. Since three tables are now regularly presented in the *Survey* (and I earnestly hope that more may be added in the future) this opportunity should be seized to highlight different concepts, rather than the same one in all three tables.

(4) I would prefer, for instance, to focus attention in the basic, detailed *Survey* table on the more conventional measurement of our current account surplus, including, however, such normal and approximately constant unilateral transfers as those represented by pensions and private remittances. Nine users out of ten, after all, adjust in this fashion the "Balance of Goods and Services" of the *Survey* and would appreciate being saved the trouble of adding—or rather subtracting—the figures themselves. I know that this would have the effect of breaking down the unity of the "Unilateral Transfers" group, but hasn't this become largely meaningless anyway, or even misleading, in view of our growing so-called lending in local currencies? These operations are, in fact, closer to grants than real loans.

(5) Such a presentation would have the additional advantage of allowing us to substitute economically suggestive signs for mere bookkeeping signs in the rest of the balance, i.e. in our capital transactions and official settlements accounts. Gold inflows, capital exports and repayments abroad, all of which, after all, signify a strengthening of our position, could be shown as a *plus*, rather than a *minus* as is now the case. Conversely, losses of gold and increases in our foreign indebtedness could be shown as a *minus* rather than a *plus*. This would be far more understandable to the layman and other balance-of-pay-

ments users, and should not befuddle for too long the trained ac-
countants and balance-of-payments builders.

The financial items "below the line" would add up to the same sum
as the current balance and show how it has been financed, rather than
given an *opposite* sign for the mere pleasure of being able to write a
zero at the bottom of all the accounts taken together.

Finally, this reversal of signs would make it easier to integrate, in
a normal fashion, the annual flows of the balance-of-payments accounts with the stock estimates of the international capital position of
the United States, as proposed in Table 2 below.

(6) The broad scheme which I propose in my first table would
pave the way for such a reconciliation and integration by including in
the capital accounts reinvested earnings and other adjustments now
left out of the *Survey's* balance-of-payments tables. I am well aware
of the lags in the availability of the necessary estimates, and would
therefore be quite prepared to accept instead highly provisional
estimates based on extrapolation from past experience until better
information can be substituted for them. This would, after all, be far
less misleading—both for analysis and policy formation—than the
total exclusion of reinvested earnings which now distorts our balance-
of-payments accounts. Such a reform would be particularly relevant
in view of our present-day problems and of current discussions relating to this very issue.

(7) Time and space limitations preclude further discussion of the
rearrangements proposed in Table 1 below. Let me merely mention the
substitution of an "Official Settlements" account for the present
"Over-all Balance" account. The difference between the two concepts
is that the first would exclude foreign *private* dollar holdings and
retain only *official* and *international* holdings (at least those of the
IMF) as deductions from our gross reserves. (New subscriptions to
the IMF capital, or other additional commitments to the Fund, should
on the other hand be added to our reserve assets, thus obviating the
unnecessary footnotes and distortions of actual gold and dollar flows
resorted to so far on such occasions). . . .

The merits of the new concept of "Official Settlements" may be
listed briefly as follows:

(a) It is directly operational, reflecting our official monetary settlements, and highlighting the role of the dollar as a reserve currency
under present gold-exchange standard arrangements.

(b) It would conform to the legal practice which makes official, but not private, dollar claims directly convertible into gold at our Treasury. Although private dollar claims may also trigger such conversions whenever (or rather after) they have been purchased by foreign central banks and thus become "official" rather than "private" holdings, so also do the dollar holdings of our own citizens; I would not suggest that the distinction between "foreign" and "resident" dollar holdings is irrelevant, but I regard the concept of net official settlements and international reserves proposed here as at least coequal in importance with the current concept of "over-all balance," which I would retain in a separate table.

(c) Finally, private dollar holdings typically fluctuate in a manner entirely different from official dollar holdings, and under very different stimuli and types of restraints; I would for this reason group them instead with other "open-market" capital transactions, as suggested by Walter R. Gardner.

The remainder of this article presented, in summary form and with explanatory comments, five basic tables designed to highlight different aspects of our balance-of-payments transactions:

(1) The first centered on the "current account" balance and its financing by (a) capital flows other than reserve movements and (b) official reserve settlements;[1]

(2) The second integrated the annual *flows* of the balance of payments (including reinvested earnings and revaluation accounts) with the end-of-year *stock* estimates of our international investment position (including gold), and highlighted the distinction between the evolution of our "net reserve position" and that of our other international assets and liabilities;

(3) The third emphasized Walter R. Gardner's concept of the "basic balance" on current account, official capital, and direct investment, and the growing role of other, so-called "open market," capital flows on the "official settlements" balance;

(4) The fourth tried to assess the impact of our military and foreign aid programs as a stimulus to exports, on the one hand, and on our dollar disbursements on the other;

(5) The fifth was designed to bring out as rapidly as possible after the end of each month an integrated presentation of the most important estimates available with only a few weeks' delay. It retained

1. See an updated version on pp. 74–75 of *The Evolution of the International Monetary System: Historical Reappraisal and Future Perspectives* (Princeton, 1964).

the traditional concept of "over-all balance" and showed it as the sum of: (a) our balance on merchandise trade; (b) partial estimates of invisible transactions, on current and capital account, available sufficiently quickly not to delay publication (such as, e.g. most of the major transactions on official account); (c) other invisible transactions, calculated as a residual item.

I stressed, in conclusion, the importance which I attached to such a comprehensive integration of all available sources of estimates relevant to the analysis of the balance of payments, but now dispersed among different series of the *Survey,* the *Federal Reserve Bulletin,* the *Treasury Bulletin,* etc., often with different definitions and little attempt at feasible reconciliation. Such integration would not only dispel unnecessary confusion and misunderstandings, but would also promote further attempts at closing or removing existing gaps, duplication, and inconsistencies in available statistics. It might even shake some other agencies into reviewing outdated forms of presentation of their own international statistics. There are far worse offenders in this area than the Balance of Payments Division of Commerce, which should, on the contrary, be congratulated for its constant and successful efforts to improve its collection and presentation of data indispensable for an intelligent handling of a problem so new and so vital to us at this juncture.

Chapter II: The End of the Dollar Gap: 1952–58

ECONOMISTS do not change their minds easily. They continued to seek explanations and remedies for a "chronic," "permanent," "structural" dollar shortage, long after our country had moved from large surpluses in its over-all balance of payments in the early postwar years to substantial and continuous deficits and reserve losses.

My resignation as Alternate U.S. Representative on the Managing Board of the European Payments Union (EPU), in the summer of 1951, was partly due to continual disagreements with my American colleagues over their refusal to countenance the gradual hardening of EPU settlement rules called for, in my opinion, by the disappearance of an over-all dollar gap in Europe, and the consequent feasibility of faster progress toward the restoration of currency convertibility. Upon my return to the United States, I found most academic, as well as governmental, economists still firmly wed to the dollar shortage theory. The following extracts reflect the evolution of my own views in this respect over the years 1952–58.

1. TWO ACADEMIC DEBATES AT PRINCETON

A. DECEMBER 1952

A conference of academic economists and governmental experts gathered in Princeton in December 1952, under the sponsorship of the Center of International Studies, to discuss the foreign economic policy of the United States on the eve of the transfer of power from a Democratic to a Republican Administration. Their debates were most lucidly summarized by Professor Klaus Knorr in a report entitled *Strengthening the World Economy* (Center of International Studies, Princeton University, February 1953).

Mr. Knorr undoubtedly reflected the prevailing opinion of economists at the time when stressing, at the outset of his report, that "assessment of the problems faced by the American foreign economic policy begins with the persistence of international financial disequilibrium in general and of the dollar gap in particular." (p. 3)

The following extracts from my own interventions struck, however, a somewhat different note.[1]

---

1. Mr. Knorr's able condensation vastly improved the style and contents of what I remember as far more verbose and rambling improvisations.

(1) The prevalent pessimism about European viability finds little basis in the analysis of balance-of-payments data.

First of all, the European deficit on current account has declined steadily since 1947 by $1 billion to $2 billion a year. From about $7 billion in 1947, it had fallen to approximately $270 million in the first six months of 1952, and all indications point to an actual surplus on current account for the second half of that year.

This trend toward readjustment was obscured by a temporary relapse in 1951, due to a totally abnormal constellation of import and export prices. Raw material prices had shot suddenly upward after the outbreak of hostilities in Korea, with a much slower rise of manufacturing prices. But the 1951 volume of European exports and imports, if calculated at *any* postwar price level except that of 1951, would have left a current account balance ranging from minus half a billion dollars to plus one and a half billion dollars, depending on the year chosen. At 1938 prices, the surplus would have reached $3 billion instead of an actual deficit of $2.9 billion. In judging the fundamental position and current prospects of the European balance of payments, we certainly should not expect a return to 1938 price levels, but it would be equally absurd to project into the future the totally abnormal price pattern of 1951.

We should also note that most European countries—Belgium, Switzerland, Portugal, Germany, the Netherlands, and the three Scandinavian countries—have progressed toward large surpluses in their current transactions. . . . The United Kingdom itself has run a current account surplus in every single year since the end of 1947, except in 1951, and is again in surplus in 1952.

On current account, therefore, we should no longer speak of a "European" deficit, but of localized deficits of a few countries explainable by obvious and localized factors, rather than by a general lack of viability on the part of Europe as a whole.

The so-called European dollar gap is no longer the product of European deficits on current account, but of the attempt of Europe to finance the deficits of its associated overseas areas. In the six years 1947–52, this financing has amounted to from four to five billion dollars. The post-1951 readjustment of Europe's terms of trade has probably brought back into equilibrium or near-equilibrium Europe's balance on current account, but aggravated at the same time the position of the underdeveloped countries. The restoration of currency convertibility in Europe may be in sight, if (1) the overseas countries restore their own equilibrium at the cost of some slowdown in their recent rate of economic development, or (2) if this development is financed, directly or indirectly, by over-all creditor countries, i.e. primarily by U.S. capital. On the other hand, if Europe itself continues to assume the main burden of financing overseas development, it will only be able to do so through the perpetuation of trade and exchange controls and currency inconvertibility. This is, in my opinion, the kernel of the problem at this stage, and the only alternatives between which we can realistically choose and determine our policy. (pp. 4–5)

(2) The spectacular expansion of European exports to 158 per cent of their 1938 volume cannot be regarded as unsatisfactory and does not suggest any serious lack of competitiveness in European prices. The main problem is not the failure of Europe to export, but its inability to convert its export earnings into dollars. Too large a portion of Europe's exports are financed by capital exports, payment agreements, amortization of debts or sterling balances, etc. The solutions cannot be found in the field of trade alone, as long as little or nothing is done to restore a multilateral system of international settlements.[2] (p. 8)

(3) *Mr. Triffin expressed his skepticism about some extreme forms of the dollar gap theory, and particularly about the view that the differential rate of productivity growth in Western Europe and in the United States can only be met by ever-increasing controls and discrimination:*

This is hardly a new problem. Such differences were probably greater among European countries themselves during the course of the Industrial Revolution than they are today between the United States and most Western European countries. They did not prevent them from maintaining not only convertibility, but even fixed exchange rates, among themselves for more than a century. I wonder what would have happened to France or Germany if they had then adopted a "sterling gap" theory, and insulated themselves from British exports of manufactures and equipment.

I would be the last to deny that growing economic rigidities would interfere today with the smooth working of the nineteenth-century methods of adjustment. I doubt, however, whether the only methods left to replace them are those of quantitative restrictions and dis-

2. See (4) below.

crimination. If the trend toward differential increases in productivity is a persistent one, such solutions would lead to *ever-increasing* discrimination, and involve in the end absurdly high sacrifices in terms of a rational allocation of resources that would certainly outweigh the advantages claimed by such policies with respect to the maintenance of employment and terms of trade. The latter arguments are far more relevant to the deflationary problem of the 1930s than they are to postwar conditions, characterized by full or overfull employment and inflationary pressures. As for terms of trade, they have deteriorated *most* for the countries which depended most on quantitative restrictions and exchange controls. This should not be surprising, as such *external* techniques of defense are usually accompanied by *domestic* policies of price controls, subsidies, and rationing designed to lower costs artificially, and to prevent domestic demand from competing for exportable products. Such policies may well have deteriorated a country's terms of trade to an even worse extent than alternative policies of domestic disinflation and exchange readjustments. One of the main handicaps of British exporters, for instance, and one of the main advantages of Belgian exporters in international trade lies in the differences of delivery dates between the two countries. This reflects different price policies which strengthen enormously Belgium's terms of trade as compared to Britain's. While other factors also played a considerable role in these differences, it may at least be doubted whether reliance on quantitative controls actually succeeded in improving the terms of trade, and whether they were really needed to avoid large-scale unemployment, or added fuel, instead, to existing inflationary pressures. Without proposing in any way an impossible resurrection of nineteenth-century techniques of adjustment, one may well question the wisdom of resurrecting the techniques of the 1930s to fight the very different problems of the 1950s. (pp. 16–17)

(4) We are much closer today to international agreement on the problem of convertibility than we were, let us say, two years ago. The interventions of the European representatives at the Mexico City conference of the IMF, the last annual report of the OEEC, and the discussions of the Commonwealth Conference in London all mark a profound disillusion with the immediate postwar policies of exchange control and bilateralism, and a new willingness to envisage a return to currency convertibility as a proximate and realistic objective of national and international policy.

We are, however, still confronted with two basically different approaches to this objective, and I suspect that much of the forthcoming negotiation of the problem this spring will revolve around this very issue, which divides sharply the most ardent proponents of convertibility, both in academic and in governmental circles.

The first, and indeed traditional, approach is that of unilateral convertibility. Each country should set its own economy in order, adjust its exchange rate—or maybe adopt a floating exchange rate—and then restore convertibility all by itself, without waiting for any similar commitment by its trade partners. The United Kingdom reluctantly followed the latter—but maybe not the first—part of this prescription in 1947, with the results that we know. A similar "dash for freedom" has been strongly advocated recently in U.K. and U.S. financial circles.

This seems to me to ignore some fundamental changes which have taken place in the last thirty years in the monetary techniques and in the economic philosophy of the major trading nations. By trading exclusively on a gold or dollar basis, the United Kingdom would become in fact a member of the dollar area, and expose itself to the same restrictions and discrimination now applied by other countries in trading with the United States. Indeed, these countries would be sorely tempted to solve their own dollar problem on Britain's back, by earning dollars from her. The United Kingdom would want to protect herself against such raids on her, by keeping the right to retaliate in kind and impose discriminatory restrictions of her own. This is probably one of the reasons why the discussion in responsible circles was very much confined to convertibility of the pound for "nonresidents." This kind of convertibility might easily lead back to the full-fledged bilateralism of the pre-EPU years, each country trying to improve its *bilateral* position vis-à-vis the convertible currency, and the United Kingdom trying to cut down its bilateral deficits with those countries which did not "willingly" retain their sterling earnings but converted them in fact into dollars.

Even a return to the traditional type of *unilateral* convertibility decisions by each country would not be devoid of similar dangers. Any country which ran again into balance-of-payments difficulties might, as in the past, suspend its own convertibility *unilaterally,* and try to extract credit and trade concessions from its bilateral creditors, while still obtaining gold payments for its bilateral surpluses with other convertible countries. Any such step, however, by a major country would put in jeopardy its own creditors who depended themselves on the settlement of their surpluses with that country for the settlement of their deficits with other countries. Inconvertibility is a highly contagious disease, requiring special measures to avoid its spread from country to country.

The second approach is through mutual, collectively organized, convertibility commitments. This approach now suffers greatly from the obvious failure of the IMF, which tried to implement it in the first postwar years. When the reasons for this failure are analyzed, however, one finds that one of them, at least, lies precisely in the absence of any such collective approach in the Fund's machinery itself. The Fund undertook individual, isolated, salvage operations designed to finance a member's deficit, but never accepted any responsibility for the maintenance of a collective system of currency transferability or convertibility. This was left as an obligation resting on each member country in isolation, but not on the Fund as such. Article VIII of the Fund Agreement, which embodied this obligation of members, was moreover subject to a wide range of exceptions and, more important, was kept under total abeyance by the untrammelled right of every country, recognized under Article XIV, to restrict and discriminate as it saw fit for the duration of a so-called postwar transition period. Full bilateralism blossomed, under cover of Article XIV, with restrictions and discrimination by the stronger as well as by weaker countries, and against the weaker currencies as well as against the hard or scarce currencies.

It has long seemed to me that the primary, even though not the only, task of an international monetary institution like the Fund is to organize the transferability of currencies on as broad a basis as possible. Bilateralism is the inevitable consequence of a system under which no country can mobilize its bilateral earnings on its debtors in order to settle its bilateral deficits with its creditors. The operations of the Fund should, in the first instance, concentrate on such arbitrage transactions rather than on deficit financing.

It is of course true that if the Fund implemented this proposal, its currency holdings would experience sharp movements in the following direction: (a) in the case of countries in approximate equilibrium, sales and purchases of their currency by the Fund would more or less balance; (b) the currency of extreme creditors, however, would be predominantly purchased from the Fund, tending to deplete and exhaust its holdings; (c) the currency of extreme debtors would be predominantly sold to the Fund, tending to exhaust such countries' quotas in the Fund.

The first case would, of course, cause no concern to the Fund, while insuring full currency transferability and multilateralism over a wide area, including a growing number of Fund members.

The other two cases would reflect the most fundamental disequilibria in the present trade and payments pattern, and give the Fund an ideal wedge to compel such extreme creditors or debtors to discuss with the Fund desirable readjustment policies—whether in the field of international credit and investment, or trade liberalization, or exchange revaluation, or domestic policies, etc. In the absence of agreement on such policies, the currency of the persistent creditor would be declared "scarce," and the currency of the persistent debtor declared in "surplus." The Fund would suspend thereupon its sales of the scarce currency and its purchases of the surplus currency, but would continue its normal operations in all other currencies. This quarantine of extreme debtors and creditors would put the problem in its true light and concentrate attention on the basic question at issue.

The dollar gap is a case in point. It is an obvious commonplace that the dollar shortage must necessarily be accompanied by *over-all* deficits—and not just dollar deficits—somewhere. The over-all surplus of the United States—or any other country—must be matched by the over-all deficits of some other countries. If these over-all debtors do not deserve financing, they should not be allowed to get it by bilateral bargaining or through the Fund. If, on the contrary, financial cushioning is desirable, as was certainly often the case in the postwar period, either as an alternative or as an adjunct to basic readjustment policies, it should be made available in multilateral form by the over-all creditor countries. The policies actually followed often fostered bilateral financing by weak countries under trade and payment agreements, because they concentrated each country's attention on the solution of its "dollar" deficit rather than of its "over-all" deficit. The dollar problem can indeed be solved by either method, but the first will end in bilaterally enforced equilibrium and inconvertibility, while a multilateral pattern of trade and payments can be restored only through the readjustment of over-all deficit and surplus positions.

The new policies which I advocate for the Fund are not a jump into the unknown. They have in fact been implemented, and fairly successfully implemented on the whole, by OEEC and EPU. The regional character of this experiment is at the same time its major weakness and its main source of strength. A close link between EPU and the Fund could easily eliminate the first without destroying the latter. This would require some reforms in both organizations, not so much in their legal statutes, but much more in their interpretation of these statutes and in the policies which they are made to serve. There is little doubt that such an approach to the problem of convertibility would rally today a very broad area of agreement among the countries of the free world. I am also convinced that it would provide the collective institutional framework which could be dispensed with in the nineteenth century, but which is indispensable to the survival of convertibility in the world of today. (pp. 21–25)

(5) [Many participants, however, objected to regional clearing arrangements, describing them as mere "gimmicks," diverting attention from "true solutions" to the "basic problems." By rendering prevailing maladjustments easier to bear, they might prevent the free world from facing and tackling the basic issues. I argued as follows against this point of view.]

Basic problems are rarely solved overnight, and I particularly doubt that any negotiation or policy readjustments now in prospect will suddenly solve and eliminate the dollar shortage problem. I reject, however, the defeatist conclusion that as long as those basic problems are not solved, there is no use in doing anything at all to adjust ourselves to existing disequilibria in the best possible manner. The transition period of the IMF has already lasted for more than the five years initially envisaged. If you cannot have full convertibility now, full bilateralism is not necessarily the only alternative left, as EPU has shown.

Call it a gimmick, if you want, say that it detracts attention from the basic problem, and that that problem is not simply a monetary one. All that is true, but the fact that a better monetary arrangement is no panacea still does not mean that you can live without any monetary arrangement—or gimmick—whatsoever, or that an absurd monetary arrangement, which needlessly reinforces bilateralism and discrimination, is then preferable to a monetary arrangement which preserves the maximum of transferability and multilateralism compatible with the underlying trade and economic pattern. (pp. 30–31)

And coming back to gimmicks, I have always insisted on this: the problem is to know in what general direction we want to move, and then to find out what the next steps are which are feasible now. We should not attempt to predict to the last detail what our tenth step will be two, three, or five years from now, because the exact nature of these final arrangements will depend a great deal on the successes and failures we have met in approaching them. We must keep our plans sufficiently broad and flexible to adjust them continuously in the light of experience.

I have always found that you will make greater and faster progress toward your ultimate goal if you first devote your efforts to bringing concrete solutions to the operational problems of the day, choosing among the various alternative solutions to such problems those which fit at the same time the general directions in which you want to go. Final fulfillment of your ultimate objective may then be reached very largely by the mere cumulative addition of those unspectacular solutions for which governments and public opinion are prepared. The EPU, for instance, has made far more progress toward international monetary integration than the Fund. And yet, the powers of the Fund —the surrender of sovereignty—are enormous *on paper,* but the members of the Fund have not wanted to use them, and the Executive Board of the Fund, therefore, never found a working majority to vote on them. If we build up an intricate mechanism much in advance of the time when it can be practically put to use, we run a great risk of finding it rusty, obsolete, and unusable by the time we are ready to put it into gear.

I am very much in sympathy with the empirical and pragmatic approach to our problem, as long as it is allied to bold and imaginative thinking and does not reflect merely inertia and cowardice. Let me add also that the absence of a realistic concern for the present often means that our most ambitious blueprints may often turn out to be either impossible daydreaming, or an unimaginative longing for the dead past. (pp. 44–45)

B. FEBRUARY 1954

The Dollar Gap. Even as late as January 1954, the Randall Commission reported to President Eisenhower and the Congress that:

> There is . . . a concealed dollar gap of some $2 billion to $3 billion annually, which would be increased if there were a change in the economic situation, such as a recession here or a deterioration in Western Europe's terms of trade. . . . Surveying the

postwar experience as a whole, the Commission believes . . .
that much remains to be done to achieve a dependable international balance. . . . This report . . . is primarily concerned
with the steps that this country can take toward solving the
world's dollar problem. . . .[1]

The economists who gathered at Princeton two weeks later, at the
invitation of Klaus Knorr, to appraise the Randall Report "had divided
opinions on the nature and persistence of the dollar gap. Some . . .
believed that there were fundamental forces at work making for a
persistent tendency toward a dollar shortage." They "seemed to support, in broad outlines at least, the Randall Report in its statements
about the causes of the dollar problem, [while] Mr. *Triffin* criticized it
for being in part unfounded in fact and unduly pessimistic in conclusion." [2] The conferees agreed, in the end, that "the latent dollar
deficiency is smaller than most people—including the Randall Commission—seem to believe," but there still "did appear to emerge consensus on the following propositions: . . . The dollar gap still
exists. . . ." [3]

Alternative Paths to Convertibility. The conferees also debated at
length the Randall Commission's misgivings about any unilateral
"dash" for convertibility by the United Kingdom, especially if confined
to external sterling convertibility by nonresidents, and maintained only
through trade restrictions on residents and/or a gradual depreciation
of the pound. "There was widespread support at the Princeton conference of the Randall Commission's view that currency convertibility
should not be pressed at the price of a general tightening of quantitative import restrictions and that efforts to diminish the use of both
instruments of control should go hand in hand." The group, however,
"was divided on the *desirability* of the regional approach" which I
had emphasized in my comments.[4]

1. *Report to the President and the Congress,* Commission on Foreign Economic
Policy (Washington, D.C., January 23, 1954).
2. *A Critique of the Randall Commission Report on United States Economic
Policy,* prepared by Klaus Knorr and Gardner Patterson on the basis of a Conference held at Princeton University, February 4–5, 1954 (International Finance
Section and Center of International Studies, Princeton University, 1954), p. 10.
3. *Ibid.,* p. 12
4. *Ibid.,* pp. 48 and 50. The distinction which I drew between convertibility and
free trade and my proposals for a fundamental revision of EPU rules, in the light of
the disappearance of the dollar shortage and in conjunction with the restoration of
convertibility by the United Kingdom (pp. 48–53), are discussed more fully in

The Adequacy of International Reserves. I should also, in all candor, mention my comments at the meeting on the adequacy of international reserves. I developed the view that "with the exception of the sterling area, which is of course a very important exception, . . . the current distribution of gold and dollar reserves among the various countries of the world is probably more adequate in relation to needs than it has been in many years. . . ." [5] I qualified this optimistic statement with a remark about the disturbing role often played, ever since 1914, by capital movements—in contrast to former days—but showed no awareness yet of the problems which I was to stress a few years later, i.e. the haphazardness and vulnerability of an international *gold-exchange* standard, crucially dependent for its performance on both persistent deficits of the reserve-currency countries and continued, unquestioned confidence in such currencies.[6]

2. THE INTERNATIONAL IMPACT OF A UNITED STATES RECESSION

The first break in the official U.S. views on the dollar shortage problem was to appear, three months later, in a Government paper on *The International Impact of a U.S. Recession*. The letdown in U.S. economic activity in the second half of 1953 had caused considerable anxiety, here and abroad, about this problem. Various studies—notably in OEEC and in Britain—concluded that any substantial recession in the United States would reactivate a latent dollar shortage, temporarily masked in recent years by a number of "abnormal" factors, such as large foreign aid programs and military expenditures by this country, etc.

The Council of Economic Advisers thus appointed in December 1953 an interagency Study Group to investigate the problem, and asked me to serve as chairman.[1] The report which we submitted to the Council on May 5, 1954, opened with the following "Summary."

(1) We have tried to estimate quantitatively the direct impact on foreign countries' gold and dollar transactions of a hypothetical decline in the United States GNP to $315 billion in 1955, i.e. a decline

---

Europe and the Money Muddle and in other parts of this volume (particularly Chapter VI, Section 1, pp. 206–15 and Chapter XI, Section 3, pp. 449–77.

5. *Ibid.,* p. 58.

6. See Part Two, below, pp. 259–63, 347–50 and *passim.*

1. The contribution of Walther Lederer to the work of the Group should be singled out for its thoroughness and foresight.

of 14 per cent in dollar terms (about 10 per cent in real terms under our price assumptions) below the record level of activity attained in the first half of 1953.

Such an hypothesis is totally unrelated to current expectations and forecasts, and is chosen only as a fair approximation to the most pessimistic estimates which might reasonably be taken into consideration in shaping governmental antirecession policies, here and abroad.

(2) A recession of this magnitude would be expected to bring about a decline of approximately $3 billion in U.S. civilian expenditures abroad on current account. One third of this decline would be made up, however, by an independent increase in planned U.S. economic grants and military disbursements, and another third by the decreased cost to foreigners of the present volume of U.S. exports of goods and services as a result of the estimated decline in U.S. prices.

The consequent net deterioration of $1 billion in the gold and dollar transactions of foreign countries would not result in a worldwide dollar shortage, but would merely reduce their gold and dollar accumulation from more than two and a half billion dollars in 1953 to about one and a half billion dollars in 1955.

(3) Foreign countries' imports from the United States and from one another would, however, also be affected by the assumed recession. The curtailment of U.S. purchases would automatically tend to reduce economic activity, prices, and import levels abroad. This automatic contractive impact could be magnified and spread from each country to the others, as has been the most usual case in past recessions, by U.S. and foreign policies of deflation, devaluation, or trade restrictions. It could, on the other hand, be moderated and localized if the countries best able to do so fought the depression through policies of economic expansion, domestically, and trade liberalization, externally.

(4) Increased emphasis on full employment and economic development throughout the world should be expected to stimulate domestic expansionary policies to fight the recession. Such policies are likely to be initiated earlier, adopted more generally, and implemented more vigorously than was the case in past recessions.

On the other hand, trade and exchange techniques of restriction, discrimination, and bilateralism have also become familiar instruments of policy and are likely to be resorted to on a much wider scale than previously, both in order to avoid a depletion of monetary reserves and to boost domestic levels of activity and employment in exporting and import-competing industries.

(5) Stabilization loans to countries with inadequate reserves in relation to depression-induced deficits in their balance of payments can play an important part in permitting or facilitating both the adoption of domestic expansionary policies and the avoidance of external restrictions and discrimination. Stabilization assistance might be made conditional upon such policy commitments on the part of the beneficiary countries.

On the other hand, the role of stabilization loans as an antirecession weapon has probably been overemphasized:

(a) With the main exception of the sterling area, current reserve levels are far more adequate than is generally realized, and are expected to rise further, even in the event of a U.S. recession, particularly in Western Europe. This will limit actual *needs* for stabilization assistance to a relatively small number of Latin American and Far Eastern countries whose economies are heavily dependent on raw material exports to the United States market. (A stabilization loan to the United Kingdom would, however, play an important role in hastening a return to sterling convertibility.)

(b) The countries most adversely hit directly by a United States recession, primarily underdeveloped countries, are likely to be also the least able to implement effective compensatory policies because of their inability to provide alternative domestic outlets for the resources previously employed in the production of export goods. This will limit greatly the *effective use* of stabilization loans for compensatory policies in the underdeveloped countries.

(c) Finally, disagreements between prospective lenders and borrowers about the soundness of the latter's monetary, fiscal, and economic policies, and therefore about their credit worthiness and repayment capacity, are also likely to limit the practical *feasibility* of stabilization assistance to some of the countries most vulnerable to a U.S. recession.

Stabilization loans must therefore be combined with, and supplemented by, other and more direct methods to avoid the spiraling of the depression through the contagion of trade and exchange restrictions, discrimination, and bilateralism.

(6) National, regional, and world-wide agreements and policies all have a useful part to play in moderating the international spread and

aggravation of a recession. No one of them can be relied upon to achieve fully its objectives. Ideally, the recession should be avoided at its very source. Insofar as this is not done, declines in income and import levels will spread the depression to other trading partners. These, in turn, should attempt to preserve economic activity and employment through expansionary policies. World-wide agreements may help them in this task by providing stabilization loans and preventing a generalized recourse to mutually destructive trade and exchange restrictions or competitive devaluations. Such agreements, however, will also be limited in scope and limited in their effectiveness. Some nations, such as the underdeveloped countries, will be unable to take effective expansionary action. Others may be unwilling to do so because of rigid fiscal policies or excessive concern for their export trade. In the latter cases, mutual trade and credit commitments may avoid the more serious adverse repercussions of the lack of universal expansionary national policies. But in practice these may prove negotiable and enforceable only on a narrower geographical basis among closely interdependent countries. Such agreements, even though unavoidably discriminatory in some respects, may still provide a useful barrier against full-fledged bilateralism. World-wide agencies should strive to limit to a minimum the discriminatory features involved, but should welcome their positive contribution to the avoidance of unnecessary bilateralism and deflationary policies.

In brief, the defense against the international spread of depressions should be a defense in depth rather than a gamble on any single "Maginot Line." The shortcomings of any one set of policies or agreements should be anticipated in advance, and partially met by other, even though less satisfactory, lines of defense, designed to minimize the consequences of the breaches of earlier and more ambitious defense lines.

(7) Current and prospective levels of U.S. expenditures abroad during the next few years, and of gold and dollar accumulation by foreign countries—particularly in Western Europe—provide a most favorable environment for bolder progress toward trade liberalization and currency convertibility, and for the development of regional and international agreements designed to consolidate such progress against the impact of future international recessions.

U.S. leadership in this field has been greatly handicapped for several years by internal conflicts of views and policies, particularly about the nature of the institutional arrangements necessary to the functioning of a multilateral trade and currency system. A clarification of these issues and an affirmative definition of official U.S. policy are urgently required to exploit the opportunity presented by the present favorable economic and political climate for successful negotiation of the international agreements involved.

We had stressed, of course, that the hypothesis of such a deep recession was "totally unrelated to current expectations and forecasts" (paragraph (1) above). In the event, economic activity recovered sharply in the latter part of 1954 and throughout most of 1955, and foreign countries' gold and dollar earnings reached more than $1.9 billion in 1955, rather than the $1.5 billion anticipated by us in the event of a deep recession. Such a modest difference might suggest that we had been wildly overoptimistic, and that a deep recession would have had a much greater impact on foreign countries' earnings. This $1.9 billion gold and dollar accumulation, however, was achieved in spite of a steep increase of more than 16 per cent (about $2 billion) in foreign countries' imports volume, which we had assumed to remain unchanged in the event of a deep recession.

Combined increases in foreign countries' imports and gold and dollar holdings thus amounted to nearly $4 billion, as U.S. economic activity recovered sharply in 1955, as against the global $1.5 billion improvement assumed by our group in the event of a deep recession.

Later years would witness a further amplification of the same trends. Foreign countries' imports from the United States were to rise phenomenally, from $12.3 billion in 1953 and $14.3 billion in 1955 to $25.8 billion in 1964, and their gold and dollar holdings from $23.3 billion in 1953 and $27.1 billion in 1955 to more than $52 billion (including $1.4 billion of the so-called "Roosa bonds") by the end of 1964.

The era of the "dollar gap" had been succeeded indeed by that of the "dollar glut."

The dragon was, however, hard to kill. The most brilliant volume of the impenitent dollar shortage theorists appeared as late as 1957, under the pen of Sir Donald MacDougall. My review of it, which follows, accented for the first time the international liquidity issue which was soon to replace the dollar gap or dollar shortage problem as the main topic of the international monetary debate, among both academic economists and government experts.

3. THE DOLLAR AND INTERNATIONAL LIQUIDITY PROBLEM RECONSIDERED

Sir Donald's book could not have come out at a more opportune moment. The Suez crisis, the European boom, the incipient United States recession, the French exchange crisis, etc., have brought back new fears of a dollar shortage and lent again some plausibility to a thesis which had long dominated postwar thinking and policies, but appeared increasingly doomed by events at the time this investigation was launched two or three years ago. The comprehensiveness of the data assembled in these 622 pages and their imaginative handling for theoretical diagnosis and policy prescription will certainly make of this volume a basic reference work for all discussions of the dollar problem in governmental as well as in academic circles.

Before launching on a rather critical discussion of Sir Donald's arguments, I should give the reader full and fair warning of my own prejudices on the matter. Having recently brought out a highly optimistic volume on the same subject, I risk being unduly unsympathetic to the moderate pessimism which pervades Sir Donald's discussion. Let me emphasize at the same time, however, that our very different appraisals of the dollar problem have still led us to very similar conclusions on matters of policy.

I

The first part of the book will be most disappointing to the dollar shortage theorists. Sir Donald shows indeed very little enthusiasm for their stock-in-trade arguments:

(1) He does not think that future American recessions are likely to be deep enough to create *by themselves* serious difficulties to the rest of the world. (They will do so, however, if they are superimposed upon a long-run adverse trend in the rest of the world's balance with the United States, or if other countries fail to build up substantial dollar surpluses and reserves in good years.)

(2) He dismisses with a shrug of the shoulders and a reference to the theory of comparative costs the "crude argument" that America's higher productivity makes all her prices lower than those elsewhere, thus making it impossible for other countries to preserve equilibrium

---

A comment on Sir Donald MacDougall, *The World Dollar Problem* (London, Macmillan, 1957), published in *Kyklos* (1958), pp. 405–18.

in their dollar transactions without recourse to trade restrictions and discrimination.

(3) He finds, moreover, little statistical evidence for the widely held thesis that the proportionate growth of productivity is normally much higher in the United States than in the rest of the world. He also disagrees with the view that United States productivity must rise more quickly because of the higher levels of savings made possible by higher levels of per capita income.

(4) He does not feel that balance-of-payments difficulties are likely to arise from the mere fact that other countries maintain higher levels of employment than the United States. He is by no means convinced, anyway, that most other countries will generally aim at higher standards of "full employment" than the United States. The United Kingdom may well prove to be in a minority in this respect.

(5) The only traditional argument retained by Sir Donald is that wages and prices may have a tendency to rise somewhat faster in the rest of the world than in the United States. He estimates, however, that hourly earnings in American manufacturing are more likely to rise, in the future, by something like 4 or 5 per cent a year rather than the 2½ per cent rate typical of normal years before the New Deal. If manufacturing productivity in the United Kingdom, for example, rose 1 per cent per annum less than in the United States, British wages could rise by 3 to 4 per cent annually without forcing prices out of line with those in the United States. Judging by postwar performance, Sir Donald considers that to limit wage increases to such a figure might not be an easy task and estimates that prices outside the United States might well tend to rise, on the average, at an annual rate 1 or 2 per cent faster than in the United States.

It becomes particularly difficult, at this juncture, to disentangle Sir Donald's factual predictions from his policy prescriptions. He would presumably agree that the "best" policy would be for the rest of the world to keep wage and price increases within the bounds fixed by comparative productivity growth in the United States and abroad—assumed elsewhere to be roughly comparable—and by the additional excess of United States wage rises over United States productivity increases. Although these limits could by no stretch of the imagination be considered deflationary, but would on the contrary still leave room for modest but persistent price rises, the task might not be "easy," and he therefore predicts the likelihood of a dollar shortage. The second-best solutions which he later develops to deal with such a shortage, however, may not prove any "easier" in the long run. Unless the United States is willing to finance indefinitely a rate of foreign inflation higher than her own, they boil down, in practice, to an alternation of temporary restrictions and discrimination on dollar trade with recurrent devaluations of the nondollar currencies. Repeated recourse to these measures, as a systematic policy for an indefinite future, could hardly fail to stimulate a permanent flight from other currencies into goods and dollars and to add immensely to the difficulties of the many countries whose social discipline and administrative effectiveness are too weak to cope successfully with the enforcement of comprehensive controls over trade and exchange transactions.

One might even wonder whether the most crucial consequences of a persistent rate of inflation higher than that predicted for the United States would not derive from its broad impact on the functioning of a money economy rather than from—and even irrespective of—its probable impact on the world's dollar balance.

II

Sir Donald's fears of a dollar shortage are primarily based, however, on a totally different line of argument, i.e. on statistical projections rather than theoretical reasoning.[1] The second half of the book projects into 1975 statistical estimates of the United States balance-of-payments receipts and expenditures under the following assumptions:

(a) maintenance of full employment—without overemployment—and of price and exchange-rate stability throughout the world, together with a doubling of production and with parallel rates of population increases in the United States and in the rest of the world; and

(b) absence of discriminatory restrictions against United States goods, or all-round trade restrictions designed to correct a dollar deficit, and of special financial assistance by the United States designed to finance it.

These assumptions, especially the latter, are admittedly unrealistic and will indeed be shown to be incompatible with the "structural" projections built on them by Sir Donald. The projections are not intended as "forecasts," but as indications of the balance-of-payments

---

1. It may be noted, in passing, that the discrepancy anticipated in the first part of the book between price trends in the United States and in the rest of the world also belongs to the realm of projections, or even of mere extrapolations of recent—and relatively short-run—statistical observations.

pressures which would be likely to arise under such circumstances and would force the rest of the world into undesired—and undesirable—policies of either deflation, or devaluation, or trade and exchange restrictions, in order to balance its accounts with the United States. Sir Donald presents "optimistic" and "pessimistic" conclusions, ranging from a $4 billion improvement to a $16 billion deterioration in the rest of the world's balance of payments with the United States, as compared with the yearly average of 1953–55.

The exercise is fascinating, and abounds with original and imaginative suggestions, theoretical and statistical, about the way in which such a problem can be handled. I cannot but confess my admiration for Sir Donald's courage and ingenuity, together with my utter inability to follow him on this road, either to agree or to disagree with him. The results of any investigation of this kind are inevitably determined by the author's intuition as to the relative significance of the innumerable factors at play and by his selection of a few of them as representative of *over-all* trends. How far into the future should we project current United States policies of agricultural subsidies and surplus disposal abroad? How long will United States imports of foreign cars continue to double from year to year? How shall we appraise the long-run price and production prospects of the fuel and raw materials needed by industry in the United States and elsewhere and the likely scope of their substitution by nuclear energy or new synthetic products?

Without entering into such speculations, let me merely list, very briefly, some of the main reasons for my skepticism before Sir Donald's projections:

(1) The "pessimistic" hypothesis from which his conclusions are derived combines extremely high estimates of United States exports of goods and services with disappointingly low estimates of total United States expenditures abroad. That this is unlikely—and indeed impossible beyond the limits imposed by previously accumulated gold and dollar reserves abroad—is readily conceded by the author, but does not infirm his argument that the inevitable equilibrium between dollar receipts and expenditures will force recourse to "undesirable" policies of deflation, devaluation, or restrictions in the world outside the United States. It does, on the other hand, stretch to the point of inplausibility the meaning of his "pessimistic" assumptions, as it assumes the ability and willingness of the United States to restrain its own domestic consumption and investment expenditures far below

its current production income. The pessimistic projection, for instance, of a $13 billion improvement in the United States trade balance combines an increase of $19 billion in exports with an increase of only $6 billion in imports. The latter increase would correspond to only 1.6 per cent of the assumed growth of gross national product, and compares with actual increases of 2.7 per cent over the period 1929–56, and 2.9 to 3.1 per cent in 1937–50, 1950–56, and 1937–56. The astonishingly low estimate of Sir Donald is based on the extrapolation of the long-term decline in the ratio of United States imports to gross national product over the period 1870–1955, which marked the transition of the United States from a relatively underdeveloped to a highly industrialized and diversified economy. Such an extrapolation appears difficult to justify, particularly in view of the near stability of this ratio in postwar years. It dropped indeed from 3.5 per cent in 1937 to a low of 2.5 per cent in 1947—when the rest of the world's exporting capacity was at an abnormally low ebb by reason of wartime destruction and postwar reconstruction needs—but recovered to 3.1 per cent in 1950 and has remained at about the same level ever since.

(2) This pessimistic appraisal of the rest of the world's exports to, and imports from, the United States is even more surprising when taken in conjunction with the assumption of a $50 billion increase in United States direct investments abroad, culminating in an annual rate of $5 billion a year in 1975. It assumes a dismally low impact of such investments on these countries' exporting capacity and on the substitutability and competitiveness with United States exports of the new production facilities stimulated by such investments.

(3) The entirety of the assumed deterioration of other countries' trade balance with the United States ($13 billion) is accounted for by the lopsided development of United States trade in manufactures, the deterioration in the food trade ($4 billion) being offset by an equal improvement in the raw materials' trade balance. United States exports of manufactures are supposed to increase by $14 billion, while her imports of manufactures increase only by $1 billion. While these figures may appear less stunning when expressed in percentages of 1953–55 exports and imports, they are nevertheless hard to swallow. They assume an increase of 180 per cent of United States manufactures exports over twenty years, simultaneously with an increase of less than 60 per cent in United States manufactures imports. The first

grew by roughly 24 per cent in volume during the last five years
(1951–56)—i.e. approximately at the rate projected by Sir Donald
in his "optimistic" hypothesis, but far below that of his "pessimistic"
one—while the second rose by nearly 75 per cent which, projected
cumulatively over a twenty-year period, would yield an increase of 800
per cent as against 175 per cent in Sir Donald's "optimistic" hypothesis and less than 60 per cent in his "pessimistic" hypothesis. In value
terms, United States manufactures imports increased indeed over these
five years by substantially more than Sir Donald's "pessimistic" hypothesis would have them grow over a twenty-year period.

PROJECTED PERCENTAGE INCREASES OF UNITED STATES TRADE IN MANUFACTURES
OVER TWENTY YEARS

	United States exports	United States imports
A. Extrapolation of actual 1951–56 rate of increase	+140	+840
B. MacDougall's projections:		
1. Pessimistic	+180	+ 60
2. Optimistic	+130	+175

This part of the analysis receives indeed a surprisingly cavalier treatment in less than five pages of a six-hundred-page volume, and is
handled nearly entirely through references to other writers' estimates.
The reason for this is not far to seek. "The very small share of imports in the total of United States manufactures means that the possibilities of expansion are large . . . [but] even if the increase were
relatively large and rapid, it would be comparatively unimportant in
dollar terms" (pp. 223–24). This reasoning is plausible in view of the
very low level of current United States imports of manufactures. It
is, however, reminiscent of that of the Egyptian Pharaoh who deemed
ridiculously modest the request of the inventor of the chess game that
he be paid one grain of wheat for the first square of the board, two
for the second, four for the third, and so on. A straight projection of
the 1951–56 rate of increase would yield, in twenty years, an expansion of more than $13 billion in United States imports of manufac-
tures. Needless to say, I would strenuously resist any invitation to
substitute any such estimate for those of Sir Donald, but I confess to
being equally unconvinced by the latter as by the first.

III

My doubts about Sir Donald's statistical projections still leave me, however, in substantial agreement with his very modest and reasonable conclusions. These are merely based on the view that the rest of the world would be unwise to predicate its policies on any confident expectation that it will continue to enjoy, over the long run, an *easy* balance of payments with the United States. If this is the gist of the book—and it is as far as its policy prescriptions are concerned—I am quite ready to concur without bothering to agree or disagree with all the theoretical and statistical paraphernalia in which it is enrobed. I am perfectly convinced that under modern institutional and political conditions, no country—not even the United States itself—can feel confident to retain at all times an "easy" balance of payments with any other country or with the world at large. Any country is always exposed to being swayed at any time by internal inflationary pressures, by foreign restrictions on its exports, by a wave of deflation abroad, etc. I also admit that the enormous weight of the United States in world trade and finance makes the rest of the world particularly vulnerable to any contraction of activity or any relapse into protectionist policies in that country. A dollar shortage, in this sense, is an ever present possibility which other countries must take into account in shaping up their own policies, both internal and external. This, I think, corresponds exactly to Sir Donald's conclusion: "The most general moral to be drawn from the analysis in this book is that governments, in framing their policies in various fields, should not overlook the distinct danger that, despite the favorable experience of recent years, a dollar problem will re-emerge in which every country is liable to be involved and which would have widespread economic and political repercussions" (p. 412).

This seems to me unexceptionable as long as it is not taken by other countries as a justification for policies which would themselves tend to resurrect a dollar shortage, nor as an invitation immediately to adjust their policies to a possible future dollar shortage while actually in the middle of a dollar plenty. Sir Donald would obviously agree with this qualification and his book is imbued throughout with a liberal outlook which brooks no sympathy for any systematic policy of permanent restrictions and discrimination against the United States, nor any illusion as to their long-run efficacy (see, e.g. pp. 388–389 and 394).

What should be done, then, to deal with a possible recurrence of the dollar shortage problem? "Reasonable" fiscal, monetary, *and* wage policies should be directed at maintaining "full employment without inflation, . . . but it may sometimes be better, if there is uncertainty about the future, to take a chance on the balance of payments, opt for a policy of growth, risk a dollar crisis, and be prepared, if necessary, to impose discriminatory import restrictions as a *temporary measure*" (p. 383; italics are mine).

Regional arrangements—such as the sterling area, the OEEC Code of Liberalization and European Payments Union, the Common Market and Free Trade Areas—should be maintained and developed in order "to prevent the reduction of nondollar trade *in a crisis* [italics mine] and facilitate the organization of temporary discrimination against the United States (and perhaps other surplus countries) while avoiding a general relapse into bilateralism" (p. 408). "It is possible that, in addition, some of the nondollar countries outside the EPU area should be associated in some way with the OEEC" (p. 411). Reforms of world-wide arrangements, such as the IMF and GATT, should facilitate—but not slow down—the adoption of such policies and aim particularly at eliciting the approval, or at least the understanding, of the United States and Canada "for any temporary discrimination against them, so that the risk of unfavourable reactions on their own policies may be minimized " (p. 411).

Other standard recommendations endorsed by Sir Donald include an acceleration of the rate of innovation outside the United States, greater stabilization of raw materials prices, increased United States Government aid to underdeveloped countries, stimulation of United States private investment abroad, but particularly a large-scale liberalization of her commercial policy and the maintenance of high and stable levels of employment. He sensibly remarks, however, that these recommendations are not new and that "other countries can hardly press for greater stability in the United States economy—the panacea most commonly proposed at the end of the war—for America's subsequent record has been good. This alone rules out any argument for permanent discrimination against her to reduce dependence on what used to be regarded as a widely fluctuating economy" (p. 413).

Another favorite panacea—"flexible exchange rates"—receives rather rough handling at the hand of Sir Donald. Nor is he very sanguine as to the short-run effects of exchange rate adjustments in general, although he regards them as more effective in the long run and as a necessity—even though a most regrettable one—in the face

of a substantial adverse trend: ". . . it should not be delayed once it
has been clearly recognized as such; for the longer it is put off the
longer it will be before a balance can be restored—if only for a time
—and the restrictions relaxed and, it is to be hoped, removed" (p.
406).

This whole analysis of exchange-rate adjustments, in Chapters xiv,
xv, and xvii and the corresponding Appendices, is both illuminating
and highly sensible. My only reservation relates to the rather pessimistic conclusion drawn from the experience of currency devaluations in
the early 1930s. It is true that the reduction in the United States'
surplus on current account was much larger in the years 1929–31
than in 1932 or later years. Balance had already been restored by
1931, at a sharply reduced level of trade, by drastic deflation and restrictions abroad, but persisted until the devaluation of the dollar in
1934, in spite of a stiff rise in United States tariffs and of the gradual
shift from deflationary to reflationary policies abroad, particularly in
the sterling area. Moreover, the trade deficit of the United Kingdom
fell from $1,800 million in 1931 to $870 million in 1933 and that of
Sweden, Norway, and Denmark from $220 million to $30 million,
while that of the six major nondevaluing countries (Germany, France,
Italy, Belgium, the Netherlands and Switzerland) rose from $270 to
$670 million. The effectiveness of exchange readjustments, more-
over, is likely to be more limited in an environment of depression and
restrictions—as in the early 1930s—than in that of generally high
and stable levels of economic activity which is assumed to underlie
this study of the dollar problem.

IV

I have left for special consideration the suggestions of Sir Donald
directed at increasing international liquidity to a more adequate level,
as I see in this problem the real crux of the world dollar problem. Sir
Donald himself comes close to this conclusion when he notes (on pp.
51ff.) that gold and dollar reserves outside the United States are
ample in comparison with imports from the United States alone. The
inadequacy of reserves in a crisis arises largely from the fact that gold
and dollar reserves outside the United States cannot be pooled to deal
with temporary deficits of the rest of the world with the United States,
but must be largely earmarked for the financing of temporary dis-

equilibria among these other countries themselves. How could we explain otherwise the often noted tendency for the rest of the world to catch pneumonia when exposed to a mere American sneeze? After all, exports to the United States account for less than 15 per cent of the rest of the world's total exports and for no more than 3 or 4 per cent of its total gross national product. A recession of even 25 per cent in United States imports would thus affect directly less than 1 per cent of other countries' gross national product. The devastating impact of United States recessions on other countries' economic activity must, therefore, be explained very largely by their indirect effects, and linked with the mutually defeating national policies and adaptations abroad whose main effect is to reduce the 85 per cent of these countries' total trade which takes place with one another, as well as of the 15 per cent of their total exports sold in the United States market. The mechanics of this contagion, however, are not confined to those arising from actual drains on monetary reserves, and this is one more reason to doubt that an increase in the price of gold—half-heartedly advocated by Sir Donald—would constitute the most logical answer to the problem. Broader arrangements for mutual assistance and coordination of policies among closely interdependent countries are certainly called for to protect their economic stability and stimulate their economic growth. This is the path successfully marked out by OEEC in postwar Europe and which is now widening into the arrangements for a European Economic Community and the proposed European Free Trade Area.

The provision of an adequate level of international liquidity is only one aspect of this broader problem, but I agree with Sir Donald that it is a crucial one. World trade and production have been rising, in recent years, at a rate of about 6 per cent a year in volume terms. A parallel growth of international monetary reserves would require annual additions of about $3.5 billion today, but of $5 billion in six years, and more than $7 billion in twelve years, if this rhythm of expansion were maintained. Current gold production contributes today only a small fraction ($500 to $600 million) of these amounts to the actual growth of world reserves. Any revaluation of the price of gold would have to be very stiff indeed to meet the problem and would promise only a temporary breathing spell rather than a permanent solution to the question of international liquidity.

The problem is not new. It was solved in the past—but always temporarily—by the gradual concentration of international reserves in the banking system first, and then in the central banks, by the growth of sterling and dollar balances as a component of international reserves alongside gold, and by the rise of the dollar price of gold in 1934. Although it is difficult to segregate the international liquidity problem as such from the lack of liquidity arising for individual countries from their own national policies, there is little doubt that it has contributed also at other times to premature or excessive recourses to currency devaluation, trade and exchange restrictions, bilateral agreements, and the spread of world deflation.

The satisfactory growth of reserves outside the United States in recent years has been fed primarily (for three fourths of the total) by a vast redistribution of United States excess reserves. Of the $13.6 billion rise in the rest of the world's gold and dollar holdings which took place between the end of 1949 and June 1956—on the eve of the Suez crisis—$10 billion was derived from the fall in the United States net reserves (gold *minus* dollar balances) and only $3.6 billion from new gold production.

The United States in turn was able to weather such a sharp fall in its net reserves both because these were largely in excess of its needs in 1949 and because most of the losses were financed by the growth of foreign dollar balances ($8 billion) and only a small portion by net gold sales ($2 billion). Yet the situation was one that caused considerable concern in some United States circles about the implications of a persistent piling up of short-term dollar liabilities abroad at a rate of $1 billion to $2 billion a year. The drain of United States reserves has been arrested, and even reversed, in the last year, but this leaves again without solution the long-run problem of providing the world with a supply of monetary reserves adjustable to the expansion of the international economy.

Dollar, sterling, or even other currency balances may, for a time, usefully supplement in this respect the insufficient resources derivable from gold production. They can do so, however, only at the cost of making the international monetary system increasingly dependent on the maintenance of confidence in these currencies and of balanced growth in the economy of the center countries. All economists concurred in the 1930s in denouncing the extreme vulnerability of such a system to arbitrary shifts from one currency into another or into gold by reserve holders, and to accidental disturbances or policy changes in the center countries. Their warnings were dramatically verified in the early 1930s by the collapse of the gold-exchange standard. More than 80 per cent of the dollar-sterling components of international monetary reserves outside the sterling area were wiped out within a few years' span, shifting the world back, temporarily and to that extent, from the gold-exchange standard to a gold bullion standard. There is no doubt that the deflationary pressures entailed by such a drastic contraction of international liquidity played their part in aggravating the world depression and in accelerating the spread of currency devaluations and of trade and exchange restrictions in the 1930s.

The ways to increase international liquidity suggested by Sir Donald all point in the right direction, but do not deal sufficiently explicitly and forcefully with this basic problem. Outside of a change in the price of gold, he recommends: (1) that each country attempt to rebuild reserves through less ambitious developmental policies in good times and through delays in the lifting of restrictions temporarily imposed during a crisis; (2) United States' stabilization loans to individual countries; (3) a greater use of sterling as monetary reserves, and a corresponding pooling of gold and dollars in London; and (4) a further expansion and more flexible use of international credit facilities, such as those available from the International Monetary Fund and the European Payments Union.

The last of these suggestions comes very close to the one which I would myself consider as the most logical, flexible, and fruitful attack on the problem, i.e. a true *internationalization* of the foreign exchange component of international monetary reserves. The creation of an international clearing mechanism would both offer the surplus countries a safe medium for the investment of their reserves, and provide the means of expanding international liquidity at a rate consonant with a maximum rate of noninflationary growth, through stabilization loans to countries encountering balance-of-payments deficits, but whose over-all policies are consistent with long-run stability and viability. Such a suggestion will probably be deemed overambitious, premature and, in any case, unnegotiable at this stage on a world-wide scale. It might, however, help provide some missing links in the ultimate shaping-up of the institutional payments framework of the European Economic Community. It might also inspire the overhauling of the European Payments Union widely regarded today as indispensable to the satisfactory functioning of the proposed European Free Trade Area.[2]

2. For a further discussion of these issues, see *Europe and the Money Muddle*, pp. 296–301 and 285–86.

V

In spite of its length, this review can still give only a most imperfect idea of the richness, soundness, and originality of *The World Dollar Problem*. Some of the 47 appendices which fill no less than 188 of its pages will prove as valuable as the text discussion itself in casting new light on such problems as the inadequacy of world reserves, the price elasticity of United States exports and imports, the secondary effects of a dollar shortage, the interrelationships between money incomes, prices, productivity, and the balance of payments, etc.

I must finally apologize for having stressed unduly in this review minor points of disagreement with Sir Donald rather than the vast area of agreement on fundamentals which exists between us. Even where I disagreed, I was always immensely stimulated by his arguments. May I express the earnest hope that many readers will wish to participate in the same happy experience, and to reach their own conclusions on the basis of a first-hand study of this most interesting contribution to one of the most controversial issues of present-day international economic policies.

Summary

Paradoxically enough, the first part of *The World Dollar Problem* is essentially devoted to a brilliant refutation of most of the traditional arguments of the dollar shortage school which dominated, for so long, postwar thinking and policies. The main reason to expect, nevertheless, a long-run trend toward a shortage of dollars is that it will not be "easy" for other countries to keep annual wage increases within the 4 or 5 per cent limit anticipated in the United States. One may doubt, however, whether the basic policies later advocated by Sir Donald—an alternation of dollar restrictions and currency devaluation in the rest of the world—would prove any "easier" in the long run when full account is taken of the probable incidence of such policies on the minimum degree of confidence required for a satisfactory functioning of monetary systems and capital markets throughout the world.

The second part of the book is likely to retain far greater attention and to be widely quoted in future discussions of the dollar problem. A most skilful and ingenious handling of a vast array of statistical data and estimates underlies "optimistic" and "pessimistic" projections ranging from an improvement of $4 billion to a deterioration of $16 billion in the over-all balance of the world with the United States in

1975, as compared to the 1935–55 average. The bulk of the projected deterioration ($13 billion out of $16 billion), however, is ascribed to the lopsided development expected in the United States trade in manufactures, and particularly to an extraordinarily low estimate of United States manufactures imports. The increase projected for these over a *twenty-five* year period is indeed substantially below that actually experienced in the *five* years 1951–56. For United States trade as a whole, moreover, the pessimistic hypothesis of Sir Donald would imply an abnormally low ratio of imports to gross national product, far below that maintained since 1950, and even inferior to that of 1947 when the world's exporting capacity was at an abnormally low ebb as a consequence of wartime destruction and postwar reconstruction needs.

One might well disagree with Sir Donald's arguments, however, and still agree with his very modest conclusions, i.e. that it would be unwise for the nondollar world to predicate its policies on any confident expectation that it will continue to enjoy, over the long run, an "easy" balance of payments with the United States. The maintenance of balance-of-payments equilibrium is likely to raise problems at times for any country. The problem may assume a new dimension, however, and involve world-wide difficulties if institutional monetary arrangements are such as to prevent an adaptation of international liquidity to the normal growth of world trade and production. Sir Donald touches on this issue at various points, but does not give it the key role which it deserves both in the explanation of the world dollar problem and in the solutions which might realistically be developed in order to meet it.

Chapter III: Issues in United States
Foreign Trade Policy: 1957 and 1962

THE FIRST of the following two papers was written at the request of the Honorable Hale Boggs, Chairman of the Subcommittee on Foreign Trade Policy of the House of Representatives' Committee, under the title *Foreign Trade Policy* (Washington, D.C., 1957, pp. 483–89). It is specifically directed at the questions raised by Representative Boggs and which were still inspired by the problems of the previous world-wide dollar shortage. The inapplicability of some of its arguments to the dollar-glut period that followed is only alluded to very briefly in the last paragraph of Section 5.

The second paper of this chapter reproduces a speech delivered at the annual meeting of the American Society of International Law, on April 28, 1962, and subsequently published in its *Proceedings* (1962, pp. 139–49).

1. NOTES ON TRADE LIBERALIZATION AND REGIONALISM

(1) There can be no doubt that the widespread use of quantitative trade and exchange restrictions abroad in postwar years has often thwarted and nullified—or even more than nullified—the tariff concessions granted to the United States under reciprocal trade agreements. It is highly tempting to conclude from this observation that we should extend our tariff bargaining process to apply to nontariff trade restrictions and indeed to other forms of impediment to international trade.

(2) Before accepting this conclusion, however, we must be clear as to: (a) the real impact of foreign restrictions and other foreign and United States policies upon our exports; (b) the actual leverage of international negotiations and agreements upon a country's policy.

(3) Paradoxical as it may sound, foreign restrictions and discrimination against United States goods have a far lesser impact on our over-all export levels than is usually imagined. The level of our merchandise and services exports is, indeed, primarily determined by our own dollar expenditures abroad and cannot exceed for long the amount of such expenditures except for relatively small additions

financed by foreign gold sales or disinvestment of previously accumulated dollar assets. Such gold sales and disinvestments financed a
modest 7 per cent of our exports in the early postwar years (1946–49).
In the following 7 years, foreign countries retained about 9 per cent of
their current dollar earnings in order to reconstitute their depleted
gold and dollar assets. The bulk of this, however, took the form of a
net inflow of foreign capital to the United States ($10 billion), and
only $2 billion was withdrawn in the form of gold purchases from the
United States, as compared to the $4.5 billion of foreign gold sales to
the United States in the years 1946–49.

Over the whole eleven-year period 1946–56, our exports of goods
and services ($196 billion) absorbed 97 per cent of the expenditures
abroad ($204 billion), the difference ($8 billion) being added to
foreign countries' gold and dollar assets.

(4) Our over-all export levels had never before been so high, indeed, as they were maintained throughout the postwar years, in spite
of generalized restrictions and discrimination abroad against all transactions involving payment in scarce dollars. Our merchandise exports
have progressed, in dollar terms, from a postwar low of 3 times their
1938 level in 1946 to nearly 6 times in 1956. In volume terms—correcting for price increases—they have ranged from a low of 1.75
times prewar in 1950 to more than $2\frac{1}{2}$ times prewar in 1956.

In the years 1946–49, however, 37 per cent of our exports of goods
and services were financed by our foreign-aid programs. This percentage declined gradually in the following years down to an almost stable
level of 10 per cent in 1954–56. This is very nearly compensated by
the current increase in gold and dollar assets of foreign countries taken
as a group, 98 per cent of our exports being currently financed in fact
by foreign sales to the United States and net foreign investments of
private United States capital. Some Asian countries, however, remain
heavily dependent on our aid—for obvious reasons related to military
and political conditions—while continental Western Europe—with
the main exception of France—was, at least until recently, adding far
more to its gold and dollar assets than the tapering-off amounts of
economic aid still directed to that area.

Broadly speaking, high and rapidly growing—by more than 31
per cent over the last 2 years—export levels are now financed overwhelmingly—up to 98 per cent in 1954–56—by our expanding levels
of imports (91 per cent) and of private capital exports (7 per cent).

(5) One may well ask, therefore, what is the actual significance to

FINANCING OF UNITED STATES EXPORTS OF GOODS AND SERVICES, 1946–56

	In billions of United States dollars						In per cent of United States exports				
	United States expenditures abroad				Foreign gold sales and dollar disinvestment	United States exports of goods and services[3]	United States expenditures				Foreign gold sales and dollar disinvestment
	Current account[1]	Private capital[2]	Economic aid and Government capital	Total			Current account	Private capital	Foreign aid	Total	
	(a)	(b)	(c)	(d = a + b + c)	(e)	(f = d + e)	(g)	(h)	(i)	(j = g + h + i)	(k = 100 − j)
Years:											
1946	7.6	0.2	5.3	13.1	1.6	14.7	52	1	36	89	11
1947	8.9	.1	8.9	17.8	1.9	19.7	45	1	45	90	10
1948	10.9	−.1	4.8	15.6	1.2	16.8	65	−1	29	93	7
1949	10.3	−.2	5.6	15.7	.1	15.8	65	−1	35	100	1
1950	12.6	1.2	3.6	17.6	−3.7	13.9	91	9	26	127	−27
1951	15.6	.6	3.2	19.3	−.5	18.8	83	3	17	103	−3
1952	16.3	.6	2.4	19.3	−1.2	18.1	90	3	13	107	−7
1953	17.3	.1	2.0	19.4	−2.3	17.1	101	3	12	114	−13
1954	16.7	1.4	1.6	19.7	−1.8	17.9	93	8	9	110	−10
1955	18.5	.7	2.2	21.4	−1.5	19.9	93	4	11	107	−7
1956	20.4	2.1	2.3	24.9	−1.5	23.4	88	9	10	107	−6
Yearly average:											
1946–49	9.4	—	6.2	15.6	1.2	16.8	56	—	37	93	7
1950–53	15.5	.6	2.8	18.9	−1.9	17.0	91	4	17	112	−12
1954–56	18.6	1.4	2.0	22.0	−1.6	20.4	91	7	10	108	−8

1. Imports of goods and services, private remittances, pensions, and other transfers.
2. Including errors and omissions.
3. Excluding military transfers under aid programs.
SOURCE: *Survey of Current Business.*

us of foreign restrictions and discrimination against dollar goods. Several aspects of the problem should be considered in turn.

(a) Foreign restrictions often constitute, to a large extent, a mere offset to abnormal levels of import demand arising from current or past inflationary trends which the country would be unable to finance in any case. The lifting of restrictions would not expand imports, as it would require the simultaneous adoption of other alternative measures —anti-inflationary policies or exchange-rate readjustments—necessary to keep the country's foreign expenditures within the limits of the foreign exchange available for their financing. To this extent, foreign restrictions do not substantially affect the over-all level of American exports.[1] Their main impact upon us derives from the fact that foreign countries may then influence the composition of their imports in accordance with some administrative criteria of essentiality rather than allow this composition to be determined by market forces in a free economy. This may, of course, introduce some disturbances in our markets, benefiting some of our producers at the expense of others.

(b) Foreign restrictions, however, tend to decrease—although as already indicated to a much lesser extent than usually imagined—the over-all level of our exports.

The main reason for this is that the resort to restrictions—in preference to alternative policies of balance-of-payments readjustment—does nothing to correct the depressive effect of internal inflation upon the country's exports, and may, in addition, discourage capital imports and stimulate capital flight. Moreover, the substitution of domestic production for prohibited imports—or of costlier imports for cheaper imports under discriminatory restrictions—adds an upward push to domestic costs and reduces further the country's competitiveness in export markets. These disadvantages, however, bear far more heavily on the restricting country itself than on its trade partners and competitors. The persistent trend for its exports to decline under such policies sets a limit to the practicable use of restrictions. An excessive postponement of more fundamental measures of readjustment would, in the end, dry up exports far below the level necessary for the financing of imports essential to the maintenance of production and economic activity.

Foreign restrictions will also reduce our export levels insofar as

1. The current high level of French restrictions, for instance, has not prevented a 50 per cent increase in French imports from the United States in 1956 over 1955.

they are used in order to accumulate or reconstitute foreign countries' gold and dollar reserves. While some international agreements might legitimately aim at preventing abuses in this respect, this has never been a serious problem for us in the past, and would be unlikely to become one in the future if it were not for the total inadequacy of current levels of gold production to supply a satisfactory rate of growth of international reserves. This difficulty has been met in recent years by an unprecedented growth of our short-term dollar liabilities, at a rate of $1 billion to $2 billion a year. These dollar balances have exactly doubled over the last 7 years, passing from $8.2 billion at the end of 1949 to $16.4 billion at the end of 1956. A full discussion of this problem and of its implications, however, far transcends the scope of this paper and bears only a distant relation to the question of foreign restrictions which we are here discussing.

(6) The maintenance of high and growing export levels by the United States depends primarily:

(a) On our own willingness to import goods and services from abroad, and to export American capital either through foreign aid or through private loans and investments. Our willingness to import is, by far, the most significant factor in the present and highly satisfactory state of our export activities. It is, in turn, dependent on the preservation of high and growing levels of activity at home and on the continuation and expansion of liberal trading policies by this country.

(b) On the ability of foreign countries to provide high and growing levels of exports at competitive prices and to attract United States capital. This, in turn, is closely related to the maintenance of high levels of activity and growth abroad, but is also dependent on the pursuit of noninflationary policies or on the willingness to offset the failure of such policies through exchange-rate readjustments rather than through restrictions and discrimination. Our concern about other countries' restrictions is, therefore, justified, but should not make us forget the far greater impact of our own policies upon our export levels.

(7) Our own influence upon other countries' policies, through bilateral or international negotiations and agreements, should be based on a realistic appraisal of the desirable and feasible objectives and techniques of such agreements.

The objectives of international cooperation among independent countries should minimize, rather than maximize, at the outset the interference of international organizations with the national process of policy-making, and respect a clear ordering of priorities inspired by both the urgency and feasibility of such interference. It would, for instance, be utopian at this stage to expect international commitments and jurisdiction to be able to preclude any and all failings of national leadership in a democratic society to preserve and enforce ideal norms of internal economic and monetary policy. Devaluation or restrictions may, therefore, become inescapable at times to correct persistent deficits in a country's balance of payments. International agreements should beware of any procedural rules and regulations that would discourage the first of these alternatives at the cost of encouraging the latter.

A total ban on all restrictions—tantamount to free trade—would, however, also be utopian at this stage. The most urgent and feasible goal of international economic policy in this respect should be the elimination of bilateralism in world trade and payments. This would restore the essential characteristic of nineteenth-century convertibility, i.e. the maintenance of competition among exporters in all third markets, and would not be incompatible with a certain measure of protection to national producers within each country's own boundaries.

The second goal of international trade and monetary agreements should be the gradual relaxation of existing restrictions, including quantitative trade and exchange restrictions as well as customs duties. These various techniques of restriction are indeed largely interchangeable, and any piecemeal attack might be useless, or worse than useless, if the ban on some restrictions merely leads to a tightening of the others. We may well have put the cart before the horse when negotiating painfully the lowering and consolidation of tariff duties before obtaining parallel commitments with respect to trade and exchange controls.

In correcting this error and broadening the scope of trade negotiations to encompass all forms of restrictions, we should, however, keep in mind the impossibility of rigidly enforcing comprehensive commitments of this sort, as long as all participating countries are not fully agreed on the alternative measures that will be taken to cushion, finance, or correct serious disequilibria in their balance of payments. The remedies to be applied will almost unavoidably have to vary with the circumstances of each case, and may have to take into account political and administrative factors limiting the actual acceptability and feasibility of strictly rational economic solutions to the problem. These considerations make it well-nigh impossible to agree in advance on clearly defined rules and commitments, and indispensable to preserve a wide latitude for negotiations on escape clauses, stabilization credits, readjustment programs, and so forth. They also suggest that the mutual understanding and effective cooperation that can be elicited in such negotiations is likely to vary in inverse ratio to the number and heterogeneity of the participating countries in the agreement. Regional agreements among highly interdependent countries can, for this reason, define far more ambitious aims and require a correspondingly greater degree of mutual cooperation and assistance than world-wide agreements among a vast number of countries having little or no familiarity with one another's problems and policies.

(8) Regional and world-wide forms of cooperation each have a role to play in harmonizing national policy decisions in an economically interdependent world. These roles should be viewed as complementary and mutually supporting rather than as antagonistic to one another.

Various arguments, however, have been marshaled up against this conclusion.

The first is that regional agreements promote discrimination against nonmember countries. This danger is certainly real, and has led a number of economists to prefer nondiscriminatory restrictions to discriminatory liberalization, and to oppose all kinds of preferential agreements up to and including partial customs unions. A full discussion of these arguments would far exceed the scope of this paper. Let me merely observe here that the liberalization of intra-European trade and payments, while admittedly discriminatory at the outset, was instrumental in reintroducing competitive forces over a vast trading area. The consequent improvement of Europe's competitive position has been followed by a gradual extension to nonmembers of the liberalization measures initially accepted only on a reciprocal basis among the participating countries themselves.[2] Intra-OEEC exports and imports nearly doubled in value between 1950 and 1956, but OEEC imports from the rest of the world also increased by more than 60 per cent in spite of the near elimination of foreign aid financing, and OEEC exports rose by 78 per cent to the rest of the world, and 130 per cent to the dollar area. This spectacular recovery of exports should do much to dispel earlier fears that European integration would develop into a sheltered, soft-currency area increasingly isolated from world trade,

2. Germany, for instance, has just announced the expansion of its dollar liberalization measures to more than 93 per cent of its imports from the United States.

and particularly from United States competition. The last two years have witnessed a particularly rapid rate of progress in the removal of European dollar restrictions and discrimination and an expansion of more than 60 per cent in imports from the United States.

A second argument against regional integration is the danger of a division of the world into a few, powerful autarkic blocs, even more threatening than national protectionism to world trade, prosperity, and peace. This fear, however, ignores the fact that there exist few, if any, areas outside Western Europe where intraregional trade would constitute more than a minor fraction of the participating countries' total trade. The EPU and the dollar area together account for nearly 85 per cent of total world trade and absorb nearly 75 per cent of other countries' exports. The maintenance of multilateral trade and payments rules by the EPU and dollar area countries would leave little or no room or incentives for bilateralism and discrimination by others. It would indeed resurrect an international trade and payments system comparable in many ways to that of the nineteenth-century gold standard, which rested essentially on the maintenance of convertibility policies by the United States and the European countries—together with their monetary areas—but did not preclude varying degrees of trade restriction and protectionism by individual countries, and of exchange-rate instability in Latin America and Asia. Similar limitations on any ideal pattern of international economic institutions are likely to remain with us as long as political and administrative difficulties make it utopian to contemplate a merger of national sovereignties into an effective world government.

Finally, we cannot forget the political implications of European economic integration for the strengthening of the free world. A weak and divided Europe would constitute a permanent danger to world peace—as it has in the past—and present a most tempting prey for outside aggression. A united Europe, on the other hand, would eliminate the traditional sources of past world wars and become a formidable deterrent to potential attacks against the West.

(9) The above considerations justify, in my opinion, the constant support given by the United States since the war to the movement toward economic and political integration in Europe. Some of the immediate and long-run implications of European integration, however, are yet to be taken into account if our own policies are to become fully consistent in this respect, and to derive from it the maximum possible benefits for us as well as for others.

First of all, we must accept less grudgingly than we have done in the past the unavoidable discriminatory features of the preferential trade or payments arrangements inseparable from such integration. These have never been questioned in relation to a full merger of political sovereignties, nor generally objected to in relation to a complete customs union. They have, on the other hand, elicited considerable opposition in many quarters against partial or progressive steps unaccompanied by firm commitments to a relatively rapid and total abolition of all trade barriers among the participating countries. We should realize that excessive rigidity in this respect might be tantamount to blocking altogether feasible progress toward highly desirable and fundamental objectives.

On the other hand, we and other countries will have a vital interest in stimulating the adoption by an integrated Europe of as liberal trading policies as possible toward the outside world. Our bargaining power in trade negotiations and our cooperation in world-wide agreements such as the IMF, GATT, and the proposed OTC should be directed toward that aim. As already suggested above, however, our ambitions in this respect will have to be tailored to the feasibility of the policy commitments and harmonization indispensable for the practical acceptability and implementation of the sacrifices of sovereignty implicit in such agreements.

Close cooperation within the Atlantic Alliance among Europe, the United States, and Canada would create a most promising framework for economic stability and growth throughout the world. This should be a prime objective of American economic policy, but is likely to depend far more on a permanent willingness to search and negotiate solutions for the new problems that may emerge than on rigid, once-and-for-all commitments implying a much larger renunciation of sovereignty than either we or our partners would be willing to contemplate at this time. This is particularly true in our case, as specific preferential agreements with Europe alone might risk embittering our relations with other parts of the free world essential to our security and to the fulfilment of the broader objectives of our international policy.

2. THE TRADE EXPANSION ACT OF 1962

Professors of economics are particularly ill-equipped to deal with the momentous issues involved in the new trade program now before

Congress. For these issues are essentially political rather than economic. They are political in two ways:

(1) From the positive side, what is at stake is not a mere trade bargain, but a long overdue adaptation of outworn, narrowly nationalistic policy instruments and institutions to the most obvious requirements of rational policy-making in an interdependent world.

(2) From the negative side, the obstacles that have postponed for so long, and at such a disastrous cost, these indispensable adjustments are also political. They can be explained only by the resistance of vested interests, and by the confusion which these have been able to perpetuate in the mind of the public and of Congress between private interests and the national interest.

The Economics of the Problem

The economic issues involved are so clear, so obvious, as to require very little explanation indeed. What is at stake is a comparison between what the United States stands to gain from an expansion in our country's exports, on the one hand, and, on the other, what it could conceivably gain from a contraction of its imports. Our merchandise exports totaled last year $20 billion and our merchandise imports $14.5 billion, i.e. we sold abroad $4 of merchandise for every $3 that we bought. Over a long period, say the last ten years, we sold abroad $175 billion of goods and bought $138 billion, giving roughly the same ratio of $4 of exports for every $3 of imports and yielding us an export surplus of $37 billion.

Let us accept provisionally at its face value the protectionists' argument that imports are a loss, rather than a gain, for our economy; and let us act accordingly. By barring foreign imports altogether, the maximum amount which we would "gain" would be $15 billion. But we would, of course, stand to "lose" $20 billion of exports. Some of our firms would lose $4 of business for every $3 that other firms might conceivably gain thereby.

I say "conceivably," for as a matter of fact three fifths to two thirds of the goods we import are not produced at all in this country. They consist of raw materials unavailable here in the quantities needed to feed our industrial plants, of tropical agricultural goods, such as bananas, coffee, etc.; in brief, of merchandise which either could not be produced here at all, or could be produced only at prohibitive costs. If we discard the "gains" that might result from sacrificing these kinds of imports—and regard them as "losses" rather than "gains," as indeed we should—only one third of our present imports, i.e. about $5 billion, could be displaced so as to create more work and employment for our own industries. But even these $5 billion of goods could be produced here only at higher costs than we now pay for them abroad, and the doubtful "gain" achieved would certainly be far more than offset by the impact of such policies upon our own sales abroad. "Finished manufactures" are, on the whole, more easily displaceable by domestic production—here and elsewhere—than foodstuffs and raw materials. Acting on this principle, we could close our market to the $5 billion of finished manufactures which we imported from abroad in 1960; but, acting on the same principle, foreigners could close their own markets to the $10 billion of manufactures which we exported to them that year.

But it is now time to consider squarely the basic and most popular argument for protection, i.e. the fact that protection creates jobs for American workers. Surely; but if this argument were really valid, the industries that we should protect are those that would create *most* jobs, *most* employment. Let us then produce bananas and coffee in American greenhouses. This would create far more employment still than the protection of industries in which we could be nearly—if not quite —as efficient as foreigners.

The basic flaw in all these arguments is that our ultimate concern is with welfare, rather than with employment as such. We want employment, but we prefer to have it where it can be most productive rather than least productive. And it is clearly more productive in the export industries, which demonstrate their efficiency by outselling foreigners in their own market, in spite of the double handicap of transportation costs and foreign tariffs and restrictions, than in those industries in which foreigners can outsell us in our own market, in spite of the similar handicaps placed upon them by transportation costs and U.S. tariffs.

The real impact of our protective tariffs is not to create jobs. It is to shift jobs around, away from our most efficient industries and toward our least efficient ones. Tariffs subsidize the latter, but by penalizing the first in two ways. They increase their production costs beyond what they would be otherwise, and they prevent us from negotiating feasible reductions in foreign tariffs and restrictions against our exports.

We stand to gain far more from expanding our sales in a large and fast-growing world market ($118 billion last year) than from attempting to close our own market to goods which we can buy more cheaply abroad than we can produce at home. If the mere logic of the case, as I have tried to summarize it very briefly and inadequately, still leaves any lingering doubts in your mind, let us look at the facts themselves, and at the experience of the United States and other countries with protectionist and liberal trade policies.

The Historical Record

The United States. The greatest cut in our imports coincided, of course, with the worst depression and the most ferociously protective tariff ever experienced by this country. Our imports were slashed by more than two thirds between 1929 and 1932, but our exports fell in roughly the same proportion. In dollar amounts, our imports declined by $3.1 billion, but our loss of exports was $3.7 billion, i.e. $600 million greater.

We pursued, in the following years, and particularly after the Second World War, the opposite policy of trade expansion, and slashed our tariffs to one third, or less, of their Smoot-Hawley levels. Our imports expanded enormously, to a near-record level last year of $14.5 billion. But our exports rose even more, to $20 billion, leaving us a $5.5 billion surplus of exports over imports. Who can believe that such a surplus could be preserved—to say nothing of its chances for expansion—if we now abandoned the policies which brought it about, and reverted to the protectionist policies whose inefficacy has been so dramatically demonstrated in the past?

Western Europe. The most spectacular evidence in favor of liberal trading policies, however, is that of postwar Europe. The great depression and the Second World War had produced the most restrictive trading system imaginable. Tariffs faded into insignificance as compared with the direct trade and exchange control measures and bilateral agreements, which stifled trade in the early postwar years.

The major achievement of the Organization for European Economic Cooperation (OEEC) lay in the progressive dismantling of these so-called "quantitative" restrictions. At first, these liberalization measures were applied only to imports from other member countries, thus resulting in discrimination against other countries' exports. But the liberalization of trade over such a wide and highly competitive area could not fail to strengthen the European economy to the point where liberalization could be extended, relatively painlessly, to imports from third countries, and particularly the United States. Europe's problem, in fact, is no longer one of trade and balance-of-payments deficits, but of excessive competitiveness in world trade, and of embarrassing increases in its earnings of gold and dollars.

What is true of OEEC is also true of its individual member countries. The German and Italian so-called "miracles" were obviously helped, and not hampered, by the liberal importing policies followed by both countries. The most protectionist of the European countries—France —lagged far behind the others in its balance of payments until 1958, but recovered nearly overnight, when the European Economic Community finally induced it to discard the crutches which had so long hampered, rather than helped, its progress.

The fantastic success of OEEC cooperation and liberalization is one of the factors that prompted the creation of the European Economic Community, and the rapid success of the latter prompted in turn the creation of the European Free Trade Area and, more recently, the historic decision of Britain and other EFTA members to join the European Economic Community. It is these developments which now force us to reconsider our own trading relations with this most important portion of the Western world. Chairman Boggs expressed this forcefully during the Foreign Economic Policy Hearings of the Joint Economic Committee of Congress, last December. Addressing Secretary Ball, he said:

> You have touched on the realities. The Common Market, whether we like it or not—and I think we like it—is a going concern. It is there; it is not a theory any more. It exists. Insofar as the Six are concerned, it has proved phenomenally successful. They are growing at a rate far in excess of the United Kingdom, considerably in excess of the home rate; the amount of internal trade has increased at a pace nobody dreamed of. The so-called adjustment devices which were established have not been used because of the sheer prosperity which resulted in the area. There is apparently no unemployment; as a matter of fact, in some places there is, as I think you know, overemployment which I think we would like to experience in the United States. (p. 347)

The European Economic Community's internal trade increased by 73 per cent in the last three years alone and its average rate of economic growth is more than twice that of the United States. The experience is so conclusive and so persuasive that the industries which, only a few years ago, insisted on a slow transition period of 12 to 15 years for the complete removal of internal tariffs, are now clamoring for an acceleration of tariff reductions. This process of acceleration was in fact started a year ago, and it is now highly probable that complete freeing of trade will be reached on or before January 1966, four to seven years ahead of the schedule initially contemplated. I feel confident that a similar shift in industrial opinion will occur here, once we engage boldly on the path of a closer association with the Common Market. Indeed, the shift may have begun already.

The economic consequences of such a revolution are momentous indeed. Let us remember that a similar movement toward a large common market, free of restrictions, was at the origin of the two great success stories of the nineteenth century, that of Germany after the *Zollverein,* and that of our own United States of America. Does anybody here think that we would be better off or, even more simply, that we would have reached the position that we now occupy in the world, if trade among our own fifty States had to overcome artificial tariff barriers between them, making it more difficult and expensive to ship goods from Connecticut to Massachusetts, and vice versa?

But the main aspects of this movement toward European integration are not economic. They are political.

Political Implications

European integration was primarily political in its objectives, and is unavoidably political in its means and its consequences. The main purpose of the promoters of the European Economic Community was, and remains, to create a United States of Europe, ending once and for all the bloody wars that ravaged Europe in the past and which you hear more and more referred to today as "civil" wars. And there is little reason to doubt that this will indeed be the outcome of European economic integration. The economic union of today is paving the way to the political union of tomorrow, just as the *Zollverein* between the former German States paved the way for the political unification of Germany a century ago. Indeed economic integration could hardly survive a prolonged lag in political integration.

This is obvious, of course, in the realm of commercial policies, but it does extend far beyond commercial policy alone. Since there will now exist only one tariff around the countries of the Common Market, and one commercial policy governing their joint relations with the rest of the world, all decisions relating to such matters will have to be reached jointly among all the members. A country encountering balance-of-payments difficulties in its relations with the rest of the world will no longer be able to protect itself through independent tariff or trade restrictions. If its difficulties are temporary, it may need and receive financial assistance from the others. If difficulties arise from divergent rates of financial expansion among the member countries, some way will have to be found to remove these divergencies, and harmonize monetary and fiscal policies throughout the Community. Finally, the removal of tariff barriers will, of necessity, involve a growing harmonization of other measures having a powerful impact on the pattern of trade, such as the structure of taxation, social legislation, antitrust policy, agricultural policy, transportation policy, etc.

Indeed, all this is already contemplated in the Rome Treaty, and work has begun on all these fronts. A joint Executive has been set up, a joint Assembly, a joint Court of Justice. And, since January of this year, more and more decisions may be taken by a weighted majority of the members, in order to escape the paralysis inevitably associated with the old unanimity rule which traditionally governs relations among sovereign national states. It is these political implications, indeed, that explain the rearguard fight of Britain and other EFTA members against their inclusion in the Community. They have now come belatedly to realize that they have far more to gain than to lose by associating with it in one form or another.

As for the United States, we were the first to realize the enormous political benefits which a European union could entail for the survival of the free world, and our Congress has long expressed itself in favor of such a movement. This does not mean, however, that we should join the European Community as a full member, and transform it from the start into an Atlantic Community. This may some day become both desirable and feasible. It is neither at the moment. First of all, our farflung world responsibilities would create for us a worse problem in this respect than that created for Britain by its Commonwealth ties. Secondly, neither Congress nor political opinion in this country would be prepared to accept as of now the vast surrenders of national sovereignty involved in full participation. The only feasible path open to us at this stage lies in the two directions which the Kennedy Administration is following:

(1) The first is the approval of the Trade Expansion Act, enabling us to negotiate effectively with the Community for a progressive, but

extensive, lowering of trade barriers, not only against our own exports to them, but against the exports of the underdeveloped nations of the world as well.

(2) The second is the broader discussion and harmonization of the policies of the Atlantic world which are already taking place in the Organization for Economic Cooperation and Development (OECD). These concentrate largely today on the devising of joint policies for the acceleration of economic growth, for a fairer sharing of development financing overseas, for mutual assistance against balance-of-payments disruptions threatening the stability of the pound, of the dollar, and, by way of consequence, of the international monetary system itself.

The Western world continues, in this manner, the unending historical process of institutional adjustment to changing needs and conditions. We have now resumed, at long last, the same evolution which erased the medieval borders of duchies, counties, and principalities to merge them into the national states of modern times. National states— at least all but the largest ones—are as obsolete today as the duchies, counties, and principalities of yesteryear. They will be merged some day into a world community, but—barring a world cataclysm—the process is likely to be a gradual one:

(a) Gradual in time: looser forms of cooperation (as in OEEC yesterday, or OECD today) paving the way for closer and closer integration (such as in the European Economic Community).

(b) Gradual in space: the Benelux Union merging yesterday with France, Italy, and Germany into the present European Community, and the European Community being enlarged tomorrow by the accession of Britain and other Western European states; while the Organization for European Economic Cooperation itself has already been transformed into the Organization for Economic Cooperation and Development through the accession of the United States and Canada.

And lurking behind, to prod us to faster action toward ultimate world, rather than merely Atlantic, unity, there is, of course, the greatest political unifier of all: the threat of an atomic suicide of the human race.

Implications for Our Balance of Payments

The considerations developed above summarize, to my mind, the most persuasive and crucial arguments in favor of the Trade Expansion Act. I should, however, add a footnote on the relevance of the Act to the solution of our current balance-of-payments problem. The accompanying Table brings out some interesting points in this respect.

INTERNATIONAL GOLD AND DOLLAR FLOWS IN 1961
(in millions of U.S. dollars)

	United States	Rest of world		
		Total	Western Europe and Canada	Other
I. Recorded U.S. Transactions	**−1,801**	**1,801**	**− 753**	**2,554**
A. Nonmilitary current account[1]	6,954	−6,954	−3,509	−3,445
B. Foreign capital[1]	577	− 577	− 393	− 184
C. U.S. capital and military expenditures (net)[2]	−9,332	9,332	3,149	6,183
1. Military expenditures	*−2,550*	*2,550*	*1,555*	*995*
2. Economic aid	*−2,831*	*2,831*	*− 388*	*3,219*
3. Private U.S. capital[1]	*−3,951*	*3,951*	*1,982*	*1,969*
II. Foreign gold, errors and omissions, and multilateral transfers	**− 616**	**1,225**	**3,752**	**−2,527**
A. Foreign gold	x	609	829	− 220
B. Errors and omissions and multilateral transfers	− 616	616	2,923	−2,307
III. Over-all balance (I + II)	**−2,417[3]**	**3,026**	**2,999**	**27**
A. Gold	− 820[3]	1,429	1,583	− 154
B. U.S. official holdings of convertible currencies	116	− 116	− 116	
C. Foreign dollar balances	−1,712	1,712	1,532	180
1. Monetary authorities	*− 455*	*455*		
2. Other	*−1,257*	*1,257*		

1. Excluding reinvested earnings and other adjustments of U.S. capital ($1,611 million in 1960, of which $1,091 million in Western Europe and Canada, and $520 million elsewhere) and of foreign capital ($109 million in 1960, of which $130 million in Western Europe and Canada, and −$21 million elsewhere).

2. Excluding military grants ($1,765 million in 1960).

3. Excluding U.S. private gold absorption ($37 million).

SOURCES: Derived from the *Survey of Current Business* (March 1962) and the *Federal Reserve Bulletin* (March 1962) estimates.

The first, certainly, is that our difficulties can no longer be ascribed to a deterioration in our trade position. While there may have been considerable justification for concern in this respect in 1959, both our merchandise balance and our current account surplus in general left near record surpluses in 1961. Excluding military expenditures, our current account surplus with the world was close to $7 billion (to which should be added another $1.5 billion of unrepatriated investment earnings and—if one wishes—another $1.5 billion of military exports under grants, making all in all a total surplus of about $10 billion).[1]

The difference—of nearly $10 billion—between our $7 billion *surplus* on nonmilitary current account transactions and our $2.4 billion *deficit* on over-all account is, of course, due primarily to the huge levels of our military expenditures abroad ($2.5 billion), economic aid programs ($2.8 billion), and exports of private capital ($4 billion). Our private capital exports are indeed probably closer to $6 billion than to $4 billion, since the latter estimate leaves out of account the reinvestment of unrepatriated earnings and the portion of "errors and omissions" which may be due to unrecorded exports of U.S. capital.

I cannot, for my part, escape the conclusion that, in the immediate future at least, any significant improvement in our balance of payments will have to come primarily from other sources than a further improvement in our record high nonmilitary current account surplus of 1961. Some redistribution of our military and foreign aid burden between us and our Allies is clearly called for, as well as some reform of existing tax provisions discouraging the repatriation of foreign earnings of American subsidiaries abroad.

In any case, the improvement must also involve primarily our payments relations with Western Europe and other industrial countries rather than with the underdeveloped part of the world. The main reason for this is that our gold and dollar outflow is entirely with the first, rather than the second, of these two broad areas. You cannot shave an egg, and there is precious little gold and dollars to be retrieved from countries that do not, in fact, accumulate them to any significant extent. Any large cut in our aid to the underdeveloped countries would be very largely matched, willy nilly, by a decline in our net exports to them, unless they can find elsewhere, i.e. primarily in Europe, an alternative source of finance for their deficits.

---

1. These are rough estimates, based on an extrapolation of 1960 estimates of unrepatriated earnings and military exports, not yet available for 1961, and making a rough allowance for the partial overlap of our military expenditures abroad and our military deliveries under grants.

As shown on line III of the table, practically all of the world's accumulation of gold and dollars last year ($3 billion) was concentrated in Western Europe ($2.6 billion) and Canada ($0.4 billion). The sources of this *increase* are worth recording, especially in view of the enormous *deficit* ($3.9 billion) of this area as a whole with the United States on nonmilitary current account and through private capital exports to this country. The difference ($6.9 billion) may be distributed as follows:

(1) $3.1 billion from direct U.S. military expenditures and capital exports to the area itself;

(2) $3.8 billion from multilateral gold and dollar receipts from the rest of the world, financed themselves from:

(a) foreign gold production ($0.6 billion);

(b) errors and omissions in the U.S. balance of payments ($0.6 billion), reflecting probably in large part unrecorded capital exports from here;

(c) the excess ($2.6 billion) of our military expenditures, economic aid, and private capital exports to the underdeveloped world ($6.2 billion) over and above the latter's deficit with us on nonmilitary current account ($3.4 billion) and from capital exports to this country ($0.2 billion).

In brief, all but $0.6 billion of the $6.9 billion gap between Western Europe and Canada's deficits and their gold and dollar accumulation can be traced, directly or indirectly, to our own exports of private capital, military programs, and foreign aid expenditures.

Two broad lines of policy emerge from this analysis. The first, and most important, is to reduce our gold and dollar losses *to Europe,* by curtailing our *over-all* military expenditures, foreign aid, and private capital exports without unleashing thereby corresponding decreases in our current account surplus. The simplest way to achieve this would, of course, be to concentrate these reductions on our *net* military expenditures in Europe and *net* private capital outflow to Europe. This could be done either through reductions in our *gross* military expenditures and private capital exports or, as the Administration is now attempting to do, by eliciting larger military expenditures and capital exports here by the Europeans. Alternatively, or rather complementarily, we could cut our aid or capital exports to other countries, if such cuts can be offset by larger, and untied, European aid and capital exports to them. In view of the need for an *over-all expansion* of economic development financing, however, European contributions should probably be regarded primarily as a way to help finance increases in our own current account surpluses in this area of the world, rather than as an invitation to any cuts in our present aid levels. Finally, I feel that we stand much more to gain from policies aiming at "untying" European aid and capital exports to underdeveloped countries, than from the "tying" of our own aid abroad. We might, to this effect, authorize the beneficiaries of our aid to use it for procurement either in the United States or in such countries as are willing to enter into reciprocal agreements regarding (a) the level of their own foreign aid programs, (b) the untying of this aid, and (c) the level of their trade restrictions against us and against the underdeveloped countries.

The second line of policy is the more traditional one of expanding further our current account surplus. It certainly needs to be pursued also with full vigor, especially as long as international considerations limit our ability to curtail drastically our foreign military programs and dictate further expansion, rather than curtailment, of our foreign aid and capital exports. Moreover, the expansion of our current account surplus would contribute also to economic recovery, faster rates of growth, and the fight against unemployment in our own economy.

Two ways are open to us to promote this objective. The first is to improve further our competitiveness in the world market, by accelerating our rates of investment and holding wage rises here somewhat below the rapid wage increases which are now taking place in Europe. The second is directly related to our trade program. We must negotiate for better access of our exports to foreign markets. Here again the problem centers on Europe rather than on the rest of the world, which would be unable to finance any substantial increases in its imports unmatched by parallel increases in its exports. Europe's import demand, on the other hand, is now stimulated by an exceptionally rapid rate of economic growth and by the resulting overemployment pressures on its own productive resources; and it would be able to finance such additional imports by merely reducing its current and excessive intake of gold and dollars ($2.6 billion in 1961). These additional imports would be of help to us, even if part of them were to come from countries other than the United States, since they would, in that case, increase the resources available to these countries to expand their imports from us.

In conclusion, Europe holds the key to an improvement of our balance of payments, but this improvement can take place through triangular arrangements involving the relations of the rest of the world both with us and with Western Europe, as well as through direct increases in our receipts from Europe or decreases in our expenditures in Europe. This applies to our trade balance as well as to our balance on military expenditures, economic aid, and private capital account. Our trade negotiations with Europe should be fitted into this multilateral pattern, encouraging, for instance, easier access to European markets for other countries' exports as well as for our own, in exactly the same way as our negotiations about a fairer distribution of defense costs and developmental aid to other countries are now already couched in such multilateral, world-wide terms.

This brings me back to my initial observation about the main significance of the Trade Expansion Act, i.e. to its efforts to adapt, after unconscionable delays, our present narrowly and inadequately national or, at most, bilateral policy instruments and negotiations to the most obvious requirements of rational policy-making in an interdependent world.

This raises still another problem, which lies outside the scope of our discussions today and which I have, in any case, explored *ad nauseam* on other occasions and particularly in my book on *Gold and the Dollar Crisis*. The restoration of full equilibrium in our over-all balance of payments will curtail drastically—by two thirds or more—the sources from which international monetary reserves and liquidity have been fed over the recent past. As stressed by President Kennedy in his first balance-of-payments message of February 1961, gold production is far insufficient today to meet in the long run the monetary requirements of an expanding world economy. And the whole fabric of our present international monetary system is now threatened, even in the short run, by its vulnerability to erratic movements of monetary reserves, as well as of private capital, among the major currencies and between such currencies and gold metal.

The consolidation of past progress and the further expansion of world trade and production urgently call for fundamental reforms of our outworn international institutions in the monetary field, as well as in the fields of trade and finance and, of course, in the military and political arenas themselves. We all know this, but have shown little willingness so far to face this challenge with the boldness which past indecision and tarrying now require, if we are finally to catch up with the fast-changing world of the twentieth century. Earlier and speedier action would have made it possible to implement at an easier, evolutionary *tempo,* the institutional changes which now loom revolutionary in character only because of the cumulative impact of past delays and inaction.

The Organization for Economic Cooperation and Development, the European Economic Community, and the Trade Expansion Act are some—although by no means all—of the instruments through which progress seems most likely to prove politically achievable at this juncture. If we refused to seize and exploit fully the opportunities which they offer us today, if we were to listen once more to the enticing song of the sirens always pleading for further delays, we would merely be storing up later and worse difficulties, not to mention the risk of being finally overtaken by catastrophic events, similar in nature to those that ushered in, some thirty years ago, the worst economic depression and the most destructive war in the world's long history.

Chapter IV: The Alternation of
Dollar and Sterling Crises: 1960–65

THE YEARS 1960–64 witnessed a bewildering succession of alternate dollar and sterling crises, made even more bewildering by the simultaneous worries, not only of Britain and the United States, but of the European Economic Community, Canada, Japan, and, of course, the underdeveloped countries of the rest of the world, about their international payments deficits.

The London *Economist* could well ask the question: Where are the surpluses?

The four papers that compose this chapter may, I hope, throw some light on this problem and help reorient national thinking and policies, here and abroad, on what is, after all, an international problem.

1. THE LATENT CRISIS OF THE RESERVE CURRENCIES

The major threat confronting the international monetary system today lies in the precarious liquidity position of the two reserve currencies of the system: the pound and, primarily, the dollar. Gold and foreign exchange reserves of countries other than the United States and the United Kingdom totaled about $42 billion at the end of 1962, of which more than half was in foreign exchange, overwhelmingly sterling and dollars. The sterling portion ($6.8 billion) was held nearly exclusively (85 per cent) by countries of the overseas sterling area and accounted for practically all their foreign exchange reserves. The foreign exchange reserves of the rest of the world—outside the United States and the sterling area—totalled about $16 billion, of which $1 billion only was in sterling ($600 million in Western Europe) and about $13 billion in dollars. The stability of the dollar is thus far more vital to the world monetary system than that of the pound, but the two are inextricably linked. Nobody doubts that a devaluation of the dollar would quickly entail a sterling devaluation as well. It is almost equally obvious that any substantial devaluation of the pound would unleash speculative move-

The Banker (London, August 1963), pp. 527–35.

ments of funds from the dollar into sterling, on a scale that would present an almost irresistible danger for the dollar itself.

To diagnose the real causes of the difficulties that have to be surmounted and indicate the directions in which appropriate solutions should be sought, a brief examination of the balances of payments of Britain and America is necessary. There are, of course, substantive differences between the two. The balance of payments of the United Kingdom on current account has been in precarious equilibrium over the past five years, with an average surplus of less than $100 million a year and wide swings from a $900 million surplus in 1958 to a

BALANCE OF PAYMENTS OF THE UNITED STATES, 1950–62
(in billions of U.S. dollars)

	Yearly average			Year			
	1950–55	1956–59	1960–62	1959	1960	1961	1962
I. Current Account	**1.4**	**2.3**	**3.7**	**−0.7**	**3.0**	**4.3**	**3.9**
II. Capital Account[1]	**2.8**	**3.5**	**6.7**	**2.1**	**6.5**	**6.3**	**7.4**
A. U.S. Government (excluding debt prepayments)	2.5	2.5	3.3	2.4	2.8	3.4	3.7
B. Dollar balances of regional and international organizations other than IMF	—	−0.2	−0.3	−0.1	−0.4	−0.4	−0.2
C. Private capital:							
Long-term	0.7	2.3	2.2	1.6	2.1	2.0	2.3
Short-term[2]	−0.5	−1.1	1.6	−1.8	2.1	1.2	1.6
III. Monetary Balance (I-II)[1]	**−1.3**	**−1.2**	**−3.0**	**−2.7**	**−3.6**	**−2.0**	**−3.5**
A. International credit transactions:							
1. Debt prepayments	—	−0.1	−0.4	−0.4	—	−0.7	−0.7
2. IMF transactions	−0.1	0.1	−0.4	−0.3	−0.7	0.1	−0.6
3. Foreign monetary authorities[3]	−0.8	−0.7	−1.1	−0.9	−1.1	−0.8	−1.3
B. U.S. gold and convertible currency reserves	−0.5	−0.6	−1.1	−1.1	−1.7	−0.7	−0.9

1. Capital imports and reserve losses are denoted by a *minus* sign.

2. Including errors and omissions as well as changes in foreign private dollar holdings.

3. Including claims recently classified as nonliquid (Treasury bonds with maturities of 15–24 months), foreign funds committed for military purchases, etc.

deficit of roughly the same order in 1960. The United States, by contrast, has shown an average surplus on current account of $2,400 million over the same period, with a rising trend from a deficit of $700 million in 1959 to a surplus hovering around $4,000 million in 1961 and 1962. (The surplus would be much larger still if account were taken of military exports under grants, and of unrepatriated investment earnings, both of which are excluded from the usual calculation of the U.S. balance of payments.)

The so-called "over-all" payments balance (which brings capital transactions into the reckoning as well) of the two countries shows a very different evolution. The United States incurred throughout the period large and persistent deficits, ranging from $3,100 million to $4,200 million a year,[1] while the United Kingdom, on a broadly similar basis of calculation, shifted from a deficit of $400 million in 1959 to a surplus of $600 million in 1962.

The "over-all deficit" concept, however, may not be the best measure of the difficulties confronting the monetary authorities of a country. For America in particular, it includes increases in short-term liabilities to private holders, but excludes parallel changes in short-term claims abroad. Thus, in general, it tends to exaggerate the actual size of the payments deficit. For the world as a whole it also tends, for the same reason, to make the sum of national deficits far larger than the sum of national surpluses. Hence, in considering the problems of the key currencies it may be more revealing to present the balance-of-payments figures in a form that brings out clearly the actual "monetary balance" that has to be settled by the monetary authorities as a result of all other parties' transactions. The payments figures for America and Britain are presented in this more enlightening form in the accompanying tables. The major change entailed is the separation of private holdings of dollar and sterling balances from official holdings: an increase in the former is treated as an inflow of short-term capital, reducing the deficit; an increase in the latter as a means of financing the deficit.

"Official settlements" among the monetary authorities are reflected mostly, with an exception noted below, in changes in "net reserves." The "gross reserves" of a country may be defined as the sum of the gold and foreign exchange holdings of the monetary authorities, plus the so-called "gold-tranche" of its quota with the International Monetary Fund. "Net reserves" are calculated by deducting from that figure

1. See remarks on page 106 regarding the adjustment of recent U.S. estimates.

BALANCE OF PAYMENTS OF THE UNITED KINGDOM, 1958–62
(in billions of U.S. dollars)

	1958	1959	1960	1961	1962
I. Current Account	**0.9**	**0.3**	**−0.9**	**−0.2**	**0.2**
II. Capital Account[1]	**−0.2**	**0.6**	**−1.7**	**0.8**	**−0.7**
A. U.K. Government	0.2	0.3	0.3	0.1	0.3
B. Sterling balance of regional and international organizations other than IMF	—	—	—	−0.1	−0.1
C. Private capital:					
Long-term	0.4	0.4	0.2	−0.2	—
Short-term[2]	−0.7	−0.2	−2.2	1.0	−0.8
III. Monetary Balance (I-II)[1]	**1.1**	**−0.3**	**0.8**	**−1.0**	**0.8**
A. International credit transactions:					
IMF	—	0.4	0.4	−1.0	1.1
Foreign monetary authorities[3]	0.4	−0.3	−0.1	—	0.3
B. U.K. gold and foreign currency reserves	0.6	−0.4	0.5	0.1	−0.5

1. Capital imports and reserve losses are denoted by a *minus* sign.
2. Including errors and omissions as well as changes in foreign private sterling balances.
3. Including, in 1958 and 1959, changes in net debt to EPU.

the gross reserves held in the country's market by foreign monetary authorities. Hence, for the world as a whole, when assets and liabilities have been offset, net reserves would broadly equal the stock of monetary gold (any discrepancy reflecting the impact of IMF transactions).

Defined in this manner, the net reserves of the United Kingdom have long been negative, but (as the table on page 107 shows) have improved substantially from *minus* $5 billion in 1957 to *minus* $3.5 billion in 1962. This improvement of $1.5 billion is equal to the algebraic sum of the "monetary" or "official settlements" of the United Kingdom over these five years. By contrast, the U.S. "net reserves" remain (as shown on p. 106) slightly positive, but have declined over the five years from $16 billion in 1957 to less than $3 billion in 1962, i.e. by about $13 billion. The "monetary deficit" of the period, however, was somewhat larger ($14.8 billion) if one includes in it prepayments of intergovernmental debts ($1.8 billion) aimed primarily at reducing the U.S. gold losses.

This computation of the U.S. deficit includes all increases in U.S.

GROSS AND NET RESERVE POSITIONS, 1957 AND 1962
(in billions of U.S. dollars)

UNITED STATES

	End of year		Change
	1957	1962	
I. Gross Reserves	**24.8**	**17.2**	**− 7.6**
A. Gold and foreign exchange	22.9	16.2	− 6.7
B. IMF gold-tranche	2.0	1.1	− 0.9
II. Reserves Liabilities to	**8.9**	**14.3**	**+ 5.4**
A. International Monetary Fund	0.2	0.8	+ 0.6
B. Foreign monetary authorities	8.7	13.5	+ 4.8
III. Net Reserves (I-II)	**16.0**	**2.9**	**−13.0**
IV. Other Liquid Assets and Liabilities	**−4.8**	**−5.5**	**− 0.7**
A. Banks' short-term assets	2.2	5.1	+ 2.9
B. *Minus* liquid liabilities to:	7.0	10.6	+ 3.6
1. International and regional organizations	*0.7*	*2.2*	*+ 1.5*
2. Private holders	*6.2*	*8.4*	*+ 2.2*

SOURCE: These estimates are derived from a Table ("Financing the U.S. Deficit, 1958–62") published in the *Federal Reserve Bulletin* of April 1963, corrected in two respects:

(1) Liquid *liabilities* to the IMF ($3.9 billion at the end of 1962) have been replaced by *net claims* on the IMF, equal to the IMF gold-tranche minus the Fund's investments in U.S. Treasury bills. The Federal Reserve Bulletin includes total liabilities to the IMF, but leaves out entirely the U.S. capital claim on the Fund.

(2) On the other hand, so-called nonliquid liabilities to monetary institutions (Treasury bonds, etc.) have been added to the Federal Reserve estimates.

liabilities to foreign monetary authorities, irrespective of their maturity. It is thus swollen by the U.S. Treasury's medium-term borrowings in foreign currency (with 15 to 24 months maturity) and by the accumulation of dollar balances earmarked for future armament purchases in the United States. These transactions were excluded last year from the estimates of the deficit compiled by the *Survey of Current Business* and regarded as capital imports "above the line." While perfectly defensible on a bookkeeping basis centering on a somewhat arbitrary distinction between "liquid" and "nonliquid" liabilities, this procedure has been criticized in many quarters, and was subsequently submitted, for revision, to a special committee appointed by the White House and headed by Dr. E. M. Bernstein. From a broader economic point of view, it would seem more appropriate to regard such transactions as means of meeting—rather than of reducing—America's monetary deficit through credit settlements rather than through gold losses.

If this point of view is accepted, the 1962 transactions of the United

UNITED KINGDOM

	End of year		Change
	1957	1962	
I. Gross Reserves	**2.4**	**3.3**	**+0.9**
A. Gold and foreign exchange	2.4	2.8	+0.4
B. IMF gold-tranche	—	0.5	+0.5
II. Reserve Liabilities to	**7.4**	**6.8**	**−0.6**
A. International Monetary Fund	0.3	—	−0.3
B. Foreign monetary authorities	7.0	6.8	−0.2
III. Net Reserves (I-II)	**−5.0**	**−3.5**	**+1.5**
IV. Other Liquid Assets and Liabilities	**−2.1**	**−2.3**	**−0.2**
A. Banks' short-term dollar assets	0.2	0.9	+0.7
B. *Minus* liquid liabilities to:	2.3	3.2	+0.9
1. International and regional organizations	0.2	0.2	—
2. Private holders	2.1	3.0	+0.9

Banks' short-term dollar assets (item IV (*a*)) include only a rough approximation arrived at by deducting from dollar assets *alone* of U.K. Government and banks (as regularly reported by the U.S.) *all* convertible currency reserves (as recently reported by the U.K.).

SOURCE: These estimates are derived primarily from the *Bank of England Quarterly Bulletin* and *International Financial Statistics*.

States "above the line" are seen to have involved an accumulation of $3.5 billion by foreign monetary authorities, of which $900 million was repurchased in gold by the U.S. Treasury. Of the other $2.6 billion (three quarters of the total) $600 million was absorbed by dollar repayments to the IMF and $700 million by advance repayments of intergovernmental debts to the United States. The remaining $1.3 billion was retained by foreign monetary authorities, either at their own initiative, or as a result of bilateral negotiations designed to slow down the U.S. gold losses.

The seriousness of this situation is highlighted by the fact that debt repayments—scheduled as well as unscheduled—to the IMF and to the United States are bound to decline sharply in the near future with the near exhaustion of the residual intergovernmental debts owed by the major surplus countries of Europe and with the rise of IMF dollar holdings to 75 per cent of the U.S. quota—at which point dollars can no longer be used for repayments to the Fund. Thus two of the main ways in which the U.S. gold stock has been shielded in recent years will no longer be open in the future. Before long America's monetary deficit will have to be absorbed almost entirely by further increases in the already swollen dollar holdings of foreign central banks and Treasuries, by borrowing from the IMF, or by running down the gold stock.

The urgency of a restoration of equilibrium in the U.S. balance of payments is therefore no longer questioned, either in the U.S. or in foreign countries. Immediately, it is the major problem confronting the stability of the international monetary system. But even the restoration of such balance will not fully safeguard the dollar if the United States remains exposed—particularly in the aftermath of a sterling crisis— to sudden or massive conversions of outstanding dollar balances and to additional outflows of speculative capital by U.S. residents themselves.

The conclusion most often derived from the above analysis is that America and Britain must bend every effort to improve their balance of payments on current account. While this is undoubtedly true— particularly for Britain—it does not take full account of a most important characteristic of the balances of payments of these two countries, intimately linked with the use of their respective currencies as "key currencies" in international holdings and settlements, official and private. This common characteristic lies in the absence of any close correlation between fluctuations in their current account balance on the one hand and their monetary balance or net reserve position on the other.

The United Kingdom, for instance, swung from a monetary deficit of $300 million in 1959 to a substantial surplus of $800 million in 1960 and back to a record monetary deficit of $1 billion in 1961, in the face of totally opposite swings in its current account balance from a surplus of $300 million in 1959 to a deficit of $900 million in 1960 and a much smaller deficit of $200 million in 1961. As for the United States, an improvement of no less than $4.5 billion in its current account from 1959 to 1962 (from a record deficit of $700 million to a near-record surplus of $3.9 billion) was accompanied by a further deterioration of $800 million in its monetary balance from a deficit of $2.7 billion to a deficit of $3.5 billion.

The official targets of the United States and the United Kingdom regarding the desired improvement of their current balance—by more than $3 billion for the U.S. and by perhaps $1 billion for Britain—are, moreover, hardly compatible with each other and with the targets simultaneously aimed at by other countries. In part, this incompatibility reflects, once again, the inconsistencies resulting from the methods

YEAR TO YEAR FLUCTUATIONS IN THE BALANCE OF PAYMENTS OF THE
RESERVE CENTERS, 1958–62
(in billions of U.S. dollars)

	1958–59	1959–60	1960–61	1961–62
I. United States: Changes in				
A. Current account surplus	−2.1	+3.6	+1.3	−0.4
B. Net capital imports	+2.5	−4.5	+0.2	−1.1
(*Of which: Short-term private capital*)	(*+1.5*)	(*−3.9*)	(*+0.8*)	(*−0.3*)
C. Official settlements (A + B)	+0.3	−0.8	+1.5	−1.4
II. United Kingdom: Changes in				
A. Current account surplus	−0.6	−1.2	+0.7	+0.4
B. Net capital imports	−0.8	+2.3	−2.5	+1.4
(*Of which: Short-term private capital*)	(*−0.6*)	(*+2.0*)	(*−1.2*)	(*+1.8*)
C. Official settlements (A + B)	−1.4	+1.1	−1.8	+1.8

Note that official settlements fluctuate, in half of the cases, in a direction opposite to that of the current account balance, but uniformly in the same direction as the capital balance, and particularly short-term private capital.

used in calculating national surpluses and deficits. But it also reflects the fact that an adequate growth of monetary reserves, for the world as a whole, is highly dependent upon continued increases in the short-term indebtedness of the key currency countries and a consequent and persistent deterioration of their net reserve position. In the longer run, however, this deterioration itself is bound to undermine the acceptability of these currencies as reserve currencies and so interfere with the satisfactory functioning of the so-called gold-exchange, or key currencies standard. When that point is reached, the world will be confronted with a choice of one of three courses:

(1) To stop, more or less abruptly, the payments deficits of the key currency countries. This, however, would itself put an end to the contribution that these deficits have made to the growth of world reserves. Moreover, in the longer run it would exercise a powerful deflationary influence not only on their own growth but on that of the world economy as a whole. Or,

(2) To resort to inconvertibility or devaluation of the key currencies, thus unleashing—as in 1931—a general collapse of a world monetary order highly dependent upon these national currencies as media for international settlements and reserve accumulation. Or, if time then permits,

(3) To make a concerted effort to solve the problem posed by the threat of liquidation of the outstanding reserve balances in national

currencies, and to avoid both its future recurrence and a threat of world deflation, by devising some other means of feeding the reserve requirements of an expanding world economy.

The solution of the immediate problem of the U.S. deficit itself can be shown to be dependent also upon such a concerted approach to the problem of world liquidity. A full re-equilibration of the U.S. balance of payments is, indeed, well-nigh inconceivable without a substantial improvement in the capital balance, and particularly the net balance of short-term capital movements. While some further improvement of the current account may be expected from the moderation of recent price and wage rises in the United States compared with those in Europe, it will probably be of modest proportion if the economy itself is expanding at a faster pace than in recent years. Moreover, as already noted, any substantial improvement would disturb the balance-of-payments equilibrium of other countries and might provoke them into actions to restore that equilibrium. In addition, some savings may be hoped for in foreign aid expenditures, but are likely to be largely offset by a decline in the amount of exports (officially estimated at $2.8 billion in 1962) financed through the aid programs. A recovery of the U.S. economy, accompanied by the increase in interest rates that such a recovery would both stimulate and make acceptable, would also have a favorable impact on private capital movements, by making the U.S. capital market more attractive both to foreign and to U.S. funds. But these potential improvements in the current and capital accounts hardly measure up to the size of America's payments problem.

Plainly, something must be done to protect the dollar against the everpresent threat of sudden or massive withdrawals of short-term funds accumulated abroad in the past under the key currencies system. This need becomes obvious if one reflects on the implications of the two following facts. First, that the major deterioration, by far, in the U.S. balance of payments arises from the spectacular reversal of the trend of net short-term capital movements (including "errors and omissions"). Secondly, that this reversal took place abruptly in 1960, i.e. with the sudden flare-up of the London gold price, and the persistent doubts that it unleashed about the future stability of the dollar. Until 1960 the United States had been a persistent and massive importer of short-term funds, as Britain had been before the First World War; this inflow helped to finance, year after year, large military expenditures, foreign aid programs and long-term capital exports, particularly direct investments. These short-term capital imports averaged $1.1 billion a year in 1956–59, and reached a peak of $1.8 billion in the year preceding the London gold crisis. They swung abruptly that year into large and persistent outflows of short-term funds, at an average rate of $1.6 billion a year over the period 1960–62, and with ups and downs that clearly reflected in part the flux of speculative expectations about the fate of the dollar. The outflow was largest, of course, during the gold-crisis year, 1960 ($2.1 billion). It subsided to $1.2 billion in 1961 with the change of Administration and the evident determination of the new authorities to preserve both the stability and convertibility of the dollar. But it moved up again to $1.6 billion in 1962 as the announced goal of restoring external payments to full balance by the end of 1963 appeared to be receding into a more distant future.

The speculative fears that explain this outflow are unlikely to be durably quelled by measures aiming exclusively at moderating immediate gold losses at the cost of further additions to the already swollen short-term indebtedness of the United States to foreign central banks and treasuries.

It has been indicated above why it will be more and more difficult to elicit international monetary cooperation, year after year, on a scale sufficient to meet a major portion of large and persistent U.S. deficits. The time has come to explore another solution. Central banks should recognize that their holdings of dollar—and sterling—balances have been built up to their present huge levels, over many years past, as a necessary consequence of the functioning of the gold-exchange standard. These balances could not be converted *simultaneously* into gold without reducing drastically the world stock of monetary reserves and bringing to an end, in fact, the convertibility and stability of the reserve currencies and of the world monetary structure erected upon them. Joint action by all countries—or even merely by the larger reserve holders—could avert such a danger, without any real sacrifice to anyone, while preserving the full value and necessary liquidity of outstanding foreign exchange reserves for the settlement of any country's future deficits in its international payments. So far as the reserve currencies—and particularly the dollar—are concerned, the removal of this threat could hardly fail to affect profoundly the speculative expectations that are one of the main roots of the abnormal short-term capital outflows of recent years. Combined with other, well-known and often-advocated measures, this new kind of international cooperation and agreements would offer at least a far more promising path toward the elimination of the U.S. deficits than do the short-term and half-hearted measures resorted to in the past two years.

Adequately protected against sudden or massive liquidation of outstanding short-term debts to central banks, the United States gold reserves should be more than adequate to meet any residual payments deficits that might still be incurred in the foreseeable future. If further assistance were to be needed, the large U.S. quota in the IMF should provide it without additional recourse to borrowings from central banks.

This is not to say that the network of swap facilities recently negotiated should be dismantled. It could, on the contrary, be used to mutual benefit to offset unpredictable, but reversible, movements of short-term funds in a world committed to currency convertibility and an increasing degree of liberalization of capital movements as well as of current transactions. But the total size of the facilities should be clearly circumscribed and they should not be used, and expanded, to meet persistent imbalances in payments.

A fundamental reorientation of the present cooperative efforts is urgently needed to achieve the following short-run and long-run objectives:

(1) To consolidate the reserve currencies against speculative fears and short-term capital outflows.

(2) To replace the deficits of the key currency countries by other, and less erratic, means of creating the international liquidity required to meet the legitimate needs of an expanding world economy.

(3) To help remove thereby major long-run as well as short-run threats to the stability of the world monetary system.

The basic elements of such a reorientation are at hand. They can be drawn and assembled from a variety of plans recently advocated by responsible statesmen and experts. What is most needed to break the present deadlock is a more constructive approach to these plans, focusing on their common and most negotiable features rather than on the contradictory and most controversial aspects of their proposals. Progress is also likely to require action on various fronts. The European Economic Community, the Paris Club, and the IMF should be regarded as complementary, rather than alternative, frameworks for feasible and necessary forms of international cooperation and commitments. Last, but not least, the proponents as well as the opponents of each solution to be explored should recognize that none can offer any ironclad guarantee of full and unqualified success in its practical operation; but they should recognize also that this should not constitute a deterrent to action and an excuse for the worst choice of all —inertia. All that can realistically be hoped for, and legitimately demanded, from the reforms to be adopted is that they offer a reasonable chance of success, and minimize, at the very least, the enormous risks of utter failure entailed, in the long or even the medium run, by the continuation of past and present policies.

2. THE END OF THE DOLLAR GLUT?

A country's balance of payments is like the weather. You can safely predict that it will change, if you wait long enough.

This, however, is one of the lessons of history—among many others, alas—which economists and statesmen find very hard to learn. Economic advice and policy are forever molded on the opposite assumption, i.e. on a long-run extrapolation of experience in the recent past. The dollar-shortage theory continued to inspire academic publications and government policies long after U.S. surpluses had been replaced by huge and increasing deficits. We are in danger of repeating the same mistake tomorrow if we don't recognize in time the signs heralding the end of the dollar glut and even a possible resurgence of substantial U.S. surpluses in world payments.

The time for such a reappraisal is not yet, but it may not be far distant. Our deficit, as usually measured, was running at an annual rate (after seasonal adjustments) of about $2 billion in the second half of last year. This is still considerable, of course, but far less than the $3.7 billion average deficit of 1958–62, and the record $4.6 billion deficit of the first half of 1963. The question is whether this spectacular recovery reflects deep-seated, durable trends, likely to persist for some time, or merely temporary factors whose cessation, or reversal, would leave us again with large and continuing deficits over the years immediately ahead.

Regrouping of Accounts

In order to throw some light on this problem, without getting lost in a welter of details, it is necessary first to regroup, in as simple and meaningful a manner as possible, the main categories of transactions underlying our over-all deficits of the last fourteen years.

The Banker (London, June 1964), pp. 351–54.

The first and most obvious distinction to be drawn is that between: (1) Our current account transactions on goods and services, including ordinary remittances and pensions; (2) our capital accounts other than reserve accounts; and (3) net reserve settlements among national and foreign monetary authorities, *plus* official prepayments of debts and military exports designed to reduce the size of such settlements and particularly of the U.S. gold losses.

Such a regrouping of our balance-of-payments accounts would immediately highlight the fact that a $5.3 billion improvement in our current account balance from 1959 to 1963 was offset by an equal deterioration in our capital accounts, leaving our settlements deficit almost unchanged at a level of about $2.7 billion.

In view of the large role played by our foreign aid in the financing of U.S. exports—particularly of surplus agricultural commodities— net outflows of official capital, however, might better be separated from our private capital exports and grouped with our current account balance, thus giving an approximate measurement of our "market" balance on current account. Exports of private capital, on the other hand, may be usefully broken down between long-term and short-term capital, including in the latter privately held foreign dollar balances and errors and omissions (whose major fluctuations seem closely associated with those in short-term capital movements).

THE U.S. BALANCE OF PAYMENTS, 1950–63
(years, or yearly rates, in millions of dollars)

	1950–58	1959	1960–62	July–Dec. 1963
I. Current Account and Official Capital	**− 400**	**−2,940**	**+1,070**	**+1,260**
A. Current Account	+2,040	− 660	+3,970	+4,930
B. Official Capital	−2,440	−2,280	−2,900	−3,660
II. Private Capital	**− 730**	**+ 220**	**−4,060**	**−3,130**
A. Long-Term	−1,310	−1,590	−2,250	−2,250
B. Short-Term	+ 590	+1,810	−1,810	− 880
III. Total = Official Settlements	**−1,130**	**−2,720**	**−2,990**	**−1,870**

Major Trends

Two broad conclusions emerge from the above table:

(1) The abnormal and unsustainable deficit in our 1959 balance

on current account and official capital has long been wiped out, and replaced by increasing surpluses.

(2) This recovery was masked, however, until very recently, by sharp increases—$4 billion or more—in our net exports of private capital, and particularly by a dramatic reversal of short-term capital movements, from large and sustained *inflows* to equally large and sustained *outflows*. These persisted throughout the years 1960-62, but have abated markedly in 1963.

(3) The combination of these two major changes has finally brought about a considerable decline in our settlements deficit from $3 billion, on the average, in 1960-62 to less than $1.9 billion in the latter half of 1963. The extrapolation of the 1963 rates of improvement in our current account and short-term capital transactions would eliminate—and even reverse—this residual deficit in a relatively short time. Although crystal-gazing is particularly hazardous in this field, let us see what are the most reasonable expectations in both respects.

Current Account and Official Capital

Probable reductions in our foreign aid programs are most likely to be closely matched by parallel reductions in the exports which they finance. On the other hand, our exports to developing countries, particularly in Latin America, may increase as a result of the unusual accumulation (more than a billion dollars) of gold and liquid dollar assets by those countries in 1963.

Our imports are also likely to rise further as economic activity continues to expand, particularly under the impact of recent tax cuts.

On the whole, however, our current account surplus—excluding government-financed transactions—is likely to continue close to the recently achieved record levels, or even higher, because of the enormous improvements which have taken place in our cost competitiveness in relation to the major industrial countries of Western Europe. We were very probably uncompetitive in the late 1950s, after the European devaluations of 1949 and the rebuilding of Europe's productive capacity. Industrial wage costs per unit of output have, however, changed very little in the United States since 1959, but are estimated to have risen by 10 per cent in England, and about 20 to 30 per cent in the major countries of the European Economic Community. The current account balance of the Community deteriorated over this period by about $3.5 billion, while ours improved by over $5 billion and was still rising at a particularly sharp pace in the closing months of 1963.

I doubt, however, whether our current account surplus can, or should, rise much further, in view of the difficulties that might be created thereby for some of our main partners in world trade. The levels already reached should be sufficient to finance adequate capital exports by us, particularly if account is taken of net reinvested earnings (about $1 billion in 1962) not usually included in our balance-of-payments estimates. Lasting equilibrium in our over-all balance should be reached primarily through a correction of the abnormally high levels of private capital outflows which are the main factor in our deficits of the last four years.

Private Capital Movements

The improvement of our balance of payments in the second half of 1963 is usually credited to the impact of the proposed interest equalization tax on U.S. exports of private capital. While this tax threat has undoubtedly helped check the extraordinary spurt in foreign security issues in our market in the first half of that year, the annual rate of U.S. long-term investments abroad—portfolio as well as direct—in the second half of the year was nearly identical to that of the previous three years.

The $900 million reduction in the net outflow of private capital is entirely accounted for by the sharp decline—by more than a half—in the net outflow of *short-term* funds, at an annual rate, from $1,800 million in 1960–62 to less than $900 million in the second half of 1963.

Short-term capital normally tends to flow toward major financial markets and did indeed do so in the case of the United States until 1960. We were a net recipient of short-term funds, at a rate of $500 million a year in the early 1950s and $1,100 million in the late 1950s. There was an abrupt change in 1960 from a record inflow of $1,800 million in the previous year to a record outflow of $2,170 million. While many factors undoubtedly played a role in this dramatic reversal, one can hardly escape the impression that it was greatly influenced by speculative movements of hot money, unleashed by the flare-up of gold prices in London and entertained ever since by recurrent rumors about possible changes in the U.S. gold prices and in the dollar exchange rate of certain European currencies. This impression is confirmed by the rise in estimated private gold absorption from about $600 million a year in 1956–59 to about $1,050 million a year in 1960–62, and by the vast inflows of short-term funds, including errors and omissions, to Europe in these latter years (about $500 million a year in Germany alone, instead of annual *outflows* of about $300 million in the two preceding years).

It is further confirmed by the sharp reduction of our short-term capital losses in 1963, as the expectations of any proximate change in gold prices and/or exchange rates were dampened by the unprecedented level of U.S.S.R. gold sales in Western markets (to finance grain purchases), by the launching of high level negotiations by the Group of Ten to consolidate the international monetary system on the basis of the present gold prices, and by the sharp reduction in Europe's balance-of-payments surpluses.

Conclusions

Huge and abnormal net outflows of short-term private capital from the U.S. account for one half to two thirds of our persistent deficits of recent years. Their cessation may now be in sight and would suffice, together with the enormous improvement which has already taken place in our current account transactions, to restore full equilibrium in our balance of payments. Further increases in our large current account surplus and/or the resurgence of normal levels of short-term capital *inflows* could easily transform our deficits of recent years into substantial surpluses.

Durable equilibrium in the world's payment pattern now hinges, to a considerable extent, on the success or failure of the Tokyo meeting, next September, and the ability of a reformed international monetary system:

(1) To deter, or offset, the abnormal outflows of short-term capital that have played such a crucial role in the balance-of-payments deficits of the U.S., and the surpluses of Europe, during the last four years.

(2) To consolidate the international reserve system against the instability imparted to it by the haphazard accumulation—or liquidation—of reserves in the form of short-term dollar and sterling indebtedness.

(3) To adjust the expansion of the international reserve pool to the full potential and requirements of noninflationary growth in the world economy, rather than to the key currency countries' surpluses

or deficits, the waves of confidence or diffidence in such currencies, and the fluctuations in gold production, U.S.S.R. gold sales, and speculative demand for gold by private speculators.

A successful outcome of the negotiations now under way is certainly of major interest to the United States today, but their failure would be as tragic tomorrow for the other countries which would be disastrously affected in the short run by a collapse of the international monetary system and, in the long run, by a possible resurgence of the dollar shortage of former years.

3. The International Network of World Payments: An Integrated Approach

Introduction

Balance-of-payments disequilibria are essentially an international problem. Yet their readjustment or financing have traditionally been, and still remain nearly exclusively today, a national responsibility.

Economists have long denounced the deflationary bias of such a system. Surplus countries are always free to pursue compensatory (neutralization or sterilization) policies which isolate their economy from unwanted external shocks, but increase correspondingly the burden of readjustment of the deficit countries, since losses of reserves may prevent the latter from pursuing similar policies as freely. From a political point of view, on the other hand, the bias may well be inflationary, as compensatory (contractionist) policies by the surplus countries are politically far less palatable, and are often more difficult to implement, than compensatory (expansionist) policies by the deficit countries. And in the end, the latter countries may be more inclined to seek relief in currency devaluation or trade restrictions than in deflationary measures.

Another source of pressures stimulating undesirable policies of deflation, devaluation, or restrictions has been diagnosed only more recently.[1] This is the incapacity of the international monetary system, as now organized, to adjust the world reserve pool available to central banks to the growing needs of world economic expansion. Here too, however, the present gold-exchange standard may foster in the short,

1. See the author's *Gold and the Dollar Crisis, The Future of Convertibility* (New Haven, 1960); and *The Evolution of the International Monetary System: Historical Reappraisal and Future Perspectives* (Princeton, 1964).

Weltwirtschaftliches Archiv (Kiel, 1964), pp. 181–97.

or even the medium, run inflationary as well as deflationary excesses whose delayed correction is apt to involve further unnecessary shocks for the economy of the countries concerned and of the world itself.

A third aspect of the nationalistic approaches which still dominate the analysis of world payments and the shaping-up of corrective policies will be discussed in this paper. It is the incompatibility of the national methods used in measuring national surpluses and deficits, of the criteria which inspire national readjustment policies, and of the official targets resulting from both of these incompatibilities.

The Incompatibility of Measurements, Criteria, and Policy Targets

In the year 1960, for instance, the "over-all" deficit of the United States, as calculated by the Department of Commerce, was estimated to be about $3.9 billion, and official policy pronouncements proclaimed that this should be primarily reabsorbed by corresponding increases in our—already considerable—current account surplus. Official British policy, at the time, targeted a current account surplus of about $1,250 million as necessary to provide for a normal level of overseas capital exports, debt repayments, and improvement of Britain's meager international reserve accounts. The 1960 current account deficit of the United Kingdom was, however, then estimated to run in the neighborhood of $1 billion, and required, therefore, in the official view, to be improved by more than $2.2 billion.

The ambition of the United States and the United Kingdom was thus to improve their combined current account balance by well over $6 billion, but no country or group of countries showed any desire to see its own current account balances deteriorate by anything approaching such an amount. Most of them indeed—with the main exception of the European Economic Community—were also concerned with excessive deficits and/or insufficient reserve levels, rather than with unwanted current account surpluses.

The present situation and policy targets of the major countries still reveal similar inconsistencies today. The United States was still worried last year by its so-called "over-all" deficit of $3.3 billion,[2] the European Community by the near-vanishing of its previous current

2. A report prepared under the chairmanship of Professor Wallich for the Republican Party still commented, on May 20 of this year, that "as far as possible, the payments deficit must be removed by an expansion of exports, along with increases in other receipts." Republican Citizens' Critical Issues Council, *The Balance of Payments and the Dollar* (Washington, 1964).

account surpluses,[3] and the United Kingdom by reserve losses and sterling liabilities increases totaling more than $400 million.

It should be obvious that national balance-of-payments targets will continue to prove incompatible with one another, and to inspire mutually defeating national policies, as long as countries measure their deficits or surpluses in a different manner, and feel that any deficit —or even merely "insufficient" surplus—in *either* their "over-all" balance *or* their current account balance must impel them to improve the latter.

Standardized Measurement

Table I brings together, in as standardized a form as is possible on the basis of published information, the balances of payments of the United States, the United Kingdom, and the European Economic Community countries, i.e. the three major economic, industrial, and financial powers of the Western World today, over the years 1958–63.

Four broad categories of transactions are distinguished:

(1) The current account balance, including private transfers.

(2) Net exports, or imports (with a *minus* sign), of official capital.[4]

(3) Net exports, or imports (with a *minus* sign), of private capital, including errors and omissions—whose major fluctuations, although not necessarily the absolute amounts, are generally thought to originate primarily in private capital transactions—and changes in *privately* held foreign balances in the reporting country's currency.

(4) Increases, or decreases (with a *minus* sign), in net monetary reserves, defined as the difference between the gross gold and foreign exchange assets of the reporting country's monetary authorities and its indebtedness—irrespective of maturities—to foreign monetary authorities.

Changes in net monetary reserves reflect the excess (or shortfall) of the current account surplus in relation to total capital exports, public and private, and are broken down between changes in the country's

3. Since substantial current account surpluses are regarded as necessary to finance, in the long run, adequate levels of capital exports and economic aid to the under-developed countries. See Mr. Robert Marjolin's speech to the European Parliament at Strasbourg, on January 21, 1964 on "The Economic Situation of the European Community in 1963 and the Perspectives for 1964."

4. Normal and recurrent transfers (shown as "pensions and other transfers" in the U.S. balance of payments) might better be included in the current account balance, but could not be isolated from other official transfers for all the countries in Table 1.

TABLE 1

BALANCE OF PAYMENTS OF THE UNITED STATES, THE UNITED KINGDOM, AND THE
EUROPEAN ECONOMIC COMMUNITY, 1958–63
(in billions of U.S. dollars)

	1958	1959	1960	1961	1962	Yearly 1958–62 average	1963
I. Current Account and Private Transfers = II + III + IV	**5.7**	**3.9**	**6.2**	**8.6**	**7.0**	**6.3**	**6.5**
A. United States	1.7	−0.4	3.3	5.0	4.3	2.8	4.9
B. United Kingdom	1.2	0.6	−0.5	0.3	0.6	0.5	0.7
C. EEC[1]	2.9	3.7	3.3	3.3	2.0	3.0	0.8
II. Official Capital Exports[2]	**3.6**	**4.5**	**4.5**	**5.4**	**5.1**	**4.6**	**5.7**
A. United States	2.5	2.1	2.6	2.5	2.4	2.4	3.6
B. United Kingdom	0.4	0.6	0.6	0.4	0.6	0.5	0.5
C. EEC[1]	0.7	1.8	1.3	2.5	2.1	1.7	1.6
III. Private Capital Exports[3]	**1.6**	**—**	**1.2**	**3.5**	**2.6**	**1.8**	**1.9**
A. United States	2.2	−0.2	4.3	3.7	4.2	2.8	3.4
B. United Kingdom	−0.4	0.2	−1.8	0.9	−0.8	−0.4	0.6
C. EEC[1]	−0.2	—	−1.2	−1.2	−0.8	−0.7	−2.0
IV. Increases in Net Monetary Reserves = I − (II + III)	**0.5**	**−0.6**	**0.4**	**−0.3**	**−0.7**	**−0.1**	**−1.2**
A. United States	−3.0	−2.3	−3.6	−1.3	−2.2	−2.5	−2.0
B. United Kingdom	1.1	−0.2	0.8	−1.0	0.8	0.3	−0.5
C. EEC[1]	2.4	1.9	3.2	2.0	0.7	2.0	1.3

1. French estimates are for the French franc area as a whole with the outside world. This underestimates the current account surplus of Metropolitan France alone and of the European Community (by about $250 million in 1961) and their *exports* of official capital (by about $1,300 million in 1961); but it also underestimates largely compensatory *imports* of private capital (more than $1 billion in 1961, including errors and omissions).

2. Includes (as a negative entry) prepayments to the U.S. of official loans and military exports, which should better be regarded as "financing" rather than "reducing" the U.S. over-all deficits and the paying countries surpluses.

3. Includes errors and omissions and changes in privately held foreign dollar and sterling holdings.

SOURCES: For the U.S.: *Survey of Current Business*, XLIV, Washington, D.C., March 1964; *Balance of Payments*, Statistical Suppl., Rev. Ed., Washington, D.C., 1963. For the U.K.: Bank of England, *Quarterly Bulletin*, IV, London, March 1964. For the EEC countries: International Monetary Fund, *Balance of Payments Yearbook*, XV, 1958–62, and XVI, 1959–63, Washington, D.C.

These estimates have been revised and brought up to date in the table on pp. 366-67 below.

gold assets, and in its net claims on (or indebtedness to) the IMF and other foreign monetary authorities. They differ in three respects from the "over-all" balance of payments reported in official U.S. and U.K. statistics:

(1) They exclude changes in foreign balances held by other than monetary institutions, those of private holders—including banks[6]— being reported under private capital movements, and those of international and regional institutions other than the IMF under official capital movements.

(2) They include changes in the U.S. *total* indebtedness to foreign monetary authorities, irrespective of maturities.

(3) They exclude, however, foreign prepayments of governmental debts to, and military imports from, the United States, shown here under official capital movements.[7]

Redefined in this manner, each category of transactions might be expected to cancel out to zero for the world as a whole, except for a net current account surplus arising from, and offset by, new additions to the world monetary gold stock. In practice, however, some discrepancies should be expected from differences in recording practices, in the timing of payments and receipts, and in the classification of some transactions as official by one of the partner countries and as private by the other.[8] Others would arise, in addition, from the unavoidable gaps and errors in the construction of balance-of-payments estimates.

Table 2 compares the gold and *net* foreign exchange gains (or losses) of the eight major countries of Table 1 with the gold and *gross* foreign exchange losses (or gains) of the other countries in the world economy. Gold estimates do indeed add up to current increases in the world monetary gold stock, and the discrepancies noted in the foreign

6. Which should be shown separately for more detailed analysis than is aimed at here, especially as they may be directly induced by the monetary authorities—to modify their own recorded reserve gains or losses—rather than by commercial consideration alone.

7. To the extent that such prepayments are prompted by a mutual desire to avoid excessive and undesirable monetary settlements, they should, however, be regarded as "financing" rather than "reducing" the U.S. deficit and other countries' surpluses. They would, therefore, have been grouped with "monetary settlements" in Table 1, rather than with "official capital" if adequate information on this score had been available from all the countries concerned. (See now: IMF, *Annual Report,* 1964, p. 76).

8. Government pensions to foreign residents, for instance, although this particular discrepancy would be eliminated if such transactions were classified under current accounts.

TABLE 2

ROUGH RECONCILIATION OF WORLD ESTIMATES OF CHANGES IN GOLD AND
FOREIGN EXCHANGE RESERVES, 1958–63
(in billions of U.S. dollars)

	1958	1959	1960	1961	1962	1963
I. Gold						
A. Western production	1.1	1.1	1.2	1.2	1.3	1.4
B. U.S.S.R. sales	0.2	0.3	0.2	0.3	0.2	0.5
C. Private absorption (−)	−0.6	−0.6	−1.1	−0.9	−1.2	−1.0
D. **Total** = increase in Western						
monetary gold stock	0.7	0.8	0.3	0.6	0.3	0.8
1. International organizations	—	0.9	0.2	−0.2	—	−0.1
2. Eight countries[1]	0.5	−0.2	0.1	—	—	0.3
3. Other countries	0.2	0.1	0.1	0.8	0.3	0.6
a. in Western Europe	*0.3*	*0.1*	*0.4*	*0.5*	*0.4*	*0.4*
b. Canada and Japan	*—*	*0.1*	*−0.1*	*0.1*	*−0.2*	*0.1*
c. Other	*−0.1*	*−0.1*	*−0.3*	*0.2*	*0.2*	*0.2*
II. Foreign Exchange						
A. Eight countries[1] (net)	−0.1	−1.0	0.4	−0.3	−1.0	−1.5
B. Other countries (gross)	−0.2	1.2	0.4	0.1	1.8	1.7
1. in Western Europe	*0.2*	*0.2*	*0.3*	*0.6*	*0.3*	*0.4*
2. Canada and Japan	*0.4*	*0.3*	*0.5*	*−0.2*	*1.0*	*—*
3. Other	*−0.9*	*0.7*	*−0.5*	*−0.3*	*0.5*	*1.3*
C. Discrepancy (A + B)	−0.3	0.2	0.8	−0.2	0.8	0.2

1. United States, United Kingdom, and EEC Countries.
SOURCE: Table 1 above and *International Financial Statistics*, Washington, D.C., May 1964, p. xvii.

exchange estimates are no larger than could be expected in view of the imperfections noted above.[9]

Before commenting on the estimates shown in these tables, one further qualification must be entered.

I shall generally comment on the combined transactions of the U.S., the U.K., and the EEC taken together, as if they represented those of the developed world as a whole in its relations with the underdevel-

9. Since the discrepancy noted is between the *net* foreign exchange gains or losses of the eight countries, and the *gross* foreign exchange losses or gains of the others, it could also originate in the use as central bank reserves of currencies other than those of the eight countries listed in Table 1. The amounts involved, however, are likely to be very small indeed, except for the impact of bilateral payments agreements.

International Financial Statistics used to publish a table on the reconciliation of gross foreign exchange assets and liabilities, but this attempt was discontinued about a year ago.

oped portion of the world economy. This is only an approximation of the truth—although a reasonably close one—since a few developed or semideveloped countries such as Canada, Japan, Switzerland, etc., should be added to the first group rather than to the second.[10] Moreover, the "overseas franc area" is unfortunately included, together with Metropolitan France herself, in the estimates for the EEC area. This has the effect of underestimating the EEC area's current account surplus (by about $250 million in 1961, for instance), official capital exports (by nearly $1.3 billion in 1961), and private capital *imports* (by more than $1 billion in 1961).[11]

Current Account and Private Transfers

The first major observation that emerges from Table 1 is that the eight countries, taken together, have maintained, throughout most of the years 1958–63, substantial surpluses on current account. These surpluses measure, in real terms, their net contributions of goods and services to the rest of the world.

For the eight countries taken together, they averaged about 0.82 per cent of GNP and 13 per cent of merchandise exports over the years 1958–62, and far more indeed for the EEC countries. The EEC current account surplus remained extremely large, and relatively stable, until the end of 1961, but has declined very rapidly since then. On the other hand, the current account balance of the U.K. improved considerably after 1960, and that of the U.S. after its all-time low in 1959. These contrasting movements can undoubtedly be related to the steep increase in EEC price and cost levels, in relation to the United Kingdom, and particularly the United States, over this period. According to the OECD statistics, the GNP price deflator rose by 13 per cent for the EEC group between 1958 and 1962—and more rapidly still in 1963—as compared to 10 per cent in the United Kingdom, and only 5 per cent in the United States.[12] Industrial wage costs per unit of output have changed very little in the United States since 1959, but are estimated to have risen by 10 per cent in England, and about

10. This could be done, but would have required more time and space than was available for this brief study, and would have complicated the main line of argument, with relatively minor gains of precision in view of the imperfection of available data.

11. The estimates in parentheses are derived from IMF, *Balance of Payments Yearbook, 14:* France, 1957–61, p. 5.

12. OECD, *National Accounts 1955–62,* Suppl. to the *General Statistics Bulletin* (Paris, March 1964), p. 9.

20 to 30 per cent—in dollar terms—in the major countries of the European Economic Community.[13] This was accompanied by an improvement of more than $5 billion in the U.S. current account balance from 1959 to 1963, and a deterioration of nearly $3 billion in that of

TABLE 3

AVERAGE RATIOS OF CURRENT ACCOUNT SURPLUS AND THEIR FINANCING
TO GNP AND MERCHANDISE EXPORTS, 1958–62

	Eight countries total	United States	United Kingdom	EEC
I. In per cent of GNP				
A. Current account surplus	0.82	0.56	0.63	1.60
B. Net capital exports	0.83	1.04	0.18	0.53
1. Official	*0.60*	*0.48*	*0.69*	*0.89*
2. Private	*0.23*	*0.56*	*−0.51*	*−0.36*
C. Monetary settlements (A − B)	−0.02	−0.49	0.44	1.07
II. In per cent of merchandise exports[1]				
A. Current account surplus	13.1	14.8	4.4	16.3
B. Net capital exports	13.5	28.0	1.3	5.4
1. Official	*9.7*	*12.9*	*4.8*	*9.0*
2. Private	*3.8*	*15.1*	*−3.5*	*−3.6*
C. Monetary settlements (A − B)	−0.3	−13.3	3.1	10.9

1. Excluding intra-EEC exports.

SOURCES: Tables 1 and 5 for balance-of-payments estimates. For GNP: *National Accounts 1955–62*, Suppl. to the *General Statistics Bulletin*, March 1964, pp. 14, 36sq. For merchandise exports of the U.S. and U.K.: *International Financial Statistics*, May 1964. For merchandise exports of the EEC to nonmembers: OECD, *Statistical Bulletins, Foreign Trade, Series A: Over-all Trade by Origin and Destination*, Paris, April 1964.

the EEC. The U.S. was very probably undercompetitive in relation to the EEC in the late 1950s, following the drastic devaluations of 1949 and the spectacular increases of Europe's productive capacity in the following years. Divergent wage and cost movements, after 1959, have altered radically this situation. The 1963 current account pattern of the eight countries certainly explains—and justifies—the EEC concern with the excessive rate of recent wage and cost increases in the Community, and the need to arrest them in order to restore a reasonable current account surplus, sufficient to finance a normal rate of capital exports by the Community to the rest of the world, and particularly to the developing countries.

13. See Marjolin, *op. cit.*

Official Capital Exports

Official capital exports by the eight countries have been kept at relatively high and increasing levels throughout the years 1958–63. They were about $2 billion larger in 1963 than in 1958, and averaged, in 1958–62, 0.60 per cent of their combined GNP and 9.7 per cent of their merchandise exports. They were highest for the United States in relation to exports (12.9 per cent), and for the EEC in terms of GNP (0.89 per cent).[14]

Private Capital Exports

The current account surpluses of the eight countries, taken together, were more than sufficient to finance their official capital exports, and exceeded them indeed by about $1.65 billion a year, on the average, over the period 1958–62. Most of this excess ($1.35 billion), however, is attributable to the EEC, and only $350 million to the U.S., the U.K. showing a small shortfall of about $50 million.

The U.S. surplus declined slightly (to about $1.35 billion) and the U.K. shifted from a small deficit to a small surplus ($170 million) in 1963. In sharp contrast with previous years, however, the much reduced current account surplus of the EEC in 1963 was about $700 million short of the amount needed to cover the area's official capital exports. This, however, was more than made up by a record inflow of private capital (more than $2 billion), thus leaving the EEC with a further increase of more than $1.3 billion in net monetary reserves.

Private capital movements—particularly short-term—are clearly the most volatile and disturbing element in the balance-of-payments network of the three areas, particularly since 1960.

Over the three years 1961–63 as a whole, they account for the entirety of the EEC net reserve gains ($4 billion) and for more than twice the U.S. net reserve losses ($5.5 billion). They similarly account nearly exactly for the successive reserve losses and gains of the U.K. of the years 1959, 1961, 1962, and 1963, and for more than twice the reserve gains of the U.K. in 1960 (see Table 4).

The breakdown of private capital movements between long-term and short-term (including, as noted above, errors and omissions and

---

14. More detailed national statistics would attribute the lion's share of official EEC capital exports to Germany. As previously noted, however, the statistics presented here exclude the enormous exports of official capital by France to the overseas franc area.

TABLE 4

SOURCES OF NET MONETARY RESERVE CHANGES, 1958–63
(in billions of U.S. dollars)

	1958	1959	1960	1961	1962	1963	Total 1961–63
I. United States	**−3.0**	**−2.3**	**−3.6**	**−1.3**	**−2.2**	**−2.0**	**− 5.5**
A. Private capital exports (−)[1]	−2.2	0.2	−4.3	−3.7	−4.2	−3.4	−11.2
B. Other[2]	−0.8	−2.5	0.7	2.4	1.9	1.3	5.7
II. United Kingdom	**1.1**	**−0.2**	**0.8**	**−1.0**	**0.8**	**−0.5**	**− 0.6**
A. Private capital exports (−)[1]	0.4	−0.2	1.8	−0.9	0.8	−0.6	− 0.8
B. Other[2]	0.8	—	−1.0	−0.1	0.1	0.2	0.2
III. EEC	**2.4**	**1.9**	**3.2**	**2.0**	**0.7**	**1.3**	**4.0**
A. Private capital exports (−)[1]	0.2	—	1.2	1.2	0.8	2.0	4.0
B. Other[2]	2.2	1.9	2.0	0.9	−0.1	−0.7	—

1. Capital exports are shown in this Table with *minus* signs, in order to bring out more clearly their relationship to changes in monetary reserves.

2. Current Account surplus *minus* exports of official capital.

TABLE 5

NET EXPORTS OF PRIVATE CAPITAL, 1958–63
(in billions of U.S. dollars)

	1958	1959	1960	1961	1962	1963
I. Long-Term	**2.5**	**1.2**	**1.8**	**1.1**	**1.6**	
A. United States	2.6	1.6	2.1	2.1	2.5	3.1
B. United Kingdom	0.4	0.4	0.3	−0.2	—	
C. EEC	−0.4	−0.7	−0.5	−0.8	−0.9	
II. Short-Term[1]	**−0.9**	**−1.3**	**−0.6**	**2.4**	**1.0**	
A. United States	−0.3	−1.8	2.2	1.6	1.7	0.3
B. United Kingdom	−0.7	−0.1	−2.1	1.2	−0.7	
C. EEC	0.2	0.7	−0.7	−0.3	0.1	
III. Total	**1.6**	**—**	**1.2**	**3.5**	**2.6**	**1.9**
A. United States	2.2	−0.2	4.3	3.7	4.2	3.4
B. United Kingdom	−0.4	0.2	−1.8	0.9	−0.8	0.6
C. EEC	−0.2	—	−1.2	−1.2	−0.8	−2.0

1. Including errors and omissions and fluctuations in *private* foreign dollar and sterling balances.

SOURCES AND OTHER NOTES: See Table 1 of this article.

privately held foreign currency balances) shows that most of these fluctuations may be ascribed to short-term capital flows. Particularly significant in this respect is the reversal of U.S. short-term capital from a record inflow of $1.8 billion in 1959 to enormous and sustained outflows of $1.6 billion to $2.2 billion in each of the years 1960–62. The role of speculation on gold and exchange rates in this reversal is confirmed by a $1.37 billion shift of the European Community from a net exporter to a net importer of short-term capital, and by the sharp rise of private gold absorption from about $600 million a year in 1956–59 to about $1.05 billion a year, on the average, in the following four years.

Net Monetary Settlements

As might be expected, the overwhelming bulk of net monetary settlements of the three areas takes place among these areas themselves. Net settlements with the outside world were relatively modest in size,

TABLE 6

COMPOSITION OF MONETARY SETTLEMENTS, 1958–63
(in billions of U.S. dollars)

	1958	1959	1960	1961	1962	1963	Total 1958–63
I. Gold	**0.5**	**−0.2**	**0.1**	—	—	**0.3**	**0.8**
A. United States	−2.3	−1.1	−1.7	−0.9	−0.9	−0.5	− 7.3
B. United Kingdom	1.3	−0.3	0.3	−0.5	0.3	−0.1	0.9
C. EEC	1.6	1.1	1.5	1.4	0.6	0.9	7.1
II. Net claims on (or debts to)							
IMF	**0.1**	**0.6**	**−0.1**	—	**0.2**	—	**0.9**
A. United States	—	−0.3	−0.7	0.1	−0.6	—	− 1.5
B. United Kingdom	—	0.4	0.4	−1.0	1.1	—	0.8
C. EEC	0.1	0.5	0.2	0.9	−0.2	0.1	1.6
III. Net foreign exchange	**−0.1**	**−1.0**	**0.4**	**−0.3**	**−1.0**	**−1.5**	**− 3.5**
A. United States	−0.7	−0.9	−1.1	−0.6	−0.7	−1.5	− 5.6
B. United Kingdom	−0.1	−0.3	0.1	0.6	−0.5	−0.3	− 0.6
C. EEC	0.8	0.3	1.4	−0.3	0.3	0.4	2.8
IV. Total = increases in net							
monetary reserves	**0.5**	**−0.6**	**0.4**	**−0.3**	**−0.7**	**−1.1**	**− 1.8**
A. United States	−3.0	−2.3	−3.6	−1.3	−2.2	−2.0	−14.4
B. United Kingdom	1.1	−0.2	0.8	−1.0	0.8	−0.5	1.1
C. EEC	2.4	1.9	3.2	2.0	0.7	1.3	11.5

SOURCES: See Table 1 of this article.

and yearly surpluses and deficits practically cancelled each other over the five years 1958–61.

This means, of course, that the net monetary reserves of the eight countries, as a group, showed no significant increase—they declined indeed very slightly—over this period. The year 1963 shows a record level of net reserve losses, but these are likely to stimulate in the near future a higher level of net spending by other areas which, on the whole, have little inclination, or ability, to accumulate large monetary reserves at the expense of consumption or investment imports.

Over the six years 1958–63, net monetary reserves of the eight countries taken together *declined* by a relatively modest amount of $1.8 billion, but this was more than covered by foreign countries' net accumulation of nearly $3.5 billion of foreign exchange claims on the eight—primarily on the United States, in the form of dollar balances —thus leaving a residue of settlements *in favor* of the eight countries by the IMF ($900 million) and in gold metal (about $760 million).

These settlements, however, are dwarfed by the size of settlements among the eight countries themselves. The U.K. increased its net reserves by $1.1 billion—nearly entirely in the form of gold—and the European Community by a whopping $11.5 billion—of which nearly $7.1 billion was in gold, $1.6 billion through the IMF, and $2.8 billion in foreign exchange.

These reserve increases of the EEC and the U.K. were clearly dependent on the even larger losses of net reserves of the U.S. (more than $14.4 billion), and the latter themselves could not have continued on such a scale if they had required equivalent gold settlements by the U.S. In fact, about half of them were covered instead by the near wiping-out of claims previously accumulated by the U.S. on the IMF ($1.5 billion) and, most of all, by a $5.64 billion increase in the U.S. net indebtedness to foreign monetary authorities, in Europe and other areas.

Conclusions

(1) The reserve movements just discussed could not, obviously, persist indefinitely on such a scale and be financed by similar means. A sharp reduction in the rate of net reserve losses by the U.S. and net reserve gains by the EEC is clearly necessary to restore a tenable balance in the future.

(2) It is highly doubtful, however, whether the corrective policies required should aim primarily at increasing much further the already ample surpluses of the U.S. on current account, or at reducing the

current account surpluses of the EEC below the very low level to which they have already dropped in 1963. On the contrary, some recovery in the EEC current account balance is clearly called for in order to finance, in real terms, the EEC contribution to the developing countries overseas. Nor is a reduction in the modest current account surplus of the U.K. desirable from this point of view.

All in all, some expansion in the current account surpluses of the eight countries, taken together, with the rest of the world should be aimed at, but should center primarily at this time on an improvement of the EEC countries' current balance.

(3) The restoration of monetary equilibrium by the U.S. should hardly be sought, alternatively, in any drastic reduction of the U.S. official capital exports to the developing countries. Nor could monetary balance for the EEC as a whole be realistically achieved through any large increase in such official capital exports, which are already the largest by far in terms of GNP.[15] For the eight countries as a whole, however, some further expansion of official capital exports to the developing countries should probably be regarded as highly desirable in the long run. This would be particularly necessary to help finance, and make possible, the larger current account surpluses of the eight countries, as a group, contemplated under (2) above. Otherwise, the current account targets of the eight countries would most probably prove incompatible with one other, tomorrow as in the past.[16]

(4) This leaves only one area of transactions to which policy action should be primarily directed. Quite clearly, the European Community should not remain a net importer of private capital, particularly on the enormous scale evidenced in recent years ($2 billion in 1963). Capital exports, particularly to the developing countries, should be encouraged, and net capital imports from the U.S. reduced well below the excessive levels of the last few years.[17]

15. About 0.89 per cent, on the average of the years 1958–62, or nearly twice as much (0.48 per cent) as the corresponding U.S. ratio. This contrast, however, is due in part to the inclusion of advance debt and military imports payments to the U.S. under official capital movements rather than under compensatory financing, and to large indemnification payments by Germany to Israel. On the other hand, the EEC contribution to development financing overseas is also much larger than suggested by the above estimates, in view of their failure to take account of France's official capital exports to the overseas franc area.

16. See pp. 119–20, above.

17. Secretary of the Treasury Dillon has long emphasized this point. See, e.g. his most recent speech to the American Bankers Association in Vienna, as reported in *The New York Times* on May 21 of this year.

This should, at first view, suggest the desirability of a hardening of interest rates in the U.S., and a lowering of interest rates in the European Community. Both the U.S. and the Community, however, have been reluctant to move sufficiently boldly in this direction, since such action would not be easy to implement in practice, and would conflict with domestic policy objectives, as long as relative stagnation and high unemployment in the U.S. coincide with booming economic activity and inflationary pressures in Europe.

The measures taken so far by the U.S. have been directed primarily —and successfully—at reducing the spurt of long-term capital exports which had taken such alarming proportions in the first half of 1963. These were brought back, in the second half of the year, approximately to the average, and still substantial, level of 1958–62.

Yet it is the movements of short-term capital which account primarily for the drastic deterioration of the U.S. over-all balance since 1960, and for its improvement in the second half of last year.[18] This improvement may continue, and even snowball, under the impact of the recent deterioration in the balance-of-payments prospects of the Community, of the current large sales of U.S.S.R. gold in the private gold market, and of continued evidence of cooperation by central banks in the efforts to preserve the present gold price and exchange rate pattern, and protect the reserve currency countries against the dangers arising from their excessive foreign short-term indebtedness.

Strong cognizance should be taken, however, of the disturbances which may be introduced in the international pattern of reserve movements by large flows of private capital, in future years as well as in the past, in response either to interest-rate differentials or to other speculative influences. These perturbing flows of short-term funds may be successfully reduced by a better coordination of interest-rate policies, but it would be exceedingly rash—and probably undesirable—to try to subordinate national interest-rate policies to this single aim, regardless of other factors which should justifiably enter into the determination of such policies.

Other measures—of a fiscal character, or in the administration of commercial bank regulations regarding reserve requirements, etc.— might be adopted, in close consultation between the monetary authorities of the countries affected by residual and undesirable capital movements.

18. See above, p. 128 and pp. 116–17.

Finally, shifts in the composition of the central banks' international reserves—among different currencies, or between currencies and gold—should at least refrain from adding to any undesirable pressures arising from private capital flows, and might even have to be undertaken in order to *alleviate* such pressures.

(5) The excessive and erratic levels of short-term indebtedness—theoretically and legally convertible at any time into gold metal—incurred by central banks to one another, under many years of functioning on an unregulated gold-exchange standard, have certainly contributed to international monetary uncertainty and to the instability of speculative capital movements in the past. Sudden or massive shifts of funds by central banks—from one currency into another, or between currencies and gold—would, of course, leave unaffected the *net* reserve position of the countries concerned in such movements. Yet, they could affect very gravely their gold holdings and *gross* reserve position, and inevitably impose, at times, highly undesirable policy reactions on the part of the countries whose gold holdings or *gross* reserves are decreasing, without forcing any policy reactions—in the opposite direction—by the countries whose *gross* reserves would increase in this process. This is another instance of the potentially deflationary bias of the present international monetary system, alluded to in the first section of this paper.

The size and composition of the combined reserves of the world's central banks, and particularly of the major reserve holders, should certainly be sufficiently coordinated over time to reconcile them with a desirable rate of growth and composition of such reserves, rather than be abandoned to the hazards of gold production in the West, of U.S.S.R. gold sales, of speculation in the gold market, of the balance-of-payments surpluses or deficits of the reserve currency countries, and of uncoordinated shifts in the composition of the other central banks' international assets.

Let us hope that the decisions at the IMF Tokyo meeting in September, and *afterwards,* will help orient international monetary reforms in such a way as to facilitate more rational and integrated solutions to these problems than those which have emerged in the past from largely uncoordinated, and mutually incompatible national policies.

4. THE STERLING CRISIS IN WIDER PERSPECTIVE

Modern cities devote as much attention today to the elimination or fireproofing of firetrap structures as to the installation of fireplugs and well-equipped fire departments. Both tasks are necessary.

The amazing degree of international financial cooperation gradually evolved to combat the recurrent dollar and sterling crises of recent years will undoubtedly continue to play a most useful role in limiting the damages of national policy mishaps in an interdependent world. It should not, however, spare the IMF and the Group of Ten from seeking ways and means to consolidate the international monetary structure of the West, and to eliminate the root causes of the crises which the present so-called gold-exchange or key-currencies standard is bound to trigger off tomorrow, as yesterday and today.

The Sterling Crisis

Causes. Academic economists—as well as speculators—are prone to blame the current sterling crisis on the uncompetitiveness of British industries in world markets, and to advocate devaluation as the most efficient and acceptable cure of the disease.

Available evidence for this view, however, is far from compelling. With the exception of 1960, Britain has maintained substantial surpluses on current account in each one of the last six years. They averaged about $450 million annually in 1958–60, and more than $550 million in 1961–63, and were approximately equal to Britain's net exports of official capital.

Net monetary reserves—measured by the difference between gross monetary reserves and liabilities to foreign monetary authorities—fluctuated widely from year to year, but improved by more than $1,200 million over the period as a whole. These fluctuations are overwhelmingly associated with massive shifts in net inflows and outflows of private capital, accounting, for instance, for about 85 per cent of net reserve losses in 1961, 97 per cent of the 1962 reserve gains, and 113 per cent of renewed reserve losses in 1963.

The current account balance admittedly deteriorated considerably in 1964, owing primarily to a sharp increase of imports. Yet, even this may reflect, in large part, speculative stockbuilding and other transactions stimulated by political uncertainties about the election,

---

The Nihon Keizai Shimbun (Tokyo, December 1964), and The Banker (London, February 1965), pp. 79–83.

TABLE 1

BALANCE OF PAYMENTS OF THE UNITED KINGDOM, 1958–64
(years or yearly averages, in millions of U.S. dollars)

	1958–60	1961	1962	1963	January–June 1964
I. Current Account and Official Capital	− 47	− 154	28	61	−863
A. Current account	444	297	658	736	−130
B. Official capital	−491	− 451	−630	−675	−734
II. Private Capital[1]	658	− 845	836	−524	218
III. Net Monetary Reserves[2]	611	−1000	864	−462	−644

1. Including errors and omissions.
2. Gross monetary reserves *minus* indebtedness to IMF and foreign monetary authorities.

and the anticipation of import restrictions and/or an ultimate devaluation of the pound. Certainly, prices and wages have tended to rise faster on the continent than in Britain in recent years, and would hardly suggest a sudden and massive deterioration of Britain's competitiveness in world markets.

This is not to say that the basic structure of Britain's balance of payments is fully satisfactory. Current account surpluses have long been uncomfortably low in relation to the level of capital exports which might correspond to the relative stage of development of the British economy. Deflationary brakes have had to be applied repeatedly to protect a totally inadequate level of monetary reserves against the vulnerability imparted to it by a staggering amount of short-term foreign indebtedness. This, in turn, has undoubtedly played a role in slowing down necessary industrial investments and modernization and the pace of economic growth in general.

Although currency devaluation might, as a consequence, become inescapable at some point, it could hardly be regarded as desirable. On the contrary, the temporary respite which it would bring about might well relieve useful pressures for overdue structural adaptations in many sectors of British industry. The main reason for the large-scale financial assistance elicited from foreign central banks to support the present exchange rate of sterling, however, lies in the catastrophic consequences that the devaluation of one of the two key currencies in world trade might entail for the other key currency and for the international monetary system itself.

TABLE 2

REPORTED LINES OF CREDIT TO THE UNITED KINGDOM
(in millions of U.S. dollars)

	Through IMF			Bilateral	Total
	From IMF holdings	From general borrowing arrangements	Total		
United States	200	—	200	1,000	1,200
Germany	—	180	180	500	680
France	—	100	100	200	300
Italy	15	5	20	200	220
Other countries and BIS	130	120	250	1,100	1,350
IMF gold	250	—	250	—	250
Total	**595**	**405**	**1,000**	**3,000**	**4,000**

Tranquilizers and Remedies. Let us give unstinted praise therefore to the amazing cooperation shown by the central banks of a dozen countries in gathering—directly and through the IMF—some $4 billion of credit lines to come to the rescue of sterling, and to scare off further bear speculation on sterling in the world exchange markets. Yet, these are admittedly in the nature of tranquilizers rather than remedies, since any credits actually used will presumably have to be repaid within a few months or, when transferred to the IMF, within a period of three to five years at most.

Nor can the 15 per cent import surcharge, or the 7 per cent Bank Rate be regarded as permanent solutions for the crisis. British authorities have been forced to give solemn assurances to GATT, EFTA, and OECD that they would remove fairly promptly a tax which clearly contravenes equally solemn previous international commitments to these organizations. As for the 7 per cent Bank Rate, it could hardly be maintained indefinitely without serious economic and political consequences, particularly by a Labor Government committed to expansionary domestic policies.

The only hope is that the brief breathing spell afforded by these measures will be put to effective use in seeking *longer-term* solutions and financial support for the two basic tasks facing the British economy and balance of payments: (1) modernization and adaptation of some industrial sectors to new technological developments and changed patterns of demand, at home and abroad; (2) strengthening of the grossly inadequate monetary reserves of Britain, particularly in view of the excessive short-term indebtedness and vulnerability to speculative capital movements inherited from the role of sterling— and the dollar—in the anachronistic gold-exchange standard whose reform is now under study.

International Perspectives

Central bankers are justifiably concerned with the inflationary trends that have accompanied the unprecedentedly fast and persistent rates of economic growth of the postwar years. They are also prone to place the blame for such trends on their colleagues rather than on themselves. The Dutch and the Germans used to blame the French, and they now all blame the Americans and the British for the "un-requited" balance-of-payments surpluses that feed the inflationary fuel in their respective countries. Yet such external surpluses are most often dwarfed by domestic credit expansion in the over-all inflationary process from which they suffer.

The international monetary mechanism itself (with temporary exceptions for the reserve-currency countries only) is strongly biased in the direction of contraction, rather than of expansion. The main reason for this has long been denounced by economists. Even moderate deficits, in relation to GNP, may threaten a rapid exhaustion of a country's reserve levels, and force it to choose between contractionist monetary and fiscal policies, devaluation or trade and exchange restrictions. Relatively large surpluses, on the other hand, may be accumulated without creating similarly effective pressures for upward currency revaluation or for trade liberalization; and their domestic expansionary impact may be counteracted to a substantial extent by so-called neutralization, sterilization, or compensatory policies.

This asymmetry between the pressures arising from balance-of-payments surpluses and deficits is further compounded by a number of other factors, such as:

(1) The tendency of "deficit" countries to react in very much the same manner to (a) losses of *gross* reserve assets, (b) declines of *net* reserve assets, even if financed by increased reserve indebtedness rather than by losses of gross reserves, (c) a deterioration of their current account balance, even if financed by capital imports rather than by net reserve losses, and, finally (d) a so-called "over-all" deficit, measured not only by reserve losses, but also by an increase in privately held short-term claims of foreigners which are nowhere registered as an accretion to reserves, but are regarded instead as capital

exports by the foreign countries concerned. This kind of international bookkeeping resulted, only last year, in worrying *simultaneously* the United States, the United Kingdom, the European Economic Community, Japan, Canada, and of course most of the underdeveloped countries, about their respective "deficits," differently defined. As *The Economist* asked whimsically at the time: "Where are the surpluses?"

(2) The tendency to seek the elimination of any of the "deficits," so diversely defined, through an improvement of the country's current account balance, even though—as has been predominantly the case for the United States and the United Kingdom in recent years—the major source of difficulties can clearly be traced to unrequited disturbances on capital, rather than current, account.

(3) The tendency to seek such current account improvement through "contractionist" credit and/or fiscal policies—or trade and exchange restrictions—rather than through currency devaluation, even when exchange readjustments might be called for by substantive changes in the trading countries' cost competitiveness in world markets.

(4) The frequent strengthening of most of the national policy biases described above by the international consultations conditioning the granting of financial assistance by the surplus countries to the deficit countries. Remedial measures can far more easily be forced by the former upon the latter than by the latter upon the former, even when the international imbalance between deficit and surplus countries might best be cured in part by more expansionist policies, upward currency revaluation and/or the liberalization of trade and capital movements by the surplus countries.

Conclusions

These remarks should *not* be interpreted as a condemnation of the remarkable development of postwar efforts at international monetary and economic cooperation, and particularly of the substantial contributions, financial and other, which surplus countries have made, and are now making, to help smooth the difficult process of international adjustment between legally independent and sovereign countries in an interdependent world. They should be regarded instead as a strong endorsement of these efforts, and as an attempt to draw attention to some of the tasks that still lie ahead:

(1) A clearer and more operational recognition of the *joint* responsibility of surplus and deficit countries alike in the correction, where

appropriate, and in the financing, where appropriate, of international imbalance between them.

(2) The elaboration of agreed, compatible criteria and targets for sustainable balance in international transactions, and of compatible national policies in the pursuit of these targets.

(3) Greater attention to capital movements as a possible source of disturbances and as a fruitful area for national and international corrective or compensatory action.

(4) An effort to reduce present institutional biases toward restrictions and devaluation, in favor of more frequent recourse to liberalization and upward currency revaluation.

(5) Last, but not least, a consolidation of our international monetary structure against glaring sources of instability, and a more systematic orientation of the process of monetary reserves creation toward the full utilization of the noninflationary growth potential of the world economy.[1]

1. Fuller evidence and documentation for some of the points briefly summarized in this article may be found in the *Weltwirtschaftliches Archiv* article reproduced above, pp. 118–32.

PART TWO

The International

Monetary System: Anachronism,

Palliatives, and Reform

Chapter V: Exchange Controls, Exchange-Rate Readjustments, and the International Monetary Fund: 1946–49

I HAVE GROUPED in this chapter a number of papers, some of them previously unpublished, written over the years 1946–49, and referring to the world-wide monetary policies of the IMF, rather than to its policies with regard to regional monetary cooperation and integration (see Part Three).

As Chief of the Latin American Section of the Board of Governors of the Federal Reserve System, I had devoted most of the years 1943–46 to studying Latin American monetary problems and helping a number of Latin American countries in radical overhauls of their monetary, exchange controls and banking systems.[1] In "National Central Banking and the International Economy" I attempted to integrate the lessons which I had learned in the process into a broad reinterpretation of the classical theory of the gold standard and some highly unorthodox policy advice for the newly born International Monetary Fund on the then burning issue of exchange controls.[2]

The next paper was written after I joined the Fund, in the summer of 1946, as Chief of the Exchange Control Division, and is also pri-

1. See, e.g. "New Monetary and Banking Measures in Paraguay," "Monetary Developments in Latin America," and "Monetary and Banking Reform in Guatemala" in the *Federal Reserve Bulletin* (January 1944), pp. 42–51 (June 1945), pp. 519–31, and (March 1946), pp. 257-88; *Money and Banking in Colombia* and *Monetary and Banking Reform in Paraguay* (Washington, D.C., Board of Governors of the Federal Reserve System, 1944 and 1946); "Central Banking and Monetary Management in Latin America" in *Economic Problems of Latin America,* ed. Seymour E. Harris (New York, 1944), pp. 93–116; *Anteproyecto de Ley Monetaria y de Régimen Orgánico de las Transferencias Internacionales* (San José, Costa Rica, December 1944); *Anteproyecto de Ley de Adhesión a los Convenios de Bretton Woods* (Guatemala, 1946); "Esbozo General de un Análisis de las Series Estadísticas Monetarias y Bancarias de América Latina sobre Bases Uniformes y Comparables" in *Memoria,* Primera Reunión de Técnicos sobre Problemas de Banca Central del Continente Americano (México, D.F., Banco de México, 1946), pp. 218–36; and (in collaboration with Henry C. Wallich) *Monetary and Banking Legislation of the Dominican Republic, 1947* (Federal Reserve Bank of New York, 1953).

2. I would like to take this occasion to stress anew my indebtedness to Dr. Raúl Prebisch's pioneering work in the same field.

marily related to my experience with exchange control problems in Latin America.

The final section of the chapter turns to the issues raised for the International Monetary Fund by the wave of devaluations triggered by the British devaluation of September 1949, and the avenues opened thereby for the elimination of exchange controls and bilateralism in world payments.

1. NATIONAL CENTRAL BANKING AND THE INTERNATIONAL ECONOMY

The growth of nationalistic policies in a growingly interdependent world is one of the paradoxes of our age. The paradox is only apparent. Interdependence has its drawbacks as well as its advantages. Far distant countries find themselves engulfed in wars which, in the past, would never have touched their shores. Economic depressions spread from one nation to the others and communicate to all the diseases contracted by a few. Nationalism can be explained in part as an effort to preserve or rebuild the crumbling natural boundaries which, in the past, isolated each country from the others and protected it from the contagion of political conflicts and economic maladjustments. The effort is often unsuccessful and self-defeating. In many cases, nationalistic measures of defense aggravate the difficulties of other countries and lead to retaliatory action which further intensifies the international crisis. The problem to which they try to give an answer, however, must be recognized as a real and challenging one. Nothing can be gained by denying or ignoring it.

Our internationalism is often short-sighted in this respect. In the monetary field, for example, we are prone to stigmatize exchange control or exchange devaluation, but slow to suggest workable alternatives

---

Published with comments by Gottfried Haberler in *International Monetary Policies,* Postwar Economic Studies, No. 7, Board of Governors of the Federal Reserve System (Washington, D.C., 1947), pp. 46–81 and 82–102; and with comments by H. D. Henderson, Thomas Balogh, and R. F. Harrod in *The Review of Economic Studies,* 14 (1946–47), pp. 58–75 and 76–97. Readers interested in the functioning of the pre-1914 gold standard may wish to consult also my study of *The Evolution of the International Monetary System: Historical Reappraisal and Future Perspectives* (Princeton, 1964), pp. 1–20 and 51–63, for a rash attempt at assembling, for the first time, comprehensive estimates of the comparative evolution of the structure of national money stocks and international reserves over a century (1815–1913), and at venturing, in this light, a radical reinterpretation of ivory tower, or armchair, abstract theorizing on the actual functioning of the so-called, or rather *miscalled,* international gold standard.

to meet or prevent in other ways the exchange shortages which bring about such measures of defense. This is undoubtedly one of the reasons why so little progress has been made in practice toward the elimination of exchange control or competitive devaluation, in spite of their general condemnation by economists and statesmen alike.

A new and more promising approach toward the problem is now in the process of effective realization. The creation of the International Monetary Fund is specifically designed to promote international monetary stability through the concerted action of all member countries. The legal powers of the Fund may be grouped into two broad categories. First of all, the financial machinery of the Fund will help the members to maintain free and stable exchanges, by supplementing their gold and foreign exchange resources in case of need. Thus one cause, at least, of monetary instability will be removed or considerably weakened, i.e. the unilateral resort to currency depreciation or exchange restrictions, for the lack of any other alternative during a period of severe, even though temporary, exchange shortages. Secondly, the Fund may exert a varying degree of influence over specific policy decisions of the member countries. In some cases, the Fund has only the power to make recommendations, or the right to be consulted. In others, such as parity changes, or the establishment of exchange control, action by a member may be subordinated to the Fund's authorization or approval.

The effective power and influence of the Fund, however, may be far greater, or far smaller, than its legal authority. Although the Fund has no right to impose domestic monetary or credit policies, it may develop a leadership and moral influence far beyond the scope of mere official, formal recommendations. On the other hand, even though the Fund can, in theory, forbid a country to engage in either currency devaluation or exchange control, such prohibition may be unenforceable, even with the best of will on the part of the member, in the face of severe exchange shortages. Currency devaluation and exchange control are often the reflection of more basic disturbances in a country's international position and cannot be eliminated as long as the root causes of those disturbances remain.

The ultimate success, or failure, of the Fund will depend, in no small part, on its ability to devise, in collaboration with member countries, workable and realistic standards of domestic, as well as of international, monetary policy. This implies a bold revision of traditional concepts and dogmas associated with the gold standard theory.

The orthodox gold standard mechanism implied a more or less passive acceptance, by each country, of automatic monetary adjustments prompted by fluctuations in the balance of payments. The same view was reaffirmed, in the twenties, by the Cunliffe Committee and played a major part in the studies and recommendations of the League of Nations in the monetary field. It was, however, in direct contradiction to the increasing trend, both in theory and practice, toward independent monetary management on the national scale.

The events of the thirties, the increasing influence of Keynesian economics, and finally the financial impact of World War II, have finally destroyed the institutional and ideological framework of the automatic gold standard. Tomorrow's currencies will be managed currencies. The only question at issue—and it is, of course, a fundamental one—is the direction toward which management will work, and the extent to which national objectives can be reconciled with international balance. Any attempt to enforce rigid solutions patterned upon orthodox gold standard doctrines would be even more futile in the postwar than it already proved to be in the interwar period.

The purpose of this paper is to review briefly the interaction between the evolution of national central banking and that of the international gold standard, to raise some important questions with relation to the actual working of the gold standard in the prewar period, and finally to outline, in conclusion, tentative suggestions with respect to the problem of international monetary stabilization.

Central Banking and the Gold Standard

The central problem of this paper is the reconciliation of domestic monetary policies with the prerequisites of international balance. In its purest form, the gold standard solved the problem automatically by eliminating one of its terms: the domestic volume of money escaped the control of national authorities, and was determined automatically by international market forces. Monetary circulation was made up of gold and subsidiary coin, and expanded or contracted, not as a result of conscious monetary policy, but in accordance with the net movements of the international balance of payments. A favorable balance of payments brought gold into the country and expanded the circulating medium. An unfavorable balance produced the opposite effect. These movements were regarded as self-readjusting through their influence on national price and cost levels and on interest rates. International balance, if disturbed, would be restored because of the effects of the ensuing domestic contraction or expansion on relative cost and interest levels at home and abroad and the resulting shifts in trade and capital movements. The automatic monetary contraction produced by gold exports would raise interest rates and attract capital from abroad. It would at the same time exert a downward pressure on domestic prices and costs, thus stimulating exports and discouraging imports. Both of these movements—capital and trade—would tend to correct the balance-of-payments deficit in which they originated.[1] A similar reasoning would show that a surplus in the balance of payments would also be self-corrective. Gold imports would expand monetary circulation, lower interest rates, increase prices and costs, stimulate capital exports and merchandise imports while discouraging exports, until foreign payments and receipts were again brought into balance.

This type of analysis, however, is based on a particularly rigid form of the gold standard, in which there exists, in practice, no national currency or national monetary sovereignty. The only circulating medium is gold itself, i.e. an international standard impervious to national manipulation or management.

The development of other means of payment, national in character, deeply modifies the functioning of the gold standard by isolating in part fluctuations in the domestic money supply from fluctuations in the balance of payments. Little attention is usually paid, in this respect, to the latent antinomy between central banking and the classical gold standard. And yet, the automatic monetary mechanism of the pure gold standard would obviously leave no room for what is today conceived as one of the primary functions of central banking action, i.e. monetary management by the central banking authorities. This oversight may be explained in part by the lack of adaptability of our dictionaries. Fundamental institutional changes are cloaked under an unchanging terminology. Just as the gold standard of the twenties was basically different from the gold standard of earlier days, the central banks of today bear little resemblance to the central banks of the nineteenth century.

Indeed the original pattern of central banking had little, or nothing, to do with monetary management, which was left, as indicated above, to the automatic regulation of the pure gold standard. The functions of

1. Modern theories of international trade and capital movements would incorporate two further major elements in this analysis. One is the elasticity of supply and demand for imports and exports, the other the direct income effects associated with balance-of-payments disequilibria.

central banks were purely ancillary ones, and even their power of issue was not designed to interfere with, or supplant, the controlling role of gold over the money supply. The shift from monetary automatism to monetary management was slow and gradual. The evolution of the Bank of England is most revealing in this respect.

The Bank Act of 1844 had as its very objective the restoration of an unmanaged gold standard, ruled exclusively by fluctuations in the balance of payments. Variations in the total note issue of the Bank of England would correspond exactly to the movements of gold itself in the reserves of the Issue Department. Any inflow or outflow of gold would produce a corresponding increase or decrease in the volume of money, just as would have occurred if the circulation had consisted exclusively of gold coin. Indeed, that was the theoretical philosophy and the practical purpose of the authors of the Act. The Issue Department of the Bank of England, therefore, played a purely passive role and could not exert the slightest influence on the volume of money.[2]

Whatever central banking functions this system left to the Bank of England pertained, not to the Issue, but to the Banking Department. No such functions, however, were originally intended by the authors of the Act. In the years immediately following the Bank Act, the Banking Department was regarded merely as a commercial bank "to be managed in the same way as any other private bank."[3] It is only gradually, and at the initiative of the Government rather than of the Bank itself, that the special position and responsibilities of the Banking Department came to be clearly recognized and accepted by the Bank authorities. These responsibilities, however, did not, even then, extend to the broad and modern concept of monetary management, but merely to the function of "lender of last resort." This function, moreover, did not imply the issue power since, in principle at least, fluctuations in the note issue continued to correspond exactly to the fluctuations in the gold assets of the Issue Department.

As "lender of last resort," the Banking Department would, through its credit and investment operations, relieve temporary shortages of

2. The only channel for interference with market forces lay in changes in the amount of the gold uncovered, or "fiduciary" issue. Outside of one brief and minor exception, no such change occurred prior to the First World War.

3. "Evidence of the Governor and Deputy Governor of the Bank of England before the Secret Committee of the House of Commons on the Commercial Distress (March 7, 1848)" in T. E. Gregory, *Select Statutes, Documents and Reports Relating to British Banking, 1832–1928*, 2 (London, 1929), p. 28.

cash in the commercial banks. In doing so, however, the Department would interfere with the process of readjustment contemplated in the gold standard theory, since it would offset the deflationary effect of a deficit in the balance of payments and, in this way, prevent its ultimate correction. The drain on the limited note reserves of the Department would continue until their exhaustion, and make impossible a continuation of its assistance to the market, except if the limitation on the fiduciary issue of the Bank were raised or suspended.[4] Thus, the "lender of last resort" operations were conceived as a mere temporary palliative, to be accompanied by other measures tending toward a fundamental readjustment similar to the one which would have taken place automatically under the pure gold standard.

The most important instrument used toward that end was the manipulation of the discount rate. Credit was made available, in times of crisis, but at higher rates leading to a general rise of interest costs and contraction of credit. In the words of the Cunliffe Committee, this would result in "a decline in general prices in the home market which, by checking imports and stimulating exports, corrected the adverse trade balance which was the primary cause of the difficulty." [5] In this way, central banks could perform their mission of lender of last resort—i.e. to provide credit institutions, in times of need, with the liquid funds necessary to tide them over temporary panics and difficulties—while still transmitting to the economy the external and self-readjusting pressures arising from balance-of-payments disequilibria under the pure gold standard system. They would cheapen and expand credit in times of favorable balances, and contract it, except for temporary assistance to the banks, in times of unfavorable balances. The general effect of this policy would be similar to the automatic results of gold inflows or outflows under a purely metallic monetary standard, at least as far as the direction of the movements was concerned.

The intensity of fluctuations, however, could be far greater, and their incidence very different, because of the gap introduced by the

4. In the first crisis following the Bank Act, the Bank refused to support fully the market until authorized by the Government to exceed its legal fiduciary issue. Similar authorizations were granted in 1857, 1866, and 1914. In the more recent period, further expansions have been made possible under the Currency and Bank Notes Acts of 1928 and 1939.

5. *Committee on Currency and Foreign Exchanges after the War, First Interim Report,* in T. E. Gregory, 2, p. 337.

banking system between gold and total monetary circulation. Under a fractional reserve system of commercial banking, and given the fairly stable ratio maintained by British banks between their cash and their deposits, the deposit component of monetary circulation would increase or decrease by several times the amount of the increase or decrease in the cash reserves of the banks. Banking expansion and contraction would also affect the cash balances of individuals and firms which, under the pure gold standard, might not have been touched, at least directly, by the monetary fluctuations resulting from disequilibria in the country's balance of payments. Finally, because of the narrow gold base which it maintained, the Bank of England, in order to defend its reserve position, was led not only to permit, but also to reinforce through its credit policies, the automatic contraction resulting from the retirement of its notes in exchange for gold. The net effect of the banking superstructure erected upon the gold standard basis, was to accentuate the violence of monetary fluctuations far beyond their normal amplitude under a pure gold circulation.

The departure from the pure gold standard mechanism, implicit in the operations of deposit banks, was carried even further under the "rules of the game" so much publicized in the twenties by central bank and League of Nations experts. "Whenever gold flowed in, the central bank was expected to increase the national currency supply, not only through the purchase of that gold, but also through the acquisition of additional domestic assets; and, similarly, when gold flowed out, the central bank was supposed to contract its domestic assets also. In this way the influence of gold movements on the domestic credit base was to be magnified, and magnified in accordance with the central bank's reserve ratio. With a ratio of 33 per cent, for instance, any net increase or decrease in the gold reserve was thus supposed to create a threefold expansion or contraction in the total credit base." [6]

The "rules of the game" were presented as synonymous with the rules of the gold standard itself. They were, of course, no such thing. On the contrary, while balance-of-payments disequilibria, under the pure gold standard, produced only an equivalent amount of expansion or contraction in the monetary circulation, they would now foster, in addition, a secondary expansion or contraction, many times the original one. This was defended as a way to speed up international readjustments and conserve the country's international reserves, but could

6. *International Currency Experience* (League of Nations, 1944), pp. 66–67.

be achieved only at the cost of much greater domestic instability.[7] No wonder that the "rules of the game" encountered increasing resistance, and that their breach became more characteristic of monetary policy than their observance.

The breakdown of the gold standard in the interwar period has often been ascribed, in part, to this unwillingness, or inability, of central banks to play the gold standard game in accordance with its supposed rules.[8] It should again be emphasized, however, that these rules deeply misrepresented the pure gold standard theory and that their observance would have meant a departure from, and not the implementation of, the classical mechanism of international adjustments. Thus, the monetary policy of the United States in the twenties has often been interpreted as a "sterilization" or "neutralization" policy, and criticized as contrary to gold standard rules. In fact, however, the total money supply (deposits and currency outside banks) increased, from June 1920, to December 1924, by $7.2 billion, or about 4.5 times the increase in gold reserves during the same period ($1.6 billion). In 1925–29, the money supply rose again by $7.6 billion in the face of a *decrease* in gold reserves. For the period as a whole, therefore, monetary circulation increased by $14.8 billion, while the increase, under a pure gold standard, would have been of less than $1.5 billion. Mr. Nurkse's discussion of neutralization policies in the United States and other countries[9] does indeed demonstrate his point, i.e. that, contrary to the "rules of the game," "central banks' international and domestic assets . . . moved far more often in the *opposite* than in the same direction." This does *not* mean, however, that the primary impact of the gold flows was fully offset or neutralized, nor even that their influence on monetary circulation was not multiplied several times by commercial banking expansion. Thus, in spite of neutralization policies, gold flows may well have exerted as great, or even greater, an influence on the money market as they would have under classical gold standard assumptions.

The most significant development of the period, however, was the growing importance of domestic factors as the final determinant of

7. This instability, moreover, will have an incidence very different from that attaching to the primary contraction or expansion associated with gold flows under the pure gold standard. It will bear especially heavily on bank borrowers and investment activities. See F. A. von Hayek, *Monetary Nationalism and International Stability* (London, 1937), pp. 25–32.

8. See especially Lionel Robbins, *The Great Depression* (London, 1934).

9. *International Currency Experience*, pp. 68–88 and 237–40.

monetary policies. While international gold flows continued to stimulate domestic monetary expansion or contraction, the total volume
of money was no longer controlled by them. Other factors, of a
purely domestic nature, contributed also to shape monetary developments in a manner totally alien both to the classical gold standard
mechanism and its "rules of the game" interpretation, or rather misinterpretation. Central bank powers were no longer used to transmit
automatically to the domestic economy the upward or downward
pressures of surpluses or deficits in the balance of payments, regardless of national policy objectives. On the contrary, central banking
policies came to be defined less and less with reference to the state of
the gold reserves or the prerequisites of international balance, and
more and more in terms of domestic price stability, the promotion of
fuller employment, etc. This tendency was greatly reinforced in the
thirties through the generalized adoption of national recovery programs, based on domestic monetary and credit expansion, behind the
protection of exchange control and currency devaluation. Thus, the
latent contradiction between the international, and automatic, monetary regulation characteristic of the pure gold standard, and the evolution toward autonomous, and discretionary, monetary management
by national central banks came to be fully realized.

The pendulum may now be swinging again in the other direction.
The experience of the thirties has demonstrated the pitfalls of monetary isolation along purely national lines and the difficulties of recon-
ciling domestic stability and prosperity with international balance.
The Bretton Woods agreements, without returning to the full subor-
dination of national monetary policies to the single goal of exchange
stability, have sought to re-establish some mechanism designed to
protect the international economy against autarkistic excesses in the
monetary field. Member countries agree to cede to the Fund a considerable measure of control over modifications in their exchange
rates or the imposition of exchange restrictions. To make possible this
partial renunciation to national monetary sovereignty, the International Monetary Fund undertakes to make available to member countries, in times of need, additional exchange reserves necessary to
finance temporary deficits in their balance of payments. The Fund,
however, does not attempt to restore a fully international and automatic monetary standard. Central banks and other national monetary
authorities are left free to determine domestic monetary policies as
long as they do not use the resources of the Fund "in a manner con-

trary to the purposes of the Fund." The success of the new institution will thus depend largely on the soundness of the national monetary policies followed by its members, and on the successful solution by each member country of the basic conflict between domestic goals of action and the preservation of international balance. Fundamental disequilibria, if not corrected by domestic measures of readjustment, would perpetuate the need for new borrowings from the Fund or would force again recourse to currency devaluation or exchange control. The only assistance provided by the Fund is a limited right of borrowing, equivalent to a mere increase in the members' international reserves, and some protection against arbitrary and damaging monetary action by other members.

No attempt is made, however, to lay down in detail "rules of the game" of the new international standard, which would prevent, or correct, fundamental international disequilibria. And yet, it is well recognized that persistent deficits in a country's balance of payments would ultimately lead to the exhaustion of its limited drawing rights on the Fund, as well as of its gold and foreign exchange reserves. Once such a situation is reached, the whole Fund machinery becomes ineffective,[10] and no paper commitments can maintain free and stable exchange rates. The problem of international disequilibria, and of their methods of correction, is thus crucial to the successful functioning of the new international monetary standard.

The Correction of International Disequilibria

In spite of the important divergences, pointed out above, between the classical gold standard theory and its modern "rules of the game" version, both types of analyses coincide in some important respects. Balance-of-payments disequilibria are ascribed to international cost and price disparities, and their correction is made to depend on the elimination of such disparities through automatic, or induced, domestic monetary expansion or contraction.

These views of the mechanism of international adjustment under gold standard assumptions are open to very grave question. First of all, they fail to distinguish between a fundamental disequilibrium in one country's international position, and world-wide disturbances in balances of payments associated with cyclical fluctuations. Secondly,

---

10. The day of reckoning could, of course, be postponed further as long as the Fund is willing and able to grant, under Article V, Section 4, additional drawing rights to meet the deficit.

the explanation of the readjustment of a country's balance of payments is vitiated by the underlying, and totally unrealistic, assumption of near-perfect competition between nations of roughly equal strength and importance in world trade.

Cyclical vs. Fundamental Maladjustments. The classical explanation of balance-of-payments maladjustments runs in terms of international price and cost disparities between *one country* and the rest of the world. While applicable to many important instances of disequilibria, this analysis does not exhaust all possible causes of deficits in a country's international transactions. The most cursory examination of statistical data clearly shows that many of the most spectacular disequilibria in balances of payments are *world-wide* in scope, and must be traced to cyclical fluctuations of an international character rather than to national price and cost maladjustments.

In the decade prior to the war, for instance, the dollar value of world trade fell by more than 60 per cent between 1929 and 1932, increased by 23.5 per cent from 1936 to 1937, and fell again by 12.5 per cent during 1938. If the major cause of these fluctuations had resided in international price and cost disparities, high cost countries would be expected to show a decrease in exports and an increase in imports, while low cost countries would show movements in the opposite direction. The striking fact, however, is that, in spite of differences in amplitude, both exports and imports moved *in the same direction* for practically all trading countries. Clearly, the major force impinging upon their trade was international in character, and associated with the world cycle rather than with individual country maladjustments.

To take a concrete illustration, Colombia lost, in the short space of three years (1929–31), 80 per cent of its central bank gold and foreign exchange reserves. Total exports fell from $122 million in 1929 to $67 million in 1932, a decline of 46 per cent. The major item of exports (about 60 per cent of total export values), coffee, suffered a reduction of 45 per cent. If this contraction in coffee exports had been due to disparities in production costs between Colombia and other major coffee exporting countries in competition with her, we would expect these other countries to have expanded their exports at the expense of Colombian producers. During the same period, however, total exports and coffee exports of all other competing coffee countries were also falling in similar, or even larger, proportions. This simultaneity in export fluctuations, both upward and downward, was also characteristic of the recovery experienced by all of them in the years 1933–37, of the 1937–40 decline, and of the record levels of export reached during the more recent war years. It might, of course, be argued that, even though no price disparity was evident as between the various coffee exporting countries, all of them were suffering simultaneously from the consequences of excessive price and cost levels as compared with the rest of the world, and that the classical prescription for readjustment still remained applicable to the group as a whole. This position, however, would be hard to defend in view of the fact that the export prices for typical coffee grades had fallen by 1930 nearly to one half, and by 1931 to not far from one third, of their 1928 level, without eliciting any substantial recovery of quantities exported.

Indeed, for most agricultural countries, large export receipts and favorable balances of payments usually coincide with high, and not with low, levels of domestic and export prices. The reason for this is that their export volume and export prices fluctuate as much, or more, with demand, as with supply, conditions. That is, they are largely determined by international, rather than domestic, factors. Major fluctuations in export values are largely the result of cyclical movements in economic activity and income in the buying countries, and not only in domestic price or cost levels compared with prices and costs in other competing or buying countries. Thus, for many agricultural and raw material countries, the international cycle is mainly an imported product. Such is also the conclusion of the League of Nations' Delegation on Economic Depressions. "General depressions would seem to result mainly from fluctuations in investment and employment in industrial countries." [11]

Whenever this is true, the classical prescription for remedial policy becomes as misleading as the diagnosis on which it is based. Deflationary efforts at readjustment by individual countries are largely self-defeating and serve as an agent of propagation of the depression, rather than as a cure for the disequilibrium. Any initial success that

11. *Economic Stability in the Post-War World* (League of Nations, 1945), p. 291. The clearest case is provided by the brief depression of 1938 in which world exports to the U.S. fell by over 35 per cent in a single year, while U.S. exports decreased only by 7 per cent. It is not denied, of course, that other factors—including price disparities—may be simultaneously operating in bringing about, or accentuating, a major depression.

they may have in curbing imports or expanding exports aggravates the difficulties in their supply and export markets, as well as in competing countries, and leads to similar, and mutually offsetting, measures of defense or retaliation. It should be noted that the argument applies equally to readaptation through currency devaluation and through internal price changes. Under the conditions described, both price deflation and currency devaluation spread from country to country and accentuate the international deflation. While some categories of exports may expand under the stimulus of price reductions, the expansion will often be insufficient to compensate for the decline in unit prices, especially in the case of agricultural or raw material exports faced with an inelastic world demand. The burden of readjustment then falls upon imports, the reduction of which further aggravates income contraction abroad and the effective demand for each country's exports.

The situation described presents a strong analogy with that of oligopoly, where efforts by one seller to cut into his competitors' markets are thwarted by the competitors' retaliation and the ensuing price war. The expansionary effect of a decline in one country's prices upon its exports is largely offset by simultaneous, or retaliatory, price decreases by competing countries. Thus, the effective elasticity of demand for one country's exports becomes merged with the much lower world's elasticity of demand for that type of product.[12] Sales can be expanded only in so far as lower prices stimulate consumption, and not through inroads into other nations' markets.

It should be noted that this analysis does not conflict in any way with the classical theory of balance-of-payments maladjustments. It merely applies to an entirely different set of circumstances. Cyclical disturbances of the kind assumed here played little or no part in classical analysis. The error made by later economists—and especially by the "rules of the game" school—was to extend to world-wide, cyclical disturbances, an analysis aimed at fundamental maladjustments between *one* economy and the rest of the world. In the latter case, moderate price changes by the deficit country may restore its normal export-import balance and share of world trade, without depressing world prices to any significant extent. This is especially true

---

12. In the case of competing oligopolists, the effective demand elasticity is similarly determined by the demand curve for the *industry* as a whole, rather than by the demand curve which would face any one seller *if* his competitors' prices remained constant.

if, as contemplated also in classical theory, its exports are broadly diversified, rather than concentrated on one or a few major items. During a cyclical depression, however, simultaneous efforts by many nations at maintaining, or increasing, their exports in the face of a shrinking world demand, merely result in an accelerated fall of prices and reduction of export proceeds all around.

Gold Standard or Sterling Exchange Standard? A second assumption underlying the classical theory of the gold standard is that of near-perfect competition between many trading nations, more or less coequal in importance. The assumption was obviously unrealistic, and many writers have in recent years expatiated at length on the central position occupied by Great Britain in the nineteenth-century functioning of the gold standard.[13] It has been suggested that that position "made the prewar gold standard essentially a sterling exchange standard system," [14] but the concrete implications of that assertion were not fully drawn. If examined, they may suggest one possible explanation both for the relative success of the gold standard in Britain and for its failure to operate satisfactorily in the least industrialized nations. In many of the latter countries, it was adhered to only sporadically, and abandoned in times of crisis. When actually enforced, it may well have retarded, rather than accelerated, the rate of their economic development. In Great Britain itself, the mechanism of balance-of-payments readjustments seems to have operated, in important respects, in a manner directly opposite to that described by gold standard theory. To a very large extent, increases in the London discount rate brought about a readjustment in the British balance of payments, not through their effects on the British economy, but through their effects on the outside world and especially on the agricultural and raw material countries.

One of the reasons for this has long been recognized. As early as 1840, it was pointed out by Tooke before a Select Committee of the House of Commons on banks of issue, that: "The effect upon the exchange of a rise in the rate of interest would be that of inducing foreign capitalists to abstain from calling for their funds from this country to the same extent as they otherwise might do, and it would operate at the same time in diminishing the inducements to capitalists in this country to invest in foreign securities or to hold foreign secu-

13. See, especially, William Adams Brown, Jr., *The International Gold Standard Reinterpreted* (New York, 1940).
14. *Ibid.*, p. xiii.

rities, and it might induce them to part with foreign securities in order to invest in British stocks and shares. It would likewise operate in restraining credits from the merchants in this country by advances on shipments outwards, and it would have the effect of causing a larger proportion of the importations into this country to be carried on upon foreign capital." [15]

This shift in international capital movements contributed powerfully to a rapid restoration of equilibrium in the exchange market. It would, however, tend to relieve, rather than accentuate, domestic deflationary pressures on the economy and, to that extent, delay or prevent the basic readjustment of fundamental price and cost disparities contemplated by gold standard theorists. It constituted, in a sense, the equivalent of the compensatory monetary policies so strongly condemned by many gold standard theorists.

Similarly, the outflow of capital in periods of favorable balances tended to check the surpluses, and thus to reduce external expansionary impacts upon the British economy. This, again, was contrary to the "rules of the game," and tantamount to the opposite policy of sterilization or neutralization of gold movements.

Debtor countries, however, did not have a similar mechanism at their disposal. Capital tended to flow toward them in times of prosperity, and away from them in times of depression, irrespective of their discount policy. The effect of such fluctuations in capital movements was to smooth down cyclical monetary and credit fluctuations in the creditor countries, but to accentuate them in the debtor countries. To that extent, the financial centers could shift part of the burden of readjustment upon the weaker countries in the world economy. Their only mechanism of defense was the policy consistently followed by the Central Bank of Argentina, in the recent past, with such remarkable success: to offset external drains from, or accretions to, its reserves, through domestic policies of expansion or contraction. This was contrary to classical orthodoxy, but in fact equivalent to the effects of the British discount rate on capital movements to and from Great Britain.

The readjustment of fundamental price disequilibria, which changes in the British discount rate were designed to stimulate, was thus thwarted and delayed by the effects of such changes on capital movements. It is still contended, however, that those basic readjustments

15. Quoted by R. G. Hawtrey, *The Art of Central Banking* (London, 1932), p. 141.

would occur in the end, capital movements notwithstanding, through the domestic effects of discount changes on British prices. The discount rate would be raised, and credit would be contracted, in order to force down excessive British prices to levels more competitive with the level of foreign prices. On the other hand, the discount rate would fall, and credit would expand, when British prices were low relative to foreign prices and tended to disequilibrate the balance of payments in Britain's favor.

It should be noted that, according to this theory, the British deficit would be corrected through a *deterioration* of the British terms of trade (i.e. a decrease in British prices relative to foreign prices), such deterioration being considered necessary to restore the international competitive position of British producers. Logically speaking, however, the opposite assumption is just as plausible. That is to say, the elimination of the deficit might also result from an *improvement* in the British terms of trade, decreasing the unit cost of imports and increasing the returns on exports.

Statistical evidence may be used to support either theory. During the interwar period, the British terms of trade consistently improved in depression and deteriorated during the upswing of the cycle.[16] Before the First World War available data are more difficult to interpret, and reveal, if anything, sharper rises in export prices than in import prices during the crest of the boom. Indices of export prices for that period, however, give relatively little weight to manufactured products and do not appear to be truly representative of British exports in general.

As far as the discount rate is concerned, the interwar period is of minor interest for the elucidation of the problem under consideration. The discount policy had ceased by then to be a major instrument of monetary control and, moreover, Britain was no longer the dominant financial center of the world. In the thirty years prior to the First World War, however, the statistical series fail to confirm the traditional view that an increase in discount rates contributed directly to a lowering of British prices relative to foreign prices. On the contrary, all major rises in the discount rate are associated with an improvement of the British terms of trade, i.e. with an increase in export prices relative

16. The ratio of export to import prices, calculated from Board of Trade indices, declined from 104 in 1923 to 98 in 1929, rose during the ensuing depression to a peak of 122 in 1933, fell to 107 in the relatively prosperous year 1937, and improved again to 116 during the 1938 recession.

to import prices.[17] The declines in the terms of trade followed the increases in the discount rate only after a considerable lag, and actually coincided with decreases in the rate. Their most obvious explanation would seem to lie in depressed business conditions in Britain, associated with the spread of the international cycle, rather than in any direct influence of the discount rate over domestic prices.

This improvement in the British terms of trade in periods of rising discount rates should not be surprising, in view of the special position of Britain as a financial center for world trade. On purely *a priori* grounds, it would appear at least as probable as the opposite pattern contemplated by the classicists. What was really discussed by them was the case of price disparities between one country and a large number of other countries, equal to the first in importance. Under that assumption, deflation by the first country would force down domestic prices and costs without affecting to any significant extent the level of prices in the rest of the world. The position of Britain in the nineteenth century was, however, a very different one. Britain was the major center of world trade and finance, and British deflationary efforts immediately affected, not only the British economy and prices, but also the economy and prices of other countries, transmitting to them the cyclical fluctuations experienced by Great Britain. Thus, the problem became essentially one, not of disparities between one country and the others, but of a simultaneous upward or downward movement engulfing most other nations along with Great Britain.

We have already seen that the most immediate effect of a rise in the British discount rates was to reverse the normal direction of international capital movements. The outflow of funds from the other countries toward Great Britain exerted an immediate downward pressure on prices and income in those countries. In fact, since the great bulk of foreign exports was financed through London, and since foreign bills far outweighed inland bills in the London discount market, a tightening in discount rates could be expected to affect the prices of foreign goods more drastically and directly than domestic prices in Britain. The reverse would be true in the case of a credit relaxation or expansion in London. These movements would be further magnified by

17. Thus, the yearly average of discount rates rose gradually from 2.9 per cent in 1885 to 4.5 per cent in 1890, while the ratio of export to import prices improved from 91 to 106. The next sustained rise in the rate, from 2 per cent in 1895 to 3.9 in 1890 was accompanied by an increase in the ratio from 97 to 114. The same positive correlation between rising rates and better terms of trade continued until the outbreak of war.

the banking contraction or expansion thus induced in the foreign countries themselves, especially as higher discount rates in those markets would tighten domestic credit without attracting, as they did in London, compensatory capital movements from abroad.

These considerations are reinforced by the fact that a large part of Britain's exports consisted of manufactured industrial products, while the bulk of her imports was composed of foodstuffs and raw materials. Lesser flexibility of demand and supply conditions could be expected to make the prices of the second category of goods especially sensitive to credit contraction and expansion, as well as to general cyclical fluctuations.

The failure of British discount policy to effect the type of readjustments contemplated in classical theory is thus easily understandable. It is due primarily to the *international* character of the London discount market, whose expansion and contraction affected foreign prices as much, or more, than British prices. It is also explainable in terms of the greater vulnerability of agricultural and raw materials suppliers, than of the British economy itself, to cyclical and credit fluctuations.

A Positive Policy for the International Monetary Fund

One main conclusion emerges from the above analysis. The "rules of the game" of the twentieth-century gold standard, no matter how valid they may be in the case of isolated fundamental disequilibria in one or a few countries' international accounts, are totally inappropriate to deal with world-wide cyclical fluctuations. The main result of "orthodox" gold standard policies, under such circumstances, was to propagate to the world at large any cyclical disturbance arising in major industrialized nations. Balance-of-payments deficits would be corrected in the end, but mostly through a general contraction in income and economic activity, rather than through direct price readjustments. Furthermore, the accompanying price changes would leave in their wake a basically unbalanced structure of international prices when the cyclical depression subsided and more normal conditions were restored.

The success of the International Monetary Fund will largely depend on the progressive development, and general acceptance, of new canons of international monetary behavior, to replace the previous "rules of the game" code. These new standards of policy should be less crude in their application, and more acceptable to the national monetary authorities of member countries. They should recognize the primacy of domestic goals of stability and high levels of economic performance, and distinguish strongly between cyclical and fundamental disequilibria in the balances of payments.

Anti-cyclical Monetary Policies. The International Monetary Fund has already proclaimed as one of its main purposes "to facilitate the expansion and balanced growth of international trade, and to contribute thereby to the promotion and maintenance of high levels of employment and real income and to the development of the productive resources of all members as primary objectives of monetary policy." [18] This formulation recognizes the basic agreement and interdependence of national and international monetary objectives. A large volume of world trade obviously contributes to domestic prosperity. Conversely, domestic prosperity redounds to the benefit of other members, by maintaining effective demand for imports and thus encouraging exports and production in other areas. The responsibility of the largest, and more industrialized, countries is especially heavy in this respect. Major depressions usually originate with them, rather than with smaller, agricultural nations, and are especially contagious internationally because of their weight in world trade and finance. The only satisfactory corrective of cyclical disequilibria in the balance of payments, not due to fundamental maladjustments in international price levels, thus lies for most nations, not in internal deflation according to the "rules of the game" recipe, but in the restoration of economic activity and purchasing power in the centers of the cyclical disturbance.

Balance-of-payments disequilibria, however, will obviously continue to occur and to threaten domestic stability, especially in countries with undiversified economies, heavily dependent on international trade and especially on one or a few export products with inelastic demand. Variations in weather and crop yields as well as cyclical fluctuations in the major world markets will result in alternate phases of favorable and unfavorable balances, reflected in inflationary and deflationary pressures on incomes, cash balances, prices, and costs. Such disequilibria would be of a temporary character, and the country should attempt to offset them, to the largest possible extent, by domestic compensatory policies. In doing so, it would also contribute to international stabilization as well as to the maintenance of domestic levels of income and activity. In the absence of compensatory action—and even worse, if the automatic upward or downward pressures are reinforced, in ac-

18. *Articles of Agreement of the International Monetary Fund,* Article I (ii).

cordance with the "rules of the game," by secondary domestic expansion or contraction—not only national, but also international balance will be needlessly sacrificed, since domestic "adjustments" to temporary disturbances of equilibrium will result in basic maladjustments, once the temporary factors cease to operate and more normal conditions are restored.

Anticyclical compensatory policies would thus, in general, contribute both to moderate national and international depressions, and to preserve fundamental international balance. Their generalized adoption, however, would tend to amplify the instability of national reserves of gold and foreign exchange. As long as the temporary factors of disequilibrium are present, reserves will move from the deficit to the surplus countries, unchecked by counteracting movements in prices, exchange rates, or national incomes. This redistribution of reserves, even though temporary, creates a serious problem. The receiving countries accumulate funds which will help them to meet later deficits, but for which they have no immediate use or need. On the other hand, the drain on the reserves of the deficit countries may be such as to make a continuation of compensatory policies incompatible with the preservation of free and stable exchanges. It is precisely this situation which the International Fund is so well organized to meet. The drain of reserves is arrested, or moderated, by an indirect extension of credit by the surplus countries to the deficit countries, through their accounts with the Fund. In this manner the deficit countries are enabled to avoid recourse to internal deflation, currency devaluation, exchange control, or other restrictive policies, while the lending of unneeded accretions to reserves by the surplus countries protects them against the contractionary effects which such measures of defense would exert on their exports and economic activity.

One of the main dangers of the system is the abuse of the Fund's credit for the financing of fundamental, as opposed to cyclical or accidental, disequilibria in a country's international account. In this case, the borrowings would assume a continuous character, and indebtedness to the Fund would pile up rapidly until the country's quota is exhausted. Adequate safeguards must be provided against such abuse of the Fund's machinery, and toward the application of effective remedial action.[19]

The first is the fullest possible use by a deficit country of its international reserves. The problem is, as yet, approached only in an in-

19. See p. 171.

direct and very incomplete manner in the Fund's charter through the application of the so-called "repurchase provisions." [20] Further progress in this direction appears highly desirable in the long run, through amendment, interpretation, or simple administration of the Fund's statutes, or through the Fund's powers of moral suasion. Such a development, however, will meet considerable resistance, based on the still prevalent misinterpretation of the role of monetary reserves. Both the public and, in many countries monetary legislation itself still regard the central bank's gold and foreign exchange reserves as the "backing" of the currency. Reserve ratios between gold and foreign exchange holdings and the central bank's note issue or total sight obligations are viewed by the public as an indication of the currency's soundness, and are generally subject by law to minimum requirements. This deep-rooted tradition bars the effective employment of reserves at the very time when they are most needed, and for the only real purpose which they can usefully serve.

This anachronistic conception of central bank reserves dates back from an entirely different institutional environment, in which gold coin effectively circulated as the ultimate legal tender, and central banks were under strict legal obligation to convert their notes into gold, not only for balance-of-payments purposes, but also for internal circulation within the country. Gold coin does not, in practice, circulate today as money, and bank notes have become the ultimate legal tender for domestic payment. The only purpose of a gold or foreign exchange reserve is to provide available resources to meet, without undue pressure on the currency, a deficit in the balance of payments.[21] All member countries should be induced to accept this viewpoint, and to liberate their reserves for effective use in case of need.

The second alternative is the recourse to foreign borrowings from other sources than the Fund itself. This would be especially valuable to meet specific rehabilitation or developmental expenditures, the financing of which is outside the scope of the Fund, and can be secured through private investments or through the help of such institutions as the International Bank for Reconstruction and Development, the Export-Import Bank, etc.

The third alternative is the husbanding of reserves for the most

20. *Articles of Agreement,* Article V, Section 7.
21. The "war chest" argument falls within the scope of this definition, although recent procedures of foreign funds controls weaken greatly the value of gold for purchases in enemy, or even neutral, countries.

urgent needs, through some priority system of exchange distribution. The very name of "exchange control" unfortunately suffices to raise such emotional reactions with many people as to prevent any serious discussion of the subject. The history of exchange control in the last two decades is such as to justify fully the condemnation of most exchange control systems used in the past. It does not, however, justify a blind excommunication of exchange controls as such, irrespective of its concrete forms and of the circumstances leading to their adoption. Exchange control was, in some cases, wilfully resorted to as a weapon of economic blackmail and aggression. In other cases, however, it was only a measure of despair, reluctantly accepted as a lesser evil under the pressure of necessity. The statesmen who introduced exchange control in so many countries were not all blackguards or fools. Their motives should be understood, and every effort should be bent to prevent abuses, or unnecessary restrictions, without sacrificing the real purposes which nondiscriminatory controls can justifiably serve. Constructive criticism may succeed where dogmatic and purely negative opposition has failed, and would probably remain as sterile in the future as it has proved in the past.

Self-denial through exchange restrictions may be preferred, both by a member country and by the Fund, to excessive borrowings, internal deflation, or exchange depreciation. Provision is already made for some such cases in the Fund agreement itself. First of all, the Fund gives the members full freedom "to exercise such controls as are necessary to regulate international capital movements" not connected with payments for current transactions or settlement of commitments.[22] Members are even prohibited, in principle, from making net use of the Fund's resources "to meet a large and sustained outflow of capital, and the Fund may request a member to exercise controls to prevent such use of the resources of the Fund. If, after receiving such a request, a member fails to exercise appropriate controls, the Fund may declare the member ineligible to use the resources of the Fund." [23]

Second, the demands made upon the Fund for a member's currency may exceed the Fund's ability to supply it. In that case, the Fund may ultimately be forced to declare such currency scarce and to ration its supply among the members applying for it. Such a declaration "shall operate as an authorization to any member, after con-

22. *Articles of Agreement of the International Monetary Fund,* Article VI, Section 3.
23. *Ibid.,* Article VI, Section 1.

sultation with the Fund, temporarily to impose limitations on the freedom of exchange operations in the scarce currency." [24]

Finally, the Fund *may* authorize a member country to "impose restrictions on the making of payments and transfers (even) for current international transactions." [25] The case would be especially likely to occur when a country has exhausted its drawing rights, under Article V, Section 3 of the Agreement, and when, at the same time, the Fund is reluctant to give, under Section 4, special approval for further borrowings. The only alternative to such authorization would then be either the enforcement of strong deflationary policies—the results of which might, in any case, prove too slow to solve the immediate exchange problem—or currency devaluation. Again, either of these alternatives would be highly undesirable in the case of cyclical or temporary disequilibria.

Exchange control may, possibly, be preferred to excessive loss of reserves and borrowings from the Fund, even before reserves and drawing rights have been exhausted. A country may feel that borrowings should not be resorted to on a very large scale for the sole purpose of financing imports of a purely sumptuary character. The Fund might concur with this view and authorize some exchange restrictions rather than force further and unwanted loans upon the country. Such an attitude on the part of the Fund's authorities would not be unlikely in view of the specific limitations placed by the Fund Agreement upon the use of the Fund's resources to finance capital outflows. While not identical, the two cases present some broad similarities. The general tenor of the Chapultepec discussions on the desirability of husbanding, for the purpose of economic development, reserves acquired in wartime would lead to the same conclusion.

The creation of the International Monetary Fund, therefore, should not be interpreted as definitely removing, even after the expiration of a transitory period, all justification for, and possibility of, exchange control measures by member countries. The Fund will greatly reduce the need for exchange control, and set up safeguards against unnecessary or discriminatory restrictions. It will not, and should not, prohibit blindly and flatly all uses of legitimate controls as an instrument of monetary policy, when temporary exchange shortages make them the only alternative to drastic deflationary policies or currency devaluation. As indicated above, price or currency adjustments may often be

24. *Ibid.*, Article VII, Section 3 (b)
25. *Ibid.*, Article

wholly inadequate to correct balance-of-payments deficits—especially in the case of agricultural or raw material producing countries, faced with an inelastic demand for their exports—except through the resulting contraction of national income and effective import demand. Moreover, since only a fraction of total income is spent abroad, the balancing of foreign transactions will normally call for a decline in the income level several times greater than the deficit to be resorbed.[26] This is clearly undesirable on national grounds and does not, in any way, lessen the unfavorable impact of import contraction on world trade. On the contrary, it aggravates the difficulties of competing exporting countries. Finally, it corrects a temporary disequilibrium at the cost of creating a fundamental one, in the other direction, once the transient factors of disturbance have disappeared. Under such circumstances, temporary and selective controls on expenditures abroad are preferable by far to indiscriminate, and multiple, income adjustments.

The efforts of the International Monetary Fund should thus be directed, not toward the simple abolition of all exchange controls, but toward the elimination of the abuses which have so often characterized them in the past.

The most patent and most crucial defect of exchange control lies in the discriminatory policies, or practices, to which it lends itself. As long as exchange is rationed on an individual basis, through arbitrary decisions of the national agencies entrusted with the application of the controls, any allocation will be open to the accusation of incompetence, favoritism, or dishonesty in the distribution of the scarce exchange among importers as well as among supplying countries or firms.[27] Such a procedure, however, is by no means inevitable. A

26. More strictly speaking, this will depend on the "marginal propensity" to import, and on the elasticity of export supply and demand.

27. International acceptance of a "previous representative period" criterion as an objective guide for allocation might help to some extent, but would be of limited value. First of all, it could not serve as a pattern for commodity allocation, since any rationing of scarce exchange *should* change the "representative" pattern of imports in favor of more essential, and against less essential, imports. Secondly, the "previous representative period" criterion tends to freeze the channels of trade in a very arbitrary and uneconomic manner. The resulting distortion and unreality will be the more marked as one must go further and further back into the past to discover a "representative" period. Structural changes brought about by the war make it extremely difficult to accept as representative not only wartime, but even prewar patterns. Difficulties are even greater in the case of the many countries in which prewar trade was already subject, since the early thirties, to import quotas and exchange control regulation.

promising alternative would be to enforce exchange restrictions through flexible, and impersonal, market forces, leaving the importers free to buy *whatever* they please *wherever* they please (presumably from the cheapest source of supply), subject only to such automatic restrictions as would normally result from the free interplay of supply and demand. More concretely, what is here suggested is that all the exchange currently available to the monetary authorities be offered for sale in the following manner.

Exchange would be freely obtainable, without previous permit or restrictions of any sort, at the normal exchange rates for payment of all essential and urgent imports or services and of contractual obligations, dividends, or reasonable amortization on approved foreign investments. The monetary authorities would undertake to sell the balance of all their current exchange receipts for payment of deferrable or unessential imports and services, again without quantitative restrictions or import permits, but through the functioning of one, or a few, auction markets. In other words, the limited supply would be distributed among the buyers, not by administrative decision, but as a result of an impersonal pricing mechanism.

In order to provide the central bank with sufficient exchange to assure the functioning of these two markets—the normal, and the auction, markets—all exchange proceeds from exports or other easily controllable sources would have to be sold, at the normal exchange rates, to the monetary authorities. On the other hand, exchange proceeds from unimportant or practically uncontrollable transactions could be freely sold and bought in a free exchange market. This would avoid giving a premium to illegal evasion, where evasion cannot be effectively checked, and would, at the same time, provide an escape valve for the control system. Capital exports, beyond those which have access to the official market, could be channelled here without harmful repercussions on the rates applying to more essential exchange requirements. The higher rates prevailing on the free market in times of crisis would, moreover, tend to discourage capital exports and encourage capital imports.

The advantages of such a plan are obvious. It would eliminate at the root arbitrary and discriminatory allocation of exchange, drastically simplify the administrative machinery, red tape and delays, and bar most of the possibilities for graft or favoritism in the distribution of exchange permits. From the international point of view, the main objection raised, quite properly, against the traditional forms of exchange control would also disappear. Nothing in the above system would tend to destroy, or even weaken, a multilateral system of world trade. No distinction need be allowed between the various currencies bid for on any auction market and, on the contrary, all auction premiums should be uniform, in percentage terms, for any one category of transactions, no matter what foreign currency is involved. The exact currency requested need not even be specified until the bidding is over and the exchange allocated. Indeed, as long as currency interconvertibility is maintained, the central bank would have no justifiable incentive to sell one currency in preference to another.[28]

Objection is likely to be raised, however, to the differential rates implied in the functioning of the auction and free exchange markets. This might be interpreted as a "multiple currency" practice, specifically outlawed by the Fund Articles of Agreement.[29]

It should be noted, first, that provision is also made in the Fund Agreement for the approval of such practices by the Fund (VIII, 3). Indeed, the Fund's approval is necessary, not only for this case, but for the more general one of any system of controls on current transactions (except as applied to scarce currencies, or under the transitional arrangements of Article XIV).

More than that, however, the exact meaning of the "multiple currency" stricture is open to question. First of all, the system here proposed does not constitute a multiple currency practice, if the term is interpreted to imply the setting up of different exchange premiums between currencies. As pointed out above, no distinction is allowed between currencies, but only between different categories of transactions, irrespective of the currencies involved.

Secondly, the auction and free market premia are completely flexible, and do not—as would *rigid* multiple rates—introduce any effective restriction on exchange transactions, independent from, and additional to, the basic and inevitable restriction resulting from the allocation of a limited quota of exchange among various claimants. Since the monetary authorities are forced, under the proposed system, to *sell fully that quota* for whatever rate the auction brings about, the rate itself does not constitute, in any way, an independent or additional restriction. Foreign exports to the country are limited only by the application of the quota, and in no way influenced by the fact that the exchange rate diverges from normal. The only significant effect

28. The case of inconvertibility is discussed on p. 163.
29. Articles IV, Section 3, and VIII, Section 3.

is a purely domestic, and entirely desirable one, i.e. the recapture by the monetary authorities of the unjustified windfall profits that would otherwise accrue to importers. It should be kept in mind that any scarcity of exchange which reduces imports below the normal demand at the official exchange rates, tends to drive up domestic prices, no matter the exchange rate charged to the importers to which exchange is allocated. In the absence of price control and rationing, the importers will be led to charge what the traffic will bear, or will distribute their short supplies in an arbitrary and capricious manner. While price control and rationing might reasonably be expected for essential goods of mass consumption, they will not, in most countries, be normally extended, and effectively enforced, to sales of luxuries and semiluxuries. Under the auction system, the importers would be forced to compete with one another for the exchange offered for sale. Such competition would drive the rate to, but not beyond, the point at which their profits will again be close to competitive levels, under competitive pricing conditions. Special problems may, of course, arise in the case of collusion or monopolistic practices by the sellers, but these would also arise under a system of administrative allocation, and can be taken care of, as far as is administratively and politically feasible, without modifying the basic mechanism of control suggested above.

It might be observed, in passing, that any system of tariff duties is equivalent to very real and rigid multiple currency practices. The very fact that objections to tariffs are so much milder than the objections to multiple exchange rates again suggests that we often tend to fight words rather than realities. Looking at the problem without dogmatic preconceptions, it will be realized that the allocation of scarce exchange through a free auction system does not add any further restrictive element, beyond that already implicit in the limitation placed on the amount of exchange made available to the market. It presents, on the other hand, the tremendous advantage of eliminating, or restricting considerably, the opportunity for favoritism or discrimination on the part of the exchange authorities.

The supervision of exchange control by the International Monetary Fund will not be limited to the avoidance of discriminatory administration of the controls. The Fund will also want to judge whether exchange control as such is justified in the concrete circumstances under which a member country requests permission to implant it. As the Fund gets under operation, it will have to develop certain general and objective criteria for granting, or denying, such requests, in order to avoid arbitrary, discriminatory, or merely haphazard decisions, which would soon breed ill will among the members and endanger their loyalty to the institution. The problem is most acute for the smaller countries, whose vote in the Fund's councils will necessarily have little weight in reaching a decision. These countries should be guaranteed an impartial treatment based on as objective rules and principles of policy as can be practically devised by the Fund.

One of the first criteria to be taken into consideration would obviously be the level of international reserves of the country requesting the authorization for the implantation of exchange restrictions. The appraisal of the adequacy or inadequacy of these reserves, from the point of view of balance-of-payments needs, obviously cannot be gauged with reference to the traditional reserve ratios, relating gold and foreign exchange holdings to note circulation or sight obligations. What is here relevant is the ability of the country to finance from its own reserves foreseeable deficits in its international transactions. From this point of view, reserves should first be expressed as a percentage of the normal requirements for payments abroad, i.e. of total annual sales of exchange by the banks. A reserve ratio of 30 per cent, for instance, would mean that the central bank could maintain a free and stable exchange market for one year in the face of a 30 per cent deficit in the balance of payments, or for two years in the case of a 15 per cent deficit. The level of reserves, calculated in this way, would indicate the breathing spell which the monetary authorities will have, while waiting for an automatic improvement in the balance of payments, in cases of temporary disequilibria, or for the readjusting effect of any corrective policy which they think advisable to adopt when the deficit is deemed to be of a persistent or fundamental nature. If the length of such breathing spell is too short, the country might be given authorization for direct restrictions over exchange sales.

Whether a 15, a 30, or a 50 per cent reserve is deemed sufficiently critical for the introduction of exchange control would, of course, depend upon the previous balance-of-payments experience of the country in question. A country subject to sudden and violent fluctuations in its export trade should be allowed a higher critical reserve level than a country with more stable sources of foreign exchange receipts. Maximum variations in exports, or exchange receipts, in the past might serve as an objective indication in helping to determine the critical reserve level.

A weaker, but still possibly valid, claim for measures of control might be made when gold and foreign exchange reserves experience a violent and sufficiently sustained decline, even though they still remain, for the time being, above the critical level agreed upon between the Fund and the member country. The argument, in this case, would be based, as in the Chapultepec discussions, upon the desirability of limiting the expenditure of reserves for luxury imports, capital flight, etc. Milder controls will suffice in this case, while stronger controls might prove unavoidable if the introduction of the controls must wait until the critical level has been reached.

As long as currency interconvertibility is maintained, no distinction need be made between the various currencies included in reserves, or between currencies and gold. On the other hand, a country should be allowed to maintain exchange freedom in general, while restricting the sales of a currency in short supply—in accordance with the criteria discussed above—provided that the currency in question cannot be procured through the Fund, or through the normal conversion into such currency of other international reserves at the disposal of the country. It would indeed be absurd to enforce general restrictions against all imports because of the unavailability of one or a few currencies only,[30] and the scarce currency clauses of the Fund Charter[31] accept, in such a case, an exception to the general principle of nondiscrimination and multilateralism.

The abuses and discriminations resulting from the blocking of some currencies cannot be blamed on the country subject to, and suffering from, the blocking. Responsibility for the maintenance of interconvertibility and multilateralism properly belongs only to the International Monetary Fund and to the blocking countries themselves.

The Fund will also want to guard against the permanency of exchange restrictions beyond the period in which they are required by the balance-of-payments situation. The system outlined above solves this difficulty without making necessary any further action by the Fund. Indeed, the control system is self-liquidating, since the auction and free market premiums would automatically decrease and vanish, as the exchange situation improves. If such improvement does not take place within a reasonable period, the disequilibrium of the bal-

30. For a discussion of this point, the reader is referred to *Economic Stability in the Post-War World* (League of Nations, 1945), pp. 245–47.
31. Article VII.

ance of payments should be recognized as fundamental, rather than temporary, and corrective measures, rather than exchange control, should be regarded as the proper remedy to adopt. The Fund might enforce this viewpoint by reviewing periodically, let us say once a year, the authorization which it grants to resort to exchange control schemes.

The above proposals are not merely theoretical. They were recently embodied in the basic monetary legislation of Paraguay and Guatemala[32] and are currently under discussion in other countries. The Guatemalan law, especially, indicates, in greater detail, the precise mechanism in which the suggestions made here can be embodied in a practical manner. Both legislations, however, express only the limitations to which these countries subjected their freedom of action on their own initiative. Further safeguards might, of course, be desirable on an international plane, through the administration of the Fund's own powers with respect to exchange control.

Fundamental Readjustments. The main emphasis of this paper has been on the inappropriateness of traditional readjustment policies as a remedy for temporary or cyclical disequilibria. The opposite danger, i.e. the failure to adopt readjustment policies in the case of fundamental disequilibria, also faces the Fund, but has been so widely discussed already that a few comments will suffice here.

In the case of a persisting disequilibrium in one country's economy, due to inflated price or income levels, corrective measures should be applied. Neither the use of the country's reserves, nor borrowings from abroad, nor exchange control bring to bear any remedial influence on the disequilibrium. While this would also be true in the absence of any International Monetary Fund, there is a danger that the financial assistance available from the Fund itself be used in order further to postpone indispensable readjustments. The country's indebtedness would then grow without lasting benefit to it, and the resources of the Fund would be wasted in a manner directly contrary to the objectives of the institution.[33] The Fund, however, can protect itself against such

32. See *Decreto-Ley No. 10043 que establece el régimen de cambios de la República del Paraguay* (Asunción, Paraguay, August 29, 1945); and *Ley Monetaria,* (Guatemala City, Guatemala, December 10, 1945). A translation of the latter legislation was published in the *Federal Reserve Bulletin* (March 1946), pp. 259-69.

33. Article I (iv) states as one of the purposes of the Fund "to shorten the duration and lessen the degree of disequilibrium in the international balances of payments of members."

abuses, not only through the ceilings placed on each country's presumptive borrowing rights, but also through the application of Article V, Section 5 of the Fund's charter.

The diagnosis of a fundamental disequilibrium, however, is not an easy task. A mere deficit in a country's balance of payments is, of course, no evidence of an excessive and untenable level of domestic as compared with international prices. Contrary to the "rules of the game" concept, it should not, therefore, be taken as a signal for deflationary policies. Compensatory action should be preferred, and supported by the Fund, whenever the deficit can be ascribed to accidental causes, such as a crop failure, or to a cyclical world depression. Similarly, a favorable balance of payments, not associated with international cost and price disparities, should not be viewed as requiring expansionary policies disruptive of domestic stability and conducive to inflationary price rises.

Before assuming the existence of a durable disequilibrium calling for corrective measures, additional evidence should be studied and weighed. Any fundamental disequilibrium should manifest itself, not only in a deficit in the balance of payments, but also in monetary and banking statistics, price and production data, etc. Such series, as well as the performance of the balance of payments, should be compared with the experience of other countries, and especially of those of similar economic structure, but subject to different domestic influences and policies. Only in this manner can a proper diagnosis be arrived at, and an adequate policy determined.

Where clear evidence is lacking, empirical decisions are unavoidable. The deficit country would probably be given the benefit of the doubt, and allowed to pursue, for a time, compensatory policies with the help of the Fund and, possibly, under the additional protection of exchange control when needed. This interpretation would later be confirmed by events if the deficit does in fact disappear within a normal period of time. It would have to be reversed, however, and corrective policies would have to be applied, if the deficits continue, piling up the country's indebtedness to the Fund, or if the need for exchange control persists, with sustained and substantial premiums on the auction and free exchange markets.

Just as a mere balance-of-payments deficit is no evidence of a fundamental disequilibrium, the absence of such a deficit is no conclusive proof of a fundamental equilibrium in a country's international position. In the absence of compensatory action by the monetary authorities, a fundamental disequilibrium may fail to be reflected in any balance-of-payments deficit, owing to the prompt transmission of external deflationary pressures to domestic prices and incomes. One of the clearest cases, in recent years, of a fundamental disequilibrium due to currency overvaluation is the experience of Belgium following the devaluation of the British pound. And yet, both the balance of trade and the balance of payments improved, rather than deteriorated, during most of the overvaluation period. The average import surplus fell from 4.3 billion francs a year in 1929–30 to 0.8 billion in 1932–34, and the international reserves of the central bank rose from 12.3 billion on the eve of the British devaluation to 13.7 billion at the end of 1933.[34] The impact of the disequilibrium was thus felt, not in a deficit in the balance of payments, but in a drastic decline in economic activity and incomes, especially in the so-called "nonsheltered" industries, in competition with foreign firms in the national or international markets.[35]

It has recently been argued that a country subject to such pressures should attempt to protect itself through domestic compensatory policies, but should not be allowed to devalue its currency unless, and until, these policies have led to an actual deficit in the balance of international payments.[36] This attitude is open to serious objections. First of all, it would lead to unnecessary disruptions, since labor and other economic factors would have to be uprooted and transferred into temporary activities, such as public works, and then returned to their normal field of employment when currency devaluation makes it again profitable and economic. Second, the scope of compensatory

34. A decline to 12.5 took place in the latter part of 1934, but is to be ascribed primarily to capital flight, prompted by the approaching devaluation of the currency.

35. See Robert Triffin, "La théorie de la surévaluation monétaire et la dévaluation belge," *Bulletin de l'Institut de Recherches Economiques* (Louvain, Belgium, November 1937), pp. 19–52.

36. See Gottfried Haberler, "Currency Depreciation and the International Monetary Fund," *Review of Economic Statistics, 26* (November 1944), 178–81. A draft of the present paper was submitted to Professor Haberler, who commented as follows on this point, in his reply: "As to your discussion of what is meant by fundamental disequilibrium, I would make this concession: If it could be shown that income effects in fact operate so fast that depreciation will not lead to an appreciable balance of payments surplus, I would not object to it. I still believe, however, that that is a rather fanciful case. I would agree however, that depreciation on the part of a small country need not be ruled out even if it led to a temporary inflow of gold, especially if that inflow was only to compensate for an outflow which has taken place some time in the past. I think I could handle all those cases with appropriate and reasonable interpretations of the balance of payments criterion."

action may be relatively limited, especially in undeveloped countries heavily dependent on the exportation of primary products. For such countries, currency devaluation will often be the most direct, or even the only effective, way of maintaining domestic levels of income.

What is true, however, is that devaluation should not be regarded as a proper and legitimate remedy for any domestic depression, whatever its origin; but neither should it be regarded as legitimate and desirable merely because a country is experiencing balance-of-payments difficulties. The Belgian case showed clear evidence that external pressures resulting from the underdevaluation of the pound with respect to the franc, were at the root of a severe domestic depression, but this evidence did not merge from balance-of-payments data. On the other hand, balance-of-payments deficits are often the result of cyclical, rather than fundamental disequilibria, and devaluation, in that case, would usually be a most undesirable remedy, from a national as well as from an international viewpoint.

Thus, the relevance of the balance of payments to the definition of a "fundamental disequilibrium" is of a subtler kind than is often imagined. There may exist a fundamental disequilibrium in a country's economy, even in the absence of any actual balance-of-payments deficit. On the other hand, a deficit in the balance of payments may be due to cyclical, or accidental, rather than to fundamental maladjustments. We might define tentatively a fundamental disequilibrium as "a maladjustment in a country's economy so grave and persistent that the restoration or maintenance of satisfactory levels of domestic activity, employment, and incomes would prove incompatible with equilibrium in the balance of payments, if not accompanied by extraordinary measures of external defense, such as a change in the exchange rates, increased tariff or exchange control protection, etc."

The latter part of this definition also suggests that devaluation is not necessarily the only, or even the most appropriate, remedy for a fundamental disequilibrium. The language of the Fund Agreement is interesting in this respect. Members agree *not to propose* a change in the par value of their currency except to correct a fundamental disequilibrium. The Fund, however, shall concur in the proposed change only if it is satisfied that the change is necessary to correct the disequilibrium (Article IV, Section 5(a) and (f)). Thus, a fundamental disequilibrium is considered by the Fund as a necessary, but not as a sufficient condition for currency readjustment. In some cases, other methods of correction may be preferable, from a national as well as from an international standpoint.

For instance, the difficulties of the nitrate industry in Chile, following the development of synthetic nitrates, were of a fundamental character and have had a deep impact on the international balance of the country. Devaluation, even though probably unavoidable under the circumstances, could not be expected to right by itself the Chilean economy. Domestic monetary and fiscal policies, changes in the tariff structure, diversification of production and modernization of industrial and agricultural techniques, possibly with foreign help, may prove better remedies than, or the indispensable complement of, currency readjustments. A specially interesting case is the one of colonial economies in which income expansion may lead rapidly and directly to balance-of-payments disequilibria, because of its effects on luxury imports, tourist expenditure abroad, capital exports, and the like, rather than because of any upward pressure on domestic wage and cost levels. Devaluation is a very blunt and indiscriminate instrument and may often be a less efficient tool than selective policies designed to plug the main leaks in the balance of payments, with a minimum impact on basic economic activities and on production and living costs.

Devaluation is also of limited value as a remedy for pervasive maladjustments, whether cyclical or fundamental, affecting simultaneously a large number of countries. Agricultural overproduction, for instance, may disrupt at the same time the international balance of all the competing countries whose exports are largely concentrated on the overproduced commodities. Concerted international action designed toward readjustment would be preferable, in this case, to cut-throat competition through lower prices or currency devaluation.

Conclusion

The classical theory of international balance and of readjustments to balance-of-payments disequilibria centers around disparities in a single country's price and cost levels with relation to the rest of the world. Under such conditions, domestic deflation—if costs are not too rigid—or currency devaluation may be able to bring about readjustment, through the restoration of the country's competitive position in world markets.

This doctrine was mistakenly extended, especially by the "rules of the game" adherents, to world-wide cyclical disequilibria, originating in one, or a few, highly developed and industrialized countries. Efforts by other countries to correct resulting balance-of-payments deficits, either through price deflation or exchange devaluation, are then thwarted because such action by any one country or group of countries aggravates the difficulties in their supply and export markets, as well as in competing countries, and leads to similar, and mutually self-defeating, measures of defense. Price deflation and devaluation spread from country to country without increasing export receipts, especially if world demand for a nation's exports is relatively inelastic. The situation presents a strong analogy with that of oligopoly, where each effort by one seller to cut into the competitors' markets is thwarted by the competitors' price retaliation. Thus, the actual elasticity of demand for one country's exports is merged with the much lower world's elasticity of demand for those products. Sales can be expanded only in so far as lower prices stimulate consumption, and not through inroads into the competitors' sales.

The main result of such policies is, therefore, to propagate to the world at large any cyclical disturbance arising in a major economic area. Balance-of-payments deficits may be corrected in the end, but mostly as the result of a general decline in income and economic activity. Furthermore, the accompanying price changes will leave in their wake a basically unbalanced structure of international prices when the cyclical depression subsides and more normal conditions are restored.

Whenever balance-of-payments disequilibria are due, not to international price disparities, but to accidental factors or to cyclical fluctuations in foreign income and demand, compensatory policies should be followed to the fullest possible extent. This requires a high level of international reserves, especially in raw material and food producing countries, and the willingness to spend these reserves liberally in times of crisis and to accumulate them during prosperous years. When reserves are insufficient, foreign or international assistance —such as that contemplated under the International Monetary Fund —would be necessary. Failing this, exchange control should be used as a third line of defense, in order to continue compensatory policies and avoid the greater evils inseparable from deflation or currency devaluation. The disadvantage of the latter policies, as compared to exchange control, is that their corrective effect on the balance of payments is likely to depend on an income contraction several times the size of the international deficit to be plugged.

Exchange control, however, should be restricted to periods of temporary exchange difficulties, and should not be used to elude readjustments to fundamental disequilibria. Even more important, the system of controls to be adopted should preserve the multilateralism and flexibility of international trade. It should not lend itself to administrative arbitrariness, rigid and uneconomic allocation of exchange, discrimination, and bilateralism. These historical evils, associated with exchange control as used in the interwar period, should not lead to a blind and dogmatic rejection of exchange control as such, but to concrete efforts to dissociate it from such abuses, and make it a fit instrument for the protection of the economy and the currency against temporary pressures on the exchange.

2. INTERNATIONAL VERSUS DOMESTIC MONEY

The topic of this paper, and its brevity, invite commonplaces. The most trite of such commonplaces is the once original observation that the gold standard was in essence an international monetary system, and that its breakdown in the interwar period represented the triumph of monetary nationalism over monetary internationalism.

Since your Chairman begged for originality in these papers, I shall try to defend exactly the opposite thesis. Paradoxical as it may sound, I submit to you that the general abandonment of the gold standard in the thirties was a reaction, not against international monetary organization, but against the lack of any such organization. I also suggest that an international monetary system cannot be approached by renunciation of national instruments of monetary policy, but implies, on the contrary, the strengthening of such instruments and their effective utilization and integration into an international policy framework. In other words, monetary internationalism must begin in the sphere of ends and policies rather than of means and techniques.

The automatism of the gold standard excluded any control, whether national or international, over monetary phenomena. It precluded, therefore, the development of an international monetary policy, by denying the means of carrying out any such policy. This *laissez-faire* attitude was defended, here as in other areas of economic life, as the sure path to economic balance and equilibrium. It is curious to reflect on the survival of this philosophy in the field of international rela-

American Economic Review, Proceedings, May 1947, pp. 322-24. For a more detailed discussion, see "Exchange Control and Equilibrium," in *Foreign Economic Policy of the United States,* ed. Seymour E. Harris (Cambridge, 1948), pp. 417-25.

tions, long after its abandoment by most economists in the field of domestic economic policies.

The prestige of the gold standard as a mechanism ensuring international monetary balance can be traced back to the classical analysis of balance-of-payments readjustments. This analysis, however, was developed in terms of a special category of disequilibria, originating in cost maladjustments between a single country and the rest of the world. It was never intended to apply to world-wide disequilibria associated with the phases of the international business cycle. The classical analysis, moreover, was greatly distorted in the twenties by the famous "rules of the game" school of monetary and central banking advisers.[1]

In the case of cyclical world-wide disturbances in balance of payments, the result of both the gold standard automatism and the "rules of the game" policies was to ensure the propagation of the cycle from the centers of cyclical disturbances to outlying geographical areas. In doing so, they accentuated rather than corrected the intensity of cyclical fluctuations the world over.

Facts proved stronger than theories and most nations finally threw orthodoxy to the winds, and embarked instead upon compensatory monetary policies, behind the protective wall of currency devaluation and of exchange or trade controls. These measures, hastily devised, and with purely nationalistic objectives and criteria of administration, were often internationally harmful and mutually self-defeating. They have, however, enriched the apparatus through which monetary policy can be made effective. The situation calls for exorcism rather than for excommunication. The new weapons should not be scrapped indiscriminately—an objective on which general agreement would, anyway, be impossible—but harmonized and integrated, through international consultation, into the implementation of internationally defined monetary objectives. This would increase their national effectiveness, as well as ensure their international usefulness.

Progress along this path will be made incomparably easier by the creation of the International Monetary Fund. The Fund quotas will decrease the need for, and offer an alternative to, national restrictions on exchange transactions. The quotas, however, may be insufficient to

---

1. I cannot elaborate or substantiate these statements here, and must refer the reader to my paper, "National Central Banking and the International Economy" reproduced above, pp. 142–77.

maintain free and stable exchange rates in cases of acute disequilibria in the balances of payments. In this case, international consultation will help select the measures most appropriate to the situation. Fundamental disequilibria cannot be corrected through exchange control measures, but call for lasting measures of readjustment, one of which may be a modification of the currency's par value. On the other hand, changes in parity would generally be inadvisable as a remedy for temporary disequilibria, since they would actually disturb the international balance of prices and costs once the temporary factors have ceased to act. As a measure of last resort, nondiscriminatory controls may then prove the lesser evil from the international as well as from the domestic viewpoint.

The task of the Fund will precisely be to examine these and other alternatives in order to reach agreement, in each concrete case, as to the most suitable policies, the extent to which action must go, and the ways to minimize harmful effects on other countries. The Fund's philosophy should not be frozen, especially at this early stage, into the rigid, ready-made formulas which have so often contributed to the sterility of previous efforts at international economic collaboration and organization. The infinite diversity of regional and other conditions which shape up a country's problem should be fully recognized. On the other hand, the imposition of exchange controls, changes in parity, and other similar measures deeply affect the economy of other countries and are of vital concern to the international community as well as to the particular country which seeks their adoption. International monetary order cannot be achieved by a return to gold standard ideals of international *laissez faire*. It implies positive action and policy, but, as distinct from the thirties, through international cooperation rather than through international anarchy.

3. The September 1949 Devaluations

The following extracts reflect my views on the policies of the International Monetary Fund on the eve of the September 1949 wave of currency devaluations, and on the "morning after."

I was, at that time, representing—in a purely technical capacity— the IMF in Europe. I was called back to Washington, however, to attend the annual meeting of its Board of Governors, participated in the staff meetings, and was present at the Executive Board's discussions during the fateful days of September 1949.

A. BEFORE

A Letter to the Managing Director

Paris, August 1, 1949

Dear Mr. Gutt:

I am mailing the accompanying paper to you exclusively. It is still in draft form, and I discussed some aspects of it with Overby and Tasca.

I find it now somewhat too verbose, since most of the introductory points I try to make appear to have become familiar to all in Washington. In any case, I would not know, from this distance, how to prepare an effective paper for the Fund, and the draft I am sending you is too much or too little for that purpose.

Cutting off the embroidery, I would summarize my views in four fundamental theses:

(1) Exchange stability, without substantial exchange freedom, is a meaningless objective to pursue. Our greatest danger is not competitive devaluation, but rather currency overvaluation buttressed by increasing controls, bilateralism, and discrimination. We must, therefore, *facilitate* rather than hamper exchange adjustments, insofar as they are conducive to an exchange rate-pattern which will hasten the dismantlement of quantitative restrictions.

While we agree with this in theory, our insistence that any exchange adjustment be *accompanied* by a commitment to a new stable rate, tends to postpone action.

Thus, flexible—but not unadministered—rates are essential, although we must take all necessary safeguards not to weaken the long-run jurisdiction of the Fund. I cannot discuss the legal aspects of this —even though I would love to—but I am afraid that mere *ex post* acquiescence in individual cases will do us more harm than good. We should have the courage of our convictions, and then get the necessary legal interpretation, or change the law. I still am not convinced that the latter is indispensable.

(2) We should create a forum for frank, regional discussion of our problems. We should inform our members of forthcoming issues, prepare with them the discussions of the Board, and ask their advice on what seems important *to them*. Otherwise, we shall never succeed in getting them to regard the Fund as a positive instrument, rather than as a hindrance, in their policy-making. Even if the countries decide to

send good *negotiators* to the Board, they will never delegate the previous *policy-shaping* functions of their Ministers of Finance or Governors of Central Banks. These people may never agree among each other even on a regional basis, but at least they will stop blaming the "Fund," and begin to realize that the trouble lies in their own midst, and that progress depends on harmonization of views at their own, policy-making level.

(3) We shall get nowhere without real and full understanding and collaboration with truly operational institutions in Europe, i.e. the OEEC and the BIS. First on our agenda is the recapture of some influence on the shaping up and actual operation of the intra-European payments scheme. I am convinced that we are no longer in a position to do so, politically and operationally, without some honest understanding with people now in charge. Fortunately, they still have something to gain in the long run from collaboration with us. But we must beware of picking a fight which we might well lose, or in which victory might be scotched for lack of experience and tradition on our part.

(4) We need more contacts here, not only at the policy-making level, but also at the level of research and operations. I am strongly of the opinion that we would have a lot to gain from some decentralization and decongestion of these services of ours, especially in the matter of current descriptive and survey memoranda. Such a move, if combined with the ones recommended above, would also facilitate greatly the hiring of an economic and efficient staff, commanding greater confidence from our members. After months of effort, I am deeply discouraged about trying to do too much here, with no material possibility of doing so. We must, however, realize also that a staff in the field is next to useless, if its work is not adequately planned, supervised, and coordinated through full-time attention at headquarters.

You will see immediately the close connection which ties together these brief and hurried suggestions. Flexible rates mean closer consultation, and more up-to-date information. All this forms a whole in the direction of regionalization, and closer effective contacts with members. The Fund must be theirs, not just ours, if it is to be anything.

You will also realize that my suggestions run directly opposite to my own personal interests. I shall be far more dependent here if we get—as we should—frequent visiting firemen from your office, taken among higher Fund officers. I am, however, deeply convinced that without some such, and urgent, reform, we are now courting disaster either at the hands of the U.S., or of the Europeans. The Fund is at stake, and I assure you it has no more faithful servant than

Yours sincerely,
Robert Triffin

Suggested Adaptations in Fund Policy

(1) The Fund might have celebrated this month the fifth anniversary of its birth at the Bretton Woods Conference of July 1 to 22, 1944. Nobody, however, seemed inclined to celebrate, and the anniversary passed quietly unnoticed. The reasons for this modesty are not far to seek. It is increasingly evident to all that the Fund has not worked so far, that it still does not work today, and that it is most unlikely to work tomorrow, in the absence of considerable reorientation in the policies followed, and in the machinery for their implementation.

(2) This should hardly be surprising in view of all that has happened since the days of Bretton Woods. The task of postwar financial and monetary reconstruction has since revealed itself as far more formidable than was then anticipated. The financing machinery of the Fund and Bank was soon overshadowed, and provisionally put into slumber, by the development of the Marshall Plan. The elaborate provisions of the Fund's agreement designed to ward off the danger of *competitive devaluations* were found powerless, and indeed somewhat paradoxical, in the face of the actual, and reverse, threat of *currency overvaluation,* propped by quantitative restrictions, exchange controls, bilateralism and discrimination. Article XIV of the Agreement robbed the Fund of any effective weapon in this respect for the duration of the so-called "transitional period." Thus the combined impact of Article XIV and the ERP program resulted in a near paralysis of the Fund's machinery, as initially set up, for the most critical years of its early existence.

(3) Some of us find easy consolation in the fact that these handicaps are temporary ones, and that the Fund will emerge from this period with its resources nearly intact, ready to take over where ECA leaves off.

I find it difficult to share, or at least to trust, such an optimistic gamble. There is no mistaking the fact that the high expectations of 1944 have been replaced by a generalized distrust of the Fund's policy

---

A memorandum, dated July 28, 1949.

and machinery. The Fund is no longer regarded as the logical instrument for monetary consultation and cooperation, and other agencies and institutions are progressively, and inevitably, filling the gap left by our enforced inactivity. There will, at the very least, be a long uphill fight to restore to the Fund the prestige and authority so vitally necessary for the fulfilment of its tasks. Moreover, the possibility cannot be ignored that, in the meantime, the present dissatisfaction may culminate into strong pressure to liquidate the Fund, or to return its functions to the U.S. Treasury, or to parcel them among other institutions. Demands for a European Stabilization Fund to succeed the Economic Recovery Program might some day combine with Latin American proposals for an Inter-American Bank, and lead to the breaking up of the Fund, or to a considerable reduction in its effective jurisdiction and influence.

(4) The Fund cannot therefore sit back and wait for its members to come back to it for leadership and assistance at some future date. It must strive immediately, with the limited means at its disposal, to win back their confidence, and restore the prestige indispensable for the fulfilment of its mission. The first prerequisite for this is a frank awareness and discussion of the criticisms directed against the Fund, in order to dispel many misunderstandings, and to seek, in collaboration with its members, whatever adaptations are necessary to make the Fund a living and workable instrument. If a bold attempt to revitalize the Fund were undertaken, the situation might still be redressed rapidly. *Most of the prevailing attacks against the Fund spring from disappointment at its performance, rather than from hostility to its principle.* The basic objective of monetary cooperation and consultation among nations has gained, rather than lost, recognition over the last few years, and the gradual disaffection from the Fund has been accompanied by the growth of parallel activity on the part of OEEC, the BIS, the regional economic commissions of the United Nations, etc. This may indicate a trend toward more manageable forms of consultations and decisions. If the Fund itself does not perform this task, it will devolve, in the end, on the big powers themselves, and especially on the United States and the United Kingdom.

I

(5) The most specific tasks assigned to the Fund in Bretton Woods may be condensed in a single formula. The Fund was created to promote both *exchange freedom* and *exchange stability*. The most per-

sistent criticism leveled against the Fund is that, when the simultaneous achievement of both appeared impossible, *the Fund preferred in fact stability to freedom.*

This choice could hardly have been a conscious one. Exchange stability is a mere shadow, empty of all substance, if quantitative restrictions and discrimination nullify the impact of exchange rates on prices and trade, and divert international transactions into bilateral channels. Our primary objective is to make exchange rates *effective,* before we can attach any importance to their stability.

(6) If we allowed ourselves to drift into the opposite position, it is because we failed to realize in time the nature, and indeed the necessity, of the choice. Obnubilated [1] by the competitive devaluations of the thirties, we did not see that the main danger confronting us today was the cancerous growth of quantitative restrictions and discrimination, and of overvalued, rather than cut-throat, exchange rates. The result has been that, behind a meaningless façade of exchange stability, world trade has moved less and less in accordance with market prices and economic incentives, but more and more in enforced conformity with administrative licensing and bilateral deals between governments. The more these trading methods become entrenched, then the more difficult it will be to retrace our steps toward a multilateral trading system. This is not only because of the vested interests created by the controls, but also because of the growing distortions in national prices and costs, which result from the replacement of free market choices by enforced State decisions.

(7) If we are to rebuild a multilateral system of trade and payments, our first and overriding objective must be the gradual relaxation and abolition of exchange controls and quantitative restrictions. There existed many excellent reasons why this may have been impossible in the immediate postwar years. They are amply discussed in various Fund documents and publications, and need not be repeated here. Circumstances have now changed fundamentally, however, at least in Western Europe. Reconstruction has made the most impressive strides and production has recovered nearly everywhere to the best prewar years. The arguments used in the past to support both the rigidity of rates and the strengthening of the controls—the second

1. This gallicism escaped me at the time, as I was writing from Paris. I have refrained from modifying in any way my July 1949 text and prefer to explain that the French word "obnubilé," meaning literally "beclouded," is widely used to indicate an overpreoccupation with some single issue, obscuring or thwarting judgment on other relevant aspects of the problem under consideration.

appearing more and more necessary to bolster the first—are fast disappearing.

(8) The liberalization of controls is inextricably tied, for most countries, with a revision of exchange rates. Pursuing either policy also means implementing the other. The accent should be put on the first, however, rather than on the second, for the revision of rates would merely *facilitate* the relaxation of controls, while the relaxation of controls would *compel* exchange rate revisions.

(9) It will not be enough for the Fund, however, to *authorize* the necessary exchange revisions. The Fund must also facilitate the process rather than hamper it by cumbersome, and often unrealistic, requirements. While stable par values must remain as a basic Fund objective, and as a definite commitment for its members, we must consider how the Fund can best promote the attainment of par values which are both stable and effective.

(10) In numerous cases, it should prove possible to shift at once from an overvalued rate to a new par value, endowed with sufficient prospects of stability. In other cases, however, the abandonment of an overvalued rate risks being considerably postponed, if it must of necessity imply a simultaneous commitment to a new, and prematurely stabilized rate.

(11) Two such cases come to mind immediately:

(a) No par value can be effectively stabilized as long as a country has not reached *internal* monetary equilibrium. We must admit that the Fund is not in a position to impose quickly and effectively an adequate anti-inflationary policy upon a recalcitrant member. We may use the Fund machinery to provide technical advice on such a problem or even to strengthen the hand of an already convinced administration in persuading its own parliament or public opinion. We cannot, in all cases, expect immediate and satisfactory results. Under such conditions, a progressive depreciation of the exchange value of the currency, which merely offsets the increase in domestic costs, could not be construed in any way as a competitive devaluation, but would be of value in avoiding a needless deterioration of exports and of the balance of payments, with its inevitable incidence in further tightening of the controls.

(b) By relaxing or abandoning quantitative controls, a country would, to that extent, deprive itself of what may be the only instrument available to it in practice to maintain rigidly any given par value. If we do not wish to hamper, or prevent, the movement for trade liberalization, we should admit its necessary consequences on the mechanism of transitional exchange arrangements. This will be all the more necessary as the consequences of mutual, or unilateral, trade liberalization are highly unpredictable after more than ten years of stifling controls and economic dislocation throughout the world. No group, or individual, no matter how fully informed he may be, would seriously dare propose, out of a blue sky, a new pattern of par values with any reasonable prospects of stability, except the kind of stability which can be enforced through quantitative restrictions and make the exchange rates themselves correspondingly ineffective.

(12) If we are, therefore, ever to grow out of the present strait-jacket of controls, and restore the real significance of exchange rates for individual importers and exporters, we should recognize openly that there exist circumstances under which the establishment of a new, and stable, par value will require some transitional period of experimentation. The objections to this course of action, however, should not be minimized. We must not open the door to competitive devaluations, nor should we give up the basic powers and jurisdiction of the Fund for the final stabilization of exchange rates by international agreement.

(13) Strong and specific provisions should therefore be made to avoid abuses of exchange flexibility:

(a) Flexibility should be limited to cases, such as those defined above, where the immediate adoption of a new par value is recognized as impossible or excessively hazardous.

(b) Even in these cases flexibility should be limited in time, and remain a *transitional* phenomenon designed to hasten, and not postpone, the fundamental objectives of exchange freedom and stability.

(c) Finally, flexibility should also be regulated in its extent, so as to avoid all dangers of competitive devaluation; depreciation should be allowed only insofar as it is necessary to offset the effect of increased costs and trade liberalization on the equilibrium of the balance of payments.

(14) It is suggested that these necessary qualifications might be handled in the following manner:

(a) The Fund would announce that there exist specific circumstances—especially the need to remove long entrenched quantitative controls—under which flexible exchange arrangements may be applied for by members as the best way to hasten the revision of a par value which is recognized as inadequate.

(b) Such arrangements would be of a transitional character, limited as to their extent and duration, and designed to lead as promptly as possible to the establishment of an *effective* par value endowed with reasonable prospects of stability.

(c) A country desiring to take advantage of these provisions would have to: (i) satisfy the Fund that a change in par value is necessary to correct a fundamental disequilibrium, and that the circumstances of the case correspond to those contemplated under (a); (ii) propose an initial *de facto* rate acceptable to the Fund; (iii) undertake to limit fluctuations in the *de facto* rate to a range agreed to by the Fund, and not to be exceeded without the consent of the Fund; (iv) recognize that the Fund's authorization for flexible rates may be suspended at any moment if, upon complaint by any member, the Fund considers that such flexibility has been abused in a manner unfairly damaging to its members; (v) commit itself to propose a new par value within a period to be agreed to by the Fund; (vi) adopt all measures necessary to permit the effective implementation and stability of such par value.

If these conditions are fulfilled, to the satisfaction of the Fund, the old par value will be suspended, and *the member will be regarded—and quite properly—as engaged in normal consultation with the Fund, for the purpose of agreeing on a new par value.*

(15) Far from weakening the powers of the Fund, such a procedure might strengthen them considerably, and be used as an instrument to bring about the effective termination of Article XIV, as provided for in the Fund Agreement.

(16) The proposal above should not be confused with a plea for "free" exchange rates, left to seek their own level without any intervention by the monetary authorities. On the contrary, the conditions listed under (14c) would make such intervention mandatory in order to preserve orderly adjustments and avoid a blind surrender to currency speculation.

(17) Neither does the proposal imply, of necessity, an abandonment of orderly cross rates. This is an entirely different and most difficult issue, which can hardly be dealt with in a general paper like the present one. Suffice it to say that the enforcement of cross rates by the Fund seems to me hardly separable from the obligations imposed under Article VIII, Section 4, of the Fund Agreement. Cross rates, just like rate stability, are a basic ingredient of orderly exchange arrangements. Both will remain meaningless, and even harmful, if they become an end rather than a means, and are artificially maintained by

restrictions and discrimination which rob them of their fundamental purposes.

II

(18) The suggestions above on Fund policy would remain unworkable in practice if they were not accompanied by other reforms designed to give more flexibility to the Fund's procedures, and especially to the existing machinery for consultation.

(19) Such reforms are anyway unavoidable on other grounds. The Fund must establish closer and more intimate contacts with its members if it is to cooperate effectively with them in their day-to-day efforts to restore domestic as well as external stability in their monetary and exchange systems.

(20) The most spectacular effort in this direction—and probably also the most promising in spite of overwhelming difficulties—is the one undertaken among OEEC countries, with the help of ECA. There is little doubt that the most significant progress made toward currency transferability and trade liberalization in the last two years, has been made by the cooperative efforts of OEEC and ECA. It is also clear that the major problem of exchange revisions in Europe is now being studied and discussed most actively in the same quarters, in close connection with the broader questions of transferability and convertibility.

The Fund has been conspicuously absent from these discussions, and especially from the elaboration and functioning of the intra-European compensations system and payment agreement. It is doubtful whether it could participate effectively, without some regionalization of the Fund machinery.

(21) This could be done fairly simply and informally, without any need for a formal revision of the statutes, if European Governors of the Fund agreed to meet in Europe at frequent intervals to discuss their common monetary problems in relation to the Fund, with a high officer of the Fund who would ensure the proper liaison with the Fund's management and Executive Board in Washington. This would have the advantage of establishing close and continuing contacts between the Fund and the people currently and actually charged in each member country with policy decisions in the monetary and exchange field.

Such meetings should prove most fruitful, especially if formal papers and procedures could be kept to a minimum, in favor of free and exploratory exchanges of views, all suggestions arrived at being presented later to the Executive Board for formal action, by the members concerned.

(22) Such meetings should be used both to inform the higher staff of the Fund of European opinions and reactions, and to inform directly European policy-makers of the problems faced by the Fund. The present attitude in Europe is too often to blame "The Fund" for anything that goes wrong. We must bring home to responsible statesmen here the real reasons for the Fund's failures or paralysis to date, and give them a chance to express their opinions, and plan their strategy at the Board level.

They must be made to feel that the Fund is an instrument which they can use positively, rather than an annoying machinery to go through *after* national decisions have already been taken. In the worst event, if they fail to agree among themselves, they will at least be more fully conscious of the real roots of their difficulties, and will not shift the blame to the Fund as a convenient scapegoat.

(23) The same procedure could be extended to other regions of the Fund's membership, whenever it appears desirable and feasible.

(24) This regionalization at the policy level could usefully be supplemented by some degree of regionalization at the staff level. A timid step in this direction has been taken already with the appointment of a few technical representatives abroad. There is a serious danger, however, that the results may prove disappointing for two reasons:

(a) These offices abroad are not staffed sufficiently to permit the effective fulfillment of the tasks assigned to them.

(b) There is still insufficient planning and coordination between the head office and the technical representatives abroad. Fuller use of the facilities thus created would require that the activity of such representatives be more adequately directed and used, under the responsibility of an officer at headquarters, specially charged with such coordination.

(25) With adequate planning and supervision from Washington, regional staff offices should be gradually and cautiously expanded to prepare in the field, in close coordination with local technicians, most of the descriptive material and data which are now prepared, far less efficiently, in Washington. This should not require an expansion of the staff, but merely a redistribution of existing staff facilities between Washington and the regional staff offices.

(26) Such regionalization would also be an indispensable pre-

requisite to the assumption by the Fund of greater operating responsibilities in the field, such as its overdue and active cooperation in the functioning of the intra-European system of payments and compensations.

Simultaneous Exchange Readjustments and Elimination of Controls

(1) The long smoldering crisis of the international pattern of exchange rates has recently broken out into the open. Substantial, and widespread, revisions in par values have been recognized as essential and opportune, and the evident truth has been strongly reaffirmed that such changes must be made through the Fund's machinery. Any other course would inevitably spell the doom of the Fund as an effective instrument for international monetary consultation.

(2) Even under the best circumstances, the modification of a member's par value will always be the most critical test of the Fund's effectiveness and right of survival. The problem which it faces today, however, is made immensely more difficult by reason of the extraordinary complexity of the present situation:

(a) The need for *simultaneous* readjustment in nearly all exchange rates, including one of the two key currencies in world trade, deprives us of the stable frame of reference from which a single currency's readjustment could be calculated with relative ease and precision.

(b) Long entrenched quantitative restrictions, exchange controls, and bilateral arrangements have completely distorted the nature of balance-of-payments equilibrium. The effect of their simultaneous—even if progressive—removal on the position of each country is impossible to gauge on any basis other than trial and error.

(c) Many countries have only just emerged from domestic inflation and are still oscillating precariously between the danger of deflation and a resumption of inflationary forces. Others are still dependent on a host of domestic controls and restrictions—of gradually weakening effectiveness—to combat the effects of excessive liquidity or latent inflation. The stability of any new exchange rate will remain in doubt as long as domestic stability has not been made reasonably secure.

(3) Under such conditions, not only is the determination of a current equilibrium rate a highly hazardous guess, but the continued appropriateness of any rate chosen will remain vitally dependent on

---

I am unable to trace the exact date of this memorandum, but it clearly must have been written shortly before or, more probably, after the preceding one with which it overlaps in part.

policies and decisions, most of which are beyond the control of the country concerned, and are likely to exhibit considerable and unpredictable shifts in the very near future. In theory, the Fund machinery is flexible enough to allow such future adaptations through the provisions of Article IV. In practice, however, the constitutional provisions of member countries and the spectacular nature of requests for currency devaluation are certain to prove a most formidable obstacle to frequent readaptations of par values once accepted by the Fund. The experience of the last two or three years is very revealing in this respect. *Desirable* rate adaptations have been much prompter and smoother in countries untied by a formal par value, and have generally been unreasonably postponed—with serious aggravation in balance-of-payments deficits, or in quantitative restrictions—in all countries which were already committed to a par value and could not change it, under the Fund's rules, without committing themselves simultaneously and spectacularly to a new par value the maintenance of which appeared exaggeratedly uncertain under present conditions.

Thus, the Fund's weapons against currency undervaluation—a purely hypothetical danger in recent years—have turned into a shield for the very real and actual abuse of currency overvaluation.

(4) Exchange rates have, indeed, exhibited a remarkable stability under this system, but few of us would be proud of this embarrassing victory, bought at the cost of increases in balance-of-payments deficits and/or quantitative restrictions and exchange controls. Moreover, exchange stability under these conditions loses all that makes it a desirable objective of monetary policy, since it is no longer the rate itself, but rather the administrative licensing decisions, that govern the actions of traders and the pattern of payments in general. While fluctuations in exchange supply and demand do not induce corresponding rate fluctuations and uncertainty, they induce the even greater uncertainty associated with the relaxing or tightening of administrative controls. Neither this, or the deterioration in the balance of payments which are the necessary outcome of currency overvaluation can be regarded by the Fund as preferable to exchange readjustments.

(5) The stability of exchange rates cannot be made again a meaningful objective of monetary policy, until the rates themselves are restored to a position of meaningfulness as determinants of individual action. This implies the progressive elimination of administrative controls over trade and payments, and this should therefore have precedence, at this time, over the long-run objective of exchange stability.

There is far too much inclination, in this connection, to adopt a defeat-ist attitude with respect to the obligation of Fund members to elimi-nate controls before March 1, 1951. While special extension, or in-troduction, of the controls may prove unavoidable, either under Ar-ticle XIV or Article VIII, the exceptional character of such departures should be strongly reaffirmed.

This is all the more so as the liberalization of controls is far from being as hopeless an objective as is sometimes assumed. Various plans —some of which are already very near to completion—are now under active consideration in OEEC and among individual European coun-tries, to implement the growing recognition that controls must soon be abolished, if they are not to become entrenched as protectionist de-vices, under pressure of vested interests, after their initial inevitable-ness from the balance-of-payments viewpoint has waned.

It is obvious, however, that substantial progress in this direction would necessitate a provisional relaxation of present commitments with respect to the stability of exchange rates. The elimination of quantitative controls would indeed deprive a country with low mone-tary reserves of the only weapon permitting the maintenance of a given level of rates. It is even submitted that this might be the best way to force realistic adjustments of rates, without direct interference with the most fundamental aspect of national monetary sovereignty.

(6) The above suggestions should not be confused with a plea for "free" exchange rates, left to seek their own level without any inter-vention by the monetary authorities. On the contrary, such interven-tion would remain essential to preserve in cooperation with the Fund the orderly character of the adjustments.

(7) It should be emphasized most strongly that this suggestion for relaxation of normal Fund procedures is purely of an emergency and transitional character. It should be closely connected with international efforts at securing:

(a) the establishment of a realistic pattern of par values;

(b) the elimination of discretionary exchange controls authorized as a *"transitional"* arrangement under Article XIV.

The system, therefore, should be designed, not to amend and re-place the relevant provisions of the Fund's Agreement, but rather to permit the full implementation of the normal Fund machinery within the shortest possible delay.

(8) International monetary cooperation within the framework of the Fund will be more necessary than ever during this period of tran-

sitory exchange arrangements. This might be ensured through special provisions along the following lines: [*The remainder of this paragraph and the following paragraphs (9) and (10) were exactly reproduced in, or from, paragraphs (13–15) of the preceding paper.*]

(11) The most difficult issue which would arise in connection with the above suggestions is that of maintaining orderly cross rates. The problem is a most complex one, a full study of which would go far beyond the limits of the present memorandum. Three remarks, however, may be helpful in the way of clarification of the issues:

(a) Each country would remain responsible for the fluctuations of its own currency, either in its market, or in the market of other participating members. Decisions to move the rate up or down should be uniform with respect to all currencies, and should be based on the fluctuation in the country's *over-all*, not bilateral, payments position.

(b) Necessary intervention in this respect should be concerted among the central banks concerned, and studied in full cooperation with the Fund.

(c) No great difficulties should arise among participating countries which agree to repurchase balances in their own currencies currently and legally acquired by the central bank of another country, and in excess of some agreed ceiling or margin. Since this is the usual case in current payment agreements—or in the absence of payment agreements—the problem of cross rates is thereby made manageable in the great majority of bilateral relations. The main exception relates to sterling, where the maintenance of cross rates by countries which are normally sterling creditors might involve a limitless accumulation of that currency without interest or repurchase provision, or necessitate administrative discrimination in favor of sterling imports and against sterling exports. It is highly doubtful whether any country should be pressed upon to maintain through such means the cross rate of any currency, the monetary authorities of which do not abide by Article VIII, Section 4, of the Fund Agreement, or are not at least prepared to enter into freely negotiated agreements with respect to the repurchase of such balances.

(12) It might further be noted in this respect that, were transferability *mutually* agreed upon, the accumulation of balances in any one currency could arise only as a result of an *over-all* deficit of the issuing country with other participants. While such deficit might justify the use of trade and capital restrictions by the deficit country, it is more difficult to defend the view that it should be financed by the

surplus partner countries. In fact, no country would be in a position to continue such financing without limit, and the practical consequence will inevitably tend to be the adoption of discriminatory practices to stimulate imports, and discourage exports, in the currency of accumulation. When this happens, the deficit will be eliminated anyway, but through an artificial bilateral balancing of trade and other international transactions. While this may help keep up the volume of trade, it is necessarily at the cost of bilateralism, discrimination, administrative interference with market forces, and a permanent disruption in the international price and cost pattern.

(13) It is believed, therefore, that the Fund's attention could be profitably directed at making progress in the following directions *and in the order indicated:*

(a) the implementation of Article VIII, Section 4, even though other instruments of quantitative controls and discrimination are retained;

(b) the progressive elimination of quantitative restrictions and discrimination, beginning with the substitution of over-all quotas for bilateral quotas;

(c) exchange flexibility should definitely be regarded as a better alternative than quantitative restrictions and should be authorized, with the precautions outlined above, as a transitional arrangement designed to permit the elimination of controls;

(d) wherever *selective* controls are considered necessary, they should be consolidated into fiscal or even tariff arrangements, acting through the price mechanism rather than through administrative interference with individual freedom and market forces;

(e) the provisions above should facilitate the emergence of a realistic—and effective—pattern of exchange rates, which is the prerequisite to the meaningful stabilization of rates, under normal Fund procedures.

B. AFTER

Taking Stock

(1) The Staff owes it to the Fund and to itself to take stock of last week's events, and to draw from this experience the lessons indispensable if the Fund is to survive as an effective instrument for international monetary cooperation.

A memorandum dated September 28, 1949.

(2) The broad results of the exchange adjustments are encouraging. The upward revaluation of the dollar in terms of most other currencies has long been advocated by the Fund, and should exercise a happy influence on the restoration of an international monetary balance. The decisions reached will also greatly strengthen the Fund's prestige with the public at large, since they were taken within the framework of the Fund machinery, and immediately after the publication of the Fund's Annual Report and the Annual Meeting of its Board of Governors.

(3) For the insiders who were in a position to follow closely the discussions of the Executive Board and of the Staff, however, the experience has been a profoundly discouraging one. It was clear from the very start that member countries were in no mood to accept any serious discussion of their decisions, and were only barely condescending to go through the formal motions necessary to avert an open violation of their obligations under the Fund Agreement. This was made amply clear both in Sir Stafford Cripps' speech and in Mr. Bolton's statement to the Board. Even when Fund approval was not required, the time allowed for discussion barred any possibility of consultation between the Fund and the member, as mandatory under the Fund Agreement.

(4) Confronted with this situation, and anxious to avoid an open flouting of the Fund's rules, the Board could do no more than approve wholesale, with a bare shadow of discussion, all the requests that poured to it during these fateful days. The Staff, on its part, adopted the same attitude, and facilitated the Board's task by adjusting exactly in each case its own recommendations to the countries' requests.

The whole procedure, therefore, became—under the pressure of circumstances—a mere sham and mockery. Responsible officials, in the Fund and in the member countries, are fully aware of this fact, and cannot but draw from it practical conclusions which must affect fundamentally the future of our institution.

(5) It is, therefore, urgent and vital for the Fund to face the facts frankly and bluntly, and to answer two critical questions:

(a) Why did the machinery of consultation break down, and could this have been avoided if a different course of action had been followed by the Board and by the Staff?

(b) Can anything be done now to repair the damage, and to salvage the Fund—in one form or another—as an effective instrument for monetary cooperation in the future?

I

(6) Let us first recognize that by September 17, 1949, nothing that could have been done either by the Board or by the Staff could have affected in the least the outcome of the consultations. Any show of insistence by the Fund on a different rate of devaluation, or even on a reasonable time for discussion, would have led merely to unilateral action, in defiance of the Fund. The real problem, therefore, is whether more effective consultation could have been stimulated *in the months preceding the formal requests for changes in par value.*

(7) This was attempted and failed, but the failure may be ascribable, at least in part, to the manner envisaged for such consultations. It is worth pondering the fact that some of the European countries which opposed most strenuously such discussions by the Board, were among the most vocal advocates of exchange readjustments in Europe. The main reason for such apparent schizophrenia is the widespread feeling that present Fund practices make it a too formal and unsafe medium for frank, but secret, exchanges of views on such delicate problems.

(8) Difficulties arise both at the Board level and at the Staff level, and force us to reconsider past methods and policies.

As far as the Board is concerned, two major considerations immediately spring to mind.

The first is that no country can be expected to delegate to its representative on the Board the task of making, or even shaping up, its monetary and exchange policy. The task of policy formation will be jealously guarded by top government leaders, and especially by Ministers of Finance and Governors of Central Banks. They will appoint as Executive Director a top-rank *negotiator,* but not a policy-maker. Especially in matters as vital as the country's exchange rate, the decision will always be taken at home, and the Executive Director will not be in a position to discuss it freely until *after* the decision is made. On the contrary, he will have to deny any intention of changing the rate, and oppose all discussion of it at the Board until he is instructed to negotiate formal and speedy Fund approval. When that stage is reached, time is of the essence and makes it nearly impossible to discuss fruitfully with the national authorities any substantial modification in their request.

(9) The second major difficulty is the regrettable but undeniable fact that many countries are reluctant to discuss fully their exchange

rate with countries which are only very indirectly concerned, but whose vote may become decisive at the Board in controversial cases. From this point of view, fuller preparation of plenary Board meetings, on a regional basis, with countries directly interested, might smooth out many difficulties, and create a better atmosphere for the meetings, without, however, challenging the authority of the Board as such to give or refuse its final approval.

(10) Both difficulties might be solved together through frequent and informal regional meetings of the Fund's Governors—mostly Ministers of Finance or Governors of Central Banks—with some top officer of the Fund who would ensure proper liaison with the Fund's management and Executive Board in Washington. This would have the advantage of establishing close and continuing contacts between the Fund and the people currently and actually charged in each member country with policy decisions in the monetary and exchange field.

Advantage would be taken of such meetings to explain and comment on recent Fund decisions of interest to the members, and to stimulate discussion of future plans and policies on matters relating to the Fund. Only then could the Fund's views and influence be brought to bear on the slow shaping up of the climate of opinion which always precedes, by far, formal and concrete decisions in the monetary and exchange field. The meetings would be all the more fruitful if formal papers and procedures could be kept to a minimum, in favor of free and exploratory exchanges of views, all suggestions arrived at being presented later to the Executive Board for formal action, by the members concerned. Both the Fund and the members would derive great benefits from such direct information and exchanges of views.

(11) At the staff level, what is needed above all else is to strengthen the practical value of our studies by obtaining the fullest collaboration possible from technicians studying similar problems in our member countries. Our studies should be helpful to them, and theirs to us. Whatever interchange of reports appears feasible should develop in time into mutual critical appraisal of technical work at the Fund and in the country concerned.

The first prerequisite for this is the extension and fuller utilization of our system of staff representatives abroad, with tighter coordination at the Washington end. The system should also provide the opportunity for the training of top regional advisers, fully familiar with local needs and conditions. Executive directors should also provide an invaluable channel for such collaboration at a higher level. Free and sincere discussion, however, would be impossible if the papers discussed were always destined to be distributed outside the Fund, or even—in some cases—to the Board itself. Any such prospect would force the Executive Director to adopt a more formal attitude in defense of his country's *official* position of the moment. On the contrary, informal and confidential contacts would be valuable for checking the Staff's information and conclusions, and to confront them with similar information and conclusions developed within the member country. There is here a most meaningful use to make of the presence in Washington of high caliber men from such varied regions of the Fund's membership.

(12) Such interchanges and cooperation should not be limited to advance discussion of par values. On the contrary, this most delicate of all problems will long remain the hardest one to handle, even with the best will of all concerned. Other aspects of each country's economy may offer better proving grounds, especially at the beginning, for the use of the technique suggested above.

(13) Absolute secrecy is the primary prerequisite for the successful implementation of this program. A second prerequisite is the drawing up of as sharp a distinction as possible between the role of the Board and the role of the Staff. The Staff must limit its competence and advice to technical matters, and must offer its suggestions in complete independence from the country's requests. In the matter of par values, for instance, the Staff should set forth its own informed opinion on the technical and economic aspects of the problem, but should leave to the Board itself the appraisal of other considerations relevant for final decision.

II

(14) The above suggestions all refer to problems of administrative methods and machinery. There is also an urgent need to re-examine past policies in the light of the experience acquired, and of the drastic revision effected in member countries' exchange rates.

(15) The Fund's Annual Report has drawn attention to the close relationship between exchange rate maladjustments and the growth of exchange controls and other forms of quantitative restrictions and discrimination. The progress made toward a more suitable pattern of rates should open the door to substantial measures of trade and exchange liberalization. It is an urgent and vital duty for the Fund not to let this opportunity pass, but to encourage and promote all reason-

able steps in this direction, made possible by the recent changes in par values.

(16) It is even submitted here that positive leadership in that direction should be one of the main aims of, and should take precedence over direct pressure for, exchange readjustments. The reasons for it are:

(a) that exchange rates are the very symbol of a member's national sovereignty in monetary matters, thus eliciting strong psychological and political resistance to outside interference;

(b) that exchange rate readjustments merely *facilitate* the relaxation of controls, while the relaxation of controls would in fact *compel* exchange rate readjustments.

(17) It will not be enough for the Fund, however, to *authorize* the necessary exchange revisions. The Fund must also facilitate the process rather than hamper it by cumbersome, and often unrealistic, requirements. While stable par values must remain as a basic Fund objective, and as a definite commitment for its members, we must consider how the Fund can best promote the attainment of par values which are both stable and effective.

(18–25) [*These paragraphs reproduce verbatim paragraphs (2–9) of the preceding paper.*]

(26) Far from weakening the powers of the Fund, such a procedure might strengthen them considerably in practice, and be used as an instrument to bring about the effective termination of Article XIV, as provided for in the Fund Agreement. Last week's experience has demonstrated amply the futility of the Fund's jurisdiction over formal requests for large, and sudden, changes in par value. Such a procedure —at least when widespread changes are necessary—gives no time for effective consultation susceptible to reverse or modify what is a major policy decision involving governmental, or even parliamentary, approval.

In contrast, Fund consultation over the management of a flexible rate, gives every opportunity for informal representations at the administrative level. Even if informal Fund advice is disregarded, forcing formal action by the Board to suspend abusive use of rate flexibility, proper notice can still be given, thus allowing more time to reach agreement between the Fund and the member.

(27) Again, the effectiveness of these policies would be greatly enhanced by closer contacts and collaboration with regional agencies or institutions such as the Council of Europe, the OEEC, the BIS, the

regional commissions of the U.N., etc., which are now actively and concretely engaged in similar, or parallel, programs of monetary co-operation and exchange or trade liberalization. It is all too obvious that the Fund has remained far too aloof in this respect, and is increasingly disregarded or forgotten in the discussion and implementation of measures which are at the very core of its objectives and jurisdiction.

(28) The creation and development of such regional contacts must necessarily imply a corresponding decentralization at the staff level. [*The remainder of this paragraph and the following paragraphs (29) and (30) repeat paragraphs (24–26) of the preceding paper.*]

III

(31) In summary, the above suggestions would imply:

(a) a clearer distinction between the responsibilities of the Board and of the Staff in the preparation of Fund decisions;

(b) emphasis on continuous, informal, consultation, as against formal action upon a member's request;

(c) greater secrecy in the distribution of important technical papers, and close cooperation with technicians in member countries, both through the Executive Director representing the country under study, and through fuller use of regional staff offices;

(d) intimate contacts and cooperation with other international and regional agencies and institutions acting in the same field;

(e) regular top level contacts, on a regional basis, with Fund Governors in member countries;

(f) primary emphasis on progress toward the multilateralization of payments and the elimination of trade and exchange restrictions, until meaningful and effective par values are restored;

(g) thorough study of the possible scope—and necessary safeguards—of flexible exchange arrangements in connection with the liberalization of trade and payments.[1]

1. For complementary suggestions to the IMF in this regard, see Chapter XI, Section 1, below, pp. 406–41.

Chapter VI: The Exhumation of Convertibility à la Key Currencies and the Oncoming of the Dollar Glut: 1953–60

THE FOLLOWING article might have been included in Part One, Chapter II, on *The End of the Dollar Gap,* with which it overlaps in large part. It is, however, included here for its relevance to the issue of institutional reforms of the international monetary system. In that respect, it is the forerunner of the later, and much expanded, analysis that appeared in *Europe and the Money Muddle* (Chapters 6–8), *Gold and the Dollar Crisis,* and in the articles reproduced below in the present volume.

1. THE ABORTIVE "DASH" TO CONVERTIBILITY: 1953

Introduction

We shall soon celebrate—unless we forget—the tenth anniversary of the Bretton Woods Conference. The hopeful plans for currency convertibility drawn up in New Hampshire have long been buried under the weight of the so-called dollar shortage which accompanied postwar reconstruction, the Korean crisis, and the first years of Western rearmament. The year 1953 witnessed, at long last, a fundamental and spectacular readjustment in the world's payments pattern. From a gold and dollar deficit of nearly $11 billion in 1947, foreign countries moved gradually to an actual surplus, before aid, of nearly $1 billion in 1953. Their gold and dollar holdings—including United States aid receipts—dropped by nearly $6 billion in the three years 1946–48, but have risen since by $8 billion, of which $2.6 billion in 1953 alone.

National and international plans for currency convertibility have thus become again, for the first time in many years, a practical policy issue. The problem was raised here, on the initiative of the United

A paper presented at the Conference of the Universities-National Bureau Committee for Economic Research, at Princeton University, May 1954, and first published under the title "International Currency and Reserve Plans," in the *Banca Nazionale del Lavoro Quarterly Review* (Rome, January–June 1954), pp. 3–20; also reproduced with a "Comment" by William A. Salant in *Policies To Combat Depression* (Princeton, 1956), pp. 377–404.

Kingdom, a little more than a year ago, but the British suggestions were received with a surprising lack of enthusiasm in the United States, in Europe, and even in England. The discussion of the plan soon revealed fundamental disagreements about the very meaning of convertibility under present economic and political conditions.

The Commission on Foreign Economic Policy, under the able chairmanship of Clarence B. Randall, devoted considerable attention to the issues involved. Its report,[1] issued last January, has done much to clarify the intimate relationship between the trade and the payments aspects of international convertibility. In the meantime, the British plan was discussed further in the Organization for European Economic Cooperation (OEEC) and at the Commonwealth Conference in Sydney. Important steps toward the broadening of currency transferability and the relaxation of dollar restrictions have also been taken in recent months by a number of major countries, particularly the United Kingdom, Germany, and the Netherlands.

The United States recession and the pending Congressional debate on the Randall Report have induced a wait-and-see attitude which has slowed down the adoption of even more spectacular decisions, both nationally and internationally. There is little doubt, however, that such decisions will soon be forthcoming, and that they will be vitally influenced by the long overdue clarification of United States policies.

The 1953 British Plan and the Randall Report

The plan presented by the British last spring rested essentially on a distinction between convertibility for residents and convertibility for nonresidents. The United Kingdom proposed to restore the convertibility of sterling earned in current transactions[2] by *nonresidents of the sterling area,* but to retain the right, for the United Kingdom as well as for other sterling area countries, to impose restrictions on all foreign transactions of their own residents. These restrictions could, of course, be imposed in order to limit the foreigners' sterling earnings

1. *Report to the President and the Congress,* Commission on Foreign Economic Policy, Washington, 1954.

2. The exclusion of convertibility for capital transactions has become generally accepted since Bretton Woods as a permanent feature of postwar convertibility plans. The practical wisdom and feasibility of this exclusion raises very complex issues which I shall make no attempt to discuss here. It might be noted, however, that the International Monetary Fund's example was not followed by the Agreement for a European Payments Union, which applies equally to all transactions among members, whether on current or capital account.

and the drain on the area's gold and foreign exchange reserves which might attend the conversion of such earnings into nonsterling currencies, particularly dollars. They could, moreover, be imposed on a discriminatory or even bilateral basis to restrict imports from the countries presenting "excessive" demands for conversion and to favor imports from the countries which retained their earnings in sterling or made use of them to expand their purchases from the area itself.

The proposal was, moreover, made conditional upon a substantial liberalization of United States trade policies and the granting of large stabilization loans or lines of credit to the United Kingdom by the International Monetary Fund and by the United States.

The major criticism leveled against the plan, both here and abroad, was that its adoption might well stimulate a new wave of trade restrictions, discrimination, and bilateralism. The Randall report agreed with this criticism and indicated that the Commission "would deplore a merely formal convertibility maintained through trade restrictions. It believes that the removal of restrictions upon trade and upon payments should go hand in hand." [3]

The European countries were particularly fearful of the implications of the British plans for the OEEC trade liberalization program and the European Payments Union. The Randall Commission expressed a similar concern about dismantling prematurely the most effective instrument for trade liberalization and currency transferability established so far: "The Union has achieved an impressive measure of success—above all, it has shown that freeing trade and freeing payment go hand in hand—and the Commission feels that it should not sponsor any measures that might wreck the Union before there is something better to put in its place." [4]

These criticisms may spring in part from an overpessimistic view of the external position of Britain and of the world's so-called "dollar shortage." [5]

In the absence of heavy balance-of-payments pressures, the current trend toward trade liberalization might be expected to develop even in the absence of formal commitments, and to be strengthened further by the proposed measures for currency convertibility.

Yet the possibility of renewed balance-of-payments difficulties,

3. *Report to the President and the Congress,* Commission on Foreign Economic Policy, Washington, 1954, p. 73.

4. *Ibid.,* p. 74.

5. See below, pp. 217 ff.

whether in Britain or in other countries, cannot be excluded. Under such circumstances, formal convertibility for nonresidents, unaccompanied by parallel commitments with respect to trade policy, might force a relapse into restrictions, discrimination, and bilateralism and destroy the progress already achieved toward a multilateral system of trade and payments.

After all, the proposed sterling convertibility already exists for residents of the United States and other "American Account" countries. Sterling earnings accruing to such residents are freely convertible into dollars. Any other country that wishes to is also free to refuse payment in inconvertible sterling, and to demand gold or dollar payment for its exports. Most countries are deterred from doing so by the realization that such a policy would generally expose them to tighter restrictions on their exports to sterling area countries, similar to the restrictions now applied by these countries against imports from the dollar area. Sterling convertibility for nonresidents is certainly not regarded as true convertibility by the United States exporters who already "enjoy" this status, and it is certainly not sought by other countries' exporters to whom this "privilege" is now denied.

These considerations explain the coolness with which the British plan was received in Europe, in the United States, and even by a large sector of British opinion. While the plan has not been formally amended, there exist numerous indications that opinion is gradually shifting, in Britain and in Europe, toward a position fairly similar to that expressed in the Randall report. To be meaningful, convertibility must apply to trade as well as payments, to residents as well as to nonresidents. This implies that progress can only be gradual and must depend on the fulfilment of certain prerequisites. "The Commission does . . . wish to emphasize its view that a strong internal economy, willing and able to control its money supply and its budget as safeguards against inflation, sufficiently mobile to make the best use of its resources, and able and willing to save in order to increase its productivity and improve its competitive position in world markets, is a prerequisite to convertibility; and that the attainment over time of these conditions should be the guide as to how rapidly full convertibility could safely be approached." [6]

These "prerequisites to convertibility" constitute, indeed, an awe-

6. *Report to the President and the Congress,* Commission on Foreign Economic Policy, Washington, 1954, p. 74.

some list, especially if they are viewed not only as once-and-for-all prerequisites for the *restoration* of convertibility, but also as permanent prerequisites for the *maintenance* of convertibility after it has been restored. Will any future lapse from internal strength automatically spell the collapse of convertibility for the country concerned? And how will the failure of some countries to reach or maintain convertibility affect the prospects for the achievement or preservation of *international* convertibility? "The Commission believes that the decisions, the methods, the timetable, and the responsibility for introducing currency convertibility should rest on the countries concerned. It recognizes, however, that currency convertibility must be examined in the light of the policies pursued by other countries, particularly the United States." [7] And it clearly thinks also that the restoration of convertibility by Britain would greatly facilitate—or even be necessary for?—its restoration by other countries, and would in turn be greatly eased "if some other of the major trading countries [were] able to make their currencies convertible simultaneously with sterling." [8]

The Report thus seems to contemplate the unilateral restoration of convertibility by each country, acting in isolation, while recognizing at the same time the interdependence among the various countries' decisions and policies, particularly the United States, the United Kingdom, and other major trading countries. The recognition of this interdependence is in happy contrast with the naive theory which still prevails in academic and business circles, and which long dominated the United States Treasury thinking, i.e. that convertibility merely depends on each country's "setting its own house in order" by stopping inflation, readjusting its exchange rate, abolishing trade and exchange controls, and requiring full gold or convertible currency settlement for its exports and other external transactions. Even a country as strong internally and externally as Switzerland still feels unable to adopt such a prescription and run the risk of generalized discrimination against its exports.

International currency convertibility cannot be restored and—even more important—maintained without the active participation and cooperation of the major trading countries. While this participation and cooperation could largely be taken for granted in the nineteenth

7. *Ibid.*, pp. 72–73.
8. *Ibid.*, p. 74.

century, they cannot be ensured today by mere unilateral decisions, but require at least a minimum of collective organization and mutual commitments.

Before discussing the nature of these commitments, we must clarify the meaning of currency convertibility, as an international policy objective. We shall then discover that the necessary commitments are far less formidable than the "convertibility prerequisites" listed in the Randall report, and which, indeed, no international agreement could ever be relied upon to enforce effectively.

Toward a Definition of "Workable" Convertibility

Currency convertibility used to be defined by the maintenance of a fixed parity or exchange rate with relation to gold or other gold-convertible currencies. It might seem rather paradoxical, therefore, to find the modern proponents of convertibility arguing in favor of flexible or "floating" exchange rates as against fixed or "pegged" rates. The reason for this shift is, of course, obvious. The fixity of exchange rates becomes largely illusory if it is preserved only through trade or exchange restrictions which control arbitrarily the access of traders to foreign exchange for each category of transactions, and may deny them the right to purchase it at any rate whatsoever. Exchange stability has little or no meaning if it is not based on exchange freedom. The latter was taken for granted in all traditional definitions of convertibility. True currency inconvertibility—as distinct from instability of exchange rates—is a relatively modern phenomenon. It might be noted, for instance, that European currencies remained convertible throughout the 1920s even though at a fluctuating exchange rate.

Here again, the Randall report marks definite progress over previous policies, and particularly over the exaggerated emphasis placed on exchange-rate stability at Bretton Woods. The Commission expresses itself as "sympathetic to the concept of a 'floating rate,' which provides alternative methods of meeting trade and exchange pressures." [9]

This seems to leave us with the elimination of trade and exchange restrictions as the modern definition of convertibility. The question arises at once whether any full elimination of such restrictions is conceivable within a foreseeable future, and whether such liberalization can realistically be confined to direct, quantitative restrictions while leaving tariff restrictions to the full discretion of each individual coun-

9. *Ibid.,* p. 73.

try. There are undoubtedly very important differences between tariff restrictions and other trade or exchange restrictions. Most of these differences relate, however, to the *domestic* impact of such measures upon income and money flows. From the point of view of their *international* impact, the differences between tariffs and trade controls are not so fundamental as to justify the definition of convertibility in terms of a full elimination of the latter without any concern for the first. High and unstable tariff levels can indeed be as, or more, damaging to international trade as moderate, nondiscriminatory systems of import or exchange controls.

Shall we therefore be pushed into a definition of convertibility which equates it to the old free trade ideal of classical economists? In this case, progress will indeed have to be gradual, and full convertibility is unlikely to reward our efforts or even those of our children and grandchildren.

Clarity of thought and effectiveness of policy both require a less ambitious definition of immediate convertibility goals. Such a definition can be found in the restoration of a *multilateral system of trade and payments,* rather than in the removal of all protection for domestic production against imports from abroad. This was indeed the meaning of nineteenth-century convertibility, which accommodated itself to varying degrees of national protection. The major differences between these age-old techniques of protection and modern inconvertibility techniques lie in the fact that the former extended protection only to the national producers and only within the protecting country's boundaries, while the second discriminate in favor of certain exporting countries at the expense of others, and try to protect domestic producers not only within the country's boundaries but in all foreign markets as well. Once adopted by a major country, such techniques inevitably spread from trading partner to trading partner, each country trying to secure special advantages to itself or being forced at least to defend its exporters against the discriminatory actions of others. International trade is then forced more and more into the straitjacket of bilateral negotiations, relegating increasingly into the background all considerations of price or quality competition and the underlying pattern of comparative costs and advantages.

The key to "workable" convertibility is not free trade—desirable as this would be—but the maintenance of full competition in third markets. Professor MacDougall's study of United States and United Kingdom exports in 1937 showed ample verification for the classical theory of comparative costs, but found that it depended essentially on *third market competition* rather than on direct trade between the two countries. "Before the war, American weekly wages in manufacturing were roughly double the British, and we find that, when American output per worker was more than twice the British, the United States had in general the bulk of the export market, while for the products where it was less than twice as high the bulk of the market was held by Britain. . . . But while in the normal textbook examples the exports of each country go to each other, the great bulk of the exports of the United States and the United Kingdom in 1937 went to third countries—more than 95 per cent of British exports of all our sample products but three, more than 95 per cent of American exports of all the products but six. It is true that each country was nearly always a net exporter to the other of products in which it had a comparative advantage, but this is of limited interest, since trade between them was in general a negligible proportion of their total consumption." [10]

Thus, the preservation—or restoration—of traditional competitive forces in international trade depends essentially on the equal access of all foreign exporters to each national market, rather than on the elimination of all protection for domestic producers within a country's own territory. The latter objective has never been achieved, and can hardly be expected ever to be fully achieved, without a political as well as economic merger among the countries concerned. Equal access to third markets has always constituted the bulk and the core of international competition.

Convertibility is not incompatible, therefore, with a certain amount of protection and restrictions. The past is, in this case, a guide to the future. The restoration of convertibility depends essentially on the elimination of discrimination and bilateralism—rather than of *over-all* protection or restrictions—from the trade and payments mechanism. This implies: (a) the ability of country A to use its earnings on countries B, C, D, etc., to settle its deficits with countries X, Y, Z, etc., i.e. full currency transferability; (b) the absence of bilateral or discriminatory trade techniques designed to shift trade artificially from low cost exporters to high cost exporters, thus distorting normal com-

---

10. G. D. A. MacDougall, *"British and American Exports: A Study Suggested by the Theory of Comparative Costs,"* Part I, *Economic Journal,* (December 1951), pp. 697–724, particularly pp. 697–99. See also below, Table 3, p. 223, column 4.

petitive forces not only between domestic and foreign producers, but in all third markets as well.[11]

The two problems are largely inseparable, as payments and trade techniques reinforce one another in this respect and can often be used nearly interchangeably to achieve the same result.

The weakness of the International Monetary Fund springs in large part from the artificial separation of these two problems—one of which was entrusted to the Fund, and the other to GATT—but even more from basic defects of the Fund's machinery in dealing with currency transferability. Countries may borrow from the Fund, but they cannot use the Fund to convert their earnings on one country into the currency needed to settle their deficit with another. Moreover, the Fund has in practice made little or no attempt to distinguish between exchange restrictions and discrimination. Organized discrimination against a "scarce currency" is theoretically provided for under Article VII of the Fund Agreement, but this provision has never been put to the test by the Fund. On the other hand, Fund members have so far retained the right to currency discrimination—against weak as well as against hard currencies—under Article XIV of the Agreement. Similar discrimination is also contemplated as a permanent feature of the Agreement under Article VIII, although its use under this Article would be subject to Fund approval.

In contrast, the remarkable success achieved by the European Payments Union is largely explainable by its comprehensive approach to the problem, encompassing full multilateralism both in trade—nondiscrimination—and in payments—currency transferability. This multilateralism, however, is confined to the relationships among member countries, and does not cover their trade and payments with other countries and particularly with the United States. Partial convertibility with the United States dollar is provided in EPU settlements, but each country is left free to regulate as it wishes its trade and payments with nonmember countries.[12]

Most of the difficulties which EPU has had to meet in its four years of operation, and most of the objections raised against it, are closely

11. This definition is very close to that proposed in the "Staff Papers" of the Randall Commission, on pp. 467-68.

12. Payments to and from nonmember countries of the sterling area are, however, channelled through the United Kingdom's account, and are subject to the same settlement rules as are applicable among members. The same applies also to all other sterling transfers.

related to these regional limitations of the Agreement. These were, however, unavoidable at the time the Agreement was negotiated. While they are probably unnecessary and even harmful under present conditions, their elimination might prove dangerous in the event of a renewed dollar scarcity, as it might then contribute to the unnecessary spread of deflationary forces and to ultimate relapse into generalized bilateralism.

The Prerequisites of Convertibility

Convertibility has been defined above as the absence of discrimination, and particularly of bilateralism, with respect to both trade and payments. While indispensable to the maintenance of international competition, such a system is also subject to a major defect. It tends to spread to the world at large any deflationary pressures arising from an economic depression or from trade restrictionism in one of the major trading centers. If each country most heavily and directly affected by the decline in this center's imports adopts *nondiscriminatory* policies —internal deflation, currency devaluation, over-all trade or exchange restrictions, etc.—to restore equilibrium in its balance of payments, it will affect unfavorably the balance of payments of other countries. These may, in turn, be compelled to adopt similar policies—or to reinforce them—thus contributing to the spiralling of deflation, devaluation, or restrictions. This process will continue until the first country's surplus is ultimately eliminated, but will involve a multiple restriction of world trade—or an extensive devaluation of currencies —which might have been avoided by direct and systematic discrimination against the surplus country alone. For this alternative to be successful, however, discrimination by the deficit countries must be directed exclusively against the *over-all* creditor country, rather than against the countries in *bilateral* surplus with them, since such bilateral creditors may themselves be in over-all deficit rather than in over-all surplus. If discrimination is left to the discretion of each individual country, acting in isolation, it will inevitably take the form of bilateral discrimination and involve even worse distortions— and, probably, a greater contraction—of world trade.[13]

13. An abundant literature has grown up around this problem and its applicability to the so-called "dollar shortage." See, in particular: E. M. Bernstein, "Scarce Currencies and the International Monetary Fund," *Journal of Political Economy, 53* (1945); Ragnar Frisch, "On the Need for Forecasting a Multilateral Balance of Payments, *American Economic Review, 37* (1947), pp. 535–51; John H. Williams, *Trade not Aid: A Program for World Stability* (Harvard University Press, 1953).

This was recognized in the "scarce currency" clause of the International Monetary Fund, but the practical implementation of such a clause would raise enormous difficulties. Public opinion in the scarce currency country is likely to pay little heed to the intricate economics of the problem and to react violently against the ganging up of other nations against its exports. The danger of retaliatory action will deter many countries from participating in systematized discrimination. This is all the more likely as such discrimination might involve the imposition of tight restrictions against essential imports from the scarce currency country while unessential imports from other countries continue to be imported freely. Countries can hardly be expected to sacrifice their own national interests in this manner for the sake of an abstract concept of international equilibrium. Certainly, the exact degree of implementation required from each participant would give rise to endless debate and controversies.

A more practical approach to the scarce currency problem lies in the extension of nondiscrimination over the widest possible area, on the basis of mutual agreements and commitments, rather than in any international quarantine of the major creditor country. The EPU experience reveals very clearly the type of commitments necessary for the effective functioning of a multilateral trading area. The creditor countries must facilitate the adoption by the debtors of *nondiscriminatory* readjustment policies:

(1) by refraining at least from hampering such policies through unnecessary trade or exchange restrictions over their own imports; definite liberalization commitments were therefore accepted by all members, but exceeded in practice by the surplus countries;

(2) by providing fractional financing to cushion moderate deficits of other members with inadequate reserves, thus allowing them to ride out temporary fluctuations in their balance of payments, or to wait for the effect of slower-acting fiscal or monetary readjustment policies;

(3) by avoiding retaliatory action against countries which may be compelled to restore restrictions temporarily because of heavier deficits, provided that:

(a) such restrictions remain nondiscriminatory among members; and (b) the restricting country submits its case to full discussion by the competent organs of the OEEC; such discussion may cover not only the external measures adopted, but also the whole range of monetary, fiscal, and economic policies of the country concerned.

From Regional Convertibility to International Convertibility

Such a close type of cooperation is hardly feasible on a world-wide basis. It is possible only among countries which are highly interdependent (exports to the EPU area account for nearly three fourths of member countries' exports), keenly conscious of their interdependence and able to understand each other's problems and policies. These factors—different in degree, but not in kind, from those underlying a fuller political union—explain the success of, and justify the need for, regional cooperation in trade and payments. The maintenance of freer trade among members constitutes, of course, a form of discrimination. Such discrimination, however, rooted in mutual commitments of the type described above, may be as justified by its broad political and economic results as the discrimination against imports from abroad, and in favor of interregional imports, implicit in present boundaries between nations. The progressive elimination, in the nineteenth century, of internal taxes on the movement of goods between cities or provinces of the same country, or the fact that national tariff walls do not apply to domestic trade, have never been objected to in the name of nondiscrimination. There is no more reason to oppose the efforts to preserve freer trade among countries which are ready to accept, to this end, mutual trade and financial commitments limiting the untrammelled use of their economic sovereignty.

Under the inflationary strains of postwar reconstruction, the sterling area and EPU arrangements provided a practical alternative, not to a better and wider system of international convertibility, but to the infinitely worse alternative of generalized bilateralism in trade and payments. They could not, however, provide a satisfactory answer to the fundamental disequilibria then prevailing between these regions and the outside world, and particularly to their trade and payments problems with the dollar area. In the sterling area, the responsibility for handling these problems centered largely on the United Kingdom, through the administration of the dollar pool and the setting up of different types of sterling accounts—American and Canadian accounts, transferable accounts, resident sterling accounts, bilateral accounts, etc.—subject to different privileges and limitations as to their transferability in payments, and implying at the same time different degrees of tightness in the administration of trade restrictions. In EPU, no such centralization was attempted, and each country was left free to handle on its own its trade and payments with nonmember countries. On the other hand—and in contrast to the exclusive use of sterling in settlement among sterling area countries—the partial gold or dollar payments involved in EPU settlements established a direct link between the position of individual EPU countries within and outside the EPU area.

Such a system may tend to stimulate discrimination against an outside scarce currency, but also tends—contrary to a widely spread misconception—to eliminate discrimination if no such scarcity exists in fact.

The stimulus to discrimination arises from both the payments and the trade rules governing the system. EPU creditors are forced to liberalize imports from other EPU members, but are left free to maintain—or liberalize—restrictions on imports from the outside. Since, however, they receive only partial gold or dollar payment for their EPU surpluses, they may be unable to finance large deficits with nonmembers requiring 100 per cent gold or dollar settlements. Even if their gold and dollar position enables them to do so, they may be alarmed by the continued growth of their EPU lending and adopt restrictions on outside imports, in order to force their residents to shift their purchases to EPU sources and thus reduce their rate of lending to the union.

Debtor countries, on the other hand, will normally prefer to incur their deficits with the Union, rather than with other countries, since the first require only partial gold and dollar payment and are, for the remainder, financed by EPU credits. These credits, however, are limited in size. When a country remains persistently in deficit with the Union, its ratio of gold to credit settlements rises steadily until the point of 100 per cent gold settlements is reached. When this occurs, the financial stimulus to discrimination disappears, and the deficit country becomes increasingly reluctant to admit freely less essential, or costlier, imports from EPU sources while continuing to restrict severely more essential or cheaper imports from the outside. On the other hand, such persistent deficits on the part of some members are reflected in persistent surpluses on the part of others. The creditors become increasingly reluctant to continue to extend larger and larger credits beyond their quotas. Since the Union, under these circumstances, is receiving 100 per cent gold settlements from the extreme debtors, its convertible resources tend to increase and to enable it to grant additional payments to the creditors either through a larger ratio of gold to credit settlements, or through some amortization of their previously accumulated claims.

The experience of EPU so far confirms these theoretical deductions. Of the $1,350 million of EPU credits initially available to them, present EPU members have used about $1,150 million and have therefore only about $200 million in all left available. For many months, France, Turkey, and Greece have been subject to 100 per cent gold settlements, and have claimed release from their trade liberalization commitments. Restrictions were also restored by the United Kingdom as long as its quota was exhausted or remained perilously close to exhaustion, and it will be remembered that, for a while, the United Kingdom also accepted sterling payment for dollar commodities bought through London. On the creditors' side, substantial amortization payments were granted to Belgium and Portugal in June 1952, and proposals now under discussion envisage both an increase in gold settlements beyond quotas and the regular amortization of long outstanding claims.

This normal evolution of the Union toward convertible settlements and nondiscrimination can only be held in check, in the long run, by a severe and generalized dollar scarcity. When this exists, most members will be anxious to preserve their exports against the tighter restrictions applied to dollar trade, and will recognize that this can be done only through mutual trade liberalization and the limited convertibility of intra-EPU settlements. When, however, the dollar position of a majority of members becomes more comfortable, the maintenance of discriminatory trade and payment rules is increasingly regarded not only as contrary to their own selfish interest, but also as unnecessary from the point of view of the group as a whole. It should be noted, for instance, that the EPU management has always prodded excessive debtors to readjust their deficits through monetary and fiscal policies. Exchange readjustments have sometimes been hinted at also, but with a discretion imposed by common sense as well as by the desire to avoid any conflict of jurisdiction with the International Monetary Fund. These pressures had a considerable influence on member countries' policies, particularly in the case of Germany and the Netherlands. They were reinforced in the first case by a special loan negotiated on the basis of an agreed readjustment program, but at no time has the EPU seriously entertained any proposals for further credit extensions to deficit countries which did not take adequate steps to readjust their balance of payments.

We may conclude, therefore, that while *formal* commitments to nondiscrimination and currency transferability are most likely to prove feasible on the basis of regional cooperation, such arrangements will tend *de facto* toward world-wide nondiscrimination and convertibility, except when discrimination against a "scarce currency" becomes the only alternative to the international spread of deflation or of bilateralism.

Even in the latter case, the maintenance of currency transferability and nondiscrimination among member countries preserves powerful competitive pressures upon the higher cost countries. It prevents them from seeking in bilateral trade and payments agreements an escape from basic economic readjustments. They can no longer extract from their creditors bilateral import credits or discrimination in favor of their exports. Moreover, the gradual liberalization of trade restrictions among members opens each market to the competition of the lower cost producers in the area, and exercises a fundamental influence on the readjustment of national price and cost patterns, indispensable to further progress toward world-wide, rather than merely regional, convertibility. There is little doubt that full competition with Belgian, Swiss, German, and other exporters over the whole EPU area has exercised upon higher cost producers a pressure equivalent, or nearly equivalent, in most cases to that of competition from nonmember countries.

Confirmation of this fact can be found in the near elimination of currency discounts and gold premia in the European free markets, and in the ease with which major steps toward trade liberalization and broader currency transferability have been absorbed in recent months. The abolition of rationing, the reopening of international commodity and gold markets in London, the merging of practically all non-resident sterling accounts—outside the dollar area—into a single transferable account system, the adoption of a similar system for Deutsche mark accounts, the liberalization of many categories of dollar imports and other transactions in Germany, Belgium, the Netherlands, etc., have already narrowed down considerably the gap between regional and international convertibility. There is every indication today that this remaining gap could be bridged if some method could be found to assuage current fears about the existence, or future resurgence, of a world-wide dollar scarcity.

International Inflation and the Dollar Shortage

A "currency scarcity" condition, i.e. the tendency for many countries to incur convergent deficits toward a single "scarce currency" country, may emerge from many different causes. A number of writers have popularized the view that a higher rate of technical advance in the United States tends to create a chronic dollar shortage. The *possibility* of such a link cannot be flatly denied on purely logical grounds. The *demonstration* of its inevitability or probability depends, however, on highly special assumptions as to the exact nature of such productivity advances, and as to their impact on prices and money wages, terms of trade, the income-elasticity of import demand, etc. It would not be difficult to construct extremely plausible models of U.S. advances in productivity the impact of which would be to reduce, rather than increase, the balance-of-payments surpluses of the United States, without exercising any generalized deflationary pressures on foreign prices, export levels, economic activity, or employment.

A dollar shortage undoubtedly tends to emerge, however, when the U.S. economy develops lesser inflationary pressures, or greater de-

TABLE 1

ESTIMATED GOLD RESERVES AND DOLLAR HOLDINGS OF FOREIGN COUNTRIES

	In billions of dollars				1953 as per cent of:		
	1928	1938	1948	1953	1928	1938	1948
1. Continental Western Europe	4.8	7.3	5.8	10.1	207	138	172
a. *France*	*2.0*	*3.0*	*0.8*	*1.1*	*52*	*35*	*132*
b. *Switzerland*	*0.2*	*0.9*	*1.9*	*2.1*	*1,080*	*230*	*112*
c. *Other*	*2.6*	*3.4*	*3.1*	*6.9*	*307*	*177*	*220*
2. Sterling area	1.4	3.9	2.9	4.0	288	104	138
3. Canada	0.4	0.4	1.2	2.4	580	610	198
4. Latin America	1.1	0.9	2.7	3.6	320	380	132
5. All other foreign countries	1.0	1.3	2.3	2.9	300	225	126
6. International	—	—	3.4	3.3	—	—	99
7. **Total outside United States**	**8.7**	**13.8**	**18.4**	**26.4**	**300**	**190**	**143**

SOURCE: *Federal Reserve Bulletin*, March 1954, p. 245.

flationary pressures, than the rest of the world. This timeworn doctrine still seems to me sufficient to explain the tendency of European countries to run into heavy dollar deficits during a period of intense inflationary pressures associated with war financing and the reconstruction of war damage, or in the course of a world depression marked by steeper price and income deflation in the United States than in most other industrial countries.

I find it extremely difficult, however, to discover any chronic dollar shortage tendency in the current pattern of world payments. Foreign countries' gold reserves and dollar holdings are estimated to have increased by about $8 billion in the last five years and $2.6 billion in the year 1953 alone. Table 1 shows that foreign gold and dollar holdings are far higher today than in any previous period. While still inferior to 1938 levels in real purchasing power, they are also far better distributed with relation to most countries' import levels and export instability than has probably been true at any time in the recorded past (Table 1).

The fears of a dollar shortage spring from the special factors underlying the present pattern of the balance of payments of the world with the United States, and particularly from:

(a) the dependence of foreign countries' current dollar earnings on large and "abnormal" U.S. expenditures for foreign aid and military procurement overseas;

(b) the expected increase in their dollar needs if present restrictions and discrimination on dollar transactions were eliminated through the restoration of convertibility;

(c) the possible impact of a U.S. depression on their levels of reserves, foreign trade and economic activity in general.

The Role of "Abnormal" U.S. Expenditure Abroad. The 1953 accumulation of gold and dollars by foreign countries far exceeds their total receipts of United States aid.[14] Even the further exclusion of U.S. military disbursements overseas would leave Western Europe and the Western Hemisphere in approximate gold and dollar equilibrium, but would leave the rest of the world with a deficit of about $1.7 billion (see Table 2).

Adding to this an estimated $0.6 billion for stockpiling purchases, the Randall report discerns in these figures a "concealed dollar gap of some $2 billion to $3 billion annually, which would be increased if

14. Other than so-called military-end-use items contributed in kind by the United States under military aid programs. This form of aid and the corresponding United States exports have been excluded throughout from the data presented in this paper, since there is every reason to assume that such items would not be imported in significant quantities by foreign countries under circumstances permitting the cessation of military aid programs.

TABLE 2

GOLD AND DOLLAR TRANSACTIONS OF FOREIGN COUNTRIES IN 1953
(in millions of dollars)

	World	Continental Western Europe	Sterling area	Canada	Latin America	Other countries	International institutions
I. Estimated increase in gold reserves and dollar holdings	**2,720**	**1,670**	**860**	**−20**	**250**	**−130**	**90**
II. Through receipts of U.S. aid, exclusive of military-end items	**1,770**	**840**	**400**	—	**20**	**420**	**90**
III. Through all other transactions	**950**	**840**	**450**	**−20**	**230**	**−540**	—
A. U.S. military purchases of goods and services overseas	2,570	990	280	150	20	1,130	—
B. Civilian transactions	−1,620	−150	170	−170	210	−1,670	—
1. Net outflow of U.S. capital	*590*	*−260*	*90*	*350*	*220*	*140*	*60*
a. government	*220*	*−110*	—	—	*340*	*−20*	*−20*
b. private	*370*	*−150*	*80*	*350*	*−120*	*160*	*60*
2. Multilateral transfers and errors and omissions	*160*	*200*	*110*	*510*	*110*	*−730*	*−40*
a. recorded in U.S. transactions	*−270*	*100*	*−220*	*410*	*130*	*−630*	*−60*
b. other	*430*	*100*	*320*	*100*	*−20*	*−90*	*20*
3. Current account with the U.S.	*−2,370*	*−80*	*−30*	*−1,030*	*−130*	*−1,090*	*−20*
a. receipts	*14,680*	*3,220*	*2,520*	*3,020*	*4,230*	*1,650*	*40*
b. expenditures	*17,050*	*3,300*	*2,550*	*4,050*	*4,360*	*2,740*	*60*

SOURCES: Data are primarily derived from official estimates of the U.S. Balance of Payments, as presented by Walther Lederer on pp. 22–23 of the March 1954 issue of the *Survey of Current Business*. Differences between total changes in estimated gold holdings as reported in the "Federal Reserve Bulletin," March 1954, p. 240, and the U.S. gold sales and purchases have been entered under "Other Multilateral Transfers," and added to the reported U.S. balance on foreign capital and gold to arrive at the "Estimated Increase in Gold Reserves and Dollar Holdings." Unilateral transfers other than aid have been included in "Current Account Receipts."

there were a change in the economic situation, such as a recession here or a deterioration in Western Europe's terms of trade. On the other hand, it should be recognized that major parts of our 'extraordinary' expenditure abroad are connected with our defense effort, and that the Western European countries' own defense programs affect adversely their trade position, by increasing their essential imports and by absorbing resources that would otherwise be available for expanding their exports." [15]

The constant reference to Western Europe in these comments leads one to suspect that the Commission was not aware of the fact that its "concealed dollar gap" concentrates nearly entirely on the Far Eastern countries, particularly Japan, whose economies have been disrupted by military events and attuned to a high rate of United States military procurement. It is, of course, obvious that these countries are not now accumulating gold and dollar *surpluses* equal to whatever the U.S. army spends there for procurement of goods and services, plus the amounts of reconstruction or defense support aid to Korea, nationalist China, etc. This becomes a "concealed dollar gap," however, only if one assumes that such expenditures are likely to be completely eliminated in time, without any corresponding offsets in foreign countries' dollar imports or exports.

Both assumptions would be extremely unrealistic. U.S. military disbursements overseas are still rising now and will at best taper off gradually, with little or no probability that they will fall down to zero in the foreseeable future. Moreover, such tapering off would simultaneously release for consumption, investment, or exports the resources otherwise absorbed in the production of the goods and services contributed under these programs. This trend would be further reinforced by the decline in foreign countries' own military budgets which would be likely under such circumstances.

The absorption of these resources into civilian production will, of course, necessitate difficult economic readjustments. For Western Europe as a whole, the problem is more likely to center on the maintenance of domestic activity and employment than on the balance of payments itself, since its current gold and dollar accumulation is already as large as the total of aid and military disbursements receipts (see Table 2, above). In the Far East, however, the readjustments will bear more heavily on the need to reduce imports or increase ex-

15. *Report to the President and the Congress,* Commission on Foreign Economic Policy, Washington, 1954, p. 5.

ports. These readjustments might spread to other areas and recreate generalized balance-of-payments difficulties with the United States if the decline in U.S. military expenditures were not offset in part by some increase in U.S. commercial imports or capital exports. Given the present rate of gold and dollar accumulation by foreign countries ($2.7 billion), however, moderate changes in U.S. export and import levels would be sufficient to absorb any foreseeable reduction in U.S. aid and military disbursements.

The Role of Dollar Discrimination. The removal of discrimination against dollar trade constitutes a second factor of fear and uncertainty in the progress toward convertibility. The Randall *Staff Papers* report that "guesses at the magnitude of the suppressed dollar demand have ranged between $1 billion and $3 billion a year; the true figure at present is probably much closer to the former than to the latter." [16]

I would myself incline to reduce even further the estimates of the real quantitative impact of dollar discrimination upon the balance of payments.

First of all, we must not forget that more than half of the U.S. exports flow to such areas as Canada, Central America, the Caribbean Islands, the northern coast of South America, Japan, the Philippines, etc., which either have no exchange controls at all (Canada and most of Central America) or which have no reason to apply discriminatory controls against dollar goods as such.

Secondly, the proportion of United States and Canadian exports in total imports of the rest of the world is now already far larger than before the war. This is true, not only for the world at large, but for all individual areas as well, with the single exception of the sterling area. The proportion is about one third larger than in 1937 for Latin American and continental EPU countries, and 20 per cent larger for the countries outside the sterling area, continental EPU, and the Western Hemisphere.

Thirdly, while the elimination of dollar discrimination will tend toward an expansion of United States exports, two other factors are now acting in the opposite direction. The reduction in foreign aid eliminates some elements of discrimination *in favor of* United States shipping and commodities previously purchased under ECA, MSA, or FOA procurement authorizations. Moreover, the recovery of produc-

16. *Staff Papers,* Commission on Foreign Economic Policy, Washington, 1954, p. 18.

tion and the abatement of inflationary forces abroad reduce foreign demand for other United States goods imported in abnormal quantities in earlier years. It should be noted that the proportion of United States and Canadian goods in the total imports of Western Europe and the sterling area has declined substantially over the past year, in spite of greater dollar availability and of the trend toward a relaxation of dollar discrimination abroad. The continuation of this trend, in a noninflationary environment, might well result primarily in price read-justments by soft-currency exporters, rather than in any large diversion in the pattern of trade. This would be all the more likely if progress toward nondiscrimination were undertaken simultaneously by all major trading countries rather than by one or a few countries alone.

For all these reasons, the relaxation of trade and currency discrimination against dollar goods is likely to have a much more moderate impact on the dollar position of foreign countries than is generally feared. In any case, the relatively small order of magnitude of its possible effects should be kept in mind. For instance, a 25 per cent increase in United States exports to the sterling area—where discrimination is most stringent and effective—would amount to about $375 million, and to a 10 per cent increase in exports to continental Western Europe and the nondollar countries of Latin America to about $250 million and $100 million, respectively, i.e. a total of about $700 million a year.

The International Impact of a United States Recession. The international impact of a United States recession could hardly be estimated in advance with any degree of precision. It may be noted, however, that the mild recession experienced since the summer of 1953 has had a far smaller impact on foreign dollar incomes than was generally expected. Gold and dollar holdings continued to rise at a rate of more than $2 billion a year throughout the period from October 1953 to March 1954. Current and prospective levels of foreign aid and military expenditures—at a rate of $4.3 billion a year—will continue for some time to act as a powerful stabilizing influence on foreign countries' dollar earnings. For the next two or three years at least, a United States recession might be expected primarily to slow down the current accumulation of gold and dollars abroad, but it is highly unlikely to resurrect any large surpluses in the United States balance of payments with the rest of the world.

The international impact of United States recessions, however, is not limited to direct trade between each country and the United States itself. Their major disruptive effects lie in the transmission of contractive forces from country to country, through their own mutual trade as well as through their trade with the United States.

The channels through which these indirect effects are propagated are of several kinds:

(1) The demand of each country for exports from other countries, and not only from the United States, may contract automatically as a consequence of the lower income levels resulting from: (a) the loss of export earnings to the United States; (b) possibly, the deterioration in its terms of trade associated with a United States recession.

(2) This will affect income levels in the supplying countries and react in turn on their own imports from the first, spreading the contraction from each country to the others.

(3) This spiral of contractive tendencies may be broken, or on the contrary accentuated, by the policies adopted in each country:

(a) Some countries may succeed, through compensatory policies, in preventing a decline in national income levels and maintaining their import demand at a higher level; their balance of payments will tend to deteriorate as a consequence, reducing previous balance-of-payments surpluses or causing a drain on their monetary reserves.

(b) Currency depreciation, tariff increases or import and exchange restrictions would, on the contrary, aggravate other countries' difficulties; they may be resorted to: (i) as the consequence of reserve losses, whether automatic or resulting from the compensatory policies above; (ii) as a substitute for such compensatory policies, in order to offset through increased exports and decreased imports the effects of the recession on economic activity, incomes and employment.

The international propagation and intensification of a United States recession can be considerably reduced by measures which will encourage and enable countries to follow compensatory policies (3a above) rather than disruptive policies (3b above) in the course of such a recession.

The difficulties of the task will be far smaller if action is taken at an early stage rather than after the recession has already been allowed to spread over a wider area.

The direct impact of a United States recession will be heaviest on the countries which are most dependent on the United States market for their exports. Canada and Latin American countries sell in the

TABLE 3

GOLD AND DOLLAR HOLDINGS, TOTAL EXPORTS AND EXPORTS TO THE
UNITED STATES IN 1953
(in billions of dollars)

	Gold and dollar holdings	Total exports	Exports to the U.S.	Per cent ratio of exports to U.S. to total exports	Per cent ratio of gold and dollar holdings to	
					Total exports	Exports to U.S.
1. Continental Western Europe and dependencies	10.06	22.2	2.51	11	45	401
2. Sterling area	4.05	18.4	1.82	10	22	222
3. Canada	2.42	4.6	2.52	55	52	96
4. Latin America	3.63	7.6	3.58	47	48	101
5. Other countries	2.90	6.0	1.47	24	48	197
6. **All foreign countries**	**23.04**	**59.0**	**11.90**	**20**	**39**	**194**
7. International organizations	3.34	x	x	x	x	x
8. **Total**	**26.39**	**59.0**	**11.90**	**20**	**45**	**222**

SOURCES: 1. Gold and dollar holdings: *Federal Reserve Bulletin*, March 1954, p. 245; 2. Total Exports: *International Financial Statistics*, April 1954, pp. 22 and 24; 3. Exports to the United States: *Survey of Current Business*, March 1954, pp. 22–23.

United States market about half of their total exports, while European and sterling area countries trade far more extensively with one another and sell only about 10 per cent of their total exports to the United States (see Table 3). This ratio is substantially exceeded by only a very few countries outside the Western Hemisphere—mainly the Philippines, India, Indonesia, and Japan. It varies, however, very greatly among individual Latin American countries, from about 25 per cent in the River Plate countries to more than 80 per cent in Mexico, Guatemala, El Salvador, and Colombia.

A 30 per cent decline in exports to the United States would therefore have a very different significance for these various countries or areas. It would correspond to only 3 per cent of over-all exports and 7.5 per cent of gold and dollar holdings for continental Western Europe, but about 16 per cent of total exports and 31 per cent of gold and dollar holdings for Canada.

There are also very great variations in the cyclical sensitivity of different countries' exports to the United States. Sterling area exports have usually been affected far more severely, and those of Canada substantially less severely, than those of other areas during past United States recessions. Exporters of wool (Australia, New Zealand, Argentina, and Uruguay), minerals (Bolivia, Chile, Mexico) and raw materials in general suffer a far heavier decline than coffee, banana (Brazil, Colombia, Central America), sugar and other food exporters.

TABLE 4

PER CENT CHANGES IN EXPORTS TO THE UNITED STATES

	1923-24	1926-27	1929-32	1937-38	1948-49
1. Continental Western Europe	− 6	−	−71	−32	−12
2. Sterling Area	−11	−18	−79	−48	−18
3. Canada	− 4	−	−65	−35	− 2
4. Latin America	+ 1	− 8	−68	−32	−
5. Other Countries[1]	− 8	−	−67	−34	− 6
6. **Total**	− 5	− 6	−70	−35	− 7

[1] Excluding Eastern Europe.

Taking into account both criteria—ratio of exports to the United States to total exports or GNP, and sensitivity of those exports to U.S. recessions—we should expect the most severe direct repercussions of a U.S. recession to concentrate on some Western Hemisphere countries—particularly Canada, Mexico, Bolivia, Chile, Argentina, and Uruguay—and on Japan, the Philippines, Indonesia, and the overseas sterling area.

International policies designed to avoid or moderate the further spread and spiralling of the depression fall into two major categories: monetary policies and trade policies.

Untied loans in convertible currencies, whether from international institutions or from high reserve countries, may be necessary to relieve these countries of severe balance-of-payments pressures and enable them:

(a) to avoid deflationary or restrictionist policies which would aggravate the depression elsewhere; and

(b) to adopt positive compensatory domestic policies designed to sustain income levels, employment and imports.

The amount of assistance required for this purpose will depend, of course, on the level of these countries' reserves. Current ratios of gold and dollar holdings to total exports now average 40 to 50 per cent for all major regions except the sterling area (see Column 5, Table 3, above). Sterling area and EPU arrangements, however, result in a considerable economy of gold and dollar settlements in intra-area trade. As long as these arrangements continue, the need for external stabilization loans will be considerably less than it would otherwise be for Western Europe and the sterling area. The resources of the IMF in gold and United States dollars—more than $3 billion—and in the currencies of other prospective creditors could provide all, or at least a considerable portion, of the residual assistance needed *and actually usable* to overcome the reserve deficiencies *arising from a United States recession.*

The latter qualifications, however, limit considerably the significance to be attached to international monetary cooperation as an antirecession device. Such cooperation may be more effective in preventing deflationary or restrictionist policies than in stimulating positive compensatory policies. The latter policies would prove very difficult to implement for many of the countries most severely affected by a United States recession, even if large stabilization loans relieved them of any anxiety about their reserve losses and balance-of-payments deficits. It is by no means easy to provide alternative employment for the men and resources left idle by the loss of export markets, especially in countries highly specialized in one or a few export products, such as tin, copper, rubber, etc.

Moreover, the ability of these countries to repay at a later stage the loans extended to them may very often be questioned by the prospective lenders. The lenders may take the view—rightly or wrongly— that balance-of-payments difficulties are aggravated during the recession, and will persist long after the end of the recession, as the result of ill-advised or irresponsible domestic policies. Disagreements on such points are likely to prove a stumbling block in many cases, especially when decisions have to be made, as is the case in the IMF by many countries with diverse geographical, historical, and economic backgrounds. They may create far lesser difficulties in more closely knit organizations—such as EPU and the sterling area—grouping countries more highly interdependent economically, more keenly conscious of such interdependence, and more familiar with one another's problems and policies.

Without minimizing the role of stabilization loans as an antirecession device, their limitations should be recognized and should prompt further efforts in other directions as well.

Commodity agreements and buffer stocks designed to reduce excessive instability in agricultural and raw material markets would be of far greater value to primary producing countries than monetary stabilization loans. The difficulties raised by such schemes are enormous, but so are their potentialities for economic stabilization and development.[17] One must regret, therefore, the rather cursory dismissal of this approach to the problem in the Randall Commission's report. Some of the Commission's recommendations, and particularly the "avoidance of actions incidental to our own commodity control and stockpile programs that would have avoidably disruptive effects upon world prices"[18] and continued consultation and cooperation with other nations to improve knowledge of world supply and demand for materials and foodstuffs, and to explore possible means of lessening instability"[19] are all to the good, but give little hope for concrete action in the near future. This conclusion is clearly shared by the Commission itself, which also recommends "a policy of encouragement of diversification of the economies of the countries now excessively dependent upon a small number of products."[20] The benefits of international specialization must, to this extent, be sacrificed to the objective of domestic economic stability. In practice, however, the costs and difficulties of diversification policies may well be as or more formidable than those of commodity stabilization.

The above measures will at best reduce, but not eliminate, the direct impact of reduced export earnings to the United States on the monetary reserves and economic activity of the countries affected. They should be coupled with other policy commitments designed to avoid, to the maximum extent, the adoption of beggar-my-neighbor policies of currency devaluation, tariff increases, trade and exchange controls, discrimination, and bilateralism, which are a major factor of propagation and intensification of international recessions. The cooperation of the major and stronger nations is particularly vital in this respect. The influence of their policies on other countries, and their ability to use alternative measures to fight depressive tendencies at home, are usually far greater than those of the smaller or less developed economies.

17. See *Commodity Trade and Economic Development,* New York, United Nations, 1953.

18. *Report to the President and the Congress,* Commission on Foreign Economic Policy, Washington, 1954, pp. 35–36.

19. *Ibid.*

20. *Ibid.*

No country, however, can be expected to renounce any means to improve its own domestic activity and employment, even at the expense of others, on the basis of Platonic appeals to international cooperation. While each of them may realize that the cumulative effect of mutual restrictions will be damaging to it as well as to others, none will feel assured that its own restraint, or lack of restraint, in this respect will decisively influence the policies of other countries. Mutual commitments, of a positive as well as of a negative nature, encompassing credit provisions together with trade provisions, remain the most promising way to promote the maximum degree of trade freedom and cooperative antirecession policies. International agreements, of the ITO or GATT type, deserve greater United States support than they have received in recent years. On the other hand, in this field as well as in the monetary field, regional organizations may develop a far closer degree of intimate cooperation among the participating countries than can be anticipated on a world-wide scale. The combination of trade, credit, and economic policy commitments and negotiations into a single institution can also contribute to greater success in all three fields, as the OEEC experiment has amply demonstrated during its brief span of years.

We have just rejoined the conclusions reached in previous sections of this paper, when we discussed the prospects of convertibility and the best means to restore and preserve it in a world of national sovereignties. Regional cooperation should be viewed as a valuable adjunct, rather than a rival, of world-wide agreements.

Conclusions

The current rate of gold and dollar accumulation in Western Europe and the sterling area, together with prospective rates of United States aid and military expenditure overseas over the next years, provide a considerable cushion against a hypothetical United States depression. We should therefore expect a continuation, and even an acceleration, of the progress already achieved in recent years and months toward currency transferability and trade liberalization.

These, however, are fair weather objectives which can only be pressed forward in an environment of high economic activity and employment. In times of depression, each nation will almost inevitably resort again to trade restrictions and currency inconvertibility in an effort to insulate its own economy from external deflationary pressures. These policies cannot be successful in the end, as each country's actions tend to aggravate the difficulties of others, widening and deepening the contractionist tendencies at work. National antidepression policies of this character have always proved in the past one of the main factors in the spread and aggravation of international recessions.

This spiral can be broken only by collective arrangements giving operational meaning to the interdependence of the various countries' policies. The avoidance of disruptive action should be made both possible and attractive through adequate access to stabilization assistance in case of need and through reciprocal guarantees against all unnecessary recourse to trade and exchange restrictions. In case restrictions become unavoidable, they should be limited in scope and time, and avoid unilateral discrimination against any country participating in the arrangements.

International cooperation of this sort is, however, extremely difficult to negotiate and implement in practice. Moderation in its aims, hopes, and promises is indispensable to avoid later disillusionment, disaffection, and retrogression. World-wide arrangements are particularly slow and cumbersome to negotiate and implement, and will necessarily remain more limited in their effective content than regional arrangements among countries which are highly interdependent on one another, keenly aware of this interdependence, readier to understand each other's problems and policies and to confide in the commitments and good faith of their partners.

Both types of approach should be developed and encouraged, and the potentialities of each should be as fully exploited as proves possible in practice. Much could be done today to improve the effectiveness of worldwide organizations such as GATT or the IMF. Much could be done also, under present favorable circumstances, to relax some of the regional limitations of the EPU and sterling area systems. Individual countries, particularly Britain, Germany, and the Netherlands, have recently taken important measures in this direction, but drastic revisions in the EPU Agreement are now long overdue to adjust it to the enormous changes which have taken place in the international pattern of trade and payments since the negotiation of the Agreement four years ago.

Major creditor nations, and especially the United States, will inevitably exercise a profound influence on the progress of other countries and of both regional and international organizations toward currency convertibility and trade liberalization. The United States has a major stake, economically and politically, in the promotion of liberal economic policies abroad and in the strengthening and development of other free nations. These objectives happily coincide with the interests of both consumers and producers in the reduction of tariff and trade barriers here, and with the need to provide increasing outlets for our exports of goods and capital.

The report of the Randall Commission on Foreign Economic Policy is now before Congress. Its obvious shortcomings as a basic document on fundamental, long-term U.S. international economic policy have attracted more attention in academic circles than its very real contribution to the clarification of urgently needed, and immediately feasible, U.S. action in the monetary and trade field. The adoption of its major recommendations would provide the necessary spark for further and considerable advances toward the rebuilding of a workable international framework for economic growth and stability.

2. The Dilemma of Convertibility: Gold Shortage or Dollar Crisis?

A. PROGNOSIS: 1957–60

My book on *Europe and the Money Muddle* concluded with a bold prediction of the imminent return to convertibility, but also of the danger that "history might easily repeat itself tomorrow if convertibility were to be restored today on the same unorganized gold-exchange standard basis" as in the late 1920s (p. 296).

I warned, on the one hand, about the excessive dependence of the international gold-exchange standard upon the mounting gold losses and short-term indebtedness of the United States,[1] and, on the other, about a possible "resurgence of deflationary trends or restrictive policies in the United States, or inflationary pressures and unilateral inconvertibility decisions in other parts of the world" (p. 274).

To help ward off either danger, I outlined, in broad terms, a number of proposals for "a true internationalization of the gold-exchange standard" (pp. 296 and 299–301), for transitional "overdraft facilities with the Fund, which could be drawn upon to cover all or part of any future decline in [outstanding dollar and sterling] balances" (p.

---

1. On this subject I concluded: "It is evident that such a movement could not continue indefinitely without eventually undermining confidence in the dollar itself" (p. 297).

301),[2] and for further regional monetary integration in Europe (pp. 280–294).

These proposals were developed in far greater detail in two articles —"The Return to Convertibility: 1926–1931 and 1958–? or, Convertibility and the Morning After" and "Tomorrow's Convertibility: Aims and Means of International Monetary Policy"—initially published in March and June 1959 by the *Banca Nazionale del Lavoro Quarterly Review,* and reproduced later in *Gold and the Dollar Crisis.*

The latter volume also includes (pp. 3–14) an abbreviated version of my testimony on the subject to the Joint Economic Committee of Congress on October 28, 1959.[3] While the Committee did not, of course, take any formal position on my proposals, it took by *unanimous* consent of both its Democratic and Republican members "the somewhat unusual course of transmitting to you for your consideration and, we hope, your comments, a copy of Mr. Triffin's statement and the transcript of the day's hearing"[4] to the President of the United States, the Secretary of the Treasury, the Chairman of the Board of Governors of the Federal Reserve System, the Managing Director of the International Monetary Fund, and the respective Chairmen of the House and Senate Banking and Currency Committees, the Senate Finance Committee and Foreign Relations Committee, and the House Foreign Affairs Committee and Ways and Means Committee.

Responses to this "unusual" step of the Committee were, alas, far less "unusual": the papers and suggestions were gratefully received and would be "read" or "carefully studied" by the agencies concerned. The only substantive comments were those of the Managing Director of the IMF, Per Jacobsson, and of the Secretary of the Treasury, Robert Anderson. Per Jacobsson's comments were candidly blunt: "I cannot see any value in Dr. Triffin's scheme as such; on the contrary, I believe that it may be positively harmful. . . . As you know, the resources of the Fund have recently been enlarged. . . . This enlargement of resources should make it possible to play its part in overcoming mone-

2. This proposal bears a striking similarity to that recently developed in much greater detail by Sir Roy Harrod on pp. 20–24 of his *Plan To Increase International Monetary Liquidity,* published (without date) by the British Section of the European League for Economic Cooperation (47 Eaton Place, London, S. W. 1).

3. For a complete text, see *Employment, Growth, and Price Levels,* Hearings before the Joint Economic Committee of Congress (Washington, D.C., 1959), pp. 2905–54.

4. Quoted from the covering letter of the Committee's Chairman, Senator Paul H. Douglas, reproduced in *Gold and the Dollar Crisis,* (rev. ed., 1961), pp. 153–54.

tary disequilibriums in cooperation with member countries, *under any foreseeable conditions* [italics mine]. . . . As far as international liquidity is concerned, I can detect no over-all problem. . . ." [5] While more temperate in tone, Secretary Anderson concurred in substance with Per Jacobsson: "In the Treasury's view, the increase in the Fund's resources . . . is sufficient to provide the degree of liquidity needed for expanding world trade *in the foreseeable* future [italics mine], and will enable the Fund to deal with the problem of temporary imbalance in international accounts which are likely to arise. . . ." [6]

The foreseeable future in question was, of course, to last little more than a year, after which frantic efforts would be devoted by the same gentlemen, or their successors, first to enlarge once more the Fund's lending resources, later to supplement them through bilateral swaps, swap-standbys, Roosa bonds, etc., and, at long last, to launch parallel and high-level investigations by the IMF and the Group of Ten "of the outlook for the functioning of the international monetary system and of its probable needs for future liquidity." [7]

The optimistic view entertained—or at least professed—by the officials until the very eve of the 1960 gold crisis was probably based on the IMF's calculation of future reserve needs and sources of supply, in *International Reserves and Liquidity*.[8] Indeed, Secretary Anderson, when answering Senator Douglas, kindly sent him "a copy of the International Monetary Fund study on liquidity in case you have not seen it." I suspect that Senator Douglas had seen it, but had rightly remained unconvinced. The Fund's forecast in effect was that the reserve requirements of the next decade would not exceed $8 billion, and that seven eighths of this amount would be provided from new gold production, "even after allowing for an increase in the present large gold hoards." [9]

I strongly questioned the bases of these calculations in *Gold and the Dollar Crisis*, raising to a range of $13 billion to $24 billion estimated increases in reserve requirements over ten years, and forecasting that

---

5. Quoted from p. 172 of *Current Economic Situation and Short-Run Outlook,* Hearings before the Joint Economic Committee, December 7–8, 1960 (Washington, D.C., 1961).

6. *Ibid.*

7. Quoted from pp. 285–86 of the *Summary Proceedings,* Annual Meeting 1963, International Monetary Fund (Washington, D.C., 1964).

8. Washington, D.C., August 1958, pp. 67–75.

9. *International Reserves and Liquidity*, p. 72.

only 29 to 55 per cent would be covered from new gold production and Russian sales, for which I accepted the Fund's estimates.[10]

The facts speak for themselves. In the five following years (from the end of 1958 to the end of 1963), i.e. only *half* of the period to which the above estimates refer, total reserves increased by $10.7 billion, of which new gold production contributed less than 12 per cent and Russian gold sales less than 15 per cent, for a total of about 26 per cent.

My last attempts to alert expert opinion, before the outbreak of the gold crisis of October 1960, were in the form of an article published in January 1960 by *The Banker* (London, pp. 13–22), under the title "Improving World Liquidity," and a reply to Mr. Hirsch's comments (*ibid.*, May 1960, pp. 352–54).

B. THE FAT IS IN THE FIRE: THE GOLD FLARE-UP OF OCTOBER 1960

A Letter to The New York Times

The delegates to the Fifteenth Annual Meeting of the Board of Governors of the International Monetary Fund (September 26–30, 1960) had hardly returned home when the official optimism that had suffused that gathering was badly shattered by the sudden flare-up of gold prices in the London market. On October 20, the dollar price of gold, which was $35.24 an once at the beginning of the week and until recently had not exceeded $35.15, jumped precipitously, if briefly, beyond $40 an ounce to settle back later in the day around $38 an ounce, i.e. 8 to 9 per cent higher than the corresponding official par value of the dollar.

The most extraordinary comment elicited by this event was undoubtedly that of our Treasury spokesman, as quoted in an Associated Press dispatch that evening: "We are watching it closely. We are wondering just what has happened. . . ."

This inane comment prompted me to write the next day the following, somewhat intemperate letter to *The New York Times*:[1]

To the Editor of *The New York Times*:

A Treasury official commented as follows on the sudden jump of gold prices in London:

10. *Gold and the Dollar Crisis*, pp. 47–53, particularly line I, 3 of Table 8, p. 49.
1. Where it appeared on Sunday, October 30.

"We are watching it closely. We are wondering just what has happened. . . ."

Just watching won't do much good, especially if the watching is done by people who can still be "wondering just what has happened," after the multiple warnings given them for more than three years that just such a crisis was bound to erupt sooner or later in the face of continued inaction by the U.S. Government.

Our persistent gold losses and increases in liabilities abroad are not new. They have now lasted for over 10 years, and took an alarming course for the worse nearly 3 years ago. All pleas for consideration of the problem and of the means to meet it have been shrugged off by the Administration, which blandly denied that there was any cause for serious concern.

The dramatic jump in London gold prices on October 20 should not be regarded with undue alarm. But it should certainly shake the complacency of our officials. This sudden break in the market can be traced to the ostrichlike attitude adopted once more by them during the annual meeting of the International Monetary Fund in Washington three weeks ago.

The absurd and blind optimism and lack of concern exhibited by them on this occasion were received with dismay by their foreign colleagues, who began to fear that we would not act in time to avoid in the end a gold embargo, and a *de facto* devaluation of the dollar.

The rise in the gold price in London could easily have been stemmed at a very minor cost in terms of gold outflow from here if the Bank of England had been encouraged to continue to regulate the market as it has so successfully done ever since its reopening in 1954. It is obvious that it received no such encouragement. There are even reasons to believe that it was informally told that we were totally uninterested in what might happen to the price of gold in the free market.

The speculative fears that have now been triggered by the do-nothing attitude of our Treasury will make official interventions on the gold market far more costly than they would have been otherwise. Yet our means of fighting such speculation are still enormous and far more than sufficient to break it.

We still have about $7 billion of so-called free gold above the amounts legally earmarked as cover for our currency. We could also, whenever we wish, draw up to nearly $6 billion, or even more, from the International Monetary Fund.

A devaluation of the dollar or—what would in the end come to the same thing—a gold embargo would be an act of sheer folly and a wanton crime against the people of this country, and against the friendly nations who have long accepted our financial leadership and placed their trust in the U.S. dollar and the integrity and intelligence of our monetary management.

Something, however, needs to be done. Brave talks and incantations about a sound dollar are not enough. The solutions are simple and obvious. They have been amply discussed here and abroad for more than a year, and have received official support in the recommendations of the Radcliffe Committee in England. Only our own Treasury and Administration have refused to show any constructive interest in a problem which is their own, and crucial, responsibility.

Robert Triffin

New Haven, Connecticut
October 21, 1960.

Congressional Hearings and Reports

A few days later, I was requested by Senator Douglas to participate again in a Joint Economic Committee's "bipartisan, factual discussion of the current economic situation, with particular reference to the balance of payments and the gold drain."

My oral statement to the Committee was reproduced on pp. 228–30 of *Current Economic Situation and Short-Run Outlook,* Hearings before the Joint Economic Committee, December 7–8, 1960 (Washington, D.C., 1961). Accompanying tables, papers ("Altman on Triffin: A Rebuttal," "The Crisis of the Gold-Exchange Standard," "The Twilight of the Gold Standard and the World Dollar Crisis"), and debate, appear on pp. 169–266 of the same volume.

The Joint Economic Committee was to continue for years its efforts to educate itself, the Congress, and the Administration on the various facets of the international monetary problem and its relationship to the protracted crisis in the U.S. balance of payments. A special Subcommittee on International Exchange and Payments was even set up under the dynamic chairmanship of the Honorable Henry S. Reuss, to study the "International Payments Imbalances and Need for Strengthening International Financial Arrangements."

A complete list of the relevant publications of the Committee is, of course, kept up to date and available from the U.S. Government Printing Office. I have extracted from this ever-growing mountain of publications the major items which some readers of this book might wish to consult. The numbers in brackets refer to the chronological order of publications by the Committee.

Employment, Growth, and Price Levels

[125]   Hearings: Parts 5 (June and July 1959) and [131] 9A (October 1959, pp. 2905-54)
[134]   Staff Report (December 1959, Chapter 11, pp. 441-88)
[135]   Committee Report (January 1960, pp. 59-61 and 90)
[144]   Study Papers (No. 16): Edward M. Bernstein, *International Effects of U.S. Economic Policy* (January 1960)
[153]   Index (December 1960)

Current Economic Situation and Short-Run Outlook

[170]   Hearings: December 7 and 8, 1960, pp. 169-266

Subcommittee on International Exchange and Payments

[182]   Hearings: May 16 and June 19-21, 1961 [2]
[183]   Report: August 1961
[224]   Studies: December 1962
[225]   Hearings: December 12-14, 1962 (particularly the excellent papers and lively debate of Fritz Machlup, Edward M. Bernstein and Harry Johnson, pp. 198-240)
[226]   Report: December 1962
[297-299]   *Guidelines for Improving the International Monetary System:* Part 1, Hearings; Part 2, Supplement; and Report (July and August 1965).

The United States Balance of Payments

[244-248]   Hearings, Staff materials, and statements by economists, bankers, and others, particularly [246] *The International Monetary System: Functioning and Possible Reform* (Hearings, November 12-15, 1963)
[259]   *The United States Balance of Payments,* Senate Report 965, March 1964

In its first report (August 1961), the Subcommittee on International Exchange and Payments concluded that "the economic objectives of

2. See also the hearings, studies, and reports published from October 1961 through February 1962 by the Subcommittee on Foreign Economic Policy [192-204], particularly [200] Peter B. Kenen, *United States Commercial Policy, A Program for the 1960's* (Washington, D.C., November 1961).

the free world are in jeopardy because its international monetary mechanism is inadequate" (pp. 1–2). After reviewing the various schemes for reform, it recommended (pp. 21–22):

(1) immediate action by the United States to "discourage destabilizing outflows of short-term capital, speculation against the dollar and speculation in gold";

(2) a "credit agreement within the IMF among the principal industrial countries" along the lines of the subsequent "General Arrangements to Borrow";[3]

(3) a prompt and continuing "study of future reserve needs."

Its second report (December 1962) expressed the belief that "unilateral and cooperative efforts of the kind undertaken to date will not suffice to eliminate the payments deficit" (p. 4), and recommended (pp. 6–9):

(1) U.S. efforts to "secure from our Western European allies a larger contribution toward the costs of mutual defense of the free world and economic aid to the developing countries";

(2) prompt and vigorous U.S. bargaining "for the reduction of the Common Market external tariff" and a request to the Common Market "to make an immediate, unilateral reduction in its tariffs on a most-favored-nation basis pending completion of the negotiations";

(3) prompt negotiation of "a payments agreement among the leading industrial countries to neutralize destabilizing short-term capital movements and to finance temporarily deficits arising from more basic factors";

(4) the assumption of leadership by the U.S. *"in establishing a mechanism which can add to international reserves* [italics mine]."

Particularly noteworthy in this latter respect were:

(a) the Subcommittee's comments on Under Secretary Roosa's advocation of "a multiple key currency reserve system. . . . This appears to be the objective of present U.S. policy, but it should be regarded as an interim step rather than a permanent system" (p. 9);

(b) its rejection of "a general gold guarantee on dollars held as monetary reserves" (p. 9), but its "willingness to consider extension of gold or exchange value guarantees . . . as part of a general multilateral payments agreement wherein similar guarantees would be offered by all participants" (pp. 8–9).

The report of the Joint Economic Committee itself (March 1964) also stressed the increased need for international liquidity (p.

3. See below, pp. 287–89.

12) and the excessive reliance of the present international monetary system on gold, the dollar and the pound sterling (p. 13). It dismissed the criticism of "some plans . . . on the ground that they would cause countries to lose a measure of monetary sovereignty." [4]

> The possibility of conflict between domestic and international policies and objectives is present under any system. And, in any system, international considerations must play a role in national policies. Under the present system, the United States has been severely impeded, in pursuing the objectives of the Employment Act of 1946, by the need to bring its balance of payments into equilibrium. To reject consideration of certain plans because they could in some ways impose new international obligations on nations, thereby limiting their sovereignty, might rule out the possibility of large gains for the sake of costs which may have little practical significance and may be substantially outweighed by the benefits. In evaluating various plans for international monetary reform, the Committee concludes that attention must be focused on matters of substance—on practical implications for the United States and other countries under various conditions of deficit or surplus in the balance of payments—and not on generalities which, while seemingly relevant and important, may serve to confuse rather than clarify the issues. (pp. 14–15)

The final recommendation of the Committee was that

> **The free world must proceed now to devise ways and means for improving its international financial organization and expanding international liquidity.**
>
> The Committee is gratified that the Administration and other nations have begun long overdue multilateral considerations of this problem. The committee urges the IMF and the Group of Ten to proceed expeditiously with their studies, and hopes that specific recommendations, sufficiently far-reaching to meet the needs of the problem, will be made at an early date.
>
> The committee, and its Subcommittee on International Exchange and Payments, have in earlier reports spelled out certain requirements for an improved international monetary system. These are (1) new arrangements should be multilateral rather

4. This was the main criticism raised against my plan by Under Secretary Roosa in "Assuring the Free World's Liquidity," *Federal Reserve Bank of Philadelphia, Business Review Supplement,* September 1962.

than bilateral; (2) credit facilities should be adequate in amount and available as needed; (3) the size of credits in relation to deficits should, by agreement, be governed by the nature of the deficit; and (4) the expansion of international reserves should, in the future, rely less on gold, the dollar, and the pound sterling, and more on the credit of a larger group of countries. The committee recommends that these general criteria form the basis of the U.S. position at the IMF and Group of Ten deliberations on problems of world liquidity. American representatives should vigorously advocate such a position and work for agreement on a draft plan for an improved international monetary system in time for presentation at the 1964 annual meetings of the Board of Governors of the IMF. The committee further recommends that the groups now considering the problem devote attention also to the functioning of the adjustment process, and in particular, to the responsibilities of both surplus and deficit countries and the role of exchange rate adjustments. (p. 19)

The latest Congressional reports on the subject (as of February 1966) are the August 1965 report of the Subcommittee on International Exchange and Payments, entitled *Guidelines for Improving the International Monetary System,* and a further report to the Joint Economic Committee, prepared by the Subcommittee's Chairman, Representative Henry S. Reuss, and by Representative Robert F. Ellsworth, and issued in December 1965 under the title *Off Dead Center: Some Proposals to Strengthen Free World Economic Cooperation.* Both of these documents succeed, to an extraordinary degree, in disentangling the major issues involved in a most complex problem and in presenting them to the public in lucid and straightforward fashion. Both, and particularly the second, also demonstrate a rare willingness to explore boldly, and endorse courageously, new and revolutionary ideas so long shrugged off as utopian and politically unrealistic by timid bureaucrats ensconced in their old routines and habits of thought.

In brief, the Congress not only showed no reluctance to accept bold leadership by the Administration on the broad issues of international monetary reform: it did indeed clamor for such leadership and for fundamental reforms rather than for the mere patchwork and palliatives which characterized the governmental approaches to the problem over the years 1961–63.

The Academic Debate

Most of the professors who testified in the Congressional Hearings showed themselves similarly sympathetic to the advocacy of revolutionary reforms in the anachronistic and crisis-prone gold-exchange standard of today.[5] The main criticism raised by a number of them against my own plan related not to its boldness, but to its timidity: they advocated a quick and radical demonetization of gold as a reserve medium in preference to the "halfway house" which I regarded as an acceptable negotiating objective for the immediate future.[6]

A review of the mushrooming academic literature devoted to the issue would be out of place here. A small portion of it fills a fat volume (446 pp.) edited by Herbert G. Grubel under the title, *World Monetary Reform: Plans and Issues* (Stanford University Press, 1963).

My own contributions to the debate are scattered among many journals, in this country, in Europe, and in Asia (Japan, India, Pakistan) and, I am afraid, are dully but inevitably repetitive in view of the need to reach each time a new audience unfamiliar with the broad issues, and to relate current crises and developments to the unchanging basic problem from which they sprang.[7] Let me merely mention here my controversy with Oscar L. Altman, Adviser on Research and Statistics at the International Monetary Fund, at a seminar organized by Seymour E. Harris at Harvard University.[8] And in the following paper I made a valiant effort to reach the famous "man in the street" in this country.[9]

5. See, for instance, the testimonies of Harry G. Johnson, Peter B. Kenen, Tibor Scitovsky, and Brian Tew in the May and June 1961 Hearings [No. 182], Theodore Geiger and Fritz Machlup in the December 1962 Hearings [No. 225], and James Tobin in the November 1963 Hearings [No. 246].

6. See, for instance, the Johnson and Kenen testimonies in the 1961 Hearings, referred to above. I later clarified my views on the subject in *The Evolution of the International Monetary System: Historical Reappraisal and Future Perspectives* (Princeton, 1964), pp. 30–32 and 48.

7. See bibliography in Appendix 2, below.

8. Oscar L. Altman, "Professor Triffin on International Liquidity and the Role of the Fund," and Robert Triffin, "A Brief for the Defense" in IMF *Staff Papers*, May 1961, pp. 151–194, and "Altman on Triffin: A Rebuttal" (*Banca Nazionale del Lavoro Quarterly Review*, Rome, March 1961, pp. 31–50). The first and the last of these papers also appear in Seymour E. Harris, ed., *The Dollar in Crisis* (New York, 1961).

9. I spoke in the same vein to a British audience on the BBC Third Programme. See "Death of a System," in *The Listener* (London, July 27, 1961), pp. 122–23. "Une interview exclusive du Professeur Triffin" published in *Combat* (Paris, October 2, 1964) was similarly designed to reach a broad audience in France. Semipopular presentations of the problem to business groups in this country are listed in Appendix 2 to this volume.

Briefing the Man in the Street

There are two ways to go broke: a slow one and a fast one. The slow way is to go on, year after year, spending more money than you earn. But if you are rich to begin with, you won't go broke very fast that way. You will pay for your overspending by depleting your bank balance and other assets and by getting loans from people who trust your capacity to repay them later.

A much faster way to go broke is to finance too much of your over-spending by short-term borrowing. Even if you stop overspending, you may then still run into serious trouble if your IOU's are suddenly presented to you for repayment at a time when your bank balance has fallen too low to cover them. If you still have other, longer-term assets in sufficient amount, you will remain perfectly solvent, but you will be confronted, nevertheless, with what is called a liquidity crisis.

This, in a nutshell, is the United States' problem today and the reason why our dollar is facing a serious threat in the international exchange markets. We have, over the past decade, spent, lent, and given away about $20 billion more than we earned and covered the difference by cash payments in gold ($6 billion) and also by short-term IOU's ($14 billion) which foreign central banks, private banks, and individuals were, until recently, quite glad to invest in, since the dollar was regarded as safer than any other currency, and even, for the time being, as safe as gold itself.

The Eisenhower Administration woke up belatedly to the problem when gold prices suddenly flared up on the London free market last October and when U.S. gold losses shot up in the following weeks to a rate of between $400 million and $500 million per month. A wind of panic blew over Washington officialdom, and hurried steps were taken or planned "to restore over-all balance in our foreign transactions."

Although the exact measures adopted may not have been the wisest ones, their objective was highly laudable. We should, of course, steer away from the slow road to bankruptcy. The trouble is that we have not given much evidence so far of any clear understanding of the liquidity, as opposed to solvency, crisis that constitutes the real and most urgent threat to the dollar and of the measures needed to combat this far greater danger.

Published under the title "The Threat to the Dollar" in *The Atlantic, 207* (February 1961), pp. 36–39.

We might well regain full equilibrium in our over-all balance of payments—we are indeed far closer to that goal already than the Eisenhower Administration seemed to suspect—and yet be faced by massive demands for conversion into gold of the short-term debts inherited from our former deficits. Such massive liquidation by foreigners of their present dollar holdings would certainly become less likely as we gave evidence of our determination and ability to put a stop to our persistent deficits of the last decade. It would still exist, however, and might be triggered at any time by speculative rumors—justified or unjustified—or, more simply, by interest-rate differentials between New York and other financial centers, primarily in Western Europe. As long as such a threat is allowed to persist, we may find ourselves unable to manage our own credit and interest-rate policies, in the best interests of our economy, without running the risks of large gold outflows from our shores and, ultimately, of a totally unnecessary devaluation of the dollar, disastrous to us and to the rest of the world as well.

Even if we chose to close our eyes to this danger, another major crisis would in time develop from the very success of our efforts to redress our own balance-of-payments position. The elimination of our deficits would indeed dry up at the source two thirds of the annual supply of monetary reserves on which the rest of the world has come to depend for the maintenance of international currency convertibility in an expanding world economy.

The present crisis of the dollar is in fact inextricably bound up with the ill-fated attempt to dig up and dust off an international monetary system which collapsed nearly half a century ago, during World War I, and which must be thoroughly overhauled in order to adapt it to present-day needs and conditions.

This international monetary system is theoretically based on the old, pre-1914 gold standard. In the decade following World War I, the "world gold shortage" was a frequent subject for discussion among academic economists and the main topic on the agenda of a long series of international conferences which culminated in the marathon debates of the Gold Delegation of the now defunct League of Nations. The "gold shortage" was temporarily solved in the meantime by the growing use of two national currencies, sterling and the dollar, as international world reserves, along with the gold, in short supply. This, however, could not be more than a makeshift. It ended, disastrously, in the early 1930s with the successive devaluations of both of these currencies and the consequent collapse of the world monetary system.

In the decade following World War II, the basic role played by gold in our international monetary system was all but forgotten. A new slogan came to dominate academic discussions and governmental policies: the slogan of the "world dollar shortage." These policies were eminently successful. They accelerated the reconstruction of war damage and the expansion of the underdeveloped economies, and stimulated a rate of growth in world trade and world production unprecedented in duration and magnitude in the history of the world.

Yet they, too, were built upon the same makeshifts as in the 1920s. They, too, threatened to end in the early 1960s in a new collapse of world trade and world currencies similar to that of the early 1930s.

This grim parallel has its roots in a common and age-old problem: the routine and inertia which tie man to his past and make him unable or unwilling to effect in time the adjustments necessary to the successful performance, and ultimate survival, of his economic, social, and political institutions in a fast-changing world.

A simple comparison may be helpful at this stage. We all know too well the need which we have to carry some amount of currency in our pockets and to keep a checking account at our bank in order to bridge the gap between paydays and to be able to pay for our groceries and other purchases. The amounts of currency and deposits which we have to hold for this purpose bear some obvious, even though fairly loose, relation to the level of our income and expenditures. In very much the same way, countries must hold, generally in their central bank, international reserves to bridge seasonal and other inevitable and unpredictable gaps between their receipts from and payments to other countries. The amounts of reserves required for this purpose also hold an obvious, although equally loose, relation to the turnover of trade and production.

Now, imagine how little trade and production could have grown in the United States over the last century if the only means of payment available to all of us, as a group, had been the number of gold coins that could be minted from the haphazard growth of gold mining in California and Colorado. This, fortunately, was never the case, either here or in any other country. Paper currency and bank deposits played, throughout, a large and growing role, alongside declining amounts of gold, silver, and other minor coin, in the national monetary system of every country. Even in the heyday of the gold standard, the total monetary gold stock of the United States, for instance—both in the form of gold coin and central gold reserves—fell from about 30 per cent of the over-all means of payment of the country in 1860 to about 8 per cent in 1914. The provision of an adequate, but noninflationary, volume of money for our expanding economy already depended then, as it still does today, upon the soundness and resiliency of our banking institutions and credit policies, rather than on any blind enslavement to the much-vaunted automatic discipline of the so-called—or mis-called—gold standard.

The basic problems which deposit banking has long been able to solve within national borders, under the guidance of national monetary authorities, still remain largely unsolved, however, as far as international payments are concerned. Or, rather, since the world has to go on, they have been solved after a fashion, but only through a succession of makeshifts and at the cost of recurrent international crises manifesting themselves in the form of widespread deflation, currency devaluations, and trade and exchange restrictions.

Under the so-called full-fledged gold standard, prevalent in the last third of the nineteenth century and until World War I, gold was used exclusively, or nearly exclusively, by most central banks as international reserves and as the ultimate means of settlement for temporary imbalance in all major countries' international transactions. The enormous gold discoveries of the mid-nineteenth century had made possible for a while the adoption of such a system, but the maintenance of adequate gold reserves by central banks the world over was fed in addition, even then, by the gradual replacement of gold coin by currency and deposits in the countries' national monetary circulation. But this latter process was bound to come to an end and did with the world-wide demonetization of gold in the 1920s and early 1930s. The world gold shortage has been with us even since, although its timing and acuity have also been vitally affected by the vast price disturbances arising from wartime and postwar inflation and from the Great Depression of the 1930s.

Over the whole period from 1914 through 1959, new gold production outside the Soviet bloc has fed considerably less than half of the average increase in the world's monetary reserves. In the fifteen years from 1914 through 1928, it accounted for only 38 per cent of reserve increases, another 30 per cent of which was derived from the withdrawal of gold coin from active circulation, and the remaining 32 per cent from the growing use of major *national* currencies—primarily sterling in those days—as *international* reserves by central banks, alongside gold itself. This custom had spread under the prodding of British currency experts and the spur of the interest that central banks could earn on such foreign exchange investments—but not, of course, on the gold kept in their vaults. Together with the flight of hot money from the war-torn and inflation-wrecked continent of Europe, it helped the British restore the pound to its prewar parity in 1925, while Continental currencies sank excessively in value under the impact of speculative money flights from the Continent to London.

This soon proved a very mixed blessing for Britain. The overvaluation of sterling or the undervaluation of other European currencies handicapped British exporters in relation to their main competitors in world markets. Europe boomed while Britain suffered from economic stagnation and unemployment. Britain, moreover, felt impelled to tighten credit and interest rates in order to attract or retain foreign funds in London and avoid unsustainable gold losses. Such monetary policies were bound to aggravate the deflationary pressures already at work on the British economy. They became, in any case, powerless to stem the flow when the later stabilization of currency conditions on the Continent triggered a massive repatriation of the funds which had previously sought refuge in London.

Continental central banks reluctantly agreed to support sterling for a while by moderating their own conversion of sterling funds into gold. This merely postponed the day of reckoning. The collapse of a bank in Vienna unleashed a new wave of currency speculation which led to further withdrawals of funds from London. On a fateful day in September 1931, Britain threw in the sponge. The collapse of the most powerful currency that the world had ever known spelled the collapse of the international gold-exchange standard itself and ushered in a long period of exchange chaos in the world's monetary relations.

A grim parallel could easily be drawn between the rise and fall of the sterling-exchange standard after World War I on the one hand, and on the other the rise of the dollar-exchange standard after World War II and the difficulties which we are facing today. Foreign funds have, ever since 1934, sought a haven in New York rather than in London. These speculative movements played a role in the consolidation of exchange rates—mostly in 1949—at levels which appear now to have undervalued European currencies with respect to the dollar. Our economy has grown, for the last ten years, at a snail's pace in contrast to the rates of growth experienced by most European countries. The repatriation of European funds which had previously sought refuge here initiated a gold outflow of more than $2 billion in 1958.

This drain was slowed down to $1 billion in 1959 and to a mere trickle in the first half of 1960 under the impact of a drastic stiffening of interest rates in this country. It again assumed dramatic and even alarming proportions, however, in the second half of last year. This was primarily, at first, the result of the lower interest rates and the darkening Wall Street outlook brought about here by an incipient recession coupled with booming activity and a tightening of interest rates in Europe. Incredible bungling by some of our Treasury officials during the September meetings of the International Monetary Fund poured oil on the fire by allowing a flare-up of gold prices in the London market, which unleashed a wave of speculative gold buying by Americans as well as foreigners. Our gold losses jumped from an average of only $25 million a month during the first half of 1960 to more than $200 million a month in the third quarter, $300 million in October, and $500 million in November; that is, to an annual rate of nearly $6 billion a year, just about equal to the amount which antiquated and ill-conceived legislative provisions leave us as "free gold" reserves.

Fortunately, other countries have as great a stake as we have in helping the United States ward off a devaluation of the dollar, which would once more usher in a long period of chaos in exchange rates, such as followed the 1931 sterling devaluation, and benefit mostly the two largest gold-producing countries in the world, South Africa and the U.S.S.R. Time is running short, however, and we are each day living more and more dangerously on the edge of the precipice.

The most feasible and constructive way to ward off the international monetary breakdown which a dollar collapse would entail would be to enlarge and streamline the present methods of operation of the International Monetary Fund. This could be done in two stages.

All that the first stage would require would be a mere declaration by the Fund that it stands ready to accept reserve deposits from its member central banks, just as our Federal Reserve System accepts reserve deposits from commercial member banks in this country. Under the rules of the Fund, such deposits would carry a gold-exchange guarantee, making them extremely attractive to central banks. They would be as safe as gold itself and as usable for payments anywhere in the world. Their conversion into any currency needed for payment would be effected most simply, efficiently, and economically by drawing a check on the paying country's account and depositing it in the account of the country whose currency was purchased.

The Fund, moreover, would be in a position to pay interest on these deposits out of the earnings derived from investment of the assets transferred to it by members in exchange for such deposits. The advantages of interest-earning, gold-guaranteed deposits with the Fund over both sterile gold holdings and exchange-risky balances in national currencies should be sufficient to induce most countries to exchange voluntarily for Fund deposits the bulk of their present foreign exchange holdings and possibly even some portion of the reserves which they now retain in gold.

Countries other than the United States and the United Kingdom would constitute, initially, the bulk of their deposits with the Fund by transferring to it the dollar and sterling balances which they now hold as part of their monetary reserves. The United States and the United Kingdom would, as a consequence, owe these balances to the Fund rather than to several scores of foreign central banks. The Fund would hardly wish to liquidate precipitously its holdings of such balances at the risk of precipitating a monetary crisis in the United States or the United Kingdom, and should not, in any case, be allowed to do so. Its right to demand repayment should be limited to a preagreed annual ceiling and should, even then, be exercised only insofar as is useful for the conduct of its own operations. In view of the vast expansion of its resources which the proposed reform would entail, it could, on the contrary, be expected to seek to expand, for several years to come, its dollar and sterling investments, thus giving us a further and useful breathing spell to bring about, in as smooth a manner as possible, the needed readjustments in our over-all balance of payments.

The United States and the United Kingdom would, in this manner, recoup the freedom of monetary management—particularly in relation to their interest-rate policies—which is now so severely handicapped by the fear of the gold losses that would accompany the liquidation of foreign-owned short-term dollar and sterling balances. As for the other countries, they should also welcome the opportunity of exchanging their bloated dollar and sterling balances for equivalent Fund deposits. They now hold large amounts of such balances in preference to gold because of the interest earnings which they carry. They do, however, expose themselves thereby to the exchange losses which would be entailed in a dollar or sterling devaluation, to say nothing of the risks of blocking or inconvertibility. Deposits with the Fund would offer them the same incentive of interest earnings—although at a slightly reduced rate—while giving them the full gold guarantees which automatically attach to all transactions with the International Monetary Fund.

This simple suggestion could be implemented all the more easily and rapidly as it does not require any amendment or renegotiation of the Fund's Articles of Agreement and as it has already received in England the unanimous blessing of the Radcliffe Committee on the Working of the Monetary System.

The second stage of my plan would require a modification of the Fund's Charter, but a very simple and unobjectionable one. The present system of arbitrary and rigid quota subscriptions to the Fund's capital should be dropped and replaced by minimum deposit requirements with the Fund. That is to say, all countries would undertake to hold, in the form of deposits with the Fund, an agreed proportion of their total monetary reserves. They would remain free to convert into gold, if they wished, any amounts accruing to their Fund deposit over and above this agreed minimum.

Such an obligation would adjust automatically and continuously each country's actual lending to the Fund according to its contributive capacity and to the need of the Fund for the currency of the particular country. It would do away with a system under which the Fund is now flooded with national currency capital subscriptions in bahts, kyats, bolivianos, and other currencies for which it has no earthly use and under which 90 per cent of its lending has in fact been made in dollars, thus aggravating our reserve losses, rather than in the currencies of the countries which were actually accumulating large reserve surpluses in their international transactions.

These proposals have been amply scrutinized and discussed in recent months, here and abroad, by academic, financial, and government experts. They obviously raise a host of questions which cannot be fully examined in this brief article. The real obstacle to action does not lie in their technical details, which could easily be modified in the course of negotiations, but in their long-run political implications. There is no denying the fact that such a reform of the International Monetary Fund could be interpreted as a first step toward the setting up of a supranational monetary authority to which central banks and governments are understandably reluctant to yield any portion of their cherished national sovereignty and independence.

Whatever one's views are in relation to this broad issue, it should be obvious that none of the measures proposed here would restrict the present real sovereignty of any country any more than it is already restricted. These measures would substitute, in a limited area, collective, mutually debated, and agreed limitations on national monetary sovereignties for the much harsher, haphazard, and often disastrous limitations now imposed upon them by chance events and by the uncoordinated use of sovereignty by several scores of so-called independent countries, with little or no regard to their compatibility and their impact on others.

Clearly, the world cannot tolerate much longer an international monetary system which has become so utterly dependent for its functioning on such accidental sources of reserve supplies as these:

(1) Gold digging in a country—South Africa—whose economic life might be paralyzed tomorrow by the eruption of racial warfare.

(2) Mr. Khrushchev's policies about U.S.S.R. gold sales to the West, which were responsible for more than a third of monetary gold increases in both 1958 and 1959 and whose abrupt cessation in 1960 contributed, at least in part, to the recent explosion of gold prices in London.

(3) The perpetuation of our balance-of-payments deficits and the continued acceptance of dollar IOU's as monetary reserves by other countries; such gold and dollar losses by us have accounted for about two thirds of foreign countries' reserve increases over the last ten years and cannot continue much longer without undermining confidence in the dollar and its acceptability as a reserve currency.

I have no doubt, therefore, that future events will push us inevitably toward a basic reform of our present international monetary system. The real question at issue is not whether the proposals outlined here, or other broadly similar ones, will be adopted in the end. It is whether political leadership in the United States and the other free countries will prove sufficiently enlightened and dynamic to adopt them in time or whether they will have to be forced upon us by new crises and upheavals such as we experienced thirty years ago, during the first years of the worst international depression that the world has ever known.

Chapter VII: The Fire Extinguishers: 1961–63

THE YEARS 1961–63 mark the gradual awakening of the officials to the amplitude of the problem raised by the anachronism, vulnerability, and ultimate unviability of our present international monetary system.

The first to be convinced were a few of our leading statesmen, such as John F. Kennedy, Prime Minister Macmillan, Under Secretary of State Ball, and Chancellor of the Exchequer Reginald Maudling.

The bureaucrats and central bankers directly in charge of operational responsibility in this area, however, were far more reluctant to change their traditional methods of operation and habits of thought. They did, nevertheless, admit the need to combat the recurrent crises that emerged, one after another, and in the process of doing so they successfully elicited from one another an unprecedented degree of international monetary cooperation and put into place, on an ad hoc basis, many cogs—small or large—of the greater reforms which they still regarded as undesirable, unnegotiable, or merely premature.

1. STATESMEN AND BUREAUCRATS

President Kennedy and Under Secretary Ball

President Kennedy's Message to Congress on the Balance of Payments and Gold (February 6, 1961) contrasted refreshingly with the drift and panic of previous official pronouncements and policies.

It emphasized the sharp deterioration of our *basic* balance in 1959, but also its recovery to "manageable proportions" in 1960. While reaffirming the need to bring these basic deficits to an end, and outlining a comprehensive program of action designed to achieve this objective within a reasonable time, the Message also diagnosed for the first time the role of short-term capital movements, and of the defects of the international monetary system itself, in the gold and dollar crisis which the free world has to face and to solve.

> Increasing international monetary reserves will be required to support the ever-growing volume of trade, services, and capital movements among the countries of the free world. Until now, the free nations have relied upon increased gold production and con-

---

The following extract is quoted from the revised edition of *Gold and the Dollar Crisis* (New Haven, 1961), pp. 179–81.

tinued growth in holdings of dollars and pounds sterling. In the future, it may not always be desirable or appropriate to rely entirely on these sources. We must now, in cooperation with other lending countries, begin to consider ways in which international monetary institutions—especially the International Monetary Fund—can be strengthened and more effectively utilized, both in furnishing needed increases in reserves, and in providing the flexibility required to support a healthy and growing world economy. I am therefore directing that studies to this end be initiated promptly by the Secretary of the Treasury.

The role which OECD might play, jointly with the IMF, in the restructuration of the international monetary and financial system was also foreshadowed in several other passages of the message:

The United States must take the lead in harmonizing the financial and economic policies for growth and stability of those industrialized nations of the world whose economic behavior significantly influences the course of the world economy and the trend of international payments.

And later on:

I earnestly request early action by the Senate approving United States membership in the Organization for Economic Cooperation and Development. The OECD, in which the industrialized countries of Western Europe, the United States, and Canada will be joined, is of vital importance for assisting, on a cooperative basis, the developing countries of the free world. It will also provide a solid framework within which we can carry out intensive and frequent international consultations on the financial and monetary policies which must be pursued in order to achieve and maintain better balance in the international payments position.

A United States Aide Mémoire on the Balance of Payments Situation, released on February 20, amplified this point by stating in unusually forceful language:

We are on the eve of creating a new phase in the history of the North Atlantic Alliance. We have new tasks; and the recovery of Western Europe in the 1950s has given us new resources. Together, the resources which we dispose are much larger than those we could command in the immediate postwar years and they are better distributed among us.

To deal with these new tasks, we must begin by recognizing that we are interdependent in all we do; and that our common burdens must be shared in a way that our people will recognize as fair. . . .

In addition, we must all come to recognize a principle on which the United States has acted in the years after the Second World War. That principle is that a sustained accumulation of gold and other international reserves by any one country is disruptive to the international community. Especially now, when trade is expanding faster than gold production, we must learn to use our reserves on a communal basis, recognizing that one nation's gain can only be another nation's loss.

It is in the light of these principles that the Government of the United States views the specific matter in hand; that is, the imbalance which has developed in the international payments situation of the Free World. The present situation is marked by a persistent basic deficit of some countries and a persistent basic surplus of other countries. This had led to a substantial increase in foreign liquid dollar holdings and, in recent years to an outflow of gold from the United States which has resulted in a reduction of United States reserves. . . .

Our common task is to design a reserves policy for the alliance which will recognize the responsibilities to the common interest of surplus and deficit nations alike. . . .

These are brave new words. They now await implementation by other countries as well as by us. Their exploration at the international level was officially, even though quietly and informally, launched a few days ago with an invitation of Per Jacobsson to the Executive Board of the International Monetary Fund to examine possible changes in IMF policy and procedures.

Prime Minister Macmillan

Britain's Prime Minister, Mr. Macmillan, stressed during his visit to Washington last April the political as well as the economic con-

---

The following extract is quoted from "After the Gold-Exchange Standard?" *Weltwirtschaftliches Archiv* (Kiel, 1961), pp. 203-04.

siderations which make it imperative for the Western nations to adjust their monetary, as well as their commercial, institutions to the common policies which they are bound to pursue if they wish to survive. He spoke forcefully about the "unsatisfactory" nature of present monetary arrangements, noting that world trade had expanded fourfold in money terms since the war, against only a doubling of the international credit base.

> All sorts of remedies are being suggested. The main difficulty about many of them is what I might call the mental hurdles which they present. . . . There seems to be something immoral in increasing the credit base by mutual agreement. It is done often enough in our internal economies; but the extension to the international field is hard to swallow. . . . Just as each individual country painfully acquired a central banking system, so there ought—ideally—to be a central banking system for all the countries of the free world.[1]

Equal emphasis was also placed by the Prime Minister on immediately feasible steps in this direction, and particularly on "the urgent need of bringing together the Six and the Seven" and of thinking "not so much nationally or even in terms of greater economic cooperation between nations but in terms of wider groupings . . . of large areas transcending national boundaries. . . ."[2]

The fulfillment of these lofty objectives and calls for action still must, however, overcome the enormous force of inertia which timorous, tradition-bound bureaucrats have always opposed to such revolutionary changes in the institutional framework and modes of thought to which they are accustomed. I don't doubt that some progress toward international monetary consolidation will emerge from the current debate, but we still run the risk, President Kennedy and Prime Minister Macmillan notwithstanding, of yielding once more to the almost irresistible temptation of confining this progress to half-way measures and stopgaps that would close, rather than open, the door to the further adjustments and historical evolution of our international monetary system indispensable to its survival in a fast-changing world.

The explorations and negotiations now under way may well uncover

---

1. "Speech by the Prime Minister, the Rt. Hon. Harold Macmillan, M.P., at the Massachusetts Institute of Technology, on Friday, 7th April, 1961," Released by Admiralty House, pp. 8 ff.

2. "Speech by the Prime Minister," pp. 6 ff.

other, and better, means of dealing with the problems which I have raised. Anybody who has ever participated in negotiations of this sort cannot but be keenly aware of the need to prune, amplify, and readjust initial proposals in the light of the unforeseen difficulties, but also of the unsuspected opportunities, which only the actual process of negotiation can bring to light. This applies to the Triffin plan as well as to the Bernstein plan and the Stamp plan. The greatest obstacle to the maximum achievement that should be hoped for and strived for, would be to freeze prematurely the path of discussion into any predetermined channel, and to close the door to a full exploration of all feasible techniques to strengthen the international monetary structure of the West, and indeed of the world itself.

Chancellor of the Exchequer, Reginald Maudling

The third annual burying of the Triffin plan, at the IMF meeting of September 1962, was rudely interrupted by the scandalous intervention of the British Chancellor of the Exchequer, who declared it "certainly worthwhile to explore this possibility" and suggested an immediate approach to it through the so-called "Maudling Plan."

The following extract from his statement to the Fund's Governors is quoted from pp. 65–68 of the *Summary Proceedings* of the meeting:

> Much . . . has been accomplished and the position of the reserve currencies and of the payments system that rests upon them is one of great strength.
>
> But we cannot be content to rest forever at this point. The Managing Director talked of "continuing to build." The "needs of our time" are changing fast as our whole world is changing. The success we have achieved—and the strength of the current position—is a basis for further advance in the future.
>
> I believe it is universally accepted that a growing volume of world trade calls in the long run for a growing volume of liquidity, even if not necessarily in arithmetic proportion. Of course there is scope for arguing at any given time whether total liquidity is adequate, or whether there is enough liquidity but unevenly distributed, or whether the liquid resources available are not themselves liquid enough. I am not concerned now with the immediate position to which I have just referred, but with the contribution that the international payments system should make in the future to the growth of world trade and production.

There are those who argue for a return to the classical gold standard. I find it difficult to accept this proposition. Either it means that the volume of world trade must be tied to the amount of gold that can be mined and acquired by monetary authorities, which seems to me a proposition that is not intellectually sustainable; or the volume of gold available must be brought in line with world reserve requirements by variations in the price of gold, and the difficulties of this course are only too clear to all of us. To quote the Managing Director's Jayne Lectures for 1961, "It is certain that gold output alone cannot be relied upon to bring about the necessary increase in the world's money supply."

At present, gold is supplemented by the two reserve currencies —the dollar and the pound sterling. But there is a fundamental difficulty about this system, namely, that the reserve currencies are short-term liabilities of the United States and the United Kingdom—one nation's reserves is another nation's debt. The rate of growth of these liabilities cannot be a matter of indifference. The process of accumulating debts can be agreeable—as we all know—especially if in the course of it we can provide a service to our friends. But the fact of having accumulated them can create inhibitions, especially if a large proportion is repayable on demand. Requests for payment may arise at times and in volumes that are determined by factors wholly outside the control of the debtor, but nevertheless that have to be promptly met. If the amounts of such currencies held as reserve assets increase too much there will inevitably be some doubt as to whether any further extension of these holdings would be prudent and practicable. The expansion of the system at any one time is therefore subject to limitations and this may inhibit the growth of world trade and production.

The gold-exchange system has already undergone extensive development in the last seventeen years, particularly in the much wider use of the dollar. But despite the many advantages of the system as we know it today, I cannot believe that its evolution can stop here, or that we already have the final answer to the longer-term problems. We shall have to be prepared to supplement present international payments arrangements if we are to make certain that they do not act as a brake upon the possible expansion of world trade and production. Indeed, the last year has already seen the scope of the system increased by valuable new ideas which must be capable of further development. The borrowing scheme, for instance, is a highly practicable arrangement for dealing with a serious threat to the international monetary system. It will enable temporarily weak currencies to be absorbed into the Fund while making available an equivalent amount of stronger currencies. But the resources made available under the borrowing scheme are not part of the normal stock of liquidity, and it is deliberately designed to be used only in exceptional and extreme circumstances.

Another valuable idea recently put forward, namely, the mutual holding of currencies, could constitute a more readily usable method of increasing the part which currencies play. But can we hope under present conditions that this would always be carried far enough, having regard to the normal inhibitions about large holdings of currencies which are temporarily surplus in the markets? Unless, therefore, we can supplement them, these two ideas will have their limitations. Is it not possible for the Fund, building on these ideas, to provide the basis of a multilateral system of a more regular and automatic character which would be capable of expansion to the extent necessary at any time? Some people have seen, for instance, in the obligations created under the borrowing scheme the germ of a truly international paper which might in due time become acceptable and transferable between the monetary authorities and so become a familiar holding among reserve assets. It would certainly be worthwhile to explore this possibility. I am myself, moreover, attracted by the thought that we might develop a system of cooperation between the leading trading countries in the form of a mutual currency account in the Fund. By this, I have in mind an arrangement of a multilateral character under which countries could continue to acquire the currency of another country which was temporarily surplus in the markets and use it to establish claims on a mutual currency account which they could themselves use when their situations were reversed. Such claims on the account would attract the guarantee that attaches to holdings in the Fund. We would hope that such a system would enable world liquidity to be expanded without additional strains on the reserve currencies or avoidable setbacks to their economic growth, and at the same time without requiring countries whose currencies were temporarily strong to accumulate larger holdings of weaker currencies than they would find tolerable.

I am not at this stage putting forward any cut and dried plan. These are not problems that can be solved by slogans or gimmicks. What I have been trying to do is to follow the logic of the argument, and I hope that these ideas that I have mentioned, and indeed any other ideas designed to solve the same real problem, will be actively studied. As the Managing Director said on Monday, "the possibilities of further action are certainly not exhausted." Nor, I hope, is the collective ingenuity of the world's leading financial authorities.

Mr. Maudling's remarks, however, were pointedly cold-shouldered by his colleagues at the Fund meeting. Even a year later, at the September 1963 meeting, the French Minister of Finance still deplored "this kind of intellectual nomadism by virtue of which one tries to escape from an existing system as soon as weaknesses become apparent in it. . . ." [3]

In the meantime, the recurring dollar and sterling crises of 1960–63 had finally stirred bureaucrats and central bankers to take a number of highly constructive steps. While still denying any need for a basic reform of the gold-exchange standard, they recognized that it had to be bolstered by new devices designed to cope with the instability of short-term capital movements. The accent was put throughout on the need to protect the reserve currencies, and the gold-exchange standard itself, against sudden shifts by reserve holders or private speculators from one currency into another or into gold. Two different methods of approach were successively developed to fulfil that aim. They are briefly summarized in the following extract from my Princeton study on *The Evolution of the International Monetary System* (pp. 26–27), and discussed further in the subsequent sections of this chapter.

The first was to increase the International Monetary Fund's lending resources, thus enhancing its ability to intervene in cases of crisis. The normal capital resources of the Fund were in-

3. *Summary Proceedings,* Annual Meeting, 1963, p. 60. M. Giscard d'Estaing followed this broadside, however, with an extremely keen criticism of the system and constructive suggestions for reform, which did not receive immediately all the attention they deserved. See below, pp. 298–300.

creased by more than 50 per cent in 1959, and a further $6 billion of resources were negotiated among the so-called Group of Ten,[4] in 1961–62, to be made available to the Fund "when supplementary resources are needed to forestall or cope with an impairment of the international monetary system . . . in the new conditions of widespread convertibility, including greater freedom for short-term capital movements."

The second approach was through less formal short-term commitments of mutual support among the central banks of roughly the same group of countries, plus Austria, Switzerland, and the Bank for International Settlements. We can range under this heading the support extended to sterling on two occasions—in March 1961 and March 1962—by a group of other central banks, the so-called gold pool in operation since December 1961, and, most of all, the vast array of bilateral swap stand-by agreements, and purchases of nonmarketable dollar and foreign-currency securities, negotiated with major financial centers in the last two years by Mr. Roosa.[5] Mention should also be made of the Monetary Committee of the EEC countries, and of Working Party No. 3 of OECD, which review periodically developments and policies bearing on international payments and monetary stability of the member countries, individually and as a group.

Considerable success was achieved thereby in offsetting and discouraging the speculative capital movements which have threatened, ever since October 1960, the two key currencies— sterling and, particularly, the dollar—on which the international gold-exchange standard is anchored. On the other hand, most of the commitments described above remain of a short-term character, subject to frequent renegotiation, and aim only at warding off future crises in the international monetary system, rather

4. The United States, the United Kingdom, Canada, Japan, Germany, France, Italy, the Netherlands, Belgium, and Sweden. Since the agreement is primarily designed to cushion dangerous capital movements between the signatories themselves, the maximum resources callable could not, however, exceed half the total, and are most unlikely to reach even that figure. For further analysis and criticism of this agreement, see my "Lendemains de Vienne: Mesures conservatoires et germes d'avenir," in Trois Etudes sur le Problème des Liquidités Internationales (Banque Nationale de Belgique, April 1962), pp. 15 and 16.

5. Operations under these agreements are summarized periodically in reports prepared by Charles A. Coombs and published in the March and September issues of the Federal Reserve Bulletin.

than at eliminating the basic vulnerability of the system which is at the root of such crises.[6]

2. THE 1961 VIENNA MEETING OF THE IMF AND THE GENERAL ARRANGEMENTS TO BORROW

A. BEFORE THE VIENNA MEETING

Although rightly credited to their main negotiator, Per Jacobsson, then Managing Director of the IMF, the "General Arrangements to Borrow" were essentially the brainchild of Dr. E. M. Bernstein, former Director of Research of the Fund.

I discussed Dr. Bernstein's proposals and presented, vainly, what seemed to me a more constructive alternative in "Two Papers on IMF Reform, the International Dollar Problem, and the Strengthening of the Monetary Structure of the West," written in the spring of 1961, while I was serving as a part-time consultant for the President's Council of Economic Advisers.

While the second of these two papers was in the form of a memorandum, specifically written for the Council (and not reproduced here), the first had been solicited by the *Quarterly Review and Investment Survey* (Model, Roland and Stone, New York)—in which Dr. Bernstein's paper had just appeared—and was published in its First Quarter 1961 issue.

I submitted both to the Council, on April 4, 1961, with the following covering note:

> These are two private papers, prepared at Yale exclusively on the basis of published information, and reflecting only the views of the author himself.
>
> It is hoped, however, that the suggestions which they embody may prove of some use in the discussions now under way in the U.S. Government and abroad regarding the awesome, but challenging, problems listed in the title.

The International Monetary Crisis: Diagnosis, Palliatives, and Solutions

The February 6 Message of President Kennedy to the Congress contrasts sharply—and refreshingly—with previous official pronouncements about the "dollar" crisis. Without denying in the least the dif-

6. For a more detailed review of the measures briefly summarized in the above text, see the excellent study of Robert Z. Aliber on *The Management of the Dollar in International Finance,* Princeton Studies in International Finance (1964).

ficulties that we still face in putting our own balance of payments in order, the President's Message puts them in their proper perspective and stresses, in particular, their relationship to some major defects in the international monetary mechanism itself. The recent dollar crisis, indeed, cannot be understood in isolation from the international monetary framework which allowed it to develop, just as it contributed over the last thirty years to far deeper and recurrent sterling crises. Even less can it be cured by unilateral United States measures without jeopardizing gravely in the future the prospects for financial stability and economic progress in the world at large, as well as in the United States.

The Message notes the paradoxical, but illuminating, fact that a record rate of over-all deficit in the latter part of 1960 coincided with a nearly all-time peak in our current account surplus, and a spectacular recovery in our basic transactions balance including foreign aid and other official capital exports and military expenditures abroad.

Two lessons emerge from this observation:

(1) We may—and have in the past—run enormous deficits in our basic transactions without being penalized and stopped by gold losses, as long as foreigners are temporarily willing to accumulate sight or short-term IOU's (or "dollar balances") in settlement of their surpluses. Thus, very few people in this country or abroad noticed—or worried about—the $10 billion deficits incurred by us over the years 1950–57. These were overwhelmingly settled in the form of dollar IOU's rather than gold payments.

(2) We and others, however, developed a near panicky attitude toward the problem when, in 1958, and particularly in 1960, large outflows and repatriation of private capital—stimulated by financial recovery, booming economic prospects, and higher interest rates in Europe—slowed down the continuous growth of short-term dollar investments here by foreigners, and led to substantial gold losses by our Treasury. Further improvements and consolidation in our basic transactions may not guarantee us against large gold losses arising from *future* conversions into gold, for similar or other reasons, of the enormous short-term claims accumulated against us as a result of *past* transactions.

In brief, the use of sterling and dollars as international reserves under the so-called "gold-exchange" or "key currencies" standard has long played havoc with the much vaunted balance-of-payments discipline supposedly forced upon all countries by the older "gold coin" or "gold bullion" versions of the traditional gold standard. The key currency countries—Britain yesterday, and the United States today— may enjoy for years the ease with which IOU settlement of their deficits give them more and more rope to hang themselves. The day of reckoning inevitably comes, however, when the rope suddenly tightens at the most inconvenient moment. Continuous discipline is replaced by temporary overindulgence, to be paid for later by a sudden and violent crisis in the international position of the key currencies. This is the consequence of the abuse of an international monetary system whose smooth functioning has become inextricably tied with unquestioned reliance on such key currencies as monetary reserves for other countries' central banks.

For the key currency countries themselves, the resulting threat takes the form of large and sudden gold outflows which may lead to an exchange-rate devaluation—as in 1931 and 1949 in Britain—or to various techniques of inconvertibility and exchange control—as in Britain again during most of the postwar years—or, at the very least, to restrictive fiscal, credit, and interest-rate policies which may be in direct conflict with internal employment and growth policies—as in Britain once more in the late 1920s and in both Britain and the United States in the very recent past.

For the world at large, the consequence of the system may become manifest in the international spread of deflation, trade and exchange restrictions, and/or chaotic exchange-rate fluctuations and competitive devaluations. There is little doubt that these typical post-1914 ills can be ascribed to a considerable extent—even though not exclusively, of course—to our obduracy in confusing international monetary order with the mere digging up and dusting off of the nineteenth-century gold standard, supplemented by the haphazard, precarious, and foredoomed use of one or a few national currencies as international reserves.

There is pretty unanimous agreement today on the need to restore over-all equilibrium in our balance of payments, and to put a stop to the indefinite piling up of more short-term indebtedness abroad characteristic of the last ten years, as well as to the more recent gold drain which was its ultimate and perfectly predictable—and predicted, may I add—consequence.

What is not so fully understood is the impact of such a readjustment upon the future growth of world liquidity.

The gold and dollar holdings of foreign countries and international institutions have grown more than satisfactorily indeed—perhaps even at an inflationary pace—over the last eleven years, from about $18 billion in December 1949 to more than $45 billion in September 1960. Of this increase of $27 billion, however, 78 per cent ($21 billion) was derived from United States net reserves losses, about 4 per cent (more than $1 billion) from U.S.S.R. gold sales in Western markets, and no more than 18 per cent (less than $5 billion) from current gold production in the West.

The broad picture is the same if we look at the increase of monetary reserves as such—excluding privately-held dollar balances, but including officially-held sterling and other foreign exchange, together with gold and official dollar holdings. Nearly two thirds of the increase of world monetary reserves over the decade of the 1950s—and as much as 92 per cent over the two years 1958 and 1959—was derived from the deterioration in the United States' net reserve position, 5 per cent from the growth of other foreign exchange reserves, 6 per cent from U.S.S.R. gold sales, and less than one fourth (24 per cent) from current gold production in the West.

Finally, and taking the world as a whole, including the United States, we find (see table) that gold production has long ceased to provide more than a fraction of reserve requirements in an expanding world economy: 43 per cent over the the whole period 1914–59, and only 33 per cent over the decade of the 1950s. The bulk of reserve increases has been fed, for nearly half a century, from a variety of expedients, makeshifts, or accidental sources, such as:

(1) The growth of foreign exchange holdings—i.e. primarily dollar and sterling IOU's—as supplementary means of reserve accumulation, alongside insufficient gold supplies (34 per cent for the period as a whole, with a peak of 59 per cent in 1950–59 and a dramatic *decrease* of 31 per cent in 1929–33).

(2) The withdrawal of gold coin from circulation and its addition to central banks' gold reserves (only 6 per cent of the over-all reserve increase for the period as a whole, but 30 per cent over the years 1914 through 1928); this, of course, came to an end in 1933.

(3) The dollar devaluation of 1933–34, which accounted for more than the total reserve increases of the years 1929–33, its impact being partly offset by the simultaneous—and closely related—wholesale liquidation of foreign exchange reserves, through their conversion into gold (see Point 1, above).

(4) In more recent years, the growing sales of U.S.S.R. gold in

SOURCES OF INCREASES IN WORLD RESERVES: 1914–59

	Total increase[1]	From Western gold sources[2]	From other sources					
			Total	Coin with-drawal	Dollar devalu-ation	U.S.S.R. gold sales	Foreign ex-change
A. In billions of dollars							
1914–28	8.5	3.2	5.3	2.5		[4]	2.8
1929–33	7.2	0.9	6.4	0.8	7.9[3]	[4]	−2.3
1934–38	7.5	6.8	0.7			−0.1	0.8
1939–49	19.1	8.7	10.4			0.3	10.1
1950–59	12.8	4.1	8.6			1.1	7.5
1914–59	**55.1**	**23.7**	**31.4**	**3.3**	**7.9**	**1.3**	**18.9**
B. In per cent of total							
1914–28	100	38	62	30		[4]	32
1929–33	100	12	88	10	109[3]	[4]	−31
1934–38	100	90	10			−1	11
1939–49	100	46	54			1	53
1950–59	100	33	67			9	59
1914–59	**100**	**43**	**57**	**6**	**14**	**2**	**34**

1. Excluding Soviet-bloc countries throughout, as well as IMF currency holdings.

2. Current gold production in the West, *minus* net sales to, or *plus* net purchases from, private channels. Large net repurchases from private channels (estimated at $1.7 billion in 1934–37) followed the sterling and dollar devaluations, in sharp contrast to the usual net absorption of gold into hoarding and private uses.

3. Calculated on the basis of the official parity change of February 1934, following the suspension of gold payments and the *de facto* dollar depreciation in 1933.

4. Included, until the end of 1933, with Western gold sources.

SOURCES: These must be regarded as only rough estimates—particularly in the early years of the table—put together from various IMF and Federal Reserve publications.

Western markets. Insignificant in earlier years, such sales contributed as much as 9 per cent of the world's reserve increases over the years 1950–59, and well over a third of the total increase in gold reserves over the four years 1956–59. Their abrupt cessation in the fourth quarter of last year undoubtedly played a role in the disruption of the London gold market in October.

Can anyone seriously argue that such a system can safely be relied upon tomorrow—any more than in yesteryears—to adjust world reserves to actual requirements in an expanding world economy and to serve as a basis for a stable and viable system of international settlements? The point to be kept in mind is not that these various sources of reserve supply taken together have failed to provide enough liquidity. They may well, on the contrary, have provided too much, particularly in recent years owing to the enormous growth of dollar balances associated with the $10 billion deficits incurred by us since the end of 1957.

The indictment of the present, unorganized gold-exchange standard is that it can only operate—and has indeed operated for nearly half a century—in haphazard fashion, creating too much liquidity at times, but only through generalized currency devaluations or through a persistent piling up of sterling or dollar IOU's, bound to undermine in the end the acceptability of these so-called key currencies as safe reserve media for the other countries' central banks. There is now general agreement in this country that over-all payments deficits must be brought to an end, but until President Kennedy's recent Message on gold and the balance of payments little thought had been given to the ultimate results upon the world at large of the consequent drying up of the source of two thirds of the liquidity increases of the last decade.

"Measures to improve international monetary institutions" are indeed the very first item of the new Administration's balance-of-payments program. "Increasing international monetary reserves will be required to support the ever-growing volume of trade, services, and capital movements among the countries of the free world. Until now, the free nations have relied upon increased gold production and continued growth in holdings of dollars and pound sterling. In the future, it may not always be advisable or appropriate to rely entirely on these sources. We must now, in cooperation with other lending countries, begin to consider ways in which international monetary institutions—especially the International Monetary Fund—can be strengthened and more effectively utilized, both in furnishing needed increases in reserves, and in providing the flexibility required to support a healthy and growing world economy."

The President's Message has finally whipped up active interest—here and abroad—in a number of proposals for International Monetary Fund reform which had, up to then, been cavalierly brushed off by responsible officials and bureaucrats.

The more modest of these—at least in appearance—are those of the former Director of Research and Statistics of the International Monetary Fund, Mr. E. M. Bernstein. Mr. Bernstein's diagnosis of the problem is strikingly similar to mine, but his plan makes no pretense of meeting the long-run liquidity requirements of an expanding world economy. This would continue to depend on future and recurrent increases in the Fund's capital, requiring each time cumbersome negotiations with several scores of countries, new international agreements among their governments, and—in most cases—legislative approval by their Congress or Parliament. Under the mechanism of the Fund, three fourths of their additional capital subscription would be in the national currency of member countries and would—in the case of most of them—merely result in flooding the Fund with currencies with which it is already overflowing and for which it will have no earthly use in any foreseeable future. What point is there in complicating to that extent the process of international negotiations for the pleasure of increasing even further the already inflated Fund holdings of cruzeiros, bolivianos, rupees, rupiahs, bahts, kyats, etc? One is forcibly reminded of the old saying: "The mountain labors, and gives birth to . . . a mouse!"

The Bernstein proposals do not address themselves to this problem, and concentrate on a more limited, but extremely important, one: that of meeting temporary disequilibria among the major trading countries themselves, and particularly of offsetting major outflows of short-term funds from one currency into another. The importance of this problem, under convertibility conditions, has been highlighted recently by our own huge gold losses of the last quarter of 1960, due nearly entirely to such movements of short-term funds from New York to other financial centers and into gold. A similar, and even more serious, crisis might threaten sterling tomorrow in the case of a reflux toward New York of the large dollar outflows which have veiled during the last year the deterioration of the United Kingdom's balance of payments on current account, just as a previous inflow of funds toward New York had partially veiled the deterioration of our own current account transactions in 1959.

Mr. Bernstein would leave untouched the basic mechanism of the Fund, but supplement it with additional machinery in the form of a subsidiary *Reserve Settlement Account,* requiring negotiation and agreement with a handful of countries only: the United States, the United Kingdom, Canada, Germany, France, etc. Each of these countries would subscribe special interest-bearing and gold-guaranteed debentures in its own currency, but the Fund would not call upon any subscribing member to take up all or part of its agreed subscription except to the extent necessary to meet large demands of such currencies by another member of the system. It might not be particularly easy to get our own Congress to approve $2.5 billion of such debentures—as suggested by Mr. Bernstein—less than two years after having extracted from it a $1.4 billion increase in our subscription to the International Monetary Fund's capital on the ground that this would solve all such problems for a long time to come. It could, of course, be agreed that we are very unlikely to accumulate in the near future any surplus that will justify a Fund's call on our debentures. The United Kingdom will be able to present the same argument in relation to the $1 billion debentures foreseen for it in the Bernstein plan. By the same token, however, this would mean that the total of $6 billion debentures to be negotiated would yield *at most* an increase of only $2.5 billion in actual resources for the Fund. In fact, the most likely outcome would be substantially less than that, since some of the participants other than the United States and the United Kingdom may also run surpluses far short of their subscriptions—or even be in deficit—while the subscription of one or a few others may fall far short of their own surpluses. Once again, the "mountain" to be negotiated may turn out in the end to yield a mere "molehill."

I certainly agree that Mr. Bernstein's plan would be better than nothing. I am afraid, however, that it may detract attention from the basic defects in our international monetary system which I have stressed above, and that by leaving untouched the Fund's machinery itself, it would perpetuate the obvious flaws in that machinery which experience has brought to light.

The amounts of each currency at the disposal of the Fund would remain dependent on advance, and necessarily haphazard, guesses about the future evolution of each country's balance of payments, and on recurrent *ad hoc* negotiations with prospective creditors. Specific action by the Fund would also remain necessary in each case to thwart —or offset—the normal tendency of members to concentrate their borrowings on the so-called "reserve currencies" or "key currencies," rather than on the currencies of the countries with over-all balance-of-payments surpluses.[1] If and when sufficient support can be gathered for amending the Fund's statutes, it would seem to me far preferable to seize upon this opportunity to simplify, streamline, and rationalize the

1. Mr. Bernstein suggests that the reserve currency countries whose currency has been regrettably requested from, and sold by, the Fund can always *offset this destabilizing action* of the Fund by subsequent drawings of the surplus countries' currencies. This is true, but remains nevertheless an unnecessarily complex and ludicrous procedure of achieving the Fund's stabilization objectives.

whole Agreement in such a way as to minimize the need for future revisions or makeshifts and for periodic renegotiation of the capital subscriptions of members.

An exceedingly simple way of fulfilling these objectives is described at length in *Gold and the Dollar Crisis* (Yale University Press, 1960), amply discussed in the *Hearings* of the Joint Economic Committee of Congress (Sessions of October 28, 1959, and December 8, 1960), and briefly summarized in simpler language in the February 1961 issue of the *Atlantic Monthly*. My proposals are still regarded in some circles —although far less generally than was the case two years ago—as dangerously radical and visionary. Yet they conform exactly to the historical line of development of monetary and banking institutions which experience has revealed indispensable to their sound operation in every country of the world, and whose first stage has already been imitated by the international monetary system itself. *Credit reserves*— in the form of foreign exchange holdings—have gradually and increasingly supplemented *commodity reserves*—in the form of gold— over the last fifty years, just as *credit money*—in the form of currency and bank deposits—had previously and increasingly supplemented and finally replaced *commodity money*—in the form of gold and silver coinage—within each country's monetary system.

The obvious danger and vulnerability arising from the unorganized creation of credit money imposed within each country, many years ago, the gradual development of central banking techniques of monetary regulation. In the international field, however, shifts between one key currency and another, or between key currencies and gold, preserve unto this day the same sources of vulnerability which marked the monetary system of the United States, for instance, before the creation of the Federal Reserve System. Something akin to a World Reserve System is still missing, and is at the source of many of the troubles that have plagued the international monetary system for nearly half a century.

This is not to say that the several scores of sovereign nations that make up our world are ready to yield their precious sovereignty to a world-wide monetary institution, endowed with powers of regulation comparable to those wielded by the present Federal Reserve System or other central banks, after many years of slow, gradual development. Neither is this necessary to restore the minimum of order indispensable to the smooth functioning of the international monetary system itself.

All that is needed is to endow the International Monetary Fund with the far more modest, but historically crucial, functions entrusted to central banks at the origin of their development. Foremost among these would be the assignment to the IMF of the role of single depository for the credit reserves of member central banks. Ideally, individual countries should cease to use *national* currencies as *international* reserves, even though this may not be achieved at a single stroke. They should be encouraged to convert their present foreign exchange holdings into international deposits with the IMF, and the volume of these should be allowed to grow over the years to the extent necessary to supply—together with available supplies of monetary gold—the reserve requirements of an expanding world economy.

This purpose could be served through a surprisingly simple reform and long overdue rationalization and streamlining of the charter of the International Monetary Fund. Stripped down to essentials, my proposals are that present capital subscriptions to the IMF be abolished —and refunded to members—and replaced by a mere obligation for each member to hold an agreed proportion of its over-all gold and foreign exchange reserves in the form of reserve deposits with the IMF. These deposits would be fully usable for settlements among central banks throughout the world and would carry—like all other Fund's assets and liabilities—a specific guarantee against exchange risks. They would, in this way, be "as good as gold" and better than the large amounts of reserves now freely retained by central banks in the form of sterling or dollar balances. They would indeed be more attractive than gold itself since they would devolve interest earnings to their holders or a participation—*pro rata* of their amount—in the earnings of the Fund.

Such a system of minimum deposits with the Fund would have two major advantages over the present system of capital subscriptions.

First and foremost, these deposits would automatically adjust to the fluctuations in the over-all reserve position of each country. The Fund's over-all resources would thus increase over the years, as the over-all level of the world's reserves increases as a result of future accretions to monetary gold stocks and of the Fund's own lending and investment operations. Most of all, the increase in deposits would concentrate on the countries which currently develop net surpluses with the world at large and whose currency is therefore most needed for international settlements.

Second, and in contrast to present capital subscriptions, these deposits would not impair in any way the liquidity and reserve position of the contributing countries. They could be used at any time, together with the other reserves held by members, to make payments anywhere in the world. They could indeed—to take an extreme case—be freely drawn down to the last cent if a country were unwise enough to sacrifice the totality of its monetary reserves to settle persistent deficits instead of correcting them in time. Yet, even in such a case, this would not affect in any way the sum total of Fund deposits—nor the corresponding assets and lending capacity of the Fund—since the decline in the over-all reserves and deposit requirements of the members in deficit would be matched and offset by corresponding increases in the reserves and deposit requirements of the surplus countries to which payment is made.

The attractiveness to central banks of interest-earning, gold-guaranteed deposits with the Fund is so evident indeed that the reform might well be initiated, if needed, without any compulsory feature whatsoever, and without requiring any renegotiation of the Fund's statutes. A mere declaration of the Fund—by way of interpretation of its charter—that it is ready to accept such reserve deposits from member central banks would, in all likelihood, induce most countries to convert into such Fund deposits a growing portion of the reserves now freely held by them in the form of foreign exchange—subject to devaluation risks—and even in the form of gold—on which they earn no interest.[2]

This would, of course, entail corresponding shifts in the ownership of the outstanding dollar and sterling balances converted by their holders into deposits with the Fund. Title to such balances would pass from several scores of foreign countries to the Fund itself. There is no reason why the Fund should wish to liquidate these balances, or modify their present pattern of investment in the New York and London money markets. It should, however, be empowered to do so in the future, but only in a smooth and progressive manner, in so far as useful for the most efficient performance of its world-wide monetary stabilization functions, and in close consultation with the monetary authorities of the countries concerned. I have suggested that this purpose could be served by giving the Fund an option—which it would rarely wish to use in full—to liquidate these investments at a maximum

2. One should note, in passing, that such a proposal was unanimously endorsed, more than a year ago, by the Radcliffe Committee on the Working of the Monetary System and received enthusiastic support from the Latin American participants at the Sixth Meeting of Technicians of Central Banks of the American Continent, held last November in Guatemala City.

pace of, let us say, 5 per cent a year. This, however, would obviously be a matter for negotiation with the United States and the United Kingdom rather than for arbitrary determination by a lonely professor at Yale.

Whatever the concrete decision arrived at on this point, it is more than evident that it would entail far less risks for the United States and the United Kingdom—and indirectly for the world's monetary system itself—than the present right—alas, increasingly theoretical —of sterling holders to require at any time the conversion into dollars of about $10.5 billion of sterling balances, and of official dollar holders to demand the conversion into gold at our Treasury of more than $10 billion of dollar balances now held by them, to say nothing of the further $7.5 billion which they might acquire from present private dollar holders abroad, in the course of their stabilization interventions on the foreign exchange markets of the world.

The recurrent sterling crises of the postwar period and the present international dollar crisis are clear evidence of the overwhelming advantages of such a long overdue reform of the gold-exchange standard for the United Kingdom and the United States. Far from implying an effective surrender of sovereignty to an international body, it would restore to both countries a freedom of monetary management—particularly in relation to interest-rate policy—which they have long lost through the gradual accumulation of an excessive level of short-term foreign indebtedness inseparable from the gold-exchange standard's reliance on *national* currencies as a supplementary source of *international* liquidity.

Yet the enormous powers which such a reform would vest in the Fund remain the major hurdle to be overcome by an effective negotiation of the reforms proposed above. The present pattern of voting power in the IMF corresponds roughly to the capital contributions of members. It gives about 26 per cent of the total votes to the United States, 24 per cent to all the nations of continental Europe put together, 12 per cent to the United Kingdom, and 37 per cent to the rest of the world.

The pattern of minimum deposits that would, in the end, replace capital subscriptions, if my plan were adopted in full, would increase sharply the relative contributions of continental Europe and the United States (to about 33 per cent each), and reduce correspondingly those of the United Kingdom (to about 5 per cent) and of the rest of the world (to about 30 per cent). A parallel change in voting power would be difficult to negotiate, and might still fail to reassure some countries about the effectiveness of their own influence on the Fund's management of the sums put by them at its disposal. It is, moreover, doubtful whether the world-wide administrative structure of the Fund could handle quickly and efficiently the numerous and delicate decisions inevitably entailed by the handling of such large sums and responsibilities.

A decentralization of the Fund's machinery is, in any case, highly desirable for a host of other reasons. Such decentralization is universally accepted as necessary for the effective organization of policy-making decisions in a national community. In our own country, all power is not vested in Washington. Some of it is left to each of our fifty states, and even to smaller administrative units such as counties, cities, townships, etc. If this be necessary within an historically integrated community, how much more necessary must it be in the initial building stages of an international monetary administration encompassing widely heterogeneous areas, with vastly different problems arising from a variegated history, and at greatly uneven stages of political, economic, and financial development.

My own feeling, therefore, is that the reforms proposed above should be implemented not only through a reform of the IMF itself, but should be inserted in part within the framework of existing, or future, regional organizations such as EEC, OECD, the Latin American Free Trade Area, etc.

The most important and immediately feasible step in this direction could be taken at the occasion of the creation of OECD. When joining that organization, the United States and Canada should also join the European Monetary Agreement and enlarge its functions along the lines described above. The members of OECD could distribute their international deposits between the IMF and an OECD monetary organization in rough proportion to their pattern of international trade and payments outside and within OECD. This would help solve, or bypass, the voting-power hurdle mentioned above, by keeping a substantial portion of the deposits under the more closely knit and more workable management of OECD. That would also give vital and powerful support to the development of the closer harmonization of "the financial and economic policies for growth and stability of these industrialized nations of the world whose economic behavior significantly influences the course of the world economy and the trend of international payments," called for in President Kennedy's Message of February 6 on the Balance of Payments and Gold.

A final word might be added about the timing of the various steps which the full implementation of the above suggestions would involve.

(1) The acceptance by the Fund itself of voluntary reserve deposits from members would require no more than a mere interpretation of its statutes, without any necessity for any formal amendments subject to legislative ratification by member countries.

In view of the benefits which the conversion of outstanding dollar and sterling balances into gold-guaranteed deposits at the Fund would entail for large dollar and sterling holders, however, such conversions should be initially subordinated to transitional *ad hoc* agreements with the major countries involved (Germany, Japan, Italy, France, etc.) regarding the cashing into gold metal of the balances which they would transfer to the Fund or continue to hold directly in dollars or sterling. These transitional arrangements would eventually be substituted by the uniform minimum deposit requirements envisaged under (2) and (3) below.

(2) The setting up of similar gold-guaranteed deposits within an OECD framework could be inserted into the revision of the European Monetary Agreement which is, in any case, to be undertaken before October 1 of this year, under the terms of the Agreement itself. Participation of the United States in the system would presumably require an Act of Congress, even though similar exchange guarantees were granted to some European countries by mere Executive Agreement under the Tri-Partite Agreement of 1936.

The OECD deposit system should contemplate minimum reserve requirements for members, similar to those suggested under (3) in order to ward off excessive conversions into gold, and to provide the keystone of the common reserve policy advocated in the United States Aide Mémoire of February 20, 1961, and broadly supported in recent official and unofficial discussions of these issues in Europe.

(3) The above measures should give the IMF the breathing space necessary to negotiate the substitution of present capital subscriptions by minimum deposit requirements as suggested above. My own feeling is that fairly modest requirements (20 per cent of over-all reserves?) would be amply sufficient to secure the Fund against excessive gold withdrawals, since the gold guarantee and interest earnings attached to Fund deposits should normally attract large voluntary

deposits to the Fund. The Fund should, nevertheless, be empowered to vary such requirements, within preagreed limits, in case of need, and particularly to apply a higher deposit ratio to future reserve increases or to that portion of each member's reserves which exceeds the average ratio of world monetary gold to world imports.

The exploration and negotiations now under way will undoubtedly uncover other, and probably better, ways of dealing with the problems raised in this paper. Anybody who has ever participated in negotiations of this sort cannot but be keenly aware of the need to prune, amplify, and readjust initial proposals in the light of the unforeseen difficulties, as well as of the unsuspected opportunities, which only the negotiation itself can bring to light. This applies to the so-called "Triffin Plan" as well as to the "Bernstein Plan." The greatest obstacle to the maximum achievements that should be hoped for and strived for, would be to freeze prematurely the path of discussion into any predetermined channel, and to close the door to a full exploration of any feasible technique to strengthen the international monetary structure of the West, and indeed of the world itself.

B. AFTER THE VIENNA MEETING

The following three papers were written shortly after the Vienna meeting.

(1) The first commented on the Vienna debate itself, and appeared initially (in German) in the *Neue Zürcher Zeitung* of October 29, 1961.

(2) The second was distributed privately and later published, together with the English version of the first article, as an Appendix to two lectures on "The Gold-Exchange Standard: Crisis and Reconstruction" in *Amerikanische Gelehrtenwoche, 1961* (Ludwig-Maximilians-Universität, Munich, 1962, pp. 189–232).

(3) The third is a "post mortem" on the "General Arrangements to Borrow" themselves and is extracted from a lecture on "The Twilight of the Gold-Exchange Standard," delivered at a symposium on International Financing and Investment, organized at the Yale Law School in the spring of 1962, and in which Per Jacobsson was one of the main participants (published for The World Community Association by Oceana Publications, 1964, pp. 18–38).

The Meeting of the International Monetary Fund in Vienna:
A Side-step in the Right Direction

Another Congress danced in Vienna last month. It too danced on a volcano.

There were, however, two differences. Congress and volcano were, this time, financial rather than political; and not even the most optimistic of the delegates could entertain the slightest illusion about the durability of what was achieved at the meeting.

The international monetary structure of the Western world remains as shaky and vulnerable today as it was yesterday, and as dependent on the luck and wisdom of American and British monetary policies, on speculative reactions to interest-rate differentials, devaluation rumors, and war fears, not to mention the Kremlin's gold sales in Western markets (which accounted last year for about 60 per cent of the increase in world monetary gold reserves).

And yet, the tone of the Vienna discussions reveals a fundamental change of attitudes which may hold great promises for future and revolutionary steps toward a long overdue reconstruction of our international monetary order. The contrast is eloquent indeed between the complacency which characterized the Fund's Washington meeting one year ago and the general recognition at Vienna of the urgent need to shore up the gold-exchange standard against future crises of the key currencies to which its fate is so intimately attached.

I

Even the official proposals of Per Jacobsson, modest as they were, reflected a keen awareness of the problem. They recognized that the progress achieved toward currency convertibility had "created new problems which the world has not had to face since the start of the Second World War." They stressed the inadequacy of the Fund's present resources to deal with these problems, in spite of the steep increases in members' quotas accepted two short years ago. They admitted that further quota increases would not provide a satisfactory solution, and called for special borrowing arrangements ensuring the Fund substantial resources in specific currencies on a scale sufficient "to convince the public that they are adequate to defend currencies from ill-advised speculation. . . . It would not . . . be sufficient to leave the actual borrowing transaction to an *ad hoc* agreement between the Fund and the lending country . . . there is great merit in an assurance that additional resources are available to the Fund for its transactions. The ready availability of resources is itself a contribution to stability and strength." Finally, "it should be part of the arrangement that the Fund would not borrow from a member country unless the country's payments and reserve position permitted this. Moreover, the arrangement would be such that any member that had lent its currency to the Fund would readily be able to obtain repayment if its own payments position changed."

If one wished to summarize in a simple institutional formula these various criteria, I submit that what they add up to might not be very different from my own proposal that each member country hold in the form of convertible deposits with the Fund an agreed proportion of its over-all monetary reserves. This would automatically ensure the Fund the currencies legitimately needed for lending, on the basis of members' over-all balance-of-payments and reserve strength, while permitting the lenders to draw freely on their deposits with the Fund as soon as a reversal in their future balance of payments and reserve position makes it at all desirable—or even indeed possible—for them to draw on their reserves to meet their own payments needs anywhere in the world.

Previous discussions at the Fund's Executive Board in Washington had initially left this point somewhat obscure, and raised doubts about the willingness or ability of the Fund to repay on demand, if needed, the amounts previously borrowed by it under stand-by agreements and re-lent to other members. These doubts need not have arisen if the stand-by commitments had been expressed in the form of minimum deposit requirements proportional to each country's over-all reserves. It would have been clear, in that case, that deposit withdrawals by countries with declining reserves would necessarily be offset—and indeed more than offset—by additional deposits from the countries with increasing reserves, and would leave unaffected the total lending resources of the Fund.

II

The reaction of some of the European countries—particularly the French, the Belgians, and the Dutch—to Mr. Jacobsson's plea was relatively disappointing. Nobody dared deny the seriousness of the problem which he had raised, but the degree of consensus achieved as to the concrete commitments that countries appeared willing to negotiate in advance of a crisis was severely limited. The French

Minister of Finance, M. Baumgartner, raised doubts about the need "to go further in this field" than central banks had proved willing to do last spring, at Basel, to fight speculation against the pound sterling. He indicated that "we do not intend any more, I believe, than some other European countries, to commit ourselves or commit this institution [the Fund] by way of an automatic or rigid solution. . . . France, like other countries, could possibly go a little beyond its present outlay, but under certain conditions." These conditions were left somewhat vague in M. Baumgartner's speech at the meeting, but spelled out far more bluntly, if less curtly, by M. Ansiaux, Governor of the National Bank of Belgium, by Dr. Holtrop, President of the Nederlandsche Bank, and by M. Baumgartner again at a special press conference. Any new resources to be contributed to the Fund should be earmarked primarily—if not exclusively—for cases when capital movements of an "arbitrary" character (i.e. not related to "unsound" policies by the United States or the United Kingdom) would threaten the stability of the key currencies and, by way of consequence, of the world monetary system itself. Countries with large and increasing reserves should, in that event, recognize a moral obligation to participate in the support operations necessary to avoid a collapse, but without binding advance commitments, and with full consultation as to amounts, terms, and conditions, including the measures to be taken by the borrowers themselves to redress their own situation. Needless to say, the assistance provided under such arrangements should include appropriate exchange guarantees for the creditors, as well as provisions for immediate repayment in case a lending country should, at a later date, find itself in a deficit position.

III

These achievements cannot but look very meager to those concerned with the basic strength and stability of our international monetary system. Yet they may be deemed an enormous advance over the complacency which marked the Fund's discussions at its Washington meeting last year.

First of all, not all countries were as negative and niggardly in their approach. The United States and the United Kingdom appeared fully ready to subscribe together some $3 billion of stand-by commitments to the Fund. While valuable in the long run, such commitments are unfortunately rather academic at this point, since the dollar and sterling balances of Fund members and of the Fund itself are already well in excess of prospective requirements for the years immediately ahead. More significant is the willingness expressed by Germany and Italy to replenish, under Article VII of the Fund Agreement, the badly depleted Fund's holdings of German marks and Italian lire.

Secondly, even the countries which now refuse to undertake firm advance commitments to the Fund are most likely to accept later, under duress, whatever arrangements may prove necessary to avoid an actual collapse in the event of a dollar or sterling crisis. The Basel operations of last spring are indicative of this mood. Central bankers will remain, until the last moment, extremely jealous of their "independence" and resist as long as possible advance commitments of any sort. But they cannot afford the currency chaos which might be triggered by a collapse of the key currencies, and may be counted upon to provide hurriedly, and with far less guarantees than those that might have been negotiated more leisurely, whatever cooperation may prove indispensable to ward off such a collapse.

Last but not least, the most powerful objections raised against the Jacobsson plan reveal, for the first time, a most necessary awareness by central bankers of the basic vulnerability of the international monetary structure of the Western world. Most of the speakers—and even those most averse to institutional reforms—referred to the dangers inherent in the present gold-exchange standard. The most scathing criticism of the system came from Dr. Holtrop, even though it was bizarrely presented by him as a refutation of the charges made against it.

> The gold-exchange standard is being blamed by some for having an inherent tendency of creating too much liquidity, thus having an inflationary bias, and by others for having been unable —or at least for being unable in the long run—to create sufficient liquidity, thus having a deflationary bias. Thirdly it is blamed for being inherently unstable. . . . [But] there is no *intrinsic* reason why the gold-exchange standard, more than a pure gold-reserve standard, should lead to an oversupply of liquidity. The history of the gold standard provides us with periods both of abundance and of shortage of gold. The gold-exchange standard may just as well bring periods of oversupply and of shortage of reserve media.

> Meanwhile we must admit that, of late, the key-currency countries have been running too high a deficit and that, consequently, we are presently faced with an oversupply of liquidity.

. . . We must yet, I think, give serious consideration to the argument that, in the long run, the present key-currency countries might not prove to be willing, or to be in a position, to increase their currency liabilities to the extent of satisfying the demand for additional reserves of the reserve-holding countries.

As for the third point of criticism—i.e. the instability of the system due to sudden and unpredictable conversions from one reserve currency into another or into gold—Dr. Holtrop recognized that this uncertainty "creates a potential threat to the stability of the system," but that "paradoxically, one might even say that the stability of the system is based upon [this] uncertainty," since full certainty about the future stability of the dollar price of gold would induce wholesale conversions of gold reserves into dollar reserves, while the certainty of a dollar devaluation would induce wholesale conversions of dollar reserves into gold. Neither of these outcomes being desirable, "it is uncertainty, therefore, that presently controls the proper [?] mixture of decisions." And he concluded, rather lamely, that "it is an intriguing question whether one should prefer uncertainty to continue its present function, or whether one should try to replace it, as would be conceivable, by some arrangement that would give more certainty, but less liberty of action."

He felt, in any case, that the Jacobsson proposals "do not give an answer to the problems I have just discussed. Additional resources would have little bearing on the stability aspect of the gold-exchange standard. They would, within the limits of the present suggestions, not offer a solution to the possible long-term problem of an insufficiency of liquidity creation. They might, on the other hand, tend to aggravate the problem of the present oversupply of liquidity."

As one of the main critics of the gold-exchange standard, I feel that I can concur nearly fully with Dr. Holtrop's analysis. My only dissent would be to question whether uncertainty presently ensures "the *proper* mixture of decisions" and to be more definitely in favor of some alternative, and less insecure, arrangement. I cannot but feel, with Per Jacobsson, that the "vivid discussions on the merits and demerits of the present system which have taken place in recent years and months . . . have been valuable . . . [and] the discussions at the present Meeting very useful and illuminating, and . . . that the work which remains to be done will increase the understanding of our common problems."

Quite obviously, the "illumination" provided by the Vienna meeting was an indispensable prerequisite to the initiation of any serious negotiation of basic reforms of our international monetary system. The Vienna discussions have made it amply clear that such reforms will have to go far beyond the "shoring up" proposals of Mr. Jacobsson. They have also brought to light a number of vital considerations which are bound to influence to a major extent the most likely path of realistic negotiations toward a feasible agreement.

IV

A large consensus seems to me to have been reached on many fundamental aspects of the problem:

(1) Nearly everybody is agreed that—in the words of the Governor of the Bank of Italy—"we should avoid solutions which imply that a return to the past is necessarily a step forward." Only a small minority of gold revaluation lobbyists and of nostalgic disciples of the myth of gold automatism would defend as desirable, or even feasible, a return to the pre-1914 gold standard and the elimination of all international reserve media other than gold metal.

(2) An even broader consensus has been reached on the risks of inflation, deflation, and instability inherent in the gold-exchange or key-currencies standard as it now operates. Many people did, it is true, emphasize that it "could" operate well *provided* that all major countries never failed to pursue vigorously and successfully "sound" national policies, and that sufficient cooperation could be elicited, in times of need, to offset undesirable capital movements between the large financial centers. History, however, offers us little comfort as to the realism of such sanguine assumptions. One might say just as well that raincoats and umbrellas could be dispensed with *if* it never rained.

(3) There is a need, therefore, to adopt new measures to protect the international monetary system against the present risks of over-liquidity, underliquidity, and instability.

(4) These measures, however, cannot—as the Jacobsson proposals did—leave intact all these sources of future crises, and be merely limited to providing the IMF with the resources necessary to enable it to salvage the key currencies from the utter collapse which such crises might entail. Prospective creditors objected to this as tantamount to signing a blank check underwriting future U.S. and U.K. policies over which they have little or no effective control.

(5) The safeguards regarded by them as indispensable fall into

three groups. First of all, any assistance provided by the creditors should be fully reversible. Any lending extended to the Fund should be fully liquid and usable to meet later reversals in the creditors' balance of payments. Second, exchange guarantees should be attached to such loans in order to protect the lenders against unilateral devaluation or inconvertibility decisions of the borrowers. Third, the arrangements arrived at must ensure proper controls over the amount of funds made available to the borrowers and over the policies which the latter will follow to preserve long-run solvency and avoid inflationary abuses of the international credit system implicit in all such proposals.

(6) Of these three conditions, the first is the easiest, and the latter the most difficult, to implement. It does indeed raise two vital questions. First, other countries must be given some effective voice on the total amount of sterling and dollar claims that they may be called upon to accumulate either directly—in the form of sterling and dollar balances held as monetary reserves by central banks—or indirectly through IMF lending or investments. Second, the countries which contribute new lending resources to the IMF must also have an effective voice over the use of these resources for other lending operations of the Fund.

Whether one likes it or not, one must recognize that prospective lenders—and particularly the major European reserve holders—feel deeply suspicious about their ability to influence the policies of the U.K. and the U.S. and the decisions of the IMF Executive Board in either of these respects. They are nearly certain, for this reason, to limit severely the amount of their advance commitments to the IMF itself. One should hope that they will not be exceedingly niggardly, but it would be oversanguine to count on contributions commensurate with the needs that a satisfactory functioning of the international monetary system is likely to require over the long run.

V

This assessment of existing and prospective attitudes toward international monetary reforms reinforces my long-standing conviction that a large part of the problem will have to be met through a decentralization of the IMF structure and operations.

The most promising avenue in this respect at the moment seems to me to lie in the creation of a European Reserve Center embodying the minimum amount, at least, of monetary cooperation and integration indispensable to the effective functioning of a European Economic Community enlarged by the accession or association of Great Britain and other Western European countries. I have little doubt that this issue will arise at an early stage of the present negotiations between Britain and the Six. It might, with goodwill and wisdom, lead to a consolidation of a badly weakened, but still highly useful, sterling system through its concatenation with the exceptionally strong currencies of continental Europe. There might thus be recreated a powerful monetary and financial center capable to resume the world-wide responsibilities and beneficial role of nineteenth century London in promoting international monetary stability and economic development.

The next step would then lie in close arrangements with the other major key-currency country and financial center, i.e. the United States. Whether these arrangements should culminate in an Atlantic Reserve Center, or be kept more flexible within the framework of the new OECD, is a question on which I would still hesitate to form an opinion at present. Even if the first of these alternatives should be aimed at, the second would probably have to precede it and help pave the way for it.

There will remain, in any case, an acute need to reinforce the IMF itself to enable it to play its proper role as the over-all coordinator of national and regional monetary policies in an interdependent world, and to facilitate settlements among the groups and countries concerned. This role should gain—and not lose—effectiveness as the IMF concentrates its full potential on it, leaving full scope to regional groups to develop the much closer cooperation and integration in solving their own problems which experience is each day demonstrating to be more and more feasible within this framework, but utopian still on a world-wide scale.

Viewed in this broad perspective, the concrete achievements of the Vienna meeting cannot but be judged exceedingly modest. Rather than a "step in the right direction"—to use a time-hallowed IMF formula—they will probably be deemed by history to have been a "side-step" in the right direction, at a time when monetary reformers should think of catching a plane, a taxi, or at least a bus, rather than merely crawling or walking toward a goal both distant and urgent.

Yet, one may be reluctantly forced to agree with Per Jacobsson's pessimistic assessment of what was actually and realistically feasible at that meeting. His keen intuition, unbounded dynamism, and extraordinary negotiating ability are among the strongest assets of the in-

stitution which he has so ably steered through many crises, potential
or actual, since the days of Suez.

A Simple Post-Vienna Proposal to Increase the Lending Resources of IMF

Proposal

(1) Amendment of the Jacobsson proposals along the following
lines might possibly revive the Vienna negotiations with better hopes
for success in the short run and greater efficacy in the long run, particularly as a first step toward a broader revamping of the IMF Agreement.

(2) The suggested agreement should be negotiated within OECD—
through the van Lennep working group—and embrace initially the
major reserve holders of OECD which are also members of the Fund,
i.e. the U.S., Canada, the United Kingdom, and the EEC countries, accounting together for 60 to 70 per cent of both the world's monetary
reserves and the total quotas in IMF (see Table 1).

(A separate protocol should associate Switzerland to the group, and
other OECD countries should also be invited to join without, however,
diluting to excess the administrative machinery of the system.)

Alternatively, the proposed agreement might be explored first in
the course of the negotiations now under way between the United
Kingdom and the EEC, and submitted by them to the van Lennep
group in Paris.

(3) The signatory countries would agree to accept net claims on
IMF—or gold-exchange certificates representative of such claims—in
settlement from either the Fund or any other signatory (or Fund
member?), without limit, provided that:

(a) They be allowed to use freely any such claims accumulated
by them: (i) for repayment of any amounts due by them to the Fund
itself; (ii) for settlements due to any other signatory, to the extent
that the ratio of such claims held by them to their gross international
reserves exceeds the average ratio for the group as a whole (see Table
2).

(b) They be allowed to demand from the IMF gold repayment of
any claims accumulated to their account in excess of whichever of the
two following amounts is the larger: (i) the amount of their Fund
quota; (ii) the amount corresponding to a uniform proportion of IMF
claims to gross reserves jointly agreed to by the group (see Table
3).

TABLE 1

INTERNATIONAL DISTRIBUTION OF IMF QUOTAS AND MONETARY RESERVES

Countries and areas	In millions of gold dollars		In per cent of world total		In per cent of signatories' total		
						Reserves	
	Quotas	Re-serves	Quotas	Re-serves	Quotas	Ex-cluding Switzer-land	In-cluding Switzer-land
1. United States	4,125	19,000	27.6	29.3	44.7	45.0	42.3
2. European Economic Community	2,606	17,500	17.4	27.0	28.2	41.5	39.1
Germany	*787.5*	*7,500*	*5.3*	*11.6*	*8.5*	*17.8*	*16.8*
France	*787.5*	*3,200*	*5.3*	*4.9*	*8.5*	*7.6*	*7.1*
Italy	*270.0*	*3,300*	*1.8*	*5.1*	*2.9*	*7.8*	*7.4*
Netherlands	*412.5*	*1,900*	*2.8*	*2.9*	*4.5*	*4.5*	*4.2*
Belgium-Luxemburg	*348.5*	*1,600*	*2.3*	*2.5*	*3.8*	*3.8*	*3.6*
3. United Kingdom	1,950	3,500	13.0	5.4	21.1	8.3	7.8
4. Canada	550	2,200	3.7	3.4	5.9	5.2	4.9
5. Subtotal	**9,231**	**42,200**	**61.6**	**65.2**	**100.0**	**100.0**	**94.2**
6. Switzerland		2,600		4.0			5.8
7. Subtotal, including Switzerland (5 + 6)	**9,231**	**44,800**	**61.6**	**69.2**	**100.0**		**100.0**
8. Other OECD countries	732	4,200	4.9	6.5			
9. Subtotal (7 + 8)	9,963	49,000	66.4	75.6			
10. Other countries	5,040	15,800	33.6	24.4			
11. World	**15,003**	**64,800**	**100.0**	**100.0**			

NOTE: These are only rough estimates derived from IFS estimates of gold and foreign exchange reserves at the end of June 1961 (except for the United Kingdom for which August estimates have been entered) and net IMF claims at the end of August 1961.

(c) Decisions relating to the implementation of this agreement, and particularly to clause (3b, ii) above be taken by weighted majority vote of the group, giving adequate recognition to the relative levels of reserves on which each country's lending commitment will be based (see comment (4) below, and Table 4).

TABLE 2

GROSS RESERVES AND NET IMF CLAIMS
(in millions of gold dollars, or per cent of total)

Countries and areas	Gross re-serves	Net claims on IMF	Ratio of IMF claims to re-serves (per cent)	IMF claims uniformly redistributed		New payment by, or reimbursement to (−) member by IMF	
				Ex-cluding Switzer-land	In-cluding Switzer-land	Ex-cluding Switzer-land	In-cluding Switzer-land
1. United States	19,000	1,206	6.4	1,405	1,324	199	118
2. European Economic Community	17,500	1,729	9.9	1,294	1,220	−435	−509
Germany	_7,500_	_695_	_9.3_	_555_	_522_	_−140_	_−173_
France	_3,200_	_437_	_13.7_	_237_	_223_	_−200_	_−214_
Italy	_3,300_	_227_	_6.9_	_244_	_230_	_17_	_3_
Netherlands	_1,900_	_226_	_11.9_	_140_	_132_	_− 86_	_− 94_
Belgium-Luxemburg	_1,600_	_145_	_9.1_	_118_	_111_	_− 27_	_− 34_
3. United Kingdom	3,500	—	—	259	244	259	244
4. Canada	2,200	187	8.5	163	153	− 24	− 34
5. Subtotal	**42,200**	**3,122**	**7.4**	**3,122**	**2,941**		**−181**
6. Switzerland	2,600	—			181		181
7. Total	**44,800**	**3,122**	**7.0**		**3,122**		

NOTE: See Table 1 above.

Negotiation of the proposed agreement might, in addition, make it necessary to provide for a gradual stiffening of qualified majority voting rules—two-thirds, three-fourths, four-fifths, or even unanimity of the total voting power—to raise beyond given percentages—20 per cent, 25 per cent, etc.—the ratio of lending commitments to gross reserves mentioned under (3b, ii).

Comments

(1) The only *additional* obligation requested from the signatories beyond those implicit in the IMF Charter would be that under clause (3b, ii). As of August 1961, it would add up to $4.3 billion—or $5.0 billion if Switzerland is included—to the lending capacity of the Fund, and even more by qualified majority vote (see Table 3).

The initial distribution of additional commitments among the sig-

TABLE 3

IMF LENDING RESOURCES UNDER THE PLAN, AT CURRENT RESERVE LEVELS
(in millions of gold dollars)

Countries and areas	Quota	20% of re-serves	25% of re-serves	30% of re-serves	New Resources		
					Up to 20% of reserves	Up to 25% of reserves	Up to 30% of reserves
1. United States	4,125	3,800	4,750	5,700		625	1,575
2. European Economic Community	2,606	3,500	4,375	5,250	1,102	1,769	2,644
Germany	*788*	*1,500*	*1,875*	*2,250*	*712*	*1,087*	*1,462*
France	*788*	*640*	*800*	*960*		*12*	*172*
Italy	*270*	*660*	*825*	*990*	*390*	*555*	*720*
Netherlands	*413*	*380*	*475*	*570*		*62*	*157*
Belgium-Luxemburg	*349*	*320*	*400*	*480*		*51*	*131*
3. United Kingdom	1,950	700	875	1,050			
4. Canada	550	440	550	660			110
5. Subtotal	**9,231**	**8,440**	**10,550**	**12,660**	**1,102**	**2,394**	**4,329**
6. Switzerland		520	650	780	520	650	780
7. Total	**9,231**	**8,960**	**11,200**	**13,440**	**1,622**	**3,044**	**5,109**

NOTE: See Table 1 above.

natories would approximate that contemplated under the Jacobsson plan, except for the mere window-dressing contribution foreseen for the U.K. under that plan.

More important, however, would be the continuous and automatic adjustment of each country's lending commitment to the evolution of its reserves and thus to its lending capacity and to justifiable demands for its currency by other Fund members.

(2) European objections to the Jacobsson plan would be met to a considerable extent:

(a) by the voting provisions under (3c);

(b) by the fact that no large sums need to be committed to the IMF in advance of actual operating requirements, and that these could be appraised by the group—together with the conditions to be attached to the additional IMF lending operations contemplated—at the time of such voting;

(c) by the fact that clauses (3a, ii), (3b) and (3c) would make obvious and automatic the liquid character of the claims accumu-

TABLE 4

INITIAL VOTING POWER
(in per cent of total)

Countries and areas	On reserve basis	On GNP basis	Uniform per country	Arithmetical average	
1. United States	45.0	64.6	11.1	40.2	
2. European Economic Community	41.5	21.7	66.7	43.3	
				Simple	Readjusted
Germany	17.8	7.9	11.1	12.3	10.2
France	7.6	7.0	11.1	8.6	10.2
Italy	7.8	3.9	11.1	7.6	10.2
Netherlands	4.5	1.4	11.1	5.7	5.1
Belgium		1.5	11.1	} 9.2	5.1
Luxemburg	3.8	0.1	11.1		2.6
3. United Kingdom	8.3	8.9	11.1	9.4	
4. Canada	5.2	4.8	11.1	7.0	
5. Total	100.0	100.0	100.0	100.0	
6. Switzerland	5.8	1.1	10.0	5.6	

NOTES:

1. A formula based on reserves alone would give excessive weight to Germany, and one based on GNP alone (1959 OEEC estimates), excessive weight to the United States. A closer approximation to a politically acceptable formula would be given by the arithmetical average in the last column. The votes of the individual EEC countries, however, might be further readjusted in accordance with Article 118 of the Rome Treaty.

2. The 5.6 per cent vote assigned to Switzerland in case of her accession to the Agreement would have to be deducted *pro rata* from the other countries, reducing to 38.0 per cent, 40.9 per cent, 8.9 per cent, and 6.6 per cent respectively, the vote of the U.S., the European Community, the United Kingdom, and Canada.

lated upon the Fund whenever needed—or, indeed, usable—for the settlement of later deficits of the lending member;

(d) by the consequent and logical inclusion of net IMF claims as part of each country's international reserves;

(e) by the fact that the initial effect of the agreement would be to authorize reimbursements of past lending to the countries which have objected most strongly to the Jacobsson plan (see Table 2, last two columns), and to demand relatively smaller commitments from them (Table 3)

(3) Clause (3a, ii) would also have the advantage of providing a

simple and logical solution, obviating once and for all the difficulties connected with the choice of currencies to be sold by the IMF in the course of future drawings. The drawing member could obtain from the IMF any currencies it wished for payment without affecting thereby the lending commitment of the countries whose currency is drawn.

(4) The distribution of voting power should logically be determined by the relative lending commitments of the signatories, and therefore by their relative reserve levels—or by their actual accumulation of net claims on the Fund if they do not choose to take full advantage of clause (3a, ii).

The *initial* distribution of voting power on this basis can be read from the last two columns of Table I, but would be readjusted periodically in the light of average claims or lending commitments over the preceding period.

Political considerations would, however, probably require some readjustment of any such simple formula, in this case as in the case of the IMF quotas. The two main problems would probably be:

(a) to find a justification for increasing somewhat the United Kingdom's vote;

(b) to reduce the margin between Germany's voting power and that of France.

An acceptable formula could probably be derived from a mixing of criteria, giving subsidiary weight to levels of trade and GNP, etc., and to an equal assignment of part of the total voting power among the signatories. The second difficulty mentioned above might also be solved by distributing the total EEC voting power among individual members of EEC in accordance with the provisions of the Rome Treaty. One of many hypothetical formulas of this sort is presented in Table 4.

Relation to a Regional European or Atlantic Monetary Arrangement

The above proposals could easily be integrated with any European or Atlantic monetary arrangement that might be adopted by the European Economic Community (enlarged by the accession of Britain and other European countries), or by OECD (to replace the expiring EMA).

The additional lending commitments suggested here could in that case take the form of *either* net claims on the IMF *or* callable deposits at the BIS (if the latter were designated as Agent for the Community or OECD), at the option of the signatories, depending on whether the additional lending resources are needed to support the currency of members of the Community (or of OECD) or of other IMF members. The acceptability of either procedure as satisfying the additional lending commitments contemplated in the Agreement might facilitate further its negotiation with European members.

The "General Arrangements to Borrow"

The need for international monetary reform, indignantly denied as recently as September 1960 by the monetary pundits assembled in Washington for the annual meeting of the International Monetary Fund, was given, one year later, top billing on the agenda of the next Fund meeting in Vienna.

What emerged from those debates, however, is not a viable long-term solution, but as Mr. Jacobsson himself tells elsewhere in this book,[1] a mere temporary respite against the unsettling impact of short-term capital movements.

According to the Fund's press release of January 8, 1962, the general borrowing arrangements concluded on that date among ten industrial countries "should make it possible to mobilize quickly large additional resources in defense of the international monetary system. The need for the assurance of additional resources arises *not* from any *failure* of the monetary system. . . . The new borrowing arrangements are designed to provide the Fund with additional resources . . . when they are needed for the purpose of forestalling or coping with an *impairment* of the international monetary system." This distinction between *failure* and *impairment* is rather subtle and puzzling to me.

Ten industrial countries have thus committed themselves to make available to the Fund in case of justified need—to be judged by them when the occasion arises—up to $6 billion in their currencies, in order to help any one of them avoid a collapse of its currency.

But this figure of $6 billion is obviously a meaningless one from an operational point of view. If some countries need assistance from the Fund, it would make no sense to have them lend to the Fund the resources which they need to borrow. The maximum conceivable scope of the new resources, therefore, is not $6 billion but at most half of this, i.e. $3 billion.

The actual distribution of these new lending commitments, however,

---

1. *International Financing and Investment* (Dobbs Ferry, N.Y., Oceana Publications, 1964), pp. 9–10.

is a most bizarre one. Six of the ten countries—those from continental Europe—are now in an exceedingly strong reserve and balance-of-payments position. In the rather distant event of a complete reversal in this position, justifying a *full* use of their borrowing facilities at the Fund, they could borrow from it about $4.5 billion. The Fund held, last December, $6.4 billion in the currencies of the other four countries, i.e. $1.9 billion more than it could be called upon to lend. Yet it now asks those other four countries to accept additional lending commitments to the tune of $3.5 billion.

Far less unlikely in the foreseeable future would be large borrowings by the four countries now in trouble, i.e. Japan—which has indeed negotiated since then for $300 million of stand-by borrowings—Canada, the United States, and the United Kingdom. These four countries could borrow up to $8.6 billion from the Fund, i.e. $7.6 billion more than the Fund's total holdings in the currencies of the other six countries. But it has asked only $2.5 billion from the latter, leaving still a shortfall of resources of more than $5 billion.

Moreover, these new lending arrangements leave intact, as Mr. Jacobsson mentions in his article, the major problems of our present unorganized and nationalistic gold-exchange standard, that is:

(1) the erratic, haphazard nature of liquidity creation under the gold-exchange or key-currencies system;

(2) the root sources of foreseeable crises in the key currencies, which the Jacobsson arrangements are designed only to salvage, rather than protect, from such crises;

(3) the long-run shortage of liquidity which is bound to arise when the key currencies no longer contribute two thirds of its current sources of supply: (a) either because they equilibrate their balance of payments, as they are urged by others, and themselves determined to do; or (b) because other central banks refuse to pile up further IOU's from them or, even worse, try to cash for gold those which they have accumulated in the past, triggering off in the process an international currency collapse *à la* 1931.

Yet, in spite of these criticisms, the Jacobsson arrangements erect an invaluable barrier against speculative movements. They will help protect us, at least for a while, against a sudden currency collapse. They give us, as Mr. Jacobsson said, a respite, but a respite to be put to use, rather than to waste.

This may well indeed be the most that could be negotiated in a hurry and time was of the essence. Moreover, as remarked by Erich Fromm in his brilliant book *May Man Prevail?*

> It is . . . one of the irrationalities of human nature that we are prone to seek for easier, short-term solutions because we are afraid of the difficulties of the fundamental and real solutions. But in individual as in social life, it is the logic of facts that determines reality, not the logic of wishful thinking.

3. The Relapse into Bilateralism and the Emergence of the Group of Ten

Bizarrely enough, no use was actually made of the "General Arrangements to Borrow" until it was finally activated to meet—in small part—the sterling crisis of November 1964.

The years 1962–64 were marked instead by the rapid mushrooming of bilateral credit arrangements (swaps, stand-bys, absorption by central banks and treasuries of nonmarketable, "convertible" and "inconvertible" U.S. Treasury bonds and notes, some payable in dollars, and others in foreign currencies) negotiated by Under Secretary Roosa with Canada, Japan, and the major reserve holders of Western Europe, by the formation of a so-called "gold pool" among the same group of countries, and active interventions by major central banks in the forward exchange market.

Interested readers will find an excellent discussion of these complicated arrangements and operations in:

(1) Robert Z. Aliber, *The Management of the Dollar in International Finance,* Princeton, 1964;

(2) "The London Gold Market," *Bank of England Quarterly Bulletin,* March 1964, pp. 16–21;

(3) the periodic review of "Treasury and Federal Reserve Foreign Exchange Operations" by Charles A. Coombs, Vice President of the Federal Reserve Bank of New York, in the March and September issues of the *Federal Reserve Bulletin* (starting with September 1962);

(4) the "Commentary" and "Analysis of Financial Statistics" which appear in each issue of the *Bank of England Quarterly Bulletin.*

Suffice it to say here that by mid-1964 the Federal Reserve had concluded short-term reciprocal currency agreements with twelve central banks (including the BIS) for a total amount of $2,050 million, and that total drawings under these arrangements had amounted to more than $1.8 billion and repayments to more than $1.7 billion. The placement of nonmarketable Treasury bonds and notes with foreign official institutions had risen over the same period to $954 million, and to $1,440 million by the end of November 1964.

These arrangements undoubtedly played a most useful and successful role in helping meet recurrent speculative crises, inspired in part by the inability of the officials to agree on the more basic reforms needed to consolidate our international monetary system. The exchange guarantees embodied in most of them overcame, to some extent, the reluctance of European central bankers to pile up more and more dollar IOU's as part of their monetary reserves. The EEC countries, for instance, slowed down their conversions into gold of their total reserve increases, from 78 per cent, on the average, in 1961–62, to 59 per cent in 1963 and 51 per cent in the first eleven months of 1964.

Yet the major reserve holders of Western Europe showed little enthusiasm for Under Secretary Roosa's vision of a future monetary system under which they might conceivably be called upon to finance indefinitely U.S. deficits through unpredictable accumulations of dollar claims, under "a constellation of special bilateral relationships between the dollar and the separate currencies of most of the other leading industrial countries." [1] Conservative bankers' fears of the inflationary potential of such a "system," may well have been excessive, but they certainly rejoined and reinforced the *political* reactions elicited by Mr. Roosa's candid description of the central role of the dollar in his planetary system: "It is a role which naturally accompanies our leading economic and political position." [2]

By the summer of 1963, therefore, European central bankers were finally ready to admit the need for a radical review of the operation of the present international monetary system, even if only to avoid the long-term implications of continued, haphazard, and precarious bilateral financing of the key-currency countries' deficits. They showed, however, a clear preference for keeping forthcoming negotiations within the framework of the Group of Ten, rather than entrusting them to the IMF, in which their voting power would be submerged by the weighted votes of the U.S. and the U.K. and by the votes of several scores of credit-thirsty underdeveloped countries.

1. Robert V. Roosa, "Assuring the Free World's Liquidity," *Business Review Supplement,* Federal Reserve Bank of Philadelphia, September 1962, p. 9.
2. *Ibid.,* p. 11.

4. The 1963 Meeting of the IMF

The first of the two following papers was written on the eve of the September 1963 IMF meeting, and the second immediately after. They were published, with minor changes, in *The Washington Post* (September 29, 1963) and *The New York Herald Tribune* (October 20, 1963).[1]

A. BEFORE: TOWARD A FATEFUL BUT DELICATE PREGNANCY

Top billing at the Sheraton Park, this coming week, will be the attempt to launch, at long last, under the aegis of the International Monetary Fund, an official study of fundamental reforms in the tottering international monetary system of the Western world.

With so many willing fathers and mothers, some offspring can be confidently expected, but the pregnancy promises to be long and difficult. There is virtually no danger of premature birth, but rather the opposite. The monetary doctors may find it extremely difficult, therefore, to eschew entirely the use of tranquilizers. Recent, and tragic, precedents should warn them, however, against the temptation to ease their job at the risk of malformation of the child. Thalidomide is definitely *not* to be advised.

The Area of Agreement

Before dwelling on such dangers, congratulations are in order, and reasons for hope should be duly stressed. Considerable progress has been achieved in the last three years toward an agreed diagnosis of the problem and even toward a clarification of alternative, and/or complementary, approaches to a viable solution.

The vulnerability of the present gold-exchange standard to speculative capital movements was recognized at the 1961 IMF meeting in Vienna, and a long list of bulwarks has been erected since then to protect it, and particularly its key currencies, against the impact of such short-run disturbances. Per Jacobsson and Under Secretary Roosa have done an admirable job in steering to success the difficult negotiations which this entailed.

The longer-run threat posed by a potential shortage of international reserves, or liquidity, is no longer denied today, even though central

1. See also "Ouvrir la porte au progrès," *Le Monde* (Paris, December 15–16, 1963).

bankers remain somewhat suspicious of its exploitation by politicians to seek in international monetary reforms an escape from the "healthy" disciplines imposed by balance-of-payments pressures upon "irresponsible," inflationary, national policies.

About 60 per cent of world reserve increases have been fed in the last five years by the continuous piling-up of dollar balances, i.e. of U.S. short-term debts, in the hands of foreign central banks. This, plus the U.S. gold losses, accounts for nearly 80 per cent of reserve increases outside the United States, which have averaged more than 8 per cent a year over the period, and a much higher rate still for the major reserve holders of Western Europe.

Central bankers are perfectly correct, therefore, in their contention that there is no world-wide shortage of liquidity today, and that the most urgent problem is to bring an end to the persistent U.S. deficits of recent years. They now admit, however, that a problem is bound to arise *if* and *when* the re-equilibration of U.S. payments dries up, at the source, three to four fifths of the current process of international reserve creation. They still insist, on the other hand, that negotiations and agreements on new sources of liquidity creation would be premature as long as they could be abused to supplement an already excessive rate of reserve growth, and to finance the perpetuation of U.S. deficits.

The Gordian knot will be cut this week through a resolution to launch a "study" of the long-range reforms required at some future date for the satisfactory performance of the international monetary system. Actual "negotiations" and "commitments" will presumably be eschewed, however, until the elimination of current U.S. deficits transforms the "potential" liquidity shortage into an "actual" one.

Agreement with the Europeans on this point was foreshadowed in the recent President's Message to Congress: "We share their view that the problem of improving the payments mechanism is one that demands careful joint deliberation. At the same time, we do not pretend that talk of long-range reform of the system is any substitute for the actions that we ourselves must take now."

The Missing Link

So far, so good. I see nothing wrong in the tentative agreements outlined above, but I hope that the proposed "study" will throw further light into some still obscure corners of the great debate.

The first is the link between our current balance-of-payments problem, and that of the British, and the question of international monetary reform itself. The sharp reversal of short-term capital movements from large and growing net inflows up to 1959 to even larger and persistent outflows since 1960 accounts for about two thirds of our recent deficits.

The major—although not the only—factor of explanation undoubtedly lies in the speculative rumors unleashed by the flare-up of gold prices in London, in October 1960, and entertained ever since by the enormous and ever-growing size of our short-term indebtedness to central banks. Speculators are far less confident than the experts in the permanence of the cooperative spirit which has restrained so far any massive conversions of such debts into gold, and continue to regard a gold revaluation, or a gold embargo, or exchange controls as a possible—even if not probable—outcome of this situation.

International monetary reform should focus initially on a removal of such threat to the stability of the dollar and of the present structure of world reserves, rather than on increasing present liquidity levels or financing future dollar deficits. The impact of such action on speculative expectations and short-term capital movements would constitute a major contribution to the elimination of these deficits themselves, and should be regarded as an essential component—along with the measures already adopted or announced by the Administration—of any program aiming at that objective. (Evidence for this diagnosis cannot be presented here, but has been summarized in a recent article of *The Banker*.[1])

Thalidomide

My greatest concern about the fruitfulness of the forthcoming debate, however, is that the reforms most easily negotiable may eschew the central problem of a rational adaptation of the process of reserve creation to the legitimate needs of the world economy, and perpetuate in fact the root causes of future crises and instability.

Gold production has long ceased (since the First World War, in fact) to provide more than a minor and ever decreasing fraction of world reserve increases. Private demand has absorbed from one half to 90 per cent of Western gold production, and U.S.S.R. gold sales in Western markets provided from about one half to two thirds of gold reserve increases, in each of the last five years. Over the period as a whole, U.S. deficits have fed nearly four fifths of total reserve increases

1. Part One, Chapter IV, Section 2, above.

outside the United States, i.e. four to five times as much as the total contribution from Western production and Russian gold sales.

To leave the process of reserve creation to be determined by such haphazard factors as gold production in a country threatened by civil war, the whims—or policies—of the Kremlin, the state of nerves of gold speculators, the size of U.S. and/or U.K. deficits, and the waves of central bankers' confidence in the dollar and/or the pound can hardly be the best way to run the world monetary system, to adjust liquidity creation to noninflationary levels of world economic growth, and to ward off future monetary crises.

Yet we shall continue to hear plausible slogans urging us "to prefer evolution to revolution, to build upon existing institutions, etc.," and damning as utopian attempts "to set up a world central bank in advance of a world government" even the most modest and practicable steps toward a more orderly system of reserve creation. To preserve intact all the present roots of instability in the system, and merely add to them additional and overlapping gimmicks such as general arrangements to borrow à la Per Jacobsson, bilateral swap agreements and medium-term or nonmarketable currency loans à la Roosa, mutual currency accounts à la Maudling, etc., etc., would give birth to a thalidomidic monster rather than to a healthy and vigorous child, susceptible of normal growth in the world of tomorrow.

Reaching for the Moon?

The alternative to such a dreary prospect is to clarify the main directions along which a rational, long-range solution should be sought, before negotiating the transitional adaptations and compromises that may prove necessary in the short run.

(1) First and foremost, the institutional machinery to be created should make it possible to adjust the over-all pace of reserve creation to the full noninflationary potential and requirements of world economic growth, rather than to the hazards of future gold production, Kremlin policies, and U.S. or U.K. payments deficits.

(2) This would certainly entail the continued use of reserve media other than gold metal alone, as a necessary component of central Bank reserves. The actual distribution of the latter between gold and other assets should be geared at filling the gap between available supplies of monetary gold and the legitimate liquidity needs of a growing world economy.

(3) Reserve assets other than gold should not be held—as they

are now—in a form that exposes their owners to the risk of unilateral devaluation or inconvertibility decisions by the debtors, and the latter to the risk of sudden and massive liquidation by the creditors.

Among the many ways in which this principle could be implemented, the simplest—though not necessarily the easiest to negotiate—would be for each country to hold the bulk of its reserves other than gold in the form of deposit balances with the IMF.

(4) This would facilitate the achievement of still another objective of a rational world monetary organization, i.e. the use of the world's thirst for reserves as a means to help finance stabilization and developmental loans, in support of mutually agreed national policies, compatible with one another and with basic objectives of noninflationary economic growth. The holding of reserve assets other than gold inevitably entails, indeed, the granting of credit to the debtor of such assets. Deposits held with a central reserve institution would permit a more rational distribution of this lending power than the direct, bilateral, and unstable accumulation of national currencies through the uncoordinated decisions of several scores of central banks.

Coming Down to Earth

Practical negotiations along these lines will admit, and even require, multiple adjustments to take account of past traditions, institutions, and habits of mind, and also of unyielding, but fast-changing, political realities.

The IMF machinery may prove too rigid, complex, and cumbersome to serve as the only channel for the implementation of the suggestions above. Particularly delicate questions would be raised by the management of its vastly expanded lending capacity, especially in view of the small voting power wielded in its Executive Board by the major creditor countries of Western Europe. Moreover, the development of the European Economic Community is most likely to entail major institutional changes in the European monetary system, and similar trends may also accompany the development of regional economic cooperation in Latin America, Africa, etc.

A decentralization of the IMF machinery would overcome both of these difficulties. The Paris Agreements of last year may give a cue to the institutional framework most likely to prove acceptable in the forthcoming negotiations. An agreement among major reserve holders —particularly the U.S., the European Community, and the U.K. as leader of the sterling system—would encompass the bulk of world reserves, and serve as an anchor and a model for the arrangements to follow with other countries.

Some attempt will most likely be made by the United States and the United Kingdom to merge the Roosa and Maudling plans as a basis for initial discussions. The nonreserve countries, on the other hand, are most likely to insist on protection against the arbitrariness and inflationary potential of continued reliance on current key-currency arrangements and their mere enlargement through further bilateral or multilateral credit lines to reserve debtors.

The Posthuma plan presents considerable merits in this respect, but will have to be pruned of the automatic lending features which make it so objectionable—and rightly so—to most central bankers, and whose complexity led one of them to describe it as requiring the setting up of an "electronic" exchange standard.

The forthcoming debate will thus be dominated by the necessity of reaching a compromise between the initial negotiating positions of the reserve-currency countries—the U.S. and the U.K.—on the one hand, and the major reserve-currency holders of continental Europe, on the other. Any such agreement would certainly be beneficial to other countries as well, but some effort should be made to avoid a mere logrolling exercise and the conflicts of interest in which it might bog down. Some uninstructed delegates, jointly appointed by other countries through the IMF, for instance, might help elevate the debate and focus it on the long-range requirements of the world at large, as well as on those of the major creditors and debtors of the outworn key-currency standard of today.

B. AFTER: THE DAWN OF AN INTERNATIONAL MONETARY REVOLUTION

The seeds of a major revolution in the world's monetary system were quietly planted last week, in Washington, at the annual meeting of the International Monetary Fund, but few people realize yet the full implications of what took place at that meeting.

The Basic Problem

The basic problem remains the one that I outlined, four years ago, before the Joint Economic Committee of Congress:

(1) Gold alone has long ceased to provide more than a minor fraction of the international monetary reserve requirements of an expanding world economy.

(2) The growing use of dollar IOU's as monetary reserves by foreign central banks has remedied that shortage in recent years, but cannot continue to do so indefinitely without undermining confidence in the dollar itself.

(3) We are facing, therefore, a most agonizing dilemma. The restoration of equilibrium in our balance of payments would dry up at the source two thirds to three fourths—even four fifths today—of the current supplies of reserve increases for the rest of the world, and unleash at some point a dangerous deflationary spiral in the world economy. Alternatively, the continuation of our deficits would be bound to trigger, sooner or later, a dollar crisis similar to that which led in 1931 to the devaluation of the pound sterling, the collapse of the international monetary system built around it, and the consequent aggravation of the world depression.

(4) We must re-equilibrate our balance of payments, but must also, in cooperation with other countries, devise less erratic and vulnerable ways to adjust the available pool of world reserves to the full potential and requirements of noninflationary growth of the world economy.

Past Roadblocks to Action

This diagnosis of a *gold* shortage was widely misunderstood at first as asserting that there already existed an actual shortage of *over-all* reserves and liquidity for the world at large. This was obviously not the case so long as U.S. deficits and growing indebtedness to central banks added each year to the over-all reserve levels of foreign countries nearly eight times the amounts derived from Western gold production.

The reality of the dollar crisis which I had predicted in 1959 was, on the other hand, widely recognized after the events that shook the London gold market in October 1960. Other countries helped us protect our dwindling gold stocks against latent or recurrent speculative attacks, and improvised to that end a whole network of defenses such as the well-publicized IMF General Arrangements to Borrow, the mysterious gold pool of central banks, and the bewildering succession of swaps, swap stand-bys and nonmarketable Treasury issues negotiated in the last two years by our imaginative Under Secretary of the Treasury.

As our deficits gave little or no sign of abating, however, foreign central banks became increasingly suspicious of the official espousal of the liquidity shortage thesis by the two major reserve debtor countries, i.e. the United Kingdom and the United States. They feared that such a one-sided argument for international monetary reform might merely constitute a thinly disguised attempt to institutionalize and perpetuate the financing of U.S. and/or U.K. deficits through indefinite increases in their holdings of dollar and/or sterling IOU's.

Finally, my 1959 proposal that all countries agree to hold a portion of their international reserves in the form of true international deposits with the IMF was widely and successfully misrepresented as implying the creation of a supranational world central bank, unworkable without the support of a supranational world government.

The Emerging Area of Agreement

All these roadblocks, except the last, have been very nearly lifted as a result of better contacts and understanding of the problem in the course of the last year, and particularly at the IMF meeting.

The diagnosis of the basic problem outlined above would meet few dissenters today. The United States has made it abundantly clear that proposed reforms of the international monetary system should in no way absolve us of the responsibility to equilibrate our balance of payments. We have also agreed with Mr. Schweitzer, Mr. Maudling, and others that future remedies should lie primarily in *multilateral* agreements rather than in further extensions of the *bilateral* agreements negotiated during the last two years. Finally we have indicated our willingness to discuss the exchange guarantees necessary to the functioning of such agreements and the limitations they may place upon capricious conversions of reserve balances from one currency into another, or into gold metal.

These subtle, but significant, shifts in past U.S. negotiating positions were matched, on the European side, by equally constructive moves on the part of France, whose willingness to cooperate had—rightly or wrongly—appeared most in doubt until then. The bold and lucid talk of the French Minister was unfortunately misinterpreted by a large portion of the American Press. A translation mishap was highlighted, out of context, to signify that the re-equilibration of the U.S. balance of payments would be "the precondition for our reaching decisions," while, in fact, the full French text took great pains to stress "agreement with the views recently and courageously expressed by authorized American sources." The speech of Mr. Dillon had, indeed, asserted, only a few minutes before, that "it is largely the prospect of the elimination of the United States payments deficit that makes it necessary and advisable to undertake these studies."

The French Minister rightly emphasized that the major question today is not that of a present over-all liquidity shortage, but relates instead to the much broader issues raised by the very functioning of the international monetary system.

His first criticism—the lack of "any automatic machinery for a prompt return to equilibrium"—endorsed, in a most cautious manner, the valid strictures raised against the haphazard use of national currencies as a substitute for gold, under the present gold-exchange standard. It did not, however, indicate any sympathy for the return to gold alone advocated by some influential Europeans—and particularly M. Jacques Rueff—on the basis of this analysis. On the contrary, the remainder of his speech aimed directly at making explicit the only realistic alternative, i.e. a concerted effort at organizing in a more equitable and sensible manner the future creation of credit reserves, as a necessary complement to the insufficient supplies of gold metal.

He criticized, secondly, the lack of reciprocity of the present system under which U.S. and U.K. deficits may be largely financed by dollar and sterling accumulation by central banks, while other countries' deficits do not enjoy similar facilities. Chancellor Maudling's proposal for "mutual currency accounts," and Under Secretary Roosa's suggestion for reciprocal currency holdings were directed, a year ago, at the very same point.

The third criticism of the present system made by the French Minister was leveled at the inequitable distribution of the burdens of international cooperation between the countries which hold a large portion of their reserves in foreign currencies, and those which keep them nearly entirely in gold metal. As Mr. Maudling remarked in his press conference, this point is unlikely to be viewed under the same angle by the reserve currency debtors (the U.S. and the U.K.) and by the reserve currency creditors. Yet, a reconciliation of these divergent viewpoints and interests might be most easily achieved if the acceptance by major reserve holders of an agreed distribution of their over-all reserves between gold and other assets served also to protect the reserve currency debtors against the threat of sudden and wanton conversions into gold of the excessive short-term dollar and sterling indebtedness incurred by them over half a century of functioning of the ill-fated gold-exchange standard.

In any case, the French Minister's suggestions had the merit of setting clearly and unequivocally some of the main problems to be solved. They coincide very largely with past proposals of the "controversial Professor Triffin," and with those portions of Professor Posthuma's plan which seemed most susceptible of rallying the greatest degree of support, last year, in the deliberations of the Monetary Committee of the European Economic Community.

Far from being negative or divisive, the French Minister's speech disentangled candidly, lucidly, and constructively from the morass of past discussions the cornerstones of the agreements most likely to prove negotiable among the ten countries actively engaged in the forthcoming exploration of world monetary reform.

The Unresolved Political Issues

Central bankers proved, once more, anxious to dispel any illusions that they might be moving toward the setting up of a "supranational world central bank" à la Triffin, inconceivable in the absence of a world government.

Such a description of my proposals is well designed to elicit emotional resistance to them, but bears no relation to those proposals themselves. Some surrenders of national sovereignty are clearly implicit in *any*, future or past, international agreements on monetary reform. They raise two questions, and two questions only:

(1) What is the actual amount of lending resources or capacity to be placed at the disposal of the IMF, or any other international group or organization?

(2) What degree of control or influence will each participating country retain on the management of these funds?

The essence of my proposals has always been that the Fund's lending capacity be fed by minimum deposit requirements, related to each country's over-all reserve level and lending capacity rather than by arbitrary, rigid, and far less liquid subscriptions to the IMF capital. The actual amount of resources assigned to the Fund could be exactly the same, whichever formula is used. If anything, the first involves a lesser sacrifice of actual liquidity by the contributing countries, and is identical to that proposed in the Posthuma plan.

The degree of control to be retained by the participating countries over their contributions raises far more explosive issues. Any rational apportionment of these contributions among the Fund's members, in accordance with each country's lending capacity and other countries' needs for settlement, will inevitably call for extensive commitments by the large reserve holders of Western Europe. On the basis of current reserve levels, more than 40 per cent of the Fund's resources should be raised from these nations, while their total voting power in the Fund is less than 25 per cent. Any conceivable increase in this voting power would still leave them with only a small minority vote in the Executive Board of the organization.

I devoutly hope that this will not deter them from enlarging substantially their present, and totally inadequate, contributions to the IMF resources. Yet a realistic appraisal of the power politics involved cannot but lead me to predict that they will wish to retain closer control over a portion at least—and probably a major portion—of the resources that will be needed in the long run to substitute for U.S. and U.K. deficits as a way to feed the desirable growth of the international reserve pool over the years to come. This is all the more probable as the largest portion of these resources will be needed to cushion temporary disequilibria in the balance of payments of the major reserve holders themselves, and particularly among the United States, the United Kingdom, and the countries of the European Economic Community.

While the IMF staff study will probably recommend—and obtain—some upward adjustments in countries' quotas and a greater flexibility in their use, the conclusions of the Group of Ten are likely to focus on the bolder reforms discussed above, without merging them fully, particularly as far as their management is concerned, into the normal machinery of the IMF.

The General Arrangements to Borrow, concluded a year ago among the same countries, will probably serve as a point of departure, but with more flexibility and built-in potential for future growth. They may also be merged with provisions for regular consultation, patterned after the experience of OECD Working Party No. 3 and of the Monetary Committee of the European Community.

Another unresolved question is that of isolating the need for an adequate growth of the world's reserve pool from any *automatic* financing of the deficit countries through a direct accumulation of balances in *national* currencies as *international* reserves. This will require to my mind reasonable limitations on the latter system, and the interposition of a multilateral reserve institution, such as the IMF, between the surplus and the deficit countries.

Revolution Through Evolution

These proposals for immediate action may, or may not, be deemed revolutionary. The changes they advocate in the international monetary system are designed to preserve it from the chaotic disruptions that threaten it, and to introduce a more orderly process of world reserve creation than the hazards of gold production in a country threatened by racial strife, the whims of the gold speculators and of Mr. Khrushchev, and the fluctuations in the U.S. and U.K. balances of payments.

Yet I'll gladly confess that I would prefer to see them implemented in a way which will facilitate, rather than hamper, future progress toward closer monetary cooperation and integration, both on a regional scale in Europe and elsewhere and on a world-wide level.

My own philosophy in this respect was expressed most forcibly, and poetically, many years ago, by Maurice Maeterlinck:

> At every crossway on the road that leads to the future, each progressive spirit is opposed by a thousand men appointed to guard the past. Let us have no fear lest the fair towers of former days be sufficiently defended. The least that the most timid among us can do is not to add to the immense dead weight which nature drags along. . . .
>
> Let us think of the great invisible ship that carries our human destinies upon eternity. Like the vessels of our confined oceans, she has her sails and her ballast. The fear that she may pitch or roll on leaving the roadstead is no reason for increasing the weight of the ballast by stowing the fair white sails in the depths of the hold. They were not woven to molder side by side with cobblestones in the dark. Ballast exists everywhere; all the pebbles of the harbor, all the sand of the beach, will serve for that. But sails are rare and precious things; their place is not in the murk of the well, but amid the light of the tall masts, where they will collect the winds of space.

Chapter VIII: Tokyo and After: 1964–?

AFTER ten months of arduous negotiations, the IMF and the Group of Ten released their two parallel reports on August 10, 1964, in preparation for the Annual Meeting of the IMF, which took place in Tokyo a little more than a month later.

I had no knowledge of either report—the secret of the two groups' deliberations was well guarded—when writing at the end of July, at the request of the London *Economist,* an article entitled "From Waterloo to Tokyo," which appeared in their August 15, 1964, issue, with the following introduction:

> Whether one regards this week's two official reports on the international monetary system as momentous or minuscule depends on the distance from which they are viewed. In close-up, their immediate impact will be as disappointingly negative as had been feared. The report of the finance ministers of the Group of Ten has, in this emasculated form approved for publication, disguised rather than resolved the major differences of approach. The second report, by the International Monetary Fund itself, has far more internal consistency, and does point the way to what would be quite radical new advances. Yet, partly in deference to the national ministers of finance whose lead it has had to follow, the IMF presents these suggestions in the most tentative and hypothetical way. For 1964, and 1965, these laborious exercises mean little.
>
> Yet on a longer view they could be seen as a turning point. When all is said and done, the hedging and the qualifications and the underlying disagreements are essentially about what kind of fundamental remedies are needed, and how soon. What does appear, for the first time in an international official report, is the acknowledgment that the present system, with its basic reliance on gold and foreign exchange balances as supplemented by largely piecemeal credits, is likely to be inadequate in the future.
>
> After a lag of five years and more, the international financial powers are in effect acknowledging much of the analysis, if not the remedies, that have been put forward most forcefully and most consistently by Professor Robert Triffin. In the following

article, Professor Triffin presents his diagnosis, and his cure, in the widest historical perspective, drawing on his new research on how the gold standard worked in practice rather than in legend.[1] We believe that this longer perspective will help bring these monetary issues into focus for many readers who are understandably bewildered by the technicalities of the current liquidity debate.

1. FROM WATERLOO TO TOKYO

Ever since the end of the First World War, monetary experts and central bankers have bent their energies on a Proustian "Recherche du Temps Perdu," trying to recapture the lost paradise of the nineteenth-century's so-called gold standard. Twice—in the late 1920s, and again in the late 1950s—their quest seemed within reach of its goal, but in each case the illusion of success was quickly shattered by the gathering clouds of a new monetary storm. The sterling crisis of 1931 spelled out the collapse of the first restoration of convertibility, and the dollar crisis of the early 1960s has finally convinced the world that the monetary order of the future cannot be found in a mere reconstruction of the past.

Gold Standard Myths

The primary explanation of the success and survival of the international monetary system of the nineteenth century lay in its ability to reform itself gradually through a slow evolutionary process—whose cumulative impact, however, was truly revolutionary. Silver coin accounted for more than a third of the world monetary stock at the beginning of the century, and for about two thirds of the additions to world money between 1815 and 1848, but declined precipitously afterwards to less than 3 per cent in 1913. The circulation of gold coin among the public probably declined in the first half of the century, swelled more than four times from 1848 to 1872, increased only very slightly from 1872 to 1892, and rose more rapidly again—by nearly 60 per cent—from 1892 to 1913.

Such sudden and massive changes in the metallic money stock—or "commodity money"—would have played havoc with the world monetary order, if they had not been largely compensated for by parallel

---

[1]. For a fuller presentation see Professor Triffin's *The Evolution of the International Monetary System: Historical Reappraisal and Future Perspectives* (Princeton, 1964).

adaptations in the creation and acceptability of "credit money," i.e. of paper currency and bank deposits. In the heyday of the so-called gold standard, paradoxically, it was in fact credit money, rather than gold, or silver, which dominated the evolution of the monetary stock, and fed the bulk of the monetary requirements of a growing world economy. After 1872, 90 to 95 per cent of the expansion of world money was derived from bank money, as against 5 to 10 per cent from silver and gold together.

High rates of economic growth were indeed reconciled with stability of exchange rates and the gold price only by the rapid growth and proper management of bank money. This could hardly have been achieved under the purely, or predominantly, metallic systems of money creation characteristic of the *previous* centuries. In truth, the nineteenth century could be far more accurately described as the century of an emerging and growing credit-money standard, and of the euthanasia of gold and silver moneys, rather than as the century of an unchanging and automatic gold standard.

The free creation of credit money by central banks of issue, in the form of currency notes, and by deposit banks, in the form of demand deposits, entailed the danger of overexpansion and bankruptcy for each issuing institution. For holders of credit money retained the legal right to convert it at will into metallic money, and they freely did so: for settlements beyond the country's borders, for wage payments and ordinary household spending, or because of diffidence about the solvency of the debtor bank. National central banking systems gradually developed in each country, and assumed growing rights and obligations to orient the creation of credit money and underwrite its ultimate convertibility into gold and foreign currencies. Central banks gradually concentrated into their own coffers more and more of the gold previously held as reserves by the deposit banks and in circulation among the public itself.

Thus the pace of total monetary expansion for all the countries adhering to the international gold standard was dependent not on the hazards of gold production alone, large as it was during the heyday of the system: gold production in the twenty-five years 1889–1913 is estimated to have nearly matched that in the previous four centuries. Monetary expansion was sustained also by this gradual shift of gold from the public and the deposit banks into the centralized reserves of national central banks.

World War Aftermaths

This slow evolutionary process had, by 1913, transformed out of all recognition the international bimetallic monetary system of 1815 into national credit-moneys linked together by their common convertibility into gold metal. The inflationary financing of the First World War and of postwar reconstruction entailed enormous and widely divergent additions to national credit money, inevitably accompanied and followed by a considerable reshuffling of exchange rates. The depreciation of continental Europe's currencies was further aggravated by vast outflows of speculative capital to the United States and Britain. Later these capital flows prompted a considerable overvaluation of the pound and a parallel undervaluation of the continental currencies. Exports, economic activity, and employment slumped into a continued depression in Britain, while booming on the continent.

The capital that had taken refuge in London then began to flow back to the continent, and additional funds moved from London to Wall Street where a speculative boom was also in full swing. The British monetary authorities tried to stop the drain on their slender gold reserves by pleading with the American authorities to keep interest rates lower than in Britain, and with the European central banks to refrain from converting into gold or dollars the vast amounts of sterling balances which they had to purchase from the markets to prevent an appreciation of their own currencies.

The first of these two techniques soon ran counter to powerful market trends and anticyclical objectives of national policy, both in the United States and in Britain. The second involved a radical shift by central banks from the traditional gold standard to the so-called gold-exchange standard, under which major gold-convertible *national* currencies—primarily sterling and the dollar—would be accumulated by central banks as legally valid *international* monetary reserves, alongside gold itself. This shift had been tentatively recommended as one of the ways to remedy the threatening gold shortage by various conferences. It had been largely implemented in the 1920s on an *ad hoc,* voluntary, basis, and had indeed contributed to hiding the underlying weakness of sterling, in the early years after World War I.

The marathon conference of the Gold Delegation of the League of Nations was still discussing the feasibility of firmer agreements to organize and consolidate the new system when the crash of a Vienna bank unleashed a new wave of speculation throughout Europe, undermining further the highly vulnerable position of sterling in the world markets. Britain threw in the sponge on September 21, 1931. Sterling's inconvertibility sounded the death-knell of the system and ushered in a prolonged period of international monetary nationalism which rekindled the economic and political crisis of the 1930s.

A Difference in Understanding

The aftermath of World War II has so far repeated, step by step, the aftermath of World War I, with the substitution of the United States for Britain as the haven for refugee capital, of the dollar for sterling as the anchor of the new gold-exchange standard, and of the international liquidity problem for the gold shortage as the recurrent theme of a frustratingly endless international monetary debate.

Fortunately, the differences are also essential. First of all, the world economy is in far better shape today than it was in 1931, and the economic and financial position of the United States far stronger than that of 1931 Britain. Secondly, the world's financial and political leaders are now keenly aware of the disastrous consequences which any repetition of the 1931 policies, or lack of policies, could entail. The latent dollar crisis of the last five years has been met by an unprecedented degree of international cooperation, and a wide array of short-term agreements among the major governments and central banks has so far shored up the new gold-exchange standard against a new collapse à la 1931.

Last, but foremost, the basic haphazardness and vulnerability of the present system of international reserve creation—and destruction—is now, for the first time, widely understood by academic economists and responsible officials alike. Who could, indeed, defend any longer a system of reserve creation under which, over the last six years, for instance, Russian gold sales in Western markets contributed more than half of the total gold reserve increases of the Western countries, and under which America's losses of net monetary reserves fed nearly three fourths of the increase in their total international reserves (in the form of dollar balances and IMF gold tranches, alongside gold itself)? How could anyone regard such a system, or rather lack of system, as a safe and rational way to regulate the increase of international reserves which must serve as the ultimate basis, particularly when currencies are convertible, for the increases in national money supplies necessary to support growing levels of production and trade in an expanding world economy? Legitimate, noninflationary reserve requirements of economic growth can hardly be defined—and met—by the algebraic additions of the monetary gold released by new production in a country threatened with civil war and by Mr. Khrushchev's sales in Western markets, *minus* the erratic amounts absorbed by private gold speculators and industrial and artistic uses, *plus* the financing of variable American and British payments deficits through voluntary, or not so voluntary accumulations of dollar and sterling IOU's by central banks, *minus* the ever possible conversions into gold metal of such IOU's accumulated over many years past.

The Reforms Needed

This is not the place to rehash once more my own proposals for a basic, and long overdue, reform of the process of international reserve creation, nor to debate the various objections raised against them. Let me simply state:

(1) That they regard as inevitable in the long run a continued growth of international credit reserves alongside gold metal reserves, just as credit money gradually supplemented, and eventually replaced, gold and silver moneys in the national circulation of each country;

(2) That they regard as especially necessary a concerted orientation of this process, aiming to adjust the total pace of reserve growth to the noninflationary growth potential of the world economy, just as the development of national credit money in the nineteenth century imposed a similar orientation, on a national scale, under the aegis of central banks or other national monetary authorities;

(3) That the partial merging of national monetary sovereignties entailed by such an evolution of our international monetary system need be no larger, and could be far better gauged and understood, than that already involved today in the bewildering overlapping of IMF quotas, general arrangements to borrow, the gold pool agreement, bilateral swaps, swap stand-bys, and the rest, to say nothing of the semivoluntary accumulation and retention, as international reserves, of national currencies always subject to devaluation, blocking, and inconvertibility by the unilateral decision of the debtor countries;

(4) That the international lending potential which would be derived from such a system should not be used blindly for automatic lending to any and all countries in deficit, but should be earmarked to support agreed policies of monetary stabilization against temporary balance-of-payments pressures, particularly in connection with capital

movements. It would thus powerfully stimulate the long run harmonization of member countries' policies, and would help to avoid unnecessary recourse to exchange restrictions, devaluation, or deflation by the deficit countries.

(5) That an orderly and adequate growth of world reserves would also provide indirect support for long-term development financing, through investments in marketable obligations of international institutions, such as the World Bank.

Taken in conjunction, the credit criteria suggested above would essentially tend to recreate some of the basic features of the adjustment mechanism of the nineteenth-century gold standard. Vast amounts of private long-term lending then cushioned, for long periods of time, the current account deficits of developing countries. Similar stabilizing capital movements could now be induced by a convincingly stable international monetary framework.

Such thoroughgoing reforms, however, are most unlikely ever to be introduced overnight, as the outcome of a grand negotiation. They will develop more gradually as the result of *ad hoc* decisions and more modest reforms. I would not, therefore, expect any radical and long-run reforms to emerge from the forthcoming Tokyo meeting. Indeed, excessive haste in the current negotiations could lead only to a premature freezing of the very limping and imperfect compromises negotiable at this juncture.

What should be hoped for instead is that full recognition will be given to the evolutionary nature of any functioning and orderly international monetary system, and to the need to orient such evolution and future reforms and adaptations through some permanent, high-level, consultative body of official experts, in close touch with the shaping-up of monetary decisions and policies in their respective countries. We may further hope that attention will center, at an early stage, on the type of techniques—such as deposits with, and investments by, the IMF and other regional monetary organizations—that can be developed most easily and adjusted flexibly to future needs. A more decentralized IMF, recognizing and encouraging openly the role of emerging regional monetary organizations and integration in Europe, Latin America, and elsewhere, would be far preferable economically—and politically—to a rump IMF overshadowed by a separate rich nations' club of the Ten or Eleven most powerful industrialized countries.

Negotiation from Weakness

A topical and ephemeral postscript to this broad excursion into a distant past and an evolving future might profitably be pondered by the Group of Ten negotiators.

The opponents of international monetary reform argued, only a year ago, that concrete negotiations should be postponed until the American balance of payments had been put in order, lest new international credit facilities be abused to finance persistent balance-of-payments deficits and monetary irresponsibility in the United States. They now argue that reforms have become unnecessary in view of the spectacular improvement in the American balance of payments and of the consequent abatement of the dollar crisis.

The full balancing of America's international transactions would, however, reduce by no less than three fourths the rate of reserve creation of recent years. Yet just this eventuality was recognized earlier as one of the major arguments for a basic reform of the present system. The need for action would be even greater if the cessation or reversal of the abnormal flow of private capital to the European continent were to lay bare the increasing deficits of Europe on current transactions. The surplus countries of today—or yesterday—might well have cause to regret tomorrow their failure to negotiate from strength, and to seize in time the opportunities open to them when their American partner negotiated, more amenably and realistically, from a position of relative, but temporary, weakness.

The precedent of Bretton Woods comes to mind in this respect. Keynes's Clearing Union plan seemed then biased in favor of prospective debtors and to entail excessive burdens for the prospective creditors. Yet the United States would have ended up in a far healthier position if it had financed a larger portion of its early postwar surpluses through the accumulation of bancor claims *à la Keynes,* rather than through long-term loans and irrecoverable grants *à la Marshall.*

2. Two Interim Reports: The Group of Ten and the IMF

I commented on the two reports of the Group of Ten and of the IMF, and on the Tokyo debate itself, in a public lecture jointly sponsored by the *Nihon Keizai Shimbun*[1] and the Japan Economic

---

1. The *Nihon Keizai Shimbun* published it from the interpreter's note in its international issue of September 22, 1964.

Research Center, at the close of the IMF meetings, and in two articles: "Post-Mortem on Tokyo" and "La guerre de Tokyo a eu lieu: Duel Giscard d'Estaing–Maudling," published respectively in Dutch in the *Elseviers Weekblad* (Amsterdam, October 30, 1964) and in French in *Le Monde Diplomatique* (Paris, October 1964).

The English text of the *Elseviers Weekblad* article is reproduced below.

POST-MORTEM ON TOKYO

Great hopes—or illusions?—were sparked, a little more than a year ago, by the setting up of two parallel investigations of the need for international monetary reform: one by the Ministers of Finance and Governors of Central Banks of the so-called Group of Ten, and the other by the International Monetary Fund. Neither of these investigations is as yet completed and the "progress reports" which summarized, last August, ten months of labor and negotiations have been deemed by most outside observers rather meager and disappointing.

The open clash of views, at Tokyo, between the Continental Europeans and the Anglo-Saxons—highlighted by the oratorical duel between Giscard d'Estaing and Maudling—might also be taken as a harbinger of further troubles. The only concrete result reached so far is a tentative agreement on extremely modest increases in IMF quotas, edged by persistent disagreement about the gold subscriptions normally entailed in such increases but which would cause further losses of gold by the United States and the United Kingdom (not only in their own behalf, but also to finance the gold subscriptions of other countries whose present reserves are largely held in the form of dollar and sterling balances). Such quota increases would undoubtedly add further to the rapidly growing arsenal of variegated weapons assembled in the last two years to fight the recurrent crises to which the fundamental haphazardness and vulnerability of the present international reserve system exposes the stability and progress of the world economy. They are *no* substitute, however, for the fundamental reforms necessary to remedy these shortcomings.

Is such an appraisal correct? I'll summarize my own views under two headings:

(1) How far have we traveled?
(2) Where do we go from here?

How Far Have We Traveled?

We have come a very long way indeed, both as to the diagnosis of the basic shortcomings of the present international monetary system and of the fundamental and revolutionary nature of the reforms that may be necessary to improve its functioning in the future. The reports of the Ten and of the Fund recognize unequivocally that:

(1) Neither gold production, nor future U.S. deficits, nor the multiplication of reserve currencies, nor present IMF credit facilities, nor the recently developed bilateral facilities for swaps and *ad hoc* support operations, can be depended upon to meet all liquidity needs in the future (see paragraphs 25(a), (b), (c), (e), and (f) of the Ten's report and page 31 of the Fund's report).

(2) "The need may in time be felt for some additional kind of international reserve asset. We think it would be timely to investigate the problems raised by the creation and use of such an asset, the possible forms it might take and the institutional aspects associated with it" (paragraph 25(d) of the Ten's report; see also page 31 of the Fund's report).

(3) "It is desirable to bring under multilateral review and appraisal the various means of financing surpluses and deficits" (paragraph 25(h) of the Ten's report), both in order to ensure that the supply of liquidity be *sufficient* to finance temporary payments imbalances and to guard against an *excessive* creation of liquidity susceptible of frustrating desirable pressures for readjustments of persistent imbalances.

It would be difficult to overstate the contrast between these statements and the complacency which prevailed, a few years ago, about the restoration of convertibility in 1958, and even only a year ago about the possibility to meet all future problems through existing mechanisms, supplemented by a mere proliferation of reserve currencies and swap facilities through uncoordinated national decisions and bilateral negotiations.

In its 1958 study on *International Reserves and Liquidity* (page 72) the IMF still argued that current gold production alone was likely to provide *seven eighths,* or more, of the estimated requirements for reserve increases over the next decade. In the six years' span 1958–63, however, Western gold production provided in fact no more than *15 per cent* of actual reserve increases and the U.S.S.R. sales about 16 per cent, leaving a gap of 70 per cent to be met by other means. The first line of defense against the reformers thus became untenable, and the second, i.e. filling the gap by further increases in traditional dollar and sterling holdings, was abandoned without a fight, in view of the enormous size of the U.S. and U.K. deficits and volatile short-term indebtedness that such a solution would entail.

A new and bewildering array of liquidity instruments was then developed under the leadership of Under Secretary Roosa: foreign currency holdings by the United States itself, U.S. medium-term and foreign-currency borrowings, reciprocal swap and swap stand-by arrangements, etc. Useful as they are—and may continue to be—to fend off short-term disturbances, and particularly those arising from speculative capital movements, they are now judged "not appropriate to meet disequilibria for more than a few months" (Fund's report, page 33), in sharp contrast with the hopes expressed, only a year or two ago, that "looking further ahead, the new arrangements also are capable of providing for a steady growth in the monetary reserves needed to service the trade requirements of an expanding world. . . . The structure . . . has already been established. Its potential capabilities for meeting the world's *longer-run* [italics mine] liquidity requirements are clearly at least as promising as any of the more familiar proposals." [1]

Most promising as planting the seeds of a gradual revolution in the international monetary system through a process of institutional growth are the suggestions of the Ten and of the Fund for:

(1) Regular interchange of data and other information and full exchange of views, providing "a basis for multilateral surveillance of the various elements of liquidity creation, with a view to avoiding excesses or shortages in the means of financing existing or anticipated surpluses and deficits in the balance of payments, and to discuss measures appropriate for each country in accordance with the general economic outlook" (Report of the Ten, paragraph 37).

The effective functioning of such a "multilateral surveillance" system could hardly fail to focus attention on the need to develop more rational guide lines for international reserve creation—or destruction

---

1. Robert V. Roosa, "Assuring the Free World's Liquidity," *Business Review Supplement*, Federal Reserve Bank of Philadelphia, September 1962, pp. 11 and 12. Mr. Roosa, however, was also among the first officials to admit as one of the "main lines of inquiry" of the Ten the possibility "to reconstitute the IMF by endowing it with the capacity to create credit and the power to allocate such credit among members": "Reforming the International Monetary System," *Foreign Affairs* (October 1963), p. 121.

—than are now provided in fact by the haphazardness of gold production in the West, of gold sales by Russia, of gold absorption by speculators, of U.S. and U.K. deficits, and of widely heterogeneous (over space) and unstable (over time) preferences of several scores of central banks for dollar, sterling, or gold as means of reserve accumulation.

(2) The immediate setting up of a "Study Group on the Creation of Reserve Assets" to report on various proposals for the creation of "some additional kind of reserve asset . . . apart from . . . gold and currency balances." (Report of the Ten, paragraphs 26–28 and 38–42. Reference might be made also, in this connection, to proposals for "long-term lending for monetary purposes" discussed in paragraphs 47 and 48.)

Obscurely alluded to in the Ten's report, but brought out into the open at Tokyo, is the opposition of views in this respect between two major proposals:

(a) the creation of a so-called "collective reserve unit," incorporating in agreed proportions a synthetic mix of the currencies of the Ten themselves—or, rather the Eleven, after the accession of Switzerland—and to be accumulated by the members of the Group in some agreed proportion to their gold reserves;[2]

(b) the accumulation by member countries, as a normal component of their international reserves, of internationally guaranteed *deposits* with the IMF, financing IMF *investments* "undertaken on the initiative of the Fund, with a main purpose of creating liquidity, and not necessarily in response to a particular balance-of-payments need" (Fund's report, pp. 38–39).[3]

Where Do We Go From Here?

Concrete progress is likely to be slow, in view of the smoldering oppositions, brought into the limelight at Tokyo, between the Anglo-Saxons, on the one hand, and Continental Europe on the other:

(1) The Europeans' concern with the *inflationary* impact of U.S.

2. The details of this proposal, spearheaded by France and the Netherlands, have not been made public, but its broad outline bears some resemblance, to say the least, to the most original feature of "The Bizarre Proposals of Dr. Bernstein for International Monetary Reform" discussed, under that title, in an article of mine for *Kyklos* (September 1964), reproduced below, pp. 327–40.

3. Sophisticated readers might see some resemblance between this proposal and that developed on pp. 104–07 and 117–19 of my book on *Gold and the Dollar Crisis* (New Haven, 1960).

deficits was countered by Mr. Maudling's opposite concern regarding the *deflationary* dangers that would arise from the present system, if the U.S. restored equilibrium—or surpluses—in its international payments, or in the event of large scale conversions of sterling or dollar balances into gold metal.

(2) The Anglo-Americans thus stressed the need to *add* to present liquidity instruments, while Giscard d'Estaing seemed to consider any new type of reserve asset as a potential—even if only partial—*substitute* for the use of dollar and sterling balances.

(3) The Europeans were understandably reluctant to abandon to the Executive Board of the IMF, in which they have only a small minority vote, the management of the extremely huge resources that they might be called upon to contribute, in the long run, for the successful functioning of the international monetary system. They looked toward a "collective reserve unit" system, organized and managed by the Ten alone, as the way out of this dilemma. The British and the Americans, on the other hand, supported by most other countries, looked askance at such a "rich man's club," and favored the use of the IMF, both by reason of their world-wide interests and responsibilities, and of their powerful voting power and influence on the Fund as contrasted with their minority position in the Group of Ten.

These opposite viewpoints must eventually be reconciled if the current negotiations are to lead to any concrete results.

The logical lines of such a reconciliation should be fairly obvious to any disinterested observer.

First of all, the Anglo-Saxons should recognize the full validity of Mr. Giscard d'Estaing's basic thesis. The fundamental weakness of the present system does not lie in any actual shortage of international liquidity, but in the haphazard process which now determines the creation—or destruction—of liquidity: "When new fiduciary means are added to gold, they should be issued in accordance with objective rules and through mutually undertaken action. . . . There should be a concerted and limited recourse to additional fiduciary means, instead of the uncertainties and instabilities of the gold-exchange standard."

Second, however, Mr. Giscard d'Estaing should be persuaded to accept the full logic of his own diagnosis. The stability of a reformed international monetary system should be protected not only against the potential inflationary impact of huge U.S. or U.K. deficits, but also against the deflationary dangers of insufficient liquidity creation, and particularly against the Damocles threat of sudden or massive liquidation of existing liquidity instruments—dollars and pounds, especially —into gold metal.[4]

Finally, the conflict of national influences upon the management of future liquidity creation can be solved in far better ways than through the politically explosive juxtaposition of a powerful "rich man's club" of the ten or eleven largest reserve holders of the world, and of a "rump" IMF. The development of *regional* monetary cooperation and integration in Europe and in other parts of the world will, in any case, inevitably entail over future years a growing decentralization of the present IMF responsibilities for world-wide policy harmonization among its member nations.

Rather than share control with the other countries of the Group of Ten over their full contributions to the future creation of international reserve assets, the countries of the European Community should divide these contributions into two parts:

(1) A substantial portion of them should be channelled into a European Reserve Fund, on which they would retain full control, and which should assume responsibility for the harmonization of monetary policies and the financing or correction of balance-of-payments disequilibria *among the EEC countries themselves.*

(2) This would reduce correspondingly the contributions which they should make to the IMF to enable it to deal with future balance-of-payments disequilibria between the EEC area *as a whole* and the rest of the world. It should make it easier to accept normal IMF rules for management of these funds, particularly as the way would remain wide open for informal advance consultation with the U.S., the U.K., and the other countries participating regularly in the meetings of OECD Working Party No. 3.

It would be overoptimistic to hope that these obvious solutions will be accepted by the Ten before several months of further squabbles around the nationalistic negotiating positions evidenced in Tokyo. It is just as obvious, however, that these positions will have to bend in the end to escape from a deadlock whose consequences would be tragic in the long, or even the short, run for each of the Ten as well as for the rest of the world.

4. See, in this respect, the suggestions developed in my article on "The Problem of International Monetary Reform: Major Questions and Prospective Initial Area of Agreement," *Banca Nazionale del Lavoro Quarterly Review* (Rome, March 1964).

P.S.   Much of what is said above was said as well, or better, by Governor Holtrop in Tokyo. I fully concur with his concern to relate the future creation of fiduciary reserve assets to "legitimate growth of demand for owned reserves" rather than to base it "wholly on the financing of payments deficits," as entailed by the functioning of the present gold-exchange standard. The fiduciary reserves created *in accordance with this criterion,* however, can certainly be properly and usefully allocated among desirable uses, in a way far more flexible than implied in the present "collective reserve unit" type of proposals. Full exploration of this thesis, however, would far exceed the boundaries of this paper, and the patience of the reader.

3. THE REPORT OF THE GROUP OF THIRTY-TWO

A third, and uninvited, report was also attracting considerable attention from the officials assembled in Tokyo. This was issued by Professor Machlup, at the conclusion of four series of sessions—at Princeton and Bellagio—of thirty-two academic economists, of widely different backgrounds and persuasions.[1]

These meetings had been organized by Professor Machlup in answer to Secretary Dillon's press announcement (at the 1963 meeting of the IMF) that no academic economist would be invited to testify before the Group of Ten, presumably because it was felt that they never would agree anyway on any practical solution of the problems under debate.

Invitations were sent to nongovernmental economists "with notoriously divergent views, . . . with an international reputation as writers or teachers, . . . from each of the eleven countries represented in the Group of Ten." [2] As stressed repeatedly by Professor Machlup, the meetings were in no way intended to reconcile, or compromise, into agreed conclusions the views of "experts known for their diametrically opposite recommendations," but rather to "interpret their disagreements in a form potentially useful to decision-makers." [3]

The purpose of the conference is an experiment: to find out whether we can identify the differences in factual and normative

1. *International Monetary Arrangements: The Problem of Choice,* Report on the Deliberations of an International Study Group of 32 Economists (Princeton, 1964).
2. *Ibid.,* pp. 8–9. See also the following pages for the full list of participants and the working methods adopted by the group.
3. *Ibid.,* p. 6.

assumptions that can explain the differences in prescriptions for solving the problems of the international monetary system. Presumably we all use the same logic. Hence, if we arrive at different recommendations, we must differ in the assumptions of fact or in the hierarchy of values. To identify and formulate these assumptions would, I believe, be a major step toward a better understanding of the present conflicts of ideas.[4]

Four broad lines of approach to monetary reform were selected for examination: a semiautomatic gold standard, the centralization of international reserves, multiple currency reserves, and flexible exchange rates. The assumptions that would logically justify the choice of each one of these approaches as most appropriate were carefully debated and set out in questionnaire form.[5] When sending out my answers to the questionnaire, I commented as follows on the procedure adopted and on my own answers.

Comments on Questionnaire

(1) I continue to feel that this questionnaire proved an extremely useful and revealing exercise, but primarily as a substitute for the psychoanalyst's couch.

By "smoking out" the hidden assumptions that would make the choice of a system "logically" justifiable, it clearly demonstrated anew what Freud had demonstrated long ago, i.e. that man's logic helps him find *ex post* rationalizations for his instinctive choices, much more than it really determines the latter:

(a) Our two proponents of the semiautomatic gold standard were primarily motivated by a deep distrust of government interference in economic life and its likely inflationary bias.

(b) Flexible rates were advocated by a much broader group, and for partly conflicting reasons: (i) *laissez-faire* preferences, similar to (a) above, but allied to a less optimistic and—to my mind, at least —more realistic appraisal of the practical feasibility and negotiability of semiautomatic gold standard disciplines, particularly in relation to wage-rate adjustments; (ii) equal—or greater—concern with dangers of deflation and unemployment as with dangers of inflation; (iii) nationalistic defense of one's own country's policies as likely to prove

4. *Ibid.*, p. 7.
5. *Ibid.*, Chapter IV, pp. 66–100.

superior to other countries' policies and to any internationally concerted policies; flexible rates thus preserving one's own country's policies against unrequited international disciplines or deflationary (inflationary) impacts from abroad.

(c) The other two solutions under examination both stress the reserve problem, rather than the adjustment problem: (i) Most of their proponents—probably all—regarded themselves as in substantial agreement, and viewed as relatively minor, or secondary, the differences between "centralized reserves" and a "multiple currency reserves" solution, particularly after the latter had been considerably amended by its proponents—under the leadership of Lutz—in a direction making it far closer to the first, and eliminating most, or all, of the instability dangers of sudden or massive shifts between different reserve assets. (ii) Preference for one of these solutions rather than the other—still accepted as a "second best"—reflected (a) primarily, a different appraisal as to practical negotiability and ease of implementation; (b) but also a greater philosophical reluctance, on the part of multiple currency reserve proponents, to full centralization of decisions in an exceedingly powerful body. (c) A more significant difference between the supporters of either of these two solutions should finally be noted: while all regarded as feasible and desirable a substantial amount of international discipline upon national policies, some (e.g. Salant and Harrod) put most of their stress on *generous* provisions for deficit financing, while others emphasized equally, or more, the need for *discretionary* lending aimed primarily at encouraging and supporting the adoption of compatible national policies.

(2) I also continue to believe that some of the (much fewer) ambiguities remaining in the present questionnaire could have been eliminated if the questions had been organized around the three "problems" rather than around the four "solutions." The first two solutions, for instance, are primarily related to the problem of adjustment, but could hardly be regarded as giving a really full and satisfactory solution to the reserves problem. On the other hand, the other two solutions are directly aimed at the reserves problem, but deal only incidentally with the adjustment problem.

Many of the elements of either of the first two solutions—fixed or flexible rates—could therefore be logically integrated with either of the other two—multiple currency reserves or centralized reserves.

Only fully and freely flexible rates, without any intervention whatsoever, would pretend to solve both problems with one single stroke, but such a solution has relatively few defenders and is, moreover, anathema to the officials.

A totally unexpected byproduct of this exercise, however, also deserves a few words of comment.

On the last day of the first Bellagio conference (January 17–23, 1964), I suggested that we might also test the degree to which we could reach consensus on our first, or second-best, answers to three very different *problems* rather than on our preference for any of the four supposed *panaceas* of the questionnaire.

To my utter surprise—and that of everybody else—the draft which I submitted in an attempt to disentangle such a consensus from our previous discussions was unanimously approved by all those present and released to the press, with minor changes, as reflecting faithfully the brunt of our discussions and of the agreement reached on the urgency and nature of a first, conservatory, step aiming at protecting the international monetary system against the most evident and immediate threat to its survival and stability.[6]

Proposals for International Monetary Reform

(1) We all recognize the existence of three separate, but interrelated problems in this area: (a) The need for relatively prompt inter-country balance-of-payments adjustments, so as to avoid the growth of cumulative disequilibrium; (b) The need for long-term adaptation of the over-all volume of world reserves to the full noninflationary possibilities of economic growth; (c) Most urgently, the need for reduction of the vulnerability now imparted to the system by an excessive overhang of international short-term dollar and sterling indebtedness resulting from past reserve accumulation by central banks (i.e. for the liquidation of the so-called "reserve currency system").

(2) Many apparent divergencies between us may reflect the fear that any attention given to any two of these three problems might divert attention from the one to which each of us, as an individual,

6. Although only ten members of the group were present when this text was formally approved, they felt confident that all the major tendencies of the group as a whole were well represented by those in attendance. Professor Heilperin—one of the two proponents of the semiautomatic gold standard—was most active in revising my original draft, and a majority of the other signatories had expressed themselves most forcefully in the debates as favoring flexible rates and/or multiple currency reserves.

attaches primary importance and has devoted most thought and attention, and which he tends as a consequence to regard as more important or urgent than the others.

(3) While essential in the long run, as well as in the short run, the problem of intercountry adjustment (a) will be less troublesome if the other two problems are also given a solution, and particularly if these solutions have favorable side effects reducing opportunities for the development of large-scale maladjustments and stimulating desirable harmonization of national policies; (b) cannot be fully solved by a once-and-for-all reform of the international institutional framework, but will continue to require careful attention to proper policy action, nationally and internationally; (c) must include appropriate use of noninflationary cushioning of temporary disequilibria, as well as stimuli for the correction of persistent disequilibria; (d) must involve more frequent and smoother exchange-rate readjustment by countries which are unable or unwilling to harmonize their national policies with those of other major trading countries; such readjustments should be less biased toward devaluation and against upward revaluations than is now the case; certain institutional reforms might facilitate the attainment of this objective; (e) might, in the view of several members, best be implemented by floating rates among such countries or groups of countries; such a system, however, would depend on a certain degree of international agreement regarding the permissible ranges of fluctuation and the intervention of central banks in the exchange markets for their own or for other countries' currencies.

(4) The solution of the second and third problems listed above (under (1)) depends to a far greater degree on institutional reforms of an international character, such as those actually on the agenda of the Group of Ten.

(5) The solution of the third problem is both more urgent and more feasible than that of the second. Although we may disagree on the proper long-term objectives and structure of reform, we would all agree on the disastrous consequences that might ensue from any massive—and self-defeating—attempt of central banks to exercise their legal right of converting into gold metal the $25 billion of national currency reserves now held by them, primarily as short-term dollar and sterling IOU's. This could be avoided by a funding of such currency reserves, barring their conversion into gold metal, but preserving their full liquidity and present exchange value for future balance-of-payments settlements.

Alternatively, the same objective could be reached by an immediate substantial increase in the dollar price of gold, which would permit the repayment in gold, at the new price, of these dollar and sterling obligations.

Mr. Heilperin would favor this second alternative, while others would favor the first. Mr. Heilperin would, however, also accept the first alternative as a second-best solution, provided that it is coupled with a flat prohibition of future accumulation of national currency reserves by central banks, apart from working balances.

Future adaptation of the world reserve pool to noninflationary growth requirements is a less urgent and more controversial issue. We all agree that any concerted action in this direction should be concerned with the danger of excessive, as well as insufficient reserve creation, and with the avoidance of the instability now involved in shifts from one reserve currency into another, from currencies into gold metal, or from gold metal into currencies.

(a) Some of us are particularly concerned to avoid the need for and dangers of international decisions in this regard: (i) Mr. Heilperin would, for this reason, entrust the whole process of reserve creation to gold production only, and to the preservation of free interconvertibility between gold and currencies for individuals as well as central banks, at a stable gold price about double the present price; (ii) Mr. Lutz and a few others would prefer the enlargement of the list of reserve currencies, coupled with gold guarantees and provisions for consolidation of past balances.

(b) Mr. Triffin and others would accept the need for international decisions in this respect, whether on a world-wide basis within the IMF framework, or by major reserve holders within the framework of the Group of Ten.

———————

Our next conference, at Princeton, on March 21 and 22, 1964, turned its attention from the problem of consolidation to that of future reserve creation. The members present, among which all conflicting schools of thought on the problem were again represented—except for the semiautomatic gold standard, defended throughout only by Messrs. Rueff and Heilperin—concurred in the following statement.

Interim Statement Regarding International Reserves

All sixteen members of the Economists' Study Group, meeting in Princeton on March 21 and 22, 1964, reached consensus on the need to distinguish three major problems about the functioning of the present international monetary system:

(1) the problem of adjustment, i.e. of correcting persistent imbalances in the payments positions of individual countries;

(2) the problem of the aggregate amounts of international reserves, i.e. of providing such amounts as would minimize inflationary and deflationary swings in the world at large; and

(3) the problem of consolidation of reserves, i.e. of avoiding sudden switches between different reserve media.

While each of these problems requires separate attention on its own merits, all three are closely interconnected. The following interim statement, focusing on a more rational organization of international monetary reserves, should not therefore divert attention from other, complementary measures of vital importance, and particularly those aiming at improving the efficiency of the adjustment mechanism.

These and other problems, such as the price of gold or flexible exchange rates, which the Group of Ten has excluded from its agenda, deserve and will receive our full attention in our next meeting. The following statements about the organization of international reserves would in any case remain valid, except under the most extreme form of a flexible-exchange-rate system (which would bar any holdings, purchases, and sales of gold or foreign exchange by monetary authorities).

(1) Monetary authorities will continue to hold international reserves. It can also be expected that the sum total of these holdings will and should expand over the years.

(2) The expansion of the world supply of reserves ought not to depend solely on the accidental conjunction of Western gold production, U.S.S.R. gold sales in Western markets, and changes in net private demand for gold.

(3) International reserve assets other than gold (designated later as "credit reserves") will therefore remain necessary as an important component in the world reserve stock. Variations in the volume of aggregate credit reserves and in their currency composition ought not to be left to unpredictable developments in the balance of payments of reserve-currency countries and to uncoordinated decisions by national and international authorities. Uncoordinated decisions may be mutually contradictory and entail excessive instability.

(4) On this account, coordinated decisions by the monetary authorities of large reserve-holding countries will be necessary regarding

(a) the volume of aggregate credit reserves, (b) the asset composition of such credit reserves, and (c) the commitments, especially as to balance-of-payments policies, of countries on which claims are accumulated.

(5) It is difficult to coordinate day-to-day decisions in this area. But the stability of the international monetary system could be improved by prior agreement among the major countries:

(a) on the long-run rates of change in total reserves held by the participating countries and on the "normal" composition of these reserves;

(b) on the terms of and criteria for extending special credit facilities that should be made available to a participating country coping with strains and crises such as may result, particularly, from international capital movements;

(c) on the choice of appropriate international bodies for taking such decisions and actions (e.g. IMF, OECD, BIS, the Group of Ten, EEC). The rates of change and the asset composition of national reserves need not be specified precisely; ranges or averages would suffice. Special credit facilities could be provided by overdraft arrangements or by relaxing the agreements on asset composition so as to permit an expansion of other countries' holdings of particular currencies.

(6) The agreements proposed in (5a) above could be implemented either through direct holdings of reserve currencies by the major monetary authorities in continuous consultation with one another, or by the indirect holding of such currencies via a reserve-deposit center. The essential issues of who lends, how much, to whom, and under what conditions, raise similar problems whichever approach is chosen.

(a) Some of us prefer, for the following reasons, a solution based on direct currency holdings by, and collaboration among, the major monetary authorities: (i) This would permit the gradual development of informal procedures for reaching consensus. (ii) It would not be necessary to determine from the start formal rules for the distribution of voting power among the participating countries, which would be difficult to negotiate. (iii) It would allow, on occasion, an individual country to go its own way.

(b) Others prefer, for the following reasons, a solution based on a reserve-deposit center: (i) The difficulties of reaching agreement and of making occasional exceptions would be no greater among national representatives on the board of a reserve-deposit center than among the same representatives meeting in continuous consultation. (ii) The reserve-deposit center could hold a wider range of assets than could individual central banks, since the latter would probably confine their holdings to major currencies. It would also avoid the need for frequent transfers of credit-reserve assets among individual central banks. (iii) In the opinion of its proponents, the reserve-deposit center would raise fewer obstacles to extending the guarantees necessary for the full acceptability of credit reserves by central banks.

(c) In view, however, of our unanimous agreement on the similarity of the problems raised by the two systems, those favoring the reserve-deposit center are prepared to accept the multiple-currency system as an intermediate step toward the deposit system, should the latter prove unnegotiable in the immediate future. At the same time, those in favor of the multiple-currency system recognize that unforeseen difficulties in reaching agreement by continuous consultation might justify and impel a later evolution toward a reserve-deposit center.

Preferences and Consensus

In the last round of meetings, held in Bellagio from May 24 to June 6, 1964, three informal polls were taken, at the initiative of Professor Robert A. Mundell. In the first poll, the sixteen participants were asked to rank thirteen alternative proposals or combinations of proposals by order of their preference. The "Triffin plan for liquidity creation combined with modified flexible rates to promote balance-of-payments adjustment" was ranked first, the "Triffin plan alone" second, and the "Triffin plan for liquidity creation combined with gold-standard rules for adjustment" third. "Modified flexible rates (wide margins and/or management) alone" was ranked fourth, and the "semi-automatic gold standard alone" last.

A second, better conceived, poll asked for separate answers to (1) the problem of balance-of-payments adjustments, (2) the desirable types of reserve media, and the regulation of their over-all growth and composition, and (3) the consolidation of outstanding reserve balances. Out of seventeen votes, fourteen were expressed throughout in favor of either adjustable pegs or wider exchange margins, centralized reserve deposits, concerted orientation of future reserve creation, and the conversion of outstanding reserve balances into IMF deposits. One of the three dissents came, naturally enough, from a lone proponent of the semiautomatic gold standard combined with an initial gold revaluation, and the other from the most obdurate advocate of flexible rates (also supported more mildly and in modified versions, such as an enlargement of exchange margins, by several other participants).

The final consensus on policy reached by the conferees is briefly summarized in Professor Machlup's report.[7] It stressed the essential distinction between temporary, reversible balance-of-payments disequilibria, calling for financing rather than adjustment, on the one hand, and, on the other, enduring disequilibria requiring a prompt initiation of adjustments—partly through more frequent exchange-rate changes—together with adequate interim financing. "The mechanism of reserve creation should be overhauled to adjust the expansion of reserves to needs . . . without inducing price inflation," and "the protection of the large outstanding foreign-exchange component of the world reserve pool against sudden or massive conversions into gold should receive a high order of priority" (pp. 101–02).

While "some members of the Group prefer a gradual transformation of the existing system, . . . many of these conferees accept—and others prefer—the centralization of reserves as a solution both to the problem of international liquidity and to the problem of confidence in reserve media. Consistent with their preference for centralization, many conferees endorse 'consolidation' proposals linked to the IMF. Under such arrangements, dollar and sterling reserves would be converted into gold-guaranteed deposits with the IMF, even in advance of more extensive reforms" (p. 105).[8]

One of the most puzzling contrasts between the officials and the academics is the unanimous sense of urgency of the latter regarding the need for consolidation of outstanding foreign-exchange reserve balances, and the total neglect of this problem by the first.[9]

To our great regret, Dr. E. M. Bernstein, former Director of Research of the IMF, and one of the most brilliant world leaders in this field, was unable to join the debate of the Thirty-Two. I reproduce below, after considerable hesitations, a rather intemperate criticism of his views, since they rightly command considerable attention in the

7. *Ibid.,* Chapter V, pp. 101–07.

8. See also Chapter I, Section 3, above, pp. 39–45.

9. The consequences of this neglect became more apparent than ever in 1965. See the article, pp. 340–45, below, on "General de Gaulle's Monetary 'Force de Frappe' and the Sterling Crisis."

U.S. Administration and give some inkling of the concrete nature of the still unpublished French proposals for a Collective Reserve Unit (CRU).

4. THE BIZARRE PROPOSALS OF DR. BERNSTEIN FOR INTERNATIONAL MONETARY REFORM

The current debate on international monetary reform has been greatly enlivened in recent months by the imaginative proposals of Dr. E. M. Bernstein for the establishment of a "composite gold standard" using as international reserve media specially created foreign exchange "reserve units," alongside of present gold holdings, IMF gold tranches and national currencies.[1] Dr. Bernstein's views deserve our most careful consideration, in view of the personality of the author —who was for many years the real brains of the IMF, and the "Eminence Grise" of his first two Managing Directors—and of their partial endorsement by French officials in the current Group of Ten discussions.[2]

Dr. Bernstein shares with most other reformers a common concern for the future growth and stability of the world reserve pool, and the adequacy of the IMF machinery for stabilization assistance, particularly to the underdeveloped countries. He also affirms, with many other writers, a preference for building on existing practices and institutions, and deprecates other attempts—including my own—for more "radical" institutional adaptations and streamlining. He shows, on the other hand, far more interest in warding off future deflationary pressures than in guarding against the inflationary dangers that might threaten the stability of the international monetary system, today or tomorrow.

The following discussion of his concrete proposals will aim pri-

1. Substantial amounts of other national currencies would also be introduced in his system, in addition to traditional dollar and sterling holdings. Dr. Bernstein's proposals have been formulated in "A Practical Program for International Monetary Reserves," *Quarterly Review and Investment Survey,* Model, Roland & Stone, New York, Fourth Quarter 1963, and in various lectures and unpublished memoranda of EMB (Ltd.) Washington, D.C.

2. The French proposals, however, eschew most of the features of the Bernstein plan criticized below, and attack indeed directly, with full Cartesian logic, the basic defects of the gold-exchange standard. They raise totally different questions which cannot be discussed here.

An article published in *Kyklos* (1964), pp. 328–45.

marily at clarifying their adequacy in relation to these broad underlying objectives of the author, and will comment only incidentally on the validity of these objectives themselves.

The Future Growth of World Reserves

Dr. Bernstein estimates at about 3 to 4 per cent a year the normal needs for world reserves growth. Since total reserves for all the countries outside the U.S.S.R.–Chinese bloc are now estimated at about $70 billion, this would mean an annual increase of $2 billion to $3 billion in the years immediately ahead. He himself quotes $2 billion as his target figure, estimates—very modestly—at $500 million the amount expected to come from gold, and considers that another $1.5 billion to $2 billion a year must be made available from other sources.[3]

The Creation of Reserve Units. The major, and most revolutionary, source envisaged to fulfill this purpose would be the creation by the eleven countries of the so-called Paris Club—the Group of Ten plus Switzerland—of a composite "Reserve Unit," consisting of a stated proportion of each of these eleven countries' national currencies. "The proportion of the reserve unit consisting of each currency would be agreed on the basis of its present role as a reserve currency and its importance in international trade and investment." [4] In a more recent version, "the present quotas in the International Monetary Fund" are suggested as "a working basis for determining the proportion of each currency in the reserve unit," although "different proportions could, of course, be fixed initially; and changes in these proportions could be made in the future. . . ." [5]

The amount of reserve units to be created would begin modestly as one ninth, but would rise gradually to one half (in the Model version) or one third (in two later versions), of the global gold reserves of the eleven participating countries (about $34.5 billion at the end of 1963). This would mean, therefore, a sudden, immediate creation of about $3.8 billion reserve units, rising gradually later to $11.5 or $17 billion, plus either one third or one half of future increases in the

3. These somewhat loose calculations and estimates are quoted from p. 6 of a paper presented on April 2, 1964, at the University of Chicago, Conference for Business Economists, and entitled "Reserve Problems and the U.S. Balance of Payments."

4. Model, Roland & Stone paper quoted above, p. 6.

5. Unpublished, but widely distributed, memorandum on "Currency Reserves and the Composite Gold Standard," March 4, 1964.

monetary gold stock of the participants. Assuming the process to be spread over ten years, and accepting Dr. Bernstein's estimate of $500 million a year for new gold accretions, gold and reserve unit holdings together would rise over the period as a whole by about $1.3 to $2 billion a year, i.e. by just about the amounts regarded by him as desirable. After the end of the transition period, however, the annual gold and reserve unit increases would fall abruptly to about $700 million a year (one third or one half more than new gold alone), unless it were decided to continue indefinitely to increase the ratio of reserve units to gold holdings.

National Currency Reserves. National currencies, and particularly the U.S. dollar, would, however, continue to be widely held and used as working balances and monetary reserves by the eleven, and even more by the other countries. Central banks would, in principle, be left free to determine their own policies in this respect, at least in the long run, but Dr. Bernstein *guesses* that Belgium, the Netherlands, Switzerland, and the United Kingdom would continue to hold about 12 per cent of their reserves—excluding reserve units—in foreign exchange, France, Germany, and Italy 15 per cent, and other countries 50 per cent or more.

These guestimates would imply an initial conversion of about $4 billion U.S. dollars into gold and reserve units. This "would not strain the reserves of the United States, particularly as the new system would increase U.S. reserves in the form of reserve units. . . . [Yet,] transitional arrangements would be necessary under which countries would agree to the gradual conversion of their present holdings of U.S. dollars into gold and reserve units." [6]

Nothing is said about the possible liquidation of sterling holdings.

IMF Quotas. The creation of reserve units would not be a substitute for needed increases in IMF quotas, and liberalization of IMF lending.

The Model article proposed that quota drawings be made fully automatic, and unconditional—except that no more than 25 per cent should be so drawn in any twelve-month period—that repayment rules be lengthened from three to four years, and that quotas be increased by about 15 per cent for all members, and by more for certain countries. In his later Chicago paper, Dr. Bernstein now recommends a 25 per cent general quota increase (by about $4 billion), considerably larger increases in the quotas of some industrial countries, and *addi-*

6. Model article, p. 8.

tional provisions for compensatory credits equal to 50 per cent of the new quotas, but entirely outside the quota system, to offset shortfalls in exports, particularly of basic commodities.

Borrowing and Reciprocal Currency Arrangements. Finally, the IMF so-called "General Arrangements to Borrow" and the vast network of reciprocal currency arrangements and nonmarketable dollar or foreign currency security issues negotiated in recent years by Mr. Roosa, would all be retained—and possibly expanded—as additional bulwarks for the stability of the international monetary system.

General Appraisal. It is not easy to appraise the probable impact of such a variety of instruments upon the future rate of growth of international liquidity. They certainly seem more likely to err—at least in the near future—on the side of inflation rather than of deflation, and to allow for too little, rather than too much, discipline on deficit-prone countries.

Secondly, they leave largely untouched the main sources of instability of the present system, i.e. the haphazardness of the creation of foreign-exchange reserves in national currencies, and of fluctuations in gold production, U.S.S.R. gold sales and private gold hoarding. If anything, they would accentuate the instability inherent in the gold component of reserves by linking directly the prospective creation of additional reserve units to the ups and downs in the accretions to the monetary gold stock itself.

Last, but not least, the $13 billion to $20 billion of new reserve units to be created would be distributed to eleven countries, most of which are the richest and most generously endowed with reserves already, but none would be made available to other, reserve-poor, countries. These, however, would benefit—along with the eleven countries—from more automatic access to larger IMF resources.

The recipients of reserve units would, of course, pay for them in their own currency, but these IOU's would not be subject to any repayment provision whatsoever. This would certainly be a valuable advantage for any recipient country which turns out to experience heavy deficits in the future, although it might be unwelcome by those which would expect larger and inflationary surpluses as a result of the excessive facilities unconditionally placed at the disposal of their partners in the Reserve Unit Club.

The Allocation of Reserve Units
Among the Eleven Countries

The allocation of reserve units among the eleven participating countries would, in fact, obey two sets of contradictory rules, whose reconciliation would introduce other complexities and oddities into the proposed system.

Initial Allocation by the IMF. The initial allocation would be determined by the agreed, fixed—although changeable by later agreement—proportions determining the actual composition of the composite reserve unit as between the eleven participating currencies. Each of the eleven countries would buy from the IMF with its own national currency, its allotted share of reserve units. The reserve units issued by the IMF would thus be backed by—and "represent"—equivalent IMF holdings of the eleven currencies according to the proportions agreed upon by members.

Reshuffling Among Members. An entirely different rule would govern the retention of reserve units by the participating countries. Each country's share would be determined as a fixed proportion of its gold holdings, and periodically readjusted to reflect any changes in such gold holdings arising from subsequent gold settlements among themselves and with the outside world.

The countries which had bought—under rule one—an amount of reserve units in excess of their share under rule two "could request the Trustee to convert sufficient reserve units into gold to reduce their holdings to the required ratio." Conversely, "countries with a deficiency of reserve units would have to transfer sufficient gold to the Trustee in return for reserve units to bring their holdings to the required ratio." [7]

These transfers of gold and reserve units would cancel out as far as the IMF, acting as Trustee, is concerned. Later adjustments to settlements among the eleven countries themselves would not be necessary since "in their transactions with each other, countries would always convert national currencies into gold and reserve units in the prescribed ratio." [8]

Further—although by no means unmanageable—complications would arise, however, as a result of gold settlements with nonparticipating countries.

7. March 4, 1964, paper, p. 7
8. *Ibid.*, p. 8.

Finally, countries could either avoid—or create, if they wish—the need for gold and reserve units transfers by shifting—unilaterally or under bilateral agreements—the composition of their reserves as between gold and national currencies.

A Hypothetical Example. These various alternatives make it impossible to determine how the system would work in practice. A highly simplified example, however, may be constructed by abstracting from the complexities arising from future shifts in members' gold holdings, and discussing only the reshuffling involved in the initial allocations of reserve units under the two rules formulated above.

The latest suggestions of Dr. Bernstein contemplate a total creation of reserve units equal to one third of the participating countries' gold holdings. Such holdings totalled about $34.5 billion at the end of last year, and would have entailed, therefore, the creation of $11.5 billion reserve units.[9]

These $11.5 billion would be allocated among the eleven countries in proportion to their Fund quotas, a special quota being assigned for this purpose to Switzerland. These proportions are shown in Column (a) of the accompanying table, and the resulting allocation—in dollar terms—in column (d).

As a result of this quota allocation, however, the United Kingdom, Sweden, Canada, and Japan would have received far more reserve units than they should hold, i.e. far more than a third of their outstanding gold reserves, while the United States, the EEC countries, and Switzerland would have received far too little (see column (e)).

Large transfers of reserve units (totalling in effect more than $2 billion) from the first group of countries to the second would be called for. If these were made against reverse gold payments, however—as they would, in principle—the proportionate gold holdings of each member would change, and a new reshuffling—in the opposite direction—would have to take place, modifying once again the gold holdings of each country, and calling for new transfers. Reshufflings would succeed each other, in an opposite direction each time, and taper off gradually until no more is called for.

9. This would, of course, be done by stages, over a period of maybe 10 years, and the total amount of reserve units to be created would presumably have increased by then, *pari passu* with the members' gold holdings. We abstract here from this, and from the gold reshuffling among members that might have occurred in the meantime, both as a result of current settlements and of the anticipated partial liquidation of outstanding dollar balances (and presumably sterling balances also, although nothing is mentioned in this respect).

Fortunately for the sanity of the Trustee and of the central banks concerned, a simple mathematical formula may be derived to short-cut this merry-go-round. The final gold holdings of each member (G) under the assumptions stated, should be equal to the sum of its initial gold position and reserve unit allotment by the Trustee $(G_0 + R_0)$, multiplied by the agreed ratio of gold to reserve units (γ) and divided

TABLE 1

THE BERNSTEIN PLAN IN ACTION
(on the basis of December 1963 quotas and estimated gold reserves)

Countries and areas	Per cent shares of			Impact of reserve unit allotments and reshuffling (in billions of U.S. dollars)			
	IMF quotas	Gold reserves	Total reserves	Quota allot-ment	⅓ of initial gold holdings	⅓ of re-shuffled gold holdings	Gold losses (−) or gains (+) (g = d − f)
	(a)	(b)	(c)	(d)	(e)	(f)	d − f
I. United States	39	45	35	4.48	5.20	5.02	−0.54
II. United Kingdom	18	7.2	6.5	2.07	0.83	1.14	+0.93
III. EEC	25	36	41	2.88	4.10	3.80	−0.92
1. Germany	7.5	11.2	15.9	0.86	1.23	1.17	−0.31
2. France	7.5	9.2	10.1	0.86	1.07	1.02	−0.16
3. Italy	2.6	6.8	6.8	0.30	0.77	0.65	−0.35
4. Netherlands	3.9	4.6	4.3	0.45	0.53	0.51	−0.06
5. Belgium	3.2	4.0	4.0	0.37	0.47	0.44	−0.07
IV. Other participants	18	12	17.5	2.07	1.37	1.54	+0.53
1. Switzerland	(6.4)	8.2	6.4	0.74	0.93	0.89	−0.15
2. Sweden	1.4	0.5	1.5	0.16	0.07	0.09	+0.07
3. Canada	5.3	2.4	5.4	0.61	0.27	0.35	+0.26
4. Japan	4.8	0.8	5.2	0.55	0.10	0.21	+0.34
Total	100	100	100	11.50	11.50	11.50	0

1. The underlying estimates are from the May 1964 issue of *International Financial Statistics*.

2. The hypothetical Swiss quota basis has been calculated on the basis of the relative share of Switzerland global monetary reserves, and is probably overestimated. A lower estimate, however, would call for even larger transfers than shown in column (g), and would not affect significantly the calculations for other members.

3. See text of this article for other qualifications, and particularly for the much larger impact of the partial liquidation—anticipated by Dr. Bernstein—of outstanding dollar balances.

by the same ratio *plus* one ($\gamma + 1$). Thus, the final gold position of each member should be equal to

$$G = (G_0 + R_0) \frac{\gamma}{\gamma + 1};$$

its final reserve units holdings should be equal to

$$R = (G_0 + R_0) \frac{1}{\gamma + 1};$$

and the difference between its initial and final gold holdings ($G - G_0$) and reserve units holdings ($R - R_0$) would indicate the transfers of gold and reserve units necessitated by the scheme. As can be read from Column (g) of the accompanying table, about $1.6 billion of gold would be paid in by the United States ($540 million), the EEC countries ($920 million) and Switzerland ($150 million) against additional purchases of reserve units, and paid out to the United Kingdom ($930 million), Sweden ($70 million), Canada ($260 million), and Japan ($340 million) against corresponding reductions in their reserve units account.

Most of the EEC countries, however, could escape the above gold losses by presenting instead a portion of their outstanding dollar holdings to the United States for repayment in gold (three fourths) and reserve units (one fourth). Dr. Bernstein anticipates that such conversions might reach $4 billion. If this guess is correct, the total drain on U.S. gold would be about $3.5 billion. It might conceivably rise to twice as much, or even more, if dollar holders developed a higher preference than assumed by Dr. Bernstein for his composite package of gold (¾) and gold-guaranteed reserve units (¼), as against unguaranteed dollars.[10] Finally, the U.S. would have to spend further amounts of gold and reserve units to acquire the "substantial amount of reserves in the currencies of other participating countries," which Dr. Bernstein regards as "essential." [11]

To guard against the excessive gold losses that all this might entail, two alternative rules are suggested. The first would be that no country should reduce its present holdings of dollars and other currencies as long as it has a balance-of-payments surplus. Alternatively, dollar holdings might be made more attractive through the conversion of

10. Similar liquidation of the relatively modest amounts of U.K. sterling balances held by other members of the Club would cause a smaller, but even less bearable, drain on the U.K. slender gold reserves.

11. March 4, 1964, paper, p. 10.

outstanding unguaranteed balances, at the option of the holders, into nonmarketable, longer-term securities, bearing agreed interest rates and exchange guarantees, and convertible before maturity whenever a country has a balance-of-payments deficit. Curiously enough, however, both rules would cease to operate at the end of the transition period—i.e. "when the final stage of the composite gold standard is in effect"—and countries would then "be under no obligation to hold any currency in any amount." [12]

The hypothetical nature of this elaborate guesswork should, however, be strongly emphasized, as each country would be free to shift at will—on its own initiative, or as a result of bilateral pressures or negotiations—from gold and reserve units into dollar (or other foreign currency) balances, or vice versa, and modify thereby out of all recognition the settlements pattern described above.

Are All These Complexities Really Necessary?

Preserving Past Techniques and Machinery. The first claim made by Dr. Bernstein in favor of his plan is that it builds on what exists, and avoids the harsh disciplines and surrenders of national sovereignty implied in the conversion of the Fund into a world central bank.

This is true insofar as all previous channels for the creation of "credit reserves" are preserved intact, or even enlarged. The establishment of the reserve unit system will be superimposed upon—rather than dispense with—IMF quotas, quota increases and general borrowing arrangements, the continued and even amplified use of national currencies as international reserves, bilateral swaps, and swap stand-by agreements, etc. One may doubt, however, whether such a complicated structure is really necessary, and whether the creation of such a new, powerful, and revolutionary technique as that of reserve units should not be designed to replace some, at least, of the techniques previously created to serve—less efficiently—the very same purpose. The time has certainly come to give some attention to the simplification and streamlining of the monstrous jumble of overlapping instruments and stopgaps inherited from past crises and hurried salvaging operations.

---

12. *Ibid.,* pp. 10–11. Except for this latter provision, the second of Dr. Bernstein's alternatives is identical—if I understand it correctly—to the creation of "reserve certificates" suggested to solve the same problem in my article on "The Problem of International Monetary Reform: Major Questions and Prospective Initial Area of Agreement," *Banca Nazionale del Lavoro Quarterly Review* (March 1964).

The most difficult decision to be faced in this respect is, admittedly, the elimination of national currencies as international reserves, except possibly for moderate amounts of working balances. This may possibly prove unnegotiable in the short run, but some attempt should be made, at the very least, to introduce a minimum of order in the over-all expansion, or liquidation, of this most haphazard and most vulnerable component of the present reserve system, rather than merely contemplate additional—and potentially inflationary—means of rescuing the currencies involved, and the international monetary system itself, from the crises which the wanton accumulation and liquidation of national currency reserves would be almost certain to unleash, in the future as in the past.

Avoiding International Disciplines on National Sovereignty. I have discussed elsewhere the reasons why the institution of minimum reserve deposits with the IMF would not involve the substantive and revolutionary surrenders of sovereignty which the emotional use of the word "superbank" or even "central bank" evokes in the mind of the reader.[13]

Far more revolutionary and unprecedented surrenders of sovereignty by prospective lenders would, indeed, be required by the Bernstein plan. Deficit countries would be assured *vast* and *automatic* access to IMF credits and, in the case of the eleven members of the Club, to reserve unit credits—without any specific repayment obligation—regardless of the wisdom or folly of their own policies, and of their acceptability to the lenders and to the international community itself.

Distribution and Maturity of the Reserve Unit Credits. The main attractiveness of the reserve unit system to hard-headed central bankers is that the resulting credit claims would be accumulated exclusively on presumably responsible club members, rather than in the presumably weaker currencies of the developing countries. The reverse of the coin is, of course, the milking of the international credits created by such a system in favor of the richest, at the exclusion of the countries most in need of such assistance.[14]

If international credits remained discretionary—as they have al-

13. See, for instance, *The Evolution of the International Monetary System: Historical Reappraisal and Future Perspectives,* Princeton Study No. 12 in International Finance (June 1964), Section III F.

14. The latter, however, would also be granted large automatic credit facilities by the IMF itself.

ways been up to now—and conditional upon the implementation by the borrowers of internationally acceptable policies, there would be no reason on earth to decree in advance that all but eleven countries will forever be barred from any access to the reserve unit credits to be established in the future in order to adjust international liquidity to the legitimate needs of world economic growth.[15]

Adequate exchange guarantees—or, *a fortiori,* gold value guarantees, as suggested by Dr. Bernstein—and guarantees against default should, in any case, go a long way to remove the lenders' reluctance to assist poorer countries, as well as the richest.[16]

Academic economists, on the other hand, may be tempted to regard the absence of any specified maturity for repayment as the cardinal virtue of the reserve unit proposal, since any such repayment would have to be offset by larger extensions of new credit in order to sustain the persistent and permanent growth of the world reserve pool, presumed to be desirable as a long-run trend over the years to come. The same purpose might be served, however, in a more traditional manner, by the accumulation of a growing investment portfolio, subject to reshuffling among various money markets in the light of the need to preserve international monetary stability, and particularly to compensate for reversible, but undesirable, movements of short-term capital.[17]

Global Amounts of Credit Reserve Creation. A system of minimum deposit reserve requirements with the IMF, combined with basically discretionary rather than automatic IMF lending, would certainly provide a smoother and more flexible method of reserve creation than the uncoordinated overlapping of reserve unit injections related to—and magnifying—the fluctuations in the world monetary gold stock, credit extensions by the IMF, and unilateral or bilateral shifts in foreign currency accumulation by central banks.

The proportion of each country's global reserves to be held in the form of IMF deposits could be readjusted, from time to time, in order to provide the IMF with the lending *capacity* deemed necessary to feed

15. There are good arguments, however, in favor of an *indirect* financing of long-term development needs, rather than for the *direct* assistance envisaged in the Stamp plan. See Section III C of my Princeton Study, quoted above.

16. *Ibid.,* Section E.

17. See again Section III C of the Princeton Study just quoted, and Section VII, 4 of "The International Network of World Payments: An Integrated Approach," *Weltwirtschaftliches Archiv* (Kiel, 1964), reproduced above, pp. 118–32.

the full potential of noninflationary growth rates in the world economy. Such deposits would automatically adjust the minimum deposits of each country to fluctuations in its own over-all reserves and balance of payments and, therefore, to the potential need of other members for settlement facilities with it.

The global resources placed thereby at the disposal of the IMF would hardly be subject to sudden and massive contraction, since fluctuations in national balances of payments and settlements could only entail a reshuffling of the Fund's deposits from the deficit to the surplus countries. These resources would increase *pari passu* with increases in the world reserve pool arising both from new gold production and from the IMF's own lending operations.

The Fund, however, would be under no compulsion to pass on automatically to prospective borrowers—through new loans and investments—every increment in its lending capacity. Its policy in this respect should take account of the over-all inflationary, or deflationary, pressures discernible in the world economy, and reflected in part in the member countries' legitimate requests for Fund assistance. The Fund might accumulate unused lending capacity—reflected in increased gold holdings—to combat world-wide inflationary pressures, and draw on it in times of depression and unemployment.

The Problem of Management. The international decisions inevitably involved in any attempt at a rational management of the world reserve pool would, just as inevitably, raise difficult questions of relative voting power for the participating countries. There is nothing new in this, and similar questions have proved soluble in past EPU and IMF operations, without any of those extensive surrenders of sovereignty which might be regarded—rightly or wrongly—as excessive or unnegotiable at the present juncture. The maximum lending capacity of the Fund would be determined by the minimum proportion of deposits to global reserves agreed to in the initial Treaty, and subject only to later agreed revisions, in exactly the same way as it has been determined in the past by IMF quotas and periodic quota increases. Further safeguards against inflationary abuses of the Fund's lending capacity could be provided in the Treaty itself.

Yet it is highly doubtful whether major prospective reserve holders —particularly in Western Europe—would be willing to entrust entirely to the IMF, as now constituted, the management of the large and constantly growing amounts of "credit reserves" that may have to be created over future years. The emergence of Working Party No. 3 of the OECD and of the Group of Ten already constitutes an operational recognition of this fact, and would be consolidated further by Dr. Bernstein's Reserve Unit Club.

It may very well be that some such group will prove necessary to orient, and manage in part, the future evolution of our international monetary system. Yet, this might reduce the IMF to a "rump" body, dealing primarily with the poorer nations of the underdeveloped world, while all major decisions are channelled through the exclusive Ten or Eleven Countries' Club.

The alternative would be a realistic decentralization of the IMF machinery itself, recognizing the useful role which regional monetary organizations could play in world-wide monetary cooperation, and for implementing among such groups as the EEC, the Central American Monetary Union, etc., a closer degree of monetary integration than is either feasible or desirable at this stage on a world-wide scale.

Since the views of a rival reformer might inevitably be biased in favor of his own plan, let me conclude instead with two recent quotations from two highly respected organs of public opinion.

The New York Times of May 25, 1964, was probably right in its news-reporting (in a dispatch from M. J. Rossant) about the prevailing mood of official negotiators regarding the international monetary system: "The prospect is that the plans for its present refurbishing will call for shiny new bumpers, brake linings, and shock absorbers. As Mr. Roosa sees it, that is all that is needed." It may have been equally right, however, in its editorial on "International Monetary Reform" of the previous day, in concluding that "it would be a mistake to rely solely on a structure that has so often survived crisis by the narrowest of margins. The very fact that the international monetary mechanism is functioning smoothly, and can be expected to cope with any immediate liquidity problem, suggests that the time is ripe for the consideration of bolder and more permanent reforms. . . . A searching examination of more revolutionary schemes, including the transforming of the IMF into an international central bank should go forward."

Two weeks earlier, the London *Economist* had drawn attention, in these terms, to a most significant and encouraging speech of the IMF Managing Director: "The . . . gloomy prospects for positive action on international liquidity were lightened just a shade this week, and from an encouraging source. M. Pierre-Paul Schweitzer, who many people frankly feared would be a consolidating rather than a reforming chief of the International Monetary Fund, has guardedly but firmly thrown the weight of the Fund on the reformist side, just as the national officials in the Group of Ten are bogged down in disagreement. While keeping to the position that liquidity is adequate now, M. Schweitzer gave a number of hard reasons why he is sure that provision for new forms of liquidity must be made in the future; and he mentioned, besides an increase in Fund quotas, two innovations that could eventually be far-reaching. The first is the possible 'acceptance by the Fund of deposits'; this looks something like a voluntary version of the Maudling plan, which has often been suggested in these columns. His second suggestion is 'the introduction of investments at the initiative of the Fund,' which probably refers to investments not in loans to underdeveloped countries à la Stamp but rather in traditional money market assets—à la Triffin. There is a possible precedent in the Fund's purchase of American Treasury bills for gold; if it did the same against its own deposits that would be the first step to real international central banking. The ministers of the Ten may have the last word this year; but a constructive blueprint from the Fund's parallel study group could help shame them into action later."

5. GENERAL DE GAULLE'S MONETARY "FORCE DE FRAPPE" AND THE STERLING CRISIS

Our anachronistic monetary system has been triggering for years repeated speculative attacks on the two reserve currencies on which it now rests to such an excessive extent: the pound and the dollar. Skilful cooperation among central banks, to an unprecedented and unexpected degree, barely avoided, two months ago, a collapse of the pound sterling. Two weeks ago, the mighty dollar itself had to weather —far more easily—the rumors let loose in Paris that de Gaulle might use to the hilt his monetary *force de frappe,* i.e. his legal right to demand from the U.S. Treasury partial, but massive, repayments into gold metal of the huge short-term U.S. debt (about $1.3 billion) held as monetary reserves by the Bank of France.

This article appeared in Italian in *L'Espresso* (Rome, January 31, 1965). See also, "Sterling, the Dollar, de Gaulle, and Gold," in *Challenge* (New York, April 1965), pp. 19–23 and "Will 1965 Repeat 1931?" in *The Reporter* (New York, April 8, 1965), pp. 27–30.

Background

These and other previous crises spring from two distinct, but closely interrelated, root-causes: the persistent balance-of-payments deficits of the U.S. and the recurrent deficits of the U.K., on the one hand, and, on the other, the haphazardness and vulnerability of the world reserve system itself.

The interrelationship of the two problems shows up in the fact that capital movements, rather than trade or current account deficits, account for most of the over-all deficits or reserve losses suffered by the United States and the United Kingdom during the repeated crises of the last five years.

This is most evident in the case of the United States, whose large and growing surpluses on current account reached a record high last year, but have been more than absorbed by huge and ever increasing capital outflows, now running at an annual rate of about $8 billion, and even close to $10 billion if we add to the official estimates—as we should—annual reinvestments of unrepatriated foreign earnings. Such an excessive drain of funds from the U.S. economy is admittedly influenced by interest-rate differentials, our tax-treatment of foreign earnings, the European investment boom linked to the formation of the Common Market, etc. It is also due in large part, however, to speculative outflows of short-term funds prompted by the growing conviction that the weaknesses of the present key-currencies system will force, sooner or later, a considerable reshuffle in the existing pattern of gold prices and exchange rates. It is certainly noteworthy that the normal *net inflows* of short-term capital toward the major money market in the world today ($500 million a year in the early 1950s, $1 billion a year in the late 1950s, and a record $1.8 billion in 1959) were succeeded by huge and persistent *outflows* ($2.2 billion in 1960, $1.7 billion in 1961, and $1.8 billion in 1962), starting with the London gold crisis of 1960.

The position of the United Kingdom is vastly different, its current account surpluses being uncomfortably small for a major financial, economic, and political power, with vast responsibilities in the world. Yet, here too, repeated crises have been primarily associated with highly volatile movements of private capital. In each of the three years 1961–63, sudden and massive shifts between net *outflows* and *inflows* of private capital accounted for as much as 85 per cent (in 1961) and

113 per cent (in 1963) of Britain's net reserve losses, and 97 per cent of her net reserve gains (in 1962). Even the huge current account deficit of 1964 has certainly been greatly influenced by *speculative* stock-building in anticipation of the election and of possible import taxes, devaluation, or restrictions.

The measures used by central banks to quell each crisis, only after it had erupted and only through relatively short-term absorption of excess sterling and dollar balances, were undoubtedly successful, but could not allay for long the fears which fed such speculative movements and the consequent U.S. and U.K. deficits. Indeed, they may even have aggravated the uneasiness of private speculators, highly conscious of the continuous growth of U.S. and U.K. indebtedness, legally convertible into gold on sight or short notice. Central banks, on the other hand, felt they could not give up such right to gold conversion without exposing themselves to unreasonable exchange risks and to an unlimited and inflationary financing of future U.S. and U.K. deficits.

De Gaulle

France's dramatic announcement of its forthcoming conversion of excess dollar balances into gold metal should be viewed in that light. The Finance Minister insisted that they were purely "technical" in character, meaning a mere "return to normalcy" in the composition of the Bank of France reserves. Reserves held in a *national* currency—be it sterling or the dollar—have long been anathema to the French, who still remember the losses incurred by them thereby on the occasion of the 1931 sterling devaluation.

Yet, the French could hardly have been unaware of the political impact of their gesture on other countries and on the much vaunted central bank cooperation which has so far preserved the exchange stability of the dollar and the pound through the willingness of all to absorb additional balances, rather than converting these and previously acquired balances into gold. Their announcement may have been timed to back up their own plan for international monetary reform, by demonstrating their readiness to convert their excess balances into gold, if the U.S. and the U.K. continue to block the French proposal for a so-called "composite reserve unit," in which sterling and the dollar would have to share their privileged reserve currency status with other major currencies, including the French franc itself. This proposal must, indeed, be most attractive to General de Gaulle himself, as it reconciles his bold, Cartesian vision of more orderly and logical monetary arrangements for the future with his emotional bias against Anglo-American domination or pre-eminence, in this field as well as in others.

Finally, on a broader and more purely political plane, the French move may add to the credibility of the General's monetary *"force de frappe,"* as a bargaining counter in other international negotiations closer to his heart and preoccupations, such as the hated NATO multilateral force (MLF) project, the neutralization of Southeast Asia, the normalization of economic and political relations with Eastern Europe, etc.

We do not have, therefore, to choose between a "technical" and a "political" interpretation of the French announcement. They constitute *complementary,* rather than *alternative,* explanations, although the forcefulness of each must undoubtedly have been weighed very differently by the technical and the political advisers of the President.

The Forthcoming Sterling Crisis

If this interpretation is correct, the speculative flurry that followed the French announcement will soon die down. The General's monetary *force de frappe* and bargaining power will not be fully and prematurely engaged—and dissipated—to force a gold revaluation and a chaotic free-for-all and *sauve qui peut* in the exchange markets. President de Gaulle is not M. Rueff.

The real danger is that this new victory of the officials over the speculators might induce anew a false sense of security and complacency, that might again delay necessary reforms of our international monetary system. The greatest threat to sterling—and the dollar—will come next spring or summer with the termination of the "six-month trinity" erected to defend it last November: six-month credit lines, six-month 7 per cent discount rate, and six-month 15 per cent import surcharge.

If this were to force a substantial devaluation of sterling—by more than 10 or 15 per cent—speculators would be practically unanimous in their expectation that other currencies would inevitably follow suit, at least part of the way. Sterling would appear safer, at least for a few months, than any currency that was still resisting devaluation. The shift of funds from dollars into sterling, not only from foreign owners, but from American firms and individuals as well, might reach such enormous proportions as to defy any likely reverse credit arrangements among the central banks concerned.

Enormous pressure will thus be put on the British authorities, particularly by the United States, to avoid any devaluation of sterling, or to limit it at least to a more modest size that would constitute a less inviting gamble for speculators. The danger is that sterling might then have to be propped up by other means, including a whole array of taxes and subsidies, or even a relapse into quantitative import restrictions and exchange controls.

The Solution

Neither of these two gloomy outcomes of the smoldering sterling-dollar crisis is as yet unavoidable, but time is running short. More sensible solutions of the problem would require:

(1) determined action by Britain—which she is clearly ready to undertake—to implement an effective incomes policy, and to stimulate the modernization of her industrial apparatus and its adaptation to new market demands;

(2) U.S. action to remove the fiscal distortions that now stimulate an excessive rate of capital outflows, and particularly the nonrepatriation of American earnings abroad;

(3) last but not least, a consolidation of *outstanding* short-term U.S. and U.K. debts to the major central banks, in ways that would preserve the *full liquidity* and *exchange value* of such dollar and sterling balances for international settlements, but rule out wanton and unsustainable conversions into gold metal.

The last of these three measures would be essential. Although it would merely formalize into binding agreements the *de facto,* but precarious, cooperation extended up to now to the U.S. and the U.K. by the major reserve holders, two obstacles have to be overcome.

One is the fear that any such consolidation would be followed by new U.S. and U.K. deficits, financed once more by renewed and inflationary outflows of short-term dollar and sterling indebtedness into the coffers of other central banks. A necessary *quid pro quo* for the acceptance of the consolidation of *outstanding* dollar and sterling balances held by the major central banks, would be an agreement specifically outlawing or limiting the *future reconstitution* of such balances, in accordance with some joint "multilateral surveillance" procedures as are already envisaged, in general terms, in the recent Group of Ten report.

A second, although far less urgent, problem lies in the need to reconcile the conflicting views of the U.S. and U.K., on the one hand, and of the continental Europeans, on the other, on the nature and management of the "new type of international reserve asset" which should, as agreed also by the Group of Ten, ultimately replace unbridled dollar deficits—which have in recent years fed close to 80 per cent of other countries' reserve growth—as a necessary supplement to gold in the world reserve system. The solution of the present conflict of views and negotiating positions on this issue would be accelerated if:

(1) the U.S. and the U.K. agreed on the need for the EEC to assume full jurisdiction and responsibility over the handling of intra-EEC balance-of-payments disequilibria, relieving the IMF of financial responsibility for the financing of such disequilibria;

(2) the EEC countries, on the other hand, agreed to channel through the IMF the resources needed to enable the Fund to deal with the disequilibria between the EEC area *as a group* and the rest of the world;

(3) all IMF members recognized the inevitability of applying different voting rules, more closely related to the relative contributions of the creditor countries, to the utilization of the *new* resources that might be made available to the Fund by the large reserve holders and surplus countries, outside the normal pattern of quotas embodied in the present Articles of Agreement.

The recurrent crises of the last four years, and the far worse crises that loom ahead, should be sufficient to elicit at long last the concrete agreements on international monetary reform so clearly called for by the agreed diagnosis of the Group of Ten and of the IMF regarding the fundamental defects and vulnerability of the present system.

The alternative to action now is another 1931 tomorrow.

Chapter IX: Updating the Triffin Plan

THE FOLLOWING TEXT of a speech delivered at the Federal Trust, in London, on May 24, 1965, and published as a special issue of *Moorgate and Wall Street* (London, Summer 1965) provides an apt—but, alas, still provisional—conclusion to an endless debate. It amends, in some important respects, my 1959 proposals in the direction of greater flexibility and negotiability.

I have always had my doubts about the truth of an old Latin proverb: *"Bis repetita placent."* The opposite English saying "Familiarity breeds contempt" is probably more realistic.

I apologize, therefore, to those of you who will find little that is really new in what I can tell you today about an old problem. I hope, however, that you will allow me to share your blame with those high officials and friends of mine who are responsible, at least in part, for the slow pace with which its solution has been gradually approached over the last six years of a dully repetitive debate.

The announced title of my talk, "The International Monetary System," leaves me in doubt also as to whether I am expected to describe to you the *present* international monetary system, or the one that may emerge *tomorrow* from the discussions now under way in the IMF and the Group of Ten. The only solution I see is to talk about both, especially since it would be impossible to talk intelligently about the second without exploring first the deficiencies of the present system which inspire the clamor for reform and the constraints which existing institutions inevitably impose upon the shape and speed of feasible adjustments.

Prisoner of his past, man has never been fully master of his future. What will be is always influenced by what is, as much or more than by what is desirable in the abstract. Before gazing into what the international monetary system of the future could be, let us see, therefore, what it is today.

What It Is

I have tried to condense into three simple tables the main highlights of our present international monetary system.

The first of these tables shows, in absolute and in percentage terms, the sources which have fed international reserve increases over the last seven years. For the world as a whole, 16 per cent has come from new gold production in the West, an equal amount from Soviet gold sales in Western markets, 8 per cent from international organizations, and 60 per cent from fast-rising reserve balances in national

TABLE 1

SOURCES OF GROSS RESERVE INCREASES, 1958–64

	In billions of U.S. $	In per cent of totals I and III
I. World	**13.6**	**100**
A. Monetary gold	**4.3**	**31**
1. From Western sources	2.2	16
a. production	*8.6*	*64*
b. private absorption (−)	*−6.4*	*−48*
2. U.S.S.R. sales	2.1	16
B. International organizations	**1.1**	**8**
1. Reserve claims on IMF	1.8	14
2. Gold sales	−0.7	−5
C. National currencies excluding EPU balances	**8.2**	**60**
1. Dollars	6.9	51
2. Sterling	0.7	5
3. Other and discrepancies	0.6	4
II. Reserves centers	**−8.2**	
III. Other countries:	**21.8**	**100**
A. Net reserve losses of reserve centers	**16.6**	**76**
1. United States	15.6	72
2. United Kingdom	1.0	5
B. International organizations	**0.3**	**2**
1. World impact (I,B. above)	1.1	5
2. Minus lending to reserve centers	−0.8	−4
a. United States	*−0.6*	*−3*
b. United Kingdom	*−0.2*	*−1*
C. Increases in world monetary gold (I,A. above)	**4.3**	**20**
D. Other currencies, and discrepancies (I,C3. above)	**0.6**	**3**

SOURCE: World reserve estimates are calculated from the revised series of the May 1965 *International Financial Statistics.*

currencies, overwhelmingly short-term dollar and sterling IOU's. If we add to this growing short-term indebtedness of the two reserve center countries of the system their losses of reserve assets, i.e. mostly gold, we find that their net reserve drains have fed more than three fourths of other countries' reserve gains, i.e. seven to eight times the amounts derived from gold production in the West, three fourths of Western gold production having been absorbed by private channels and particularly by the tripling or quadrupling of speculative gold hoarding purchases ever since the October 1960 gold flare-up in the London market.

The second table illustrates the impact of these movements upon the net reserve position of the two reserve centers of the system. The

TABLE 2

U.S. AND U.K. MONETARY RESERVES AND INTERNATIONAL INVESTMENT POSITION, 1957–64
(in billions of U.S. dollars)

	United States			United Kingdom		
End of year	1957	1962	1964	1957	1962	1964
I. Net monetary reserves	**15.9**	**3.5**	**0.3**	**−4.2**	**−2.8**	**−5.1**
A. Gross assets:	**24.8**	**17.2**	**16.7**	**2.4**	**3.3**	**2.3**
1. Gold	22.9	16.1	15.5	1.6	2.6	2.1
2. IMF reserve position	2.0	1.1	0.8	—	0.5	—
3. Foreign exchange	—	0.1	0.4	0.8	0.2	0.2
B. Liabilities (−) to:	**−8.9**	**−13.7**	**−16.4**	**−6.5**	**−6.1**	**−7.4**
1. IMF	−0.2	−0.8	−0.8	−0.3	—	−0.5
2. Foreign monetary authorities	−8.7	−12.9	−15.6	−6.2	−6.1	−6.9
II. Other international assets and						
liabilities (net)	**28.9**	**46.6**			**7.4**	
A. Short-term	**−4.7**	**−1.9**			**−2.6**	
B. Long-term	**33.6**	**48.6**			**9.9**	
1. Official	13.6	16.0			−4.4	
2. Private	20.0	32.5			14.3	
a. portfolio	*0.3*	*2.9*			*6.3*	
b. direct investment	*19.7*	*29.6*			*8.0*	
III. Total	**44.8**	**50.1**			**4.6**	

SOURCES: This table attempts to present in comparable form estimates derived from the following sources: (1) the *Survey of Current Business* estimates of the U.S. balance of payments and international investment position; (2) the *incomplete* estimates of the U.K. international investment position published in the March 1964 issue of the *Bank of England Quarterly Bulletin,* from officially reported gross monetary assets, and from rough estimates of the evolution and breakdown of short-term liabilities pieced together from various tables of the *Bank of England Quarterly Bulletin,* particularly in an article on "The Balance of Payments: Methods of Presentation" (December 1964 issue, pp. 276–86).

United Kingdom's liabilities to foreign monetary authorities have, of course, long exceeded its gross monetary reserves, but this excess indebtedness has risen sharply in the last two years from $2,800 million to $5,100 million. As for the United States, its net reserves have fallen even more precipitiously, from $15,900 million at the end of 1957 to less than $300 million at the end of last year and $100 million in February of this year.

That this process cannot continue indefinitely is now universally admitted. What is not sufficiently perceived as yet is that it has already killed and buried the gold-exchange standard of yesteryear. This standard rested indeed, as its name implies, on the reserve holders' confidence in their unqualified right and ability to convert, on sight and at will, their gold-exchange balances into gold metal. This has long ceased to be true for sterling, but the restoration of sterling convertibility reopened an indirect channel from sterling to gold, via the gold-convertible dollar. This channel has now been heavily clogged, to say the least, by Mr. Roosa's success in eliciting from major central banks precarious restraints on such gold conversions, and by the opprobrium now attached to noncompliance with these "voluntary" restraints. Our old friend, Sir Roy Harrod, was the first to characterize these moves, many years ago, as institutionalizing the inconvertibility of the reserve currencies through gentlemen's agreements.

Such agreements and cooperation are soundly based on what has become the golden rule of international monetary behavior and the only chance of survival of our international monetary system: "Don't rock the boat in which we are all sitting!" The trouble is that these gentlemen's agreements remain, as of now, threateningly precarious and short-term, particularly whenever the passengers disagree stubbornly with the pilot—the U.S.—or the copilot—the U.K.—regarding the speed and direction imparted by them to the common skiff. Any passenger may take the risk of rocking the boat by trying to jump out, if he feels that it is being driven at reckless speed, in the middle of a thick fog, in a northerly direction when he wants to go south or, even worse, toward an area strewn with reefs.

The full implications of this curious breed of international monetary cooperation, however, were not fully perceived at first. They have unfortunately been thrown into a cruelly sharp light by President de Gaulle's speech of last February. The survival of the gold-exchange standard has now become dependent on the *political* willingness of foreign countries to finance, through their own monetary issues, the deficits of the countries whose *national* currency is accepted by them as international reserves. Compliance with such a system becomes more precarious every day, not only because the growing illiquidity of the reserve debtors throws increasing doubts upon the ultimate exchange value of such unguaranteed claims, but also because central banks are being called upon to finance debtor countries' policies in which their own governments have no voice, and with which they may profoundly disagree.

The second of the three tables distributed to you shows, for instance, that U.S. net reserve losses of $12,400 million, over the years 1958–62, helped finance an increase of nearly $10 billion in U.S. direct investments abroad. President de Gaulle objects to having his own Bank of France finance—through the accumulation of dollar IOU's—what he calls "a sort of expropriation" of his country's business firms. He recognizes that foreign monetary lending to the U.S. has also "facilitated and favored . . . the multiple and considerable assistance provided by the United States to many countries for development purposes," but it is no secret that he does not particularly enjoy exposing himself to the accusation of helping finance our military assistance to Chiang Kai-shek, the escalation of the war in Vietnam, our ill-fated intervention in the Dominican Republic, etc.

This national and international politicization of the gold-exchange standard explains the queer and unprecedented incursion of Heads of State into esoteric problems traditionally abandoned to the technical officials of their Central Banks and Ministries of Finance. The recent "summit clash" between President de Gaulle and President Johnson— needless to say, the ordering of these two names is purely chronological—probably reflects a justified and growing impatience with the slow progress of these technicians in the Group of Ten negotiations, and a lurking feeling that the international monetary problem has become far too serious to be left indefinitely to monetary experts!

More than four years have elapsed since our late President Kennedy announced, in his first Message to Congress on the Balance of Payments and Gold, that he was "directing that studies to this end [of basic international monetary reform] be initiated *promptly* by the Secretary of the Treasury," and since your own former Prime Minister, Mr. Macmillan, condemned the "unsatisfactory" nature of present monetary arrangements and pleaded for the creation of "a central banking system for all the countries of the free world." Presidents Johnson and de Gaulle; Prime Minister Wilson; former Chancellor

Maudling; former Secretary of the U.S. Treasury, Mr. Dillon; the French Minister of Finance, M. Giscard d'Estaing; the Vice President of the European Economic Community's Commission, M. Marjolin; two successive Managing Directors of the International Monetary Fund, Mr. Jacobsson and M. Schweitzer, and many others, have since joined the growing chorus of the reformers.

One might have thought, last August, that they were on the verge of success, when the IMF and the Group of Ten issued two parallel reports endorsing unanimously two boldly revolutionary steps toward a fundamental reform of our international monetary machinery.

Recognizing that prospective gold production would be vastly insufficient to assure a satisfactory growth of world reserves in future years, that the pound sterling and the U.S. dollar could no longer safely fill the whole gap between available gold and legitimate reserve needs in an expanding world economy, and that the multiplication of reserve currencies was both unlikely and undesirable—as it would multiply already existing sources of instability and vulnerability of the system—they established a Study Group on the Creation of Reserve Assets "to investigate the problems raised by the creation and use of . . . some additional kind of reserve asset, the possible forms it might take and the institutional aspects associated with it."

The second major conclusion of the Group of Ten was that "the process of adjustment and the need for international liquidity are closely interrelated. . . . The need being to supply sufficient liquidity to finance temporary payments imbalances without frustrating the required process of international adjustment in individual countries, it is desirable to bring under multilateral review and appraisal the various means of financing surpluses or deficits." Steps were therefore recommended to "provide a basis for multilateral surveillance of the various elements of liquidity creation."

The Managing Director of the IMF, M. Schweitzer, has repeatedly confirmed, in several speeches over the last few months, "the emerging consensus among the international community that the creation of international liquidity, like the creation of domestic liquidity, should become a matter of deliberate decision," rather than be left—as of now—to the hazards of current gold production, U.S.S.R. gold sales, speculators' gold purchases, U.S. balance-of-payments deficits, and uncoordinated decisions by scores of central banks regarding their further accumulation of dollars or the cashing of outstanding dollar balances into gold metal.

Each of these two major conclusions and proposals—the creation of a new type of reserve asset and the organization of multilateral surveillance of the various elements of liquidity creation—marks indeed a revolutionary break with past attitudes on the problem.

Two further points should be noted.

One is the concrete proposal of the IMF for "investment operations . . . undertaken on the initiative of the Fund, with a main purpose of creating liquidity, and not necessarily in response to a particular balance-of-payments need," and for the financing of such investments, at least in part, by members' liquid "deposits" with the IMF, "according to suitable criteria," and with characteristics similar to the present gold tranches, "which permit them to be considered as part of a country's reserves." These commonsense proposals by responsible officials should, of course, be carefully distinguished from identical, but utopian, suggestions of irresponsible academics, and most of all from the notorious Triffin plan, of which the least said the better.

The other point I wish to note is the actual implementation, on an *ad hoc* basis, of what I described in 1959 as "the keystone" of my proposals, i.e. "the substitution of IMF balances for balances in national currencies, i.e. mostly dollars and sterling, in all member countries' monetary reserves." [1] This was done, indeed, on the occasion of each sterling crisis, the sterling balances initially acquired by central banks being in each case reimbursed a few months later by IMF drawings, and converted into equivalent increases in the creditor countries' gold tranches with the Fund. The General Arrangements to Borrow were essentially designed to pave the way for similar operations in the event of U.S. drawings on the IMF's depleted resources in European currencies.

Over the five years 1960–64, about $2.1 billion of dollar and sterling balances have been converted into IMF gold tranches by other Fund members, of which $1.6 billion by the six countries of the European Economic Community. Such was indeed the purpose and destination of the $1 billion drawing of the U.K., last November, and 70 per cent, or more, of the new $1.4 billion drawing of two weeks ago.

Such conversions of national currency reserves into true international reserves are now undertaken only after, rather than before, the eruption of the crises triggered by the present system. They do, however, build up precedents which may later be integrated, on the basis of experience, into an institutional framework designed to prevent

1. *Gold and the Dollar Crisis*, p. 102.

such crises *ex ante,* rather than to cure them *ex post,* and which would implement concretely the broad agreements of principle reached last summer by the Group of Ten and the IMF.

What It Could Be

After having described what the present system *is* and the agreements of principle already reached about the broad direction of the reforms unanimously recognized as indispensable, let me now try to outline first the simplest and most efficient way in which these agreements could be concretely implemented. The proposals which I shall put before you may carry at times an uncomfortable aroma of wide-eyed idealism and woeful ignorance of practical, negotiating realities. But this theoretical exercise should nevertheless provide us with badly needed guide lines before we turn to the more pedestrian task of seeing how they can best be approximated in real life, by men prisoners of their past prejudices and illusions, and how they can help reconcile the various plans—academic and official—now under discussion into a workable synthesis, giving proper weight to conflicting points of view and interests.

Let me first brush aside, however, the most attractively simple plan proposed so far: that of our good friend, M. Rueff. Acutely aware of the mistakes that man has always made—and will continue undoubtedly to make—in his management of monetary affairs, he would boldly rule out, at least in principle, any such management altogether. Monetary reserves would be strictly confined to gold metal alone and their future growth would be abandoned to the hazards of Western gold production, of Russian gold sales to the West, and of private purchases of this fascinating metal by speculators as well as by industrial and artistic users. M. Rueff, however, has never been able to explain, to my own satisfaction at least, how the algebraic sum of those hazards would automatically measure the "objective needs" for world reserves.

The second—and admittedly the most difficult—problem of international monetary management is the preservation or restoration of equilibrium in each country's balance of payments. This would also be solved magically by M. Rueff, "in less than three months," if all surpluses and deficits were immediately and religiously settled in gold, rather than financed through international credit. This "very audacious prediction" is apparently predicated, not on the discipline or policies which such a straitjacket would impose on central banks—again, M. Rueff has no faith in monetary management—but simply because such a form of settlement "will exert its own influence by the transfer of purchasing power which is the result of the transfer of gold . . . I have never seen," says M. Rueff, "a country with a real system of international payments in which the deficit stays for more than three months after it has re-established the balance of purchasing power; I mean suppressed the inflationary excesses." I am very much afraid, however, that inflationary excesses will not be exorcized by what M. Rueff calls the old rule of the gold standard, i.e. "of creating money only against gold or bills in national currency, [but not] against any assets in dollars." [2] National currency assets of central banks have certainly been as potent an inflationary factor, to say the least, in many countries as their accumulation of dollar assets. And many countries, including France, have repeatedly experienced severe balance-of-payments difficulties over far more protracted periods than three months, even though they never enjoyed with the world tailors of M. Rueff's parable the exorbitant privilege of paying for their deficits with their own IOU's.

Lurking behind M. Rueff's simple rule is the far more drastic, but unattainable, will-o'-the-wisp of outlawing conscious national as well as international monetary and credit management from the horizon of our central bankers. I am very much afraid, however, that these problems will not yield overnight to the magic wand of any "invisible hand" or automatic gold transfers. We may distrust the management of man over his own affairs, but neither God nor Gold will manage them for him.

Finally, M. Rueff regretfully concedes now that his proposed reform would require a doubling of the present gold price. If, however, the gold standard could be trusted with the *automatic* virtues ascribed to it by M. Rueff, the overnight doubling of world gold reserves would certainly open the gates wide to an immediate tidal wave of inflation. What would happen after that is anybody's guess, but only the most bizarre and haphazard coincidence between "objective needs" and the totally unrelated sources of gold supply noted above could protect the world against inflationary excesses or deflationary shortfalls.

This obvious point has, it is true, repeatedly been conceded by M. Rueff to his opponents. He would meet it through international agreements absorbing the gold profits of two of the more than one hundred countries of the present world through gold repayments—at half their

2. All the above quotations are from M. Rueff's special interview by *The Economist* of February 13, pp. 662–65.

current gold parity—of outstanding dollar and sterling debts to central banks. Other countries would presumably be expected to sterilize also their gold profits through the amortization of outstanding debts of their governments to their own central banks. Future excesses or shortages of gold supply in relation to noninflationary growth needs would also have to be met through deliberate tinkering by several scores of central banks with the automatism of the pure gold system.

All these agreements and deliberate decisions, however, are the very antithesis of the only virtue ascribed by M. Rueff himself to his system, i.e. its automaticity. If such agreements are needed in any case, they can certainly be put to better uses than the digging of larger holes in the ground, in South Africa as well as in Fort Knox.

Such was, in any case, the conclusion unanimously reached and unequivocally affirmed, last summer, both by the Group of Ten and by the IMF reports. I endorsed it, in advance, in my 1959 proposals for world monetary reform and see all the less reason to abandon it now as the doubling of the gold price would in fact penalize all those who have cooperated in making the present system work—no matter how imperfectly—and reward those who refused such cooperation and have kept, or converted, most of their reserves into gold hoards. It would be hard to conceive of a worse preface, and of a more effective deterrent, to the maintenance and intensification of international cooperation which M. Rueff himself recognizes as indispensable to the successful implantation and smooth functioning of his own system.

Having thus neatly demolished both the gold-exchange standard of yesterday and the pure gold standard of M. Rueff, what are we left with? "Assez taillé, mon fils, maintenant il faut recoudre!"

Let me start with a commonsense observation, which should serve as a benchmark for all practical proposals for international monetary reform:

"No satisfactory outcome is possible which does not recognize . . . that the supply of reserves must be a matter of concerted international decision. . . ."

I find this a particularly happy formulation, especially as it is not mine, but that of M. Schweitzer in a recent speech to the Economic and Social Council of the United Nations. Moreover, the principle which it expresses was unanimously, if implicitly, agreed upon last summer already by the Group of Ten, under the less happy vocable of *"multilateral surveillance."*

The easiest and most efficient way to implement it has also been outlined already in the last Annual Report of the International Monetary Fund. It is essentially identical with the double-barrelled proposal for Fund deposits and investments which I outlined, several years ago, in *Gold and the Dollar Crisis*.[3] "Investment operations . . . could be undertaken on the initiative of the Fund, with a main purpose of creating [needed] liquidity, and not necessarily in response to a particular balance-of-payments need. . . . Any acquisition of assets by investment would tend to put a strain on the Fund's resources and create a need for additional resources." A portion, at least, of such resources, and probably a very substantial one, could be derived from the accumulation by IMF members (all, or some) of a portion of their total reserves in the form of IMF "deposits" endowed with appropriate liquidity and exchange-value guarantees.

The most conservative people in this group should be reassured at once about the "revolutionary" character of this proposal. Such Fund deposits and investments would not involve "any sharp break with the past," but would, on the contrary, "build upon what already exists."

IMF *deposits,* endowed with full liquidity and exchange-value guarantees are already accepted as a respectable component of many countries' international reserves, under the barbaric denomination of "Fund Gold Tranche Positions," recently replaced, in the Fund's literature, by the simpler and more enlightening one of "Reserve Positions in the Fund." They already reached, as of last March, the respectable total of $4,185 million.

IMF *investments,* on the other hand, have also been built up already to the more modest amount of $800 million, but have been confined so far to gold-guaranteed investments in U.S. government securities, imaginatively undertaken under the scarce currency clause of the Articles of Agreement long after the dollar had ceased to be a scarce currency, for the professed purpose of increasing the Fund's earnings, rather than to increase world reserves or reduce the U.S. gold drain. Similar investments will, however, be expanded in the near future, in order to alleviate the unfortunate impact of the increase in members' gold subscriptions on the slender gold reserves of the United States and the United Kingdom.

The further expansion of Fund deposits and investment for the purpose of concerted reserves creation raises four major questions which I shall briefly discuss in turn:

3. New Haven, 1960, pp. 102–20.

(1) What should determine the global amount of such deliberate increases of the world reserve pool?

(2) Who should hold the new IMF deposits to be created, and under what conditions?

(3) How should the corresponding Fund investments be distributed among members and, again, under what conditions and for what purposes?

(4) Last, but not least, who shall decide?

In brief, who will decide who will lend, how much, to whom, and under what conditions?

The Global Pace of Reserve Growth. Whoever decides should obviously try and adjust the over-all pace of reserve creation in such a way as to stimulate a maximum use of the noninflationary potential for world economic growth. This means essentially that the pace of reserve creation should be stepped up whenever recognized as necessary to combat any pervasive deflationary pressures that might arise in the world economy, and that it should be slowed down, or even reversed, in the opposite case of pervasive inflationary trends.

World trade and production have increased in postwar years— even in real terms—at unprecedentedly fast and steady paces, ranging roughly from 5 to 6 per cent a year, or even more. I do not believe for an instant, however, in any rigid, mechanical connection between such economic growth rates and the need for the expansion of monetary reserves. Some of my readers seem to have been misled in this matter by the fact that, in *Gold and the Dollar Crisis,* I followed, but mostly to criticize it, this Fund's approach to the problem in its 1958 study on International Reserves and Liquidity, and suggested, as an anti-inflationary safeguard, that a presumptive ceiling be established by treaty on the annual increase of the Fund's global loans and investment portfolio, and that qualified—rather than simple majority —votes be required in order to permit increases beyond this presumptive ceiling.

The Distribution of Deposit Obligations Among Fund Members. To be acceptable by members, as part and parcel of their international reserves, IMF deposits must be endowed with appropriate exchange-value and liquidity guarantees.

All Fund transactions are now denominated in "gold dollars," protecting them against any unilateral devaluation of the paper dollar, or indeed of any other currency. There is, therefore, no need for innovation in this respect. One might even question whether some sort of "unit of account" guarantee, patterned after that of the old EPU, or the one that will soon have to be defined by the EEC, might not meet the problem just as well, or better.

The liquidity of the Fund's deposits might best be defined in terms of their immediate and unquestioned acceptability by creditors from debtors, in all international settlements. If appropriately guaranteed against exchange and default risks, there is no reason to think that any creditor would turn down such deposits in settlement of its claims, particularly as they should carry, in addition, some modest interest earnings. Yet some obligation might have to be spelled out contractually in advance, until all nations become fully familiar with the system and its actual operation.

The actual composition of world reserves might be used as a guideline to determine, at each point of time, the agreements that might be needed in this respect. At the end of last year, for instance, the world reserve pool totalled about $69 billion, of which $41 billion was held in gold, and $28 billion in credit reserves, i.e. in foreign exchange—primarily dollars and pounds sterling—and IMF reserve positions. In order to guard the system against a (presumably undesirable) contraction in world reserves, it might have seemed desirable, therefore, to require all Fund members to hold no more than 60 per cent of their reserves in gold metal, and at least 40 per cent in credit reserves.

In order to simplify the exposition, allow me to bypass for the moment the role of national currencies as credit reserves, and to assume that all credit reserves should be held in the form of deposits with the IMF. It would, even then, be unnecessary to impose a rigid ratio of 60 per cent gold and 40 per cent IMF deposits upon all Fund members, whose chosen ratio of credit reserves to total reserves varies widely, at present, from 7 or 8 per cent, for instance, in the case of the United States and the United Kingdom to 85 per cent in Japan.

There would be no need to interfere with each country's decision in this respect as long as the result of their combined choices remained compatible with the desired level of world reserves. If, however, these combined choices were to result in an excessive demand for a limited stock of monetary gold, enforcing thereby an undesirable contraction, or even merely an exceedingly slow growth in world reserves, some action would have to be taken. The problem might possibly be met by an acceptable increase in the interest rate paid by the Fund on its deposits. If this were insufficient, however, it might prove necessary to enjoin the countries with the lowest percentage of IMF deposits to their total reserves from lowering it further, and even to require them to increase it.

If, on the other hand, as is far more probable in the long run, the combined decisions of reserve holders were to result in large transfers of gold to the Fund in exchange for Fund deposits, this would not create any inflationary dangers, since the Fund could merely sit on its gold holdings. Its lending potential would undoubtedly rise, but its actual use would remain limited anyway by the wisdom of the Fund's traditionally conservative management, and by the presumptive ceilings and voting rules embodied in the revised Articles of Agreement. Interest rates on deposits might be lowered and, in some distant future, Fund members might even possibly give some thought as to whether the continuation of a rigidly guaranteed minimum price to gold producers and gold hoarders constitutes a boon, or a hindrance, to national and international monetary management, and promotes a wise use or a senseless waste of the world's productive resources.

They are unlikely to ask themselves this question, however, in the foreseeable future. Sterile gold hoardings may continue to be preferred by some to guaranteed and interest-earning IMF deposits, because of the fear that the most sacred Treatise—including the Articles of Agreement of the Fund—might be jettisoned in the event of a world war. The IMF deposits might become blocked, at the most inconvenient time, for those who find themselves on the "wrong" side of the fence.

Another type of guarantee might prove useful indeed to overcome this fear, wherever it exists. Any country could request the Fund to deposit within its own territory a portion of the Fund's global gold holdings roughly proportional to its share in the total deposits of the Fund.

The Fund's guarantees to depositors, however, cannot be any better than the Fund's own assets, and might prove impossible to honor in full, in the case of defaults by its debtors. To guard against this, all Fund members might agree to channel through any defaulting country's deposit account with the Fund all payments to be made to it in the future by any of them, until the default is fully covered. Such a guarantee would thus rest, not on the borrowing countries' commitments, but on those of all Fund members, and on their interest in assuring the ultimate worth of their own claims on the institution.

Taken together, such guarantees would erect, indeed, stronger safeguards for the Fund's depositors than any ever devised in past international lending operations.

Let us note, finally, that an agreed percentage of minimum deposits with the Fund—in relation to each country's global reserves—might in time be substituted advantageously for the Fund's General Arrangements to Borrow, and even for the cumbersome and wasteful procedure of capital subscriptions and periodic quota increases that now feed the lending potential of the institution. Each member's contributions would, in this way, adjust automatically to the fluctuations of its balance-of-payments and reserve position and, therefore, of its lending capacity. The net claims accumulated on the Fund would, moreover, as is already the case now, remain perfectly liquid and usable to meet later deficits. The Fund would eschew, however, the absurdity of having to channel through the parliamentary or congressional procedures of scores of countries the vote of millions, or billions, of perfectly useless cruzeiros, bahts, and other kyats, on the occasion of each increase in its capital. It would also spare itself the ingenious acrobatics through which it now has to elude the deflationary impact of gold subscriptions, not only on the subscribing members, but also on the depleted gold reserves of the United States and the United Kingdom.

The Distribution of Fund's Loans and Investments. The more conservative members of this audience will be happy to hear that I do not propose any revolutionary revision of the present lending procedures of the Fund. I am particularly wary myself of the suggestions of my old friend, and former chief at the Fund, E. M. Bernstein, for a substantial increase in the automatic borrowing rights of Fund members. Such automaticity might well be considered indeed, but only for moderate amounts, and relatively short-time maturities, designed to meet unforeseen situations and to provide the time necessary for a deliberate examination of a country's problem and for the reaching of joint agreements on the amounts and purposes of the Fund's assistance. But it would be revolutionary and utopian, indeed, to expect the lenders to accept large automatic commitments to finance blindly the future deficits of all and any country, without regard for the wisdom or folly of the policies which may be at the root of these deficits.

This is precisely the point at which the need for the growth of world reserves may be met in such a way as to promote and support indispensable readjustment policies, by surplus as well as by deficit countries, depending on the circumstances of such imbalances in world payments. Multilateral surveillance should—the Group of Ten has already told us—apply to the financing of individual countries' deficits as well as to the global pace of all forms of reserve creation.

If this financing were to remain constricted—as it has largely been so far—to medium-term loans, of three to five years' maturity, the gross lending that would prove necessary, year after year, to offset repayments and feed desired increases in world reserves would soon exceed all reasonable needs and uses for such medium-term assistance, while far more crying needs for longer-term development financing would remain starved for adequate sources of funds.

I am well aware, of course, of the traditional objections to the use of liquid monetary deposits for long-term financing of this sort, either by commercial banks, or even by national central banks. These objections, however, would be totally irrelevant—as brilliantly shown by Professor Machlup—to the operations of a world-wide reserve center, such as that recommended here. The inflationary dangers of long-term lending—as well as of short-term lending, for that matter —should be adequately guarded against through the over-all ceilings, discussed above, on the Fund's portfolio increases, limiting those to agreed requirements for reserve growth. As for the danger of illiquidity, usually associated with long-term loans, it could not arise under the proposed system. The world pool of reserves being destined to grow overtime, with little or no probability that circumstances would ever require a sudden or massive contraction, the Fund should never have to face any drastic reduction of its deposit liabilities, forcing it to liquidate any substantial portion of its global assets. Balance-of-payments settlements among IMF reserve holders will reshuffle the Fund's deposit liabilities among its members, but should not reduce their total amount.[4]

Yet there exist some valid reasons to limit the maturity of Fund loans and investments. The first is that such limitations will provide added flexibility for shifting the Fund's assistance from some countries to others, whose needs may be greater and exceed what the Fund can currently contribute from desirable increases in the total pool of world credit reserves.

4. This would not be strictly true if surpluses centered on countries with low ratios of IMF deposits to total reserves, and deficits on countries with high ratios. The problem would then have to be met through a reduction of the IMF gold reserves in the short run, and in the long run by the provisions, discussed on pp. 358–59. above, designed to prevent an undesirable contraction in the world reserve pool.

A second reason why the Fund should not engage directly in long-term development lending is that such lending requires a very different type of knowledge and expertise than those that should be relevant to its primary tasks and purposes, i.e.: (a) a rate of creation of over-all world reserves most appropriate to sustain noninflationary rates of economic growth; (b) a distribution of its corresponding lending power designed to stimulate the adoption and implementation of desirable readjustment policies by the beneficiaries; (c) the reshuffling of such lending that may be needed to compensate large, but reversible, movements of private capital, particularly among major monetary and financial markets whose general policies are consonant with longer-term equilibrium in their balances of payments.

The bulk of the Fund's assistance to long-term development financing should thus, in all probability, be channelled through—and cushioned by—intermediary institutions, specialized in such long-term lending. The Fund might, for instance, distribute its investment portfolio between marketable obligations of international institutions, such as the International Bank for Reconstruction and Development, and other short-term or medium-term investments in the major financial centers—New York, London, Paris, Frankfurt, Amsterdam, etc.—enabling these to engage more boldly and actively in long-term lending, in the knowledge that temporary pressures on the country's reserves would be offset by a reshuffling of the Fund's own investment portfolio. Such reshuffling would be particularly appropriate to meet the objectives now served by the Fund's General Arrangements to Borrow.

Who Shall Decide? Last, but certainly not least, is the question of the appropriate machinery through which agreements are to be hammered out on all these issues calling for joint decisions among several scores of theoretically sovereign and independent, but factually interdependent, countries. Logically, the IMF should obviously be the main instrument to be used to that end. Yet some of the main reserve holders of Western Europe strenuously object to relinquishing to the Executive Board of the Fund the management of the vast sums which they might be called upon to contribute in future years to the growth of world reserves. The EEC countries alone are already now holding close to two thirds of the net claims that finance the lending operations of the IMF, but they wield only 15 per cent of the voting power in all Fund decisions. The distribution of voting power in the Fund is indeed primarily determined by the relative size of each country's quota. Quotas, however, are tantamount to lending commitments for the creditor countries in the Fund, and to borrowing rights for the others. It is not difficult to understand the objections of the continentals to a system which rewards equally with voting power the obligation to lend and the right to borrow, especially at a time when the camp of the prospective borrowers includes not only several scores of less developed countries, but also the United States and the United Kingdom, which alone command more than twice as many votes in the Fund as the six EEC countries together.

I have long recommended two parallel solutions to this worldly problem. The first is to encourage a substantial decentralization of the Fund's operations and responsibilities, through positive encouragement to regional monetary cooperation and integration such as is being rapidly developed today in EEC and in Central America. This could indeed help to couch readjustment advice to individual countries in more realistic terms, and to avoid excessive criticism of the Fund by countries which now bear little or none of the responsibilities for such advice and financing.

Article 108 of the Rome Treaty provides a most realistic model for such decentralization. Any disequilibria among the EEC countries should be dealt with primarily by the EEC itself, and financed through a joint European Reserve Fund, as long advocated by Jean Monnet's Action Committee for the United States of Europe. This would reduce to a more manageable size the contributions which these countries should make to IMF to cover disequilibria between the EEC area as a whole and the rest of the world.

A further, and not unreasonable, compromise might be to observe the voting procedures of the Articles of Agreement for normal quota drawings financed out of present capital subscriptions and future quota increases, but to establish a special open-market committee to manage the investments financed from voluntary "deposits" additional to the quota subscriptions of the Articles of Agreement, and to give adequate recognition to the relative size of these deposits in determining the relative voting power of the depositors.

Coming Down to Earth

This bare outline has purposely skirted many complexities arising from vested national interests, real or imaginary, in the preservation of some features of the present system, and from the need to provide a smooth transition from past habits and institutions to those that should gradually emerge tomorrow, in the light of practical experience and *ad hoc* precedents, as well as of purely logical and abstract theorizing.

In order not to abuse your patience, I shall single out only one, but maybe the most crucial, of such problems: the need to deal with outstanding sterling, and particularly dollar, balances traditionally integrated into the international reserve system which we have inherited from the past.

Let me observe, first of all, that the key-currency role of sterling and the dollar in private trade and finance is quite independent of their reserve currency role for central bankers. The use of both currencies in the first of these two roles long preceded, and will long survive, their use in the second. In fact, the attractiveness of both sterling and the dollar as a key currency for private traders and investors is increasingly endangered today by the creeping exchange restrictions imposed by the U.S. and the U.K. on bank lending and other capital movements, in order to stem the gold outflows to which a reserve currency is necessarily exposed as a result of conversions into gold of reserve balances accumulated abroad over many years past.

This constitutes indeed one of the major dangers today to the stability of the pound and the dollar, and of an international monetary system so closely tied to the fate of these two currencies. The third of the three tables illustrates this point, alongside many others on which time will not permit me to comment.

The reserve losses of the United States over the last five years stem largely from a spectacular reversal in the international movement of short-term capital. We were receiving up to 1960, as should be expected in the case of a major financial center, persistent *inflows* of short-term funds, averaging more than $1 billion a year in the late 1950s, and which reached a peak of $1.8 billion in 1959. This was succeeded by abnormal, but persistent, net *outflows* throughout the years 1960–64, averaging more than $1.4 billion a year, i.e. a total shift of about $2.5 billion in our average net balance.[5] This is more than twice our net reserve losses of last year ($1.2 billion).

Although various factors, including interest rates, have undoubtedly played a large role in this dramatic reversal, closer analysis leaves

---

5. J. L. Stein arrives, through a far more ambitious regression analysis, at an identical estimate of the impact of speculative pressures on short-term capital flows. See his "International Short-Term Capital Movements," *American Economic Review*, LV (March 1965), pp. 40–66, particularly p. 41, p. 64, and Table 2 on p. 65.

little doubt about the importance of the speculative attitudes unleashed by the 1960 gold flare-up in the London market. The outflow reached a peak ($2.3 billion) in that year, and can be largely explained by an unprecedented inflow of short-term funds into Germany ($1.1 billion) in anticipation of a revaluation of the mark, and into private gold purchases ($1 billion, i.e. nearly double the previous years' average) in anticipation of a revaluation of gold. It was at a low (only $260 million) in 1963 when gold and exchange-rate speculation was strongly discouraged by the unanimous rejection of gold revaluation by the Group of Ten and by unprecedentedly large gold sales by the U.S.S.R. in Western markets ($550 million, i.e. more than twice the previous years' average).

There can be very little doubt, I think, that our residual deficit would soon disappear, and even probably be replaced by large surpluses, if agreement could be reached, along the lines which I shall presently describe, in order to delay for many years to come, or even forever, any expectation of a gold revaluation. This could hardly fail to induce a substantial disgorging from the enormous gold hoards accumulated by speculators over many years past, and particularly since 1960.

The case of Britain is not so clearcut as that of the United States. Current account surpluses in the British balance of payments have fluctuated widely over the past seven years, and have often been insufficient to finance official grants and capital outflows. Yet, here too, net reserve movements show little or no correlation with the fluctuations in the current account balance, but often a striking parallelism —until 1964—with net inflows and outflows of private capital, and particularly short-term funds. Net reserve losses of $1,600 million in 1961 and 1963 were associated with net outflows of $1,500 million of short-term capital, while the $770 million reserve gain of 1962 was practically equal to net short-term capital inflows of $750 million, and the $820 million reserve gain of 1960 was dwarfed by net short-term capital inflows of more than $2 billion.

Speculative movements of short-term funds are clearly one of the dominant factors in the balance-of-payments problems of the two reserve centers of the gold-exchange standard. The threat which they constitute to the stability of the system would be substantially reduced if it were agreed that *any contraction as well as expansion, of the world reserve pool should be a matter for joint decisions* by, at least, the major reserve holders.

TABLE 3

BALANCES OF PAYMENTS OF THE UNITED STATES, THE EUROPEAN ECONOMIC
COMMUNITY AND THE UNITED KINGDOM, 1958–64
(in billions of U.S. dollars)

	1958	1959	1960	1961	1962	1963	1964
I. Current account and official capital	**2.4**	**−0.6**	**1.6**	**3.0**	**1.7**	**0.7**	**2.6**
U.S.	−0.8	−2.5	0.8	2.6	2.1	1.5	4.0
EEC	2.4	1.8	1.8	0.6	−0.5	−0.8	—
U.K.	0.8	0.1	−1.0	−0.2	—	—	−1.4
A. Current account and private transfers	5.5	3.8	6.1	8.6	7.0	6.5	8.4
U.S.	1.5	−0.7	3.2	4.9	4.3	4.9	7.4
EEC	2.8	3.8	3.4	3.4	2.0	1.0	1.5
U.K.	1.2	0.7	−0.4	0.3	0.7	0.7	−0.5
B. Official transfers and capital	−3.1	−4.4	−4.6	−5.6	−5.3	−5.8	−5.8
U.S.	−2.3	−1.8	−2.4	−2.3	−2.2	−3.4	−3.4
EEC	−0.4	−2.0	−1.6	−2.8	−2.6	−1.8	−1.5
U.K.	−0.3	−0.6	−0.6	−0.5	−0.6	−0.7	−0.9
II. Private capital	**−1.7**	**−0.1**	**−1.2**	**−3.6**	**−2.5**	**−1.9**	**−3.9**
U.S.	−2.2	0.2	−4.4	−3.9	−4.4	−3.5	−5.2
EEC	0.2	—	1.4	1.2	1.2	2.1	1.8
U.K.	0.3	−0.3	1.8	−1.0	0.7	−0.5	−0.5
A. Long-term	−2.5	−1.4	−1.5	−0.9	−1.4	−2.4	−3.5
U.S.	−2.6	−1.6	−2.1	−2.2	−2.6	−3.2	−4.1
EEC	0.5	0.6	0.9	1.0	1.3	1.0	1.3
U.K.	−0.4	−0.4	−0.2	0.3	—	−0.2	−0.7
B. Short-term	0.8	1.3	0.3	−2.7	−1.1	0.6	−0.4
U.S.	0.3	1.8	−2.3	−1.7	−1.8	−0.3	−1.1
EEC	−0.2	−0.6	0.5	0.2	−0.1	1.1	0.5
U.K.	0.7	0.1	2.1	−1.2	0.7	−0.3	0.2
III. Net monetary reserves (= I + II)	**0.8**	**−0.7**	**0.4**	**−0.6**	**−0.8**	**−1.2**	**−1.2**
U.S.	−3.0	−2.3	−3.6	−1.3	−2.2	−2.0	−1.2
EEC	2.6	1.8	3.2	1.9	0.7	1.3	1.8
U.K.	1.1	−0.2	0.8	−1.1	0.8	−0.5	−1.9

TABLE 3 (*continued*)

	1958	1959	1960	1961	1962	1963	1964
A. Reported reserve assets	1.2	−1.2	2.4	1.2	−1.1	0.9	1.0
U.S.	−2.3	−1.0	−2.1	−0.6	−1.5	−0.4	−0.2
EEC	2.8	0.1	3.6	2.2	0.4	1.5	2.0
U.K.	0.7	−0.3	0.9	−0.4	—	−0.2	−0.8
1. Gold	0.5	−0.2	0.1	—	—	0.3	0.4
U.S.	−2.3	−1.1	−1.7	−0.9	−0.9	−0.5	−0.1
EEC	1.6	1.1	1.5	1.4	0.6	0.9	0.9
U.K.	1.3	−0.3	0.3	−0.5	0.3	−0.1	−0.3
2. Convertible currencies	0.5	−1.3	2.1	0.6	−0.8	0.6	0.7
U.S.	—	—	—	0.1	—	0.1	0.2
EEC	1.0	−1.2	1.9	−0.2	—	0.5	0.5
U.K.	−0.5	−0.1	0.2	0.6	−0.8	−0.1	—
3. IMF reserve position	0.2	0.3	0.2	0.6	−0.3	—	−0.2
U.S.	—	—	−0.4	0.1	−0.6	—	−0.3
EEC	0.2	0.2	0.2	0.9	−0.2	0.1	0.6
U.K.	—	0.1	0.4	−0.5	0.5	—	−0.5
B. Liabilities to IMF	−0.1	0.3	−0.3	−0.6	0.6	—	−0.5
U.S.	—	−0.3	−0.3	—	—	—	—
EEC	−0.1	0.3	—	—	—	—	—
U.K.	—	0.3	—	−0.6	0.6	—	−0.5
C. Other assets and liabilities (net)	−0.4	0.2	−1.6	−1.2	−0.2	−2.1	−1.7
U.S.	−0.7	−0.9	−1.1	−0.7	−0.7	−1.6	−1.0
EEC	—	1.4	−0.4	−0.3	0.2	−0.2	−0.1
U.K.	0.4	0.2	−0.1	−0.2	0.2	−0.3	−0.5

SOURCES: These estimates have been pieced together, in as comparable a form as possible, from the more detailed estimates published in *International Financial Statistics*, the current IMF *Balance of Payments Yearbook*, the *Survey of Current Business*, the *Bank of England Quarterly Bulletin*, the *Monthly Report of the Deutsche Bundesbank*, and other official publications.

As of last December, for instance, the $24 billion of credit reserves held in foreign exchange were overwhelmingly made up of dollar ($15 billion to $16 billion) and sterling (about $7 billion) claims. One of the major and most urgent objectives of any sensible reform should be to prevent any sudden or massive contraction of this large component of world reserves through wanton conversions into gold metal, which their holders are now legally entitled to claim, but which would nevertheless prove both disastrous and impossible in practice if they made any extensive use of this legal right.

This unenforceable right to gold conversion should be abandoned in favor of feasible and adequate guarantees regarding the future exchange value of such claims and their continued usability in all balance-of-payments settlements. The cleanest way to achieve this objective would be to exchange all unrequired dollar and sterling balances of central banks for guaranteed deposits with the IMF, whose unqualified transferability for all balance-of-payments settlements would be based on the obligation discussed above of all reserve holders to retain a certain portion of their global reserves in the form of credit reserves rather than gold. [The same objective could, however, be served through the conversion of unrequired sterling and dollar balances into reserve certificates, with similar exchange value and transferability guarantees, although this would require additional provisions regarding the appropriate distribution of credit reserves between dollar and sterling certificates by each individual reserve holder.]

This leaves unresolved the question of eventual amortization of the U.S. and U.K. indebtedness transferred to the IMF [or converted into reserve certificates]. Since the need for any massive contraction of existing reserves can be ruled out in practice, not only as unnecessary but even as highly undesirable, any systematic provisions for contractual amortization of the resulting indebtedness of the United States and the United Kingdom should be regarded as equally unnecessary and even undesirable. Yet, amortization might be required from them in the two following cases:

(a) Whenever feasible and desirable to finance later surpluses of the debtor country. This provision would be particularly useful and appropriate in the event of large movements of private funds between the two reserve debtors themselves. The IMF, for instance, would be able to compensate such movements by an opposite reshuffling of the official dollar and sterling balances transferred to it initially, without exposing itself either to gold losses or to the need for invoking the General Arrangements to Borrow in order to obtain the necessary financing from either the U.S. or the U.K.

(b) In moderate amounts, compatible with international stabilization objectives, whenever desirable to enlarge the ability of the IMF to lend to other deserving countries whose need for credit is greater than that of outstanding reserve debtors.

The lack of any explicit discussion of this problem of *outstanding* reserve currency balances by the Group of Ten constitutes undoubtedly the most glaring gap in their report of last August.

The *future* use of sterling and dollar balances as normal feeders and components of world reserves also presents a major hurdle to the negotiators of the Group of Ten. Even though it has already been agreed by them that "multilateral surveillance" should apply to all forms of reserve creation, the U.S. and the U.K. are reluctant to abandon the privileged position enjoyed by them in the past through the use of their national currencies as international reserves. Some Colonel Blimps even seem to regard it as a matter of national prestige to have their country's national IOU's float precariously in the coffers of foreign central banks. Yet, the constraints which possible conversions of such IOU's into gold metal imposes upon the freedom of monetary and economic policy in the U.S. and the U.K. are likely to prove increasingly burdensome in the future, while the chances of any substantial piling-up of further dollar and sterling balances in other countries' reserves are bound to become increasingly slimmer.

This does not mean, however, that the role of dollar and sterling balances in the world reserve system could be entirely dispensed with. They will retain, at the very least, an important function as working balances, to be used by central banks for daily interventions in the exchange market. This would, of course, remain true even if agreement were to be reached, as suggested above, for the concentration of all credit reserves in IMF deposits. Surplus countries would deposit in their account with the Fund unrequired foreign exchange balances bought from the market in excess of normal requirements for working balances. Deficit countries, on the other hand, would purchase from the Fund—against corresponding debits in their deposit account —the foreign exchange necessary to reconstitute their depleted working balances. Because of their wide use as key currencies in private trading and financial transactions, the dollar and the pound would retain the major role which they have traditionally played in this respect, although other currencies would not be barred from such use also.

Any attempt to preserve the use of national currency balances as international reserves—except for such moderate working balances— would complicate immensely the implementation of the "multilateral surveillance" principle agreed to last summer, without benefiting in any way either the United States or the United Kingdom if multilateral surveillance is to be equally and effectively enforced upon them as upon other countries. As long as credit reserves are held exclusively in the form of Fund deposits, as envisaged above, joint agreements need cover only the distribution of such deposits among reserve holders, and of correlative Fund loans and investments among prospective borrowers and financial outlets. If, however, direct dollar and sterling holdings are now retained alongside IMF deposits as normal components of each country's credit reserves, multilateral surveillance decisions will inevitably have to consider also the distribution of these three types of reserve media both between creditors and between debtors, and to assure the compatibility of this double distribution pattern. Each and every country will have to be induced to adjust the over-all amount of its credit reserves between IMF deposits, dollars, and sterling in such a way that the combined result of their separate decisions will produce the agreed constellation of financing for the U.S., the U.K., and other Fund members. Even worse, frequent, and often large, fluctuations in every country's global reserve holdings will force constant and complicated reshufflings, matching separately the dollars, sterling, and IMF deposits unloaded by the countries in deficit with the dollars, sterling, and IMF deposits absorbed by the countries in surplus.

I cannot, therefore, but agree with those who consider that dollars and sterling should be replaced, rather than merely supplemented, by the new type of international reserve asset whose creation is now being studied by the Ossola Committee. The seeming endorsement of this view by Prime Minister Wilson, at the conclusion of his conversations with General de Gaulle, two months ago, is particularly encouraging in this respect. The French themselves, on the other hand, have indicated that they would have no objection to the continued use of sterling and dollar reserves by countries traditionally regarded as forming part of the sterling and dollar areas.

A compromise might be reached, therefore, under which the new system proposed above would be initially negotiated and fully implemented only by the major reserve holders of the Group of Ten, and would leave most other countries free to retain, as now, a substantial portion of their reserves in the form of dollar and sterling assets. The total amount of national currency reserves, including working balances, held at the end of last year by all the less developed countries taken together totaled about $6.9 billion, i.e. 10 per cent of the world reserve pool. Since these countries are most unlikely to run large surpluses in the foreseeable future, the total amount of reserves which they might choose to accumulate in national currencies—or, for that matter, in gold—would be equally unlikely to endanger seriously the stability of the system as a whole.

Let me, in conclusion, add a few words about what is commonly regarded, even by its sympathizers, as the major obstacle to the acceptance of the Triffin plan. Hard-headed realists, as well as antiquated nationalists, fear that it would involve large and unprecedented surrenders of national sovereignty to a supranational world central bank, which could not operate effectively without the support of a world government.

These fears are totally groundless.

The IMF would, it is true, be a "lender of last resort," but this has been true from the very inception of the Fund, eighteen years ago. Neither the present nor the reformed IMF, however, would have any right to dictate individual countries' policies, nor any means to guarantee the stability and long-run equivalence of the national currencies of its members. These would remain free, as they are now, to reject the Fund's policy advice and to pursue whatever policies they wish, even if this involved in the end their inability to escape a devaluation of their currency.

Actual surrenders of sovereignty to the Fund would continue to depend on the amount of lending potential contributed to it by its members. The fact that some of these contributions would take the form of "deposits" rather than capital subscriptions would not reduce in any way the sovereignty of anybody, since these deposits would be at least as liquid as the present capital subscriptions, and any increases would have to be agreed upon by the contributors just as is the case now for periodic increases in the Fund's capital.

The U.S. and the U.K. would, it is true, renounce the expectation of being able to palm off their short-term IOU's upon the world reserve pool. But they would also be protected against massive and unsustainable conversions of their past IOU's into gold metal. Who can doubt that this would restore to them a greater freedom of monetary management than they now enjoy? The threat of future gold conversions is certainly far greater today than the likelihood of any substantial piling-up of more dollar and sterling balances by the major reserve holding countries of Western Europe.

These large reserve holders, on the other hand, would give up their present legal right to wanton conversions of past dollar and sterling balances into gold metal. But they already know that this right has become largely theoretical and that its actual use could only precipitate devaluation, inconvertibility, or gold embargo decisions by the debtors. My proposals would safeguard them against such dangers, preserve the full liquidity of outstanding dollar and sterling balances for the purpose of international settlements, and protect each of them against the deflationary or inflationary pressures which the liquidation or accumulation of such balances by others can now unleash at any time upon the world monetary system. Note that none of them can escape such pressures by its own freedom of action. The fact that Dr. Holtrop can choose to accumulate his country's surpluses in gold rather than in dollar reserves does not protect the Netherlands against the inflationary pressures resulting—in his view—from the excessive financing of U.S. deficits by other central banks.

Finally, the underdeveloped countries could only, of course, welcome the expansion of the Fund's lending capacity, and particularly its indirect channeling into development financing via the Fund's investments in the IBRD, other international lending agencies and the major financial markets specialized in long-term lending.

If time had permitted, I would have concluded this talk with a brief discussion of the ways in which the various plans talked about today—the Stamp or Wilson plans, the CRU plan, the Maudling plan, the Posthuma or Blessing plans, the Bernstein plan, etc.—fit into the synthesis which I have just outlined.

But time is running short, for us here today, as well as for the negotiators of the Group of Ten. I hope we shall all make good use of it in our ensuing debates, and that our success may inspire our official colleagues to speed up the pace of their own discussions and escape the fate of their unlucky predecessors of the Gold Delegation of the League of Nations, some thirty-four years ago, on September 21, 1931.

———

The most courageous of my readers may also wish to consult two other studies covering the same ground as this one, but with somewhat different emphasis.

"Guidelines for International Monetary Reform" was written in the summer of 1965 at the request of the Honorable Henry S. Reuss, chairman of the Subcommittee on International Exchange and Payments, and attempts to give specific answers to the crucial questions raised by the Subcommittee, particularly with regard to U.S. national interests and the future role of the dollar in the international reserve system. See pp. 164–184 of the Sub-committee's *Hearings,* Part I (July 27–29, 1965).

In a memorandum prepared in December 1965 at the request of the United Nations Economic Commission for Latin America, and discussed at headquarters with the Commission's Staff and a number of government representatives from various Latin American countries, I reviewed once more the whole problem of international monetary reform, with special emphasis on the interests of underdeveloped countries in the negotiations now in process. I also spelled out in greater detail the new proposals outlined in the present paper with respect to the handling of outstanding and future balances in national currencies used as monetary reserves by central banks. See "International Monetary Reform," in the March 1966 issue of the *Economic Bulletin for Latin America.* My proposals differ substantially, in both respects, from those seemingly favored at the moment (February 1966) by the United States and the European Economic Community, but rejoin some of the preoccupations expressed by Representatives Henry S. Reuss and Robert F. Ellsworth in their December 1965 report to the Joint Economic Committee entitled *Off Dead Center: Some Proposals to Strengthen Free World Economic Cooperation.*

PART THREE

Regional Monetary Integration

MY INTEREST in *regional* monetary integration springs from a deep and old conviction as to its necessary role in the planning and implementation of effective *world-wide* monetary integration. The rationale of this view is the main topic of Chapter 7 of *Europe and the Money Muddle* (pp. 234–68, particularly 256–68) and of the two articles grouped in Chapter X below.[1]

The other three chapters discuss the concrete application of this approach to the problem of monetary integration in Western Europe, Latin America, and Africa.

1. See also "Universalisme et régionalisme sur le plan économique," *Revue Economique et Sociale* (Lausanne, September 1959), pp. 43–51.

Chapter X: Internationalism and Regionalism in World Policies and Institutions

1. ECONOMIC INTEGRATION: INSTITUTIONS, THEORIES, AND POLICIES

William Diebold, Jr., *Trade and Payments in Western Europe: A Study of Economic Cooperation, 1947–1951,* New York, Harper & Row (Council on Foreign Relations), 1952, 488 pp. $5.00.

Robert Marjolin, *Europe and the United States in the World Economy,* Durham, N.C., Duke University Press, 1953, 106 pp. $2.00.

James E. Meade, *Problems of Economic Union,* Chicago, University of Chicago Press, 1953, 102 pp. $1.75.

I

Each of the three books reviewed below makes a very distinct contribution to the fast-growing literature on economic integration.

Diebold's book is primarily a historical and critical account of the postwar negotiation of intra-European trade and payments agreements.

> The pages that follow are, with few exceptions, concerned with those proposals that actually reached the tables of cabinets and conferences. What governments have not done is as important a part of this account as what they have done. . . . This book is an account and an analysis but not a prescription. It does not attempt to provide the "right" solution for Western Europe's problems. . . . It is simply an attempt to help understand the events of these four years. (pp. 6–7)

Taken as such, this book must be counted an outstanding success. Diebold takes us to the international conference table, and resurrects for us in lively fashion the negotiating processes through which agreements were reached or shipwrecked. I know of no clearer and more comprehensive explanation of the successive agreements for multilateral compensation and intra-European payments, or of the gradual development of the OEEC codes for the liberalization of trade and in-

---

A review article for *World Politics* (July 1954), pp. 526–37.

visible transactions, or of the failure of more ambitious plans for customs unions, tariff preferences, or structural integration by economic sectors.

In sharp contrast with Diebold, Meade purports only to discuss, in the strictest academic manner, the abstract issues involved in economic unions. "It is the general principles of economic union rather than their application to a particular union which I intend to examine" (p. 9). His abstractions, however, fit admirably the general positions adopted by Britain toward the very concrete issues involved. Progress toward integration should be slow and gradual, building on institutions already at hand (p. 84), and within the framework of an Atlantic Union of America, Britain, and continental Europe, rather than of Western Europe as such (p. 9). In the best tradition of British political economy, Meade's "general theory" glorifies as eternal truth the particular approach of an able and well-meaning Englishman to one of the major problems confronting his country and the world today.

His main theme is that the full potentialities of economic union cannot be realized without "an integration of the market for the factors of production, as well as for their products," that the latter "would involve serious limitations upon the intervention of national governments in domestic markets for particular goods and services," and that the first would similarly require a considerable surrender of national sovereignty to the Union authorities with respect to the choice of financial weapons for economic stabilization and general fiscal measures for influencing the distribution of income and property (pp. 82–83).

The logic of Professor Meade's arguments is unimpeachable. All it demonstrates, however, is that far-reaching surrenders of sovereignty over domestic as well as external economic policy would be necessary *to maximize the benefits of economic union.* For instance, the full advantages of free trade may be thwarted by divergencies between social and private costs—the external economies or diseconomies dear to Pigou—by differential taxation—or subsidization—of particular commodities, by monopolistic restrictions on output, etc. All this is undoubtedly true but, as Meade himself points out, the United States economy itself would fail to pass the rigorous integration test proposed by the author, i.e. the full equalization of market prices with "marginal utilities to consumers and marginal costs to society." Such an achievement would certainly be far beyond the reach of any administrative or political machinery conceivable today within a single country as well as among independent countries. If Utopia is set up as the goal of economic integration, it is easy to demonstrate how difficult and improbable its achievement is. I cannot but agree with Marjolin and Diebold, who both distinguish integration as an *end* —i.e. the achievement of full economic unification—and as a *process* —i.e. "all the steps taken toward this objective, even though they may fall very short of the final objective" (Marjolin, pp. 40–41; Diebold, p. 8).

The Secretary General of the OEEC presents a far less ambitious, but on the whole far better balanced, discussion of European integration than either Diebold or Meade. His brief sketch of the OEEC and EPU machinery and methods of operation highlights the essential features which explain both their achievements and their limitations. The parallels drawn between the OEEC, the European Coal and Steel Community, and the Council of Europe are very brief, but extremely revealing, particularly in connection with the vital distinction emphasized by Marjolin between the legal and practical implications of the unanimity and majority rules in the operation of international organizations.

The historical summary of Europe's achievements under the Marshall Plan, and of the difficult problems raised by the rearmament program adopted after the outbreak of the Korean War, is followed by a keen analysis of the long-run task of maintaining a satisfactory pace of economic expansion throughout the free world, together with a tenable equilibrium among the dollar area, Europe, and the underdeveloped countries. The policy conclusions of this part of the book go far beyond the historical analysis of Diebold and the theoretical analysis of Meade. I find myself in close agreement with Marjolin's concrete suggestions for complementary policies of international development by North America, Europe, and the underdeveloped areas, even though I sense more pessimism on his part about the so-called "dollar shortage" problem than can be justified either by facts or theory.[1]

II

All three authors find it hard to dissociate their concept of "economic integration" from the "free trade" ideal of classical economics.

[1]. See my paper on "International Currency and Reserve Plans," presented at the Second Conference on Policies to Combat Depression, Universities-National Bureau of Economic Research, Princeton, N.J., May 1954.

This is particularly true of Diebold, who reflects in this the prevalent attitude of American policy-makers toward the problem. Economic integration is discussed almost exclusively in terms of the removal of national barriers to trade or payments. The success of economic integration is measured by its success in lowering trade and currency barriers in general, not only among the members of the area but also with countries outside the area. The pros and cons of regional integration revolve mainly around Viner's distinction between the "trade-creating" and "trade-diverting" effects of a customs union. Diebold's conclusion is therefore a very guarded one: "It cannot be taken for granted that the dynamics of E.P.U. will make Western Europe better able to participate in a larger, freer trading area. Some elements in it promote that objective; others hinder it." (p. 415)

Meade recognizes the same problem, but only to exclude it from his analysis.

> I shall consider only the economic relationships between the countries forming the union and not their relationships with the countries outside the union. . . . By neglecting the very existence of countries outside the economic union, I shall be considering the advantageous effects of the union in creating trade and shall be neglecting the possibility that the union merely makes matters worse by diverting trade. (p. 8)

Having thus narrowed down the problem to that of free trade, he immediately broadens his horizon, however, by relating free-trade objectives to the goal of economic stabilization.

> We consider a group of countries which are coming together to form an economic union. They wish to raise their economic efficiency and so their standard of living by creating a large free-trade area and perhaps also by creating a large area within which factors of production can freely move to the most productive employment. They wish to do this in a way which is at least compatible with the avoidance of domestic booms and slumps and with the maintenance of equilibrium in their balances of payments. . . . In modern economic conditions this would be desirable on purely economic grounds which are too familiar to need repetition. In modern political conditions it is also, I am glad to say, a *sine qua non* without which countries would be unwilling to participate in any economic union. (pp. 6 and 33)

Finally, Marjolin's integration objectives are even broader.

> Let it be clear that all the objectives I have stated—nondiscrimination, freedom of transaction and transfer on current account, stability of exchange rates, controlled freedom for capital movements—are subject to the overriding consideration that the modern world cannot stand a large amount of unemployment for any length of time. Furthermore . . . the basic condition for the survival of our free societies is a dynamic, continuously expanding economy. (p. 82)

Meade and Marjolin both derive the same practical conclusion from their analyses. The complete abolition of trade barriers among independent countries would be inconceivable today without simultaneous agreements on the coordination of other phases of their economic policy—internal as well as external—designed to replace trade restrictions as a means toward other fundamental objectives related to the level of economic activity and employment, the pace of development, national security, etc. Such objectives have far more influence on modern governments and public opinion than does the rational allocation of resources which is the basic aim of free trade.

Second, the pursuit of these objectives by international cooperation and agreements—rather than by national policy—requires such vast commitments and surrenders of sovereignty as to rule out their sudden and radical implementation. A gradual, step by step, approach remains the only possible one for a long time to come.

III

We cannot rest content, however, with such a vague policy prescription. We can give it a far more concrete content on the basis of both theoretical analysis and historical experience. The following suggestions may appear as obvious and trite to some readers as they do to me. Yet they are still hotly opposed by many excellent minds in both academic and government circles.

(1) First of all, progress toward freedom of trade and payments can hardly be achieved, and particularly consolidated, by unilateral national action. This has long been recognized in the tariff field, and has prompted both bilateral and multilateral negotiation of tariff agreements, binding the partners to *simultaneous* and *reciprocal* commitments. We cannot rely on Platonic appeals to international co-

operation to prevail upon the national interests which are necessarily the first preoccupation of national governments. Desirable tariff action can only be made attractive, and undesirable action unattractive, from the national point of view through a system of collective agreements making the benefits of trade liberalization for each country dependent on its own trade policy toward the others.

What is true in the tariff field is equally true with respect to direct trade or exchange controls, including the multiple techniques of currency inconvertibility which have cropped up in the last twenty-five years. Marjolin rightly points out, in this connection, the contributions made by EPU

> to the cause of world convertibility by experimenting with mechanisms which I personally believe to be not only valid but necessary for the whole world. The E.P.U. system, which includes both rules and safety clauses, is based on an international agreement. This is the great superiority of the E.P.U. system over the gold standard. There was never any agreement between countries using the gold standard, whereas the E.P.U. is a system of simultaneous commitments. This essential feature explains a great deal of its success. It would be extremely difficult, if not impossible, to bring any country to give up restrictive practices, monetary or commercial, if it did not feel with some degree of assurance that the other countries were going to do the same. In other words, it is much easier to get all the countries to agree together to a measure of freedom in trade and payments than to agree one after the other. I cannot help feeling, therefore, that this system of simultaneous and reciprocal commitments holds great promise for the future. (pp. 83–84)

(2) Extensive trade and exchange commitments will still remain dependent, however, on other measures of cooperation designed to moderate the impact of external fluctuations on the domestic economy of the countries entering into such agreements. Complete freedom of trade and payments could not be achieved and maintained, and should not even be sought, in the absence of cooperative measures of a positive nature designed to cushion temporary fluctuations in the countries' balances of payments, and to facilitate desirable methods of adjustment to long-run fluctuations of a more fundamental character. The success of EPU in the elimination of all trade and currency discrimina-

tion among members, and in the progressive liberalization of other nondiscriminatory restrictions, is intimately related to:

(a) the provision of stabilization credits—both automatic and discretionary—by the creditor countries to the debtor members of the system;

(b) the willingness of the creditor countries to speed up their own liberalization measures beyond the formal commitments agreed to by all members, and to release temporarily from such commitments partner countries which encounter heavy balance-of-payments pressures;

(c) the willingness of all countries to submit to international discussion and scrutiny the whole range of their economic policies, internal as well as external, which may have a bearing on persistent or excessive balance-of-payments disequilibria threatening either the liquid resources of the Union or the continued progress of its members toward trade liberalization;

(d) the existence of a highly effective machinery for continuous consultation and negotiation among members, both at the technical and at the highest policy-making level, on the problems confronting the organization.

(3) Such extensive commitments, negotiations, and coordination of national policies are hardly feasible or desirable at this stage on a world-wide basis. Nor can they, even on a regional basis, aim at a total elimination of all trade barriers and protectionist measures. Three different levels of cooperation should be recognized as equally desirable in the interests of economic efficiency, stability, and development:

(a) the full integration of economic policy which can be achieved only on the basis of political unity, and which alone can ensure the total elimination of all trade and exchange restrictions within the national boundaries;

(b) the incomplete, but still intimate, integration of economic policies which is feasible among countries that are highly interdependent, keenly conscious of this interdependence, and easily amenable to close cooperation because of the similarity of national viewpoints and policies resulting from a common geographical and historical background and a relatively homogeneous stage of economic development;

(c) the looser agreements which prove both necessary and feasible

on a world-wide basis as a framework for national or regional decisions and policies.

The degree of coordination to be pursued at each one of these
three levels should depend upon a weighing of the advantages and
urgency of centralized decisions against the real costs and friction inseparable from such centralization. Internationalism is not desirable
per se. A fishing rights convention among the Scandinavian countries
should not be forced to wait upon the agreement of a landlocked
country, such as Switzerland, or even of a far distant country, such
as Australia. Many issues of trade or exchange policy arise primarily
among a limited group of countries and can be most fruitfully explored first through regional negotiation. About 70 per cent of Latin
American trade takes place within the Western Hemisphere, and two
thirds of EPU trade within the EPU area. Considerable progress may
often be achieved with greater ease and speed by direct discussion
among the countries most vitally concerned and should not be delayed
or impeded unnecessarily by insistence on a worldwide negotiation of
all the issues involved. The IMF consultations on the September 1949
devaluations, for instance, could have been far more significant, and
less purely formal, if they had been preceded and prepared by more
careful exploration at the regional level, before being brought up to
the Fund's Executive Board for decision. World-wide cooperation and
agreements are certainly essential to avoid or resolve world-wide
conflicts of interests, but they should not be overburdened with issues
which can best be handled by a more limited negotiation among the
countries most directly concerned.

The advantages of the regional approach are all the more evident
when, as indicated above, agreements are dependent upon the acceptance by all participants of positive, long-range commitments about
financial assistance, coordination of domestic monetary and fiscal
policy, etc. To insist here upon world-wide agreements will often be
tantamount to blocking action altogether.

Similar remarks apply to the substantive content, as well as to the
geographical scope, of international agreements. We should be ready
to exploit every area of feasible agreement rather than to insist on an
"all or nothing" procedure, which usually ends up with "nothing"
rather than with "all." The two criteria which should determine the
choice of objectives at any point of time are: (a) the relative urgency
of the cooperative measures aimed at; and (b) the feasibility of agreement. The EPU negotiation, for instance, centered primarily on the

elimination of bilateralism, i.e. upon the restoration of competition among all participating countries' exporters over the whole EPU area. The harmfulness of bilateral negotiating techniques had become evident to all, and complete agreement proved feasible on this point. The second objective of EPU was the removal of all direct trade and exchange restrictions on intra-European trade. This was far more difficult to achieve in view of the heavy balance-of-payments pressures to which many countries were still subject at that time. Only gradual progress could be achieved, with a 50 per cent liberalization target at first, rising quickly to 60 per cent, and later to 75 per cent of each country's private import trade. Even then, escape clauses had to be provided and were temporarily resorted to, at one time or another, by many of the participating countries.

The definition of ultimate integration goals is far less significant in practice than a clear order of priority among the objectives to be pursued. I would personally rank them roughly as follows:

(a) the immediate and complete elimination of all *bilateral* trade and exchange restrictions;

(b) the extension of *nondiscrimination* over as wide an area as is made possible by the policy commitments which can be negotiated among members, or by the *de facto* policies followed by nonmembers;

(c) the gradual relaxation of other forms of *restrictions* and trade protection, and particularly of direct, administrative trade and exchange controls;

(d) the avoidance of unnecessary fluctuations in exchange rates.

I have an uneasy feeling that world-wide attempts at postwar cooperation followed exactly the reverse order, negotiating exchange-rate commitments before tariff commitments, tariff commitments before the liberalization of other forms of restrictions, the liberalization of restrictions before the elimination of discrimination, and the elimination of discrimination before the elimination of bilateralism. The latter—most urgent and feasible—fields for effective cooperative action were therefore left fallow, thus stimulating the regional forms of cooperation which are responsible for most of the postwar progress toward economic integration, trade liberalization, and currency convertibility.

(4) This gradual and flexible approach to the ultimate ideals of international economic integration carries with it some implications totally alien to the pure logic of classical, or neoclassical, political economy. I shall mention only one of these by way of example.

Regional agreements, such as a customs union or preferential tariff area, have been subjected to heavy criticism because of their discriminatory, or trade-diverting, implications. Even the milder forms of regional integration implicit in the present OEEC trade code and EPU settlement system undoubtedly stimulate to some extent a diversion of imports from lower-cost suppliers outside the area to higher-cost suppliers within the area. If we accepted the full logic of this kind of reasoning, however, we should roundly condemn not only regional integration but national integration as well. If a tariff wall could be erected around each one of our forty-eight states, many of them would probably buy from cheaper sources of supply outside the United States goods which they now import from higher-cost suppliers within the United States. The elimination of such uneconomic trade-diversion could be carried even further through the erection of nondiscriminatory tariff walls around each one of our three thousand counties.

In pure economics, I would agree with Professor Viner's criterion and weigh in each case the advantages of the trade-creating impact of integration against the disadvantages of its trade-diverting impact. Very clearly, however, national boundaries and tariff walls have never been chosen, and could never be chosen, on such a basis. And yet they are usually accepted by the economists as a valid test in defining discriminatory or preferential trade practices. Mutual tariff or trade liberalization within the sterling area or EPU area is regarded as discriminatory, and therefore bad, but the absence of tariffs or other trade controls between northern and southern France is taken for granted and escapes condemnation by the economists as a "discriminatory" trade practice.

Such contradictions can be resolved only if trade liberalization is considered in its full economic, administrative, and political context. Mutual commitments, ranging over a wide area of economic policy, are indispensable to the success and consolidation of trade liberalization measures, particularly under present-day conditions. The economically undesirable trade-diverting effects of regional agreements must be weighed not only against their trade-creating effects, but also against the stability and security which they provide against sudden, unilateral changes of policy by the partner countries. The gradual elimination, in the nineteenth century, of internal barriers to the movement of goods within each country's national borders could hardly be regarded as a retrogressive step in their economic life. We are witnessing today the gradual development of free—or at least freer—trade areas across national borders, on the basis of reciprocal commitments involving various degrees of surrender of national economic sovereignty. I have far more confidence in the continued progress of these forms of international cooperation, rooted in practical considerations of each participant's national interests and of the feasibility of administrative and political implementation, than I have in universal agreements that are based on abstract economic ideologies and extremely difficult to negotiate and administer effectively in practice. Economic integration is a process of growth and may easily be smothered rather than accelerated by premature, over-all landscaping.

To conclude with an old French saying which might be worth some meditation in our State Department as well as in our universities: "Le mieux est souvent l'ennemi du bien."

2. The Size of the Nation and Its Vulnerability to Economic Nationalism

Orthodox economic advice is once more being spurned by the statesmen. The Common Market Treaty has already been signed, and negotiations on the establishment of a European free trade area are moving rapidly toward a successful conclusion. The specters of discrimination and trade diversion have been unable to block the path toward regional liberalization and to push the nations toward the highroad of world-wide liberalization under the auspices of GATT or of the ITO.

The economists, however, are gentle fellows who take such rebukes in their stride, and are quite willing—even anxious—to try and find belated economic justifications for the decision of their governments to do the opposite of what they had wanted them to do. Keynes did this in the 1930s and I suspect that we may have been assembled here for a similar face-saving operation.

Let us not indulge once more in our favorite pastime and take the classical economists as the villains of the play. They cannot be blamed for our former misgivings and hostility toward preferential—or discriminatory—trade liberalization, customs unions, etc. They were indeed remarkably silent on such topics, as well as on the broader theme assigned to us here: "The Economic Consequences of the Size of Nations." Their main contention was that any nation, whether small or

Presented at a Round Table of the International Economic Association, in Lisbon, September 11–18, 1957, and published in *The Economic Consequences of the Size of Nations,* ed. Austin Robinson (Macmillan, 1960), pp. 247–64.

large, has a selfish interest in pursuing free trade policies, whether other nations wisely follow the same path or foolishly allow themselves to be lured away from it by protectionist fallacies. If, however, we were able to conjure up their spirits among us today and to ask them pointblank to express an opinion on the "economic consequences of the size of nations," I have little doubt as to what their answer would be. After having assumed everything else to be equal, they would probably point out that the larger the nation the larger the area over which free trade would be guaranteed by political organization in a world of nation states. They would also point out, I am sure, that if each nation state acted rationally and embraced free trade, little or no damage could be done by the existence of separate political sovereignties and that the size of nations would then be irrelevant to their economic prosperity.[1]

The adoption of protectionism by any one state, however, does damage to others as well as to itself, since it deprives them of opportunities for profitable exchange and specialization, based on comparative costs and advantages. Everything else being equal—once more—the smaller nation will be more vulnerable than the larger nation to the action of its neighbors, since its ability to concentrate on, and exploit to the full, the lines of production for which it is best fitted by natural advantages will be more dependent on its freedom of access to foreign markets for its exports and imports. Who can doubt that minuscule Luxemburg is more vulnerable to other nations' nationalism than the gigantic United States?

Aspects of Vulnerability

This vulnerability expresses itself in a great variety of ways. A high level of foreign restrictions is the most familiar, but by no means the most important, of its manifestations. A second is the fact that the individual country is exposed at all times to sudden and unpredictable shifts in the level of these restrictions. This has become of paramount importance in a world in which the age-old, and relatively stable, techniques of tariff protection are now supplemented by quantitative trade and exchange controls, far more rigid in their incidence and subject to day-to-day changes of an administrative character, bypassing the slower channels of parliamentary decisions and renegotiation of tariff treaties. A third is the growth of bilateral trade and payments

---

1. Even then, however, the size of nations would still have been regarded as relevant to the mobility of factors of production.

techniques, in which naked bargaining power supplants price and quality competition as a determinant of each country's trade pattern. Finally, the course of economic events in a small country may be vitally affected even by the *internal* policies adopted by its trade partners. If it wishes to avoid recourse to trade restrictions or currency devaluation, it will be forced to adjust its own internal policies to theirs, or at least to eschew any faster rate of monetary expansion with relation to production and liquidity requirements than that prevailing beyond its national borders.[2] This may be regarded by outsiders as a desirable discipline, preventing the adoption of irresponsible inflationary policies, and it is sometimes pointed out that a small country enjoys in this respect a real advantage over a large country because of its inability to seek a practical escape from such discipline through protectionist restrictions and economic isolation. Its smallness thus protects it from the follies in which a larger country may indulge more easily! This type of argument, however, is at best more convincing to outside judges than to the national authorities concerned. And it certainly glosses over the fact that the small nation may thereby be forced to adjust its policies to the inferior, as well as to the superior, wisdom and administrative capacity of other countries.

Implications for Policy

The vulnerability of the small nation to economic nationalism still plays only a minor role in shaping up the policy prescriptions of traditional international trade theory. First of all, it is often assumed (as already observed above) that each country will have a selfish interest in free trade anyway, no matter what other countries do. This might be true if other countries adopted, once and for all, a given and unchanging level of protection in their international trade relations. It may not be true, however, if other countries' policies exhibit frequent and violent shifts, making them highly unstable and volatile markets for the exports of their trade partners. Switzerland, for instance, might have a natural advantage in concentrating an even larger share of its productive resources on the manufacture of watches for export and in supplying a correspondingly larger share of its home requirements of other goods through imports rather than from home produc-

2. The emergence of balance-of-payments problems plays here a role similar to that of interbank clearings—and the inability of an individual bank to create legal tender—in preventing an overexpansion of credit by an individual bank relative to the pace of expansion of other banks, within the same country or monetary area.

tion. This advantage might not be decisive, however, and a certain degree of protection and insulation from world trade might well become advisable if, in fact, its export markets for watches fluctuate violently from year to year, and bring back recurrent waves of unemployment for highly specialized workers and equipment which cannot be shifted easily and quickly into other occupations. One might presume, however, that these considerations would not go unperceived by private firms, although the spread of unemployment insurance schemes would tend to create divergencies between private and social calculations in this respect.

The second, stock-in-trade argument of traditional economics is that there is little that a country can do to influence the policies of others, and that insofar as such influence exists it only reinforces the argument for liberal trading policies. Protectionism tends to spread and invites retaliation, while liberal policies have also a tendency to spread and may be generalized and consolidated through the most-favored-nation clause or through world-wide agreements of the ITO, or GATT, variety. The validity of this argument was far greater in the nineteenth century than it is today. It rested very largely indeed on the tacit assumption that all countries choose only between more or less *restrictive* policies, but do not resort to *bilateral* restrictions and discrimination. The situation became very different with the generalization of bilateral techniques in world trade and payments. Even a small country could now influence greatly the restrictions applied by other countries to its exports, depending on whether or not it agrees to engage in bilateral negotiations with them. The refusal of Italy to conclude a bilateral agreement with the United Kingdom in 1947, for instance, might have deprived that country of the bulk of its export markets for fruit and vegetables which the United Kingdom was in a position to buy elsewhere, or do partly without in accordance with the "austerity" policy to which it was driven by its balance-of-payments difficulties. There were many economists in those days to recommend that Italy put "its own house in order," restore the convertibility of the lira, and refuse to accept payment for its exports in inconvertible sterling. If this advice had been heeded, Italians would probably have had either to eat their lemons and drink their Chianti, or to find substitute markets for them in the few hard-currency countries then in existence—and absorbing normally little more than 10 per cent of Italy's exports—or to accept severe unemployment, or to reshuffle fundamentally their production and export pattern to adjust it to generalized discrimination against Italian exports by the soft-currency areas—normally accounting for nearly 90 per cent of Italy's export trade. None of these solutions could be deemed very attractive or promising. In the short run, bilateral trading itself would result in a less wasteful allocation of Italy's resources than the very low levels of trade that would ensue at first from the adoption of such policies. And in the longer run the painful overhauling of Italy's trade and production pattern, necessary to maintain lira convertibility in an inconvertible Europe, would have had to be undone and reversed in order to readjust Italy's economy to the more normal conditions brought back by Europe's recovery.

Nineteenth-century techniques of trade negotiation were indeed attempted, and improved upon, during those days to deal with this kind of problem. Their success was very modest, however, and the reasons for this cannot all be ascribed to temporary postwar dislocations. The liberal philosophy of limited interference by the government in economic life (internal as well as external) and the ignorance of modern techniques of intervention—such as direct controls, rigid inconvertibility techniques, bilateral trade and payments agreements, etc.—narrowly limited in former days the likelihood of large-scale divergencies in the monetary evolution of the major trading countries and in their national price and cost levels. The harmonization of policies could be left, to a considerable extent, to the spontaneous interplay of market forces. The residual role left to international negotiation and agreements was a relatively modest one and could be handled by comparatively simple techniques, centering upon the conclusion of tariff treaties and their generalization through the most-favored-nation clause

The broadening of the horizons of economic policy—to include as objectives a maximum rate of employment and growth, the stabilization of prices, the improvement of working conditions, assistance to weaker economic sectors, etc.—and of the instruments of control or intervention at the disposal of national states have increased enormously the tasks that must be performed today by negotiated, rather than spontaneous, policy harmonization among independent economic sovereignties. The problems raised by such harmonization are basically different from those analyzed by the classical economists, and cannot be handled or understood through the use of the traditional tools of economic theory. They refer to the reconstruction of the stable institutional framework for international trade and payments which the classicists assumed as a datum and a point of departure for their investigation, rather than as a problem for economic policy.

The reconstruction of such a stable framework involves essentially the acceptance by independent countries of certain limitations on their economic sovereignty, or, in less resounding words, of certain constraints on the manner in which they will make use of this sovereignty. It is a dangerous illusion that strict limitations on the use of *external* policy tools—such as exchange-rate determination, tariffs, import restrictions, exchange controls, discrimination, and bilateralism—can be effectively negotiated and implemented without parallel agreements of a more positive nature about mutual assistance or escape clauses in case of difficulties, and even about a minimum of harmonization in the area of *internal* economic policies insofar as these have direct and important repercussions upon the countries' balance of payments.

The OEEC-EPU experiment, and the area covered by the more recent negotiation of the Common Market Treaty, abundantly confirm this conclusion. They also make clear why success is more likely to be reached first by regional, rather than universal, organizations and institutions. The mere administrative burden involved in continuous consultation and reconciliation of divergent interests and points of view is a first and immediate handicap to world-wide cooperation. The depth and comprehensiveness of feasible cooperation and commitments will, moreover, be in inverse relation to the number and heterogeneity of the participants in such discussions. The implication of these facts is obvious. While exploiting to the fullest possible extent the opportunities for world-wide agreements, we cannot neglect the greater potentialities opened up by regional agreements for more intimate forms of cooperation and harmonization of policies among countries highly interdependent, keenly conscious of this interdependence, and better prepared for such coordinated action by a common geographical and historical background and a relatively homogeneous stage of economic development. Various levels of economic integration are perfectly reconcilable with one another and may indeed reinforce one another. Agreements of the IMF or GATT type can be complemented by closer and closer forms of association, ranging from those of the Atlantic Community, for instance, to intergovernmental agreements of the OEEC and EPU type, down to supranational groupings like the European Coal and Steel Community, economic unions *à la* Benelux, and finally the complete merger of sovereignty of the nation state.

The Bogey of Trade Diversion

This commonsense conclusion would indeed belabor the obvious, if common sense had not been strongly challenged and clouded over here by ingenious economic arguments stressing the dangers and pitfalls of customs unions and other "discriminatory" arrangements among independent countries. Bizarrely enough, none of these economists appears to be disturbed by the discriminatory implications of national boundaries themselves, and none has followed his own line of reasoning to its logical conclusion and argued for the breaking up —in the name of nondiscrimination—of national economic areas into smaller economic areas delineated by provincial, municipal or even (why not?) individual household boundaries.

The traditional argument against customs unions was formulated long ago and most lucidly, if succinctly, by Professor Viner. Customs unions may be good or bad depending on whether or not their "trade-creating" impact outweighs their "trade-diverting" impact. Let us suppose, for instance, that Germany can produce cars more efficiently than France, but less efficiently than the United States. A customs union between France and Germany would be good, according to Viner's concept, if it induced Frenchmen to shift from French cars to German cars, but bad insofar as it induced them to import from Germany cars that would otherwise be imported from the United States.[3]

Professor Haberler later made use of the same criterion to justify the ITO distinction between trade preferences and customs unions. The reduction of duties under preferential regimes is likely to be predominantly trade-diverting, "because there is a natural tendency to reduce trade barriers only for those commodities which do not actively compete with domestic production." On the other hand, "a customs union will always be to some extent, possibly to a large extent, trade creating." Yet Professor Haberler recognized that "in Europe the policy of regional trade liberalization (implying, though it does, discrimination against the United States, Canada, Latin America, Japan, and others) has had some success and has gone beyond trade diversion, creating additional trade between the European countries. Fortunately, however, the discrimination against the United States, Canada, Latin America, has become progressively less severe because restrictions on

---

3. See Jacob Viner, *The Customs Union Issue* (New York, Carnegie Endowment for International Peace, 1950).

imports from dollar countries have been reduced and currencies have become more freely convertible." [4]

This latter observation illustrates, to my mind, the fact that the main argument for regional economic integration lies outside the scope of mere economic reasoning of a static character. The lowering of restrictions on imports from nonmember countries and the gradual extension of currency convertibility may well be a byproduct of regional integration rather than an independent and fortunate accident. The trade-creating and trade-diverting effects of regional integration cannot be fully appraised by looking only at the immediate and direct trade concessions incorporated in a regional agreement. Indirect effects and policy incentives are far more significant for arriving at a broad judgment of the over-all impact of the agreement on future trade patterns.

Let us first accept the Viner-Haberler argument at face value, and see whether we cannot make at least a tentative guess as to the probable balance of trade-creating and trade-diverting impacts in a concrete case. Continental OEEC countries, together with their overseas territories, absorbed in 1955 about 58 per cent of these countries' total exports. Sterling area markets absorbed another 16 per cent, making a total of 74 per cent, as against 8 per cent of total exports going to the United States and Canada, 6 per cent to Latin America, and 13 per cent to the rest of the world.[5] The proportion of EPU markets in individual countries' exports exceeded 70 per cent in all cases but three—Turkey, Italy, and Switzerland—and ran as high as 94 per cent in the case of Ireland (see Table 1). Everything else being equal, therefore, one might expect that the area of trade amenable to "trade creation" under the EPU type of regional liberalization is about three times as large as the area susceptible to "trade diversion" under these arrangements.

Everything else was far from equal, however, in 1949. Restrictions on hard-currency imports from nonmembers, and particularly from the dollar area, were about as stringent as they could be before the es-

4. *Foreign Economic Policy:* Hearings Before the Subcommittee on Foreign Economic Policy of the Joint Committee on the Economic Report, 89th Congress (Washington, D.C., 1955), pp. 501, 505, and 507–08.

5. These proportions are almost identical to those of 1950, dispelling the notion that the OEEC-EPU system tended to isolate Europe from world trade and to result in a major distortion of trade patterns. Comparisons with 1937, however, show a substantial increase in Europe's exports to its overseas territories, at the expense of exports to the "rest of the world," i.e. to countries outside EPU and the Western Hemisphere.

TABLE 1

PERCENTAGE DISTRIBUTION OF OEEC AND STERLING AREA EXPORTS IN 1955

Exporting countries and areas	To EPU markets			Other			
	Continental OEEC and dependencies	Sterling area	Total	Total	U.S. and Canada	Latin America	Other
Austria	62	9	71	28	5	4	19
Belgium	63	13	76	25	12	4	9
Denmark	43	37	80	19	6	4	9
France	68	11	79	21	5	5	11
Germany	59	13	72	29	7	8	14
Greece	60	12	72	29	13	1	15
Italy	47	15	62	37	9	10	18
Netherlands	55	21	76	24	7	5	12
Norway	43	29	72	29	10	6	13
Portugal	54	21	75	25	11	5	9
Sweden	52	26	78	22	6	6	10
Switzerland	49	13	62	38	13	9	16
Turkey	42	8	50	51	16	—	35
Subtotal	**58**	**16**	**74**	**27**	**8**	**6**	**13**
United Kingdom	27	48	75	25	11	4	10
Ireland	5	89	94	6	3	—	3
Sterling area	**24**	**49**	**73**	**26**	**11**	**2**	**13**

SOURCE: *International Financial Statistics.*

tablishment of EPU. Imports from these sources were severely limited to essential goods and raw materials for which there existed no substitute sources of supply within the EPU area. The scope for further "trade diversion" was thus extremely narrow, while that for mutual "trade-creating" concessions was enormous.

The same observation casts serious doubts on the practical relevance of Professor Haberler's commonsense expectations that preferential concessions—short of a full customs union—are likely to concentrate on "those commodities which do not actively compete with domestic production." In any case, the rapid expansion of trade liberalization commitments to categories of goods accounting for 50, 60, 75, and finally 90 per cent or more of total imports from other members, made it increasingly difficult to pick and choose these categories in such a way as to exclude goods competing with domestic production.

The trade-diverting argument is, moreover, open to broader objections and limitations on general grounds of economic theory. Let us, for the sake of concreteness, examine the implications of a preferential reduction of tariffs between France and Germany. Is it conceivable that France will be able to grant to Germany significant concessions leading to a substitution of German goods for American imports rather than for French-produced merchandise? This would presuppose the existence of severe customs duties or other restrictions on goods which, in spite of these duties and restrictions, France herself still does not produce domestically. In other words, it presupposes a high level of *ineffective* protectionism by the French. Is it not far more likely that the highest duties will be encountered on goods whose home production can be stimulated thereby rather than on goods which France does not produce anyway?

Restrictions may be imposed by France, however, for other than protectionist reasons, e.g. for balance-of-payments reasons. In this case, trade-diverting concessions to Germany become possible. The *quid pro quo* of such concessions, from the French point of view, would be similar concessions by Germany opening the German market to additional exports from France. If, however, the French balance-of-payments difficulties are due to *over-all* inflationary pressures, i.e. to the financing of expenditures in excess of maximum production, the concessions obtainable from Germany would be of little value to the French. If their economy is already fully employed, an expansion of exports to Germany—accompanied by a reshuffling of import sources, but not by an over-all increase in imports—could be effected only at the cost of a decline in French exports to other areas, or of an aggravation of internal inflationary pressures in France. Such a situation would create few incentives for mutual trade concessions of the "trade diversion" variety.

These observations seem to me to restrict to a special case the Viner fears about the impact of preferential tariff reductions or elimination. They would be most relevant in a situation in which all partners suffer simultaneously from balance-of-payments difficulties *and* unemployment, arising from uncompetitive cost levels or exchange rates. They would have far less relevance to a situation in which duties and restrictions are prompted by protectionist motives or by balance-of-payments difficulties originating in *over-all* inflationary pressures rather than in price distortions.

This distinction is all the more significant as the trade diversion argument loses much of its force in the first of the three situations distinguished above, i.e. when balance-of-payments deficits coincide with unemployment. In such a case, trade diversion would improve both employment and the balance of payments of the partners to the preferential agreement. France and Germany, for example, would both reduce their imports from the United States—while keeping their *over-all* import levels unchanged—and would export more to one another, without subjecting themselves thereby to shortages or upward price pressures susceptible of bringing a reduction in their exports to the United States.

The simultaneous abatement of unemployment pressures and balance-of-payments difficulties would then tend to reduce two major incentives to restrictions and discrimination against nonmember countries. The trade-creating and trade-diverting impacts of regional integration cannot be fully appraised by looking only at the initial pattern of trade concessions incorporated into a regional agreement. Indirect effects and policy incentives must also be taken into account, including particularly the allocation of the balance-of-payments improvements resulting from trade diversion to the reduction of initial import restrictions against nonmember countries.

The Bogey of the Sheltered High-Cost Area

These favorable effects of trade diversion upon employment and the balance of payments would taper off, however, as full employment is approached throughout the territory of the participating countries. Further expansion of intraregional trade would then be accompanied by overemployment pressures, price increases, and a reduction of exports to the outside world. The union might develop into a high-cost area, increasingly cut off from world-wide competition by inflationary developments at home behind the barrier of higher and higher restrictions against imports from the outside.

Let us first remember, however, that the net impact of regional integration on the members' cost level will be the result of two contrary types of price pulls. Prices will be pulled upward by trade diversion, but downward by trade creation. The creation of competitive conditions throughout the European territory would expose each industry to competition from the most efficient producers in Europe. One suspects that, as of today, there exist relatively few categories of goods for which no European producer offers competition as strong as American production itself. The Belgian steel industry, the German electrical and chemical industries, watch and precision instruments in Switzerland, etc., are as (or more) efficient as their American counterparts and would exercise powerful pressures for competitive readjustments in European cost levels. The mere elimination of bilateralism sufficed to reintroduce these competitive forces via the competition of exporters throughout the EPU territory. Excessive national cost levels had to be readjusted to preserve exports even before protective restrictions were themselves reduced under the OEEC trade liberalization program. The dismantlement of protection will be carried out further under the common market and free-trade area provisions. Progress will be slower in this respect—extending over a period of 12 to 17 years—but it is worth noting that the mere signature of the treaties will constitute from the start a powerful spur to the most efficient producers to increase their production capacity and develop their export markets, in the knowledge that such expansion will no longer risk being arrested by a sudden tightening of controls, but will in fact be assisted by the gradual elimination of existing restrictions.

In the longer run, the maintenance of competitive cost levels will depend, of course, on the comparative evolution of monetary, fiscal, and price policies within and outside Europe. The question should therefore be raised as to whether regional integration is likely to strengthen, or to weaken, monetary discipline in the participating countries.

Two possibilities should be sharply distinguished in this respect.

The first is that of a free-trade area or customs union accompanied only by a minimum of monetary integration among the participating countries. I mean by this the type of monetary integration now embodied in the European Payments Union or the European Monetary Agreement. These arrangements are primarily designed to eliminate bilateral techniques in payment,[6] but leave each country fully responsible for the conduct of its monetary policy and the financing of its balance-of-payments deficits within as well as outside Europe. Under such conditions, monetary overexpansion in any one country, relative to the others, rapidly leads to unsustainable balance-of-payments deficits and reserve losses, and forces the adoption of "corrective" measures indispensable to arrest the drain on reserves. In the absence of a customs union, these measures may take the form of trade and ex-

6. Widespread alarm was expressed in 1949 and 1950 concerning the "excessive" credit facilities of the EPU arrangements. These were totally unfounded and have been amply refuted by later events. See *Europe and the Money Muddle* (New Haven, 1957).

change restrictions, behind the protection of which inflationary forces may be allowed to proceed to a considerable extent until their final impact upon export and import levels becomes economically and politically unbearable. The free-trade area eliminates this possibility as far as regional trade is concerned, and authorizes only the tightening of restrictions on imports from nonmembers, i.e. on a minor portion of the deficit country's total trade. The Common Market Treaty goes even further, since it involves the adoption of a uniform tariff which cannot be changed at the discretion of any single country.

Under such conditions, the deficit country will have no alternative left but to readjust its internal policies and cost level or to devalue its currency. Monetary discipline will therefore be far stronger than in the absence of regional integration. The participating countries will have to "keep in step" with one another, and the pressures which will force them to do so will concentrate upon the more inflationary, or less deflationary, countries of the group.

The second possibility is that of closer forms of integration, culminating in a unification of monetary responsibilities and policies among the participating countries, and excluding exchange readjustments among them. The over-all pace of expansion would, in this case, be determined by collective decisions—involving a greater or lesser degree of *a priori* centralization or *a posteriori* negotiations—rather than automatically by the policies of the more conservative countries in the group. Regional integration of this kind will make it easier for the group as a whole than it was for individual countries to isolate themselves from more deflationary, or less inflationary, policies followed in the rest of the world. Regional integration decreases the vulnerability of the participating countries to foreign shocks. It gives them the means of protecting themselves from the impact of other countries' follies or wisdom, increasing their ability to follow wiser or more foolish policies than those prevailing in the outside world. Whether acquiring such mastery over its own destiny would be a gain or a loss for Europe is a question on which statesmen are likely to feel the least need for the opinion of their economic advisers.

The Bogey of the Large Autarkic Blocs

The various considerations outlined above seem to me to create a far stronger presumption in favor of regional agreements than that which might emerge from a purely static and exclusively economic interpretation of the balance between their immediate trade-creating and trade-diverting impacts. Yet it is still no more than a presumption, which may be strengthened or weakened by the concrete circumstances surrounding actual experiments in economic integration. If, for instance, regional integration tended in fact to divide the world into rival blocs bent on protectionist, autarkic policies, we would view it with much greater misgivings than if it created instead a large and stable area of freer trade, gradually drawing nonmember countries into its orbit.

Postwar integration has clearly developed in the latter, rather than the former, direction. Formal cooperation among OEEC countries was extended through EPU to an area whose total trade accounts for nearly 60 per cent of world trade. Harmonization of this area's trade and payments policies with those of the United States and Canada would cover about 80 per cent of world trade, and would be tantamount to establishing a universal framework for world trade and monetary settlements. The regional approach would blend, in this case, into the world-wide approach to economic cooperation.

Regional economic integration is indeed unlikely to lead to the formation of rival autarkic blocs for the simple reason that this would require a most radical upheaval in the world trade pattern. The formation of EPU was greatly enhanced by the fact that exports to the EPU area have long accounted for 70 to 75 per cent of the total exports of most EPU countries. This was already true in prewar days when currency convertibility prevailed and discriminating trade and exchange restrictions were at a minimum over most of the present EPU area.

Trade patterns in other parts of the world are very different indeed. A Latin American union, for instance, would regulate only 10 per cent of the total exports of its members. Even a Western Hemisphere bloc would include only 53 per cent of the participating countries' exports, and substantially less than this (43 per cent) for the southern countries of the group, whose main export markets (47 per cent) are in the EPU area itself (see Table 2). For reasons amply discussed above, effective regional agreements are likely to be concluded only among countries closely interdependent on one another, and this would seem to preclude the duplication of EPU types of arrangement in other parts of the world.[7]

7. This is not to say, however, that other countries might not find it useful to conclude different types of arrangement aiming primarily at strengthening their bargaining position in trade negotiations with nonmember countries.

TABLE 2

REGIONAL DISTRIBUTION OF WORLD EXPORTS IN 1954
(in per cent)

Exports from	Exports to			
	World	EPU area	Dollar area	Other countries
EPU area	58	73	11	15
Dollar area	27	34	50	16
Other countries	16	51	22	27
World	**100**	**60**	**23**	**17**

NOTE: Exports to (first column) and from (last row) the world are given in per cent of world totals. The other data are given in per cent of each area's total exports to the world.

SOURCE: Derived from GATT estimates in *International Trade*, 1955 (Geneva, GATT, May 1956), pp. 201–203 and 222–23.

The impact of European integration on trade and payments arrangements in the rest of the world may indeed help us resolve a rather puzzling question. What is *international*, as distinct from *national*, convertibility? One swallow does not make a summer. But *how many* swallows are needed to make a summer? The preservation of convertibility by one or two countries obviously does not ensure international convertibility. Just as obviously, however, we would not regard the maintenance of inconvertibility by Paraguay or Honduras as a fatal flaw in the armor of international convertibility. Even the nineteenth-century gold standard rested essentially on the adherence of the United States, Western Europe, and its dependent monetary areas, but did not preclude various degrees of restrictions and protectionism by individual countries, and of exchange rate instability by many countries in Latin America and Asia.

I have discussed elsewhere[8] the reasons why the elimination of bilateralism, rather than of protectionism, should be regarded as the primary criterion in the definition of convertibility, if the latter is not to become confused with the old ideal of free trade. The significance of regional European integration for international convertibility flows from this observation. European integration does not rule out protectionism in the rest of the world—nor indeed by Europe itself—but it

8. "International Currency and Reserve Plans" in *Policies to Combat Depression* (National Bureau of Economic Research, Princeton, 1956), and *Europe and the Money Muddle,* Chapter 7.

greatly reduces the probable scope of bilateralism in the world at large.

No country has a direct interest in discrimination, i.e. in shifting its imports from less costly to costlier sources of supply, except as a means to extract from its trade partners similar discrimination in its own favor, or to protect its exports against unfavorable discrimination by them. The EPU Agreement, however, together with the nondiscriminatory policies generally pursued by the dollar area effectively safeguard against discrimination 85 per cent of the EPU countries' exports, and preclude the use of discrimination as a weapon for expanding these exports. All other countries together absorb only 15 per cent of EPU countries' exports, and their own exports account for only 20 per cent of total world exports (see Table 2). This leaves relatively little room for discrimination, particularly if one considers that profitable discrimination requires in each case mutual action by at least two countries.

EPU countries have, moreover, an interest in avoiding discriminatory arrangements concluded with third countries at one another's expense. Recent EPU consultations have been dealing with this problem and have already led to a substantial contraction of credit margins in payments agreements with nonmember countries, to a large decline in the number of such agreements, and to the adoption of transferable EPU currencies for settlements with inconvertible countries. The main concern underlying residual bilateral payments provisions is to guarantee debt repayment by the partner country rather than to promote a further expansion of exports through discriminatory trade and payment practices.

The increasing reluctance of EPU countries to perpetuate bilateral trade and payments agreements makes it correspondingly difficult for third countries to maintain such agreements with their major trading partners. Since the overwhelming bulk of their own trade is with the EPU countries, the United States, and Canada, the remaining opportunities for discrimination and bilateralism are becoming so scant as to be of little significance for world trade and payments in general. The essential point is that the broad direction of the international trade and payments system toward or away from convertibility is determined by the policies of the major trading nations. These can force their weaker partners into convertibility as well as into inconvertibility, but the smaller countries cannot exercise the same influence upon the larger ones.

This is why firmer, *de jure* arrangements among the latter are both necessary, under modern conditions, and sufficient to restore and maintain international convertibility. Trade and payments relations not covered specifically by these agreements will depend on the *de facto* policies pursued by the countries concerned, but will offer few opportunities, incentives, or pressures for discrimination and bilateralism, except as a protection of last resort against the international spread of deflation or restrictions.

Such a mixture of *de jure* and *de facto* convertibility may not be sufficient, of course, to ensure the continued progress of trade liberalization and exchange-rate stability among all the countries of the world. Broader negotiations, within the framework of the OTC and the IMF, will retain a major role in this respect, but will be helped rather than hindered by the closer degree of cooperation and integration which may be achieved under regional agreements.

Conclusion

Progress toward freer trade involves essentially the acceptance of specific limitations on the interference of political power in economic life, as a way to defend the interests, real or fancied, of the group subject to that political power. The acceptability of such limitations, and their political feasibility, have always depended in large part on the existence of alternative ways of achieving the same objective. Complete and irrevocable commitments to free trade are therefore hardly encountered historically except within areas subject to the same political sovereignty, i.e. within the confines of the nation state. The dismantlement of local barriers to trade followed indeed, rather than preceded, the withering away of local or provincial autonomy and the assertion of full sovereignty by national governments. The economists are prone to accept meekly—and sometimes unconsciously—these political developments as valid criteria for economic policy. A general rise in French tariffs against imports from foreign countries will be regarded as nondiscriminatory, even though it implies a corresponding increase in existing discrimination between external trade and the trade of, let us say, northern France with southern France.

This is, of course, perfectly illogical and completely indefensible, on theoretical as well as on historical grounds. If various countries are ready to accept a partial pooling of their economic sovereignty sufficient to eliminate or even reduce national barriers to their mutual trade, the results of these arrangements cannot automatically be labeled as more discriminatory than those involved in the maintenance of separate *national* customs areas, merely because the latter rest on a full merger of political, as well as economic, sovereignty. The economic significance of national boundaries may change as a result of economic integration as well as of political integration among the participating countries.

Economic incentives to integration are closely linked with the degree of economic interdependence between various geographical areas and of awareness of this interdependence on the part of their residents and political leaders. These incentives (together with parallel political incentives arising from the awareness of political interdependence) must be sufficient to overcome the emotional and administrative obstacles to the acceptance of advance commitments to certain lines of action and policy or to collective procedures for the adoption or harmonization of later decisions. Both of these factors point in the same direction. The need for integration is greatest, the obstacles to integration are least, and integration is therefore most likely to be achieved among areas closely interdependent on one another, keenly conscious of this interdependence, and better prepared by geographic proximity and a common historical heritage for a sympathetic understanding of each other's problems and policies. Integration at the national level, within the political boundaries of nineteenth-century nation states, could serve reasonably well the needs of a world where *lassez-faire* traditions circumscribed narrowly the intervention of state authorities in economic life and minimized the chances for large-scale maladjustments in the international trade and payments pattern. The enormous growth of national interventionism in economic life has increased correspondingly the scope of such maladjustments while reducing or distorting automatic mechanisms of readjustment based on market forces. Conscious policy integration can no longer stop at the national boundaries, and cannot be approved or condemned on the basis of a narrowly economic appraisal of its trade-diverting and trade-creating impact. The fundamental dilemma of international economic relations in this twentieth century lies in the inadequacy of national sovereignty as a framework for policy decisions and their administrative implementation in an interdependent world. This dilemma cannot be resolved overnight through a sudden and radical transformation of our institutions and habits of thought. The days of a world government are not yet at hand. The mushrooming and overlapping of international and regional institutions since the Second World War are both bewildering and disappointing to the logical mind. This proliferation, however, merely reflects our persistent efforts to remedy the partial failure of previous, half-hearted gropings after new forms of political organization necessary to reach and implement collective decisions where their need is sufficiently felt to overcome old prejudices and inertia. The ambitious framework of universal cooperation, indispensable as it is in many cases, often limits feasible coordination to *ad hoc*—and often *ex post*—attempts to smooth out conflicts of views and interest on specific issues and proposals. Regional cooperation, on the other hand, is far more likely to succeed in developing habits of continuous consultation and negotiation over a broader range of governmental responsibilities; and it may, if successful, gradually evolve toward the actual merging of areas too small and too interdependent on one another to preserve national welfare and security on the basis of national sovereignty exercised within present political boundaries.

We have long been familiar with the first problem, but we still fail to see clearly the full implications of the second for the reorientation of international economic theory as well as international economic policy.

Chapter XI: European Integration

THE PAPERS reproduced in this chapter are extracted from the enormous mass of unpublished studies and memoranda which I prepared over the years 1947–58 for the IMF, the Economic Cooperation Administration (and its successor agencies), the OEEC, etc., on the preparation, negotiation, and reform of the European Payments Union. They should be read, or consulted, only by students interested in the negotiating process itself. Other readers will find the highlights of the story in the other sections of this chapter and on pp. 128–36 and Chapters 4, 5, and 6 of *Europe and the Money Muddle*.

I. THE IMF MISSES THE BUS . . .

The European Payments Union is universally credited today as having been the main instrument through which European countries succeeded in shedding the bilateral straitjacket of the early postwar years and in restoring, by 1958, trade liberalization and currency convertibility not only within Europe itself, but also in their relations with the rest of the world. Many academic economists and government experts, however, were far from enthusiastic, in the late 1940s, about the proposals from which EPU was to emerge, after three years of bitter and protracted debate, in the summer of 1950. Nationalist planners saw in trade and exchange restrictions, discrimination, and bilateral negotiations indispensable bulwarks against the transmission of deflationary pressures from the surplus countries to the deficit countries. Internationalists and *laissez-faire* economists, on the other hand, violently denounced the danger of dividing the world into autarkic blocs, and/or spreading inflation from the weaker to the stronger countries, thus creating a sheltered, high cost area condemned to increasing protectionism and discrimination against outside competition and resulting balance-of-payments deficits.

These contradictory viewpoints coalesced into an unholy alliance and common opposition to my repeated attempts, over the years 1947–49, to organize, under the aegis of the IMF, a multilateral system of European settlements. The first three memoranda which I prepared for the Fund are reproduced below, in order to illustrate the techniques which I proposed and the economic and political problems which they tried to overcome. Later memoranda and discussions, too repetitive or technical for inclusion in this volume, are then briefly summarized in order to complete this record of failure, and to explain how the Fund was finally banished—or banished itself—from the major and most successful drive to implement its very objectives.

A. THE UNRESOLVED PROBLEM OF FINANCING EUROPEAN TRADE

The Problem

Present plans relating to the European Recovery Program concern themselves primarily with the financing of the participating countries' deficit toward the United States and, in part, toward other Western Hemisphere countries. Little attention is being paid to the problem of facilitating the expansion, or even the maintenance, of trade among the European countries themselves.

The exact nature of the difficulty of financing inter-European trade is not always clearly understood. It is sometimes assumed that a general payment agreement is needed to induce European countries to permit the transferability of current account balances, or their convertibility into gold or dollars. Such convertibility, however, already exists in a majority of cases under present payment agreements, insofar as balances in excess of debit ceilings must be, and are currently, settled in gold or convertible currencies. The real problem is to make such convertibility possible or, alternatively, to limit the exercise by surplus countries of their convertibility claims through other methods than trade restrictions by debtor countries and the elimination, or near elimination, of bilateral deficits and surpluses.

Paradoxical as it may seem, the network of bilateral payments agreements concluded in the postwar years filled that very function of avoiding, or at least postponing, pressures for bilateral balancing of trade. Their effectiveness in this respect, however, was limited by the size of the credit ceilings granted under the agreements, and was further restricted by the bilateral character of these credits. By the fall of 1947, the effective credit or debit balances under existing payment agreements tended more and more to exceed the bilateral ceilings, and forced a resumption of gold settlements. The decline in European trade in the latter part of 1947, reversing the remarkable

---

Excerpts from a memorandum prepared for the IMF in September 1947, and released on December 16, 1947

growth since the end of the war, is probably due in part to this progressive paralyzation of the payment agreements mechanism.

As long as gold and dollar reserves remain at their present low level, only further credits can relieve the pressure for bilateral balancing of inter-European trade. Insofar as this pressure expresses itself in the curtailing of luxury imports or other nonessential expenditures, something may be gained by it. Even then, however, the economic resources so released may lack the flexibility that would be necessary for their employment in more essential activities. Lace workers will not mine coal, nor will vineyards be turned into wheat fields. Moreover, such diversion would often be uneconomic in the long run. While efforts should be made to expand essential production, and to divert to other markets—especially the U.S.—the exportation of luxury goods, this policy has its limitations and could hardly be counted upon to produce by itself the bilateral balance of trade which is sought. Such balancing will involve primarily discrimination among export markets and sources of imports, to divert sales and purchases from their most economic pattern into the artificial directions required for bilateral compensation.[1]

Each country will cut essential, as well as nonessential, imports from countries with which it is running a deficit, and increase imports, whether essential or not, from countries with which it has a surplus. The result will be a diversion of imports both from lower to higher cost sources, and from essential to nonessential goods. It may also mean an absolute decrease in the over-all volume of trade. Exports from countries enjoying an over-all surplus in Europe will be especially affected, slowing down their own recovery as well as that of their customer countries. Insofar as the Marshall Plan will provide financing primarily for imports from the U.S., goods previously bought in Europe will now be bought in the United States at higher cost, enhancing inflationary pressures in that country, retarding the recovery of production in Europe, and increasing the dependence of European countries on the American economy both as a source of imports and as an export market.

To avoid these harmful consequences of an enforced bilateralization of trade, two things are necessary:

(1) Credits are necessary to prevent trade from degenerating into barter deals.

---

1. This argument was addressed to my staff colleagues, most of whom were then opposed to any plan that would help finance "unessential" trade and production.

(2) Such credits should be of a multilateral character in order to avoid a similarly artificial fitting of trade balances to bilateral credit facilities.

On the other hand, deficit countries should not be relieved of the pressure to curtail all unnecessary imports, so as to hasten economic rehabilitation and the readjustment of their balance of payments. The achievement of this aim supposes again two prerequisites: (1) an over-all ceiling on the credits extended to them; (2) the multilateralization of these credits, so as to avoid their compulsory use for less essential imports from the lending countries.

The multilateralization of the credits granted is, therefore, nearly as important as the concession of the credits themselves. As far as U.S. loans are concerned, it means adequate provision for the financing of so-called "off-shore" purchases, as well as of purchases in the American market. As far as European credit arrangements are concerned, it means the multilateralization of the payments agreements under which such credits are now granted.

Multilateralization of European Payments Agreements

. . . As a first step, the present credit commitments—or debit availabilities—under existing payment agreements should be transferred from individual countries to all participating countries as a group. That is to say, the sum total of the credits opened in favor of a country, e.g. France, by all other participants in the agreement, could be used without distinction by France for settling balances with any or all of the participating members, irrespective of the bilateral distribution of the original credit ceilings. Or, to look at it from the creditor's point of view, the total of the credits opened by a country, e.g. Belgium, in favor of all other participants in the agreement, would be available without distinction to any or all of them for settling balances with Belgium. Only in this manner, can the flow of trade be freed from the artificial channels traced by the pattern of bilateral credit facilities.

This substitution of a general, multilateral agreement for the present network of bilateral agreements would find its most practical expression in the creation of a European Clearing Union. The total credit commitments made by each country to other Clearing members would be paid into the Clearing in its own currency, and the country would receive an equivalent balance in the Clearing which it could then use to settle current account deficits with *any* Clearing member.

That is to say—and this is the essence of the "multilateralization" aimed at—France's deficit with Belgium, for instance, could be financed beyond the present ceiling in the bilateral Franco-Belgian agreement, the Clearing drawing for this purpose on the credit accumulated by other countries against Belgium or against the unused credit commitments made by Belgium to other countries.

The payments would be made most simply by debiting the paying country's balance in the Clearing and crediting the balance of the receiving country. Balances in the Clearing could thus most conveniently be expressed in an inter-European unit of account, rather than in various national currency units, since they are in fact expendable to pay debts in all or any one of the participating countries. This essential aspect of the Clearing's mechanism could be dramatized by the introduction of an inter-European currency unit, equal in value to one American dollar, and called, let us say, "European dollar" or "interfranc." All balances in the Clearing, i.e. the Clearing's liabilities, would be computed uniformly in terms of that currency.[2]

The assets of the Clearing, on the other hand, would necessarily remain in the various currencies of its members. Whenever a country makes a transfer through the Clearing, the Clearing authorities must register the corresponding shift in assets from the currency of the receiving country to the currency of the paying country.

At the time they enter the Clearing, all countries will already have accumulated net creditor or debtor positions under their present bilateral agreements. This will influence the initial position in two ways:

(a) The balance of each country in the Clearing will be larger, or smaller, than its quota by the amount of net credits, or net debits, previously accumulated;

(b) The distribution of the Clearing's assets among the various currencies of its members will also differ from the quotas, assets being larger in the currencies of debtor countries, and smaller in the currencies of creditor countries.

2. While limited at first to a mere bookkeeping function, this new currency unit might later serve as a basis for further monetary integration in various directions—such as a limited exchange guarantee for inter-European loans—if the movement toward European cooperation succeeds in gathering momentum. [Regarded as wildly "utopian" at the time, this suggestion was actually implemented in later years through the international flotation of "units of account" loans, totaling today some $70 billion. Professor Fernand Collin, President of the Kredietbank of Belgium, should be credited for the imaginative and untiring leadership which finally prevailed over the derisive skepticism and apathy with which the banking and financial community first greeted his initiative.]

A simple example of this mechanism is presented in Appendix I, and a concrete example based on actual clearing balances as of June 30, 1947, in Appendix II.

The first result of this multilateralization of the payments agreements will be to increase the financial assistance of European creditors to European debtors, by promoting a fuller utilization of credit commitments up to the sum of each country's ceilings under present payments agreements, whatever the bilateral pattern of trade surpluses and deficits. As a consequence, the currency of creditor countries will tend to become scarce in the Clearing and, if no way is found to replenish the Clearing's holdings, the multilateral utilization of the Clearing's balances will have to be suspended with respect to payments in the scarce currencies and limited to payments in those that are not scarce.

Without external aid, therefore, the effectiveness of the Clearing in establishing a true multilateral system of payments is likely to be extremely short-lived. This may be one of the reasons why the prospects of a broad agreement on the matter have been waning ever since European countries began to realize that additional American aid was unlikely to be forthcoming for the financing of the Clearing.

If the Fund, therefore, deems it worthwhile to promote the multilateralization of European payment agreements, it can help in making the proposal workable as well as attractive to the European nations.

Replenishing of Scarce Currencies in the Clearing

The exact nature of the outside assistance required for the functioning of the Clearing mechanism described above should first be made clear. Since exports from European countries to European countries are also, by definition, imports to European countries from European countries, inter-European trade is necessarily in over-all balance and would not seem to require any financing from outside sources. Nevertheless, some financing, whether inter-European or foreign, is required for three reasons:

(1) Some European countries have a net over-all deficit toward other European countries;

(2) After excluding these net balances, each country's imports from Europe are offset by equivalent exports to Europe, but imports from any one individual country may exceed exports to that same country, and cannot, in the absence of multilateralization, be settled by the export balances toward other countries;

(3) Even that portion of inter-European trade which is bilaterally balanced over the year may give rise to seasonal or temporary imbalance during the year.

At the peak rate of trade reached in the last quarter of 1946, the total value of trade between the nine major Marshall Plan countries would run in the neighborhood of $4,500 million a year. Of this, about $860 million represented the net balance between European creditor and debtor countries on trade account, $440 million the bilateral deficits offset by bilateral surpluses, and $3,200 million the portion of trade which was bilaterally balanced.

If a drain on existing gold reserves is to be avoided, even the last item requires some financing in order to take care of seasonal fluctuations. Such financing, however, would be limited to a very small fraction of the total trade involved, and would be automatically liquidated over the year. The same would be true of the second item, i.e. the bilateral deficits multilaterally offset, if a multilateral clearing system were established. The main complication comes from the first item, i.e. the net over-all inter-European deficit, which must be financed in its entirety, and which can be liquidated only, within the inter-European framework, through a reversal of the net surplus or deficit position of member countries. In the absence of special provisions in this respect, the cumulative impact of these net deficits and surpluses leads to the exhaustion of the deficit countries' credit availabilities and to a similar exhaustion of the Clearing's holdings in the currencies of the surplus countries. The final result is the paralyzation of the whole clearing mechanism owing to the persistence of the net over-all inter-European surplus and deficit positions, and of the confusion between financing (item 3) and clearing (items 1 and 2) requirements.

The crucial problem thus boils down to the limitation and financing of the net European deficits. In the absence of fundamental or structural disequilibria, such deficits would be offset by surpluses toward other areas, especially the Western Hemisphere, and could be settled from the proceeds of such surpluses. This is not the case at the moment. The French deficit in Europe, for instance, coincides with an even larger deficit toward the American continent. If American aid to France exceeded the latter deficit and were made available for "offshore" purchases in Europe, the problem could be solved. It is, however, unlikely that offshore financing will be provided on a sufficient scale to eliminate all difficulties in this respect. The countries which experience a persistent deficit in their European transactions will thus probably remain in need of additional financing beyond the aid received from the U.S. under the European Recovery Program.

On the other hand, if the dollar deficit of the countries which accumulate a net surplus in their European transactions is fully met by American aid, these countries will be enabled to finance such surpluses themselves, without any deterioration in their over-all reserve position. They would, however, accumulate dollar debts toward the U.S., in exchange for soft currency claims against their European debtors. This would not be a very attractive proposition, and reluctance on their part should be anticipated, especially as they may feel that even the mere maintenance of their present reserve position would leave them in a very vulnerable situation.

The first step toward a logical and acceptable solution of the problem would be to define, for each European country, the maximum deficit which could be reasonably and safely incurred. The second step would be to apportion the burden of the necessary financing, after deduction of the portion financed by the United States under the ERP. Thus, assuming that the dollar deficit of European countries will be adequately covered by ERP aid, the Fund could limit its transactions with European countries coming under the program to the sale of currencies other than dollars. Moreover, the aggregate of such sales would remain governed by the present yearly maximum of 25 per cent of each country's quota, or any other stricter limitation that the Fund might feel justified to enforce in practice in view of the direct American aid.

The sale of European currencies by the Fund would initially be similar in effect to further credit extensions by the countries the currency of which is sold by the Fund. The difference, however, is that the resulting claims which they would accumulate would be general claims against the Fund, rather than specific claims against the borrowing countries. While the real burden on their economy would be the same, such a form of financing would, of course, be far more attractive to the European surplus countries.

From the point of view of the Fund, these operations would result in a shift of assets from relatively hard to relatively soft European currencies. This, however, is implicit in the very purposes of the Fund's mechanism, and is similar to the present concentration of sales upon the dollar, and of purchases on the weaker member countries' currencies. Indeed, the situation would be improved insofar as sales would now be distributed among a large number of currencies.

We must also envisage the hypothesis, however, that the ERP aid may not be fully adequate to meet all legitimate European dollar needs. In that case, the Fund might be called upon to sell dollars, as well as European currencies. The danger is, however, that if dollar sales are treated exactly in the same way as the sale of other currencies, all countries will continue, as they do now, to concentrate directly their demands upon the dollar, with a consequent acceleration of the trend toward a dollar scarcity. As long as drawing rights on the Fund can be exercised *indifferently* in any currency whatsoever, members will have a strong preference for buying the Fund currency for which their relative need is greatest, and will be reluctant to decrease their right to dollars by purchasing other currencies.

In order to avoid this and maintain a better distribution in its transactions, the Fund could exercise its discretionary powers in exchange transactions to make a distinction between dollar requests and requests for other currencies. Requests would be granted fairly liberally for any currency whatsoever, including the dollar, insofar as the Fund's holdings of the applying member's currency will not, after the transaction, exceed 75 per cent of the member's quota. On the other hand, dollar requests would be scrutinized much more severely than requests for other currencies, whenever the Fund's holdings of the member's currency already exceed, or would exceed after the transaction, 75 per cent of the member's quota.

The practical result of this would be to give the creditor members of the clearing a strong inducement to extend additional credits to other clearing members through sales of their currency by the Fund, and to give the debtor members of the clearing an incentive to apply for needed European currencies without feeling that this will automatically reduce their chances to obtain dollars from the Fund.

The advantages of the system for the Fund are evident. The present situation leads inevitably to the concentration of practically all currency sales upon a single currency, the dollar. A restoration of a multilateral system of payments in Europe would avoid this danger and increase substantially the effectiveness of the Fund's resources. It would at the same time lessen the tendency of the Fund to become merely another dollar-lending agency, and bring its operations into closer conformity with the purposes of the Agreement as envisaged in Bretton Woods.

The Role of the Fund

It should be noted that the method suggested here for the Fund's transactions in Europe is independent of the creation of a European Clearing Union. The Fund, however, is vitally interested in a restoration of a multilateral system of international settlements and thus in the broadening of the present bilateral agreements into a true multilateral clearing system. A first step in this direction, even though a very modest and imperfect one, has been taken with the formation, this month, of a limited compensation system between Belgium, France, Italy, Luxemburg and the Netherlands. The Fund could hardly remain aloof from this experiment. It should, on the contrary, endeavor to broaden it both geographically and operationally. The original projects from which the agreement evolved all contemplated that the system would be operated by the Fund itself. It would be desirable to have the Fund replace the BIS in the operation of the plan.

A general European Clearing, based on the multilateralization of the present bilateral payment agreements would, of course, involve many, and daily, operations among members, entirely independent of transactions between members and the Fund. It would be highly desirable to have the general supervision and centralization of these operations, if not their execution itself, entrusted to the Fund. This would give us precious information on the current evolution of international payments in Europe, and on the development of situations which make likely future calls for transactions with the Fund. Finally, it might also be possible to use such a Clearing Union for a preliminary screening and study of such requests.

Appendix I

A simple example may facilitate concrete understanding of the functioning of a European Clearing.

Let us assume three countries with the following mutual credit-debit ceilings (translated into dollars) under existing payment agreements:

1. Belgium-France: $80 million
2. Belgium-Italy: $30 million
3. France-Italy: $60 million

The quotas in the Clearing would be as follows:

1. Belgium: $80 million + $30 million = $110 million
2. France: $80 million + $60 million = $140 million
3. Italy: $30 million + $60 million = $ 90 million

Before any transaction has been made, the Clearing's position would be:

TABLE A

Assets (in individual currencies, converted into millions of European dollars)					Liabilities (in millions of European dollars)	
Received from	In Belgian francs	In French francs	In Italian lire	Total	Due to	Amount
Belgium	110			110	Belgium	110
France		140		140	France	140
Italy			90	90	Italy	90
Total	110	140	90	340	Total	340

If, however, either before or after the creation of the Clearing, France had already drawn $60 million on Belgium, Belgium $10 million on Italy, and Italy $30 million on France, the position would be as follows:

TABLE B

Assets					Liabilities		Net Creditor (+) or Debtor (−) Position
Received from	In Belgian francs	In French francs	In Italian lire	Total	Due to		
Belgium	110	+60	−10	160	Belgium	160	+50
France	−60	140	+30	110	France	110	−30
Italy	+10	−30	90	70	Italy	70	−20
Total	60	170	110	340	Total	340	0

Vertical columns, under assets, show the amount of each country's currency still available in the Clearing. The amount received from each country in its own currency corresponds to its quota, the amounts shown as received in other currencies correspond to credits granted to (+), or received from (−), other countries, and for which the respective claims or liabilities are transferred to the Clearing. The

liabilities of the Clearing to each country express that country's outstanding drawing right. Finally, the difference between such liabilities
and the country's quota reflects its net credit or debit position under
the agreements.

Appendix II

Example Based on Actual Status of Agreements as of August 31, 1947

Tables I and II correspond to Tables A and B in Appendix I, but
are based on the actual status of the Agreements between twelve
European countries as of August 31, 1947 of this year. Several
countries, however, had in fact overdrawn their account. Such overdrafts are not entered in Table II, but are shown separately in Table
III. Table IV shows the net creditor or debtor position of each country, i.e. the sum of the net positions within the limits of the agreements
(Table II) plus the net positions outside such limits (Table III).
Finally, Table V compares the unused bilateral credit under each
payment agreement to the original credit ceiling.

Table I indicates the theoretical maximum of credits made available
under the agreements. Since the same amounts always appear twice,
however, and since it is impossible for the same country to be simultaneously a creditor and debtor vis-à-vis the same partner, the maximum of available credits is only half of the total shown, i.e. $659
million of the $1,317.9 million shown in the table.

In practice, however, the bilateral character of the agreements prevents anything approaching a full utilization of the credit margins.
Of the theoretical maximum of $659 million, only $271 million net
had been utilized up to August 31. It should be noted, however, that
the gross cumulative drawings were certainly far in excess of this
figure, but were reduced to the lower amount through fluctuations and
reversals of net positions over the period of the agreements.

Table III indicates the extent to which mutual credits were overdrawn as of the same date (August 31, 1947). It is striking to note
that such overdrafts totaled $144 million, bringing up total credits to
$411 million (Table IV), or more than 50 per cent above the credits
used within the limits of credit ceilings. Eighty per cent of the total
overdrafts, however, represent excess drawings by the United Kingdom, and may have been in part the object of informal understandings
amounting in fact to an increase in credit ceilings. In the case of
Belgium, it is known that the credit ceiling was raised on September 9
from $20 to $109 million.

Table IV shows the net position of the various countries, whether within or beyond the credit ceilings of the agreements. Seven countries, Belgium, Switzerland, Norway, Sweden, Portugal, the Netherlands, and Austria, were in a net credit position, and five countries, Denmark, the United Kingdom, France, Italy, and Germany (French Zone) in a net debtor position. The concentration both of creditor and debtor positions is indicated by the fact that three countries accounted for more than 85 per cent of the total net credits (Belgium, 37 per cent; Switzerland, 28 per cent; and Norway, 21 per cent), and three other countries for more than 98 per cent of the net debits (Denmark, 39 per cent; U.K., 37 per cent; and France, 22 per cent).

Table V compares, for all bilateral debtor positions, the amount of the original credit ceiling and the unused amount as of August 31, 1947. It can be seen that in a large number of cases, credit ceilings were nearly exhausted or even overdrawn, especially with respect to credits extended by Belgium. The network of bilateral credit agreements was rapidly approaching a state of paralysis, from which it could be saved only by new credit extensions or by the multilateralization of the agreements.

[These lengthy tables have been omitted here, their details being of no interest to today's readers. The above comments, however, give the main documentation used in support of the proposals above.]

B. MULTILATERALIZATION OF EUROPEAN PAYMENT AGREEMENTS AMONG FUND MEMBERS

Introduction

The restoration of a multilateral system of payments in Europe would constitute a first-rate contribution to the attainment of the Fund's objectives. It would also be a demonstration of the vitality and effectiveness of the new Organization for European Economic Cooperation.

The American and European Governments have been exploring possible solutions of this problem through the use of offshore purchases and of the local currency equivalent of American aid to Europe. Both Americans and the Europeans, however, are preoccupied with the need to avoid any appearance of arbitrary action or political pressure by the American ECA administration in the use of such powerful instruments.

Memorandum to the IMF dated May 7, 1948 (tables omitted).

It would be particularly unfortunate if the Fund remained aloof from a problem so essential to the fulfillment of its purpose. It could, indeed, play here a most important role which, when added to the use of ECA aid, could ensure the success of a bold and ambitious plan of multilateralization, and would correspond fully to one of the most basic objectives of the institution as defined at Bretton Woods. This would, at the same time, provide the Fund with an objective and workable criterion for its policy in Europe during the transition period.

The main advantages of multilateralization over a mere extension of new credit facilities would be:

(a) to make further use of already existing credit arrangements among the European countries themselves;

(b) to discourage uneconomic or unessential intra-European trade now fostered by the bilateral character of present credit arrangements;

(c) to make progress toward ultimate currency convertibility, by ensuring immediately the maximum degree of transferability compatible with the special circumstances of the transitory postwar period.

Nature and Size of the Problem

The core of any multilateralization scheme is the pooling of all the lending commitments (and borrowing facilities) under payment agreements, irrespective of the bilateral margins which now limit their effective use, and distort the European trade pattern. In other words, the credit margins granted by Belgium, for instance, could be drawn upon indifferently by any and all other participating countries within the limits of each country's total debit ceilings. Similarly, the various credit facilities conceded to the Netherlands by the various participants could be used against any and all of them, irrespective of the bilateral limits in the present agreements.

Such a multilateralization plan presents two technical difficulties:

(a) the concentration of drawings on one or a few creditor countries, and the consequent exhaustion of their credit commitments;

(b) accumulating deficits of the weakest debtor countries, and the consequent exhaustion of their drawing rights.

These two difficulties are of a very different nature and require entirely different solutions. The second problem is a *credit* problem rather than a multilateralization problem, and already exists in acute form under the present bilateral arrangements. Its solution, moreover, can never become automatic. No country can be assured in advance that credits will always be extended to it to the full measure necessary to finance any future deficit in its balance of payments, irrespective of its own efforts, or lack of efforts, to redress its situation.

On the other hand, it would be desirable that any given pattern of credits actually granted be placed on a multilateral basis, i.e. be made available for payments to any other country participating in the plan. The maximum amount of external aid necessary to permit this can be exactly calculated for any given level of credit margins agreed upon. If net deficits and net surpluses within Europe were fairly evenly distributed, the multilateralization of the present bilateral credits would not necessitate any external aid. In fact, however, there is a marked concentration of the intra-European surplus and debit positions. If the credit margins were multilateralized, drawings by the deficit countries, even within such margins, would concentrate on one or a few creditor countries and exceed the credit commitments accepted by the latter. The worst case would be the case in which all countries but one concentrate their drawings on the remaining member. External aid would then be necessary *up to the difference between the total of these convergent drawings and the over-all credit commitments of the country on which the drawings are made.*

This would be most likely to occur with respect to Belgium. The maximum limit of the external aid that might be required to solve this problem within the present credit margins would be $338 million. This is calculated as follows:

(a) The total credit rights of all countries, except Belgium, are $350 million.

(b) The unused credit commitments of Belgium, to be deducted from the above, are $12 million, leaving a maximum uncovered need of $338 million.

A Possible Fund Solution

External resources of $338 million would therefore be sufficient to multilateralize the *present* credit margins among Fund members. This sum could be provided from purchases of Belgian francs (or other currencies) from the Fund, opening to Belgium (or other countries) additional dollar resources from the Fund if and when her balance of payments requires it. To the extent that such need does not arise, there would be no consequent sales of dollars by the Fund, but the building up of a net creditor position by Belgium with the Fund. In this case, the $338 million limit mentioned above would remain unused by a corresponding amount.

The Fund's ERP decision opens the door to such an arrangement. It should be complemented, however, in three ways:

(a) The sale of scarce European currencies by the Fund would have to be assured in order to remove all bilateral obstacles to compensation.

(b) In order to limit financing by the Fund such sales would, however, be made only when the creditor countries' commitments have been exhausted.

(c) The purpose of a Fund's transaction under this arrangement would not be to extend additional credit facilities to the countries whose currencies it buys, but merely to provide the currencies needed to permit the continued use of existing credit margins on a multilateral basis. Indeed, while the choice of the currency (or currencies) to be sold by the Fund would be determined by the pattern of intra-European payments, the choice of the currencies acquired by the Fund in exchange is theoretically indifferent to the solution of the multi-lateralization problem.

In practice, however, participant countries would have to commit themselves in advance to effect such transactions with the Fund as may be required for the functioning of the multilateral clearing plan, i.e. to procure from the Fund the needed European currencies. Such commitments might most logically be accepted in proportion to the comparative net debits incurred by the participants toward the clearing. They would not be required to sell additional amounts of their currencies, but merely to transfer such amounts from the clearing to the Fund. This transaction would not give them any automatic increase in their credit facilities, but would merely decrease their ultimate liability to the clearing, and increase it correspondingly toward the Fund.

Advantages and Limitations of the Proposal

The adoption of such a scheme would present obvious advantages, both to creditor and to debtor countries, and also to the Fund:

(a) The creditor countries would receive net credits against the Fund, convertible in dollars, for any surplus in excess of their credit commitments. In practice, this would restore from their point of view the convertibility of other European currencies.

(b) The debtor countries could mobilize any credit balances or credit margins remaining in their accounts with some countries, to pay countries with which their credit margins are already exhausted.

In fact, this would release for all of them taken together, drawing rights amounting to $350 million and which they are practically unable to use under present bilateral arrangements.

(c) The Fund would gain initially through a better diversification of its operations which would approximate the pattern contemplated in Bretton Woods, as against the present concentration of its sales on one currency only, i.e. the U.S. dollar. It is true, of course, that on the second round the European currencies sold might, to a greater or lesser extent, come back to the Fund against dollar disbursements. Some residue of European currency sales, however, would remain, insofar as dollars are not needed by these countries in equal amounts to finance balance-of-payments deficits toward the dollar area. In such a case, the recent Fund decision on dollar sales to ERP countries would preclude them from having access to the Fund's dollar resources. Finally, even if dollars were drawn in each case, and for a corresponding amount, the total dollar disbursements involved would still be limited by the size of the credit margins between participant countries.[1]

This method of intervention would still not solve, however, the difficulties of a deficit country which has exhausted all its drawing rights. Moreover, deficit countries might be reluctant to incur a dollar obligation to the Fund, in order to procure European currencies. Finally, they would be reluctant to abandon the bargaining advantages, real or fancied, associated with a bilateral system of negotiation both as to trade and payments. A further incentive would be needed, and might be provided, e.g. by making some further credits available to debtor countries, beyond the limits of the present credit margins. Unless some other source of external aid can be found, these additional credits would have to come mainly from the European creditor countries themselves, in connection with a revision of the present, and largely haphazard, pattern of credit margins.

Conclusions

(1) The maximum external aid necessary to ensure the fullest multilateral availability of any given pattern of credit margins can be exactly calculated. Under present credit margins, the theoretical limit —unlikely to be fully reached in practice—would be $338 million.

(2) The exhaustion of their credit margin by the deficit countries

---

1. As indicated above, the maximum theoretical limit, under the present pattern of credit margins, would be $338 million.

raises an entirely different problem, which is one of over-all credit facilities, rather than multilateralization. This second problem cannot be solved automatically and once and for all. The permanent solution lies in the restoration of over-all, but not bilateral, balance-of-payments equilibrium. Further credits may be required in the meanwhile, but their amount will necessarily depend on the prospective lenders' appraisal of the efforts made by each country to redress its situation.

C. THE OEEC PLAN FOR THE FINANCING OF INTRA-EUROPEAN PAYMENTS, 1948–49

Introduction

One of the fundamental purposes of the Fund, possibly the most important of all during the present so-called transition period, is "to assist in the establishment of a multilateral system of payments in respect of current transactions between members and in the elimination of foreign exchange restrictions which hamper the growth of world trade."

The Fund could not therefore remain a disinterested party to the major effort in this direction undertaken in Europe this year, under the auspices of the OEEC and with the powerful backing of all the ECA resources and planning. The difficulty of the task is amply demonstrated by the fact that after five months of continuous and arduous negotiations, and in spite of ECA prodding and financial cooperation, the agreement reached so far on the multilateralization of intra-European payments is still of the most limited and provisional character. We must frankly face the fact that the ultimate failure to achieve better results would almost certainly spell the doom of any hopes that the Fund, left to its own resources, could make any substantial progress for a very long time to come toward the realization of its objectives in Europe. The continued aloofness of the Fund from the present negotiations in Paris would, moreover, constitute the gravest threat to its prestige and influence on the European continent. It would be most difficult to explain how the Fund could remain a passive observer to the major attempt made so far to fulfil one of the main objectives of Bretton Woods.

A memorandum to the IMF, forwarded on October 12, released on November 8, 1948, and applying to the multilateralization of newly negotiated bilateral "*drawing rights*" and *conditional aid* the proposals for Fund drawings previously developed for the multilateralization of bilateral payments agreements and *credit margins*.

This is all the more so as the intervention of the Fund might prove to be the only practical manner to break the deadlock which now opposes the ECA and the OEEC and threatens to paralyze the implementation of an agreement which cost so much effort to achieve. While a compromise has finally been reached to permit the initiation of the program, the real difficulties have not been solved, and are due to reappear in later negotiations.

Before examining possible procedures for such an intervention, it is necessary to summarize, at least briefly, the character of the present draft agreement, with all its successes and shortcomings.

In brief, the cooperation of European countries in providing the means to finance intra-European payments seems to me to have exceeded all reasonable expectations. The scale of the United Kingdom's contribution to the solution of this problem is especially adequate and generous.

On the other hand, progress toward effective multilateralization of payments remains disappointingly small. Indeed it might be said that at the very moment when bilateral payment agreements have become paralyzed owing to the exhaustion of available credits, ECA dollars will be used to revitalize them through a whole network of bilateral counterpart grants, totaling more than $550 million a year.

The Distribution of Counterpart Grants

Total ECA aid is supposed to cover the foreseeable deficit of the participating countries ,taken as a group, toward the Western Hemisphere. The distribution of ECA aid among the various participating countries is also based, initially, on each country's Western Hemisphere deficit. This leaves entire the problem of financing the deficits incurred by some participating countries toward other participating countries.

The first possibility explored in Paris to solve this second problem was the technique of off-shore purchases in Europe itself. Thus a surplus country like Belgium would have seen its Western Hemisphere deficit covered in part through direct dollar allocations, and in part through dollars spent in Belgium by ECA in payment for goods purchased there for shipment to European deficit countries. On the other hand, direct allocations to the deficit countries covering their Western Hemisphere deficit would have been supplemented by off-shore financing of their additional deficit in intra-European relations.

For various reasons, this procedure was discarded in favor of an entirely different one originally suggested by Mr. Tomlinson, the U.S. Treasury representative in Paris. European countries feared that the off-shore procedure would be a very cumbersome and limiting one, in view of the rules established by Congress with respect to the use of ECA dollars in off-shore operations. They also felt that the procedure would imply exaggerated interference by ECA in their foreign trade and commercial policies. The ECA itself shared some of these misgivings and wished to promote more flexible, and less discretionary, methods, which would contribute to the liberalization and multilateralization of trade channels through the cooperative efforts of the European countries themselves.

This led to the adoption of the so-called counterpart grant technique, adopted in principle at the end of July, and embodied about a month ago in a formal decision of the OEEC Council on the distribution of American aid (see Appendix 2 [omitted here]). Briefly, each country would receive a direct dollar allocation covering either its Western Hemisphere deficit, or its over-all deficit,[1] whichever is smaller. European surplus countries would, in addition, receive a conditional allocation equal to their European surplus (the sum of their direct and conditional allocations thus covering their Western Hemisphere deficit), subject to their own financing of such surplus in the form of counterpart grants to their European debtors. European deficit countries, on the other hand, would, by the same token, be covered for their over-all deficit: (a) through direct ECA aid as far as their Western Hemisphere deficit is concerned, and (b) through the above counterpart grants insofar as their intra-European deficit is concerned.

To take a concrete example, a country with a Western Hemisphere deficit of $250 million, but a European surplus of $200, would receive the difference, i.e. $50 million, in the form of unconditional dollar allocation, and the rest ($200 million) in the form of a conditional dollar grant, subject to an equivalent extension of counterpart grants in its own currency to its European debtors. On the other hand, a country which experienced a deficit both toward the Western Hemisphere (of, let us say, $1 billion) and toward other participating countries (of, let us say, $300 million) would receive the first amount in direct ECA dollar allocation, and the second through counterpart grants in the currencies of its European creditors.

1. Excluding, however, for the time being, deficits or surpluses with other non-participating countries that are not members of the sterling area.

This procedure necessitated previous agreement on the size of both the Western Hemisphere deficit and of the intra-European surpluses and deficits of each participating country. Such an agreement was of course most difficult to arrive at, each country having the greatest financial interest in overestimating its deficits, and underestimating its surpluses. It is therefore no small achievement that final agreement was ultimately reached—subject only to minor qualifications—on the distribution of direct aid and counterpart grants.

TABLE 1

PROPOSED DISTRIBUTION OF DIRECT AID AND COUNTERPART GRANTS
(in millions of U.S. dollars)

Countries	Direct ECA aid	Counterpart grants given (−) or received (+)	Net aid to be received
European creditor countries:			
Belgium	250	− 207.5	42.5
Italy	601	− 20.3	580.7
Sweden	47	− 25.0	22.0
Turkey	50	− 19.7	30.3
United Kingdom	1,263	− 282.0	981.0
Bizone	414	− 10.2	403.8
Total	**2,625**	**−564.7**	**2,060.3**
European debtor countries:			
Austria	217	+ 63.5	280.5
Denmark	110	+ 6.8	116.8
France	989	+323.3	1,312.3
Greece	146	+ 66.8	212.8
Netherlands	496	+ 71.7	567.7
Norway	84	+ 31.8	115.8
French Zone	100	+ 0.8	100.8
Total	**2,142**	**+564.7**	**2,706.7**
Total	**4,785**[1]	x	**4,785.0**[1]

1. Including $18 million for Trieste.

Before drawing on their counterpart grants, the participating countries must, however, first make use of other existing resources available to them, i.e. their credit balances under existing payment agreements after deduction of amounts considered necessary as working balances. The addition of such existing resources changes substantially the pattern of over-all financing facilities available to debtor countries. Thus, to the $282 million of sterling contributed by the United Kingdom as counterpart grants, must be added an estimated $220 million of existing sterling balances also available for financing the participating countries' net deficit toward the sterling area. Taking these balances into account, the resulting intra-European financing facilities and liabilities under the scheme are as follows:

(in millions of U.S. dollars)

A. Available means	
Austria	63.5
Denmark	6.8
France	323.3
Greece	86.8
Italy	35.7
Netherlands	126.7
Norway	31.8
Sweden	35.2
French Zone	0.8
Total	**710.6**
B. Liabilities	
Belgium	207.5
Turkey	0.7
United Kingdom	502.0
Bizone	0.4
Total	**710.6**

The over-all totals correspond fairly closely to the estimated over-all disequilibrium in intra-European payments over the year ($672 to $814 million). If the local currencies made available under the plan were fully transferable among the participating countries, the cooperation of ECA and OEEC could be said to have attained a most unusual degree of success in providing adequate financing both for intra-European trade and for trade with the Western Hemisphere. In any case, this first effort of the OEEC should already be credited with having brought forth an unhoped-for degree of cooperation on the part of the participating countries, and especially of the United Kingdom.

There remains now to examine the shortcomings of the plan, and to explore methods by which these could possibly be remedied in order to give its full value to the cooperative effort already achieved, and to hasten the restoration of sound and flexible currency mechanisms in Europe, in conformity with the Fund's objectives.

Bilateral Shortcomings of the Present Plan

One of the motives which prompted the substitution of the present counterpart grant plan for the offshore purchase technique was the desire to set up a flexible and truly multilateral system of intra-European payments, in preference to rigid administrative and *ad hoc* decisions. The full multilateralization and transferability of at least the counterpart grants formed therefore an integral and essential part of the initial projects. This feature, however, met determined opposition, as well as support, in Committee meetings, and the final plan emerged in very emasculated form.

The only automatic compensations allowed are the so-called first category compensations (i.e. involving all-round reductions in balances) which have proved so disappointing under the Basle compensation mechanism. Even with respect to first category compensations, special authorization of each debtor country will be necessary for the use of its counterpart grant facilities beyond its bilateral deficit during the previous month (the counterpart grants being, in addition, to be used only after the exhaustion of other existing resources under payment agreements).

The overwhelming bulk of possible compensations belongs, however, to the so-called second category group, and here previous acceptance by all interested parties remains necessary as it was under the original Basle scheme. The only commitment in this respect is a general declaration of intention that all will "cooperate fully in facilitating, having regard to all the circumstances, any reasonable propositions put forward to them by the Agent for compensations." In the case of refusals, the Agent will report to the OEEC the motives given for such refusals, when authorized to disclose them; otherwise, the OEEC "may, if it thinks it necessary, request the contracting party concerned to give it further information."

The report of the Trade and Payments Committees to the Council included, in addition, a somewhat cumbersome arbitration procedure ending before the Council itself, to take care of complaints arising from refusals to authorize second category compensations. It is significant that these provisions had to be stricken out because of disagreements within the Council itself.

Ironically enough, the present draft convention on compensations even finds it necessary to state that "nothing in this Article shall *prevent* any contracting party from intimating to the Agent that it is prepared to accept, without prior reference, any second category compensations which may be arranged by the Agent."

The disappointment of ECA, when confronted with these proposals, is therefore understandable. Indeed, they are tantamount to using ECA dollars as a basis for a whole new set of bilateral agreements at the very moment when previous bilateral agreements had become paralyzed because of the exhaustion of the surplus countries' credits. This explains the delays of ECA in accepting the OEEC draft proposals. A compromise has now been reached, the exact details of which are not yet available at this time, but which seems designed primarily to permit the immediate initiation of the plan, leaving the unresolved, and most substantial, differences to later negotiations.

No grave problem would arise from the lack of transferability if the various bilateral grants could have been based on correct estimates of the bilateral deficits to be financed. At best, however, any advance estimates of this sort are necessarily subject to a large margin of error. More important is the fact that the final distribution of the grants was determined largely by a hard process of bargaining among the various countries, and distorted from the start by the vinculation of the grants to the distribution of ECA aid.

Thus, the need for Belgian francs was estimated at about $254 million and will probably exceed this sum. Since, however, Belgium was to receive total ECA aid of only $250 million, and wished to reserve some of this for domestic investment needs, the final assignment of counterpart Belgian francs was limited to $207.5 million. On the other hand, the United Kingdom made available $282 million, in addition to the $220 million of sterling available as credit balances under existing payment agreements. The total of $500 million of sterling thus available is generally thought to exceed substantially the sterling needs of the participating countries.

It is perfectly understandable, therefore, that Belgium led the fight for multilateralization and that the United Kingdom showed the greatest reluctance to accept binding and automatic commitments in that respect. Indeed any automatic transferability would, almost certainly, lead to transfers of sterling to Belgium, and to subsequent gold or dollar payments by the United Kingdom to that country. The U.K. points out that this would be caused by the very generosity of the sterling grants and by the inadequacy of the Belgian francs grants.

On the other hand, the absence of transferability is a big blow to the hopes of overcoming the present bilateral distortions in intra-European trade. Countries short of Belgian francs, but well provided with sterling grants, will have to curtail more essential imports from Belgium while buying less essential ones from the sterling area. They are all the more likely to continue these latter purchases as their sterling resources are in the nature of grants, which they would have little reason to keep unutilized. If they did—which is still conceivable since the grants will not lapse at the end of the present ECA year—difficulties would arise between ECA and the U.K., because the financing by ECA of the British dollar deficit is in part conditional upon the sterling counterpart grants, and these cannot be said to have been effectively realized if the sterling remains unused.

On the other hand, the total dollar allocations to creditor countries are based, in theory, on estimates of these countries' deficit toward the Western Hemisphere. The United Kingdom will probably argue[2] that its dollar needs are the same, whether or not European countries make use of the sterling counterpart. This would, of course, come close to nullifying the distinction between the conditional and the unconditional parts of the total dollar allocation.

In truth, the distribution of aid was certainly influenced by the size of the counterpart grants. It is obvious, for instance, that Belgium would have received substantially less than $250 million, if it had not been for the size of the counterpart grants requested from her and to which she gave her consent. And indeed, even on purely economic grounds, there will normally exist some relationship, even though far short of a complete parallelism, between the level of a country's unrequited exports and the size of its Western Hemisphere deficit. If the United Kingdom imported more from, or exported less to, Europe it could, at least to some extent, import less from, or export more to, the Western Hemisphere. Thus, the nonutilization of the sterling grants corresponding to the conditional part of American aid would undoubtedly give grounds to the ECA for reopening the question of the dollar allocations to the United Kingdom.

The adoption of bilateral principles in the OEEC plan, and the unbalanced character of the counterpart grant allocations are the result of a complicated interplay of national interests and policies.

The interest of debtor countries was to receive as large, and as transferable, grants as possible. They knew, however, that the actual

2. [It did, and most forcefully!]

size of the grants which they could obtain would depend in part on the extent of their transferability. It was quite clear that the United Kingdom could afford only much smaller grants if full transferability conditions were to be attached to the system. Some debtor countries, therefore, preferred to sacrifice the transferability of the grants for the sake of a larger amount. Others, however, chose the opposite path, either because of the greater acuteness of their need for the less available currencies (especially Belgian francs) or because they hoped that their direct dollar allocations would be greater if their counterpart grants were made lower. This latter expectation, in turn, was based on the assumption that the total dollar allocation to creditor countries would vary with the size of the counterpart grants they consented to make, so that smaller counterpart grants would result in a shift of dollar allocations from the creditor to the debtor countries.

Creditor countries also adopted different attitudes toward the problem, depending on their individual circumstances and on their assumptions regarding the division of dollar aid. Quite obviously, Belgium would favor, and the United Kingdom oppose, transferability because the relative scarcity of Belgian francs with respect to sterling would lead to a conversion of sterling into francs and, ultimately, to gold payments by the United Kingdom to Belgium. The United Kingdom might have avoided, or at least minimized, this danger, while still accepting transferability, by making her counterpart grants as small as possible. If it had been perfectly clear that the size of the grants would not affect in any way the total amount of ECA aid, this decision might possibly have been taken. The United Kingdom, however, reasoned that larger grants to Europe—financed in part by the sterling area—would elicit a larger volume of conditional ECA aid. Moreover, the United Kingdom was emotionally opposed to transferability, after the brief and disastrous convertibility experiment of last year, and preferred to demonstrate its spirit of European cooperation through larger sterling grants, which would at the same time facilitate the expansion of sterling export markets on the continent.

Belgium was, of course, the main champion of transferability, since it definitely served its own interests. In determining the size of grants, it acted on the same assumption as the United Kingdom—i.e. that larger grants would gain it a larger volume of ECA aid—but only up to the point where she could hope to push such aid and to use it in fact, considering the programming limitations of the Act. The main difference from the United Kingdom in this latter respect is that eligible imports, under the ECA Act, are needed by Britain in far greater volume than is the case for Belgium. The Belgian contribution was thus kept at a relatively low level, because of the more limited size of Belgium's import needs for programmed commodities.

Italy's policy was primarily determined by her desire to keep as large a national currency counterpart as possible, for domestic stabilization and investment. This aspect of American aid had been widely publicized and even led to special legislation to govern the use of the so-called "lire fund." While the same considerations were also influential in Belgium, Italy seems to have assumed that the size of total ECA aid would not be materially affected by the size of its own counterpart grants, and that, in consequence, any increase in its grants would be accompanied by a nearly equivalent shift from unconditional to conditional ECA allocations.

If the interpretation above of the participating countries' policies is correct, it is to be regretted that ECA could not have exerted greater influence on obtaining a more balanced allocation of counterpart grants, by making it clear that its total dollar aid to each country would be directly correlated to the size of such grants, but only insofar as the grants corresponded to imports of a broadly similar degree of essentiality—at the margin—to the deficit countries.

A sound solution of the European payments problem would require: (1) an effective multilateralization of the intra-European payments system, i.e. the equalization of the utility of trade within Europe, at the margin; and (2) in the long run, but only in the long run (i.e. let us say, at the expiration of ECA), an equalization at the margin of the utility of intra-European and extra-European trade.

Neither condition is fulfilled by the present draft agreements. The first is certainly defeated by the bilateral character of the counterpart grant arrangements, especially in view of the probable overflow of sterling and deficiency of Belgian francs. The second cannot, and should not, be made immediately effective, and would depend on the relative adequacy of intra-European and Western Hemisphere financing facilities. For obvious reasons, the second must outrun the first for some time to come and this is precisely the purpose of the ECA program.

For the duration of the program, two basic difficulties should be reconciled as far as possible:

(1) The debtor countries should be free to base their European

import program on criteria of essentiality, irrespective of any bilateral financing facilities or lack of facilities.

(2) The creditor countries should be able to count on an adequate financing of their over-all Western Hemisphere deficit, provided that they extend sufficient—but not conditional on excessive—financial aid to their European debtors.

In order to prepare progressively for the end of the ECA program, the intra-European financing facilities should also be progressively scaled down, together with the ECA dollar aid.

The compromise arrived at on October 5 between ECA and OEEC is not likely to provide an adequate and lasting solution to these problems, and especially to the first one. The question is certain to reappear again in the most acute form later in the year, and especially when new allocations are made for 1949–50. At such a time, the Fund will again have a unique opportunity to break the threatening deadlock through the effective use of the machinery which was set up at Bretton Woods for this very purpose.

Possible Methods of Fund Intervention

The intervention of the Fund would necessitate special arrangements with ECA and OEEC, the exact terms of which raise many, but not insuperable, problems of a legal nature. These legal aspects of the question are bypassed in this paper for the sake of clarity.

The kernel of the difficulty remains that discussed in RD 463 and RD 605.[3] That is to say, the multilateralization of the grants might lead to convergent drawings upon some, relatively scarcer, currencies in excess of the amounts made available under the OEEC scheme. On the other hand, as long as no country is permitted to draw in excess of its over-all grant facilities, some currencies would remain idle in the pool. The problem boils down, therefore, to ensuring through the Fund the convertibility of the latter into the first. For the system to be automatic, the countries whose currencies are not fully used would have to commit themselves to draw upon the Fund, at the direction of the Agent, to obtain the currencies which are needed. Conversely, the Fund would have to provide some assurance that the necessary transaction will be authorized under the conditions specified in the multilateral agreement.

3. The two preceding papers in this chapter.

This raises a number of problems, the most important of which may be:

(a) How can the Fund give such assurance in view of the discretion which it must retain over its operations and the use of its resources?

(b) What amounts are likely to be involved?

(c) Will this mean a drain on the Fund's dollar resources during the life of ECA?

(d) Will member countries accept to draw upon their quota in the Fund for this purpose?

A. The main objection of the Fund to automatic, or semiautomatic, drawings is the fear of giving a country additional credit facilities which may be used to finance fundamental disequilibria and decrease the pressures which might lead to their correction. It is most important to note, however, that the present proposal does *not* increase the credit facilities at the disposal of any one country. It merely shifts their use from a bilateral to a multilateral basis. Moreover, the control of the Fund would be ensured at two stages: (1) in the periodic discussion of the amount and distribution of counterpart grants by OEEC and ECA; (2) through the provisions of the agreement designed to prevent or correct abuses of the facilities of the system for financing fundamental disequilibria.

B. For the year 1948–49, the total of net counterpart grants amounts to the equivalent of $565 million. The addition of other so-called "existing resources" (available credit balances) would raise this sum to $710 million. The total errors involved in the bilateral distribution of these facilities among the participating countries might conceivably reach, or even exceed, $100 million. The main problem will probably be the relative oversupply of sterling and the correlative scarcity of Belgian francs.

There is every reason for the Fund to help in multilateralizing a reasonable pattern of intra-European grants or credits. Indeed, if the distribution were estimated as competently and honestly as is possible, the cost of meeting unforeseeable imbalance would be very small indeed. Estimates should moreover be currently revised and corrected as experience is gained with the handling of the system. Currencies which remain unused, and converted through the Fund mechanism, should be provided in lesser amounts in subsequent or revised allocations, and should cease to accumulate to the Fund's holdings. Multilateralization could then be effected with only minor cost of Fund resources and through the full utilization of the Fund's information and technical experience in improving constantly the mechanism of intra-European payments.

C. It need not be assumed that the whole of the sums estimated above will mean an immediate and equivalent dollar drain upon the Fund's resources, contrary to the policy adopted in Europe for the duration of ERP. What is initially involved is an acquisition of certain European currencies, in exchange for other European currencies. It is true, however, that, on a second round, the countries the currency of which has been sold by the Fund would have semiautomatic access to the Fund's resources, including dollars, if necessary to finance a balance-of-payments disequilibrium. The latter condition might well constitute a first brake on the withdrawal of dollars, especially as the Western Hemisphere deficit of these countries is supposedly covered by ECA allocations, and as they will have every reason to maintain their actual dollar deficit as close as possible to the ECA estimates so as to husband their own dollar resources—including their net creditor position against the Fund—to smooth out the much greater difficulties to be anticipated when ECA aid is discontinued. Such a policy (which the Fund may help press upon them) would be entirely consistent with the NAC (National Advisory Council) views on the use of Fund dollars.

A second brake is the fact that some countries at least would not become immediately eligible for automatic access to the Fund's dollars, because the present holdings of the Fund in their currency exceeds 75 per cent of the quota.

Finally, it should be remembered that if a country did in fact experience a serious dollar shortage in its balance of payments, drawings upon the Fund might in any case be regarded as perfectly legitimate. The main difference is the fact that countries which have acquired a creditor position against the Fund would not be debarred from financing through the Fund capital movements as well as deficits in current transactions. Requests of this sort, however, would be most unlikely under present-day conditions and some formal commitments from the countries concerned not to use their legal rights in this respect during the ECA period should not be too difficult to obtain.

D. The last question is probably the most difficult to solve. European countries will be most reluctant to incur a dollar obligation toward the Fund for the sole purpose of multilateralizing their commitments in Europe. Indeed this multilateralization itself may be regarded as a sacrifice of bilateral financial pressures advantageous to their own export trade.

There are reasons, however, which might prompt them to accept such multilateralization in the end, if the Fund can be relied upon to participate in its implementation.

First of all, serious difficulties may be encountered by some countries in providing in fact the export surplus envisaged in the present OEEC plan. If they were to fail, and if the ECA insisted on the conditional character of the supplementary allocations, the only way to maintain these would be to accept the transferability of their counterpart grants. Nothing would be gained, of course, if such transferability resulted in a direct and immediate dollar drain on their resources, but the intervention of the Fund would substitute for this a future commitment, and one which need not necessarily be expressed in dollars.

The question would be more complex if the grants were in fact fully utilized, but only by reason of their bilateral character. This would be the case, for instance, if France decided to use its sterling grants to the full, even for less essential imports, while being forced to curtail more essential imports from Belgium for lack of adequate facilities in the latter country's currency. This is precisely the drawback of the bilateral character of the grants, and one of which ECA must be acutely conscious. Less essential trade would be stimulated at the expense of more essential.

This would be so completely in opposition to the principles openly professed by OEEC and ECA that some reaction should normally be expected, especially as this unwanted shift of imports would obviously be detrimental to the debtor countries. Unfortunately, the alternatives are far from clear. If France, for instance, insisted on the multilateralization of her sterling grant, the United Kingdom might—and quite reasonably—claim that the level of the sterling grant should be revised downward. If a corresponding part of the conditional dollar allocation were, as a consequence, shifted from the U.K. to France, the advantage to France would be evident, but the U.K. might legitimately protest that the curtailment of her exports to France does not permit a corresponding increase in her exports to—or decline in her imports from—the Western Hemisphere, and that consequently the decrease in her conditional ECA grant should be less than the saving in her sterling counterpart grant. In such a case, France would lose more sterling than she would gain in Belgian francs, and her decision would be at least doubtful. Some ECA pressure may, therefore, prove well-nigh indispensable to prevent a collusion of both debtor and creditor countries to finance, through American aid, bilateral arrangements which each may, for different reasons, regard as being in its own interests.

On the other hand, the reluctance of European countries to incur dollar obligations and to encumber their later access to the Fund's resources is perfectly understandable. Special provision might prove necessary in this respect and might possibly involve the use of the waiver clause with respect to drawings originating directly in the multilateralization agreement. Finally, the difficulties would also diminish if repayments could be made, under some conditions, in the currencies purchased. Such a possibility is now being studied by the Legal Department. It would, of course, be very greatly enhanced if some European currencies were declared technically convertible, in the special meaning of the Fund Agreement, through renunciation of the benefits of Article XIV.

Conclusions

The suggestions above raise so many difficulties as to make a do-nothing attitude a most tempting one. We must, however, face the fact that we are now offered a unique opportunity to develop a systematic policy in Europe, with the powerful backing of ECA and of OEEC. If such an opportunity is missed, the chances of restoring a multilateral exchange system in Europe will be immeasurably weakened, and the Fund will anyway be bypassed in the fulfillment of one of the essential objectives which prompted its creation.

The danger of competitive currency depreciation in Europe is not a very serious threat at the moment. The opposite, and more real danger of currency overvaluation is one which the Fund is not very strongly equipped to fight. Our main job, indeed, for some years to come, will probably be the gradual elimination of exchange restrictions. This, however, is most unlikely to be realized through a country-by-country approach. The abolition of exchange controls by one country will often be dependent on the simultaneous renunciation of controls by other partner countries. Our best hope to achieve results is to increase progressively the sphere of multilateral payments, in accordance with OEEC and ECA objectives.

If we fail in this, the Fund will not necessarily save the resources that might have been employed in such a task. It will probably continue to finance *ad hoc* operations of an emergency character, without making any frontal attack, or achieving any substantial results, in the fulfillment of its fundamental objectives and purposes.

D. THE LATER COURSE OF DISCUSSIONS AT THE FUND

New arguments for postponement of action by the Fund along the lines proposed above were brilliantly developed by the Fund's staff in a memorandum discussing the "prerequisites for currency convertibility."

I tried to answer these arguments in a paper on "Interconvertibility, the Fund, and OEEC," dated November 25, 1948, by showing that they referred primarily to a unilateral declaration of general [worldwide] convertibility by a single country acting in isolation. What is more relevant to the present OEEC problem is the interconvertibility of a limited group of currencies, undertaken simultaneously. Interconvertibility within any given group of currencies is possible if it is compatible with the *over-all* equilibrium of each member of the group with the rest of the group taken as a whole.

While OEEC countries were admittedly far from such equilibrium in 1948, inconvertibility and bilateralism were not the inescapable, or even the best, solution to the problem. Financial assistance—available on a large scale under the ECA and OEEC schemes—could be so devised as to support immediate progress from narrow bilateralism to at least regional liberalization and interconvertibility, and to recreate desirable pressures and incentives for general monetary and exchange readjustments, indispensable [in the longer run] to the restoration of fundamental equilibrium in the balance of payments.

It is also important, in this connection, to distinguish between inconvertibility and nondiscrimination. Inconvertibility may aim at two results, and two results only:

(1) To force other countries to accumulate, against their wishes, the currency of the inconvertible country, i.e. to extend to it an interest-free loan to finance its bilateral deficits toward these countries. This can hardly be considered as a net gain for a group of countries, taken as a whole;

(2) To force other countries to shift their exports from the inconvertible country toward other areas, and their imports from other countries to the inconvertible country, in order to avoid the necessity for the above accumulation. This is, of course, a most uneconomic procedure and would tend, in the end, to force international trade

into the straitjacket of strict bilateral balance between each pair of countries.

This was well understood by the London *Economist* which argued on August 9, 1947 (pp. 228–39), that the villains of the piece (in the Anglo-American Financial Agreement) were not the convertibility, but the antidiscrimination provisions. Indeed, discriminatory practices—whatever the other objections to them—can be far less lethal than inconvertibility, insofar as they can be used to promote semi-multilateral, rather than strictly bilateral equilibrium.

In practice, and in accordance with the above reasoning, sterling was soon made *administratively* transferable, rather than strictly inconvertible, the main purpose of the arrangement being to prevent transfers that might lead to a transfer of sterling into gold or dollars (mainly transfers into Belgian francs). This could not, however, solve the difficulty mentioned in the *Economist* article, i.e. the increasing difficulty of buying "imports except for payment in hard currencies."

It should be remembered that the acceptability of a currency for international transfers does not depend on mere permission by the monetary authorities of the issuing country. Other countries will refuse to accept such currency transfers in payment for their own exports, if they are not assured of the opportunity to use it (immediately or later on, as the need may be) for payments to their own creditors. In the end, the convertibility of a currency will depend essentially on the over-all equilibrium of the issuing country. If such equilibrium does not exist, neither convertibility nor inconvertibility can permanently persuade other countries to finance indefinitely the disequilibria of the issuing country. If, on the other hand, the issuing country is in over-all equilibrium, transferability of its currency should raise little difficulty.

In summary, the danger of a premature declaration of interconvertibility may well be matched by the danger that continued inconvertibility offers a dangerous escape from more basic monetary, budgetary, and exchange readjustments necessary to the restoration of fundamental equilibrium. Inconvertibility may, in some cases, be *an* answer, but definitely is not *the* answer to over-all balance-of-payments disequilibria.

While placing more and more stress on the desirability of exchange-rate readjustments and the mopping-up of excess liquidity inherited from latent inflation, rationing, and price controls, I also tried, in the same memorandum and in subsequent ones, to devise concrete operational techniques—scornfully dismissed as "gimmicks" by their opponents—susceptible of reintroducing pressures and incentives for the adoption of such policies by members and of facilitating progress from bilateralism to regional liberalization and interconvertibility. One of these was destined to play a key role in the later EPU agreement. It was the so-called "matching credits" formula, under which intra-European disequilibria would be settled simultaneously partly in gold and partly through credit claims *multilaterally* usable by the creditor to settle later deficits within the area.

A joint memorandum, described as "A Staff Proposal" emerged from a new round of staff discussions in Washington, and was transmitted to the Executive Board on March 8, 1949. It endorsed an enlarged, *tripartite* financing formula, under which (a) one third of the disequilibria would be settled through "conditional aid" allocations of dollars from an unallocated pool of Marshall aid funds earmarked for the purpose, (b) another third, through gold or dollar settlements or drawings on the IMF, and (c) the remaining third, from the "matching credits" mentioned above.

Discussion of this memorandum by the IMF Executive Board elicited, once more, broadly favorable statements by most of its members, but it was felt that the proposals should be referred to ECA and the OEEC for further appraisal and negotiation before the Board itself could take any concrete action on them. Indeed, the commitments (financial and other) envisaged in the Staff proposals would have to be undertaken primarily by ECA and the European countries, rather than by the Fund; and the IMF offices in Washington had long been deserted in favor of the Chateau de la Muette in Paris by the main negotiators of the intra-European payments plans and their technical experts.

The estrangement of the Fund from the negotiations that ended in the establishment of the European Payments Union deepened in the course of the following months, with the growing hardening of the conflict between ECA, which represented the United States in the OEEC negotiations in Paris, and the Treasury, which dominated the U.S. representation in the Fund's Board in Washington. The Treasury representatives conducted a bitter rearguard fight, in the Fund and elsewhere, against the EPU proposals advanced in Paris by the ECA. Eventually, ECA won the battle, the end-result of the Treasury's opposition being merely to keep the Fund aloof from the latest phases of the negotiations and to exclude it for years from any participation and representation in the ECA Agreement and administrative machinery.

In the summer of 1949, I was asked by the U.S. Government to join the ECA staff in Paris to help in the drafting and negotiation of an agreement along the lines of my previous IMF memoranda. I did so in December of that year, after having failed also to gain any acceptance by the Fund for the views expressed on the eve and the morrow of the September 1949 devaluations.[1]

2. . . . And ECA Catches It

A. POINTS FOR DISCUSSION ON THE PROBLEM OF CURRENCY TRANSFERABILITY IN EUROPE

[The following memorandum, prepared in the weeks following the September 1949 devaluations, summarized the main issues involved in the transferability debate and presented a number of new suggestions that were to be pressed successfully by ECA in later negotiations (particularly the consolidation of outstanding bilateral debts, the organization of compensations "over time" as well as "over space," a faster rate of liberalization by excess creditors, increasing ratios of gold settlements by debtor countries, provisions for so-called "structural" surpluses and deficits).]

(1) Full transferability of currencies in Europe, at least for current payments, is generally accepted in ECA and OEEC circles as a desirable objective for the immediate future.

(2) Discussions, however, have floundered so far because of a deep cleavage of opinion on the implications of transferability within the group on the problem of dollar convertibility. The U.K. has generally been in favor of transferability, but with the proviso that the issuing countries should not be obliged to redeem into gold or dollars balances of their currency accumulated by foreign countries. This view is unacceptable both to ECA and to the accumulating countries, since the latter would then be forced to finance, without any limitation whatsoever, other countries' deficits with them, or to stop such accumulation either through a breaking of cross rates or through the adoption of discriminatory exchange and import controls. Both methods would lead to an artificial balancing of trade, and the second

1. See above, pp. 179–200.

would have the further disadvantage of raising production costs and living costs by the amount of the price differentials which quantitative discrimination is designed to overcome.

(3) These difficulties, however, have been greatly diminished as a result of recent currency readjustments and of the general progress of domestic monetary stabilization in most European countries. It is clear, in any case, that the general acceptance of transferability is linked to at least some degree of partial convertibility of accumulated balances.

(4) The risks of "premature" convertibility have been generally exaggerated since the ill-fated—but also ill-prepared and truly premature—convertibility experiment of sterling in 1947. It is often argued that the prerequisites for convertibility imply *the pre-existence of such a pattern of (bilateral) trade and payments as would permit the restoration of convertibility, at current exchange rates and with current domestic monetary policies, without entailing any serious risks of gold or dollar losses.* Such a formula, however, would define the *consequences,* rather than the *prerequisites* of convertibility, since such a pattern is most unlikely to emerge spontaneously except under the spur of the incentives and discipline created by convertibility itself. Production and *over-all* exports can recover to extraordinary levels without bringing any nearer the fulfillment of such conditions. This is clearly revealed by the experience of European countries in the last two years.

(5) This is not to deny the reality of the problem, and the need for some true prerequisites for convertibility. These would include notably: (a) a reasonable restoration of physical productive capacity, and satisfaction of emergency postwar needs for re-equipment and re-stocking; (b) the adoption of monetary policies consonant with convertibility, and especially the elimination—or control [1]—of latent as well as current inflation.

(6) The *over-all* production and balance-of-payments position of the U.K. compares favorably with its prewar position, equilibrium being now achieved on current balance-of-payments transactions. Even the dollar gap is broadly comparable with prewar, the basic

---

1. The full elimination of inflation would permit the elimination of controls over current transactions, while the continuation of latent inflation might require continued controls, quantitative or otherwise, on the use of excess liquidities, but not necessarily *bilateral* or *discriminatory* controls.

difference being that debt repayments—especially of sterling balances —and new investments—especially in the sterling area—now exceed the British bilateral surpluses with nondollar areas, and cause a direct drain on the dollar resources of the U.K. Before the war, these surpluses were, on the contrary, a source of dollar earnings for the United Kingdom, permitting the compensation of the current deficit with the dollar area.

Ninety-six per cent of the over-all dollar drain in the first half of 1949 was associated with such capital exports and debt repayments. A more moderate rate of capital exports and debt repayments would undoubtedly permit full participation of the U.K. in *mutual* undertakings for the restoration of transferability and convertibility in Europe.

(7) Convertibility, as here defined, does not necessarily imply the immediate removal of all exchange controls and other restrictions on current transactions, whether with the Western Hemisphere, or even in intra-European relations. This is also a desirable objective, and one toward which considerable progress should be effected in the immediate future, through simultaneous, mutual steps of trade and payments liberalization.

As, or more urgent, however, is the removal of all the pressures toward *bilateral* balancing of accounts, inherent in the present trade and payments mechanism.

(8) The most glaring of these pressures is a country's refusal to redeem balances in its currency currently acquired by another country, except through increased sales of its own goods to that particular country.[2] The latter country is then led to follow discriminatory import, and possibly export, policies, irrespective of prices, qualities, or needs, in order to avoid indefinite accumulation of the inconvertible currency.

(9) Only slightly less obvious and objectionable is the policy of other countries which, while accepting to redeem their balances above a bilaterally agreed margin, apply discriminatory restrictions on their imports from countries with which the margin is reached, so as to avoid in fact any gold payments.

(10) In both cases, the result is an artificial and costly balancing of international accounts along bilateral lines. The main difference is

2. This may be qualified, of course, by transferability with a limited number of other countries, either on an automatic or on an administrative basis.

that, in the first case, the main burden of such balancing is thrown on the surplus country, instead of remaining the responsibility of the deficit country.

(11) The most promising approach, at this time, toward the elimination of such bilateral pressures—but not of the pressures for the over-all balancing of accounts—would be the *multilateralization* of gold payments over as broad a regional area as possible. That is to say, no country would be called upon to pay gold to settle a bilateral deficit, but only as necessary to settle an over-all net deficit toward all other participants as a group. Similarly, no country would be entitled to receive gold payments to settle a bilateral surplus, but only to settle an over-all net surplus toward all other participants as a group.

Mutual commitments to this effect among the bulk of OEEC members would eliminate one of the main incentives to bilateral, discriminatory administration of exchange controls and other restrictions, and would foster substantial progress toward multilateral, rather than bilateral, balancing of trade and payments.

(12) Such a system would not necessarily lead to an expansion of gold and dollar payments in intra-European trade. On the contrary, some of these payments, which are now taking place in isolated bilateral relationships, would be economized through the offsetting of bilateral surplus and deficit positions, preliminary to any such payments under the suggested arrangement.

(13) Gold payments would then be required from any country only to the extent that it maintains with the rest of the group an over-all deficit for which it cannot find voluntary financing either in the capital markets, or from intergovernmental or international loans. No country would be barred from raising funds in this manner, nor from correcting its over-all deficit through changes in its domestic policies, or in its exchange rates, or even possibly in its system of over-all exchange and import controls. The only recourse excluded is that of *forcing* other countries to choose between unlimited financing of their debtors or the adoption of discriminatory controls in their favor.

(14) Debtor countries can therefore escape all gold and dollar payments in Europe by eliminating their net over-all deficit in intra-European relations. Such an extreme result, however, would be far from desirable, not only from the surplus countries' point of view, but also from that of the European debtors themselves.

Both groups of countries will, in the long run, profit from multilateral balancing of their accounts on a world basis, rather than on a regional basis. In some cases (Denmark is an outstanding one) any artificial balancing with other European countries alone would require drastic—and catastrophic—modifications in the country's economic structure. Thus, even though recognizing the need for an over-all balance between Europe as a whole and the rest of the world, taking into account available capital imports, there should remain room for some offsets between intra-European surpluses and extra-European deficits, and between intra-European deficits and extra-European surpluses, on the part of individual countries. What may be true is that the scope for such offsets may be less than in prewar and that some structural changes may be needed to take this limitation into account.

(15) Further economy in gold payments, especially in view of the low level of European reserves, would result from the setting up of moderate credit margins designed to cover over-all temporary imbalance (of a seasonal character, for example), or to cushion more permanent deficits until corrective measures have had time to produce their effects.

Room should be left also for normal capital movements from the relatively stronger countries to those relatively less developed or reconstructed. As indicated above, this should normally take place through the capital markets rather than through any permanent clearing machinery. For the remainder of the ERP period, however, necessary financing designed to reconstruct war-shattered economies cannot so be placed on a commercial basis. Conditional aid and drawing rights could properly be integrated into the clearing machinery, in order to facilitate its initial operation under the special difficulties inherited from the war. They should, moreover, be used to elicit from the more prosperous countries a reasonable amount of noncommercial contributions complementing the American effort. These contributions could be built up from the existing network of bilateral payment agreements and credit margins, with two basic modifications: (a) a full multilateralization of such margins, in order to avoid unnecessary bilateral bias in the administration of remaining trade and payments controls; (b) a partial consolidation of old balances, and readjustment of over-all margins into a less haphazard pattern than the present one.

(16) The Basle system of intra-European compensations has not yet been able to solve these problems in a satisfactory manner, and voluntary compensations—of so-called "second category"—have re-

mained extremely limited. The reluctance of the countries to use the system more fully is due especially to the fact that extensive compensations would tend to concentrate all creditor-debtor relationships between the stronger surplus countries, on the one hand, and the weaker deficit countries on the other. Both groups object to such an arrangement which would benefit exclusively the intermediate countries, the latter cancelling hard currency indebtedness with soft currency claims.

(17) On the other hand, full multilateralization of debit and credit margins under present payment agreements would require a solution of the possible gap between the credit commitments of the surplus countries and the use of credit margins by the deficit countries. If numerous, even though small, deficit positions happened to concentrate upon a single, or a few surplus countries, the credit commitments of the latter might be exhausted even though no deficit country has yet exhausted its own borrowing facilities. This central problem of a multilateral system of intra-European payments and credits is discussed at length in IMF memoranda RD-463 of December 16, 1947, RD-605 of May 7, 1948, RD-770 of November 25, 1948, and RD-809 of March 8, 1949.[3]

(18) The machinery of the Fund could here be used to excellent avail, as indicated especially in RD memoranda 463 and 605. The currency of countries whose credit commitments have been exhausted could be sold by the Fund against the currencies of debtors, without increasing in any way the borrowing facilities of the latter. Such sales would merely permit the multilateral use of already existing credit facilities, which would otherwise remain on a bilateral basis.

The systematic use of such transactions would require the preliminary acceptance by participating countries of two special commitments:

(a) They would have to commit themselves to request from the Fund the scarce European currencies needed by members (up to their credit margins), this obligation being distributed, in case of need, among the net debtors in proportion to these debts. The scarce currencies thus obtained from the Fund would be ceded to members in exchange for the repurchase of equivalent balances in the national currency of those debtor countries.

(b) To lessen the burden on the countries which are thus forced to increase their indebtedness to the Fund (always repayable in gold

3. See above, Chapter XI, section 1.

or convertible currencies), the countries whose currency is bought from the Fund should undertake to reverse the operation at a later date if the debtors become able, within a specified period of time, to offer repayment in the scarce European currency. These repayments would be used by the scarce currency country to repurchase from the Fund the debtor's currency previously sold to the Fund, thus reversing entirely the initial Fund transaction and restoring the original position of both members in the Fund.

(19) Further highly desirable features would include:

(a) Specific provisions and authority to bring pressure for the re-adjustment of excessive deficit or surplus positions through changes in fiscal, credit, and monetary policies, in exchange rates, etc. An automatic commitment for the liberalization of at least quantitative controls should be imposed on excess creditors as a condition for gold payments to them by other members.

(b) Other provisions designed to serve the same objective might increase gradually the ratio of gold payments to borrowing facilities for the settlement of deficits, as the borrowing ceiling is approached by a debtor. Conversely, this ratio would decrease for a creditor as his over-all surplus position is built up and approaches the maximum commitment accepted by him.

(c) Finally, the provisions regulating gold payments to intra-European surplus countries might attempt to take into consideration their normal needs for non-European currencies, considering their economic structure and normal markets for imports and exports, and the probable availability of surpluses in such currencies to be con-tributed by intra-European debtors.

(20) The International Monetary Fund owes it to itself and its members to promote the general objectives which the suggestions above seek to serve. If other methods are deemed preferable, the Fund should propose and support them.

If, however, the Fund agrees in general with what is proposed here, it could play a most useful role in enlarging the scope of possible multilateral settlements both within and outside Europe.

(21) *In summary:*

(a) The progress of European reconstruction and stabilization makes it possible to take now, on a mutual basis, a number of measures to ensure the *immediate transferability,* and the *progressive convertibility* of European currencies.

(b) Further delay can only freeze trade and payment channels into an artificial pattern molded upon the absence of such transferability and convertibility, and aggravating the difficulties and dislocations attendant upon their restoration at a later date.

(c) It is suggested above that considerable progress toward our ultimate objectives could be made through the multilateralization of gold payments and credit margins in Europe.

(d) Actual settlements of *over-all* surplus and deficit positions would be based on a combination of gold payments and multilateral credits, in varying proportions.

(e) Specific provisions would put additional pressure on members to correct persistent trends toward excessive surplus or deficit positions.

(f) The IMF can play a vital part in enlarging the scope of such a multilateral system of settlements and in linking it with other countries outside the system.

(g) *The one mistake which the Fund cannot afford is to continue to remain officially indifferent to such problems, and to the attempts made elsewhere to find practical solutions of immediate, even though gradual, applicability.*

B. INITIAL PROPOSALS FOR A EUROPEAN CLEARING UNION

Concrete proposals for negotiation by ECA were briefly summarized in the following note, dated December 22, 1949:

(1) full transferability of European currencies, at least on current account, through application of the following principles;

(2) full multilateralization of gold points;

(3) full multilateralization of credit margins and incorporation of all European payments agreements into the system;

(4) all debits and credits to be established with central clearing, in a common unit of account carrying with it an exchange guarantee, and with the joint, solidary guarantee of all participants;

(5) further backing of above obligations through the constitution of a reserve fund, partly in dollars;

(6) building up of a dollar pool through allocation of intra-European dollar aid to the clearing, and requirement of fractional gold or dollar payments by debtors, beyond temporary swing margins,

the proportion of such payments increasing as the deficit increases;

(7) fractional gold payments to creditors, in proportion decreasing as the surplus increases;

(8) over-all quota in European currencies of each debtor to be based on some proportion of its over-all intra-European trade, plus tapering off amounts corresponding to structural deficits and financed by ECA allocations to the clearing;

(9) need for administrative, as well as automatic mechanisms designed to correct excessive credit or debit positions;

(10) as a consequence of the above: (a) immediate and full *multilateralization* of remaining exchange and import restrictions; (b) substantial *liberalization* of such over-all restrictions.

Numerous hurdles still had to be overcome before full agreement could be reached on the concrete provisions of a European Payments Union. The main phases of the negotiation are briefly summarized in my volume on *Europe and the Money Muddle*, pp. 161–68. The final agreement (summarized in the same volume, pp. 168–79) differed very little, however, from the initial proposals outlined above.

3. FROM EPU TO EUROPEAN MONETARY INTEGRATION: HOPES, DISILLUSIONS, AND ACHIEVEMENTS

The EPU Agreement had to be renewed and revised yearly to adjust it to the fast-changing pace of Europe's payments problems. These year-to-year adaptations were the main topic of a long series of studies and memoranda, official and unofficial, which I prepared over the years 1951–58. These would make very dull reading today, and only two are reproduced below.

My broad approach to these ephemeral, transitional arrangements was dominated, however, by longer-run considerations. I had conceived, from the very beginning, the EPU Agreement as only the first of many steps on a long road toward the eventual integration of European monetary policies and institutions. My concrete proposals for annual revisions of the Agreement kept in view this ultimate aim as well as the day-to-day problems of current EPU operations.

This long-run strategy is reflected in the following memorandum transmitted to ECA in November 1951, upon my return to academic life (at Yale), after several years of national and international civil service and negotiations on these issues in Washington and in Europe.

A. THE PATH FROM EPU TO EUROPEAN
MONETARY INTEGRATION

Introduction

Upon my return from an extended assignment in Europe, first for the International Monetary Fund and later with ECA, I have been asked to draw from my experience in the negotiation and management of EPU some suggestions as to how we might best pursue our general objective of promoting closer European integration in the monetary field. This problem is especially important on the eve of the mandatory revision of the EPU agreement, after the first two years of operation.

The present paper is therefore narrowly limited, and highly subjective, in content. It does not touch, except incidentally, on the problems connected with rearmament. Neither does it attempt to deal extensively with the substantive problems of EPU or of monetary integration in general. It centers instead on problems of strategy and tactics in a negotiation which will continue to be a most difficult and delicate one.

My own position in this respect derives entirely from concrete experience in similar negotiations over the past three years. I was lucky enough to establish, slowly and gradually, very intimate and confident contacts with some, at least, of our major European partners at the technical level: people like Marjolin, Figgures, and Selleslags in the OEEC Secretariat, Roll and Bridge for the U.K., Frère and Ansiaux for the Belgians, Calvet for the French, Posthuma and Keesing for the Dutch, Carli for the Italians, Bauer and Rossy for the Swiss, etc. Many of these people were just as sincere as ourselves in their devotion to European integration, but they were at the same time in a better position to appraise the risks inseparable from such a program and the way in which political doubts and fears, at the governmental level, might best be overcome in their respective countries. I have not the slightest doubt that the success of the EPU negotiations and of its functioning during the first year of operations is due, to a very large part, to the frankness and sincerity of the relations thus established among top EPU technicians. I put a great deal of stock, therefore, in what I have learned from them of the best chances of, and major obstacles to, the achievement of full monetary integration in Europe.

The latter objective is here accepted as a datum of U.S. policy. In particular:

(1) I take it that our European integration program is not an alternative to, but on the contrary an integral part of, our broader aims of world-wide economic cooperation. This may well be worth emphasizing, since EPU has long been regarded by some of its opponents as a rival to the IMF, and by some of its proponents as directed toward equilibrating *each* European country's *regional* balance of payments with the rest of Europe, rather than its *over-all* balance of payments in a world-wide system of multilateral trade. I firmly believe:

(a) that world-wide cooperation is served—and not undermined—by a certain degree of decentralization, promoting a closer integration between neighboring countries than would be either objectively desirable or politically feasible in a broader framework;

(b) that closer regional integration will also be served in the long run—and not undermined—by an open-door policy, taking advantage of every opportunity for multilateral trading among the various regional groups. We must certainly recognize the full impact of the so-called dollar shortage on such possibilities, but we should not assume that this should lead to bilateral balance in each country's transactions with the dollar area.

Both points would necessitate fuller developments, far beyond the narrow limits of the present paper. Suffice it to say here that the insufficient clarification of these issues is probably responsible for:

(a) the needless conflicts which have arisen between proponents and opponents of EPU in the U.S. Government, and the present lack of cooperation between EPU and the IMF;

(b) the avoidance by EPU of some major issues underlying present balance-of-payments disequilibria, and in particular the scant attention given to exchange-rate policy and to the problem of sterling transferability;

(c) much of the current confusion on the issue of settlements beyond quotas.

(2) It is also believed that the present emphasis on the problem of European rearmament should not detract from, but if possible add to, our drive for European integration. We may, it is true, find it easier at times to apply *bilateral* pressure on each European country to increase its rearmament effort, and this may tend to slacken our efforts to build up a more viable European economic and political structure, or incline us toward measures or policies which may provide short-cuts toward defense financing, but at the cost of weakening or destroy-

ing the progress already achieved toward European integration. I am convinced that this can only end, within the near future, in the progressive disaffection and demoralization among our European allies, and in a consequent strengthening of isolationist sentiment in the United States. The initial building up of the Atlantic coalition certainly requires a large degree of U.S. leadership and financing, but its ultimate viability certainly depends on Europe's own determination to defend itself, and this determination in turn depends on the confidence of Europeans in their own strength and future.

(3) A third preconception is that very fast progress—faster than most Europeans now believe—can be achieved toward an extremely close degree of European monetary integration, but that success or failure may depend nearly as much upon our *strategy* as upon our *objectives* in promoting such policies. It is from this point of view that I would like to review below the major achievements and failures of EPU in its first year of operation.

EPU's Achievements Toward Monetary Integration

(1) The most significant achievement of EPU, from a long-run point of view, lies in the administrative rather than in the financial field. It is the extraordinary degree of cohesion and influence developed nearly overnight by its Managing Board. Throughout the first year of operations, all MB decisions, without a single exception, have been unanimous, although only a majority vote is required. No decision was ever postponed or eluded because of a lack of such unanimity. All MB decisions or recommendations were fairly promptly endorsed by the Council and accepted by the countries concerned. This is an outstanding record, especially when viewed against the background of the interminable and often sterile discussions of the Payments Committee during the preceding two years.

Among the reasons for this success are:

(a) First, and probably foremost, the fact that the MB brings together in Paris once or twice a month top policy-makers in the monetary field, rather than instructed delegates or representatives. The same man participates in MB discussions, and also participates at the top level in the day-to-day shaping of his own country's monetary policy. He soon discovers how valuable the MB pooling of information and coordination of policies can be to help him discharge his national responsibilities. He realizes similarly how his own policy decisions or advice may contribute to such coordination or, on the contrary, raise insoluble problems in EPU. In fact this combination on the same heads of international and domestic responsibilities has clearly resulted in having Board members promote an international viewpoint at home as much or more as defend their national interests at the Board meetings. The outstanding examples of this frame of mind came to the fore during the discussion of the French and British surpluses during the first months of EPU, of the Belgian surpluses last summer, of the revision of the Dutch quota in June, of the regulation of capital movements by the Swiss, of the revision of EPU interest rates, of the development of the German crisis, etc.

(b) Another potent factor is the separation effected in the EPU statutes between political and technical responsibility for major decisions. On all questions of some importance, the MB can only issue recommendations to the OEEC Council. This apparent source of weakness has proved in fact to be a cause of strength for the MB. If the Board's decisions were final, no member could vote on any measure without being sure of the concurrence of his government. In many cases, this would have produced a complete deadlock, as it did in the old days of the Payments Committee. In the Managing Board, unanimous decisions have been reached time and again with the agreement of, let us say, the Danish member, although such decision was not to the liking of the Danish Government, and was later criticized and opposed by the Danish delegate in the Payments, or in the Economic, Committee of OEEC. Indeed, there have been cases where the MB recommendation was supported only by a minority in these Committees, but the opposition was divided among delegates arguing for widely different solutions of the problem. In the absence of unanimity these Committees could not modify the MB recommendations to the Council. Unanimity, it is true, was still required at the Council level, but by the time the MB recommendations reached it for final decision, the impossibility of reaching agreement along different lines had been amply demonstrated, and in many cases agreement with the MB was still better than no agreement at all.[1] In many cases, also, the recommendations were addressed primarily to one country and could be followed by that country even in the absence of a Council decision.

(c) A third reason is that the MB succeeded, more and more, in acting in a most unspectacular and discreet manner. Whenever possible they avoided the technique of formal recommendations—requir-

1. Similar remarks could be applied today (in 1965) to the catalyzing role of the Commission in EEC policy formation.

ing channelling to the Council via the Trade and Payments and Economic Committees—and resorted instead to making their recommendations known to the countries concerned merely by communication of the minutes of the meetings and personal interviews with the countries' representatives. This often proved a most effective shortcut, saving a lot of discussion, publicity, and ill will on the part of the countries concerned.

(d) Credit must also be given to the sincerity, imagination, and driving power of the personalities involved. Calvet, Ansiaux (and Figgures for the Secretariat) were particularly outstanding in this respect.

To summarize, the influence of the MB was mostly due not to its statutory powers, but rather to the absence of such powers. The comparison with the IMF is of great significance here, on all four points mentioned above. It is also worth noting that this influence came most unexpectedly, all countries—with the single exception of Belgium—having fought tooth and nail throughout the negotiation of EPU against the U.S. view favoring a strong and powerful management. The success of the MB grew out of experience rather than legal commitments.

(2) In the financial field, the substitution of multilateral for bilateral settlements facilitated a rapid expansion of trade on a sounder pattern, while at the same time: (a) reducing by two thirds (from 32 per cent to 9 per cent) the recourse to U.S. financing of intra-European disequilibria; (b) raising from 2 per cent to 42 per cent the financing of gross deficits by multilateral offsets of bilateral surpluses and deficits (At the end of September, 80 per cent of the deficits were covered by multilateral offsets and reversals of positions.); (c) liquidating over 15 months 47 per cent of the monetary intra-European debts accumulated under the previous bilateral agreements; (d) substituting multilateral claims and credits, freely usable throughout the EPU area, for bilateral claims and credits whose effective use depended, to an ever-growing degree, on bilateral, discriminatory techniques designed to twist the normal and most economic pattern of trade.

(3) In the commercial field, EPU succeeded in: (a) eliminating overnight all financial incentives to bilateral discrimination; (b) reducing from 50 per cent to 25 per cent or less the degree of trade restrictions maintained by all important EPU countries. This was all the more unexpected as many countries had freely predicted that they

would be forced to restore restrictions as soon as their gold free tranche had been exhausted. In the event, large gold payments were made to EPU (up to 60 and 80 per cent in the Dutch and German cases) without any restoration of restrictions. Only long after the German quota had been exhausted were restrictions reintroduced by Germany, under strict OEEC supervision.

(4) European cooperation in EPU was also marked in: (a) the quick and successful handling of the German problem, which allowed German production and exports to continue their amazing rate of recovery in the face of a most stringent exchange crisis; (b) the objective examination of the Greek, Austrian, and Turkish problems, and the courageous recommendations made to these countries even though the Board well knew that the request to EPU was in fact a request for American, rather than European, assistance; (c) the discreet, but effective influence of the MB on other countries' policies, particularly the Netherlands and Denmark.

Failings of EPU and Major Threats to its Viability

(1) The major failings of EPU arise mostly from the problems left unsolved at the time of its creation, and particularly from the smoldering conflicts between the regional and the world-wide approach to monetary reconstruction:

(a) The relationships of EPU to the IMF were left totally undefined, and mutual suspicions prevented any realistic cooperation between the two institutions;

(b) As a result, EPU eluded consideration of all problems directly related to the IMF jurisdiction, and particularly: (i) the problem of exchange rates; (ii) the problem of sterling transferability.

(c) Finally, the conflict between the proponents of soft settlements and the defenders of hard settlement terms was also left partly unsolved, and the issue was never fully clarified. The resulting uncertainty for both creditors and debtors remains as a major reason of diffidence toward the maintenance of the EPU arrangements.

(2) The major threat to EPU certainly lies in the continuing uncertainty surrounding various phases of its operations. We must realize, more clearly than we do, that EPU cannot live and progress indefinitely on the basis of American decisions and financial support. Its viability and future depend primarily on the loyalty and confidence of its members, and on their own desire to strengthen it and use it as a means toward monetary integration in Europe.

European monetary leaders, however, are predominantly of a conservative frame of mind, which finds its expression in the very strict rules governing the operations of most European Central Banks. Open-end commitments and uncertain assets are anathema to this system, deeply ingrained in the European mentality and in the structure of European financial and monetary institutions.

As long as EPU assets and liabilities are left vague and uncertain, and EPU rules of operations subject to constant interference and revisions, there will always lurk in the background some desire to liquidate the organization in order to end these uncertainties.

ECA should, therefore, devote major efforts to clarifying such rules and commitments, even where this implies a final arbitration between divergent philosophies and trends in Washington. I would mention particularly in this respect:

(a) the uncertainty still surrounding the definiteness of our capital commitments, particularly in the case of liquidation. We should attempt to clarify at an early opportunity: (i) the exact grounds on which we might object to liquidation; (ii) the exact amount which we would claim the right to block in the case of a liquidation to which we object. Our major reason for retaining our present powers in this respect was certainly to prevent *premature* liquidation, which France was, for a long time, suspected to favor. We should realize, however, that our present interpretation of the agreement gives us the power to make EPU illiquid and even insolvent if we block more than $236 or $271 million at liquidation. Rather than deterring liquidation, this may well tend to prompt it on the part of creditors who will wish to avoid building up claims on an insolvent institution. We should therefore indicate, at the beginning of the forthcoming negotiation of EPU's revision, that we shall eliminate this uncertainty as soon as agreement is reached on the future shape of a permanent EPU. We might possibly go as far as to withdraw our right to block convertible assets and substitute instead a provision allowing for the distribution of convertible assets as long as such distribution takes place in accordance with revised statutes on which full agreement has been reached among Europeans and between Europeans and ourselves. Such an advance promise—and such a bargaining weapon—might prove most effective in the negotiation of the EPU revision;

(b) the need for an early decision in the matter of settlements to creditors in excess of their quota;

(c) stricter rules regarding the right of individual withdrawal or suspension;

[(d) the final elimination of the initial balances technique of 1949–50, with its attendant impact on EPU's capital and convertible assets. This was eliminated already at the occasion of the June 1951 revision, thus removing one of the major dangers of disaffection toward EPU.];

(e) the creation of a Special EPU Assistance Fund, contributed by EPU members themselves and under the control of the MB. In order to prompt this, and to eliminate the present uncertainties regarding the use of our own Special Assistance Fund, we might turn over to EPU the remainder of this latter Fund, up to an amount matching the contributions of the Europeans themselves to the build-up of such a Fund.

(3) Another source of uncertainty lies in the initial confusion into EPU itself of two very separate functions: (a) a *permanent* system of monetary settlements among members, with cushioning credits of a temporary character; (b) a *temporary* system of grants in aid, to assist reconstruction (initial balances) or rearmament (burden-sharing contributions). Both functions are essential, but they obey very different motivations, and fall into two very different fields of competence. The first function relates primarily to monetary and financial decisions, of the competence of Central Banks and monetary experts. The second involves top political decisions at a very different level. The Managing Board is ideally suited to the first, and extremely inept with respect to the second.

Again, the elimination of the initial balances technique has brought a definite gain in this respect. Burden-sharing contributions should similarly be decided within the NATO framework and should not call for any discussion or review by EPU itself. They should be channelled anonymously through EPU, together with all other payments and very much in the same way as Red Cross contributions, for instance, now affect EPU settlements without ever coming to the specific attention of the EPU authorities.

Progress of EPU Toward Fuller Monetary Integration in Europe[2]

Once the above uncertainties and causes for disaffection are removed, the evident value of EPU to its members will ensure their loyalty and their desire to strengthen and develop it themselves, as required by the logic of events. I, for one, feel confident that this will transform fairly rapidly EPU into a Central Reserve Bank for Europe, and may even end up in something approximating a single currency area.

If the U.S. wishes to encourage such a development, however, great tact and discretion must be used in our handling of the problem. A European Central Bank cannot possibly be imposed upon Europe by outside pressure. To be successful, such an institution will need the full and sincere support of its members, and this is possible only if it grows out of European consciousness of the services it can render.

Any spectacular or grandiose plan which we would ourselves initiate and propose would be greeted by amused skepticism at our naïveté. Even if we could succeed by financial pressure in extracting some formal agreement, open or concealed opposition would soon whittle it down to a mere paper institution, without life or drive of its own. Witness again the sterility of such a theoretically powerful institution as the IMF.

What can we do therefore to encourage European monetary integration?

(1) First, throw our support behind any European initiative which may well be expected to develop in this direction, as a consequence of other plans such as the European Army, the Schuman Plan, etc. Such support, however, should not take the form of direct political or financial pressure from the outside.

(2) Consolidate the EPU, and refrain from too frequent interference—or threats of interference—with its functioning, except on the few major issues which would fundamentally affect our national interests and policies.

(3) Take advantage of any concrete problems arising in EPU to support concrete solutions which will, in fact, gradually assemble all the materials needed for a central banking institution. This would imply advance consideration and planning of such problems as can

2. The following remarks were intended to deter ECA from a spectacular initiative to earmark up to $1 billion of Marshall aid as capital fund for a European Super-Central Bank to be created in 1952.

be foreseen, and careful weighing of alternative solutions in the light of our long-run objective. In negotiation, however, each solution would be defended exclusively on its *ad hoc* merits with relation to the concrete problem at hand. I can only sketch here, in way of examples, the forms which such a policy might take:

(a) We should be concerned with the gradual building up of a joint reserve fund for Europe. Such centralization of reserves is certainly one of the first prerequisites and functions of a European Central Bank. This could be initiated by offering creditors beyond quotas higher terms of settlement if they agree to accept such settlements in the form of convertible accounts, rather than cash.[3] Great care should be taken to allow maximum discretion and flexibility in the rules governing such accounts. They should, at the outset, be fully guaranteed by the corresponding gold and dollar assets economized by the shift from cash to convertible account settlements. As confidence grows, the percentage of such reserves may gradually be lowered to levels which experience indicates as leaving a safe margin for liquidity. Unspectacular in itself, the convertible account technique would set in motion the very mechanism out of which modern banking actually developed over the course of history.

(b) We should be concerned with strengthening the centralized resources which EPU can place at the disposal of its members in case of need.

The convertible account technique would already constitute a step in this direction. The building up of a Special EPU Assistance or Reserve Fund would constitute an additional means to the same end. Yet it could easily be presented as a means to replace, and absorb, our own Special Assistance Fund, and as a *quid pro quo* in favor of weaker countries at the occasion of the definition of rules of settlement protecting creditors beyond quotas.

(c) We should be concerned with the development of the MB influence on members' policies. A good beginning has already been made in this direction. The use of methods (a) and (b) above would reinforce this influence by placing at the disposal of the MB larger financial resources to back up its advice to members. At some future time, a U.S. stabilization loan, or automatic rediscounting facilities with the IMF, could further strengthen those resources. As for EPU

---

3. The reader may note the similarity between this proposal and my later suggestions for minimum IMF deposits or reserve certificates, inconvertible into gold metal, but fully usable in all balance-of-payments settlements.

creditors, MB influence could be gained on their policies by retaining for the MB the right to modify settlement terms beyond quotas against any member whose policies are deemed improper by the MB or the OEEC. (Special rules would be necessary to circumvent the veto of directly interested parties. I have offered some suggestions in this respect in my paper on "The Adequacy of EPU Convertible Assets.")

(d) We should be concerned with encouraging, in the longer run, greater stability in intra-European exchange rates, or even the emergence of a single European currency. This is still a distant objective, and possibly even a questionable one. Any such stabilization is only conceivable after a better and stabler equilibrium has been reached in Europe. In the meantime, exchange flexibility, rather than stability, should probably be encouraged.

In the longer run, however, the above policy could be implemented gradually in the following manner:

(i) Encourage and legalize the use of the EPU unit of account as a form of exchange guarantee for all intra-European loans or investments corresponding to EPU objectives, i.e. moving from the stronger to the weaker members of EPU. Such loans or investments might, in addition, be protected against unilateral action in the field of exchange controls.

(ii) Whenever countries reach the stage of formal stabilization of their currencies, secure agreement, whenever possible, on the adoption of a new national currency unit, equal in value to the EPU unit of account. Since this may appear utopian, I may state here that top policy-makers of the only two countries with whom I once broached this possibility, accepted it nearly immediately as a very practical suggestion which they would be ready to back up at the proper time. They recognized a new currency unit as indispensable anyway, the present currency units being far too low for the convenience of transactions.[4]

While the new currencies would remain purely national in law, exchange fluctuations would be greatly discouraged by the mere similarity of their valuations. A shift from par with the EPU unit and with other currencies to 90 per cent of par would elicit far more public attention and opposition than a change from one arbitrary figure to another (i.e. from 314 to 349 francs per dollar). The experience of

4. The redefinition of the French franc, in December 1958, implemented in part these proposals, informally discussed with French technicians and officials in 1949 and 1950, and further expanded in the various articles quoted below.

Latin American countries is most eloquent in this respect, currencies at par with dollar (in Cuba, Panama, Guatemala, and the Dominican Republic) or carrying a simple, traditional relationship to the dollar (Haiti, Honduras, Salvador) contrasting sharply in their stability with all other Latin American currencies. Economic or geographical factors fail totally to account for this contrast.

Countries adopting similar currency units could also grant, on a mutual basis, intercirculation privileges to such currencies. They could be shipped back to the country of origin whenever they tended to accumulate in another country's central bank. Resulting accounts intervening in the meantime among the central banks concerned would, of course, carry the same exchange guarantee as all other accounts already passing through EPU at the present time.

At a later stage, even domestic contracts might gradually be allowed a similar guarantee through an EPU denomination clause. This may indeed prove the only way to restore capital markets in Europe, and might provide governments with a far more attractive source of financing than the printing press. Even though still cheap financially, recourse to the printing press has become so costly politically (overthrow by Parliament), economically (immediate price rises, wage claims, and capital evasion) and socially (strikes and social discontent) that even the weakest governments have preferred in recent years the unpopularity of drastic taxation programs to the onus of new central bank advances.

(e) The gradual implementation of these various *ad hoc* solutions to concrete operational problems would not only pave the way toward the creation of a Central Bank for Europe. They would indeed embody already most of the substance of central banking. Whether these developments would lead in the end to a formal renunciation to national currencies in favor of a single European currency issued by a single European Central Bank would, of course, depend on the progress toward a European federation in other fields. We might feel sure, at least, that monetary integration would already be far ahead, and would lead the way, rather than obstruct progress, toward federation in other directions.

Summary and Conclusions

Practical progress toward European monetary integration can best be promoted, as far as U.S. policy is concerned, by a series of unspectacular moves, strengthening and consolidating EPU, and offering *ad hoc* solutions to its concrete operational problems. The following measures only indicate a few examples of such concrete solutions, guided and buttressed by a long range policy:

(1) clarification of the relationship between EPU and the IMF, particularly with respect to: (a) a more active exchange-rate policy; (b) the problem of sterling transferability; (c) IMF operations involving European members or European currencies;

(2) clarification of the American reserve relating to the U.S. contribution to EPU's capital;

(3) an early decision on the problem of settlements beyond quotas;

(4) strict adherence to a clear distinction between the permanent settlement functions of EPU and the problems of political or military assistance and grants in aid, arising in OEEC or NATO;

(5) exercise of great restraint by the U.S. in EPU matters not directly related to our vital interests and policies;

(6) constitution of a joint European reserve fund via the technique of convertible accounts;

(7) further strengthening of EPU's influence on members through the building up of an EPU reserve fund for special assistance within the framework of agreed programs for monetary and economic rehabilitation;

(8) gradual development of the EPU unit of account into a form of exchange guarantee for desirable capital movements, and into a center of attraction for currency stabilization.

B. MAJOR PROPOSALS FOR EPU AND IMF REVISION

The following memorandum, prepared for OEEC on August 8, 1952, indicated how this broad approach could be concretely implemented on the occasion of current revisions of the EPU Agreement.

Introduction

(1) The physical recovery of Europe, under the aegis of the Marshall Plan, may be regarded as having reached, or even exceeded, its objectives. Monetary recovery, however, still lags far behind and the consequent inability of Western Europe to restore the satisfactory functioning of a market economy continues to threaten the stability and unity of the free world.

(2) Some of the difficulties may be ascribed—particularly in the U.K. and France—to continued inflationary pressures, aggravated by, or arising from, the heavy requirements of the defense program.

There is no easy way out of these difficulties, but they are better understood today than before and courageous efforts have begun, and must be continued, to bring into balance the internal economy of all European countries. These efforts may be greatly helped, or flouted, by the solution, or lack of solution, of other economic problems of an international character. Only the monetary aspects of these problems are discussed here. It should be clear, however, that this is only part of the over-all policies which must be pursued. The insufficient level of monetary reserves in most countries, for instance, would be less worrisome if recent and violent fluctuations in raw material prices and terms of trade could be reduced by international cooperation. Economic progress is, moreover, dependent on the elimination of political tensions and fears, and on greater political unity both within Europe and between Europe and other parts of the world.

(3) In the international monetary sphere, most of our major problems can be traced back to one common root cause: the failure to restore a multilateral system of settlements. The International Monetary Fund assumed that such a system would exist, but left essentially to *individual* countries the responsibility of re-creating it. The transitional period foreseen in Article XIV of its Articles of Agreement has come to an end; but it is abundantly clear that, in the absence of new and more constructive policies, the normal provisions of the Fund will remain confined to the handful of countries (El Salvador, Guatemala, Mexico, Panama, and the United States) which accepted them initially by renouncing the right to invoke Article XIV.

(4) In the absence of a multilateral system of settlements, postwar trade fell into the opposite extreme of strictly bilateral arrangements, with all the economic waste, economic warfare, and disincentive policies which such a system implied. The sterling area alone escaped some of the worst features of such a system, but under conditions which constantly tended to widen the gulf between it and the rest of the world and which, as a consequence, threatened repeatedly the cohesion of the area itself.

(5) The European Payments Union succeeded equally in restoring a multilateral system of settlements between the countries of OEEC, including also indirectly the whole of the sterling area. Fractional gold settlements introduced, in addition, a first approach toward convertibility in the relationships among European countries and between the continent and the sterling area. The regional nature of this agree-

ment, however, gradually led to difficulties very similar to those which plagued the sterling area itself. The viability of EPU was threatened last year by the problem of persistent creditors, and the present difficulties of some extreme debtors currently threaten the collapse of the trade liberalization program or, alternatively, of EPU itself.

(6) The principle of multilateralism and nondiscrimination among members, which is the cornerstone of both the sterling area and EPU, must gradually be extended to the relations with other areas, and particularly the United States, if the world is not to relapse into narrow bilateralism through the breakdown of the regional agreements. This objective must therefore be assigned top priority in international monetary policy.

(7) One possible approach would be the integration of the United States and other third countries within the EPU system. This would mean, in practice, the demise of the IMF and such a solution (a) would be politically difficult; (b) would carry a serious risk that present IMF assets—including $1.5 billion in gold, $1.5 billion in U.S. and Canadian dollars, and other relatively hard currency holdings—might be dispersed among the contributors and creditors of the IMF, rather than held available for international cooperation; (c) would introduce in EPU many of the defects, which have made IMF a particularly cumbersome and unmanageable instrument for negotiation and cooperation.

The alternative is to retain in EPU the many advantages of a regional, closely knit, organization for handling most European monetary problems, and to relate it closely to a rejuvenated IMF, to handle the monetary problems arising between EPU and third countries, particularly the United States.

(8) A legal revision of EPU is bound to take place in any case during the first half of 1953. A legal revision of the IMF Articles of Agreement appears equally desirable and could easily get the necessary support from members. If necessary Parliamentary action appears too slow or difficult, however, most of the following suggestions could be implemented by a more flexible interpretation of the statutes, and announced in a general policy statement early next year.

(9) The present suggestions do not imply any final judgment on the possibility or timing of any general move toward currency convertibility. They would remain valid irrespective of whether convertibility is, or is not, adopted at this stage.

First of all, the return to convertibility by one or a few countries only, on a unilateral basis, would aggravate enormously these countries' difficulties. Other countries would try and earn scarce gold or dollars from them, and restrict bilaterally their imports from them in order to develop the necessary bilateral surpluses. The disastrous and short-lived attempt of the United Kingdom to restore convertibility in 1947, in advance of other countries, is most illuminating in this respect. It must be clearly realized that multilateralism cannot be restored or preserved by unilateral action on the part of one or a few countries. Convertibility is synonymous with multilateralism only when its obligations are simultaneously accepted by all major trading areas.

In the absence of such simultaneous commitments, the first countries to restore convertibility would expose themselves to new difficulties, and their failure to overcome them would probably end up in a new wave of bilateralism, destroying the real, if insufficient, progress of the last two years in the direction of multilateral settlements.

Second, even if convertibility were simultaneously restored by all major countries, the whole edifice would remain most vulnerable to individual defections from the system. A relapse into inconvertibility by an individual country would deprive its creditors of the earnings needed to settle their own deficits in other relations, and make it difficult or impossible for them to maintain the convertibility of their own currency. An individual defection from convertibility would, therefore, constantly threaten to pull other countries into the same path and to spread inconvertibility from one country to the others. Specific measures to allow each country to mobilize its bilateral earnings to settle its bilateral deficits constitute an indispensable discipline for the maintenance of multilateral convertibility in the modern world. Suggestions in this respect will be made below in Section I (1) and Section II (3) of this paper.

(10) The following proposals are mostly based on the analysis above, but they incorporate also three other conclusions, of a general character, from our postwar monetary experience:

(a) The maintenance of international equilibrium in the balances of payments cannot be made to depend *exclusively* on internal readjustments, particularly when these appear, rightly or wrongly, to threaten the maintenance of satisfactory levels of employment and economic activity. If external measures of readjustment must be allowed, preference should generally be given to: (i) market methods, such as tariff or exchange readjustments, over administrative methods such as quantitative restrictions; (ii) to restrictions which remain multilateral in character rather than to discrimination or bilateralism. Proposals II (1) and (5) are based on this view.

(b) A flexible system of multilateral settlements demands for its working large monetary reserves or capital movements, or both, in order to cushion temporary fluctuations and to give the necessary time for required policy readjustments. This inspires proposals I (3, 4, 5, 6) and II (3 and 4).

(c) Finally, the success of international cooperation at this stage depends essentially on mutual negotiations and compromise, rather than on legal jurisdiction. Where fifty countries are involved, negotiation and meaningful compromises acceptable to all are particularly difficult. Regional negotiation should be preferred to world-wide negotiation whenever regional problems or conflicts of interest are at stake. An agreement on fishing rights need not await agreement by landlocked countries like Bolivia or Switzerland, nor even probably agreement between Iceland and Australia. This observation underlies proposals I (2) and II (2) and is particularly relevant in connection with current efforts and achievements in the development of economic and political integration among the nations of Western Europe. Regional integration can be made, and should be made, a step toward, rather than away from, world-wide cooperation in the economic as well as in the political field.

(11) Some particular proposals would require lengthy developments, explanations, and justifications, far beyond the scope of this paper. These could best be brought up after the discussion has proceeded further and informally, at a purely technical level. The following notes have been inspired by the hope and desire to suggest a first draft program susceptible of eliciting a maximum degree of agreement among all interested parties. Comments, criticisms, and additions would be most welcome as a basis for further drafts, including amendments as well as clarification of the views here put forward for discussion.

I. A Revision of EPU

(1) The *automatic clearing* of bilateral balances into a net position determining the size and direction of monetary settlements constitutes a most essential contribution of EPU to the restoration of a multilateral system of trade and payments. Such clearings are indis-

pensable to escape from strict bilateralism as long as convertibility is not restored. They will remain just as indispensable as a discipline of convertibility, when restored, and in order to avoid a relapse into bilateral, rather than multilateral, convertibility. The danger of bilateralism will remain as long as all major countries are not firmly, permanently, and effectively committed to the total elimination of trade and exchange restrictions for residents as well as nonresidents.

(2) The *Managing Board* must also be retained as the most effective instrument yet devised for:

(a) the discussion and gradual harmonization of monetary policies —of extreme creditors as well as debtors—insofar as necessary to avoid a deterioration and ultimate breakdown of multilateral settlements in Europe;

(b) the programming and financing of Special Assistance operations in favor of members in difficulties, avoiding to the maximum possible extent the restoration of trade and exchange restrictions in Europe;

(c) negotiation and cooperation with respect to the mutual relaxation of exchange restrictions, and eventually readjustments in the pattern of exchange rates. (Prior regional discussion of such matters appears as the only way to implement concretely the IMF jurisdiction in these respects and to escape from the empty formalism which characterized the September 1949 "consultations" on par values and the 1952 "consultations" on the removal of exchange restrictions.)

(d) the preparation and implementation of further progress toward (i) general convertibility, and (ii) European monetary integration.

(3) On the other hand, the *credit provisions* of EPU will have to be overhauled drastically to make the institution viable, and to adjust it to any new developments, favorable or unfavorable, in the hoped for progress toward general convertibility.

The necessary credit provisions of a permanent EPU are discussed below in the order of priority to be assigned to them in the long run. Provisions under A and B would appear necessary under any conditions. Provisions under C and D would depend on the rate of progress actually achieved toward general convertibility and the elimination of the dollar gap.

A. *More adequate provisions for Special Assistance loans are urgently needed:*

1. to reconcile maximum progress toward convertibility—and

the general hardening of settlements—with the need to help individual countries in difficulties and avoid unnecessary relapse into trade and exchange de-liberalization;

2. to back up the efforts of members and of the Managing Board to bring about desirable readjustments in internal and external monetary and financial policies as a workable alternative to trade and exchange restrictions;

3. to promote the development of EPU into an effective instrument for monetary integration in Europe.

B. *Provision is also needed, in any case, for swing credits,* of an effectively temporary character, in order to complement present monetary reserves and inadequate capital mobility. The level of these reserves and capital movements is now far too low for the effective discharge of their proper function, i.e. to cushion sudden balance-of-payments deficits:

1. of a temporary, reversible character, making it undesirable to adopt any "corrective" measures, external or internal, inappropriate to long-run equilibrium;

2. of a more persistent character, while the proper corrective measures are being taken and given time to produce the desired readjustments.

Failing such swing facilities, any sudden deficit in the balance of payments—whether or not it calls for corrective measures—risks being met primarily by new restrictions which could otherwise be avoided.

All or part of the automatic credits provided for in EPU should take the form of such swing credits and require gradual amortization over twenty-four (or twelve) months whenever they have been outstanding for more than one (or two) years, i.e. to the extent that they are not amortized by reversals of positions under the cumulative principle of EPU. The proceeds of such amortization could either be used to strengthen the EPU liquidity or to make *pro rata* amortization of the longer standing claims of extreme creditors.

C. If normal quota credits, of an automatic character, are maintained—which would depend on the rate of progress toward convertibility and the elimination of the dollar gap—the following amendments should be introduced:

1. In order to eliminate some of the absurdities of the present

regional criteria for borrowing rights and lending commitments:

(a) to replace cash payments to creditors—at least beyond quotas—by payments in convertible accounts usable to meet deficits outside as well as within the EPU area, but only to meet deficits;

(b) to require EPU debtors to use their net earnings outside the area, partly or wholly, for amortization of their EPU debts.

2. In order to strengthen further the convertible assets of EPU.

(a) to generalize past (pre-June) *ad hoc* decisions relating to settlements to Belgium, Switzerland, Portugal, etc. beyond quotas in the form of a systematic commitment by all members: (i) to accept 50 per cent settlements of their surpluses beyond quotas, up to one-half of the quota itself; (ii) to accept 70 per cent settlements of further surpluses for a second supplementary tranche equal also to one-half of the quota.

This would mean the doubling of the creditor quotas, but with cumulative settlements of 50 per cent instead of 40 per cent. It would remove in practice all threats to EPU liquidity, even in the face of strong convergence of diffused deficits toward a few creditor countries only, and would permit 100 per cent settlements beyond twice the quota level (see 3 below);

(b) to bring up correspondingly cumulative debtor settlements from 40 per cent to 50 per cent by a new schedule of 10, 30, 50, 70, and 90 per cent settlements in each tranche, without modifying, however, the over-all level of debtor quotas.

3. In order to remove present uncertainties of a disruptive character with respect to post-quota settlements to creditors:

(a) to provide for presumptive payments of 100 per cent (or 90 per cent) in convertible accounts for surpluses in excess of twice the quota;

(b) under condition that agreement be reached between the Organization and the creditor on its commercial and financial policies insofar as they affect the level of such surpluses;

    (c) with rediscounting of such convertible accounts with the IMF in case of need, if the EPU convertible assets fund had fallen temporarily to too low a level at the time of drawings. (This would be most unlikely, except as a result of Special Assistance operations.)

D. In the event that a further unexpected deterioration in the European dollar position made it necessary to amplify rather than reduce—as now hoped—the EPU credit facilities, it is suggested that all or part of outstanding EPU debts be funded over a 5- or 10-year period with gradual amortization, thus reopening initial quota facilities (by an amount substantially larger than the amounts funded).

(4) Greater efforts should be made to restore normal capital movements as an alternative to official quota credits. This restoration, including the commercialization of outstanding EPU credits, would be helped by:

(a) a substantial increase in interest rates for debts or claims outstanding for more than two years;

(b) the authorization for the parties concerned to denominate in units of account private loans or investments certified by the Managing Board as being of a reequilibrating character from the point of view of the Union's operations. This would merely extend to private capital movements the exchange guarantee which now attaches already to the equivalent EPU accounts which such capital movements might replace.

(5) The use of third currencies in EPU settlements could greatly stimulate European trade with third areas, where such trade is now constricted by efforts at bilateral balancing. A separate Memorandum [MBC(52)52] has been submitted in this respect. Particularly valuable in the long run would be the acceptance by EPU of working balances on behalf of nonmembers for transferable settlements with EPU countries.

(6) Note that the liquidity of EPU and its consequent ability to provide Special Assistance to members, would be greatly enhanced by:

(a) the amortization of outstanding debts under (3) B;

(b) the payment of extreme creditors in convertible accounts in lieu of cash under (3) C, 1 (a);

(c) the extra amortization of EPU debts by outside earnings under (3) C, 1 (b);

(d) the additional commitments of creditors under (3) C, 2 (a);

(e) the additional cash settlements by debtors under (3) C, 2 (b);

(f) the rediscounts with the IMF under (3) C, 3;

(g) the reduction of EPU positions consequent on (4);

(h) the dollar component of working balances constituted under (5).

(7) Important implications of the above strengthening of EPU upon the development of closer monetary integration in Europe lie outside the scope of this memorandum.

II. A Revision of IMF

(1) The present attitude of the IMF toward *the problem of par values* must be radically changed to restore the initial significance and basic purposes of the par value concept.

The Fund now insists on the adoption of par values by every country, and accepts as par values the most fanciful declarations of members (while France, Italy, and Canada are penalized by ineligibility because they have no par value, the Fund recognizes the par value of 31 Chilean pesos per dollar, although this rate applies only to a few categories of transactions, other effective exchange rates ranging—and fluctuating—from 19.37 to 136 pesos per dollar). The cumbersome and spectacular procedure for changes in par values results mostly in delaying desirable adaptations and stimulating recourse to trade and exchange restrictions, without giving the Fund any real control over exchange rates. This was clearly demonstrated during the purely formal "consultations" of September 1949.

It is not the Fund that should plead and press for the definition of a par value, but the countries themselves. The international recognition of their exchange rate as a "par value" should be the final consecration of a prior *de facto* stabilization of the rate and reflect confidence in the future maintenance of this rate without excessive trade and exchange restrictions. The acceptance of a rate as par value should therefore have as consequence a freer access to the Fund's resources under conditions which minimize the dangers of an excessive immobilization of the credit granted.

In the meanwhile, desirable rate adaptation and exchange liberalization should be facilitated by the acceptance of rate flexibility in consultation with the Fund. These consultations could, even under the present Articles of Agreement, involve two stages:

(a) immediate agreement between the Fund and the member that the old par value is inadequate and incompatible with "fundamental equilibrium," and should therefore be suspended;

(b) protracted consultations between the Fund and the member on the definition of a new, and maintainable, par value. During these consultations, which could extend over several months, or even years, the member would be free to vary its rate as needed. In case of abuse, however, the Fund could make informal representations to the member and, as a last resort, the Executive Board could, upon the complaint of another member, decide that this flexibility is abused in a manner damaging to other members, and enjoin the country from allowing further depreciation. In case of final disagreement or noncompliance, the member could ultimately be suspended from membership, as is the case now.

(2) The need to *decentralize* the administration and functioning of the Fund will be readily admitted. This is generally indispensable in order to simplify the Fund's tasks and, particularly, to substitute the fruitful methods of joint consultation and negotiation for the sterile assertion of legal jurisdiction of a formalistic character.

Wherever regional monetary organizations exist (as now in Europe) or are created later, the negotiation of purely regional problems and the spade work preparatory to broader decisions should be delegated to the regional organizations. This would apply, for instance,

(a) to most *preliminary* discussions of exchange-rate adjustments for non-key currencies;

(b) to *mutual* commitments with respect to exchange liberalization;

(c) to exchange transactions among members of a regional organization, including both automatic credits and special assistance operations. Fund representatives should take part in discussions about the latter, and the regional organization should have access to Fund rediscounts when necessary to preserve its liquidity.

This decentralization would obviously imply a drastic revision, and curtailment, of the activities of the International Monetary Fund Executive Board. While alternates might possibly remain in permanent residence in Washington—but mostly as regional advisers and contact men, rather than as a Board—full Board meetings should be called only two or three times a year, and should be attended by top officials of member countries carrying continuing daily responsibility for monetary management and policy with their respective governments. These meetings would review the work of the regional bodies and fix ceilings for rediscounts applicable during the intervals separating such meetings.

Finally, more flexible procedures for exchange readjustments on the part of other small countries should be defined, so as to liberate the staff from overconcentration on minor problems. This would allow both a reduction in personnel and greater attention to more fundamental problems of a broader character and importance for the ultimate success of the institution.

(3) Emphasis in *Fund transactions* should shift from individual salvage operations to triangular or multilateral operations designed to maintain a multilateral framework for monetary settlements. Apart from special assistance to over-all debtors, the Fund should give maximum attention and automaticity to the mobilization of bilateral earnings necessary to cover bilateral deficits in other directions. This is not borrowing, but transferability. The implications of such operations for creditors and debtors will be considered presently:

A. *For creditors.* If as a result of mobilization and special assistance operations, the borrowings tend to concentrate on the currency of one, or a few, over-all creditors, the IMF will confront the familiar *scarce currency* problem. The following suggestions are offered in this respect:

1. a maximum strengthening of the convertible assets, in the form of gold or creditor currency contributions to the capital of the Fund;

2. the right for the creditor to cast its vote against special assistance operations, or in favor of a stricter handling of "superabundant currency" cases (see (3) B below);

3. some increase of voting rights for extreme creditors;

4. creditor quotas should be explicitly recognized as defining a minimum, rather than maximum, commitment. If lending tends to rise beyond the quota, the creditor will have to choose between the following alternatives:

   (a) to retain full protection against discriminatory action by other members, provided that: (i) agreement be reached between him and the IMF on liberalization measures—including tariffs—or other means to reduce its surpluses; or (ii) failing such agreement, acceptance by the creditor of further lending under conditions to be negotiated;

   (b) to refuse both liberalization and further lending, losing in this case all protection against discrimination directed at preventing continued surpluses without forcing a general contraction in world trade. Discrimination would therefore be allowed only as a defensive measure of last resort after all other ways of remedying the situation have been fully explored.

B. *For debtors.* If, on the other hand, the *over-all* deficits of a country tend to produce a situation in which the Fund accumulates the debtor's currency at an excessive rate or in excessive amounts, the following steps could be taken by the Fund:

    1. First, the Fund must receive assurances from the member that its indebtedness will be settled by gradual amortization, over an agreed period (three to five years?) if it is not reduced under normal repurchase provisions by a reversal of the deficits and the consequent improvement in the member's reserves;

    2. Second, the Fund might request immediate fractional payments in accordance with some graduated scale similar to that of EPU;

    3. Third, the Fund may insist on joint consultation on the measures to be adopted by the member to correct its persistent deficits;

    4. As a weapon of last resort, and failing agreement on 3, the Fund may declare this particular currency "superabundant" and limit or exclude its eligibility for mobilization operations.

C. Note that the system above would reintroduce in the IMF operations some essential features of the Keynes Clearing Union Plan. Bilateral payment agreements, even if not specifically outlawed, would become very nearly unworkable, as well as unnecessary and unattractive, if the bilateral creditor were forced to mobilize its bilateral earnings with the Fund before being allowed to borrow through sales of its own currency. On the other hand, the Fund would not be compelled to rediscount earnings corresponding to a creditor's over-all surplus, since such a creditor could not then demonstrate his need for obtaining another currency from the Fund. This might also help avoid the emergence of a "scarce currency" situation.

D. With respect to EPU members, or members of a similar regional organization, the rediscounting should ideally take place between EPU itself and the Fund, and the present Fund limitations on borrowings (25 per cent of the quota yearly) should be applied to the total of the members' quotas ($2.8 billion) rather than to individual quotas. Until a legal revision of the Agreement makes this possible, the same criteria could be applied in using systematically the present waiver clause, and the rediscounts could be granted:

1. either to EPU creditors on the basis of their convertible accounts in EPU (see Section I above, (3) C, 1);
2. or to the EPU debtors, who would commit themselves in EPU to request such rediscounts *pro rata* of their indebtedness, and to use the proceeds to amortize part of such indebtedness.

(4) At a propitious time, the Fund might also back up a general move toward convertibility in Europe by participating, along with other countries or institutions, in the necessary stabilization loans. Such stabilization loans could be made to, or through, EPU, rather than directly to an individual EPU member.

(5) The Fund's jurisdiction in the handling of GATT problems should be enlarged. A "low tariff club," for instance, might be operated along the following lines:

(a) Preferential reductions of duties among the members of the club would be authorized as a *substitute* for present quantitative discrimination against the dollar area and other third countries;

(b) Pending the formation of a full Customs Union, tariff duties against nonmembers could be maintained at a higher level than the preferential duties among members only on balance-of-payments grounds, i.e. only insofar as justified by the persistence of Europe's dollar deficit. As this deficit declines, the outside tariffs would be brought down gradually toward the level of the internal tariffs. In other words, the present GATT rules on quantitative restrictions would be applied instead to tariff techniques, the latter being substituted to the maximum extent for the first.

(c) These balance-of-payments criteria would continue to be determined by the Fund as under the present GATT rules.

(6) It is finally suggested, in tactical preparation for the above developments, that OEEC extend immediately to the Fund an official invitation to appoint a permanent observer to take part in the work of the OEEC Council and general Committees, particularly with reference to payments problems and to the discussions on financial stability.

C. THE UNITED KINGDOM SCUTTLES THE BOAT

I have recounted elsewhere[1] the United Kingdom's abortive "dash for freedom" of 1953 and its later successful fight for the liquidation of EPU. I tried vainly, until the very last moment, through a series of letters and notes to my British friends then actively engaged in these negotiations, to ward off this fateful break in the close monetary cooperation which a revamped EPU could have preserved between the United Kingdom, the emergent European Economic Community, and the other countries of OEEC.

I suggested, in essence, a merger between the EPU and EMA Agreements, the replacement of residual EPU "automatic" credits by "discretionary" credits or "credit lines," and the financing of such credits through minimum deposit requirements related to each country's global reserve level. Such a revision of the EPU Agreement had long been overdue, anyway, and would have helped consolidate—through various collective guarantees that need not be spelled out here—the proposed restoration of currency convertibility by Britain as well as by other major European countries. There is little doubt that British initiative in this direction would have been welcomed by most EPU members, many of whom viewed indeed with serious misgivings the precarious character of a convertibility system based on unilateral (even though simultaneous) and unilaterally revocable national decisions.

The huge and persistent deficits of the United States in later years removed, for some time at least, the danger of any unilateral relapse into inconvertibility by Britain as well as by other OEEC countries. The scuttling of EPU at the end of 1958, however, eliminated one of the most powerful links that still preserved a high degree of active, continuous, monetary consultations and cooperation between the United Kingdom and the emergent European Economic Community. The mere "restoration" of international currency convertibility, on the haphazard basis of the old gold-exchange standard, was also at the origin of the recurrent sterling and dollar crises of the years 1960–65.

Both of these consequences may be deemed unfortunate in retrospect, and might have been avoided by an evolutionary reform of the

---

1. See particularly Part Two, Chapter VI, pp. 00–00, above; *Europe and the Money Muddle*, pp. 209–20; and my review of Graham L. Rees, *Britain and the Postwar European System* (Cardiff, 1963) in *The Journal of Political Economy* (October 1964), pp. 517–18.

EPU Agreement aiming at organizing the continued cooperation of Britain, the European Economic Community, and the United States in the achievement and consolidation of a rational system of worldwide convertibility and reserve creation.[2]

4. MONETARY POLICIES AND INSTITUTIONS OF THE EUROPEAN ECONOMIC COMMUNITY

The creation of the European Economic Community has given a new impetus and new dimensions to concrete planning for European monetary integration. Such integration has indeed become well-nigh necessary for the survival of economic union among the Six, and its feasibility will be enhanced by—and facilitate—further progress toward the ultimate goal of political union in the Community.

My memoranda to the Commission, outlining concrete alternative approaches toward this objective, cannot be published at this time, but are rooted in the analysis presented in my published work, and particularly in "Intégration économique européenne et politique monétaire," [1] which develops much further and integrates into a broader framework the proposals advanced in *Europe and the Money Muddle* (particularly pp. 287–94) and in *Gold and the Dollar Crisis* (pp. 131–44).

2. See, for instance, my inaugural Wicksell lecture on *The Future of the European Payments System* (Stockholm, Almquist and Wiksell, 1958).

1. In *La Restauration des Monnaies Européennes* (special issue of the *Revue d'Economie Politique,* December 1960), Paris, Sirey, 1960, pp. 58–81. See also among other articles in French:

"Système et politique monétaires de l'Europe fédérée," *Economia Internazionale* (Genoa, February-March 1953), pp. 207–14;

"La monnaie et le Marché Commun—Politiques nationales et intégration régionale," *Cahiers de l'Institut de Science Economique Appliquée,* No. 74 (Paris, December 1958), pp. 1–17;

"La Communauté Economique Européenne et la coopération monétaire internationale," Rapport présenté à la Xème Table Ronde des Problèmes de l'Europe, Bâle, 8–10 novembre, 1962; reproduced in *Problèmes de l'Europe* (Paris, 1963).

Chapter XII: Payments Systems
in Latin America

1. THE EUROPEAN PAYMENTS UNION
AND LATIN AMERICA

The United Nations Economic Commission for Latin America asked me, in the summer of 1952, to explore the possibilities for some form of Latin American participation in the EPU compensations and settlements system.

A series of notes on the subject were consolidated in a memorandum published on March 4, 1953, by the United Nations Economic and Social Council.[1] The suggestions outlined in this memorandum, and previously discussed with the EPU Managing Board in Paris were implemented, but only very partially, beginning in August 1952.[2]

2. MONETARY COOPERATION IN LATIN AMERICA

The success of EPU, however, was also eliciting growing interest in Latin America—particularly under the prodding of the U.N. Economic Commission for Latin America—for the establishment of a Latin American payments union.

I discussed various aspects of this problem and alternative lines of approach in successive Meetings of Technicians of Central Banks of the American Continent, and of the Center of Latin American Monetary Studies (Centro de Estudios Monetarios Latinoamericanos; CEMLA).[1]

The first concrete step toward Latin American monetary cooperation was the establishment, in the summer of 1961, of a Central American Clearing House to facilitate payments and eschew unnecessary and costly recourse to foreign currencies in settlements among

1. U.N. publications reference: GENERAL, E/CN./12/299, 4 March 1953.
2. See the Annual Report of the EPU Managing Board for 1951–52, p. 53; for 1952–53, p. 73; for 1953–54, pp. 78–79; for 1954–55, p. 26; for 1955–56, pp. 24–25; for 1956–57, p. 39; and for 1957–58, p. 28.
1. See, e.g. "Latin America in World Trade and Payments," *Fifth Meeting of Technicians of Central Banks of the American Continent, 5* (Bogotá, Colombia, Banco de la República, 1957), 93–115; and "Una Cámara de Compensación y Unión de Pagos Latinoamericana, in *Cooperación Financiera en América Latina* (México, CEMLA, 1963), pp. 95–117.

the central banks of the area. The immediate and spectacular success of this experiment (in which I took a very modest part in various preparatory meetings) induced CEMLA to reopen the problem, on a broader front, at its seventh meeting, in Mexico City, in September 1962.[2]

The paper I presented on that occasion ("A Latin American Clearing House and Payments Union") was severely criticized by the IMF technical staff in a report widely distributed in June 1963 and later reproduced in the IMF *Staff Papers* (November 1963). The attitude of the IMF, however, underwent considerable change in later months, and its representatives expressed full support for the unanimous resolution adopted at the Seventh Meeting of the Central Bank Technicians of the American Continent (at Rio de Janeiro in October 1963) in favor of a more active exploration of the problem at a negotiating level.[3]

An all-inclusive Latin American arrangement, along the lines proposed in the Mexico and Rio meetings mentioned above, appeared very problematical or far-distant at best, as long as some of the major countries of South America had not succeeded in controlling the raging inflation and balance-of-payments crises in which they were so deeply involved.

I prepared, therefore, at the request of the Central Bank of Venezuela a recasting of my previous proposals, designed to facilitate a gradual approach toward the ultimate objectives of Latin American integration, and focusing particularly on some steps susceptible of more rapid negotiation and implementation among the countries of the Caribbean area.

A. TOWARD A LATIN AMERICAN MONETARY ORGANIZATION

The spectacular success of regional economic and monetary cooperation and integration in Western Europe since the end of World War II has long spurred similar efforts in other regions, and particularly in Latin America. Most of these efforts, however, have been

2. More important, it led to the signature on February 5, 1964, of an "Agreement for the Establishment of the Central American Monetary Union." The Agreement entered into force, after ratification by the signatory central banks, on March 20 of the same year.

3. See the first paper below.

Published in Spanish in *Integración de América Latina*, ed. Miguel S. Wionczek (México and Buenos-Aires, Fondo de Cultura Económica, 1964) pp. 264-70.

thwarted so far by divided counsel, both among the countries concerned and on the part of international organizations and consultants.

In the monetary field, the opposition to regional organization sprang largely from the fear that regional agreements would weaken balance-of-payments barriers to domestic inflationary pressures, and involve discriminatory trading and settlements provisions, incompatible with world-wide currency convertibility and an economic allocation of the participating countries' productive resources.

These fears were by no means groundless, particularly as initial proposals tended to copy too slavishly the *early* provisions of the European Payments Agreement, based as they were on multilateral clearing and partial credit settlement of *bilateral* balances arising from a complex network of bilateral payments agreements. These initial EPU provisions were totally overhauled in later years, as Europe moved from bilateral shackles to near-convertibility. Balances notified to the Agent for compensation no longer arose from bilateral agreements, but from normal interventions of central banks on the foreign exchange markets in support of exchange-rate stability. Convertible currency settlements shifted from a 50 per cent to a 75 per cent basis, and would have progressed to 100 per cent if the EPU Agreement had not been prematurely terminated at the insistence of the United Kingdom. Debtor balances were, moreover, regularly amortized, rather than left pending until the debtor country shifted to a surplus position within the region.[1]

The resurrection of the initial EPU provisions in the early proposals for a Latin American Payments Union were indeed a sheer anachronism in a world which had progressed, in the meantime, from early postwar bilateralism to substantial currency convertibility.

Far less valid were the arguments leveled against Latin American integration on the basis of the admittedly low level of intraregional trade in Latin America. These arguments implicitly assumed that this low level of intraregional trade was a normal and desirable phenomenon, reflecting Adam Smith's famed invisible hand and the most economic allocation of the area's geographical resources. Any regional integration measures could only—so the argument ran—distort the natural pattern of trade, increase production costs, and lower economic welfare throughout the area.

Such views reflected, of course, a naively narrow economic viewpoint. The absurdly low level of trade within the region is very largely

---

1. See *Europe and the Money Muddle*, pp. 218–20.

the product of an infrastructure—in such fields as transportation, banking, entrepreneurship, capital financing, etc.—historically developed by foreign (primarily European and U.S.) interests to promote their own food and raw material imports from the area and seek outlets for their own exports. The resulting bias in favor of extra-area trade, and against intra-area trade, was no God-given phenomenon, but a byproduct of history, calling for specific policy measures aiming at correcting the lopsidedness and uneconomic character of such a trade pattern.

Such correctives were all the more necessary in view of the additional bias resulting from *national* protectionist policies adopted by Latin American countries. Even when justifiable on an "infant industry" argument basis, such policies should have been applied only against the more developed countries, but not against neighbors suffering from the same "infant industry" handicap. Insofar as *nondiscriminatory* protection did not actually stave off *all* imports in favor of national production, it did actually discriminate in favor of better placed developed countries' exporters, and against exports from other underdeveloped countries in the area.

The clarification of this issue—important as it may be for the academic economist—had probably little influence on the governmental debate itself. Far more important, from this point of view, were (1) the drafting of new proposals, eschewing the pitfalls denounced above in the original ones; and (2) the spectacular success achieved in Central America by their actual implementation.

The new proposals established a sharper distinction between the clearing of compensable surpluses and deficits on the one hand, and the settlement or financing of residual imbalances on the other.

A clearing mechanism for central banks could demonstrably shave off the unnecessary commissions and exchange costs now involved in triangular settlements via New York or other financial centers. While such benefits would admittedly be very modest at the start, the clearing machinery would provide an institutional framework on which other, and far more significant, measures of cooperation could be grafted. The exchange guarantees implicit in the adoption of a joint unit of account could be supplemented by solidary guarantees, effective safeguards against default, etc., and remove major obstacles to the granting of credits to a country in difficulties, both by other members and by countries outside the area itself. Clearing operations could also be facilitated by, and invite, the maintenance of some portion of each country's international reserves in the form of working deposits with the Clearing, without decreasing in the least the liquidity of such reserves for balance-of-payments settlements. Such deposits would, in turn, provide the Clearing with a mass of maneuver which need not be kept permanently 100 per cent in foreign currencies, but could be used in part for short-term stabilization loans to member countries.

If one were to indulge in long-term dreams about a still distant future, one might even contemplate the ultimate development of such a system toward fuller monetary integration among the participating countries, just as central banks originally developed—on the national scale—from similar, and initially modest, deposit and clearing functions, through a natural and logical process of institutional growth.

The clearing, deposit, and credit mechanism briefly outlined above escapes the major criticism levelled against *automatic and narrowly intraregional* credits, patterned upon the haphazard development of intraregional surpluses and deficits. Credits would be, with minor exceptions, discretionary, rather than automatic, and depend on mutual agreement regarding the borrowing country's monetary policies, internal as well as external. They would be granted to support overall stabilization policies, rather than to finance intraregional deficits only. They would be derived from the deposits of all countries, *pro rata* of their actual reserve strength, rather than financed on a far less liquid basis, and only by countries in surplus within the region, regardless of their *over-all* balance-of-payments and reserve position.

To take a concrete example, automatic lending and borrowing criteria based on *regional* surpluses and deficits would entail persistent lending by one of the poorest countries in Central America, Honduras, to one of the richest, El Salvador, merely because the most economic use of the two countries' factor endowment normally promotes a pattern of production and trade in which important Salvadorean foodstuff and raw material import needs can best be satisfied by imports from Honduras, while fewer Honduran needs can be met economically from Salvadorean sources. There is no reason why financial arrangements should be specifically designed to discourage such trade, desirable from both countries' point of view, as long as Honduras fully complies with its trade liberalization and preferential commitments under the Latin American Free Trade Area and Central American Integration Treaties.

Credit provisions under regional payments agreements should be geared to the *over-all* balance-of-payments and reserve needs and capabilities of the member countries, using temporary surpluses and unused reserves of some to help cushion temporary deficits of others. Such credits should, moreover, remain discretionary, rather than automatic, in order to promote the harmonization of national monetary policies indispensable to the correction of persistent balance-of-payments disequilibria and to the successful implementation of member countries' trade and exchange liberalization commitments vis-à-vis one another.

The scope of such cooperation will, of course, be far more limited among underdeveloped countries with low levels of reserves and mutual trade than among the richer and more closely integrated economies of Western Europe. Much of the monetary stabilization assistance which they could profitably use will have to be sought, tomorrow as today, from outside sources, and particularly from the International Monetary Fund. Mutual credit arrangements, modest as they have to be, could nevertheless prove of enormous value in improving relations between the Fund and the underdeveloped countries and avoiding unjustifiable policy conflicts and bitterness. The case of a country in need of assistance would normally be discussed first among the members of the regional organization, and these would have to agree on the policies which the prospective borrower should pursue in order to justify the assistance required. If such agreement is reached, they would both risk their own lending resources in the proposed stabilization intervention and support jointly a request for complementary assistance or underwriting by the IMF. This would strengthen the hand of the borrowing country in its negotiations with the Fund, and help the Fund itself formulate policy programs—and conditions—more acceptable to the members of the area, and better adjusted to economic and political circumstances which non-area members may be less able to gauge correctly and realistically.

On the other hand, the members of the area would no longer be able to indulge in irresponsible criticism of the Fund for subordinating its assistance to reasonable conditions, on which they would also have to insist themselves to minimize the risks attendant to their own participation in the stabilization program and maximize its chances of success.

The recent weakening of long-standing prejudices against regional monetary cooperation and integration, however, can only be ascribed in part to the persuasiveness of such abstract arguments. As, or more, influential has been the undeniable success of actual regional agree-

ments devoid of the monetary discrimination features of the initial
EPU Agreement. As already mentioned above, later revisions of EPU
had already adjusted it, to a considerable extent, to the requirements
of world-wide currency convertibility. The European Monetary Agreement completed this adaptation at the end of 1958, while loosening
also to a regrettable degree methods of monetary integration that
would have bolstered, rather than hindered, the viability of currency
convertibility in Europe. Wide-ranging techniques for mutual help
and monetary integration have also been incorporated in the Treaty
of Rome and developed further in the Action Program of the European
Economic Community.

The Central American Clearing House, which I helped draft in
1960–61, has been widely applauded as an undoubted success, not
only by the participating central banks, but also by private bankers
and traders in the area, and by the IMF itself. The association of
Mexico, last year, gave further evidence of the confidence so rapidly
and deservedly gained by this institution, and this example of Mexico
may soon be followed by other countries, such as Panama, Colombia,
and Venezuela.

In any case, the October 1963 Meeting of Central Banks Technicians of the American Continent witnessed, for the first time in twelve
years of vain, and sometimes bitter, debates, a *unanimous* interest in
the opening of concrete negotiations aiming at a creation of a Latin
American Clearing or Payments Union, along the lines briefly summarized above and described in greater detail in the study which I
presented to the CEMLA meeting in Mexico in September 1962.

A meeting of African and European monetary experts, convened
in January of this year in Tangiers by the United Nations Economic
Commission for Africa, also rallied complete *unanimity* around my
proposals for regional monetary cooperation in Africa. The initial
steps envisaged in Tangiers, and submitted to the VIIth ECA session
in February 1964, for prompt negotiation and implementation, are
relatively modest and take full account of the uncertainties still surrounding the future political and administrative structure of the new
African nations. Yet the Tangiers Agreement also outlines ambitious
guidelines for future progress toward closer monetary cooperation
and integration, and aims at creating institutions susceptible of favoring such progress through a logical process of internal growth, similar
to that from which central banking systems actually developed, on a
national scale, in the nineteenth century.

The unanimity achieved at the experts' level, both in Rio and in Tangiers, and the encouragement given to the participants by the IMF observers at both meetings, create a new and promising climate for the intergovernmental negotiations which are now opening. Let us hope that they will attack the problem in the same constructive spirit, eschew spectacular, but divisive and ultimately sterile, political slogan-eering, and concentrate on laying as rapidly and solidly as possible the groundwork for future Latin American and African monetary co-operation and integration, within the world-wide framework of a more flexible, decentralized, and realistic IMF machinery.

B. INTERNATIONAL MONETARY ARRANGEMENTS, CAPITAL MARKETS, AND ECONOMIC INTEGRATION IN LATIN AMERICA

Introduction and Summary

The title of this paper is so ambitious as to recall Pico della Mirandola's treatise *"De omni re scibili,"* and Voltaire's suggested addition: ". . . *et de quibusdam aliis."*

Its contents, however, will be more modest. I certainly don't know everything that there is to know or might be learned about these three topics, and I did not have time to find out enough about them in the brief time allotted to me to prepare for this meeting. I shall therefore concentrate on what I know already—or think I know—and on draw-ing attention to those questions which seem to me most deserving of further investigation at this time. I shall focus throughout on prospec-tive policies, of a concrete sort—even if not necessarily ripe for im-mediate action—rather than on pure research, although the latter may be as, or more, essential in the long run, and should probably receive equal attention in CEMLA's planning.

An agonizing reappraisal of Latin American international trading and monetary policies and institutions has become particularly urgent in view of current developments and future prospects abroad in this field. Let me note particularly:

(1) In the private sector: The rapid recovery of European capital

---

A paper prepared at the request of the Banco Central de Venezuela for discussion at the eighth meeting of CEMLA in Caracas, in November 1964, and published in Spanish in the *Revista de Economía Latinoamericana* (Caracas, Venezuela, January 1964), pp. 1–55; and in English in the *Journal of Common Market Studies* (Oxford, 1965), pp. 70–104.

markets, both as an outlet for investments and as a source of funds. New opportunities emerge here especially from the development of the Euro-dollar (and Euro-sterling) markets, and from the increasing pace of security flotations in foreign currencies and in the so-called "unit of account."

(2) In the public sector: The expansion of regional cooperation, and even integration, not only in the field of trade, but also in:

(a) the cushioning of balance-of-payments disequilibria: IMF "General Arrangements to Borrow," gold pool, Basle agreements, Roosa stand-by credits, mutual aid provisions of the Rome Treaty, Cámara de Compensación Centroamericana, etc.;

(b) the mutual confrontation of monetary, fiscal, and economic policies bearing on such disequilibria, in order to determine the appropriateness of the support given under (a): Economic Policy Committee and Working Party No. 3 of OECD, Monetary Committee and numerous other Committees of the European Economic Community, etc.;

(c) current studies and planning of more ambitious institutional reforms aiming at the further broadening and consolidation of the developments above: Committee of Multilateral Surveillance and Study Group on the Creation of Reserve Assets of the Group of Ten, Council of Central Bank Governors, and European Reserve Fund project of the six EEC countries, Agreement for Establishment of the Central American Monetary Union, proposals for IMF reform, etc.

These developments offer to the Latin American countries and their Central Banks new challenges and opportunities which will be briefly discussed below under the following headings:

(1) foreign investment of Central Banks reserves;

(2) Latin American security flotations in foreign markets;

(3) Central Bank arrangements in support of mutual trade;

(4) Central Bank arrangements in support of currency convertibility and stability.

Feasible international agreements, in all four of these respects, will often impose difficult, but inevitable, compromises between desirable geographical extension and desirable deepening of mutual commitments: the wider the extension, the shallower the depth is likely to be, and vice versa. Fortunately, the mutual benefits derived in the past from the coexistence of the IMF, the OECD, the EEC, the Benelux, and the Belgo-Luxemburg Economic Union amply demonstrate the complementarity, rather than incompatibility, of concentric regional approaches to world-wide economic cooperation. This is likely to prove true in Latin America, as well as in Europe, and in other parts of the world. Care should be taken from the very beginning, however, to keep open all avenues to the future broadening, as well as to the future deepening, of the initial agreements that prove feasible.

I. Foreign Investment of Central Banks' Reserves

A. The Problem

The total monetary reserves of the Latin American countries (including Jamaica) were estimated last June at about $2,800 million: (1) $1,165 million in gold; (2) $117 million in IMF gold tranches; and (3) $1,520 million in foreign exchange, overwhelmingly held in dollars in the United States.

The close links between Latin American countries and the United States amply justify the investment of such a large proportion (54 per cent) of Latin American monetary reserves in the form of dollars. They might even, *ex post,* throw doubts on the wisdom of sacrificing potential earnings on the still large proportion (42 per cent) retained in gold, primarily as an edge against a possible (but highly improbable) devaluation of the dollar.[1]

The difficult responsibilities now involved in the choice between earnings and security might, however, be eluded in the future, if current explorations about the functioning of the international monetary system were to lead to the creation of new types of reserve assets, carrying both earning power—although at lower rates—and exchange guarantees. Such a possibility, including particularly proposed reserve deposits with the IMF, is now under active discussion, both in the Fund and in the Group of Ten, and should deserve greater attention—and, in my opinion, support—on the part of the Latin American Central Banks.

In the meantime, the possibility of maximizing earnings on Central Banks' foreign exchange investments also deserves careful consideration, in view of the increased competition for such investments in the United States and of the emergence of new market instruments (Euro-dollars, Euro-sterling, unit-of-account securities and deposits) in other

---

1. Even moderate earnings, at compound rates, on Latin American gold investments since 1934 would have exceeded by far any conceivable losses from a dollar devaluation. An amount of $1 billion would produce in twenty years, if invested at 2 per cent, earnings of $486 million, and if invested at 3 per cent, earnings of $806 million.

major financial markets, increasingly used today by even the most conservative central banks.[2]

B. *Possible Solutions*

(1) As a minimum approach to the problem, involving no commitments whatsoever on the part of the participants—except for the insignificant costs involved—the Central Bank officers charged with the main responsibility of deciding on foreign exchange investments should attempt, on a mutual basis, to exchange as full information as possible on: (a) actual earnings on their outstanding investments of different types and maturities; (b) potential earning opportunities on other types of investment, which may have come to their attention, and their reasons for rejecting them if more favorable than those under (a).

(2) Slightly more ambitious, but potentially most valuable, particularly to the smaller countries, would be the formation of a Joint Agency for such investments. Participating Central Banks would designate one of them—presumably the largest investor—as Agent for all, with respect to the investment of a substantial portion (at least 25 per cent?) of their total reserve funds. An Advisory Investment Board, composed of the responsible officers of the participating banks, would meet periodically to review available investment opportunities and give, or review, its instructions to the Agent. These instructions, however, need not be identical. The investment pattern might vary from bank to bank, and each Central Bank might modify its instructions to the Agent, even in the intervals between the Board's meetings.

The main advantages of such a system, under which final decisions would remain entirely in the hands of each participant and carried out for its own account, would be to increase their information and bargaining power through joint action, bearing on larger amounts of funds.

(3) These benefits could be further expanded, however, if (possibly after an initial trial period on the above basis) the functions of the Agent were gradually enlarged:

(a) by agreeing jointly on the range and types of investment shifts which could be initiated by the Agent himself, with or without prior discussion and agreement by the participants;

---

2. Rates in excess of 2.5 per cent are currently available on large Euro-dollar demand deposits subject to 48-hour notice for withdrawals, and rates in excess of 4 per cent, or even 4.5 per cent, on time deposits.

(b) by the pooling of agreed investments and of the corresponding risks and earnings, *pro rata* between the participants. The participation of each Central Bank in the joint investments agreed would then be expressed in the form of convertible deposits, possibly of different maturities, denominated either in U.S. dollars or in another jointly agreed unit of account (see Section III B (3) below). Such a pooling method could, of course, be introduced by stages, and apply only to a portion of the total investments, the remainder continuing to run for each participant's separate account, as explained above.

The main advantages of such an enlargement of the Agent's functions—and particularly of pooling arrangements—would be to offset against one another divergent fluctuations in the participants' investment accounts, thus enabling the Agent to save charges on investment shifts, and to increase earnings through the lengthening of maturities, without any sacrifice of actual liquidity for the individual participating Central Banks.

(4) Even the pooling system just described would *not* involve any credit commitments *among* the participating Central Banks, the investments being placed in their entirety on the U.S. market (and possibly other major financial centers) in accordance with the decisions and delegations of power jointly agreed among the members. This being the case, all the agreements discussed so far could realistically be kept open for participation by any Latin American country that wished to join them, either initially or at a later stage.

Such broad inclusiveness might not be regarded as realistically feasible, at this stage at least, if a further—and highly desirable—dimension were added to such agreements, in order to make room for *mutual investments and credit commitments among the participating countries* themselves. The actual attraction of such operations, and their attendant risks, would inevitably, and rightly, be appraised differently by each member, depending on the composition of the group as a whole. Such mutual investment and credit arrangements are most likely, in practice, to prove inseparable from other and broader agreements encompassing mutual trade policies and commitments, the harmonization of monetary and other policies affecting the balance of payments, or even in some cases still more ambitious aims of economic and monetary union, such as are now being actively pursued among the Central American countries (see below, Sections III and IV).

This is a primary example of the conflict between depth and extension briefly alluded to in the Introduction of this paper.

II. Latin American Security Flotations in Foreign Markets

Two main reasons for introducing this topic, even if only very briefly and inadequately, are:

(1) The enormous and rapidly increasing amounts of expatriate Latin American capital make it imperative to study whether and how recent trends in this respect might be slowed down or reversed, in support of currency stability and economic development in Latin America.

(2) The reactivation of European capital markets offers new opportunities for raising capital abroad—from foreign funds as well as from expatriate Latin American funds—for Latin American development.

A. *Expatriate Capital from Latin America*

Reported net outflows of Latin American capital are estimated to have averaged more than $100 million a year in the last eight years, and to have reached $300 to $400 million both in 1961 and in 1962. A large, but undetermined, proportion of "errors and omissions" probably reflects additional, unregistered movements of domestic funds. If both were added together, the average net outflow of Latin American funds would be estimated at more than $600 million a year in the period 1956–63, with peaks of about $850 million both in 1961 and in 1962. Assuming, more conservatively, that only half of errors and omissions reflect domestic capital outflows, guesstimates of total net outflows of Latin American capital would show a rise from about $270 million a year in 1956–60 to more than $600 million yearly in 1961 and 1962, and a grand total of close to $3 billion over the last eight years alone (See Table 1).

More careful investigation of all available sources of estimates would be necessary to check these rough calculations, and particularly to suggest any plausible order of magnitude for the outstanding stock of expatriate Latin American capital, including pre-1956 outflows and cumulative unrepatriated earnings and capital appreciation over many years past. One may hazard the guess that the total could hardly be inferior to $5 billion, and might be considerably in excess of that figure.

Reported Latin American assets in the United States alone, excluding central banks' dollar holdings, were estimated at about $3,400 million at the end of last year (Table 2). Considering that a sub-

TABLE 1

BALANCE OF PAYMENTS OF LATIN AMERICA (EXCLUDING CUBA), 1956–63
(in millions of U.S. dollars)

| Periods | Current account | Capital Imports | | | | | | Monetary reserves |
| | | Total net | Foreign funds | Domestic funds, errors and omissions | | | |
				Total net	Domestic funds	Errors, omissions	
Year							
Average 1956–63	−1,019	1,000	1,619	−618	−106	−512	−18
Average 1956–60	−1,061	1,087	1,576	−489	−51	−438	25
Average 1960–62	−906	721	1,411	−689	−193	−496	−184
1960	−986	1,035	1,387	−352	131	−483	48
1961	−1,067	945	1,788	−844	−383	−461	−122
1962	−664	185	1,057	−872	−328	−545	−479
1963 (p)	−125	406	838	−432	−14	−418	281
Totals: 1956–63	**−8,149**	**8,003**	**12,949**	**−4,946**	**−847**	**−4,099**	**−145**
1956–60	−5,307	5,433	7,879	−2,446	−254	−2,192	126
1960–62	−2,717	2,164	4,232	−2,068	−579	−1,489	−553
1963 (p)	−125	406	838	−432	−14	−418	281

SOURCE: Economic Commission for Latin America, *Economic Survey of Latin America, 1963* (provisional text, United Nations: E/CN. 12/696/Add. 2, July 1, 1964, Vol. III, p. 139).

stantial portion of capital evasion may elude reporting in the U.S. and be channelled also toward other countries from which future disclosures appear least likely, estimates for total Latin American assets abroad might be raised, e.g. by 50 per cent or even 100 per cent to roughly $5 billion or $7 billion.

The convergent results of these two independent approaches cannot strengthen very greatly confidence in such dubious "guesstimates." Yet the order of magnitude of any reasonable guess of Latin American expatriate funds is, in any case, large enough to justify more determined attempts than have been made so far to try and induce some repatriation as a source of development financing and, in some cases, of strengthening of inadequate reserve levels.

The ineffectiveness of exchange restrictions in this respect is amply demonstrated by these estimates themselves. Realistic planning should

TABLE 2

REPORTED LATIN AMERICAN ASSETS AND INVESTMENTS
IN THE UNITED STATES
(at the end of 1963, in millions of U.S. dollars)

I. Long-Term	**1,393**
Direct	112
Portfolio	1,281
II. Short-Term Assets and U.S. Govern- **ment Obligations**	**3,396**
III. Total (I + II)	**4,789**
IV. Central Bank Holdings (approximate)	**1,400**
V. Private (III − IV)	**3,400**

SOURCES AND NOTES:

1. Lines I–III: *Survey of Current Business*, August 1964, p. 24.

2. Line IV: Total foreign exchange reserves of Latin American countries at the end of 1963 are estimated at $1,505 million in *International Financial Statistics*, November 1964, p. 17. Sterling holdings of Latin American monetary authorities are estimated at the equivalent of $61 million at the same date, and total (private as well as official) Latin American dollar claims on U.K. banks at $174 million (Bank of England, *Quarterly Bulletin*, September 1964, pp. 240 and 242). The rough estimate of $1.4 billion official dollar holdings retained above assumes that a total of $105 million of reserves are held in sterling and other currencies.

focus instead on the methods that have proved successful over recent years to solve similar problems in Europe, i.e. (1) the restoration of currency convertibility and exchange stability at realistic exchange rates; (2) regretfully, fiscal amnesty for past, untraceable, evasions of existing regulations; (3) international loan flotations, with adequate exchange-rate guarantees. Some suggestions relating to this third point will be briefly outlined presently.

B. *Reactivation of European Capital Markets*

The Euro-currencies market, already referred to in Section I above as an outlet for investments, should also be regarded as an important source of short-term funds for Latin American borrowers. The last *Annual Report* of the BIS (p. 130) estimates that: "All in all, a figure of about $7 milliard—of which some $5 milliard actually in U.S. dollars—would seem to be a reasonable estimate of the net volume of

Euro-currencies at the end of September 1963." The BIS also reports (p. 135) that "Over 30 per cent of recent fiscal borrowers of Euro-dollars (considerably less in the case of other Euro-currencies) appear to have been resident outside Western Europe and North America." Japan is often mentioned as such a borrower, but little mention has been made of Latin American borrowings. Borrowing rates are reported to range from about 4½ per cent to 6 per cent.

Of particular interest to Latin America is the establishment in Luxemburg, a few months ago, of the Atlantic Community Development Group for Latin America (ADELA) with a nominal capital of $40 million, of which $16 million has so far been subscribed by some fifty industrial and banking concerns. ADELA's activities will be directed mainly to providing equity capital, but also to investing in fixed-interest securities or in completely new projects.

One should also note the rapid extension, in recent years, of security flotations, deposits, and loans in European units of account. A dozen or more banking institutions—from Germany, the Netherlands, Italy, Great Britain, Belgium, Luxemburg, etc.—have participated in such unit-of-account flotations on behalf of both private and public institutions in Portugal, Norway, Denmark, Italy, etc., for a total amount so far of about $70 million. Unit-of-account securities, with maturities up to 20 years, and interest rates ranging around 5½ per cent, are generally quoted well above par on the financial markets.

The New York Times reported only two weeks ago (November 10, 1964) a step which it quoted as "the first concrete demonstration that the birth of a genuine wide capital market is at hand." Three British banks and five Luxemburg banks are heading an underwriting syndicate of 57 banks (from Belgium, France, Germany, Italy, the Netherlands, Sweden, Denmark, Norway, and Britain) for the flotation of a fifteen year, 5½ per cent, $30 million Euro-dollar loan to the European Coal and Steel Community.

The time has certainly come for Latin American countries to take cognizance—as Japan has already done—of the opportunities presented by such developments, and by others *expected in the very near future,* for seeking in Europe, as well as in the overburdened U.S. market, additional sources of financing for healthy development projects.

The regional agreements discussed in other sections of this paper may also, at a later stage, play a useful role in enhancing Latin American credit abroad and lowering the costs of such borrowings. Of particular interest in this respect would be the possibility of offering to foreign investors joint, solidary guarantees by the group on approved borrowings by its members.

III. Central Bank Arrangements in Support of Mutual Trade

A. Introduction

Mutual trade among Latin American countries constitutes only a small fraction (about 9 per cent in 1962) of their total trade. This is often quoted as an argument demonstrating the insignificance of proposals such as those that will be outlined presently, but should, on the contrary, be viewed as an indication of the existence of a large pool of untapped trading opportunities which could be developed in the future.

The present trading patterns of the Latin American countries cannot be regarded indeed as the God-given result of an unchangeable geographical distribution of factor endowments and productive resources. It has been strongly biased in favor of extraregional trade and against intraregional trade by historical factors such as:

(1) the development of each country's production, transportation, and financing infrastructure by European and North American capital and entrepreneurship, primarily interested in Latin American exports of raw materials and agricultural produce and in Latin American outlets for the manufacturing products of Europe and the United States;

(2) the equal application of tariff and other restrictions, by each Latin American country to all other countries, under the most-favored nation clause of tariff agreements, irrespective of the degree of development of the partner countries. Thus, protectionist restrictions that might—or might not—be justified by the "infant industry" argument were applied against the infant industries of sister nations in Latin America as well as against the industrially developed nations of Europe and North America. Insofar as this protection was often of very limited effectiveness, it encouraged imports from the latter countries, while handicapping severely the development of adequate markets for Latin American production.

The special provisions in favor of mutual trade among the Latin American countries will not, of course, induce any large development of mutual trade in the bulk of their traditional exports—such as coffee, for instance—whose main outlets will continue to lie outside the area itself. They might play a crucial role, however, in the development of new industries, and in the consequent diversification of Latin American production and trading patterns.

The results of the determined and intelligent efforts pursued in this direction by the small countries of Central America would confirm this judgment. While their external trade remained practically stagnant between 1957 and 1962, their mutual trade more than tripled over the same period, and accounted in 1962 for about 10 per cent of their total trade, as against only 3.6 per cent in 1957.

This is not the place to discuss all the variety of measures which might be used in pursuance of such policies. Our discussion will be limited to the role which arrangements among central banks could play to help in the financing of mutual trade expansion, to stimulate such expansion through cost reductions, and to save, in the process, avoidable transaction costs in foreign currencies. These opportunities arise primarily from the possibility of compensating:

(1) over space, each country's bilateral deficits with some of its partners against its bilateral surpluses with others;

(2) over time, seasonal and other fluctuations in each country's over-all receipts from, and payments to, its area partners.

Both types of compensations would bypass foreign exchange costs now attendant upon immediate bilateral settlements, usually effected in dollars through New York banks. These savings could be passed on to the trading community through reductions in exchange charges and margins, and contribute thereby to the profitability and expansion of mutual trade.

For the sake of concreteness, precise proposals are developed below in relation to the financing of mutual trade among the Caribbean countries, which have manifested an active interest in such cooperation. They could, of course, be readjusted to include some other neighboring countries, and to establish similar arrangements among the Southern countries of the continent. It would seem highly desirable, at this stage, to concentrate initial integration efforts on manageable areas grouping only a small number of countries highly conscious of their interdependence, and not too dissimilar in their economic and monetary policies and experience. This, I feel, is one of the lessons to be derived from the success of Central American integration efforts as well as of those of the European Economic Community. Neither the first nor the latter would have made as much progress as they have, if they had waited for all other countries of Latin America or Europe to join them before taking any step toward closer cooperation and integration among themselves.

A *concentric, decentralized* approach toward Latin American integration will remain necessary for many years to come in order to exploit fully the different willingness and ability of different nations to merge some portions of their economic sovereignty for the sake of greater effectiveness in its very use. The existing Central American group, for instance, must retain its separate identity if it is to implement as rapidly and efficiently as possible its plans for full monetary and economic union among its members. It could, however, participate with a less closely integrated Outer Caribbean group of countries in joint payments agreements embracing all the countries of the Caribbean area. Finally, this broader Caribbean group itself could join with other Latin American countries—or, when it is formed, with a Southern Continental Group—into still more modest initial agreements, such as those outlined in Sections I and II above.

Only at a later stage, as and when each of these groups moves toward more intensive mutual agreements and commitments, could closer links be established also between them, so as to maximize the geographical extent as well as the actual content of feasible cooperation and integration in the Latin American area as a whole.

B. *A Caribbean Payments Union?*

One of various possible alternative schemes for a Caribbean Payments Union is outlined below, in order to help gauge the feasibility of opening, as soon as possible, formal negotiations aiming at an early agreement implementing the above suggestions.

For the reasons already mentioned, such a Caribbean Payments Union should be built upon two separate groups:

(1) A *Central American group,* based on the commitments already incorporated in the Cámara de Compensación Centroamericana and the Acuerdo para el Establecimiento de la Unión Monetaria Centroamericana, and composed of Guatemala, El Salvador, Honduras, Nicaragua, and Costa Rica;

(2) An *Outer Caribbean group,* composed, at the very least, of Mexico, Venezuela, Colombia, and Jamaica.

The above listing of countries should not be regarded as exclusive. The absence of a Central Bank has constituted, up to now, the main obstacle to full participation by Panama in the Central American efforts at monetary integration, but ways and means should be sought to associate Panama with these arrangements. As for the Outer Caribbean group, it should certainly remain open to later accession by the Dominican Republic, Haiti, and hopefully Cuba when present political obstacles to such a step can be lifted. Judging from available trade estimates, however, it seems that Ecuador might well wish to participate, from the start, in the Caribbean group, which has absorbed in recent years one half, or more, of its exports to Latin America and provided well over 60, or even 70, per cent of its imports from Latin America.

The following discussion will refer to available 1962 trade estimates for these ten countries, including Ecuador, but excluding provisionally Panama, the Dominican Republic, Haiti, and Cuba. It will focus on the arrangements that might be considered for the formation of an Outer Caribbean Group and its relations to the existing Central American Group, but will refrain at this stage from suggesting amendments to present arrangements among the latter countries.

As already noted above, mutual trade among the Central American countries alone already accounts for about 10 per cent of their total trade, as against only 3.6 per cent in 1957. In sharp contrast, mutual trade in the proposed Outer Caribbean Group represented in 1962 less than 1 per cent of the total trade of these countries, certainly far less than would correspond to a rational allocation of resources through more active trading within the area.

A similar contrast exists between the two groups with respect to the amount of trade which could be cleared by mutual compensations of each country's export claims and import debts. In the Central American Group, such compensations could be applied on a yearly basis to more than three fourths of total intraregional trade, leaving less than one fourth to be settled through transfers of reserves from the net debtors to the net creditors (Table 4, lines I, A, B, and C). Compensable trade in the Outer Caribbean group is only about 60 per cent of mutual trade, and would even drop to little more than 40 per cent if Ecuador did not participate.

Initial clearing opportunities in a broad Caribbean Group would cover nearly two thirds of mutual trade, and save settlement costs—in foreign exchange—on more than $100 million per year, leaving only $27.3 million—instead of $79.9 million—of net settlements to be effected by Guatemala ($12.9 million), Costa Rica ($3.9 million), Nicaragua ($2.5 million), Colombia ($3.2 million), Ecuador ($2.3

TABLE 3

INTRA-CARIBBEAN EXPORT MATRIX, 1962
(in millions of U.S. dollars)

TO \ FROM	Central America					Outer Caribbean area				
	Guatemala	El Salvador	Honduras	Nicaragua	Costa Rica	Mexico	Venezuela	Colombia	Ecuador	Jamaica
I. Central America	**3.4**	**18.7**	**12.9**	**3.5**	**1.8**	**9.4**	**4.5**	**1.8**	**0.1**	
1. Guatemala	x	7.6	3.2	0.4	0.1	3.6	1.2	0.3		
2. El Salvador	2.5	x	9.3	1.9	1.2	2.0	0.5	0.5		
3. Honduras	0.8	6.0	x	0.2	0.2	0.9	0.2	0.4		
4. Nicaragua	0.1	3.3	0.2	x	0.3	1.5	0.8	0.6	0.1	
5. Costa Rica	0.1	1.8	0.2	1.0	x	1.4	1.8			
II. Outer Caribbean Area	**0.1**	**0.1**	**3.1**	**0.7**	**1.1**	**6.8**	**6.2**	**2.6**	**3.1**	
6. Mexico	0.1		1.0	0.2		x	0.1	0.1		
7. Venezuela		0.1	1.1	0.1		4.4	x	1.0		
8. Colombia				0.2	1.1	1.7	1.5	x	3.1	
9. Ecuador						0.7	3.3	1.5	x	
10. Jamaica			1.0	0.2			1.3			x
III. Total	**3.5**	**18.8**	**16.0**	**4.2**	**2.9**	**16.2**	**10.7**	**4.4**	**3.2**	

NOTE: These estimates, assembled from the *Statistical Bulletin for Latin America* (Vol. I, No. 1, pp. 134–36) and *Direction of Trade* (Annual 1958–62 and monthly 1964 issues), are incomplete for Guatemala, Nicaragua, and particularly Jamaica, for which no estimates of exports to other countries listed are reported in these sources.

million), and Jamaica ($2.5 million), in favor of Mexico ($14.7 million), Honduras ($7.2 million), Venezuela ($4.0 million), and El Salvador ($1.4 million).[3] It should be noted, however, that these estimates, based on available f.o.b. export estimates for 1962, might be substantially modified—upward and downward—by the inclusion of missing estimates, by changes in trade patterns and, particularly, by the inclusion of other so-called "invisible" services and capital transactions.

In order to take full advantage of these opportunities for compensations, and minimize the need for cash settlements, agreements would be necessary on: (1) normal provisions for so-called *interim finance* between settlement dates; (2) provisions for the *settlement of residual net creditor and debtor positions*.

In the European Payments Union, net positions were calculated only once a month, full financing being assured in the interim between monthly settlement dates, and partial financing being continued afterward and made initially repayable only through later reversals in a country's net position—from deficits to surplus, or vice versa. At a later stage, however, regular amortization provisions were introduced to accelerate repayments and reopen the quotas blocked by persistent deficits or surpluses.

In Central America, net positions are calculated weekly, with full interim finance within each week, and full financing—up to modest quotas of $500,000 per member—afterward, and periodic full settlements twice yearly.

A special problem may arise whenever the borrowing rights of deficit countries happen to concentrate on one, or a few, creditors, exceeding the latter's lending commitment. This was covered in EPU by the constitution of a capital fund, contributed by the United States out of Marshall Plan allocations. In Central America, it is covered by additional voluntary lending by the extreme creditors and/or rationing of the deficit countries' use of their normal borrowing rights.

Similar, or different, solutions might be adopted, singly or in combination, for the financing of intra-Caribbean trade. For concreteness and simplicity's sake, only one will be retained below, but could be considerably amended, or even thoroughly overhauled, in the course of actual negotiations.

3. See Table 4, lines IV, A, B, and C: third column for the area as a whole, and following columns for individual countries' estimates.

TABLE 4

INTER-TRADE, POTENTIAL COMPENSATIONS, AND NET BALANCES IN 1962 CARIBBEAN TRADE
(in millions of U.S. dollars)

	TOTALS			COUNTRIES									
	Central America	Outer Caribbean	Total	Guatemala	El Salvador	Honduras	Nicaragua	Costa Rica	Mexico	Venezuela	Colombia	Ecuador	Jamaica
I. Within Central America													
A. Total Trade	**80.6**		**80.6**	**14.7**	**33.6**	**20.1**	**7.4**	**4.8**					
Exports (−)	40.3		40.3	3.4	18.7	12.9	3.5	1.8					
Imports (−)	−40.3		−40.3	−11.3	−14.9	−7.2	−3.9	−3.0					
B. Total compensations	**61.6**		**61.6**	**6.8**	**29.8**	**14.4**	**7.0**	**3.6**					
Exports	30.8		30.8	3.4	14.9	7.2	3.5	1.8					
Imports (−)	−30.8		−30.8	−3.4	−14.9	−7.2	−3.5	−1.8					
C. Net balances	**19.0**		**19.0**	**7.9**	**3.8**	**5.7**	**0.4**	**1.2**					
Surpluses	9.5		9.5	—	3.8	5.7	—	—					
Deficits (−)	−9.5		−9.5	−7.9	—	—	−0.4	−1.2					
II. Within Outer Caribbean area													
A. Total trade		**37.4**	**37.4**						**7.0**	**11.6**	**8.9**	**8.6**	**(1.3)**
Exports		18.7	18.7						6.8	6.2	2.6	3.1	
Imports (−)		−18.7	−18.7						−0.2	−5.4	−6.3	−5.5	−1.3
B. Total compensations		**22.6**	**22.6**						**0.4**	**10.8**	**5.2**	**6.2**	
Exports		11.3	11.3						0.2	5.4	2.6	3.1	
Imports (−)		−11.3	−11.3						−0.2	−5.4	−2.6	−3.1	
C. Net balances		**14.8**	**14.8**						**6.6**	**0.8**	**3.7**	**2.4**	**(1.3)**
Surpluses		7.4	7.4						6.6	0.8	—	—	—
Deficits (−)		−7.4	−7.4						—	—	−3.7	−2.4	(−1.3)
III. Between the two areas													
A. Total trade	**20.9**	**20.9**	**41.8**	**5.2**	**2.6**	**4.7**	**3.5**	**4.9**	**10.7**	**5.8**	**3.1**	**0.1**	**(−1.2)**
Exports (−)	5.1	15.8	20.9	0.1	0.1	3.1	0.7	1.1	9.4	4.5	1.8	0.1	—
Imports (−)	−15.8	−5.1	−20.9	−5.1	−2.5	−1.6	−2.8	−3.8	−1.3	−1.3	−1.3	—	−1.2

	1	2	3	4	5	6	7	8	9	10	11	12
B. Total compensations	**7.2**	**7.8**	**15.0**	**0.2**	**0.2**	**3.2**	**1.4**	**2.2**	**2.6**	**2.6**	**2.6**	**(1.2)**
Exports	3.6	3.9	7.5	0.1	0.1	1.6	0.7	1.1	1.3	1.3	1.3	—
Imports (−)	−3.6	−3.9	−7.5	−0.1	−0.1	−1.6	−0.7	−1.1	−1.3	−1.3	−1.3	—
C. Net balances	**13.7**	**13.1**	**26.8**	**5.0**	**2.4**	**1.5**	**2.1**	**2.7**	**8.1**	**3.2**	**0.5**	**0.1**
Surpluses	1.5	11.9	13.4	—	—	1.5	—	—	8.1	3.2	0.5	0.1
Deficits (−)	−12.2	−1.2	−13.4	−5.0	−2.4	—	−2.1	−2.7	—	—	—	(−1.2)
IV. Within Caribbean area												**(−2.5)**
A. Total trade	**101.5**	**58.3**	**159.8**	**19.9**	**36.2**	**24.8**	**10.9**	**9.7**	**17.7**	**17.4**	**12.0**	**8.7**
Exports	45.4	34.5	79.9	3.5	18.8	16.0	4.2	2.9	16.2	10.7	4.4	3.2
Imports (−)	−56.1	−23.8	−79.9	−16.4	−17.4	−8.8	−6.7	−6.8	−1.5	−6.7	−7.6	−5.5
B. Total compensations	**73.6**	**31.6**	**105.2**	**7.0**	**34.8**	**17.6**	**8.4**	**5.8**	**3.0**	**13.4**	**8.8**	**6.4**
1. Sum of above	68.8	30.4	99.2	7.0	30.0	17.6	8.4	5.8	3.0	13.4	7.8	6.2
Surpluses	34.4	15.2	49.6	3.5	15.0	8.8	4.2	2.9	1.5	6.7	3.9	3.1
Deficits (−)	−34.4	−15.2	−49.6	−3.5	−15.0	−8.8	−4.2	−2.9	−1.5	−6.7	−3.9	−3.1
2. Area Positions	**1.2**	1.2	6.0	—	4.8	—	—	—	—	—	1.0	0.2
Surpluses	2.4	0.6	3.0	—	2.4	—	—	—	—	—	0.5	0.1
Deficits (−)	−2.4	−0.6	−3.0	—	−2.4	—	—	—	—	—	−0.5	−0.1
C. Net balances	**27.9**	**26.7**	**54.6**	**12.9**	**1.4**	**7.2**	**2.5**	**3.9**	**14.7**	**4.0**	**3.2**	**(2.5)**
Surpluses	8.6	18.7	27.3	—	1.4	7.2	—	—	14.7	4.0	3.2	2.3
Deficits (−)	−19.3	−8.0	−27.3	−12.9	—	—	−2.5	−3.9	—	—	—	(−2.5)

Sources and notes:

1. These estimates, assembled from the *Statistical Bulletin for Latin America* (Vol. I, No. 1, pp. 134–36) and *Direction of Trade* (Annual 1958–62 and monthly 1964 issues), are incomplete for Guatemala, Nicaragua, and particularly Jamaica, for which no estimates of exports to other countries listed are reported in these sources. Addition of missing estimates would probably increase compensations, and reduce correspondingly net balances, not only for these countries, but also for their trading partners.

2. Potential compensations, for each country, are equal to either total exports, or total imports, whichever are smaller. Horizontal additions show potential compensations for each area.

3. Net surpluses obviously equal net deficits within each area (lines IC and IIC and Column 3 throughout), but not in trade between areas (Columns 1 and 2 of lines IIIC and IVC.)

4. Potential compensations increase with the size of the area, not only through the summation of compensations shown under I, II, and III (line 1 of IVB), but also through compensations between each country's net surplus (or deficit) within its subarea with its net deficit (or surplus) in trade with the other subarea (see line IVB2, reflecting opposite balances in lines IC or IIC and line IIIC).

5. The net balances in line IVC, arrived at in this manner, correspond, of course, to the excess of exports or imports in total area trade (lines A).

(1) *Lending Commitments*

(a) Each participating country will be called upon to grant the Cámara de Compensación, at the beginning of each year, an interim finance *normal credit line* equal to the full amount (or to 50 per cent?) of gross claims registered with the Cámara in the preceding year. In the initial year of the system, this normal credit line would be calculated on the basis of each country's gross exports to other participants in the last year for which estimates are available.

(b) In the event of a convergence of borrowing rights upon one or a few extreme creditor countries, the latter will extend a *supplementary line of credit* to the Cámara, up to 50 per cent (or 100 per cent?) of their normal quota.

(c) Each country will be entitled, however, at its own discretion to grant additional credits to the Cámara, to the extent needed to cover operations, but also to limit its total credits to a ceiling equal to x (5?) per cent of its gross monetary reserves (gold, IMF gold tranche, and foreign exchange holdings of the monetary authorities).

(2) *Borrowing Rights*

(a) Each participating country will be granted, at the beginning of each year, a *normal borrowing line* with the Cámara equal to the full amount (or to 50 per cent) of the gross claims accumulated by it with the Cámara, or by the Cámara on it, during the previous year, whichever amount is smaller *and thus proved compensable*. In the initial year of the system, this normal borrowing line will be calculated on the basis of each country's gross imports from, or exports to, the other participants—whichever amount is smaller—in the last year for which estimates are available.

(b) In the unlikely event in which provisions (1b), (1c), and (2a) above failed to avoid fully the emergence of a "scarce currency" condition in the Cámara, the latter will either reduce *pro rata* the borrowing rights of each member, or demand that their use be combined with partial cash settlements satisfactory to the extreme creditors.

(c) If, on the other hand, the resources of the Cámara permit it, supplementary interim credits may be granted on an *ad hoc* basis, to the debtors whose credit line is threatened with exhaustion.

The latter possibility (2c) is indeed far more likely to emerge in fact than the opposite danger of a "scarce currency" condition. As may be seen from the accompanying table (Table 5), initial "normal" lending commitments to the Cámara would total close to $40 million

TABLE 5

PROPOSED INITIAL LENDING AND BORROWING LINES FOR INTERIM FINANCE

Areas and countries	In millions of U.S. dollars						Unadjusted total lending commitment in % of reserves (g)
	Borrowing line (a)	Lending commitment			Total readjusted (e)	Monetary reserves (f)	
		Normal (b)	Supplementary (c)	Total (d = b + c)			
I. Outer Caribbean area	**15.8**	**34.5**	**17.2**	**51.7**	**48.9**	**1,558**	**3.3**
A. Internal	11.9	18.7	9.3	28.0			
1. Mexico	*0.2*	*6.8*	*3.4*	*10.2*			
2. Venezuela	*5.4*	*6.2*	*3.1*	*9.3*			
3. Colombia	*3.1*	*2.6*	*1.3*	*3.9*			
4. Ecuador	*3.2*	*3.1*	*1.5*	*4.6*			
5. Jamaica							
B. With Central American area	3.9	15.8	7.9	23.7			
1. Mexico	*1.3*	*9.4*	*4.7*	*14.1*			
2. Venezuela	*1.3*	*4.5*	*2.2*	*6.7*			
3. Colombia	*1.3*	*1.8*	*0.9*	*2.7*			
4. Ecuador		*0.1*		*0.1*			
5. Jamaica							
C. Total (A + B)	15.8	34.5	17.2	51.7	48.9	1,558	3.3
1. Mexico	*1.5*	*16.2*	*8.1*	*24.3*	*24.3*	*506*	*4.8*
2. Venezuela	*6.7*	*10.7*	*5.3*	*16.0*	*16.0*	*776*	*2.1*
3. Colombia	*4.4*	*4.4*	*2.2*	*6.6*	*6.1*	*122*	*5.4*
4. Ecuador	*3.2*	*3.2*	*1.6*	*4.8*	*2.5*	*50*	*9.6*
5. Jamaica						*104*	
II. Central American area with Outer Caribbean area	**3.6**	**5.1**	**2.5**	**7.6**	**3.8**	**234**	**3.3**
1. Guatemala	*0.1*	*0.1*		*0.1*	*0.1*	*78*	*0.1*
2. El Salvador	*0.1*	*0.1*		*0.1*	*0.1*	*65*	*0.2*
3. Honduras	*1.6*	*3.1*	*1.5*	*4.6*	*1.2*	*25*	*18.4*
4. Nicaragua	*0.7*	*0.7*	*0.3*	*1.0*	*1.0*	*41*	*2.4*
5. Costa Rica	*1.1*	*1.1*	*0.5*	*1.6*	*1.2*	*25*	*6.4*
III. Total (I + II)	**19.4**	**39.6**	**19.8**	**59.4**	**52.8**	**1,792**	**3.3**

1. Column (a): 1962 imports from, or exports to, the area, whichever is smaller (*net* surpluses of Colombia and Ecuador with Central America have been included in their "internal" borrowing line).

2. Column (b): 100 per cent of 1962 exports to the area.

3. Column (c): 50 per cent of column (b), callable only in case of concentration, to avoid a "scarce currency" condition.

4. Column (e): same as column (d), except for underlined estimates reflecting countries' right to reduce their lending commitment to 5 per cent of their total reserves.

5. Estimates under II do not include existing, or future, lending commitments and borrowing rights of Central American countries with respect to their mutual trade (see text of this article).

6. Minor discrepancies in additions due to rounding-off errors.

(column b), while lending commitments by the Cámara to its members would total less than half that amount (column a).

Moreover, recent trading patterns strongly suggest that the two countries with the largest lending commitment (Mexico and Venezuela) would also be most likely to be major net creditors in the Cámara, and would not therefore make any large or continuing use of their borrowing rights. The borrowing rights of all other members taken together would be only about $11 million, while the normal lending commitments of Mexico and Venezuela alone would be about $27 million. The proposed system is therefore highly conservative and errs in the direction of extreme caution for the maintenance of untrammelled and fully multilateral use of members' borrowing facilities. One might well be inclined, on the basis of this analysis, to recommend some scaling down of lending commitments, or some increases in borrowing rights.

While not opposed to such readjustments, I do not wish to propose them here, for the following reasons:

(a) I feel it preferable to start conservatively with a "fool-proof" system, opening the door to later expansion in the light of experience, rather than exposed to the risk of requiring later contraction and retrenchments;

(b) *Ad hoc,* rather than automatic, increases in borrowing facilities would be useful as a stimulus to policy confrontation and harmonization, to the maintenance of confidence among members, and as preparing the ground for the more extensive use of discretionary credits contemplated under Section IV below.

(3) Earnings, Guarantees, and Settlements

The account of each participant should be handled in the same way as any checking account of a firm or individual with its bank, being credited immediately for each check drawn by another participant in its favor, and debited for each check drawn by it in favor of others.

Interest should be paid, through monthly debits, on the net debt of each participant to the Cámara, at a rate approximately equal to the average interest available on investments of similar duration in the New York market. (Different rates would apply therefore, depending on the length of time the participating country has been in net debt to the Cámara.) The Cámara's earnings would be similarly credited to members, *pro rata* of their net claims, at interest rates varying with the length of time such claims have been outstanding. The costs of operating the system would be borne by all members, *pro rata* of the turnover of their transactions with the Cámara.

All accounts would be denominated in a special unit of account, guaranteeing the Cámara and its members against any unilateral changes in exchange rates. The simplest solution would be the adoption of the U.S. dollar as a measuring rod in this respect. A more logical, but somewhat more complex, solution would be to define a Caribbean unit of account ("pesal"? or "libral"?) in a way similar to the definition of the EPU unit of account,[4] i.e. in such a way as to keep it at par with whichever member's currency remains most stable in the future in relation either to gold, or to the U.S. dollar. A third possibility would be to select as currencies of reference for such a definition the major world currencies in which Latin American Central Banks invest their reserves. As of now, this last proposal would, of course, merge in practice with the first.

Exceptionally strong guarantees against default would result from a commitment of all members to channel through its Cámara's accounts any and all payments to a member in default, until such default is fully covered and extinguished.

Finally, all net debts and claims would be fully settled at the end of each year (or twice a year?), in U.S. dollars or other currencies acceptable to the Cámara's creditors. To facilitate such settlements, the due date for net debtors should precede by a few days the due date for payments by the Cámara to the net creditors. Any delays or credits to debtors in a weak reserve position would be granted only on *ad hoc* basis, and are discussed in Section IV below, which deals with foreign exchange, rather than local currency, credits among members.

(4) *Relations with the Banking and Trading Community*

Further precisions about concrete operations, and particularly about their linkage with the banking and trading community, should benefit from the experience of the Cámara de Compensación of Central America.

Certainly, one of the major aims should be to help stimulate mutual trade in the area by passing on to private traders—and, through them, to ultimate producers and consumers—the savings derived from its compensations system.

4. See Jean L. Blondeel, "A New Form of International Financing: Loans in European Units of Account," *Columbia Law Review* (June 1964), pp. 995–1011.

The Cámara would deal exclusively with participating Central Banks, rather than with commercial banks or the public. Payment instruments eligible for settlement through the Cámara would normally[5] include: currency and bank notes, checks, documents originated from letters of credit liquidations, payment orders, and other documents resulting from payments or liquidations among the Central Banks. Caribbean checks, similar to the "Cheque Centroamericano," could also be issued by each Central Bank to all who have to make payments within the area. They would be cashable without charge at any central or commercial bank within the area, and would be channelled through the Cámara de Compensación by any Central Bank which ultimately acquires them. Centroamerican checks are now cashable without any charge whatsoever, a small charge (one fourth of 1 per cent, with a minimum of $0.20 and a maximum of $25.00) being paid by the buyer. (While such checks are now issued in local currency, the Central Banks of countries in which there are no exchange restrictions might well consider the advisability of selling similar checks with a unit-of-account denomination, as an alternative to checks in dollars or other foreign currencies freely purchasable anyway by their residents in such a case.)

Member banks should agree, in view of attendant savings on transaction costs, to make necessary arrangements within their own territory to reduce to jointly agreed margins—lower than on foreign currency instruments—banking charges or commissions on the purchase or sale of such payment instruments through commercial banks or other authorized exchange dealers. The Cámara itself would credit the depositing Central Bank, and debit the Central Bank of the drawer, at the par value between local currencies and the unit of account. As pointed out in a recent paper of Dr. Jorge Gonzalez del Valle, former director of the Central American Clearing House: "although the member central banks remit compensable documents directly between themselves, in practice it is the commercial banks which negotiate with the public the greater volume of documents compensated through the Cámara. Normally, the commercial banks obtain a credit on account from their respective central banks for documents expressed in other Centroamerican currencies which they channel through their local clearing house. In consequence, the member banks centralize the compensable documents negotiated in their respective banking systems since they act as agents of the Cámara de Compensación

5. See, however, the last paragraph of this subsection (4) below.

Centroamericana." (*Problemas de Pagos en América Latina,* CEMLA, 1964, pp. 52–53).

There is no *a priori* reason to limit the use of compensable instruments to current exchange transactions only. Indeed, any limitation of this sort would be difficult to implement in countries in which there exist no exchange restrictions or controls; and it would be highly undesirable to require the introduction of such controls as a condition for participation in the proposed system. All legal transactions within the area—whether on current or capital account—should, therefore, be eligible for settlement through the Cámara.

On the other hand, the exchange controls in existence in member countries should be respected by other members, and by the Cámara itself. This may exclude, in some cases, the eligibility of currency notes for settlement through the Cámara, although less stringent limitations have proved feasible in Central America. It would also require prior validation of payment instruments by the national exchange control authorities, for all transactions requiring such prior authorization, before the respective instruments are accepted by the partner country's Central Bank and transmitted by it to the Cámara to be credited to its account.

(5) *Institutional Framework*

The establishment of a Caribbean compensations system need not involve, at least at the start, any change in the very successful operation of the already existing Cámara de Compensación Centroamericana. Compensations and settlements among the Central American countries themselves may continue as at present, even though later adjustments may be deemed desirable by them in the light of the experience acquired with the Caribbean compensations system proposed here.

The Cámara de Compensación del Caribbe would thus have as members: (a) the Central Banks of the so-called Outer Caribbean group, for all their transactions with Central America as well as within the Outer Caribbean Area, and (b) either the individual Central Banks of Central America, or the Cámara de Compensación Centroamericana, for all transactions between the Outer Caribbean members and Central America.

Close cooperation and exchange of information between the two Cámaras would, in any case, be necessary in order to take advantage of all possible compensations opportunities within the Caribbean Area.

Actual transactions between such a small number of accounts would not require any large bureaucracy. Just as the Bank of Honduras performs such operations as *Agent* for the Cámara Centroamericana, one of the Caribbean Central Banks should be designated as *Agent* by the participating members. (In view of its geographical position, and relative size, the Central Bank of Venezuela might be a logical choice, especially if it were also entrusted with the Agency functions discussed in Section I above.)

The Agent would report to, and receive instructions from, a Managing Board on which each member Central Bank would designate a representative. (Alternatively, a single member from the Cámara Centroamericana might exercise the representation of the five Banks of Central America.)

(6) *Further Provisions*

It would be premature to burden this paper with more details on other—even though important—matters that would have to be negotiated if the suggestions above succeed in eliciting sufficient interest to trigger such a negotiating process.

In the meantime, competent officials from prospective member Banks might study with greater profit the relevant provisions of the European Payments Union Agreement, and particularly of the Cámara de Compensación Centroamericana.

IV. Central Bank Arrangements in Support of Currency Convertibility and Stability

A. Introduction

The suggestions outlined in Section III refer only to mutual settlements within the Caribbean area, and to short-term credits in national currency, of a very modest size indeed, and mostly automatic in character.

As, or more, important in the long run would be the development of monetary cooperation of a broader type, providing for mutual offsets of compensable fluctuations in member countries' balances of payments with the world at large and, therefore, in their gold and foreign exchange reserves. The purpose here would not be merely the expansion of mutual trade, but the strengthening of currency convertibility and stability in general and mutual assistance in the financing of soundly based policies for economic development.

Appropriate instruments for this purpose, and particularly the norms governing lending commitments and access to borrowing, could hardly be based on any mechanical observation of mere intra-area surpluses and deficits.

The first reason for this is that surpluses or deficits in such a small portion of each country's total trade and payments would often bear no relationship whatsoever to its over-all payments and reserve strength, its lending ability or its need for borrowings. It has already been noted, for instance, that one of the poorest countries in the area would be likely to emerge as a net creditor and be forced thereby to lend to far richer neighbors, if regional payments positions were to serve as criteria for lending obligations and borrowing rights.

The second reason is that any large automatic borrowing rights related to a country's external payments position—whether within the region, or even with the world at large—might underwrite and reward the inflationary policies of some members, involve unacceptable credit risks to other members of the group, and weaken in any case the reserve position of the latter.

These were, indeed, the main arguments that blocked agreement on previous projects for regional payments arrangements in Latin America. The proposals now to be outlined, however, embody a very different approach which was debated at length, and received general support, in the last Rio de Janeiro Meeting of the Central Bank Technicians of the American Continent. In conclusion of these debates, the delegates unanimously agreed to ask CEMLA to study further "the various possibilities of establishing new mechanisms of compensation and credit, taking account of the views expressed in this meeting . . . to communicate its studies to the Central Banks and other interested organizations, and to consult them on the advisability of calling a meeting of high officers of Central Banks in order to determine whether the basis existed to carry out concrete proposals at the level of political decision." The view was also expressed that "something more than studies was necessary, i.e. that the latter should aim at rapid action. In general terms, the meaning of the discussion was that it was urgent to arrive at concrete action and implementation." [6]

The IMF delegate at the meeting welcomed this new approach to an old problem, "expressed the very favorable attitude of its institution to follow closely and support . . . the studies that have been decided and the later steps that may be agreed." [7]

6. *Relatoría* del Dr. Márquez, in *Problemas de Pagos en América Latina* (CEMLA, 1964), pp. 294–95.

7. *Informe General* del Dr. Copete Lizarralde, *Supplemento al Boletín Quincenal* (CEMLA, November 1963), p. 394.

The debate revealed the concern of delegates to keep the door open to the eventual participation of all Latin American countries to the proposed clearing and credit institution, but also to recognize present obstacles to such participation on the part of some countries, and the appropriateness of immediate action, on a subregional scale —as in Central America—to be gradually amplified as conditions permit. The convention for compensations and mutual credits negotiated last year between the Bank of Mexico and the five Central Banks of the Cámara de Compensación Centroamericana was quoted as a concrete example of such broadening of initially more limited agreements.

B. Concrete Proposals

The concrete proposals outlined below—as supplementary to those in Section III above—follow exactly the path recommended in Rio de Janeiro. They would associate to Central America and Mexico the other countries of the Caribbean area, in a compensation and credit system aiming at *general* currency convertibility and stability, rather than at automatic financing based on regional criteria and stimulating undesirable distortions and discriminations in the production and trading pattern of the countries concerned.

Their presentation might best begin with an outline of the lending *commitments* that might be reasonably accepted by members, and that will determine the lending potential available to the institution. Only then shall we be in a position to discuss the most fruitful use of such lending potential and the conditions that should determine individual members' prospective *borrowing rights*.

(1) Members' Commitments

The members' commitments might best be grafted on those already suggested in Section I, i.e. on their agreement to hold an agreed proportion of their over-all monetary reserves in the form of international deposits with a joint institution. The only difference in members' commitments would be that they would now authorize this institution not only to invest such deposits in foreign financial markets, but to use a portion of them for investments within the area itself. This, however, is a vital difference that would, in all likelihood, limit to subregional groups—as already indicated above—the immediate acceptability of such a system. The discussion that follows will refer therefore to the same group of Caribbean countries retained, for the sake of concreteness, in Section III. While other countries might join in the 25 per cent deposit system outlined in Section I, it is assumed that only the Caribbean countries would participate from the start in the internal investment operations described below.

Member countries would undertake to maintain in the form of guaranteed international deposits with the Cámara 25 per cent at least of their gross monetary reserves. They could draw freely at any time on such deposits, in U.S. dollars or other internationally traded currencies in which the Cámara would keep its investments, in order to make payments anywhere in the world. Their only obligation would be to keep such deposits at, or above, 25 per cent of their gross reserves, but (a) they could freely draw upon any amount in excess of this minimum 25 per cent; (b) even if they always kept their deposit at this minimum figure, they could still draw on it to finance one fourth of their gross payments abroad, parallel with the use of their other reserves for the remaining 75 per cent; (c) deposits with the Cámara could therefore theoretically be drawn to the last cent, just as other reserve assets, in the extreme hypothesis of a total exhaustion of a member country's gross reserves.

If the latter extreme hypothesis (under c) were to be retained as a practical working hypothesis, and applied to all the members of the Cámara, there would, of course, be no room for any diversion of the Cámara's investments from foreign currency investments to investments within the area itself. Such diversion can be contemplated, however, without weakening in any way the reserve position of the participants as long as the intra-area investments of the Cámara: (a) are adequately protected against risks of default or excessive immobilization; (b) do not exceed in toto 25 per cent of the bare minimum to which the sum of the participating countries' international reserves might possibly be allowed to fall in the most pessimistic hypothesis worth retaining as a practical guide for policy action.[8]

The most extreme drop in the gross monetary reserves of the Caribbean area, over a period of more than thirty years, was one of about 47 per cent, from December 1957 to September 1962 (See Table 6). This was probably the largest decline ever recorded, except for the 1929–33 collapse, and most of it (87 per cent) was due to totally abnormal reserve losses of a single country from an all-high peak, following the collapse of a previous dictatorial regime, and

8. Note that the lowest sum to which the *combined* reserves of members might fall over any period is larger than the sum of the minimum reserves to which individual countries' holdings might have fallen during the same period.

TABLE 6

CARIBBEAN AREA MAXIMUM RESERVE LOSSES: DECEMBER 1957 TO SEPTEMBER 1962
(in millions of U.S. dollars)

Areas and countries	December 1957	September 1962	Reserve gains (+) or losses (−)
I. Outer Caribbean area	**2,172**	**1,114**	**−1,058**
1. Mexico	475	359	−116
2. Venezuela	1,459	515	−944
3. Colombia	145	122	−23
4. Ecuador	39	41	+2
5. Jamaica	54	77	+23
II. Central America	**157**	**128**	**−29**
1. Guatemala	75	40	−35
2. El Salvador	42	33	−9
3. Honduras	16	13	−3
4. Nicaragua	11	22	+11
5. Costa Rica	13	20	+7
III. Total	**2,329**	**1,242**	**−1,087**
IV. Total, excluding Venezuela	**870**	**727**	**−143**

SOURCE: *International Financial Statistics.*

strongly influenced by an exceptional combination of events, such as large speculative and investment capital inflows during the Suez crisis and later speculative panics triggered by the Cuban revolution and the fears of its spread to other countries in the Caribbean area. Even then, the reserves of all the other countries of the area taken together did not fall by more than about 16 per cent of their previous peak level.

In the light of this historical record, the Cámara could probably invest a substantial proportion (certainly up to one third, or even one half) of members' deposits within the area itself, without endangering in any way its ability to meet later withdrawals of such deposits in the foreign currencies most used for external settlements. Full use of this margin should not, however, be contemplated at the start. Far more modest levels of operation should first be experimented with, both in order to acquire the experience necessary for a prudent and fruitful use of this new technique, and to build up full confidence in the management of the funds entrusted to the Cámara.

It is, therefore, suggested to limit initially to a highly conservative ceiling of, let us say, 5 per cent (or 10 per cent?) of total reserves, i.e. 20 per cent (or 40 per cent?) of the total deposits with the Cámara, the maximum amount that could be invested by it within the area, the remaining 80 per cent (or 60 per cent?) of deposits being obligatorily invested in major foreign financial centers, in accordance with the criteria and procedures suggested under Section I above. As of June 1964, such a ceiling would have released about $90 million (or $180 million) for possible credits and investments within the Caribbean area (See Table 7, last line of columns 4 and 5).

TABLE 7

PROPOSED MINIMUM FOREIGN EXCHANGE DEPOSITS WITH CÁMARA
AND CEILINGS ON INTERNAL INVESTMENTS
(in millions of U.S. dollars)

Areas and countries	June 1964 reserves	Minimum deposits		Internal investment ceilings			
		Initial	Ultimate	Initial		Ultimate	
				A	B	A	B
I. Outer Caribbean area	**1,558**	**389**	**779**	**78**	**156**	**260**	**389**
1. Mexico	506	126	253	25	51	84	126
2. Venezuela	776	194	388	39	78	129	194
3. Colombia	122	30	61	6	12	20	30
4. Ecuador	50	12	25	2	5	8	12
5. Jamaica	104	26	52	5	10	17	26
II. Central America	**234**	**58**	**117**	**12**	**23**	**39**	**58**
1. Guatemala	78	19	39	4	8	13	19
2. El Salvador	65	16	32	3	6	11	16
3. Honduras	25	6	12	1	2	4	6
4. Nicaragua	41	10	20	2	4	7	10
5. Costa Rica	25	6	12	1	2	4	6
III. Total	**1,792**	**448**	**896**	**90**	**179**	**299**	**448**

1. All calculations are based on the June 1964 monetary reserves estimates of *International Financial Statistics* (November 1964 issue).

2. Minimum deposits are assumed to be fixed initially at 25 per cent (column 2), and ultimately at 50 per cent (column 3) of each country's monetary reserves.

3. Internal investment ceilings are assumed to be fixed:

a) initially at on fifth of minimum deposits, i.e. 5 per cent of gross reserves (Hypothesis A, column 4), or two-fifths of minimum deposits, i.e. 10 per cent of gross reserves (Hypothesis B, column 5);

b) ultimately at either one third of enlarged minimum deposits, i.e. one sixth of gross reserves (Hypothesis B, column 6), or one half of minimum deposits, i.e. one fourth of gross reserves (Hypothesis B, column 7).

4. Minor discrepancies in totals are due to rounding off.

Provision should be made in the initial agreement, however, for later expansions of this ceiling, by qualified (two thirds?) majority vote, up to a maximum of, let us say, one third (or one half?) of total deposits, to be reached only by gradual steps over a period of no less than five years. At current levels of reserves, this would correspond to a total margin of about $150 million (or $225 million) (one third or one half of last line of column 2).

Similar provisions could also be made, however, for raising from the initial 25 per cent to 50 per cent (or even more) the proportion of their reserves to be held by members with the Cámara.

If *both* of these provisions were later used to the maximum extent contemplated here, the maximum internal lending potential of the Cámara could ultimately reach—on the basis of current reserve levels—a sum of $300 million ($450 million), i.e. one sixth (or one fourth) of the members' total reserves, the other five sixths (or three fourths) being retained in gold and foreign exchange (see last line of columns 6 and 7).

Further increases to the one third (or one half) level mentioned above as still within conservative safety margins, should probably remain subject to a unanimous vote, and undertaken only in preparation for full monetary union if such a step appeared desirable and politically feasible in a more distant future. At that point, however, different guide lines should become more appropriate and relate instead external reserve requirements to such traditional criteria as annual imports from outside the area, sight liabilities of a federal central banking system or of the consolidated monetary and banking system of the area as a whole, etc.

Such horizons of policy are still far too remote at this stage to deserve consideration in this paper, oriented toward immediately feasible action.

(2) *Access to Credit*

Members' access to credit would be limited, first, by the Cámara's maximum lending potential derived from members' commitments as discussed above. It will also have to be limited, however, by further provisions designed to protect the creditors against undue risks and to channel the available lending power of the Cámara in the most fruitful directions, rather than waste it in the underwriting of unviable national policies.

Guarantees against exchange and default risks have already been discussed in Section III B (3) above. Default risks, however, would be totally covered, and more than covered, here by the fact that borrowing members would normally hold foreign exchange deposits with the Cámara for an amount several times larger than their total borrowings from it. The Cámara should be instructed, by the initial Agreement itself, to deduct automatically from any member's deposit the full amount of any debt of the member to the Cámara that has not been repaid before, or at, the date of maturity.

The normal borrowing quota of each member in good standing would be determined by applying to its minimum deposit with the Cámara the same percentage that the Cámara itself is authorized to invest within the area, i.e. if the suggestions described under (1) above are accepted, initially one fifth (or two fifths?), and ultimately one third (or one half?) of its minimum deposit. In terms of each country's total reserves, these percentages would be equivalent to 5 per cent (or 10 per cent?) and ultimately one sixth (or one fourth?) of each country's gross reserves.

Table 7 indicates the presumptive, normal access of each country to the Cámara's credit, as calculated on the basis of its reported June 1964 reserves.

For the reasons already discussed above, and generally endorsed at the last meeting of Central Bank Technicians in Rio, access to these credits should not be automatic, but should be made subordinate to agreement on the borrowing country's needs and stabilization policies. An additional and powerful reason for nonautomaticity is to enable the Cámara to grant occasionally credits *in excess* of its presumptive quota to any country experiencing special payments difficulties, but whose policies are fully endorsed by the other participating countries.

Among the various techniques that might be followed for the granting of such credits, one of the most flexible ones would be to credit the Cámara's deposit of the borrower not only with the foreign exchange resources deposited by him, but also with the counterpart of short-term, or medium-term securities—to be amortized gradually by quarterly installments—issued by it to the Cámara, and negotiable with other member Central Banks, or even with commercial banks and the public. While this negotiability provision might appear somewhat academic at first, the various guarantees attached to such securities should make them in time extremely attractive to investors, and initiate the way toward the development of open-market operations and other capital transactions in the area. Sales by the Cámara or the Central Banks to commercial banks and the public might help mop up excess liquidity in times of inflationary pressures. Markets might even be found abroad, strengthening in this case the gross reserve position of the area as a whole.

Within the area, Central Banks in a reasonably strong reserve position might accept additional commitments to use a proportion of any reserve increases for the acquisition of such securities, with the understanding that in the event of later declines in their reserves they could sell them back to the Cámara or to other member Banks whose reserves were increasing.

Various guide lines might be agreed upon in advance in order to facilitate and expedite the negotiating process entailed by *ad hoc,* discretionary, decisions on the granting of credit by the Cámara. For instance:

(a) Credits should be granted only to a country whose over-all reserves are decreasing, or are well below the Group's average in relation to imports or other relevant criteria.

(b) Automatic, or semiautomatic, credit lines could be established in advance—making use of IMF experience in the granting of standby agreements—to cover declines in reserves clearly seasonal or temporary in character.

(c) Thorough scrutiny of a country's policy should be necessary only when the temporary nature of reserve declines is seriously in doubt, and particularly when such declines coincide with domestic inflationary developments, such as rising prices and/or large increases in internal bank credit.

(d) Criteria should be tightened whenever necessary to protect the Cámara's own reserve ratio of gold and foreign exchange assets to its total deposit liabilities. The criteria suggested above imply the maintenance by the Cámara of an initial reserve ratio of at least 80 per cent (or 60 per cent?) and an ultimate ratio of two thirds (or one half?). Since, however, the actual ratio may vary not only as a consequence of new lending operations, but also as a result of deposit withdrawals—in cases of reserve declines for the Group as a whole—escaping any control by the Cámara, a logical inference from the above criteria would be for the Cámara to suspend temporarily all new credit operations whenever its actual reserve ratio falls below the ratio suggested in the text, i.e. initially below 80 per cent (or 60 per cent), and ultimately below two thirds (or one half).

(e) The lending potential of the Cámara may often prevent it from granting as full and generous assistance to a member as would be deemed desirable in view of that member's needs and policies. The Cámara should, in such cases, support the member's request for parallel assistance by the IMF, in order to supplement the credits which it is itself willing and able to grant. Such a procedure, similar to that foreseen in the Rome Treaty establishing the European Economic Community (Article 108, 2, a), would have the triple advantage: (i) of suggesting to the IMF authorities policy conditions more realistically adapted to the Latin American scene than those that might otherwise come out of the Washington deliberations; (ii) of enhancing the persuasiveness of Latin American advice by backing it up with some resources—even if modest in amount—from the area itself; (iii) of reducing thereby clashes of views (too frequent in the past) between the IMF and public opinion in Latin America.

Summary and Conclusions

Rapid and momentous changes have recently taken place and are still in progress in the areas of currency stabilization, balance of payments, liberalization and reactivation of capital markets, reciprocal credits among central banks, mutual policy confrontations and consultations, negotiation of further and wide-ranging reforms in the international monetary system, etc. These developments are followed and pushed with unexpected vigor by responsible monetary authorities in the European Economic Community and the other major OECD countries associated in the so-called Group of Ten.

Highly ambitious measures of a similar kind have been in progress also among the republics of Central America, and have proved extraordinarily successful. The rest of Latin America, however, has failed to develop so far any active and constructive policies in these matters, even though its own future will be profoundly affected thereby.

The present paper has focussed attention on a number of *concrete* proposals, suggested by these developments and susceptible of *early negotiation and implementation*.

The steps proposed in the first two Sections involve *no mutual credit commitments* whatsoever and should, therefore, prove acceptable to most, or even all, countries of Latin America. They aim (1) in *Section I:* at diversifying the present pattern of reserves investment abroad, and at maximizing earnings on such investments; (2) in *Section II:* at reducing the recently increasing net outflows of expatriate capital from Latin America, at stimulating partial repatriation of such funds and, more generally, at exploring more systematically the new opportunities for foreign borrowings arising from the reactivation of European capital markets (Euro-currency markets, security flotations in foreign currencies and in units of account, etc.).

The intraregional *credit commitments* and inseparable measures of *policy harmonization* involved in the last two Sections are not likely to prove immediately negotiable among *all* Latin American countries, and have been explored primarily in the context of the Caribbean area. They could, however, be adjusted to similar subregional agreements among other countries, and should, in any case, preserve opportunities both (a) for later linkages or mergers between such subregional groups; and (b) for closer monetary integration, or even monetary unions, among countries where such ambitious sovereignty mergers appear politically feasible and desirable. This is the main reason for preserving the identity of the present Central American group in a broader Caribbean payments agreement.

While Section III focuses on *local currency* credit lines in support of mutual trade only, Section IV envisages broader forms of cooperation involving *foreign exchange* credits, offsetting national fluctuations in monetary reserves and bolstering mutually acceptable policies of economic development, currency convertibility, and exchange-rate stability.

One should mention, in addition, the desirability of studying further, and coordinating if possible, the future attitude of the Latin American monetary authorities and governments in current and forthcoming explorations and negotiations regarding world-wide reforms of the international monetary system and of the IMF.[9]

The program above is bound to appear too ambitious and/or premature to many. I sincerely and profoundly believe the opposite to be the case. The negotiating process is always so slow, anyway, that the real danger, tomorrow as yesterday, is "too little and too late" rather than "too much and too soon."

As pointed out repeatedly in the last meeting of Central Bank Technicians in Rio de Janeiro, it is high time to bring to the negotiating table these issues which have been bogged down for more than a decade in the morass of academic studies and inconclusive meetings

9. See my paper on "International Monetary Reform," dealing specifically with this point and prepared at the request of CEPAL, in the *Economic Bulletin for Latin America* (United Nations), March 1966.

at the technical level. This can only be done if the present debate succeeds in instilling in some of you a sufficient conviction and feeling of urgency to induce you to take an active leadership, within your own country and with your colleagues in other Latin American countries, toward the actual negotiation of such agreements.

As for those who still hesitate to accept the responsibilities which the world is thrusting upon them, I would urge them to give these— or other similar—proposals a trial, and to insist only on flexible provisions for amendment or termination of, and withdrawal from, the agreements to be negotiated, if experience reveals fatal defects in their practical functioning. The risks involved in such *action* are certainly far smaller than those which *inaction*, at this stage, is bound to entail, both in terms of actual losses and of missed opportunities.

The dreary drifting of the interwar years into competitive deflation, devaluations, and restrictions was largely the product of such inaction or, more precisely, of the inability of national countries to negotiate successfully the reciprocal commitments necessary to ensure the co-ordination and compatibility of national policy objectives and instruments. The contrasting and unprecedented growth rates sustained in the postwar period by most European countries—particularly those of the European Economic Community—can largely be ascribed to the workability and fruitfulness of such reciprocal commitments and agreements, whose effectiveness has not only belied the pessimistic prognostications of skeptical opponents, but even exceeded the most optimistic hopes of their proponents.

Nothing is certain in this world of ours, but faced with such unavoidable uncertainties we should follow the bridge-player's maxim: "When in doubt, lead trumps!" rather than the defeatist French proverb: "Dans le doute, abstiens-toi!"

Chapter XIII: Keeping Humpty Dumpty
Together in Africa

EFFECTIVE monetary cooperation among the newly independent nations of the African continent raises difficulties, political and administrative, as well as economic, incomparably greater than in Latin America and, *a fortiori,* in the European Economic Community. It is with great reluctance and skepticism, therefore, that I finally agreed, in the summer of 1963, to study this problem for the United Nations Economic Commission for Africa. My report to the Commission, reproduced immediately below, concluded nevertheless that a determined effort should be made immediately to arrest the frightening process of disintegration then under way, and to pave the way toward later, and broader, regroupings of existing African monetary areas in connection with other agreements, particularly in the trade field.

The two papers that follow reproduce the text of my report and follow its fate in the course of the following debates and negotiations.

1. Report on the Possibilities of Establishing a Clearing and Payments Union in Africa

I. Introduction

(1) Resolution 87 of the fifth session of the Economic Commission for Africa "requests the Executive Secretary to undertake a study of the possibilities of establishing a clearing system within a payments union between the African countries and to submit the study to the Commission at its seventh session."

(2) A parallel resolution, adopted at the Conference of Heads of African States, invites ECA "to request its Executive Secretary to give . . . all the necessary support and assistance which it may require . . ." to a Commission of Experts "charged to study, in collaboration with governments and in consultation with the Economic Commission for Africa, *inter alia* the following questions and submit their findings to Member States:

Prepared in August 1963 at the Addis Ababa headquarters of the United Nations Economic Commission for Africa, and published as Annex VI of U.N. Document E/CN.14/262, February 4, 1964.

(f) the establishment of an African Payments and Clearing Union;

(g) a progressive freeing of national currencies from all non-technical external attachments and the establishment of a Pan-African monetary zone."

(3) The present paper suggests initial procedural steps to implement resolution 87(V) and outlines, in very broad and provisional terms, some of the possibilities that might be studied in this respect by the group of experts mentioned under II(7) below.

(4) Attention is centered exclusively on the possibility of payments and monetary arrangements, although the feasible and desirable shape of such arrangements will obviously be determined overwhelmingly by broader political and economic developments, such as the formation of customs unions, etc., which are the subject of a separate ECA study.

II. The Need for Immediate Action and Planning

(5) The African continent is now broken up into about twenty currency areas, some of which are confined to the national territory of Member States, others joined in broader monetary unions and/or closely linked to outside currencies, such as the pound sterling, the French franc, etc. The situation is also a highly fluid one, bound to evolve rapidly under the opposite pressures of nationalistic feelings, of aspirations toward African unity, and of the emergence of regional customs or economic unions among some of the countries of the area. This fluidity makes it extremely difficult to devise concrete and feasible solutions for the African payments problems, since such solutions must adjust to, and are inevitably dependent upon largely unpredictable developments in the economic and political fields, both within and outside Africa. Yet it is also a most compelling argument for concerted thinking and planning designed to facilitate later progress in these broader fields, rather than hamper it through the haphazard creation and entrenchment of vested interests and of institutions or agreements unsuited to the longer term goals of African economic growth.

(6) Two initial procedural steps are suggested to develop the recommendations to be presented to the Economic Commission for Africa:

All central banks and monetary authorities of member countries should be requested to forward to the ECA Secretariat:

(a) a copy of all laws and regulations governing the operation of

their monetary system, banking institutions, foreign exchange transactions, and payments agreements, with such comments as they deem
appropriate;

(b) information about proposed reforms or agreements now under
consideration in these same fields;

(c) information about the major difficulties and obstacles encountered by them in their international payments, both within and
outside Africa, and of the measures which they would consider appropriate to eliminate or reduce such difficulties and obstacles.

(7) The documentation thus assembled should be forwarded, together with the present study, to a selected group of monetary and
financial experts, to be discussed in a joint meeting to be held in
Tangier. This group would be charged with the preparation of concrete recommendations for the implementation of resolution 87(V),
to be submitted to the next meeting of the Commission.

(8) The report of the experts should be forwarded, with ECA's
comments and recommendations, to all Member countries and to the
Organization of African Unity.

III. A Charter for African Monetary Cooperation

(9) A charter for African Monetary Cooperation should attempt
to lay down, as early as possible, the major guide lines which should
serve as a framework for future agreements. Such a Charter might
include, for instance:

(a) a definition of major objectives, such as the adaptation of
national monetary and payments policies, institutions and regulations
to cooperative endeavors and agreements to raise African living standards through the expansion of production, investment, trade, and
capital flows throughout the area;

(b) as means to these ends, commitments to re-examine periodically existing payments restrictions and discrimination with a view
to their progressive elimination on a reciprocal basis, and to foster
mutual assistance agreements and policy coordination to overcome
balance-of-payments obstacles to such liberalization;

(c) a commitment to seek and develop such agreements on as
broad a geographical basis as possible;

(d) the recognition of the role which regional agreements among
limited numbers of countries can play, at least in a transitional period,
to develop among them more intensive forms of cooperation and

integration than would be immediately possible on an all-African scale;

(e) agreement on the need, however, to frame such regional agreements in such a way as to avoid all unnecessary discrimination against nonmembers, and to facilitate their later merger into broader agreements as soon as feasible (a desirable operational procedure in this respect would be to submit such agreements to some all-African consultative group, one month before their entry into force, for mutual consultation on feasible and desirable revisions or expansions);

(f) finally, the establishment of some all-African consultation machinery in the monetary and payments field, to foster the above objectives (see IV below).

(10) This Charter for Monetary Cooperation should form only a chapter of a broader Charter for *Economic* Cooperation, encompassing other fields as well, and particularly trade and investment agreements.

IV. An African Monetary Council

(11) The central banks—or other monetary authorities—of the continent should establish regular contacts in order to implement the objectives of the proposed Charter, and to suggest such later revisions as may appear desirable in the light of experience. The Governors of Central Banks of Latin America, for instance, meet once a year and those of Western Europe as often as once a month. The Latin American Central Banks have also established a permanent Center of Monetary Studies (CEMLA) for the centralization and dissemination of information to member banks and for the training of their officers and employees. They have also organized, since 1946, biannual Meetings of Central Bank Technicians of the American Continent to confront mutually their problems and experiences in the field of monetary policy.

(12) An African Monetary Council, composed of the Governors of Central Banks or other monetary authorities, could be set up to develop similar cooperation in Africa. They could meet regularly, at least once a year, and organize a permanent secretariat to centralize and disseminate useful information on African monetary legislation and developments, arrange training courses for central bank personnel, etc. *Ad hoc* meetings of governors or other major officials might also be called from time to time to deal with special problems that might

arise, and particularly to review proposed regional agreements, as suggested under III 9 (e) above.

(13) The secretariat of the Council might be most economically set up initially at the headquarters of some existing African organization, such as the United Nations Economic Commission for Africa; or—after they have begun effective operations—the Organization of African Unity, or the proposed African Development Bank. African cooperation in other closely related fields, such as trade and finance, will require the further development of parallel contacts in these fields. Joint meetings of Ministers and Central Bank Governors will also be necessary to prepare or adopt important decisions and agreements exceeding the competence of Central Banks alone, but closely related to their activities and responsibilities.

V. Clearing and Payments Agreements

(14) The suggestions above would help pave the way for future progress toward increasing monetary cooperation among the African countries. The specific agreements that might be concluded could only be shaped up by the member countries themselves and could hardly be realistically predicted or proposed in the present study. All that can be done at this stage is to outline some of the major types of agreement that should be explored and that might progressively become feasible and negotiable, whether on an all-African or on a regional basis.

Clearing Functions

(15) Suggestions for an African Clearing or Payments Union are most often prompted by the realization of the spectacular success achieved in this respect in postwar Europe by the functioning of the European Payments Union between 1950 and 1958. There is, however, no parallel between the European payments problems of those days and those of Africa today. Europe had emerged from the war with a score of inconvertible currencies and rigid national exchange control legislations which would have paralyzed international transactions altogether except for the conclusion of more than a hundred bilateral payments agreements, regulating settlements between each European country and its trading partners. These bilateral agreements facilitated settlements between each pair of countries separately, but left each country unable to mobilize its surpluses with one trading

partner to finance deficits with another. The main purpose of EPU was to permit such mobilization through the multilateral clearing of bilateral surpluses and deficits against one another, and to facilitate thereby—and through a host of other provisions regarding mutual credits and policy consultations—the gradual elimination of exchange-restrictions and controls on European trade and other transactions.

(16) The success of EPU paved the way for the restoration of currency convertibility on a broader, world-wide basis, in 1958, and for the simultaneous liquidation of EPU, whose initial main function had therefore become unnecessary. The disappearance of EPU as a focus for European monetary cooperation and integration may nevertheless be deplored, but these desirable and endurable aspects of the Union were partly preserved through the simultaneous establishment of the European Monetary Agreement and, particularly, through the expanding work and responsibilities of the Monetary Committee of the European Economic Community.

(17) The African problem today is totally different from that which confronted Europe in 1950. First, trade among African countries themselves still constitutes only less than 10 per cent of their total trade, as against two thirds (or thereabouts) in the case of Western Europe, and the bulk of this intra-African trade is concentrated among small and widely separated clusters of countries, such as those of North Africa, for instance, and the trade between South Africa and the Federation of Rhodesia and Nyasaland at the other end of the continent. While this should act as a spur, rather than as a bar, to the efforts to develop a more normal level of trade flows between neighboring countries, it nevertheless limits severely the feasible scope and significance of an African clearing union in the years immediately ahead.

(18) Fortunately, an African clearing machinery is far less essential today to African countries than a European clearing system was to the European countries ten or fifteen years ago. Virtually all the African trade is stipulated today—as is also the case outside Africa —in the convertible currencies of major trading countries (pounds sterling, French francs, and dollars, particularly). The earnings of any country in any one of these currencies can be readily converted in other currencies needed for payment with the exception of a still significant portion of the French franc earnings of the countries belonging to the franc zone.

The main problem is not that of currency inconvertibility, but of the *over-all* payments difficulties of some countries and of the exchange restrictions which these difficulties impose upon them.

(19) There exist nevertheless powerful arguments in favor of the early creation of an *African Payments Union*. The immediate benefits of such a Union would admittedly be minor: it might reduce slightly the costs of exchange transactions between one currency and another, and open up some opportunities for slightly more profitable investment of a portion of each country's foreign exchange reserves. The main significance of the Union, however, would be to give concrete expression to Africa's gropings for effective cooperation in this field, and to set up *immediately* on an *all-African* basis, and *without costs or risks to anybody,* an institutional machinery susceptible of far larger and more fruitful developments in the future.

(20) As a minimum initial step, the African Payments Union would merely open a new opportunity to its members, on a purely voluntary basis:

(a) As regards *trade with nonmembers,* each member country would be allowed to exchange convertible currencies earned or accumulated by it for other foreign currencies needed for payment. This would shave African countries' exchange transactions costs by offsetting, for instance, the sterling surpluses and French franc deficits of some countries or currency areas with the sterling deficits and French franc surpluses of other members.

(b) As regards *trade among African countries or monetary areas,* any member could be credited by the Union with its convertible currency claims on another member, and these credits could be used to settle any convertible currency debt incurred toward another member. This type of transaction would in fact obviate any actual use of foreign currencies in the settlements to be effected.

(21) The maximum and most efficient use of these clearing facilities would involve the maintenance by each member of minimum working balances in convertible currencies with the Union. Payments could then be effected readily by debits to the member's account rather than require simultaneous and equivalent transfers of other currencies by the payer to the Union.

(22) Whenever advantage would be taken of these working deposit facilities, unused deposit balances would initially be retained by the Union in the currencies deposited, the exchange risk continuing to run for the depositing country itself, exactly as would be the case

if the exchange assets had been retained directly abroad, rather than transferred to the Union. Alternatively, some arrangements could be worked out to denominate such working balances—or any portion of them—in a common unit of account, sharing exchange risks among the depositors on a *pro rata* basis, expanding the scope of possible clearings, and permitting a more flexible and profitable pattern of investment of the exchange resources of the Union.

(23) The initial Agreement might allow each depositing country to specify the terms under which it wishes to operate in this respect, but it may be hoped that familiarity with these arrangements would induce most, or all, of them to shift gradually to the broader type of arrangements outlined in the preceding paragraph.

(24) In all events, the clearing arrangements proposed so far would *not* involve any credit operations among the member countries. The exchange resources transferred by them to the Union would be fully used for balance-of-payments settlements, or retained abroad as exchange reserves in convertible currencies, thus eschewing the assumption of any credit risks not implicit already in the retention of foreign exchange reserves abroad by each of them separately and directly. Nor would any compulsion be involved in these arrangements, designed only to offer members new opportunities, to be used or ignored at their own discretion. This is essential in order to facilitate a general acceptance of the African Payments Union provisions by all African countries or monetary areas, without sacrifice of any one's sovereignty and present currency links with other countries, and without assumption of any additional exchange or credit risks.

(25) The immediate benefits of such a riskless all-African agreement would be correspondingly modest, but they might be progressively supplemented and expanded, either on an all-African or on a narrower regional basis, by further agreements of the type discussed below. Most of all, the early setting up of an African Payments Union would provide the institutional contacts and machinery necessary to induce and implement such further cooperation and integration among the African countries.

Interim Finance for Intra-African Settlements

(26) The European Payments Union included, among other and more comprehensive credit provisions, automatic credit facilities postponing at least to the end of each month the due date of settlements for intra-European transactions. Similar provisions have been re-

tained, on an *ad hoc* basis, in the European Monetary Agreement.

(27) Similar facilities might be grafted on an African Payments Union Agreement, either on over-all basis, or by separate agreements within regional groups of more closely interdependent trading countries.

(28) Such interim finance agreements could be couched in many alternative forms, of which only the most modest and most easily negotiable will be discussed here.

(29) Each participating country in such agreements might agree, for instance, to extend to the African Payments Union a line of credit, up to an agreed percentage of its gross receipts from other members in a previous reference year, postponing for a period of one to three months any payments due to it by other participating members. Conversely, it might be authorized automatically, upon simple request to the Union, to postpone for a similar period any payments due to other participating members.

(30) In order to preserve fully the multilateral charter of these credit facilities, the line of credit automatically available to each country as a borrower would have to remain substantially lower than the line of credit granted by it to the Union as a lender. (This results from the fact that many countries might be simultaneously in deficit toward *a few,* and wish to concentrate the use of their borrowing lines to make payments to these few countries, thus exceeding the latter's total lending commitments, as occurred repeatedly during the functioning of the European Payments Union.) Alternatively, of course, some working capital might be assigned to the Union for this purpose from some outside sources, as was done in the case of the European Payments Union.

(31) The use of the credit lines proposed above could also be married, on a proportional basis to be agreed upon, with immediate cash payments in convertible currencies for part of the settlements due.

(32) In any case, the due date of repayment to the Union by the debtor members should precede by a few days the due date of settlements by the Union to the creditor members.

(33) Finally, all credits and debts should carry—as in the European Payments Union—an exchange guarantee, concretized by the adoption of a single unit of account, and a solidary guarantee of all obligations to the Union to cover the possibility of any default by any one of its debtors.

Mutual Assistance Pacts

(34) More intimate and ambitious forms of payments and credit arrangements could be required and negotiable only in connection with parallel agreements for extensive trade and exchange liberalization and tariff reductions or elimination among the participating members.

(35) The experience of both OEEC and EEC suggests that such agreements need the support of *mutual assistance and policy consultation* provisions to enable countries in temporary difficulties in their balance of payments to honor nevertheless their commitments, without excessive and unnecessary recourse to escape clauses.

(36) Indeed, while the elimination of restrictions among participating members would constitute a powerful stimulus to a general expansion of their trade and production along more rational and economic lines, reduce wastes and costs, and strengthen thereby the competitiveness and balance of payments of the *group as a whole* with the outside world, these benefits would not be distributed equally among all the countries concerned. The new export opportunities created may lend themselves to more immediate exploitation by some countries than by others, depending on the nature of the productive processes involved and of the initial differences in cost patterns hidden by the restrictions and brought into the open by their elimination.

(37) Until needed adaptations have been effectively carried out—through a redirection of investments, a rationalization of production, and, in some cases, through exchange-rate readjustments—a few countries may even suffer an absolute deterioration in their balances of payments.

(38) Escape clauses from liberalization commitments would have to be available in such cases to the countries in difficulty, but their actual use could be avoided, or minimized, if temporary financial assistance is extended to them by the members who benefit most, and most rapidly, from the liberalization measures adopted, and have the greatest and most immediate interest in their maintenance.

(39) Yet even such members cannot be expected to extend indefinite credit assistance to a country which would remain in persistent deficit, without making the necessary effort to redress its situation. Borrowing rights, therefore, should not be automatic, except possibly for moderate amounts and short-term maturities (three months?) designed primarily to allow the time needed for discussion and negotiation. The extension of substantial credits, with longer-term maturities

(from one to three or five years?), should be coupled with mutual agreements among members about the policies to be pursued by the borrower in order to redress its payments imbalance in the manner least prejudicial to other members, and about the policies to be pursued by the lenders themselves to ease the process of adjustment and the repayment of the obligations contracted.

(40) In brief, mutual credit provisions should be designed in such a way as to elicit from all members a sufficient degree of policy harmonization to ensure, in the long run, a viable equilibrium in the members' payments position.

(41) This equilibrium itself should not aim at straitjacketing, in separate compartments, the payments balance of each member country with the rest of the trading group, on the one hand, and with the rest of the world, on the other. The most economic and desirable trade pattern of any country will normally involve multilateral offsetting between its deficits with some trading partners and its surpluses with others.

(42) Borrowing rights and lending obligations cannot, therefore, be related exclusively to a country's deficits or surpluses within Africa alone, and even less within a subregion of Africa. No country should be barred from borrowing, nor, *a fortiori,* forced to lend, solely because it happens to provide more exports to its neighbors than it is able to procure needed imports from them. The adoption of intraregional balance-of-payments criteria to determine borrowing rights and lending obligations would be all the more haphazard when applied to countries which carry only a very small fraction of their total trade and capital transactions with one another, and whose payments position is, therefore, overwhelmingly dependent on their extraregional transactions. The poorest country might be required, in that case, to lend to the richest, and the financial incentives and deterrents created by such a system could only promote a most absurd and wasteful distortion of normal and desirable trade patterns.

(43) A member country's need for assistance—or its ability to provide assistance to others—should therefore be determined by its *over-all* payments and reserve position, as suggested in paragraph (45) below.

(44) Legitimate needs of some countries for such financing are, unfortunately, likely to exceed the total lending capacity of other members. Every effort should be made, therefore, to obtain outside

the member countries, as large a portion as is feasible of the resources needed for the functioning of the system:

(a) through specific assignment of foreign aid funds to such a purpose;

(b) through the collective raising of funds abroad, with the mutual and solidary guarantee of all participating countries;

(c) through joint approach to the IMF, supporting a request for drawing by the member in need, indicating the policies commonly agreed upon to help correct the member's deficit, and suggesting, whenever appropriate, the utilization of other members' currency contributions to the IMF as a partial source of financing for the proposed transaction.

(45) Finally, mutual assistance *stricto senso* might be financed most logically through the acceptance by members of a minimum deposit obligation with the African Payments Union, equal to an agreed percentage of each participating country's gross international reserves. The acceptance of such a deposit obligation by members would in no way infringe upon the availability and liquidity of their reserves, whenever needed for payments, since their deposit obligation would always decrease *pari passu* with their global reserves, whenever such payments are actually called for. Deposits with the Union would always be as liquid and usable as deposits in London, Paris, or New York. Under the normal provisions of the Payments Union—such as those outlined under paragraphs 22–24, above—this liquid availability would be guaranteed by the fact that the Union would indeed retain abroad, on the major money markets of the world, the full counterpart of its deposit liabilities to the members of the Union.

(46) The provision just mentioned would be relaxed, within the limits of prudence, with regard to the compulsory deposits maintained with the Union by the members of a mutual assistance pact. The *global* reserves of members—and, therefore, their global deposits with the Union—would be less unstable than the reserves and deposits of each, taken separately. It should, therefore, be possible for the Union to invest a prudent portion of its over-all assets in the form of short- or medium-term loans or investments in favor of members, while retaining abroad a level of reserves amply sufficient to meet any likely contraction in the global level of deposits maintained with it by all its members.

(47) Various alternative clauses might be written into the agree-

ment to guard against any assumption of excessive risks in this respect. To give only one example, qualified majorities (two thirds, three fourths, or even unanimity) might be required to approve loans whose effect would be to reduce the ratio of foreign exchange reserves to deposits below 75, 60, or 50 per cent.

(48) Recourse to this procedure might also be linked with IMF standby agreements, guaranteeing in advance the intervention of the IMF to relay the loans granted on the basis of compulsory deposits with the African Payments Union, in the event of a later excessive depletion of the latter's foreign reserves counterpart.

(49) Finally, the development of separate regional agreements of this sort, encompassing in the end most or all of the members of the African Payments Union, might create gradually the conditions necessary to the successful negotiation of wider agreements, aiming at partial or total mergers of the regional groups initially created, or at a more decentralized system under which regional groups would retain their identity, but have access to the African Payments Union itself, as a lender of last resort, under conditions to be negotiated in the light of available needs and resources, and of the growing agreement and trust of African countries and monetary areas in their respective policies and mutual commitments.

Monetary Unions

(50) A number of African countries preserved, after independence, the more intimate monetary links previously established among them by sterling area and French franc area arrangements. This is particularly true of the West Africa and Equatorial Africa Monetary Unions whose charters define in precise and workable terms the conditions necessary to reconcile full monetary integration with national political sovereignty, and preserve in addition the unconditional convertibility of the Unions' currencies with the French franc. In former sterling area countries, independence has generally been accompanied so far by a total break-up of the former monetary unity, except as long as political federation was preserved, as in the case of the Rhodesias and Nyasaland, where it appears most unlikely to survive the break-up of the Federation. On the other hand, effective monetary union has been preserved in East Africa after the accession of Tanganyika and Uganda to independence, and negotiations in process for the formation of an East African Federation contemplate the maintenance of full monetary union for the area.

(51) Stringent conditions, involving a partial merger—rather than surrender—of national monetary sovereignty, are of course necessary for the functioning of a monetary union. Agreement must be reached on the practical organization of joint decisions and common institutions, assuring a sufficient harmonization of monetary and credit policies to avoid an excessive or persistent spread of inflationary, or deflationary, tendencies from some members of the Union to the others. Such safeguards, however, are clearly in the interest of each of the participants, and merely impose contractually upon them the kind of policy restraints that market forces themselves would otherwise impose upon them as long as they remained determined to avoid the economic waste and political dangers arising from domestic inflation and external instability of their currency. It can also be shown that the effectiveness of monetary policy in fighting either inflation or deflation and in promoting economic growth increases considerably with the expansion of the monetary area covered by such policy.

(52) There are, therefore, powerful arguments favoring the maintenance, or creation, of monetary unions, whenever it is possible to elicit from members the political wisdom and courage necessary to overcome the short-term difficulties involved in reaching and implementing such agreements. Fortunately, nationalistic pride, prejudices, and vested interests have had no time as yet to entrench themselves deeply in Africa, and the common fight for independence has created strong bonds among all Africans and a deep aspiration for unity among their political leaders and their people. This is a foundation on which to build, but many difficulties—of a practical, rather than ideological, nature—will have to be solved, and will impose, in most cases, the adoption of a pragmatic and gradual approach, testing the viability of proposed monetary unions and their adaptation to local conditions, before full and irrevocable commitments can be realistically negotiated among prospective members.

(53) Such a gradual process might evolve, in a natural manner, from the mutual assistance pacts suggested above. Every participating country might retain, initially, its own currency and its full control over its own monetary and credit policy, agreeing only to the minimum deposit obligation characterizing such mutual assistance pacts.

(54) *Ad hoc* agreements for policy adaptation and harmonization would, however, be necessary on the occasion of each recourse by a country to the mutual assistance of others. They would, each time, create precedents, the accumulation of which would facilitate their

progressive institutionalization into agreed criteria and procedures for *joint* policy decisions. At the same time, the proportion of gross reserves to be maintained in the form of deposits with the Union could be progressively enlarged until they culminate in a full pooling of the participating countries' monetary reserves. The successful maintenance of exchange-rate stability between the national currencies concerned could, at some point, be consolidated and dramatized through the adoption of equivalent monetary units where such do not exist already and their intercirculation at par throughout the Union's territory.

(55) The way would then be paved for the final stage of a full currency merger, in which a single, common currency would be issued under the responsibility of a federal banking system. (Long-term stabilization loans might be necessary at this stage to equalize the contribution of each member country to the joint international reserves of the system, *pro rata* of the currency issues whose liability is transferred from the previous national banks of issue to the new federal institution.)

VI. Links to Major World Currencies

(56) The agreements outlined above should aim at facilitating transactions not only among their participating members, but also with nonmembers. This is generally understood and accepted by all, of course, insofar as relations with nonparticipating African countries are concerned, but the same point of view should be adopted towards non-African countries which constitute today more than 90 per cent of African export outlets, and will continue to provide for many years to come the major markets by far for African production, and the major sources of African imports of goods and of capital, public and private.

(57) Such arrangements with major world trading countries and financial centers as already exist should not therefore be lightly condemned or broken up. Efforts should be directed, on the contrary, at expanding and revising them in the future, to take account of new developments and opportunities arising from political and economic changes within and outside Africa. Such revisions should aim particularly:

(a) at reflecting in a realistic manner both the national sovereignty of all participants and the inevitability of adequate consultations and agreements in all transactions and arrangements involving major credit or assistance commitments, particularly of a long-term or open-end character;

(b) at reducing and eliminating as rapidly and completely as possible the elements of discrimination which they now involve among African countries. Several provisions of the recent Treaty of Association with EEC, and the accompanying comments of responsible EEC and African officials, offer grounds for optimism in this respect;

(c) at enlarging the scope and sphere of application of such agreements, insofar as possible and useful:

(i) The association of African countries with the European Economic Community, for instance, may offer increasing opportunities in the future to broaden in a more profitable and less discriminatory manner some of the links now maintained by these countries with national European countries. The full extent and direction of these opportunities will depend, however, on future developments, and particularly on the strengthening of monetary, economic, and political integration, both among associated African members and within the EEC itself.

(ii) On the other hand, these arrangements inevitably involve some discrimination in favor of the Associated Members which may be highly harmful to other countries, both in Africa and elsewhere. Negotiations between EEC, the United Kingdom and other countries are bound to create new situations and new opportunities to solve these problems, both through the broadening of existing agreements and through the revision of present EEC tariff, fiscal, and other provisions which have a major incidence on the underdeveloped countries' trade.

(iii) Sectoral trade and investment agreements regarding particular projects and industries of major interest to both associated and non-associated countries, might be particularly useful in this respect, and should be inserted into development plans cutting across present boundaries between countries or regional groups.

(iv) All African countries should participate actively in the various negotiations, agreements, and institutions designed to reconcile and integrate sub-regional, regional, and world-wide efforts at cooperation, and to broaden progress toward economic liberalization, cooperation, integration, and material help, on as wide a basis as possible. The forthcoming United Nations Conference on Trade and Development should play a major role in this respect.

VII. Conclusions

(58) Early action and planning are urgently necessary to ward off a further disintegration of the economic and monetary links of African countries with one another and with the outside world, and to set in motion an opposite process of increasing cooperation and integration aiming at accelerating the pace of useful trade, investments, economic development, and social progress in Africa.

(59) Regional agreements among more closely interdependent countries, keenly conscious of this interdependence, and better prepared by historical and geographical links to understand and trust each other's policies and commitments, can assign themselves, in this respect, more immediate and more ambitious aims than is yet possible on an all-African basis. There is, however, no necessary opposition or dilemma here between more intimate regional links on the one hand, and looser but geographically wider forms of association, on the other. On the contrary, the experience of postwar Europe makes it abundantly clear that both types of agreements can be couched in such a way as to complement and bolster one another. Regional agreements should be outward-looking as well as inward-looking, and be framed with a view to avoid unnecessary discrimination in the short run, and facilitate in the long run progress towards broader cooperation and integration on as wide a basis as proves politically feasible.

(60) A Charter for African Monetary Cooperation and an African Monetary Council might serve as initial instruments to guide future planning and agreements in the monetary field, and emphasize the long-term requirements of African solidarity that need be kept in mind by the framers of regional agreements and of national policies.

(61) The establishment of an African Payments Union among all or most African countries should be negotiable in the immediate future, as it need not involve any sacrifices or risks for any of the participants. While its immediate benefits would also be correspondingly modest, the Union would create a machinery for joint action of a concrete sort, and facilitate the later negotiation and implementation of more ambitious agreements, in the monetary and financial fields, both on a regional and on a wider scale.

(62) In brief, African countries should lose no time in exploring all avenues for fruitful cooperation among them and with other countries. Feasible agreements among limited groups of countries should not be sacrificed or unduly postponed for the sake of the broader but

less immediately attainable aims of all-African or world-wide unity. On the other hand, such regional agreements should be framed from the start—and revised, whenever necessary—in such a way as to facilitate, rather than hinder, parallel negotiations exploiting to the fullest possible extent, at every point in time, existing or future opportunities for fruitful cooperation on a wider and wider scale among countries and regional groups, both within and outside Africa.

Appendix: The African Currency Scene Today

(1) There are, as of now, January 22, 1964, thirty-five independent countries and about twenty colonies or territories in Africa, with twenty-six separate currencies. This situation is bound to evolve rapidly, however, with the accession of new countries to full independence, and the further probable breakdown of some of the monetary links inherited from colonial times. Most of the new currencies which have emerged so far have preserved their former parity with the European currencies to which they were previously linked, and are predominantly, or exclusively, backed by foreign-exchange reserves in these same currencies. The development of national monetary institutions and policies, however, will inevitably affect the evolution of the new countries' balances of payments and make it difficult, at times, to preserve the full stability and convertibility of their currencies into one another and into the major world currencies. It has been possible in some cases, and it may still be possible in others, to ward off these dangers through contractual arrangements for monetary unions, involving the coordination of national monetary policies under the aegis of joint, federated monetary authorities and institutions. Such arrangements undoubtedly strengthen greatly the efficacy of monetary policy and its ability to promote agreed economic objectives, such as the maintenance of price stability, high rates of economic activity and development, etc. They also presuppose, however, full and continuous agreement on such objectives and on the means necessary to achieve them, and require in effect a merging of the national monetary sovereignties of the participating members.

(2) The 55 countries and territories of Africa may be classified, as of today, in seven major groups: the former French, British, and Belgian areas, the Spanish peseta and Portuguese escudo areas, the South African rand area, and the countries with a longer tradition of national monetary independence.

I. *The Former French Area* includes eighteen countries and two territories, but only ten separate currencies, of which four are closely linked to the French franc through the so-called CFA (*Communauté Financière Africaine*) arrangements.

A. *The* CFA *Franc Zone* encompasses twelve countries and two territories, with four separate currencies, with the same name (CFA franc) and exchange valuation (CFAF = 0.02 French franc = 0.00405099 U.S. dollar). Their free interconvertibility into French francs is guaranteed by an overdraft on the French Treasury, made possible through the acceptance of common rules and joint authorities and institutions regarding the issue of the CFA currencies.

    1. The *Banque Centrale des Etats de l'Afrique de l'Ouest* is entrusted with the issue of a CFA franc which circulates as legal tender in seven countries: Dahomey, the Ivory Coast, Mauritania, Niger, Senegal, Togo, and Upper Volta.

    2. The *Banque Centrale de l'Afrique Equatoriale et du Cameroun* issues the CFA franc in circulation in five other countries: Chad, the Central African Republic, the Congo (Brazzaville), Gabon, and Cameroun.

    3. The *Institut d'Emission Malgache* issues the currency of Madagascar, and replaces the *Banque de Madagascar et des Comores,* whose currency circulates in the Comoro islands.

    4. The currency of the island of Réunion is issued by the *Institut d'Emission des Départements d'Outre-Mer.*

B. *Five other countries* have adopted separate national currencies since independence. Four of them, however, maintain close financial links with France, and belong to the French Franc Zone:

    1. Algeria, whose franc is at par with the French franc;

    2. Mali: Mali franc (= CFA franc);

    3. Morocco: Dirham (= 0.197609 U.S. dollar);

    4. Tunisia: Dinar (= 2.38 U.S. dollar);

    5. Guinea, which has left the French Franc Zone: Guinea franc (= CFA franc).

C. *The Djibouti franc* (= 0.00466435 U.S. dollar) circulates in French Somaliland, but is not part of the French Zone, although Djibouti is a French territory, closely linked with France itself.

II. *The Former British Area* includes eight fully independent coun-

tries and six territories, with currencies still more or less closely linked
with the pound sterling.

A. Nine are grouped under two separate *currency boards* and one
Central Bank, ensuring full convertibility into sterling of the
three currencies issued by them, but this situation is likely to
evolve rapidly toward the creation of independent national or
federated—at least in East Africa—monetary systems.

1. The *East African Shilling* (= U.K. shilling = 0.14 U.S.
dollar) circulates in Kenya, Uganda, Tanganyika, and
Zanzibar (also in Aden).

2. The *Central African Pound* (= pound sterling = 2.80
U.S. dollar) circulates in Northern Rhodesia, Southern
Rhodesia, and Nyasaland.

3. The *West African Pound* (= pound sterling = 2.80 U.S.
dollar) circulates in Sierra Leone and Gambia.

B. *Four other separate currencies* circulate in the rest of the former
sterling area:

1. Three of them, the *Ghanaian, Nigerian, and Libyan*
pounds, are at par with sterling.

2. A *rupee* (= 0.21 U.S. dollar) circulates in Mauritius and
the Seychelles islands.

III. *The Former Belgian Franc Area* now includes two separate currencies:

1. The Congo franc in the Congo (Leopoldville) (with a
buying rate of 0.0066667 U.S. dollar and a selling rate
of 0.0055556 U. S. dollar).

2. The franc of the Rwanda-Burundi monetary union (nom-
inally at par with the Belgian franc = 0.02 U.S. dollar).

IV. *The Spanish Peseta* (= 0.0166667 U.S. dollar) circulates in the
Spanish Sahara and the Spanish Guinea colonies.

V. *The Portuguese Escudo Area* includes an Angolan and a Mozam-
bique escudo, while the Portuguese escudo itself circulates in the other
four "overseas provinces" of Cabinda, Portuguese Guinea, Cap Verde
and Sao Tome, and Principe islands. The escudo is valued at about
0.0348 U.S. dollar.

VI. *The South African Rand* (= 1.40 U.S. dollar) circulates in
South Africa, South West Africa, Basutoland, Swaziland, and Be-
chuanaland.

VII. There remain five other independent countries, with separate
currency units:

1. The Egyptian pound ($=2.87156$ U.S. dollar) in the United Arab Republic;
2. The Sudanese pound ($=2.87156$ U.S. dollar) in the Sudan;
3. The Ethiopian dollar ($=0.40$ U.S. dollar) in Ethiopia;
4. The Somalo ($=0.14$ U.S. dollar) in Somalia;
5. Liberia actually uses as its basic currency the U.S. dollar itself, but circulates also national Liberian coins and will shortly issue Liberian currency notes.

2. Unanimity in Tangier and Discord in Tokyo

Initiatives looking toward the development of an African Payments and Clearing Union did not originate from outside experts. They emerged from the Africans themselves, during the March 1963 meeting of the Economic Commission for Africa and the first Summit Conference of the Heads of States, a few months later at Addis Ababa.

The two resolutions unanimously adopted at such a high political level were unavoidably couched in very broad terms, and expressed a deeply-felt aspiration rather than any concrete and operational plan for action. They called for the meeting of a commission of economic experts to examine their possible implementation and submit their findings to Member States.

Such a commission assembled in Tangier in January 1964 and substantially endorsed with a rare unanimity the proposals which I had developed, at the request of ECA, in a draft report submitted to the commission.

These proposals were admittedly very modest in their initial ambitions, and advised a progressive, but immediately operational, approach toward the ultimate goals of African monetary cooperation and integration.

They aimed, first of all, at arresting the frightening process of monetary disintegration, restrictions and bilateralism that was rapidly sweeping the continent. By December 1963, Africa and the adjacent islands counted no less than three scores of political or administrative entities, of which thirty-five "sovereign states," with thirty-three distinct currencies. Decisions already adopted by some of the newly independent states promise to enlarge to at least thirty-eight the number of African currencies in use this year (1965). Bilateral agree-

Published in German in *Internationales Afrika Forum* (Munich, March 1965).

ments, of varying scope and effectiveness, are also mushrooming in alarming proportions and creating further distortions and rigidities in the African trade and payments system.

First things must come first. I found it difficult to believe that this divisive process, whose roots are political as well as economic, could be totally reversed overnight by any grandiose payment scheme encompassing the whole of Africa, and requiring firm and long-term credit and institutional commitments among desperately poor countries, whose mutual trade and economic interdependence are still, in most cases, next to negligible. I envisaged therefore a progressive approach, based on:

(1) a determined attempt to preserve and consolidate remaining subcontinental monetary and economic unions, to develop mutual clearing and credit arrangements among their members, and to increase their independence from former colonial bonds and influences without weakening useful trade and credit links with their main export outlets and sources of capital outside Africa;

(2) the immediate establishment of cooperative arrangements for monetary and economic research and its diffusion among members, the training of monetary and banking personnel, the interchange of information and experience among responsible officials, etc., with the active assistance and cooperation of the International Monetary Fund;

(3) the immediate creation of a Clearing and Payments Union for the exchange or compensation, on a voluntary basis, of any convertible currencies or bilateral claims and debts arising from members' international settlements, both inside and outside Africa;

(4) the immediate drawing up of an African Monetary Charter and establishment of an African Monetary Council, to guide the above activities and ensure their compatibility with the ultimate goals of increasing closer monetary cooperation and integration, on as wide a basis as possible, among all African states willing to participate in such arrangements;

(5) the latter goals would then be implemented, in a gradual manner, but as rapidly as possible, through the negotiation of interim credit commitments and mutual assistance pacts among the various African states and Monetary Unions, up to and including any geographical extension and/or ultimate mergers of the latter which time proved economically desirable and politically feasible.

These proposals were debated and scrutinized at length by the Committee of Experts which assembled in Tangier in January 1964.

This led to a useful clarification of the most realistic timing of future negotiations on these various points, and of the concrete steps that should be taken to implement them and increase the flow of information necessary for their guidance.

What was truly extraordinary, however, and really stunning to all participants, was the degree of frankness and good will which marked these discussions among delegates from countries with widely divergent viewpoints on the problems involved. The final and *unanimous* adoption of a lucid, forceful, and operational report certainly came as a total surprise and most heartening encouragement to all of us.[1]

The Economic Commission for Africa seems to have been equally surprised at receiving so speedily, at its sixth session, in February 1964, a report which had not been expected to be completed before its seventh session. It nevertheless endorsed, unanimously also, a broad-ranging resolution calling, among other things, for a first meeting, before the end of the year, of the African monetary authorities, to consider the documentation and suggestions already assembled, and further information and studies that would still be prepared in the meantime.

The meeting did take place in fact, on the occasion of the annual gathering of the IMF and IBRD in Tokyo, last September, and found itself rather suddenly confronted with new, and ambitious, proposals of the ECA Secretariat for a full-fledged Payments Union, to be set up along the lines of the defunct European Payments Union. These proposals were incorporated in a carefully written document, remarkable for the ingenuity and imagination with which it attempted to adapt to totally different problems and circumstances the complex structure of the EPU system. This inevitably entailed, however, additional and baffling complexities which could hardly be fully digested and agreed upon in the short time available to the delegates.

While in full sympathy with the hopes of the Secretariat to accelerate the drive for African unity in monetary affairs, I very much feared the divisive political, and even emotional, reactions which such a document might elicit from unprepared delegates, with deeply divergent viewpoints and interests regarding the attractiveness of such extensive credit commitments and administrative machinery.

---

1. See *Report of the Expert Group on an African Payments Union*, U.N. Document E/CN.14/262, February 4, 1964; and "Utilité et Possibilité d'une Union Africaine des Paiements," *Banque Centrale des Etats de l'Afrique de l'Ouest*, No. 106, May 1964.

In the event, the actual outcome exceeded my most pessimistic expectations. According to the meager reports that filtered to the outside world, the debate began, proceeded, and ended in complete confusion and bitter opposition between warring factions, and was even unable either to reveal or to conceal utter failure through the innocuous "agreed" press communiqué, usual in such cases.

This is a sad ending for the Africans as well as for their friends abroad. They can only hope that it will not be really THE END, but a challenge that will spur renewed and more realistic efforts to implement, at long last, the resolutions of the 1963 ECA session and of the Summit Conference of the Independent African States.

Conclusion:

See Introduction.

Appendix

1. A SIMPLIFIED SCHEME FOR THE INTEGRATION OF MONETARY AND INCOME ANALYSIS: CREDIT, MONEY, PRODUCTION, PRICES AND BALANCES OF PAYMENTS IN OEEC COUNTRIES, 1948–56

I. Purposes

The main purpose of this study is to provide a systematic analysis of money and credit developments for the OEEC countries, comparable from year to year and from country to country, and fully integrated with other OEEC estimates of national product and expenditure. The system will also yield, as a byproduct, broad and comparable estimates of balances of payments and net international monetary reserves.

Needless to say, such statistical estimates will require careful interpretation in the light of a more detailed knowledge of each country's problems and policies. They should, nevertheless, stimulate a more systematic and comparable presentation of OEEC studies of individual member countries, particularly with relation to external balance and internal financial stability. They may also serve as background for the discussion of financial assistance to member countries and of the recourse to escape clauses from liberalization commitments.

Sections II and III below will be primarily of interest to the statisticians charged with the formulation of the estimates themselves, and may be skipped over rapidly by other readers. Section IV indicates some of the limitations flowing from the statistical sources and methods used. Section V discusses briefly the theoretical background and implications of the method used, and its relevance to policy analysis. Section VI summarizes the main results of the application of the method to OEEC data for the period 1948–56. Finally, Section VII extends the analysis to a review of comparative price and exchange-rate changes over the same period.

Prepared for the OEEC in February 1958. The suggested study was published by the OEEC in 1960 under the title, *Statistics of Sources and Uses of Finance, 1948–58*. An earlier and briefer version of the present paper was published in the Proceedings of the *Fifth Meeting of Technicians of Central Banks of the American Continent, 4* (Bogotá, Colombia, Banco de la República, 1957), 293–311, with a Spanish translation in the same volume, pp. 313–32 and in *Estadística* (Washington, D.C., December 1958), pp. 532–46. This statistical presentation was later adopted for regular use and publication by the Central Banks of Honduras and Peru and by CEMLA for its annual review of *Aspectos Monetarios de las Economías Latinoamericanas*.

II. Brief Description of Method

Two sets of estimates (Income Analysis and Monetary Analysis) are presented for each country. They are shown first in value terms, measured in millions (or billions) of national currency units (Table 1).[1] To facilitate intertemporal and intercountry comparison, the income estimates are next expressed in per cent of the previous year's gross national product at market prices, and the monetary estimates in per cent of money supply at the end of the previous year (Tables 1a).

Income Analysis

The excess of *Expenditure* during the current year (item 2) for consumption and domestic capital formation over the previous year's *Gross National Product* (item 1) is shown as an *Expansionary Impulse* (item 9), absorbed by:

A. *Production Growth* (item 10), i.e. the increase in GNP measured at the previous year's prices;

B. *Excess Demand* (item 11), reflected in:

    1. the nominal rise in GNP values, resulting from the increase in the current year's prices over the previous year's prices (item 12);

    2. the excess (item 13) of imports of goods and services (item 27) over goods and services exports (item 28).

Monetary Analysis

The second set of estimates (Monetary Analysis) applies a parallel analysis to the financing of this Expansionary Impulse, and to the ways in which the purchasing power thus created or released was absorbed by production growth, price increases, and external deficits.

Total Monetary Financing (item 22) parallels in this analysis the concept of Expansionary Impulse (item 9) used in income analysis. For the economy as a whole, intersector lending cannot be the source of such financing since it can only reshuffle money balances among the different sectors of the same national economy. The only possible sources of financing are:

I. *Current Credit Monetization* (item 14), i.e. the injection of new money into the economy by:

    A. *External Credit Monetization* (item 18), i.e. net foreign disinvestment—grants or borrowings from abroad, or liquidation of

---

1. Reference numbers have been changed to correspond to those in the tables subsequently published in *Statistics of Sources and Uses of Finance, 1948–58* (Paris, OEEC, 1960) which supersede the few tables initially attached to this paper and which are omitted here

assets previously accumulated abroad—by the nonbank sectors of the economy;

B. *Internal Credit Monetization* by the national monetary and banking system (item 15), i.e. that portion of the expansion in the system's internal assets, or gross lending (item 16), whose counterpart appears in an increase of the money supply, or in a decrease of the system's net gold and foreign assets, rather than in an expansion of its internal liabilities other than money (minus item 17).

II. *Relative Contraction of Monetary Liquidity* (item 19), i.e. the activation of money supply through the increase in the velocity of money or, in other words, through a reduction in the ratio of money to GNP. This may be measured by subtracting from the previous year's money supply the money supply corresponding to the current ratio of money to GNP applied to the previous year's GNP.[2]

The total amount of money currently created by credit monetization (item 14) or released by liquidity changes (item 19) does not determine the final change in the country's money supply. A certain volume of money may also be created by the excess of current exports of goods and services over goods and services imports (*minus* item 26) or, on the contrary, absorbed by the excess of current imports over exports (item 26). In the first case, net foreign exchange receipts are surrendered to the banks against an equivalent amount of local currency. In the second case, national currency is surrendered to the banking system in payment for the foreign exchange needed for settlements abroad. The destruction (or creation) of money by external deficits (or surpluses) is thus identical to these external deficits (or surpluses) themselves, as recorded in item 13 of Income Analysis.

The internal absorption of money by production growth and price increases, on the other hand, is not equal to the total impact of these upon expenditure, but only to a proportion of such impact corresponding to the current monetary ratio. Items 23 and 25 are thus equal to items 10 and 12, *multiplied* by this monetary ratio.

The sum of items 25 and 26 measures the amount of money absorbed by "excess demand" (item 24) and is closely related to item 11 in income analysis. Excess imports (item 13 = item 26) are common to both item 11 and item 27, but the monetary impact of price increases on money supply is only a fraction of their impact upon current expenditure. The same remark applies to the impact of production growth on money sup-

---

2. The Tables of *Sources and Uses of Finance* show instead the contraction of liquidity as the shortfall of the *actual* increase in money circulation (item 21) in relation to the increase which would have been required if the ratio of money to GNP had been maintained at the previous year's level (item 20).

ply (item 23) and on expenditure (item 10) and similarly explains the difference between total monetary financing (item 22) and the expansionary impulse (item 9).

Finally, items 30, 32, and 33 indicate how the external deficit on goods and services was financed. The foreign exchange used in settlements abroad must indeed have been derived: (a) either from net unilateral transfers from abroad (item 30), primarily composed of American grants in aid and private donations; or (b) from other net foreign disinvestment—borrowings or liquidation of assets abroad—by the nonbank sectors of the economy (item 32); or (c) from a decline in the net gold and foreign-exchange assets of the banking system (item 33).[3]

(It should be noted that it is precisely the sum of items 30 and 32 which make up the external credit monetization recorded under item 18 above. If we wished to attach a normative—but narrower—connotation to the concept of "excess demand," we might exclude from it the excess expenditure financed by foreign grants and by the net borrowings or disinvestments abroad of the nonbank sectors of the economy. The term "excess demand" would then be redefined to designate only the portion of expenditure absorbed by price increases and declines in bank reserves. Item 18 would then be deducted from items 9, 14, and 22, and items 30 and 32 similarly deducted from items 22, 24, and 26.)

III. Sources

All the present tables[4] except those for Belgium and the Netherlands are derived from published and readily available international sources.

National Account Estimates

All the income analysis estimates are taken or calculated from the national accounts estimates of OEEC published in the 1957 edition of *Statistics of National Product and Expenditure, 1938 and 1947 to 1955,* brought up to date and revised in current OEEC *General Statistics.* The estimates of production growth are, of course, derived from the estimates of national product and expenditure at constant prices, but recalculated in terms of the previous year's prices rather than at 1954 prices. The impact of price increases is measured by comparing the actual value of the GNP of the current year at current prices with its calculated value at the previous year's prices.

Monetary Estimates

The estimates of money supply are simply taken from the *International Financial Statistics* of the International Monetary Fund, and the monetary

3. The sum of items 32 and 33 is shown in *Sources and Uses of Finance* as the decrease in the country's net foreign assets (item 31).
4. Omitted here; see *Sources and Uses of Finance.*

ratio is derived from these and from the OEEC estimates of gross national product at current market prices (item 1).

International Financial Statistics is also the source of the other estimates needed to complete the monetary analysis. Unilateral transfers from abroad (item 30) are the sum of private and official donations in the IFS balance of payments statistics. The "monetary surveys" of IFS are used to estimate: (a) changes in the net foreign assets of the monetary and banking system (item 33); (b) changes in the banks' gross domestic lending (item 16); and (c) changes in the banks' internal liabilities other than money (item 17).

Finally, changes in the net foreign asset position of the nonbank sectors of the economy (item 32) are obtained residually by deducting from excess imports (item 13) the amounts financed by unilateral transfers (item 30) and by changes in net bank reserves (item 33). The sum of items 30 and 32 gives us the total net foreign disinvestment—or external credit monetization—of the nonbank sectors of the economy (item 18).

The estimates thus derived are probably far from satisfactory in some cases, and should be carefully checked and revised with the help of published or unpublished national data. Their main weakness lies in the fact that the IFS monetary surveys do not always isolate fully foreign from domestic assets and liabilities. This is particularly the case for foreign liabilities, some of which may be included together with domestic assets under "unclassified liabilities."

While this defect should, and can easily, be remedied, it may not be as fatal to the analysis as might seem at first. The distinction between external (nonbank) and internal (banks) credit monetization is indeed affected in some cases by procedural or accounting differences between foreign disinvestment by banks and by nonbanks. An IMF loan, for instance, may be reflected either in item 18 or in item 15, depending on whether the loan is made directly to the Treasury or channelled through the Central Bank. The distinction, in any case, is irrelevant for the measurement of current credit monetization (item 14) which groups together internal and external credit monetization and is the most significant for monetary analysis.

A Shortcut Method

This observation leads to another remark which will provide the analyst with either a method to crosscheck his results or, at least, with a shortcut method of arriving at the broad aggregates most useful for economic analysis.

Current credit monetization (item 14) may indeed be derived as a residual item from the estimates of total monetary financing (item 22) and liquidity changes (item 19) for which the only original estimates required are money supply and national account estimates of GNP and expenditure at current and constant prices. Internal monetization (item 15) may then be obtained also as a residual from total current monetization (item 14) and external monetization (item 18).

In the accompanying tables, these shortcut methods have been used both to check the estimates derived from the IFS monetary surveys and to complete the tables for the years previous to the publication of these surveys. The few, and usually minor, discrepancies revealed in this manner are noted in the tables.

Belgian and Netherlands Estimates

The monetary estimates for Belgium and the Netherlands are the only ones for which national sources have been used in preference to IFS sources, after 1949 for the Netherlands, and after 1950 for Belgium. We hope to follow the same procedure for other countries, but began with Belgium and the Netherlands for the following reasons. First, the central banks of both countries already publish estimates which lend themselves particularly to—and indeed have inspired in part—the development of the analysis presented here. Second, the IFS monetary survey for the Netherlands has been revised considerably for recent years, but does not provide comparable information for the years previous to 1954. Finally, the analysis carried out for Belgium on the basis of the IFS monetary surveys reveals particularly large discrepancies with the estimates arrived at by the residual method described above, and the IFS notes that "the data in the Monetary Survey cannot be reconciled with those reported in the other sections." Full reconciliation could be effected, on the other hand, by using estimates regularly published in the *Bulletin d'Information et de Documentation* of the National Bank of Belgium.

IV. Qualifications and Warnings

First of all, the present estimates are obviously subject to the same margins of error as the original estimates from which they are derived.

We should note, second, the element of arbitrariness involved in the strategic role given here to the concept of money supply and in its isolation from the other domestic liabilities of the monetary and banking system. Some of these—time and saving deposits, for instance—are far more "liquid" than others—such as the banks' capital and surplus—and may indeed be closer, in that respect, to money than to the latter. The country analyst will certainly want to watch carefully any large fluctuations in item 17 of the tables, and to break it down into various components in order to be able to diagnose any significant build-up of "quasi-money" or "secondary liquidities" whose later monetization by their holders would lie outside the control of the monetary and banking authorities. The Bank of the Netherlands has paid particular attention to this problem, in view of its incidence on the possible emergence of "latent" inflationary forces, and included among "secondary liquid resources" some official securities as well as time and foreign currency deposits.

At the other extreme, the Bank of Italy stresses currency notes rather than money supply in its analysis. One reason for this emphasis may be to stress the responsibilities of the central bank rather than of the banking system as a whole in the development of monetary disequilibria. Another may be that currency circulation may be more closely related to price developments and may constitute a first approximation of money supply in the hands of households, as distinct from deposit money used primarily by business firms.

The choice of "money supply" in our analysis is dictated primarily by the desire to present comparable data for all OEEC countries. This precludes any recourse to an enlarged concept of liquidity, as the definition of quasi-money necessarily differs widely from country to country. The "monetary ratio" based on the traditional concept of money supply also seems to show a greater degree of stability over time than a "liquidity ratio" grouping near-money together with money supply. In some countries, however, the use of the narrower concept of "currency circulation" may well deserve more careful consideration than it generally receives today.

One may note, in passing, that the enlargement of the liquidity concept in monetary analysis has been the subject of considerable controversy in the Netherlands. Its merit is to draw attention, at an early stage, to the development of an inflationary potential, but it may be argued also that the latter should still be distinguished from the development of the more active and immediately inflationary forms of liquidity constituted by currency and demand deposits.

We should finally mention a definite shortcoming of our method which could be eliminated but only at a disproportionate cost in terms of added complexities in calculations and presentation. The "monetary ratio" used in the tables relates money supply *at the end of the year* with the GNP *for the year as a whole*. This is necessary for a correct and precise aggregation of the various sources of monetary financing, and the reconciliation of this aggregate with the ways in which it is absorbed by production growth, price increases, and external deficits. One might, alternatively, calculate the monetary ratio on the basis of annual averages of money supply, and introduce a corrective factor for its reconciliation with the other data. The gains which might be expected from this alternative method, however, would hardly be worthwhile, particularly in view of the other accidental, and practically unaccountable, sources of fluctuations in the monetary ratio. (See below, pp. 557–59.)

V. Theoretical Considerations and Policy Implications

The Algebraic Model

The two statistical models discussed in this paper are nothing more than a series of balance equations, which may be written very simply as follows:[5]

(1). An over-all economic equation:

$$X - Y_0 = (y - y_0)p_0 + (p - p_0)y + D, \text{ or}$$

item 2 − item 1 = item 10 + item 12 + item 13, meaning that the excess of expenditures during the current year over the previous year's GNP must be reflected in production growth,[6] price rises,[6] and the external deficit on goods and services (any of these quantities may, of course, be negative, but the algebraic identity above must be verified in any case).

(2). An over-all financing equation:

$$F = F^i + F^e + F^m = \mu_0(y - y_0)p_0 + \mu_0(p - p_0)y + D, \text{ or}$$

item 22 = item 15 + item 18 + item 19 = item 23 + item 25 + item 26, meaning that total monetary financing (or the sum of internal credit monetization, external credit monetization and liquidity financing) is absorbed by the impact of production growth, price rises, and the external deficit upon the country's holdings of money.

(3). An external financing equation:

$$D = F^e - N^e, \text{ or}$$

5. Capital letters represent yearly flows (X = total expenditure, Y = GNP at market prices, and D = external deficit on goods and services) or stock changes (M, A, L, and N representing respectively annual changes in the money stock, and in banks' gross assets, gross liabilities, and net assets; the same letters preceded by Σ designate stock values at the end of the current year), all valued at current prices. Small y's refer to GNP measured at *constant* prices, and p_0 to the GNP price deflator of the preceding year, i.e. to the ratio of the preceding year's prices to the current year's prices. The Greek letter μ indicates the monetary ratio of the current year $\frac{\Sigma M}{Y}$ and μ_0 that of the preceding year. Finally, superscript i and e designate the internal and external components of the variable.

6. For this identity to hold, production growth ($y - y_0$) must be valued at previous year's prices (p_0) and price increases ($p - p_0$) applied to current year's production, or *vice versa*. A more correct procedure would, of course, use previous year's weights both for production growth and price rises, and introduce a third, neutral term reflecting the impact of price changes upon production changes. The equation would then read:

$$X - Y_0 = (y - y_0)p_0 + (p - p_0)y_0 + (y - y_0)(p - p_0) + D$$

The resulting gain in precision, however, would be negligible in most cases and would hardly justify the added complexities in calculation, and particularly in the presentation of the results.

item 29 = (item 30 + item 32) + item 33, meaning that the external deficit on goods and services must be financed externally by the net foreign disinvestment of the nonbank sectors of the economy, plus the decline in the banks' net gold and foreign assets.

Let us note the exact meaning of the financing concepts used:

$$F = F^e + F^i + F^m, \text{ where}$$

(1) F^e = item 18 = item 30 + item 32 = unilateral transfers from abroad, *plus* the decline in the net foreign assets position of the nonbank sectors of the economy;

(2) F^i = item 15 = item 16 + item 17 = $A^i - (L^i - M)$, where A^i represents the increase in the gross internal assets of banks and $L^i - M$ the increase in their internal liabilities other than money;

(3) F^m = item 19 = item 20 - item 21 = $M_0 - \mu Y_0$, where M_0 represents money supply at the end of the preceding year, μ the ratio of money supply at the end of the current year to the current year's GNP, and Y_0 the previous year's GNP.

Simpler Versions of Monetary Analysis

The total assets of any banking system (ΣA) must always be equal to its total liabilities (ΣL), and annual increases in gross assets (A) equal to annual increases in gross liabilities (L). A number of statistical models of monetary analysis (in Latin American countries, for instance, and in France) have long analyzed on this basis any increase of money supply into increases of internal origin and of external origin. These models are based on the following distinctions:

(1) all changes in assets and liabilities are classified into internal and external changes in assets (A^i and A^e respectively), and internal and external changes in liabilities (L^i and L^e);

(2) changes in internal liabilities are classified into changes in money (M) and changes in internal liabilities other than money ($L^i - M$).

Using the notation N^e to designate an increase in *net* external assets ($A^e - L^e$), and N^i to designate an increase in *net* internal assets ($A^i - L^i$), we note that any change in net internal assets must be offset by an opposite, but equal, change in net external assets:

$$N^i = A^i - L^i = -N^e, \text{ or}$$
$$A^i - (L^i - M) - M = -N^e, \text{ or}$$
$$-A^i + (L^i - M) + M = N^e, \text{ or}$$
$$M = A^i - (L^i - M) + N^e$$

But $A^i - (L^i - M)$, i.e. the excess of gross internal lending over the increase in liabilities other than money has been defined above as "internal credit monetization" (F^i). We may thus rewrite our last equation:

$$M = F^i + N^e$$

and analyze any change in money supply into a change of internal origin (internal credit monetization) and a change of external origin (net purchases of external assets by the banking system). We may, alternatively, analyze the impact of credit monetization by banks into an increase in money and a decline in the banks' net reserves:

$$F^i = M - N^e$$

Or we may, finally, explain a decline in the banks' net reserves by the excess of credit monetization over the amount of money which the public is willing to add to its previous money holdings:

$$-N^e = F^i - M$$

Relation of the Two Models

The statistical scheme presented in this paper merely relates these simpler versions of monetary analysis to production and price changes and to the balance of payments on goods and services (or excess of over-all expenditure over GNP).

For this purpose, two links are necessary. The first is the concept of external credit monetization by the nonbank sectors of the economy (F^e), necessary to bridge the gap between the change in the net external assets of banks (N^e) and the external deficit on goods and services (D). While the decline in the net external assets of banks is equal to the excess of internal credit monetization by banks over the increase of money supply ($-N^e = F^i - M$), the external deficit on goods and services is the excess of current internal *and* external credit monetization over the increase in money supply ($D = F^i + F^e - M$).

The second link that must be introduced is the impact of changes in the monetary ratio (μ), and is necessary to relate money changes to production growth and price increases. An actual increase in expenditure may indeed be financed by drawing on existing cash holdings as well as by net borrowings abroad and from the banks. The importance of this source of financing will be seen later (see Section VI) to have been particularly large in the postwar years for the countries in which "latent" or "repressed" inflation had been previously built up through effective price controls and rationing.

Brief Considerations on the Role of Liquidity in the Analysis

We have seen above that current increase in money supply may be equated either to current credit monetization by banks *plus* the increase (or *minus* the decrease) in their net foreign assets, or to current monetization, internal and external, plus the country's surplus—or *minus* its deficit —on goods and services:

$$M = F^i + N^e = F^i + F^e - D$$

There remains to relate money supply changes to changes in prices and production. If people retained a fixed and unchanging ratio of cash to GNP (measured at current prices), any increase in money supply could be broken down into:

(1) a portion related to production increases and equal to $\mu_0 (y - y_0)p_0$ (item 23 in the tables); and

(2) a portion related to the impact of price increases upon GNP, and equal to $\mu_0(p - p_0)y$ (item 25 in the tables).

This is not the case, however, and changes in the monetary ratio of cash to GNP must consequently be brought into the analysis. This is done in the tables by including in the concept of total monetary financing (item 22) the amounts of money released for expenditures by the current contraction of monetary liquidity (item 19). Conversely, any increase in the monetary ratio must lead to a corresponding deduction from current credit monetization in order to arrive at the concept of total monetary financing, since the new money created is, to that extent, sterilized for the time being and exercises no impact on the level of expenditures.

An enforced increase of the monetary ratio resulted in wartime and early postwar years from the policies of "latent" or "repressed" inflation pursued in most countries during that time. The later relaxation of price controls and rationing led to predictable declines in the monetary ratio whose impact must be added to that of current credit monetization as a source of financing for production growth, price increases, and balance-of-payments deficits.

The monetary ratio is also subject to other, fairly predictable, fluctuations. It shows a long-run growth trend in countries in the course of economic development (see item 35 in the tables for Turkey, Portugal, and Italy) as a more comfortable level of cash balances is one of the conveniences which people will wish and be able to afford with an increase in per capita incomes. Economic development may, to this extent, be financed in part from current credit monetization without inflationary incidence on prices and the balance of payments. On the other hand, the monetary ratio being much lower in the underdeveloped countries than in the developed countries, a smaller portion of current monetization will be absorbed by addition to cash balances in the first countries than in the latter. Any given amount of credit monetization not absorbed by production growth will then tend to have a much larger inflationary impact in underdeveloped than in developed countries.

The monetary ratio also fluctuates in a predictable direction in the course of the business cycle. It is highest in years of low economic activity and employment, as in the 1930s, and tends to contract in boom years such as 1956. Changes in the monetary ratio may also tend to defeat anticyclical measures designed to contract or expand current credit monetization through changes in interest rates or quantitative credit controls.

Outside of growth trends and cyclical fluctuations, changes in the monetary ratio may help us diagnose a situation of monetary disequilibrium. As noted above, an abnormally high monetary ratio is usually associated with a state of "latent" inflation. Conversely, an abnormally low monetary ratio will often accompany the opposite situation of rapid, open inflation creating widespread distrust toward the national currency. The current impact of current credit monetization upon price rises and foreign deficits will be slowed down in the first case, and accelerated in the latter. The later return to monetary equilibrium and a more normal monetary ratio will, on the other hand, create added difficulties for the countries which have to re-absorb latent inflation as well as to arrest current inflation, but it will facilitate the task of the countries in which a reconstitution of normal cash balances will permit either a noninflationary absorption of current monetization or a quick recovery of foreign exchange reserves, or both. (The so-called "Poincaré miracle" of France in 1926–28 illustrates this point even more dramatically than the progress toward monetary equilibrium in the same country in 1949–50 and in 1953–55.)[7]

Finally, other and less predictable variations in the monetary ratio may be due to certain lags in economic adaptations, to institutional changes in banking and payments habits, to significant shifts in income distribution—between firms and households, or among different income groups—to statistical errors in GNP estimates, etc. Most of these changes, however, operate relatively slowly and the monetary ratio normally shows a high degree of stability from year to year, particularly in developed countries which other criteria would lead us to regard as close to monetary equilibrium. Among the OEEC countries, for instance, Germany, Italy, the Netherlands, and Switzerland show a maximum divergency of 2 per cent or less from average over the period 1953–55. This is a far smaller order of magnitude than that of observed variations in other coefficients often used in income analysis, such as the propensity to save or to import, etc.

This suggests a possible alternative method of handling liquidity changes in the analysis. A "normal" monetary ratio may be guessed at on the basis of past experience, "excess liquidity at the beginning of the current year" substituted for "contraction of monetary liquidity" (item 19) as a factor

7. The same phenomenon was repeated under de Gaulle, the monetary ratio rising from about 0.31 in 1958 to more than 0.38 in 1963, in spite of cyclical influences running in the contrary direction.

of monetary financing, and "excess liquidity at the end of the current year" added to Production Growth and Excess Demand as a factor of absorption of monetary financing.

Income and Monetary Analyses

The income and monetary analyses presented in the accompanying tables summarize different, but closely related, facets of the same reality. The monetary analyst may be prone to assign a dominant role to the concept of monetary financing and to underestimate possible conflicts between the use of monetary financing as a policy instrument and the simultaneous pursuit of other targets of economic policy. The income analyst, on the other hand, centers his attention on consumption, production, investment, imports, and exports as the key factors in the situation. He often ignores the "boundary conditions" imposed upon it by the limitation of the external means of settlement necessary to finance foreign deficits, and neglects the possible use of monetary financing as an instrument of policy. Current credit monetization and liquidity changes are treated as "irrelevant variables" adjusting passively and automatically to the gap between production and expenditure. This may, of course, be correct if the monetary authorities remain completely supine, and make no attempt to influence economic development by resisting or compensating the inflationary or deflationary pressures arising from the behavior of certain economic sectors. The task of the monetary analyst, however, is precisely to bring into light the potentialities and limitations of the monetary weapon as a policy instrument and the possible consequences of alternative decisions in the monetary and credit fields.

Income analysis will be useful therefore in explaining the pressures—inflationary or deflationary—confronting the monetary authorities, while monetary analysis will help indicate the reactions of the monetary and credit systems to these pressures and the final impact of these reactions on economic developments.

Causality, Equilibrium, and Policy Analysis

The way in which statistical estimates are presented in the accompanying tables might suggest to the reader a direction of causality running from the top to the bottom items in the tables, i.e. from the Expansionary Impulse, or from Total Monetary Financing to production, price, and balance-of-payments adaptations. The unavoidable use of shortcut methods of exposition in various parts of this paper—and particularly in Section VI below—might reinforce that impression.

The system, nevertheless, is perfectly compatible with an opposite interpretation, explaining the Expansionary Impulse and the amount of Monetary Financing by pressures arising from production growth, price changes and balance-of-payments developments. All that it implies is the inevitability of adjustment between the top items and the bottom items of the tables. Only the economic context can help us determine to what extent the first moved in response to the latter, and the latter in response to the first.[8]

From a policy point of view, however, the elusive distinction between cause and effect will often be far less relevant than that between desirable policy *targets* and available policy *instruments*. Monetary and fiscal instruments may well, for instance, be the best available instruments to fight inflationary developments arising from sources totally unrelated to the credit and fiscal fields—a wage-price spiral, or an abnormal and temporary increase in foreign demand for scarce export products, for instance.

The monetary analysis presented here stresses the role of monetary financing as an instrument of economic policy. Three major qualifications need be stressed in this respect.

(1) The assignment of a "correct" value to this instrument constitutes a *necessary,* but not a *sufficient* condition for the simultaneous attainment of multiple policy targets, such as a maximum rate of production growth, internal price stability, and balance-of-payments equilibrium. Any excess of monetary financing over this "correct" value must inevitably give rise to over-all inflationary pressures reflected in price increases, or balance-of-payments deficits, or both. Any shortfall with respect to the "correct" value, on the other hand, will be accompanied by over-all deflationary pressures, reflected in price and/or production declines, and/or balance-of-payments surpluses. A "correct" value of monetary financing, however, will not ensure the achievement of all three policy objectives, as such financing may spill into price rises and/or balance-of-payments deficits rather than sustain the desired growth of production. Other policy instruments must therefore be used, in conjunction with monetary financing, in order to further the fulfilment of multiple policy targets.

(2) The choice of both targets and instruments of policy may be influenced by a great variety of considerations, and restricted in fact by certain "boundary conditions" or other considerations, of a less rigid character, such as the ease with which such policies may be implemented in a given environment. A few examples will clarify this point.

Strict external equilibrium on goods and services account may be both

8. Price rises may, for instance, be initiated by negotiated wage increases, underwritten by a monetary expansion prompted by a concern to avoid a decline in employment. They may, on the other hand, follow such an expansion and prompt later readjustments in wages. Similarly, a sharp deterioration of the balance of payments may, in some cases, be clearly traceable to unfavorable developments abroad and, in others, to inflationary developments at home. The timing of the changes in disaggregated national series—money stock, prices, and wages, for instance, or import prices, export prices, and domestic prices—international comparisons of price changes, etc. may help throw light on the problem.

undesirable and unnecessary, if financing is easily available, at moderate economic and political costs, to cover excess imports susceptible of accelerating the pace of economic reconstruction and development. On the other hand, a surplus on goods and services may become desirable or necessary if such financing is unavailable and the country needs or wishes to repay previous borrowings abroad, increase its foreign investments or reconstitute adequate levels of monetary reserves.

Full price stability may be very difficult to maintain—together with fixed exchange rates and an unchanged level of trade and exchange restrictions —if the existing price level does not correspond to competitive equilibrium with prices outside the country, or if the latter are currently moving sharply upward or downward. A more realistic price target, particularly for a small, open economy, may be to "keep in step" with international price developments.

Finally, a maximum rate of growth or of employment can hardly be defined with reference to physical capacity alone. Less than full physical capacity may be accepted as a satisfactory target in order to preserve some degree of flexibility and mobility in the economy and to reduce pressures for wage increases in excess of productivity growth.

(3) The amount of Total Monetary Financing is the sum of various components, all of which are not equally amenable to policy control by the monetary authorities. These may influence in various ways—through interest rate policy, for instance—but cannot fully determine the level of external credit monetization, the changes in monetary liquidity and the changes in bank liabilities other than money. This influence may be strengthened by measures designed to strengthen confidence in the currency, and to approximate a "normal" level of monetary and quasi-monetary liquidities. Yet, the effectiveness of monetary policy will probably have to depend, to a major degree, on the ability of the monetary authorities to use movements in "gross bank lending" as an offset to undesirable developments in the other components of total monetary financing. In an inflationary environment—characterized by an active demand for bank credit —the main requirement will be the assertion of a sufficient degree of control over the private banks' lending policies. In a deflationary environment, on the other hand, the willingness of the banks to lend may be thwarted by the dearth of demand by credit-worthy borrowers. In that case, the achievement of a desirable level of monetary financing may require that the state itself step in as a willing borrower and engage in deficit financing. Whether this is dubbed "monetary" or "fiscal" policy is irrelevant, since what is involved in any case is a joint decision by the Treasury and the banking authorities.

We may finally observe that such over-all "quantitative" fiscal and credit policies may be complemented by "selective" policies in both fields. The pattern of such selective policy instruments should be chosen in the light of income analysis—and particularly of the comparative evolution of consumption and investment expenditures—and of a breakdown by economic sectors of both income and monetary analysis. The global estimates presented in this paper should, therefore, be supplemented at a later stage by such a breakdown of the estimates among the major sectors of the economy.

VI. Brief Interpretation of Results

The accompanying tables are mainly designed to be used in the preparation of country studies, reviewing major economic and financial developments and policies since the war in each of the OEEC countries. Only a few comments will be offered here on the broad indications that may be derived from the estimates relating to monetary analysis. In order to facilitate their interpretation and comparison, the major aggregates arrived at are presented, in a highly simplified form, in the accompanying charts [omitted here].

The first column of the Charts refers to the *sources* of monetary financing. One curve represents total monetary financing (item 24 of Tables 1a), and the other current credit monetization (item 14). The difference between the two curves reflects the impact, positive or negative, of changes in liquidity (item 21).

The following columns refer to the *absorption* of monetary financing. The second column compares total monetary financing with excess imports of goods and services (item 28). The difference between the two curves thus represents the impact on money supply of internal production and price changes (sum of items 25 and 27). Finally, the third column compares the latter internal impact with the impact of price changes only (item 27). The difference between the two curves then shows the absorption of money supply by production growth (item 25).

Sources of Monetary Financing

Total monetary financing, for the period 1948–56 as a whole, was substantially lower—and sometimes negative—in Germany, Switzerland, Sweden, and Belgium than in the other countries. It was highest in Turkey, Austria, Norway, France, and Italy. The gradual abatement of inflationary forces in nearly all countries, but particularly in the latter, is reflected in the sharp declines of the early postwar years. The Korean inflationary spurt, the post-Korean downward readjustments and the renewed upward pressures accompanying the recent development of prosperity into boom are also noticeable for most countries.

There is a fair parallelism throughout between total monetary financing and current credit monetization. The difference between the two curves is accounted for by the drawing down or reconstitution of the ratio of cash balances to GNP.

The drawing down of cash balances is larger and more persistent in the Northern countries (the United Kingdom, Denmark, Norway, Sweden, and the Netherlands), particularly during the early postwar years. It reflects the gradual absorption—by production growth, price increases, and balance-of-payments deficits—of the previous latent inflation inherited from wartime and early postwar financing, rationing, and price controls. This source of monetary financing tends to taper off, as previously built liquid balances are absorbed during the Korean upsurge of prices, production, and foreign deficits. It tends to reappear, however, both within and outside the Northern group at the end of the period, reflecting the increase in the velocity of circulation, characteristic of the boom phase of the cycle.

The opposite movement—reconstitution of cash balances—follows the Einaudi reforms in Italy and characterizes Italian developments throughout, with a lag during the Korean crisis, made up in the following year. This long-run trend toward higher liquidity is typical of the transition from an underdeveloped to a developed economy with higher and better distributed income levels.

A substantial reconstitution of cash balances also follows the return of currency confidence in Austria, after the drastic curtailment of credit expansion in 1952–53.

The French monetary evolution is characterized by the alternation of hoarding and dishoarding waves, influenced by current developments in credit and prices. Immediate postwar dishoarding continued later than in Italy and was stopped only during the 1949–50 progress toward monetary stabilization. It reappeared during the Korean credit and price inflation, and was followed by a reconstitution of cash balances after the Pinay stabilization. Later data will probably show a re-emergence of currency flight in 1957 and a reverse trend in 1958. [This guess was confirmed indeed by later events.]

Liquidity movements are much milder throughout, as might be expected, in the countries closest to full monetary equilibrium: Belgium, Switzerland, and Germany.

Absorption of Monetary Financing

(1) A close correspondence is marked everywhere, and throughout the whole period excepting the Korean crisis, between total credit monetization and balance-of-payments deficits on goods and services. This reflects the open character of the European economies, and the quick spilling out of expansion or contraction of purchasing power into foreign deficits or surpluses, as well as into domestic price increases or decreases. External

deficits and surpluses, moreover, have a one to one impact upon money supply, while the impact of internal price or production movements upon money holdings is far smaller and depends on the current monetary ratio in each country.

The large balance-of-payments deficits of the early postwar years were, of course, made possible by the American aid which financed them. The counterpart of this aid is also included here in the estimates of credit monetization, and helps maintain an abnormally high level of "excess demand." The estimates of excess demand (item 27 in the tables) so defined should not, however, be given a normative connotation of "undesirable" inflation, since they include high levels of reconstruction and investment expenditures which American aid was precisely intended to stimulate and finance. In the current analysis for future years, it will probably be preferable to exclude unilateral transfers from the calculation of both credit monetization and external deficits.

(2) The discrepancy between total monetization and balance-of-payments deficits (in the second column of the charts) reflects internal adjustments, i.e. the impact on money supply of price rises and production growth. This combined impact is generally smaller and less volatile than the external impact of monetization on the balance of payments. It rarely exceeds 10 per cent a year, except in the immediate postwar years—when inflationary forces were particularly strong and their price impact reinforced by the activation of the latent inflationary fuel inherited from the previous years of rationing and price controls during the Korean crisis, and in a few countries where inflation was more obdurate.

These internal adaptations are broken down, in the third column of the charts, between price and production movements. Both are generally positive throughout. Production movements, reflected in the discrepancy between the two curves, are less volatile, of course, than price fluctuations, and subject to more definite physical limitations, expressing a full capacity ceiling. Price increases were largest in the early postwar years and during the Korean crisis. They tapered off substantially in the following period, but regained some impetus with the development of the European boom during the last two years.

The price curve shows a striking parallelism between fluctuations in the various countries. It reflects largely international movements, encompassing also the United States. The amplitude of the movements, however, varies from country to country depending on their terms of trade—whose influence was particularly marked for Sweden and Norway at the top of the Korean boom—and on the pace of domestic inflation. These international price discrepancies were one of the main factors influencing, although often with considerable delay, the extent of exchange-rate readjustments. This aspect of the problem will be examined in the next section of this paper.

VII. Monetary Financing and Cost Competitiveness as Explanatory Factors in Balance-of-Payments Fluctuations

Theoretical Considerations

In spite of the many criticisms that may be leveled against it, the theory of cost competitiveness (i.e. the purchasing power parity expressed in terms of GNP prices) retains considerable interest for the analysis of long-run fluctuations in balances of payments and exchange rates. In the analysis of short-run movements, however, the impact of cost competitiveness may be overshadowed by that of monetary financing, particularly in a world where trade and exchange controls and international assistance programs may interfere considerably with the classical mechanism of balance-of-payments adjustments. An integration of these long-run and short-run factors of analysis is attempted below, and will help us interpret the comparative evolution of prices, exchange rates, and balance of payments over the period 1948-56.

A. Cost Competitiveness

The theory of cost competitiveness tries essentially to define an "equilibrium exchange rate" by estimating the exchange-rate adjustment necessary to offset a divergent evolution of national prices and costs and to restore the same conditions of international competitiveness as those which prevailed in a base period in which equilibrium is supposed to have existed.

The main difficulties or insufficiencies of this theory result from:

(1) the difficulty of choosing a base period in which "equilibrium" was clearly realized;

(2) the difficulty of identifying a current position of equilibrium with the actual balance of payments, in view of:

(a) the compatibility of such equilibrium with "desirable" surpluses or deficits financed by "desirable" movements in monetary reserves and other capital accounts;

(b) the incidence on the current balance of payments of a country of other factors than cost competitiveness, such as (i) its own level of trade and exchange restrictions; (ii) trade and exchange restrictions abroad; (iii) the current state of overliquidity or of underliquidity in the country and abroad; (iv) the current development of inflationary or deflationary financing in the country and abroad; (v) changes in tastes and production capacity in the country and abroad; and (vi) other structural changes in the current balance of payments, such as may result from changes in investment earnings from abroad, as a consequence of changes in their levels, or rates of return.

These deficiencies make it extremely difficult to relate current balance-of-payments fluctuations to the discrepancies observed between actual exchange rates and the cost competitiveness exchange rate calculated on the basis of this theory. Yet the theory retains a considerable degree of interest for long-run analysis. The statistical data presented below will show that:

(1) The enormous discrepancies that may develop over time in the evolution of national prices are brought down to very moderate proportions when national price indices are translated into cost competitiveness indices.

(2) Most of the discrepancies in cost competitiveness indices are susceptible of a reasonable interpretation and explanation in the light of the factors mentioned above.

(3) Residual large descrepancies will usually suggest at least the direction and rough order of magnitude of existing disequilibria, calling for correction.

B. *Monetary Financing*

For short-run analysis, however, a different approach strongly emerges from an examination of the tables presented in this paper. These show indeed a much stronger correlation between yearly balance-of-payments fluctuations and monetary financing than between such fluctuations and the changes in national price levels.[9] The main elements of explanation may be described as follows:

(1) The level of total monetary financing is subject only to very broad limits, related to the continued acceptability of the national currency in payments. It must, however, by identity, be reflected either in production changes, price changes, or balance-of-payments deficits (or surpluses) on goods and services account.

(2) Production changes move within a relatively narrow range, limited upward by physical capacity, and downward by the open character of the European economies and the consequent pervasiveness of international influences on any one country's production.

(3) National prices are also strongly influenced by the evolution of prices in other OEEC countries and in the other major world trading countries, particularly the United States. This limits particularly the likelihood of price decreases much larger than abroad. National prices expressed in national currencies, however, may rise much more than foreign prices if the link between the first and the latter is broken by a tightening of trade and exchange restrictions. Any persistent or large discrepancy in national price levels, however, is likely to be offset in time by exchange readjustments, as each country will want to maintain at least a minimum export level sufficient, together with other sources of financing, to pay for imports necessary to economic development and the satisfaction of essential consumption

9. For further study of this important empirical and theoretical point, see above Chapter I, Section 2.

needs, and whose substitution by domestic production would be either impossible or too costly or too time-consuming.

(4) External surpluses on goods and services are subject only to very broad limits, as long as countries do not impose generalized restrictions on their exports. These limits derive from the impact of such surpluses on spendable incomes and money supply, and on the consequent impact on the country's prices and cost competitiveness.

(5) External deficits, on the other hand, are limited by the availability of reserves and foreign loans or grants. These limits were relatively high in the days of the Marshall Plan, and remain relatively high for year to year movements.

(6) The above considerations lead to the following explanatory schema, which will be checked below against available data and estimates.

(a) Annual production increases together with price rises in the OEEC area would, on the average, absorb 6 to 10 per cent of existing money supply.

(b) If monetary financing is substantially inferior to that amount, the difference is primarily reflected in balance-of-payments surpluses, which may be large—up to 25 per cent or more of money supply—and persist for several years.

(c) If monetary financing is substantially superior to that amount, the difference is likely to be reflected first in external deficits, financed by foreign aid, borrowings and reserve losses. These resources are, however, limited, even though they were abnormally high in the years of the Marshall Plan. Thus, persistent or large monetary financing, in excess of sustainable reserve drains and disinvestment—together with monetary requirements associated with production growth and internationally shared price increases—tends to force a tightening of trade and exchange restrictions and to spill into national price rises larger than the rises in international prices. The economy becomes increasingly uncompetitive in world markets, and the maintenance of export levels sufficient to finance essential imports finally imposes readjustments in exchange rates.

The above process may be delayed, as it was in wartime and in the immediate postwar years, by price controls and rationing. The overliquidity imposed thereby on the economy, however, will in time weaken production incentives and may, if carried to extremes as in Germany, lead to a total currency collapse. In less extreme cases, the gradual build-up of overliquidity will, in time, make the effective maintenance of controls more and more difficult, and their evasion or relaxation will appear as monetary financing, together with current credit monetization.

(d) We are thus led back to emphasize cost competitiveness as a long-run trend in balance-of-payments adjustments, subject to the qualifications mentioned under Section A, above, on Cost Competitiveness. The analysis summarized under Section B, on Monetary Financing, integrates more explicitly in the over-all analysis the short-run factors of disturbance listed under A, except the last two which usually relate to even longer, or highly disturbed, periods such as the effects of World War II on the structure of investment earnings.

Interpretation of OEEC Data, 1948–56

A. Cost Competitiveness and Long-Run Trends in the Balance of Payments

The usefulness and limitations of the cost competitiveness theory is eloquently brought out by a comparison of Charts II and III [omitted here], which respectively present national price indices and cost competitiveness indices for thirteen of the OEEC countries.[10]

The spread of national prices (Chart II), in per cent of 1938, ranges from a minimum of 161 to a maximum of 19,000 in 1947, and from a minimum of 189 to a maximum of 75,000 in 1956. Obviously, the countries at the upper end of this range would have seen their exports dwindle to nothing if the bulk of their price increases had not been absorbed by exchange readjustments. Even these would not have sufficed to restore export competitiveness in relation to the rest of the world, and particularly to the United States, if national prices had not also risen there very sharply since 1938.

The combined result of European price rises, United States price rises and exchange readjustments on cost competitiveness is depicted in Chart III. The previous spread of national prices is reduced, through the effect of the latter two factors, to a range of only 77 to 174 in 1947, and 68 to 146 in 1956.

For nine of the thirteen countries listed, the 1956 spread is only from 68 to 89 and probably reflects in large part the structural changes brought about by the war in the invisible items—particularly overseas investment earnings—of their balance of payments, together with the deterioration in Europe's terms of trade in relation to the late 1930s. Three of the five countries at the top of the range—Switzerland (89), Sweden (85), and Portugal (81)—are nonbelligerent countries, whose internal economy and external investment position were least affected by the war and its aftermath. They were, on the other hand, too closely dependent on their European

10. Germany is not listed in view of the difficulties created by territorial changes and the currency reform in linking together prewar and postwar GNP and price estimates. On the basis of the "working estimates" of the OEEC Secretariat, Germany's competitiveness index would be the lowest in Europe. This result corresponds to what would be expected in view of the large and persistent German surpluses and of the vast *overvaluation* of the mark in the base period. A few other countries (Iceland, Ireland, and Luxemburg) have also been left out here, both in order to simplify the charts, and because of their small size—magnifying the importance of other factors such as terms of trade—or the uncertainty of basic GNP estimates.

trade to be able to isolate themselves totally from European price movements. We thus find their competitiveness index about halfway between the indices of most other OEEC countries and the United States index.

TABLE 1

NATIONAL PRICE INDICES AND COMPETITIVENESS INDICES FOR OEEC COUNTRIES:
1947 AND 1956
(1938 = 100)

Country	In 1947		In 1956	
	Price index	Competitiveness index	Price index	Competitiveness index
Switzerland	(168)	(99)	(189)	(89)
Sweden	161	103	239	85
Portugal	[210]	[110]	225	81
Denmark	(191)	(105)	285	88
Italy	4,266	81	6,124	86
Norway	(185)	(88)	294	78
United Kingdom	181	86	270	72
Austria	[249]	[77]	747	71
Netherlands	(219)	(87)	312	68
Turkey	(418)	(108)	(704)	(146)
Greece	[19,117]	[139]	74,988	131
France	(1,031)	(174)	(2,671)	(123)
Belgium	(348)	(136)	425	116

NOTES:
1. The competitiveness indices are the national price indices (based on OEEC estimates of GNP at current and constant prices) deflated by the United States price index and by indices of exchange rates vis-à-vis the United States dollar.
2. Figures in round brackets make use of unofficial OEEC estimates and those in square brackets of unpublished working estimates of the Secretariat.
3. The base period is 1937 (rather than 1938) for Austria, and 1938–39 for Sweden.

The competitiveness indices of Denmark (88), Italy (86), and Norway (78) are substantially higher than those of the United Kingdom (72), Austria (71), and the Netherlands (68). One may note that the first three of these countries have tended to be persistent debtors, and the last three persistent creditors, on goods and services account in recent years. The United Kingdom and the Netherlands were, moreover, the two European countries whose balance of payments was most unfavorably affected by losses of overseas investments and other invisible earnings as a result of wartime and early postwar developments.

In brief, the actual discrepancies between cost competitiveness indices for these nine countries in 1956 are all contained within a relatively narrow range and reflect both real differences in the structural impact of the war upon their balance-of-payments position and a small residue of cost overcompetitiveness or undercompetitiveness, apparent in current trends toward surpluses or deficits in their international transactions.

Only four of the thirteen countries listed had a competitiveness index higher than 100, thus suggesting an overvaluation of their currency with relation to 1938. The first three (Turkey, Greece, and France) were experiencing extremely large deficits in their balance of payments and the French franc was devalued, in effect, by 20 per cent in 1957.[11] It is also

TABLE 1A

COST COMPETITIVENESS INDICES: 1956, 1959, AND 1962
(1938 = 100)

Country	1956	1959	1962
Switzerland	89	87	(90)
Sweden	88	90	96
Portugal	85	81	(82)
Denmark	88	87	95
Italy	84	81	87
Norway	79	78	80
United Kingdom	73	74	78
Austria	71	72	78
Netherlands	69	70	77
Turkey	144	66	(75)
Greece	131	122	128
France	124	103	111
Belgium	116	114	116
European Economic Community	**82**	**77**	**84**
European OECD	**79**	**74**	**80**

NOTES:

1. See Table 1.

2. Based on latest revisions of GNP estimates in *General Statistics, National Accounts* (OECD, Paris, March 1964).

11. [The subsequent devaluations of Turkey (in the latter part of 1958, in 1959, and in 1960) and of France (in December 1958) confirmed *ex post* this diagnosis, made in February 1958. Table 1A, newly prepared for this volume, derives from revised and more recent estimates new cost-competitiveness indices for 1956 (as in Table 1), 1959 (the year of unprecedented U.S. deficits on current account), and 1962. A general reduction in European competitiveness (or overcompetitiveness) is clearly noticeable between 1959 and 1962, and was accompanied by parallel reductions in Europe's current account surpluses, and improvements of the U.S. current account balance. The spread between individual country indices was also substantially smaller in 1962 than in 1956, thus confirming the long-run predictive value of the cost competitiveness analysis.]

likely that 1938 is a poor reference basis for the latter currency which was probably undervalued at that time after the cascade of devaluation experienced by it in the years 1936–38.

The cost competitiveness index of Belgium (116) is more difficult to interpret. It has remained nearly stable around that level ever since 1950—with a maximum of 119 in 1952, and a minimum of 114 in 1954—and has coincided with persistent surpluses in the Belgian balance of-payments. The rapid development of the Belgian Congo's resources is certainly one of several explanatory factors, especially in contrast with the deterioration of the overseas position of countries like the United Kingdom and the Netherlands. More importance should probably be attached, however, to the marginal position of many Belgian exports in world trade, and the sensitiveness of their prices to cyclical conditions. The base year 1938 was particularly unfavorable in this respect, while Belgian exports have enjoyed persistently booming export markets throughout the postwar period. Finally, reference should be made to the maintenance of tight monetary policies in Belgium and to the considerations developed below on the impact of monetary financing upon the balance of payments of OEEC countries.

B. *Monetary Financing and Short-Run Fluctuations in the Balance of Payments*

Annual deficits and surpluses on goods and services are compared, in Table 2, to the annual amounts of monetary financing.

The correlation between these two variables is well marked throughout, but is particularly striking in the last five years. Surpluses are uniformly associated with monetary contraction or with moderate amounts of monetary financing (less than 10 per cent of money supply) absorbed by production growth and price increases. Deficits coincide similarly with monetary financing in excess of such amounts. The largest surpluses coincide with monetary contraction, and the largest deficits with the largest amounts of monetary financing.

The correlation is less close for the early years, particularly 1948, 1949, and 1951. Production and especially price movements were extremely disparate in 1948 and 1949, and absorbed a similarly disparate amount of total monetary financing. These discrepancies in the evolution of national prices gave rise, in turn, to differential exchange-rate readjustments during this period. This is particularly the case for France and Austria, whose deficits were *relatively* small in relation to monetary financing during this period, but which experienced also larger price rises and currency devaluation than the other countries.

The correlation between monetary financing and the balance of payments was the lowest in 1951 because of the highly abnormal price and terms of

TABLE 2

MONETARY FINANCING AND ANNUAL SURPLUSES OR DEFICITS ON
GOODS AND SERVICES, 1948–56
(in per cent of money supply at the end of the preceding year,
and number of countries in each group)

Monetary financing	Surpluses			Deficits			Total
	20% or more	10–20%	0–10%	0–10%	10–20%	20% or more	
I. Four years, 1948–51							
from −10 to 0			3	2			5
from 0 to 10		2	6	4			12
from 10 to 20			2	10			12
from 20 to 30				3	6	1	10
above 30					4	4	8
II. Five years, 1952–56							
from −20 to −10	4	3					7
from −10 to 0		4	9				13
from 0 to 10			14	4			18
from 10 to 20				11	7		18
from 20 to 30				2	4		6
above 30					2	1	3
Totals:							
1948–51	0	2	11	19	10	5	47
1952–56	4	7	23	17	13	1	65
Total of surpluses and deficits:							
1948–51		13			34		47
1952–56		34			31		65

trade fluctuations arising from the Korean war, and which affected very differently the various countries, depending on the general structure of their balance of payments. Sweden and Norway, for instance, accumulated larger surpluses than would have been expected in view of their monetary financing, as their prices rose further than in other countries, and their terms of trade improved because of abnormally high earnings on their raw material exports and shipping services.

The closer correlation between monetary financing and the balance of payments over the years 1952–56 reflects the return to more normal conditions and the predominance of international over national factors in the evolution of the various countries' prices. The main exception which may be detected in a closer examination of country data is the moderate size of external deficits in relation to monetary financing in the Turkish case during the years 1955 and 1956. This again related to the much steeper price rises experienced by Turkey in recent years and which are reflected in our previous analysis of cost competitiveness (see above).

VIII. Unfinished Business

The present draft is highly tentative and should be regarded primarily as a starting point for future work.

First, the estimates themselves should be checked and completed, insofar as possible, with the help of country specialists at OEEC and of the national statistical offices in member countries.

Second, the global estimates presented here should be broken down among the main sectors of the economy, and particularly among the central government, the local authorities and the private sector of the economy. (A breakdown between firms and households would be extremely useful, but would be next to impossible in view of the limitations imposed by the nature of available statistical information.) Two or three statistical examples, based on British, Netherlands, and Norwegian estimates, are now under preparation, and will be issued in a separate paper for comments and criticism.

Third, the monetary estimates presented here might also be broken down for each country so as to reflect the relative role of different financial institutions, and particularly the degree of control of the central bank over the private banks, and the manner in which such control is achieved and maintained.

Finally, we would welcome any criticism and advice of OEEC country desks and of national experts, as well as their interpretation and explanation or correction of the estimates summarized in the accompanying country tables, in the light of their own knowledge of major developments and policies in each country. The information thus assembled would be used in the preparation of country studies summarizing the postwar monetary evolution in the OEEC countries. These studies might be issued as part of the Tenth Annual Report, or as a separate OEEC document.

2. A Surfeit of Triffin: Chronological List of Publications

1935

"Les mouvements différentiels des prix de gros en Belgique de 1927 à 1934. Calcul et interprétation d'indices de groupes comparables," *Bulletin de l'Institut des Sciences Economiques,* Louvain, May 1935, pp. 267–95.

1937

"La théorie de la surévaluation monétaire et la dévaluation belge," *Bulletin de l'Institut de Recherches Economiques,* Louvain, November 1937, pp. 19–52. (Spanish translation in *El Trimestre Económico,* Mexico, April–June 1948, pp. 91–149.)

1940

Monopolistic Competition and General Equilibrium Theory. Cambridge, Harvard University Press, 1940.

1941

"Monopoly in Particular-Equilibrium and in General-Equilibrium Economics," *Econometrica,* April 1941, pp. 121–27. (Summarized in Report of Fifth Annual Research Conference on Economics and Statistics of the Cowles Commission for Research in Economics held at Colorado Springs, July 3–28, 1939.)

1942

1. "Reply" to Sidney Weintraub's article on "The Classification of Market Positions: Comment," *Quarterly Journal of Economics,* August 1942, pp. 673–77.
2. Review article of William H. Nicholls, "A Theoretical Analysis of Imperfect Competition with Special Application to Agricultural Industries," *American Economic Review,* June 1942, pp. 359–62.

1943

El Régimen Monetario Orgánico de la República del Paraguay, Asunción, Paraguay, Editorial Guarania, 1943.

1944

1. "New Monetary and Banking Measures in Paraguay," *Federal Reserve Bulletin,* January 1944, pp. 42–51.
2. *Ley Orgánica del Banco del Paraguay y Ley de Bancos,* Asunción, Paraguay, La Colmena, 1944.
3. *Money and Banking in Colombia,* Washington, D.C., Board of Governors of the Federal Reserve System, 1944. (Spanish translation: *La Moneda y las Instituciones Bancarias en Colombia,* Bogotá, Colombia, Banco de la República, 1944.)
4. "Central Banking and Monetary Management in Latin America," *Economic Problems of Latin America,* ed. Seymour E. Harris, New York, McGraw-Hill, 1944, pp. 93–116.
5. *Anteproyecto de Ley Monetaria y de Régimen Orgánico de las Transferencias Internacionales,* San José, Costa Rica, December 1944.

1945

"Monetary Developments in Latin America," *Federal Reserve Bulletin,* June 1945, pp. 519–31.

1946

1. "Monetary and Banking Reform in Guatemala," *Federal Reserve Bulletin,* March 1946, pp. 257–88.
2. *Monetary and Banking Reform in Paraguay,* Washington, D.C., Board of Governors of the Federal Reserve System, July 1946.

3. "El Funcionamiento Histórico del Patrón Monetario Internacional," *Memoria,* Primera Reunión de Tecnicos sobre Problemas de Banca Central del Continente Americano, México, D.F., Banco de México, 1946, pp. 218–36.

4. "Ocho Puntos Presentados por el Dr. Robert Triffin sobre la Definición de Desequilibrio Fundamental," *Id.,* pp. 259–62.

5. "La Política Monetaria y el Equilibrio Internacional," *Id.,* pp. 286–308.

6. "Esbozo General de un Análisis de las Series Estadísticas Monetarias y Bancarias de América Latina sobre Bases Uniformes y Comparables," *Id.,* pp. 410–30.

7. *Bretton Woods Legislation in Latin American Countries,* in collaboration with Henry Wallich and Alice Bourneuf (unpublished).

8. *Anteproyecto de ley de adhesión a los convenios de Bretton Woods,* Guatemala (unpublished)

1947

1. "International versus Domestic Money," *American Economic Review,* Proceedings, May 1947, pp. 322–24.

2. "National Central Banking and the International Economy,"
> (a) with "Comments" by Gottfried Haberler in *International Monetary Policies,* Postwar Economic Studies No. 7, Washington, D.C., Board of Governors of the Federal Reserve System, September 1947.
> (b) with "Comments" by H. D. Henderson and others, in *The Review of Economic Studies, 14* (1946–47), 53–112.
> (c) Spanish translation in *El Trimestre Económico,* January–March 1948, pp. 569–645.

1948

"Exchange Control and Equilibrium," *Foreign Economic Policy for the United States,* ed. S. E. Harris, Cambridge, Harvard University Press, 1948, pp. 417–25.

1950

1. "Aspects de la reconstruction monétaire de l'Europe,"
> (a) *Revue d'Economie Politique,* Paris, May 1950, pp. 5–36. (Introductory report at the Congrès des économistes de langue française, 1950).
> (b) Also reproduced with minutes of ensuing discussion in the *Rapport du Congrès des économistes de langue française, 1950,* Paris, Recueil Sirey, 1950.

2. "La multilatérisation progressive des devises en Europe," *Economia Internazionale,* Genoa, May 1950, pp. 501–28.

3. "Monetary Organization in Western Europe," with Summary of Discussion by T. Wilson and F. A. G. Keesing, in *Tracing a New International*

Balance, International Study Conference, Netherlands School of Economics at Rotterdam, Leiden, Steinfert Kroese, 1950, pp. 19–37.

4. "Les Etats-Unis et la coopération monétaire internationale," *Société Belge d'Etudes et d'Expansion,* No. 142, Liège, August–October 1950, pp. 603–06.

5. "Schumpeter, souvenirs d'un étudiant," *Economie Appliquée,* Paris, July–December 1950, pp. 413–16.

6. "Observations," in Robert Mossé, *La Monnaie, Bilans de la connaissance économique,* Paris, 1950, pp. 134–47.

1951

1. "Institutional Developments in the Intra-European Monetary System," *Money, Trade, and Economic Growth,* in Honor of John H. Williams, New York, Macmillan, 1951, pp. 33–57.

2. *Full Employment Objectives in Relation to the Problem of European Cooperation* (in collaboration with Nicholas Kaldor, Anthony Crosland, and Richard Downing) Secretariat General of the Council of Europe, Strasbourg, 1951.

3. "L'Union européenne des paiements," *Comptes-Rendus des Travaux de la Société d'Economie Politique de Belgique,* No. 204, Bruxelles, April 1951.

4. "L'Union européenne des paiements," *Revue Economique Franco-Suisse,* Paris, August–September 1951, pp. 201–02.

1952

1. "Monetary Reconstruction in Europe," *International Conciliation,* New York, Carnegie Endowment for International Peace, June 1952.

2. "Strengthening the Free World Economy," Discussion participant; remarks summarized in Klaus Knorr's Report. Princeton University Center of International Studies, February 1953.

3. *The European Payments Union and Latin America* (Limited OEEC distribution, Paris, July 1952).

1953

1. "L'Etalon monétaire européen depuis la Guerre," *L'Intégration Economique de l'Europe,* ed. Lucien de Sainte-Lorette, Dotation Carnegie pour la Paix Internationale, Paris, Presses Universitaires de France, 1953, pp. 117–88.

2. "Système et politique monétaires de l'Europe fédérée." *Economia Internazionale,* Genoa, February–March 1953, pp. 207–14.

3. *Monetary and Banking Legislation of the Dominican Republic, 1947,* (in collaboration with Henry Wallich) Federal Reserve Bank of New York, August 1953.

4. *Proyecto de Ley para Instituciones Bancarias,* (in collaboration with Paul Vinelli) Tegucigalpa, Honduras, September 1953.

1954

1. "International Currency and Reserve Plans,"
   (a) *Banca Nazionale del Lavoro Quarterly Review,* Rome, January–June 1954, pp. 3–20. A paper presented at the Conference of the Universities-National Bureau Committee for Economic Research, Princeton, May 1954.
   (b) Also published with a "Comment" by William A. Salant in *Policies to Combat Depression,* Princeton, 1956, pp. 377–404.
   (c) French translation in *Problèmes Economiques,* Paris, November 23, 1954, pp. 1–11.
2. "Economic Integration: Institutions, Theories, and Policies," *World Politics,* July 1954, pp. 526–37.
3. "Convertibilité ou intégration?" *Economie Appliquée,* Paris, October–December 1954, pp. 359–75.
4. "Die Konvertibilität und die innereuropäische Wirtschaftliche und finanzielle Zusammerarbeit," *Aussenwirtschaft,* Zürich, December 1954, pp. 215–23.

1955

"Adjusting Features in the Mechanism of the Balance of Payments and Exchange Rates," *Foreign Economic Policy.* Hearings before the Subcommittee on Foreign Economic Policy of the Joint Committee on the Economic Report, November 9, 1955, Washington, D.C., U.S. Government Printing Office, 1955, pp. 131–55.

1956

1. "Effrondrement et relèvement de l'économie européenne: 1947–1954," *Economie Appliquée,* Paris, January–June 1956, pp. 5–65.
2. "La politique monétaire d'après-guerre aux Pays-Bas," *Economie Appliquée,* Paris, January–June 1956, pp. 68–105.
3. "Convertibilité monétaire et intégration économique en Europe occidentale," *Economie Appliquée,* Paris, October–December 1956, pp. 619–58.
4. "La Política Monetaria Nacional e Internacional a Mediados del Siglo," *El Trimestre Económico,* Mexico, October–December 1956, pp. 448–57.

1957

1. "Integración y Convertibilidad Monetaria. Perspectivas Actuales y Programa de Acción," *Moneda y Credito,* Madrid, March 1957, pp. 3–21.
2. *Europe and the Money Muddle: From Bilateralism to Near-Convertibility, 1947–1956,* New Haven, Yale University Press, 1957.
3. "Notes on Trade Liberalization and Regionalism," *Foreign Trade Policy,* Subcommittee on Foreign Trade Policy of the Committee on Ways and Means, Washington, D.C., U.S. Government Printing Office, 1957, pp. 483–89.

4. "A Simplified Scheme for the Integration of Monetary and Income Analysis,"

> (a) *Fifth Meeting of Technicians of Central Banks of the American Continent, 4,* Bogotá, Colombia, Banco de la República, 1957, pp. 293–311.

> (b) Spanish translation, *Id.,* pp. 313–32 and in *Estadística,* Washington, December 1958, pp. 532–46 (see 1958, no. 5).

5. "Latin America in World Trade and Payments," *Fifth Meeting of Technicians of Central Banks of the American Continent, 5,* Bogotá, Colombia, Banco de la República, 1957, pp. 93–115. (Spanish translation, *Id.,* pp. 117–42.)

6. "The Size of the Nation and its Vulnerability to Economic Nationalism," Presented at the International Economic Association Conference, Lisbon, 1957, and published in *The Economic Consequences of the Size of Nations,* ed. Austin Robinson, New York, St. Martin's Press, 1960.

7. Review of Richard N. Gardner's "Sterling-Dollar Diplomacy" in *The Yale Law Journal, 66* (1957), pp. 474–76.

1958

1. *The Future of the European Payments System,* Wicksell Lectures 1958, Stockholm, Almquist and Wiksell, 1958.

2. "The Dollar and International Liquidity Problem Reconsidered," *Kyklos, 11,* Fasc. 3 (1958), pp. 405–18.

3. "L'oece, la Communauté Européenne et la zone de libre échange," *La Suisse et l'Intégration Européenne,* Geneva, Institut Universitaire des Hautes Etudes Internationales, July 1958, pp. 16–21.

4. "La monnaie et le Marché Commun. Politiques nationales et intégration régionale," *Cahiers de l'Institut de Science Economique Appliquée,* No. 74, Paris, December 1958, pp. 1–17.

5. "Un Esquema Simplificado para la Integración del Análisis Monetario y de Ingresos," *Estadística,* Washington, December 1958, pp. 532–46.

1959

1. "The Return to Convertibility: 1926–1931 and 1958–? or, Convertibility and the Morning After,"

> (a) *Banca Nazionale del Lavoro Quarterly Review,* Rome, March 1959, pp. 3–57.

> (b) Italian translation in *Moneta e Credito,* Rome, 1959.

> (c) French translation: "Le Retour à la Convertibilité," in *Bulletin SEDEIS,* Paris, June 1959, pp. 1–31.

2. "To-morrow's Convertibility: Aims and Means of International Monetary Policy," *Banca Nazionale del Lavoro Quarterly Review,* Rome, June 1959, pp. 131–200. (Italian translation in *Moneta e Credito,* Rome, 1959.)

3. "El Dólar en la Economía Internacional," *Los Pagos Internacionales y*

la Política Monetaria, by Arthur W. Marget and Robert Triffin, Mexico, Centro de Estudios Monetarios Latino-Americanos, 1959.

4. "Universalisme et régionalisme sur le plan économique," *Revue Economique et Sociale,* Lausanne, September 1959, pp. 43–51.

5. "Statements and Discussion of the International Monetary Position of the United States,"

    (a) *Employment, Growth, and Price Levels,* Hearings before the Joint Economic Committee of Congress, October 28, 1959, Washington, D.C., U.S. Government Printing Office, 1959, pp. 2905–54.

    (b) Reprinted in *Money and Economic Activity,* ed. Lawrence S. Ritter, ed., Boston, Houghton Mifflin, 1961, pp. 435–45.

1960

1. "Improving World Liquidity," *The Banker,* London, January 1960, pp. 13–22 and June 1960, pp. 352–54. (Spanish translation in Supplement to *Boletín Quincenal,* Centro de Estudios Monetarios Latino-Americanos, Mexico, March 1960, pp. 49–54.)

2. "La Situazione e la Politica Monetaria degli Stati Uniti," *Stato Sociale,* Turin, No. 1, 1960, pp. 24–39.

3. *Statistics of Sources and Uses of Finance, 1948–58* (in collaboration with Geer Stuvel and OEEC staff) Paris, Organisation for European Economic Co-operation, 1960.

4. *Gold and the Dollar Crisis: The Future of Convertibility,* New Haven, Yale University Press, 1960.

5. "Le crépuscule de l'étalon de change-or,"

    (a) *Comptes Rendus des Travaux de la Société Royale d'Economie Politique de Belgique,* No. 272, Bruxelles, June 1960.

    (b) *Annales d'Economie Politique,* Paris, 1959–60, under the title "L'Avenir de l'étalon monétaire international."

6. "Rasgos Distintivos del Mecanismo de Equilibración de la Balanza de Pagos y los Tipos de Cambio," *Moneda y Crédito,* Madrid, June 1960, pp. 3–16.

7. "Statement and Supporting Papers (including 'The Twilight of the Gold Standard and the World Dollar Crisis'), and Discussion," *Current Economic Situation and Short-Run Outlook,* Hearings before the Joint Economic Committee of Congress, December 7 and 8, 1960, Washington, D.C., U.S. Government Printing Office, 1961, pp. 169–260.

8. "Intégration économique européenne et politique monétaire," *La Restauration des Monnaies Européennes* (Special Number of *Revue d'Economie Politique,* December 1960) Paris, Sirey, 1960, pp. 58–81.

1961

1. "The Threat to the Dollar," *The Atlantic,* Boston, February 1961. (Italian translation: "La Vera Minaccia al Dollaro," *Mercurio,* Rome, September 15, 1961, pp. 37–40.)

2. "The International Monetary Crisis: Diagnosis, Palliatives, and Solutions,"

(a) *Quarterly Review and Investment Survey* (Model, Roland, and Stone) New York, First Quarter 1961

(b) *Employment in the Dynamic American Economy,* Congressional Record, Proceedings and Debates of the 87th Congress, First Session, Washington, 1961, pp. 72 ff. (with Congressional comments).

3. *Gold and the Dollar Crisis: The Future of Convertibility,* revised and expanded edition, New Haven, Yale University Press, 1961.

(a) Japanese translation, Tokyo, 1961.

(b) Spanish translation, Mexico, D.F., Fondo de Cultura Económica, 1962 (see 1962, no. 12)

(c) French translation, Paris, Presses Universitaires de France, 1962 (see 1962, no. 13).

4. "A Brief for the Defense," *Staff Papers,* International Monetary Fund, May 1961, pp. 192–94.

5. "Death of a System," *The Listener,* London, July 27, 1961, pp. 122–23.

6. "The International Monetary Position of the United States,"

(a) *The Dollar in Crisis,* ed. Seymour E. Harris, New York, Harcourt, Brace and World, 1961, pp. 223–42.

(b) Mark and Slate, *Economics in Action,* 2nd ed. Belmont, Calif., 1964.

7. "Altman on Triffin: A Rebuttal,"

(a) *The Dollar in Crisis,* pp. 277–94.

(b) *Banca Nazionale del Lavoro Quarterly Review,* Rome, March 1961, pp. 31–50.

(c) Italian translation in *Moneta e Credito,* Rome, June 1961, pp. 196–215.

8. *El Caos Monetario: Del Bilateralismo a la Casi Convertibilidad en Europa, 1947–1956* (Spanish translation of *Europe and the Money Muddle,* with new introduction) Mexico, D.F., Fondo de Cultura, 1961.

9. "Nach der Wiener Tagung des Internationalen Währungsfonds,"

(a) *Neue Zürcher Zeitung,* October 29, 1961.

(b)Japanese translation in *Nihon Keizai Shimbun,* October 1961.

(c) unpublished typescript: "A Side Step in the Right Direction," November 1961 (see 1962, no. 7).

10. "Grandeur et décadence de l'étalon-or,"

(a) *Revue Economique et Sociale,* Lausanne, October 1961, pp. 269–78.

(b) *Stato Sociale,* Turin, 1961, pp. 827–38.

11. "After the Gold-Exchange Standard?" *Weltwirtschaftliches Archiv,* Kiel, December 1961.

12. "The Presentation of U.S. Balance of Payments Statistics, General Comments," *American Statistical Association 1961: Proceedings of the Business and Economic Statistics Section,* pp. 51–57.

1962

1. "Balance of Payments Problem," *Yale Daily News,* January 1962.

2. Numerous lectures and interviews published in Japanese in February.

3. "Comments on Proposals for the Reorganization of the Monetary Situation," *Economic Journal,* March 1962, pp. 244–49.

4. "Lendemains de Vienne: Mesures conservatoires et germes d'avenir," *Bulletin d'Information et Documentation de la Banque Nationale de Belgique,* April 1962. (Dutch translation: "Na de conferentie van Wenen: Beschermende maatregelen en grondslagen voor de toe Komst," *Tijdschrift voor Documentatie en Voorlichtichting van de Nationale Bank van Belgie,* April 1962.)

5. "L'Ordre monétaire de Michel Heilperin et la double fonction de l'étalon monétaire de Per Jacobsson." Published with preceding item in *Trois Etudes sur le Problème des Liquidités Internationales,* Brussels, Banque Nationale de Belgique, April 1962.

6. "The Gold-Exchange Standard: Crisis and Reconstruction," and

7. "The Meeting of the International Monetary Fund in Vienna: A Side Step in the Right Direction," *Amerikanische Gelehrtenwoche, 1961,* Munich, Ludwig-Maximilians-Universität, 1962.

8. *Crisis and Reform in the International Monetary System.* Kingston, Canada, Queen's University, Winter 1962.

9. "The Twilight of the Gold-Exchange Standard," *International Financing and Investment,* Proceedings of the 1962 Conference on International Trade and Investment conducted at the Yale Law School World Community Association, Oceana Publications, 1964.

10. "The Trade Expansion Act of 1962." *Proceedings of the American Society of International Law,* 1962, pp. 139–49.

11. "The Adjustment Mechanism to Differential Rates of Monetary Expansion among the Countries of the European Economic Community." (in collaboration with Herbert Grubel), *Review of Economics and Statistics,* November 1962, pp. 487–91.

12. *El Oro y la Crisis del Dólar.* Spanish translation of *Gold and the Dollar Crisis,* Mexico, D.F., Fondo de Cultura Económica, 1962.

13. *L'Or et la crise du dollar,* French translation of *Gold and the Dollar Crisis,* Paris, Presses Universitaires de France, 1962.

14. "The Complementary Roles of National Policies and the International Institutional Framework in the Functioning of the World Monetary System," *Kautilya,* Bangalore, India.

15. *The Role of Credit Policy and the Banking Structure in the Economic Development of Panamá,* Panama, Ministry of Finance, May 1962.

1963

1. *La Communauté Economique Européenne et la coopération monétaire internationale.* Rapport presenté à la Xe Table Ronde des Problèmes de l'Europe, Bâle, 8–9–10 novembre 1962; reproduced in *Problèmes de l'Europe,* 1963.

2. *L'Etalon monétaire du XXe siècle.*

    (a) Conférence au Collège de France le 29 mars 1963.

    (b) Republished by Institut de Science Economique Appliquée, Paris, 1963.

    (c) German translation: "Die Währungsordnung des 20. Jahrhunderts," in *Inflation und Weltwährungsordnung,* Erlenbach-Zürich and Stuttgart, Eugen Rentsch Verlag, 1963.

3. *O Nomismatikos Kanon Tou Eikostou Aionos,* Greek translation of Conference in Athens, based on preceding item, Athens, 1963.

4. "The Latent Crisis of the Reserve Currencies." *The Banker,* London, August 1963. (German translation: "Die Latente Krise der Schlüsselwährungen," in *Neue Zürcher Zeitung,* August 2 and 3, 1963.)

5. "Fund Will Consider Fiscal Reform Study," *Washington Post,* September 29, 1963.

6. "World Liquidity—A Concerted Effort," *New York Herald Tribune,* October 20, 1963. (abridged version of "The Dawn of an International Monetary Revolution.") (German translation: "Der Beginn einer internationalen monetären Revolution," in *Amerika Handel,* November 1963.)

7. "Integración Económica Europea y Política Monetaria," *Coordinación Monetaria Regional,* Mexico, CEMLA, 1963, pp. 43–63. (Spanish translation of no. 8, 1960.)

8. "Una Cámara de Compensación y Union de Pagos Latinoamericana," *Cooperación Financiera en América Latina,* Mexico, CEMLA, 1963, pp. 95–117.

9. "Ouvrir la porte au progrès," *Le Monde,* Paris, December 15–16, 1963, p. 7.

1964

1. *Report on the Possibilities of Establishing a Clearing and Payments Union in Africa,* United Nations Economic and Social Council, E/CN. 14/262, February 4, 1964 (prepared in August 1963 for U.N. Commission for Africa). (French translation: *Rapport sur les possibilités d'établir une union de compensation et des paiements en Afrique,* Banque Centrale des Etats de l'Afrique de l'Ouest, Document No. 103, February 1964.)

2. "The Problem of International Monetary Reform: Major Questions and Prospective Initial Area of Agreement," *Banca Nazionale del Lavoro Quarterly Review,* Rome, March 1964, pp. 88–106. (Italian translation:

"Il problema della riforma del sistema monetario internazionale: questioni fondamentali e prospettive di una prima area d'accordo," in *Moneta e Credito,* Rome, June 1964, pp. 208–27.)

3. "Triffin's Proposals for International Monetary Reform," in "Plans for Increasing International Liquidity," *Banking,* April 1964, p. 131.

4. "Hacia una Organización Monetaria Latino-Americana," in *Integración de América Latina: Experiencias y Perspectivas,* ed. Miguel S. Wionczek, Mexico and Buenos-Aires, Fondo de Cultura Economica, 1964, pp. 264–70. (See also item 2 under 1966.)

5. "The End of the Dollar Glut?"

    (a) *The Banker,* London, June 1964, pp. 351–54.

    (b) Japanese translation in *Nihon Keizai Shimbun,* Tokyo, April 1964.

    (c) German translation: "Von dem Enden des Dollarüberflusses?" in *Neue Zürcher Zeitung,* April 28, 1964.

6. *The Evolution of the International Monetary System: Historical Reappraisal and Future Perspectives.*

    (a) Princeton Studies in International Finance No. 12, Princeton, 1964. (Private printing for Fifth Seanza Central Banking Course, Karachi, 1964)

    (b) Excerpts in Joint Economic Committee, Subcommittee on International Exchange and Payments, *Hearings,* Part 2, July 27–29, 1965, pp. 368–96.

7. "From Waterloo to Tokyo," *The Economist,* London, August 15, 1964, pp. 657–59. (Spanish translation in *Revista del Banco de la República,* Bogotá, Colombia, August 1964, pp. 1010–14.)

8. "Decentralized IMF Necessary; Europe Should Create Own Fund," (Summary of a lecture given in Tokyo during the IMF 1964 annual meeting) *Nihon Keizai Shimbun* International Weekly Edition, September 22, 1964, pp. 3–5.

9. "Le duel Maudling-Giscard d'Estaing a clarifié la situation en vue d'une réforme," *Le Monde Diplomatique,* Paris, October 1964, p. 11.

10. "Post-Mortem on Tokyo," *Elseviers Weekblad,* Amsterdam, October 30, 1964.

11. *Vida Internacional de las Monedas,* Mexico City, CEMLA, 1964.

12. Interventions, and particularly debate with Jacques Rueff, at the Congrès des économistes de langue française, 1963, in *Problèmes de l'Organisation Monétaire Internationale,* Paris, Editions Cujas, 1964, pp. 18–24, 110–17, and *passim.*

13. "The Bizarre Proposals of Dr. Bernstein for International Monetary Reform," *Kyklos,* Fasc. 3, (1964), pp. 328–45.

14. "The International Network of World Payments: An Integrated Approach," *Weltwirtschaftliches Archiv,* December 1964.

15. "Une interview exclusive du Professeur Robert Triffin," *Combat,* Paris, October 2, 1964.

16. "International Monetary Arrangements, Capital Markets, and Economic Integration in Latin America." Spanish translation in *Revista de Economía Latinoamericana, 13,* Caracas, 1964; and English text in *Journal of Common Market Studies,* Oxford, 1965, pp. 70–104.

17. "The Sterling Crisis in International Perspective." *The Banker,* London, February 1965, pp. 79–83. (Spanish translation in *Suplemento al Boletin Quincenal,* Mexico City, CEMLA, January 1965.)

18. "The International Economic Community and the Problem of International Monetary Reform," *Währungspolitik in der europäischen Integration,* ed. Heinrich Rieber and Lutz Köllner, Baden-Baden, 1964, pp. 43–54.

1965

1. "General de Gaulle's Monetary Force de Frappe and the Sterling Crisis," (Italian translation in *L'Espresso,* Rome, January 31, 1965).

2. "African Monetary Cooperation," (German translation in *Internationales Afrika Forum,* Munich, March 1965).

3. "Sterling, the Dollar, de Gaulle and Gold." Published with 1965, no. 4 in *Challenge,* NYU, April 1965. (Spanish translation in *Suplemento al Boletín Quincenal,* Mexico City, CEMLA, March 1965.)

4. "Gold, Rueff, and de Gaulle,"
   (a) Italian translation in *L'Espresso,* Rome, February 28, 1965.
   (b) Dutch translation in *Elseviers Weekblad,* Amsterdam, March 20, 1965.

5. "Will 1965 Repeat 1931?" *The Reporter,* April 8, 1965.

6. "The International Monetary System,"
   (a) *Moorgate and Wall Street,* London, Summer 1965.
   (b) Joint Economic Committee: Subcommittee on International Exchange and Payments, *Hearings,* Part 2, July 27–29, 1965, pp. 350–67.
   (c) Spanish translation in *Información Comercial Española,* October 1965, pp. 131–44.

7. "International Currency and World Trade," *The Listener,* London, June 17, 1965 (Triffin interviewed by J. R. Sargent).

8. "Guidelines for International Monetary Reform," Joint Economic Committee: Subcommittee on International Exchange and Payments, *Hearings,* Part 1, July 27–29, 1965, pp. 164–80.

9. "La banquise a enfin craqué!"
   (a) Italian translation in *L'Espresso,* Rome, October 24, 1965.
   (b) German translation in *Neue Zürcher Zeitung,* Zurich, October 22, 1965.

1966

1. "International Monetary Reform," *Economic Bulletin for Latin America,* United Nations, Economic Commission for Latin America, March 1966.
2. "Toward a Latin American Monetary Organization," *Latin American Economic Integration,* Miguel S. Wionczek, ed., New York, Praeger, 1966.
3. *Wegweiser vom Währungswirwarr,* Berlin, Berlin Verlag, 1966.